Hodges'
Harbrace
Handbook

fourteenth edition

Hodges'
Harbrace
Handbook

fourteenth edition

John C. Hodges

Suzanne Strobeck Webb
Texas Woman's University

Robert Keith Miller
University of St. Thomas

Winifred Bryan Horner
Texas Christian University

HARCOURT COLLEGE PUBLISHERS

Fort Worth   Philadelphia   San Diego   New York   Orlando   Austin   San Antonio
Toronto   Montreal   London   Sydney   Tokyo

Publisher: **Earl McPeek**
Market Strategist: **John Meyers**
Developmental Editor: **Michell Phifer**
Project Editor: **Jon Davies**
Art Director: **Sue Hart**
Production Manager: **Angela Williams Urquhart**

Cover image: © Copyright Ernst Haas/Tony Stone Images

ISBN: 0-15-506765-6

Library of Congress Catalog Card Number: 00-102333

Address for Domestic Orders
Harcourt College Publishers
6277 Sea Harbor Drive
Orlando, FL 32887-6777
800-782-4479

Address for Editorial
Correspondence
Harcourt College Publishers
301 Commerce Street, Suite 3700
Fort Worth, TX 76102

Address for International Orders
International Customer Service
Harcourt, Inc.
6277 Sea Harbor Drive
Orlando, FL 32887-6777
407-345-3800
(fax) 407-345-4060
(e-mail) hbintl@harcourtbrace.com

Web Site Address
http://www.harcourtcollege.com

Harcourt College Publishers will provide complimentary supplements or supplement packages to those adopters qualified under our adoption policy. Please contact your sales representative to learn how you qualify. If as an adopter or potential user you receive supplements you do not need, please return them to your sales representative or send them to: Attn: Returns Department, Troy Warehouse, 465 South Lincoln Drive, Troy, MO 63379.

Printed in the United States of America

0 1 2 3 4 5 6 7 8 9   039   9 8 7 6 5 4 3 2

Harcourt College Publishers

Preface

A compact yet comprehensive guide, *Hodges' Harbrace Handbook,* Fourteenth Edition, offers practical, well-organized, and easily accessible advice for writers. Specific examples throughout the book demonstrate the principles of writing that are applicable to both course work and professional tasks, and frequent cross-references establish how these principles inform each other.

The fourteenth edition is a complete revision of the thirteenth. While recognizably the same book that generations of writers have come to trust, the handbook is now easier to use and understand. We have improved upon or added the following features.

New to This Edition

1. Bulleted lists begin each chapter, providing users with a quick reference to what each chapter includes.

2. Clear explanations give the reasons or purposes for specific elements of grammar, punctuation, style, and mechanics. Students write better when they understand the reasons behind the rules. In this spirit, grammatical and rhetorical terms are defined when they are first used, reducing the extent to which students will need to consult the glossary.

3. The information devoted to writing with computers has significantly increased. Computer boxes highlighting discussions involving electronic composition are placed throughout virtually every chapter of the book, and computer icons highlight additional references to computers. The increased emphasis on the computer as a writing and research tool is most evident, however, in chapters 8, 37, and 38.

- Because of the ease computers bring to using graphics in documents, chapter 8, "Document Design," now offers advice on using such elements as charts, maps, drawings, and photos and on constructing Web pages as well as on using the computer to format a paper and to submit it electronically.
- Chapter 37, "Research: Finding and Evaluating Sources," has an expanded, integrated discussion of searching the World Wide Web and other electronic sources throughout the research process. This extensively revised chapter reflects research showing that many students turn to the Web as their primary source of information but need advice on how to determine the credibility of Web sites. In addition, the chapter provides clear explanations on how to find and evaluate sources that cannot be accessed electronically, such as the texts of most books and many journal articles.
- Chapter 38, "Research: Using and Citing Sources," now includes many more examples of how to cite electronic sources.

4. Expanded discussions of writing difficulties common to dialect and to English as a Second Language are placed in context rather than in a separate chapter. This decision is in response to current national demographics as well as to our determination not to make international students feel as though their needs were addressed as an afterthought. Many of the problems identified by our globe icon are problems that American English–speaking students face as well, so this icon does *not* mean that a concept relates only to ESL students.

5. The first seven chapters in the Grammar section have been expanded to include more discussion of complex grammatical concepts as well as more examples for illustrating these concepts and more exercises to practice mastering them.
   - Because students have various kinds of difficulties understanding the distinct functions of adjectives and adverbs, chapter 4 now includes a practical explanation of how to recognize and use adjectives. In addition, the chapter now discusses adjectives before it discusses how to recognize and use adverbs.

- Because understanding the functions of the various types of pronouns will aid students in choosing proper case, chapter 5, which has been retitled "Pronouns and Case," now includes expanded information discussing pronoun functions as well as how pronouns are used in sentences.
- Chapter 7, "Verbs," has also benefited from a thorough restructuring that logically organizes the forms, functions, and tenses of verbs. The chapter also addresses how verbs should be used in sentences.

6. Chapter 19, "Good Usage," has been extensively rewritten to help students write positively to and about all people. It now offers advice not only about handling matters of gender in language, but also about including members of all races, classes, ages, and orientations. The topics of dictionary use, usage labels, and style are given their own sections.

7. Chapter 31, "Working with Paragraphs," now focuses on unity, coherence, and how paragraphs are developed through details and examples. Paragraphs illustrating rhetorical strategies, such as comparison and contrast, now appear in chapter 32, "Planning and Drafting Essays," because students are most likely to find these strategies useful when developing their essays. Chapter 32 also includes a fuller discussion of prewriting.

8. Advice about writing introductions, conclusions, and titles has been moved from chapter 32 to chapter 33, "Revising and Editing Essays," because this information is more likely to benefit students when they are working with material they have already drafted. Once again, three versions of a student essay are included—together with comments generated by peer review—to illustrate the process of writing an essay. In addition, chapter 33 now includes a new section offering advice on how to benefit from peer review.

9. Chapter 35, "Reading and Thinking Critically," now includes more information about enthymemes and warrants as well as a fuller discussion of the difference between fact and opinion.

10. Chapter 36, "Writing Arguments" now contains a fuller discussion of how credibility, reason, and emotion contribute to persuasion as well as a fuller discussion of the types of claims that may be asserted in argumentation. There is also an expanded explanation of Rogerian argument.

11. Chapter 38, "Research: Using and Citing Sources," contains a new MLA sample paper analyzing the rhetorical and political implications of a controversial memoir by Nobel Peace Prize winner Rigoberta Menchú. The discussion of documentation in this chapter illustrates recent changes in MLA and APA styles.

12. Chapter 39, "Writing for Special Purposes," has been revised with evolving classroom practices and assignments in mind as well as new challenges for writing in the workplace. The chapter now includes an introduction to literary theory and a new student essay using reader-response theory to analyze a novel. Moreover, an undergraduate grant proposal illustrates the documentation style of the Council of Biology Editors (CBE).

In addition to these major changes, we have:

- updated existing examples that illustrate the various concepts of writing and added several models of student work;
- increased the number of sample sentences that are revised with handwritten corrections to illustrate the principles being taught;
- increased the number of exercises that encourage students to write or to revise in context;
- included advice for students in chapter 34, "Writing under Pressure," not only about the essay exam but also about other kinds of writing for deadlines;
- added directories for MLA- and APA-style documentation in chapter 38 in order to help students find the model entries they wish to consult; and
- given a new title, "Writing," to the former "Larger Elements." Although the entire handbook concerns writing

to some extent, "Writing" serves as the heading for the seven chapters that address how to plan, research, and develop writing beyond the sentence level in order to make the purpose of these chapters more readily apparent to students.

Those familiar with past editions of the handbook may appreciate the new four-color-process design, which offers a clearer and more varied palette for the various boxes, screens, icons, and annotations that contribute so successfully to the visual display and accessibility of this edition. Another notable design feature is that a large decorative letter marks each of the six divisions of the handbook, allowing for immediate identification of the section for the reader.

Although we have considerably expanded the section covering the writing process, *Hodges' Harbrace Handbook* remains a handbook first and a rhetoric second. Where we have changed chapter titles and subtitles, we have tried to make the book easier for instructors to teach from and for students to use. In doing so, we have worked hard not to compromise its well-established integrity, but rather to improve it. As a result, the new edition responds to the changing needs of writers in the twenty-first century.

The following supplements accompany *Hodges' Harbrace Handbook,* Fourteenth Edition.

Instructor Supplements

Instructor's Manual
Harcourt Brace Guide to Teaching First-Year Composition
Harcourt Brace Guide to Teaching Writing with Computers
Harcourt Brace Guide to Writing across the Curriculum
Harcourt Brace Guide to Peer Tutoring
Harcourt Brace Sourcebook for Teachers of Writing
Diagnostic Test Package
Transparency Masters
Instructor's Correction Chart
Exercise Bank (available in print and on disk for PC or Mac)

Student Supplements

College Workbook
Basic Writer's Workbook
ESL Workbook
Working Together: A Collaborative Writing Guide
The Resourceful Reader
Hodges' CD-ROM
Hodges' WebCT

For additional information on these and other supplemental materials for *Hodges' Harbrace Handbook,* please visit the *Harbrace* Web site at http://www.harcourtcollege.com/english.

Acknowledgments

For the material on English as a Second Language, we are indebted to Kelly Kennedy-Isern of Miami Dade Community College. Her special expertise added much to this edition of *Hodges' Harbrace Handbook.*

The following individuals gave us their advice and experience, which shaped the fourteenth edition.

Specialty Reviewers

For *argumentation:* Marie J. Secor, Pennsylvania State University. For *research:* Helen J. Schwartz, Indiana/Purdue University; James Lester, Austin Peay State University; Joe Law, Wright State University; and Jan Malcheski, University of St. Thomas. For *composition:* Christine Farris, Indiana University at Bloomington; Erika Scheurer, University of St. Thomas; and Victor Villanueva, Washington State University. For *grammar:* Dennis Baron, University of Illinois at Urbana-Champaign; Chris Collins, Cornell University; John Peters, California State University at Northridge; Mary Ramsey, Georgia State University; and Gilbert Youmans, University of Missouri at Columbia. For *literary theory:* Michael C. Jordan, University of St. Thomas.

Class Testers

Vicky Anderson, Loyola University of Chicago; Nancy Ellis, Mississippi State University; and Cecile Anne de Rocher and Tammy Cole of Georgia State University.

Handbook Reviewers

Adrienne Acra, Old Dominion University; Brian Anderson, Central Piedmont Community College; Brenda Ayres, Middle Georgia College; Kirsten Benson, University of Tennessee at Knoxville; Anne Bliss, University of Colorado at Boulder; Mona Choucair, Baylor University; Kurtis Clements, University of New Orleans; Karen Weaver Coleman, Reading Area Community College; Margaret DeHart, Trinity Valley Community College; Cynthia Denham, Snead State Community College; Brenda Dillard, Brazosport College; Janet Eber, County College of Morris; Patrick Enright, Northeastern State University; Karen Grossaint, Regis University; Kim Haimes-Korn, Southern Polytechnic State University; Nels Highberg, University of Illinois at Chicago; Mary Hurst, Cuyahoga Community College; Wendell Jackson, Morgan State University; Maggie Jenkins, Pellissippi State Technical Community College; Peggy Jolly, University of Alabama at Birmingham; Yvonne McDonald, Milwaukee Area Technical College; Susan McKay, Weber State University; Gwendolyn Morgan, Clark Atlanta University; Sue Munn, Floyd College; Deborah Normand, Louisiana State University; Sue Pine, Florida Community College at Jacksonville; Zaide Pixley, Kalamazoo College; Katherine Raign, University of North Texas; Porter Raper, Portland Community College at Cascade; Denise Rogers, University of Southwestern Louisiana; Paula Ross, Gadsden State Community College; Donna Schouman, Macomb College; Brian Shelley, Campbell University; Sylvia Shurbutt, Shepherd College; Terry Spaise, University of California at Riverside; Rebecca Stout, Texas A&M University; Tracy Thornton, Old Dominion University; Richard Viti, Southern Illinois University; Mike Williams, New Mexico

Junior College; and Wanda Williams, Jefferson State Community College.

Focus Group Participants

Linda Hill, Sheila Fox Miller, Mary Ann Robinson, Rosia Wade, Celia Wood, and Stephanie Brook Woods of Hinds Community College; Michalle Barnett, University of Alabama at Birmingham; Tim Barnett, Northeastern Illinois University; Donna Gessell, North Georgia College and State University; Fred Green, Floyd College; Kirsten Komara, University of Evansville; Jack O'Keefe, Daley College; Donna Singleton, Reading Area Community College; Julie Hagemann, Purdue University at Calumet; Sylvia Stacey and Richard F. Tracz of Oakton Community College; Susan Giesemann North, University of Tennessee; and Jane Wagoner, Wilbur Wright College.

Survey Participants

Alabama Southern Community College, Alvernia College, Arkansas State University, Auburn University at Montgomery, Berry College, California State University at Fullerton, Central Michigan University, Christian Life College, Clark Atlanta University, Cleveland State Community College, College of Lake County, Colorado Northwestern Community College, Community College of Philadelphia, Concordia College (New York), Darton College, Delaware State University, Delaware Technical and Community College, Delta State University, Diablo Valley College, Florida Community College at Jacksonville, Florida Metropolitan University, Floyd College, Fugazzi College, Gadsden State Community College, Georgia Perimeter College, Georgia State University, Glendale College, Glendale Community College (California), Grace College, Grossmont College, Harold Washington College, Illinois Central College, Jamestown College, Jefferson State Community College, Kalamazoo College, Kalamazoo Valley Community College, LIFE Bible College, Louisiana College, Louisiana State University, Louisiana State University at Eunice, Loyola University of Chicago, Macon State

College, Maine Maritime Academy, McNeese State University, Meredith College, Modesto Junior College, Montana State University at Billings, Montana Tech of The University of Montana, Mount Mercy College, Mountain Empire Community College, New Mexico State University, Northeast Iowa Community College, Northeast Louisiana University, Notre Dame College of Ohio, the Ohio State University at Lima, Otero Junior College, Owensboro Community College, Paine College, Reading Area Community College, Riverside Community College, Rowan University, Saint Joseph's University, Saint Martin's College, Shasta College, Sojourner-Douglass College, Southeast Community College, Stephen F. Austin State University, Suffolk County Community College, Texas Southern University, Unity College in Maine, University of Alabama at Birmingham, University of Evansville, University of Hawaii at Manoa, University of Maine at Farmington, University of New Orleans, University of Northern Iowa, University of West Alabama, University of Wisconsin, Urbana University, Ursinus College, Weber State University, and West Hills Community College.

For the daunting task of copyediting the manuscript, we thank Mary Stoughton.

For the details from research to manuscript preparation, we are indebted to Judith Bean, Kim Allison, and Kay Robinson of Texas Woman's University. For their support we thank: Suzann Buckley, Dean of Arts and Sciences, and Hugh Burns, Chair of English, Speech and Foreign Languages at Texas Woman's University; and Ralph Pearson, Vice President for Academic Affairs, and Michael Mikolajczak, Chair of English at University of St. Thomas.

Finally, we wish to give special thanks to the editorial, marketing, and production staff at Harcourt College Publishers: Claire Brantley, Acquisitions Editor; Michell Phifer, Senior Developmental Editor; John Meyers, Marketing Strategist; Jon Davies, Project Editor; Sue Hart, Senior Art Director; Angela Williams Urquhart, Production Manager; and Linda Beaupre, Assistant Manager of Art and Design, who created the cover.

Contents

G Grammar

Ⅿ   Mechanics

P : **Punctuation**

Spelling and Diction

Effective Sentences

Writing

Grammar

Chapter

1

Sentence Sense

Sentences are the basic units of language that we use to make statements, ask questions, or express commands. When we write sentences rather than say them, we observe certain customs that tell us where they begin and where they end: we capitalize the first letter of the first word; we place a period (or question mark or exclamation point) at the end. Writing a clear, precise sentence is an art, and one way to master that art is to understand how the various parts of a sentence work together and to use that knowledge to refine your efforts—to revise—so that each sentence says exactly what you want it to say. (For explanations of any unfamiliar terms, see the Glossary of Terms.)

Careful study of this chapter will give you a clearer understanding of

- what the parts of a sentence are,
- how the parts of a sentence work (**1a** and **1b**),
- what the various classes of words are (**1c**),
- how to use certain groups of words (**1d** and **1e**), and
- how to recognize different kinds of sentences (**1f**).

An English sentence divides into two parts.

COMPLETE SUBJECT	+	COMPLETE PREDICATE.
The **plate**	+	**is** clean.
Gabriel	+	**replaced** the bulb in the lamp.

The largest **dog**	+	**was judged** Grand Champion.
A **bird** in the hand	+	**is** worth two in the bush.
The **child**	+	carefully **placed** a dime on top of the quarter.
Our former **dean,** Professor George Smithers,	+	**donated** his entire library to the university.

These parts, the subject and the predicate, are the two essential elements of an English sentence. The **subject** is what the sentence is about and answers the question *Who?* or *What?* The **predicate** says something about the subject (see 1a) and contains a word that expresses action or state of being—a verb. In the sentences above, the boldfaced words identify the subject and the verb. So *replaced* expresses the action the subject, *Gabriel,* took. The verb *is* in the first sentence links the subject, *plate,* with *clean* to express the state of the plate, and so on. The pattern is **SUBJECT + PREDICATE,** which is the usual order of English sentences.

1a Verbs form the essential part of the predicate of a sentence.

A verb is a word that expresses action or state of being and that often, but not always, ends in *-s* or *-ed.*

Chandra **writes.** [verb by itself]

Chandra **writes** clearly. [verb plus a word that describes, limits, or qualifies (modifies) the verb]

Verbs can be compound, that is, composed of more than one verb.

> Chandra **writes** and **speaks** clearly.

You will sometimes find that a verb has more than one word. An additional verb, a helping verb, is often called an **auxiliary** or *verb marker.* The verbs *have* and *be* are auxiliaries and follow the pattern of **AUXILIARY + VERB.** Verbs such as *can—could, may—might,* and *shall—will* (**modal** verbs) follow the same pattern and express such things as ability or possibility; *shall—will* expresses future tense. (See chapter 7 for a complete discussion of verbs.)

> The film **had started** by then.
>
> She **will be arriving** at noon.
>
> Mara **should go** now.

Other words sometimes intervene between the auxiliary and the verb.

> I **have** not **bought** my ticket.
>
> Television **has** still not completely **replaced** radio.

Phrasal verbs   Verbs that combine with words such as *at, in, out, up,* and the like (often called **particles**) function in the same ways that single-word verbs or verbs with auxiliaries do. However, the meaning of the combined verb is different from that of the single-word verb. For example, the meaning of the verb *turned* is different from the meaning of the combination *turned out.*

> Martha **turned** the car **out of the way.** [prepositional phrase modifying the verb *turned*]
>
> Nothing **turned out** the way she expected. [phrasal verb meaning *happened*]

Some examples of verbs with particles are *look up, burn down, phase out, turn off, watch out, put off, try on.* In sentences such as the following, a phrasal verb can sometimes be separated from its accompanying preposition.

She **looked up** the word in the dictionary. [The parts of a phrasal verb are usually side by side.]

She **looked** the word **up** in the dictionary. [The word the verb acts on may come between the parts of the phrasal verb.]

OR

She **looked** it **up** in the dictionary.

The meanings of phrasal verbs can be found in a good ESL dictionary, such as *The Longman Dictionary of Contemporary English.* This type of dictionary will also tell you whether the phrasal verb can be separated. Make sure you do not rely on a translation dictionary for this type of activity. (See chapter 19, pages 267–68 for a list of ESL dictionaries.)

Although most phrasal verbs can be separated, there are some that cannot: *back down, off, out; call on; drop out (of); fool around (with); get along (with); grow up; keep on; look out (for); put up with; run into, out of; watch out (for).*

1b Subjects, objects, and complements can be nouns, pronouns, or word groups serving as nouns.

Nouns name persons, places, things, ideas, animals, and so on. **Pronouns** stand for nouns. Normally, nouns and pronouns that come after the verb and that are influenced by it or complete its meaning are called **objects** or **complements.**

Sentence Sense

(1) Subjects of verbs can be nouns, pronouns, or noun phrases.

Grammatically complete sentences contain a subject. Except for commands or requests (imperatives) in which the subject, *you,* may be understood, those subjects take the form of nouns, pronouns, or groups of words serving as nouns. In the following sentences, the subjects are in boldface and the verbs are in italics.

> **Georgia** *produces* delicious peaches.
>
> *Does* **South Carolina** also *produce* peaches?

Subjects of verbs may be compound.

> **Georgia** and **South Carolina** grow peaches. [compound subject]

In commands or requests, the subject is often understood.

> [**You**] *Take* my luggage to my room. [command]
>
> [**You**] Please *come* to see me when you're in town. [request]

To identify the grammatical subject of a sentence, find the verb and then use it in a question beginning with *who* or *what,* as shown in the following examples.

The runner leaped the hurdle.	The book was read by Nan.
Verb: **leaped**	Verb: **was read**
WHO leaped? **The runner** (not the hurdle) **leaped.**	WHAT was read? **The book** (not Nan) **was read.**
Subject: **runner**	Subject: **book**

Subjects usually come before verbs in sentences. In questions, however, and after the words *there* and sometimes *it* (these are called **expletives**—words that fill out a sentence without altering its meaning), the subject comes after the verb.

> **Was** the **book** interesting? [verb + subject—a question]
>
> There **were** no **refusals.** [there (expletive) + verb + subject]

It **is** not easy **to study** on a sunny spring day. [it (expletive) + verb + infinitive subject]

(2) Objects of verbs are nouns, pronouns, or word groups serving as nouns.

Direct objects

Verbs that express action often require a noun or a pronoun— a **direct object**—to receive or show the result of the action. (See **7a(4)**.) In the following sentence, the objects are in bold-face.

Martin bought three **books.** [direct object: *books*]

To identify a direct object, find the subject and the verb and then use them in a question ending with *whom* or *what,* as shown in the following example.

Juana silently took his hand.

Subject and verb:	**Juana took**
Juana took WHAT?	**hand**
Direct object:	**hand**

Direct objects in sentences like the following are directly affected by the action of the verb.

Hurricane Andrew ravaged Miami. [The subject, *Hurricane Andrew,* acts. The object, *Miami,* receives the action.]

Knowing how to change a verb from *active* to *passive voice* can also help you identify an object. When you make an active verb passive, its object becomes the subject of the passive verb. The original subject is either omitted or incorporated into a phrase beginning with *by.* (See the examples on pages 114–15 and 128 of chapter **7** and in **29d(1)**.)

Active   The blizzard **buried Chicago.** [*Chicago* is the direct object of *buried.*]

Passive	**Chicago was buried.** [*Chicago* is the subject of *buried;* the original subject is omitted.]
Passive	**Chicago was buried** by the blizzard. [The original subject is incorporated into a prepositional phrase.]

A form of *be* (such as *is, are, was*) is added when an active verb becomes passive.

Indirect objects

Sometimes an **indirect object**—a word that shows to whom or for whom the action occurred—comes between the verb and the direct object.

> Martin bought **me** three **books.** [indirect object: *me;* direct object: *books*]

Like the subjects of verbs, direct and indirect objects can be nouns, pronouns, or groups of words used as nouns.

Some verbs (such as *bring, buy, give, lend, offer, sell, send,* and *take*) can have both a direct object and an indirect object.

> Linda gave Felipé a new bicycle. [subject + verb + direct object: **Linda + gave + bicycle.**]

> Linda gave a bicycle TO WHOM? **Felipé** [indirect object: **Felipé**]

Direct and indirect objects of verbs can be compound.

> He eats only **vegetables** and **fruit.** [compound direct object]

> We offered **Elena** and **Octavio** a year's membership. [compound indirect object]

(3) Subject and object complements may be nouns, pronouns, word groups serving as nouns, or adjectives.

Nouns, pronouns, and words that limit, identify, or qualify nouns and pronouns (adjectives) are used as subject and object complements. (See **1c**.) A **subject complement** refers to, identifies, or qualifies the subject and helps complete the meaning of the forms of *be* (*am, is, are, was, were, been*), linking verbs (such as *become, seem*), and sensory verbs (such as *feel, look, smell, sound, taste*). When verbs do not take direct objects, they are often called **intransitive verbs.** (See **7a(4)**.)

Leilani is my **sister.** [*Sister,* a noun, identifies *Leilani,* the subject.]

Violence became **inevitable.** [*Inevitable,* an adjective, describes or qualifies *violence,* the subject.]

The rose smelled **sweet.** [*Sweet,* an adjective, describes *rose.*]

An **object complement** refers to, identifies, or qualifies the direct object. Object complements help complete the meaning of verbs such as *call, elect, make, name,* and *paint.*

Today, we call Einstein a **genius.** [*Genius,* a noun, is an object complement renaming *Einstein.*]

The benefits make the job **desirable.** [*Desirable,* an adjective, is an object complement describing *job.*]

(4) Word order determines the meaning of a word in a sentence.

Becoming thoroughly aware of English word order—usually **SUBJECT + VERB + OBJECT** or **COMPLEMENT**—will help you recognize subjects, objects, and complements. If you look carefully at the five most common sentence patterns, you will see how important word order is and how a change in word order results in a change in meaning. Notice also that when you turn a statement into a question, the subject and verb may be reversed and the direct object does not always take the position indicated by the basic pattern.

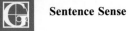
Pattern 1	**SUBJECT + VERB.**

 s   *v*
Most parents worry.

 s   *v*
The air in the room smelled.

Variant	*aux* *s* *v*

Do parents worry?

Pattern 2	**SUBJECT + VERB + OBJECT.**

 s   *v*   *do*
My cat terrorizes their dog.

 s   *v*   *do*
Their dog terrorizes my cat.

 s   *v*   *do*
A Chinese skater nearly won a gold medal.

Variant	*do* *aux* *s* *v*

What did a Chinese skater nearly win?

Pattern 3	**SUBJECT + VERB + INDIRECT OBJECT + DIRECT OBJECT.**

 s   *v*   *io*   *do*
Lissa showed Aaron her prize.

 s   *v*   *io*   *do*
Professor Crowl taught me physics.

Variant	*do* *aux* *s* *v* *io*

What did Professor Crowl teach me?

Pattern 4	**SUBJECT + LINKING VERB + SUBJECT COMPLEMENT.**

 s   *v*   *sc*
Derek is Marcus's son.

 s   *v*   *sc*
Joe DiMaggio was a hero.

Variant	*sc* *v* *s*

What was Joe DiMaggio?

Pattern 5	**SUBJECT + VERB + DIRECT OBJECT + OBJECT COMPLEMENT.**

        s   *v*   *do* *oc*
Marcus named his son Derek.
    s   *v*   *do*   *oc*
We called Joe DiMaggio a hero.

Variant   *oc* *aux* *s*   *v*   *do*
What did they call Joe DiMaggio?

EXERCISE 1

Label all subjects and verbs (including auxiliaries) in the following sentences.

1. Some companies require no real safety compliance.
2. Safety regulations once ignored become useless.
3. The workers must take off their normal clothing and put on protective gear.
4. The company has suffered a disaster.
5. In the newspaper article, the journalist gives us a detailed description of the latest industrial accident and its environmental consequences.
6. Clean air and a safe environment make workers confident and keep management satisfied.
7. The new manager suggests that the employees revise their former work habits.
8. The company has not always sought suggestions from workers.
9. There was one astonishing and peculiar suggestion.
10. Safety regulations, particularly government rules, give workers a sense of security but can be difficult to understand.

EXERCISE 2

Label all direct and indirect objects and complements in the sentences in exercise 1.

E X E R C I S E 3

Identify the basic sentence patterns (and any variations) of the sentences in exercise 1.

1c Understanding the traditional parts of speech provides vocabulary for discussing writing.

Verbs, nouns, adjectives, and adverbs (called **vocabulary** or **lexical words**) make up more than 99 percent of all words listed in the dictionary. But pronouns, prepositions, and conjunctions—although few in number—are important because they are used over and over in speaking and writing. Interjections express such feelings as surprise. Prepositions and conjunctions (called **function** or **structure words**) connect and relate other parts of speech. Prepositions, conjunctions, and interjections do not change form or function. (For a summary of the form changes of the other parts of speech, see inflection in the Glossary of Terms.)

The chart below shows the forms and functions of the various parts of speech in a sentence. These forms and functions are also discussed on the following pages. (See the corresponding entries in the Glossary of Terms as well.)

To demonstrate a computer program to her friends, my sister patiently gave them detailed directions.

	Form	Function	Part of Speech
To demonstrate	infinitive	modifies *gave*	adverb
a	invariable	determiner	adjective (article)

computer	singular	modifies *program*	adjectival noun modifying *program*
program	singular	obj. of infinitive	noun
to	invariable	connector	preposition
her	possessive	modifies *friends*	pronoun
friends	-*s* (plural)	obj. of preposition	noun
my	possessive	modifies *sister*	pronoun
sister	singular	subject	noun
patiently	-*ly* ending	modifies *gave*	adverb
gave	past	predicate	verb
them	objective	indirect obj.	pronoun
detailed	-*ed* ending	modifies *directions*	adjective
directions	-*s* (plural)	direct obj.	noun

Here, one part of speech—the noun (a naming word that forms the plural with -*s* and the possessive with *'s* or *s'*)—is used as a subject, a direct object, a modifier, and an object of a preposition.

A dictionary labels words according to their parts of speech. Some words have only one classification—for example, *notify* (verb), *sleepy* (adjective), *practically* (adverb). Others have more than one label because they can function as two or more parts of speech. The label of a word therefore depends on how it is used in a given sentence. For example, the following sentences show how the word *up,* usually viewed as an adverb or preposition, can be used as almost any of the parts of speech. (It cannot be used as a pronoun or conjunction.)

They dragged the sled **up** the hill. [preposition]

She follows the **ups** and downs of the market. [noun]

"They have **upped** the rent again," he complained. [verb]

Kelly ran **up** the bill. [part of a phrasal verb]

The **up** escalator is broken again. [adjective]

Hopkins says to look **up** at the skies! [adverb]

The following chart lists some words showing the common endings that mark different parts of speech.

Verb	Noun	Adjective	Adverb
correlate	correlation	correlated	
motivate	motivation	motivational	motivationally
	motivator		
	motive		
negotiate	negotiation	negotiated	
	negotiator		
progress	progress	progressive	progressively
recognize	recognition	recognizable	recognizably
		recognized	
sense	sensation	sensory	
	sense		
validate	validation	valid	validly
	validity		

(1) Verbs have traditionally been defined as words that show action or being.

notify, notifies, is notifying, notified
write, writes, is writing, wrote, has written

Verb-making suffixes are *-ize* and *-ify:* terror (noun) becomes *terrorize, terrify* (verbs); *real* (adjective) becomes *realize* (verb).

A verb can consist of one or more words, and it forms an essential part of the predicate. (See **1a**.)

He **is writing** those dull stories again.

A new street gang **terrorized** our neighborhood.

I **tripped** on the step and **stumbled** into the room.

Phrasal verbs (verbs combined with prepositions) function just as single-word verbs do. (See **1c(6)**.)

Joseph **turned out** the light.

Verbals are words derived from verbs but used as nouns, adjectives, or adverbs. A **gerund** is a verbal noun ending in *-ing*. It functions like any other noun. An **infinitive** is a verbal signaled by *to* and used as a noun, an adjective, or an adverb. A **participle** is a verbal adjective ending in *-ing* or *-ed*.

Using a computer is simple. [gerund]

I love **to run.** [infinitive]

I stop at **blinking** lights. I bought a **used** computer. [participles]

(2) Nouns have traditionally named persons, places, things, ideas, animals, and so on.

nation, nations, nation's, nations'
woman, women, woman's, women's
kindness, kindnesses
Carthage, United States, William, NASA
breakthrough, buddy system, sister-in-law

Noun-making suffixes are *-ance, -ation, -ence, -ism, -ity, -ment, -ness,* and *-ship: relax* and *depend* (verbs) become *relaxation* and *dependence* (nouns); *kind* and *rigid* (adjectives) become *kindness* and *rigidity* (nouns).

A noun may function as subject, object, complement, appositive (a word or phrase that supplements the meaning of a noun), and modifier, as well as in absolute expressions (phrases that are grammatically independent of the rest of the sentence) and in direct address (expressions directing speech to particular persons). The articles *a, an,* and *the* signal that a noun is to follow (a *chair,* an *activity*).

Russell sent a **check** to the **Alzheimer's Foundation.**

Groups of words such as *father-in-law, Labor Day,* and *swimming pool* generally refer to a single thing and so are classified as *compound nouns.*

 Count/Noncount Nouns (See 22a(1) *for the use of articles.)*

Count nouns are words that represent individual items that can be counted and cannot be viewed as a mass, such as *book, child,* or *atom.* Count nouns can be either singular or plural and, when plural, are preceded by words such as *few, a few, many, a number,* and *several.* Use either indefinite (*a, an*) or definite articles (*the*) with count nouns.

Noncount nouns, such as *humor* or *furniture,* represent an abstract concept, a mass, or a collection and do not have an individual existence. Modifiers such as *much* or *a little* can be used with noncount nouns, but *a* or *an* never can. Noncount nouns cannot usually be plural.

(3) A pronoun is a word that can substitute for a noun or a noun phrase—a noun and any of its modifiers.

I, me, my, mine, myself; you, your, yours, yourself
he, him, his, himself; she, her, hers, herself; it, its
we, us, our; they, them, their, theirs

this, these; who, whom, whose; which, that
one, ones; everybody, anyone

Pronouns change form according to their function. You cannot add anything to a pronoun to make it into another part of speech, and you cannot create a pronoun or use any other word as a pronoun. (See chapter 5.)

She sent **it** to **them.**

Someone said **that.**

(4) Adjectives modify or qualify pronouns and words, phrases, or clauses used as nouns.

shy, sleepy, attractive, famous, historic
three men, *this* class, *another* one
young, younger, youngest; good, better, best

Adjective-making suffixes are *-al, -able, -ant, -ative, -ic, -ish, -less, -ous, -y: accept* and *repent* (verbs) become *acceptable* and *repentant* (adjectives); *angel* and *effort* (nouns) become *angelic* and *effortless* (adjectives).

Generally, adjectives appear immediately before the words they modify, including before gerunds. (See page 15.)

Certain expensive parts make this imported car a poor choice.

The **unusual** prickling of my scalp warned me of the danger. [*Prickling* is a gerund.]

In the following example, the adjective *graceful* functions as a subject complement, a word that modifies the subject and helps complete the meaning of the sentence. (See 4a and chapter 7.)

In competition, gymnasts must look **graceful.**

The articles *a, an,* and *the* are often classified as adjectives although they are very different from typical adjectives such as *tall* and *happy* and are more properly called **determiners**— words that point to nouns. Nouns that function as modifiers are also often reclassified as adjectives. (See 1c(2).)

Sentence Sense

(5) Adverbs modify verbs, adjectives, and other adverbs.

rarely saw, call *daily, soon* left, left *sooner*
very short, *too* angry, *never* shy, *not* fearful
practically never loses, *nearly always* cold

The adverb-making suffix is *-ly: rare* (adjective) becomes *rarely* (adverb).

Luis **rarely** saw his sister.

Kendra was **too** short to reach the top of the cabinet.

Li **nearly always** turns her work in on time.

Adverbs also modify verbals, phrases, or clauses used as nouns, adjectives, or adverbs.

They wanted to leave **soon.** [modifies the infinitive *to leave*]

The book **almost** under the sofa is the one I want. [modifies the phrase *under the sofa*]

Understandably, my family was concerned about me, but they needn't have worried. [modifies the independent clause *my family was concerned about me*]

Sometimes an adverb does not modify any word in the sentence. When that is the case, it is said to modify the sentences as a whole and is called a *sentence modifier.* It is separated from the rest of the sentence by a comma.

Honestly, Jo wasn't speeding.

In fact, I wasn't even there.

(6) Prepositions set up relationships between words.

on a shelf, *between* us, *because* of rain
to the door, *by* them, *before* class

In addition to establishing relationships, prepositions have objects. The object of a preposition is usually a noun or a pronoun (except when the preposition is part of a phrasal verb such as *look up*).

Some Common Prepositions

about	beneath	in	regarding
above	beside	inside	round
across	between	into	since
after	beyond	like	through
against	by	near	to
among	concerning	of	toward
around	despite	off	under
as	down	on	unlike
at	during	out	until
before	except	outside	up
behind	for	over	upon
below	from	past	with

The preposition establishes a relationship such as space, time, accompaniment, cause, or manner between the object of the preposition and another part of the sentence. A preposition combined with its object (and any modifiers) is called a **prepositional phrase.**

> **With** great feeling, Martin Luther King, Jr., expressed his dream **of** freedom. [*With great feeling* tells us about King's manner, and *of freedom* makes the kind of dream specific.]

A preposition may follow rather than precede its object, and it can be placed at the end of the sentence.

> What were you thinking **about** yesterday? [*What* is the object of the preposition. COMPARE Yesterday, you were thinking about what?]

Some prepositions, called **phrasal prepositions,** can contain more than one word.

> **Except for** the last day, it was a wonderful trip.

The following list contains the most commonly used phrasal prepositions.

Sentence Sense

Phrasal Prepositions (Two or More Words)

according to	by way of	in spite of
along with	due to	instead of
apart from	except for	on account of
as for	in addition to	out of
as regards	in case of	up to
as to	in front of	with reference to
because of	in lieu of	with regard to
by means of	in place of	with respect to
by reason of	in regard to	with the exception of

 Some prepositions, such as *by/until* and *except/besides,* pose special problems. *Until* indicates a continuing situation that will come to an end at a definite time in the future. *By* indicates an action that will happen at or before a particular time in the future.

I will finish my work **by** six o'clock.

I will be away **until** next Tuesday.

Besides means *with* or *plus* and usually "includes," while *except* means *without* or *minus* and usually "excludes."

Besides a salad, we had soup and crackers.

We had everything we wanted **except** a salad.

(For other problems with prepositions, consult the Glossary of Usage or one of the ESL resources listed in chapter 19 on pages 267–68.)

(7) Conjunctions are connectors.

cars *and* trucks; *neither* Martha *nor* Debbie
after Lisa graduated; *why* the dog ran away

Coordinating conjunctions and **correlatives** join sentence elements (single words, groups of words lacking a subject or predicate—phrases—or groups of words having a subject and a predicate—clauses). (See **26c**.)

| coordinating | *and, but, for, nor, or, so, yet* |
| correlative | *both—and, either—or, neither—nor, not only—but also, whether—or* |

in the boat **or** on the pier

will try **but** may lose

neither Ana **nor** Miguel

Subordinating conjunctions join subordinate clauses to independent clauses. (See **1e**.)

I worked **because** Dad needed money.

The river rises **when** the snow melts.

Subordinating Conjunctions

after	in case	supposing that
although	in that	than
as (far/soon) as	inasmuch as	though
as if	insofar as	till
as though	lest	unless
because	no matter how	until
before	now that	when, whenever
even if	once	where, wherever
even though	provided (that)	whether
how	since	while
if	so that	why

Words like *consequently, however, nevertheless, then,* and *therefore* (adverbial conjunctions—see the list on page 53) sometimes link independent clauses.

> Olivia had begged to register for the class; **therefore,** it was odd that she was often absent. [A semicolon is required before and a comma after this use of *therefore;* see **3b** and **14a.**]

(8) Interjections are expressions of surprise or strong feeling.

Interjections can be followed by an exclamation point or by a comma.

> **Oops! Oh,** that's wonderful.

EXERCISE 4

Identify the part of speech for each word according to its use in the sentence.

1. We floated down the river toward the whitewater rapids.
2. Neither danger nor fear could keep our friends from joining us on this trip.
3. Phyllis picked Terry to be her companion on the river and then tried to pick on her until the trip was over.
4. She criticized Terry's paddling technique, chided her behavior, and offered herself as a model specimen of the ideal outdoor athlete.
5. To avoid Phyllis, Terry helped the guides during lunch and when they set up camp every evening.

1d A phrase is a group of words that can function as a single part of speech.

A word group that does not have a subject or a predicate and that functions as a single part of speech (noun, verb, adjective, adverb) is a **phrase.** Phrases that function as adjectives or adverbs often expand a short, simple sentence. (See **1c(4–5).**)

Phrases are generally classified either by their function (verb, noun, appositive, absolute, or prepositional phrase that acts as an adjective or adverb) or by their form (gerund, infinitive, participle).

Type of Phrase by Function	Examples
Verb phrases	The flowers **have wilted.**
	Have you **watered** them?
	Gerald **has looked up** the word.
	I **might have been told.**
Noun phrases	**The heavy frost** killed **fruit trees.**
	They elected Alexandra **vice president.**
Appositive phrases	John, **my brother,** is here today.
	June 21, **the longest day of the year,** is my birthday.
Absolute phrases	**The lunch having been packed,** we were ready to go.
	The star gymnast left the building, **reporters following her eagerly.**
Prepositional phrases	Parking **on campus** is prohibited.
	We were racing **against time.**

Noun phrases serve as subjects, objects, and complements, while **verb phrases** serve as predicates. **Prepositional phrases** modify nouns, pronouns, adjectives, adverbs, or verbs, and **absolute phrases** modify sentences. **Appositive phrases**

Sentence Sense

substitute for and expand the meaning of nouns: Millicent, *my oldest sister.*

Type of Phrase by Form	Examples
Gerund phrases	**Swimming across the lake** is fun.
	They loved **playing in the water.**
Infinitive phrases	He wanted **to start immediately.**
	He asked me **to go with him.**
Participial phrases	**Exploring the beach,** we found many treasures.
	The picnic ground, **covered with trash,** looked pretty bad.

As you learn to recognize phrases, give special attention to verb forms in word groups that are used as nouns, adjectives, or adverbs. Although such verb forms (called **verbals**) are much like verbs because they have different tenses, can take subjects and objects, and can be modified by adverbs, they can serve only as modifiers or noun phrases.

Students **standing around** did not ask questions. [participial phrase, *standing around,* modifying the noun *students*]

Some organizations serve their communities by **picking up trash** on nearby highways. [gerund phrase, *picking up trash,* serving as the object of the preposition *by*]

We just received the forty new computers **ordered for an open access lab.** [participial phrase, *ordered for an open access lab,* modifying the noun *computers*]

To graduate early had become a necessity for Marissa. [infinitive phrase, *to graduate early,* serving as the subject of the sentence.]

CAUTION Infinitives, participles, and gerunds cannot function as the verb in a sentence.

(1) Phrases may be used as subjects and objects.

Gerund phrases are always used as subjects or objects, and **infinitive phrases** often are (although they can also function as modifiers). A **prepositional phrase** can also occasionally serve as a subject or object ("*After supper* is too late!").

Nouns	**Phrases Used as Subjects or Objects**
A talented **singer** practices constantly.	**Singing beautifully** requires constant practice. [gerund phrase—subject]
She likes **collaboration.**	She likes **to work in a group.** [infinitive phrase—direct object]
He works best in **silence.**	He prefers silence for **working efficiently.** [gerund phrase—object of a preposition]
She wants only two things: a **degree** and **admission** to law school.	She wants only two things: **to graduate and to go to law school.** [infinitive phrases in a compound appositive]

An **appositive phrase** identifies, explains, or supplements the meaning of the word it refers to.

Johnnycake, **a kind of cornbread,** is a New England specialty.

(2) Phrases may be used as modifiers.

Prepositional phrases nearly always modify nouns or verbs, and **infinitive phrases** can also function as modifiers.

Sentence Sense

Participial phrases generally modify nouns, and **absolute phrases** function as adverbial modifiers. (See sentence modifier in the Glossary of Terms.)

Adjectives	**Phrases Used to Modify Nouns**
It was a **sad** day.	It was a day **for sadness.** [prepositional phrase]
A **destructive** tornado roared through the city.	**Destroying everything in its path,** a tornado roared through the city. [participial phrase containing a prepositional phrase]
My **wet** clothes felt cold.	**Soaked with water,** my clothes felt cold. [participial phrase containing a prepositional phrase]

Adverbs	**Phrases Used as Adverbial Modifiers**
Spend **wisely.**	Spend **by making wise decisions.** [prepositional phrase]
She sang **joyfully.**	She sang **to express her joy.** [infinitive phrase]
Today I could feel the warm sun on my face.	**My eyes shaded against the glare,** I felt the warm sun on my face. [absolute phrase]

The preceding examples demonstrate that although phrases function like single-word modifiers, they are not merely substitutes for single words. Phrases can express more than can be packed into a single word: they can highlight the main idea or deemphasize less important information.

Placing a phrase at the beginning or end of a sentence gives extra emphasis to it. Generally, unless there are reasons for placing them elsewhere, phrases occur immediately before or after the word they modify.

EXERCISE 5

Work through all of the sentences in this exercise, doing first part A and then part B.

A. Underline each phrase in the following passage.
B. Note whether the phrase functions as a noun, an adjective, an adverb, or an appositive.

[1]Within the past few years, more science fiction movies, many of which deal with issues surrounding the Internet, have appeared at theaters. [2]This increase has occurred despite science fiction's previous reputation, negative but perhaps accurate, which suggested that most of its fans were incredibly brainy but socially inept teenage boys. [3]Such a reputation, whatever its negative overtones may have been, is currently undergoing a change. [4]Indeed, some movies, including the films *Hackers* and *The Net,* directly contradict the implications suggested by this reputation, and they suggest that such young men are "cool," particularly if they have computer expertise. [5]In fact, this trend may be changing primarily because the use of computers is more common and popular than ever before.

[6]Although computers, too, are often associated with brainy young men, sociological reality is changing this notion as well. [7]In fact, the heroines of several recent films depicting the near future are brainy young women, one example being the female lead in *Hackers.* [8]Indeed, her character, surrounded by teenaged male geniuses, is the one who possesses the most sophisticated computer knowledge. [9]This increase in female roles and characters may help account for the genre's ever-increasing popularity.

1e Recognizing clauses helps in analyzing sentences.

A clause is a group of related words that contains a subject and a predicate.

(1) Independent clauses can stand alone.

An **independent clause** has the same grammatical structure as a simple sentence; both contain a subject and a predicate. In the example below, the independent clauses are in bold.

> **The boy chased the dog.**
>
> **He couldn't catch him.**

Independent clauses can be combined with other independent clauses or with dependent clauses to form sentences.

> **The boy chased the dog,** but **he couldn't catch him.** [two independent clauses]
>
> Although the boy chased the dog, **he couldn't catch him.** [a subordinate clause and an independent clause]

(2) Subordinate clauses must be attached to an independent clause.

A **subordinate clause** is a group of related words that contains a subject and a predicate but cannot stand alone. In the example below, the subordinate clause is in bold.

> Maria received the gold medal **because her performance was flawless.**

Subordinate clauses provide additional information about the independent clause and establish the relationship between the additional information and the independent clause. A subordinate clause is grammatically dependent and functions within a sentence as a modifier or as a subject or object.

> The last ship carrying passengers had recently arrived in the Ross Sea, **which was closed by ice most of the year.** [clause modifying *Ross Sea*]
>
> I needed to get to the meeting early **because I wanted to pick my seat.** [clause modifying the entire independent clause *I needed . . . early*]

Astronomers don't know **what black holes really are.** [clause serving as the direct object of *know*]

A subordinate clause usually begins with a conjunction that introduces, connects, and relates the clause to other words in the sentence. A **subordinating conjunction** is a word such as *after, when, because, although.* (See **1c(7)**, page 21 for a list of subordinating conjunctions.)

Relative pronouns also serve as markers of those subordinate clauses called **relative clauses.** (See chapter **5**, page 74.)

that	which	whom, whomever
what	who, whoever	whose

Subordinate clauses used as subjects or objects

Nouns	**Noun Clauses**
The **testimony** may not be true.	**What the witness said** may not be true. [subject]
We do not understand their **motives.**	We do not understand **why they did it.** [direct object]
Send the money to **charity.**	Send the money to **whoever needs it most.** [object of the preposition]
Karen's **protest** worried me.	The fact **that Karen protested** worried me. [appositive]

When no misunderstanding would result, the conjunction *that* before a noun clause can often be omitted because it is understood.

I think they were wrong.

Subordinate clauses used as modifiers

Two types of subordinate clauses—adjectival clauses and adverbial clauses—serve as modifiers.

Adjectival clauses Any clause that answers the questions *which one, what kind of,* or *how many* about a noun or a pronoun is an adjectival clause. Such clauses, which nearly always follow the words they modify, usually begin with a relative pronoun but may sometimes begin with words such as *when, where,* or *why.*

Adjectives	Adjectival Clauses
Nobody likes **malicious** gossip.	Nobody likes information **that pries into people's private lives.**
Some **sensible** students study for tests beginning on the first day of classes.	Students **who know how to make good grades** study for tests beginning on the first day of classes.
My sister lives in a **peaceful** town.	The town **where my sister lives** is peaceful.

A relative pronoun (*who, whom, that, which,* and so on) can sometimes be omitted from an adjectival clause if it is not used as the subject.

> Mother Teresa was a woman the whole world admired. [COMPARE She was a woman *whom I admired.*]

Adverbial clauses An adverbial clause usually answers the questions *where, when, how,* and *in what condition* about a verb, an adjective, an adverb, or even the rest of the sentence in which it appears. Adverbial clauses are ordinarily introduced by subordinating conjunctions.

Adverbs	Adverbial Clauses
As a result, the company hired six new writers.	**Because its annual report was criticized,** the company hired six new writers.
He packed for his vacation **quickly.**	He packed for his vacation **after he called a taxi.**

Some adverbial clauses may omit words that are obviously understood (elliptical clauses). (See **25b(3)**.)

ITEM CHARGED

Patron: Lesilyn Ellinwood
Patron Group: SMWC Undergrad

Due Date: 12/15/2004 02:00 AM

Title: Bonhoeffer, exile and
                martyr / Eberhard
                Bethge ; edited and with
                an essay by John W. de
                Gruchy.
Author:
Call Number: BX4827 .B57B39
Enumeration:
Chronology:
Copy: 1
Item Barcode: 30000000315734

If I can find a cheap place to live, I'll spend the summer at the shore. **If not,** I'll have to stay home and swelter in the city. [Clearly implied words are omitted.]

E X E R C I S E 6

A. Underline the independent clauses in the following paragraph.
B. Place brackets around the subordinate clauses and label each as a noun clause, an adjectival clause, or an adverbial clause.

[1]The late 1970s are most often remembered for disco music and polyester styles, tacky as they may have been. [2]Still, an aggressive kind of music, different from the popular disco styles, was coming out of Austin, Texas, at the time. [3]This new sound—punk—had grown out of the music of other bands, earlier British punk bands. [4]A club named Raul's became very popular, spawning a surge in the local music scene, and very soon Austin was swamped with new bands, all playing their original songs to devoted fans as well as other musicians.

[5]The punk movement, ever in opposition to disco, took on a decidedly nonpolyester look. [6]In fact, the look was very different, usually consisting of a torn white T-shirt, scruffy jeans, a leather biker jacket, spiked hair, and safety pins, many of which were strategically placed.

[7]The movement thrived in Austin for about seven or eight years, but was hindered by the closing of Raul's, which had been sold by its aging owner. [8]While this event reduced the number of places where new bands could play, fresh, original music continued to live in Austin, a town still known for being on the cutting edge of music.

1f Sentences may be analyzed by form and function.

The form of a sentence is identified by the number and kinds of clauses it contains. The function of a sentence refers to its purpose.

(1) There are four sentence forms.

a. A **simple sentence** consists of a single independent clause.

   I [subject] **totaled my car.** [A simple subject is followed by a predicate containing a verb and a direct object.]

b. A **compound sentence** consists of at least two independent clauses and no subordinate clauses.

   I totaled my car, so **I bought a new one.** [A comma and a coordinating conjunction (*so*) link the two independent clauses.]

c. A **complex sentence** has one independent clause and at least one subordinate clause.

   Because I totaled my car, I bought a new one. [A subordinate clause—signaled here by *because* and ended by a comma (see **12b**)—precedes the independent clause.]

d. A **compound-complex sentence** consists of at least two independent clauses and at least one subordinate clause.

   I totaled my car, so I bought a new one, **even though I had planned to wait.** [*So* connects the two independent clauses; *even though* signals the subordinate clause.]

(2) Sentences have four functions.

English sentences make statements (**declarative**), ask questions (**interrogative**), give commands or make requests (**imperative**), and make exclamations (**exclamatory**).

Declarative	He answered a hard question. [statement]
Imperative	Answer the question now. [request or command]
Interrogative	Did he answer the hard question? He answered, didn't he? He answered it? [questions]
Exclamatory	What a hard question you asked! And he answered it! [exclamations]

Be aware of the forms and functions of the sentences you read and note how writers achieve particular effects. (See chapter **30.**) In your own writing, think about what you want your readers to understand and revise each sentence to express your thoughts most effectively.

E X E R C I S E **7**

This exercise is an opportunity to practice what you have learned throughout this chapter by analyzing the following passage.

A. Identify the form (simple, compound, complex, or compound-complex) of each sentence.
B. Identify the function (declarative, interrogative, imperative, or exclamatory) of each sentence.
C. Identify and label the independent and subordinate clauses.

[1]Certainly something had to be done. [2]Just think: Matthew and Nathan had told me four times in as many minutes just how bored they were and how much they really didn't appreciate it. [3]I have to think of something for them to do, I mused, looking at the pile of books on the table in front of me, since whether they were bored, or I was bored, or we were all bored, I was sure of one inescapable fact: I had to finish reading six chapters for an exam the following day.

[4]As I saw it, the best way to handle their boredom was to get them to go outside and play; I suggested this because I was at my wits' end, and I was relieved when they hurried outside.

[5]In fact, they were ecstatic! [6]Had they been, perhaps, waiting until I gave them my seal of approval? [7]Were they behaving like frustrated, lazy couch potatoes merely because they were afraid they'd anger me by asking to go outside? [8]At that point, I decided it was time for a break, so I, too, went outside and joined in their fun.

E X E R C I S E **8**

A. Write a sentence for each of the types listed below.

1. A simple sentence that makes a statement
2. A compound sentence that makes a statement
3. A complex sentence that makes a statement
4. A simple sentence that gives a command

5. A compound sentence that gives a command
6. A complex sentence that gives a command
7. A simple sentence that asks a question
8. A complex sentence that asks a question
9. A compound-complex sentence that makes a statement
10. A simple sentence that is an exclamation

B. Identify the independent and subordinate clauses in your sentences and label the subordinate clauses as noun, adjective, or adverb.

Chapter
2 Sentence Fragments

The information in this chapter can help you

- recognize fragments and
- revise fragments resulting from incorrectly punctuated phrases (**2a**) and clauses (**2b**).

A **fragment,** an incomplete sentence starting with a capital and ending with a period, is usually avoided in college and professional writing. Fragments lack a subject or verb, or both, but can still be difficult to recognize within the context of surrounding sentences.

> He enjoys flowers and shrubs. **Which help screen his yard from the street.**

> **Having driven across the desert.** We enjoyed the cool weather.

Fragments are often phrases or clauses beginning with a word (subordinating conjunction or relative pronoun) that marks them as subordinate. In the above examples, the fragments (in bold) can be corrected by substituting *they* for the subordinator to make an independent sentence or by connecting the phrase to an adjoining sentence.

> He enjoys flowers and shrubs. **They help screen his yard from the street.**

> **Having driven across the desert,** we enjoyed the cool weather.

 Sentences in English must contain a stated subject unless the sentence is an imperative where *you* is the understood subject. Omitting the subject can result in a fragment.

The class w
^Will begin the test at ten.

Begin the test at ten. [imperative, implied *you*]

CAUTION Since fragments are generally considered errors in college writing, it is safer not to use them at all. You may wonder, however, why you often see fragments in the books and magazines you read. Professional writers sometimes deliberately use fragments for literary emphasis, in dialogue, as answers to questions, as transitions, and as exclamations. Fragments are also characteristic of advertising.

> **Understand? Unbelievable! No pain, no gain.** [colloquial use of question with an implied subject (*you*), of exclamation, and of phrases]

> "Tom, when is Camilla leaving for spring break?" "After she gets her car serviced." [colloquial use of a subordinate clause as an answer to a question]

> I don't remember a world without language. From the time of my earliest childhood, there was language. **Always language, and imagination, speculation, utters of sound. Words, beginnings of words.** —SIMON J. ORTIZ [Literary use of phrases. Repetition links the first fragment to the preceding sentence and telegraphs Ortiz's emphasis in the second fragment.]

It is risky to rely on a grammar checker to find fragments. To do that, checkers compare verbs with groups of words that begin with a capital letter and end with a period. When they find a match, they allow the group to pass as a sentence, often even if it begins with a subordinating conjunction. The group may falsely be marked as a fragment if it does not contain a word the checker recognizes as a verb. Thus, computer

2. *Attach the fragment to a related sentence. This method establishes a relationship between the fragment and the sentence it is attached to.*

Archeologists excavating ancient cities carefully brush dirt from the artifacts. *, using* **Using paintbrushes for that purpose.**

Later, Raymond began to tap out the rhythm. *, first* **First on the table and then on the counter.**

My department is looking for a new teacher. *, preferably* **Preferably a writing teacher.**

Mai was the first woman to be elected president of her class. *and* **And tapped for Mortar Board.**

I am interested only in the properties of citrus fruits. *such* **Such as lemons, oranges, and grapefruit.**

EXERCISE 1

Rewrite the following fragments as complete sentences.

1. Many painkillers sold over the counter are anti-inflammatory drugs. Such as aspirin, ibuprofen, ketoprofen, and naproxen sodium.
2. People take anti-inflammatory drugs for various types of pain. For headaches, for joint pain, and for muscle aches.
3. Be aware of drug interactions with anti-inflammatory drugs. To avoid the harmful effects of mixing prescription and over-the-counter painkillers.
4. People who regularly take prescription medications need to be particularly careful. Reading the warnings on the bottle first and then consulting a doctor before taking an anti-inflammatory drug.

5. Anti-inflammatory drugs may interact with certain prescription medications. Such as blood thinners, blood pressure medications, and steroids used for asthma or arthritis.

6. Although an asprin taken daily benefits the blood flow to the heart. It can also thin the blood too much if taken with a prescribed blood thinner.

7. Anti-inflammatory drugs taken with blood thinners and blood pressure medications can increase the risk of bleeding. And raise blood pressure.

8. Taking high doses of anti-inflammatory drugs with steroids may result in ulcers. Because these two types of drugs can thin the lining of the stomach.

9. Anti-inflammatory drugs can cause stomach irritation and bleeding. Especially if mixed with three or more alcoholic beverages during the day.

10. Aspirin can also hinder the absorption of pills taken for diabetes. Leading to significantly decreased blood sugar.

2b You can revise subordinate clauses mistakenly punctuated as sentences in at least three ways.

You can attach them to the sentence they logically belong to by removing the subordinating word or by reducing the clause to a single-word modifier. (See chapter 4.)

1. *Attach the fragment to a related sentence.*

They tried to understand Arturo's objections., which ~~Which~~ were unreasonable.

Arturo discovered that he had made serious mistakes. when ~~When~~ **he forgot to deposit a large payment from a customer and when he wrote a check for more money than he had in the bank.**

OR

Arturo discovered that he had made serious mistakes. **When he forgot to deposit a large payment from a customer, and ~~when~~ he wrote a check for more money than he had in the bank.** [The colon (**17d**) serves as a coordinator, so the subordinating conjunctions are deleted.]

2. *Remove the subordinating word and supply the missing elements.*
They tried to understand Arturo's objections. *The objections* ~~Which~~ were unreasonable.

Arturo   discovered   that   he   had   made   serious   mistakes.
He
~~When~~ he forgot to deposit a large payment from a customer, and ~~when~~ he wrote a check for more money than he had in the bank.

3. *Reduce the fragment to a modifier and include it in the related sentence.*
They tried to understand Arturo's *unreasonable* objections. ~~Which were unreasonable.~~

forgetting to deposit payments and writing overdrafts were
Arturo discovered that ~~he had made~~ serious mistakes. ~~When he forgot to deposit a large payment from a customer and when he wrote a check for more money than he had in the bank.~~

 When the subordinate clause comes first, it is usually separated from the independent clause by a comma. When the subordinate clause is in the second part of the sentence, a comma is not used. Never use a semicolon between a subordinate clause and an independent clause.

> Before Mark goes to bed, he always brushes his teeth.
> [subordinate clause + comma + independent clause]
>
> Mark always brushes his teeth before he goes to bed.
> [independent clause (no comma) + subordinate clause]

Finding and fixing fragments

Before you begin to follow the steps below, locate a potential trouble spot by finding a subordinating word or an expression that introduces an example or a list, or else pinpoint a sentence that seems to have more than one verb or one in which you do not recognize any verb at all. Then apply these tests.

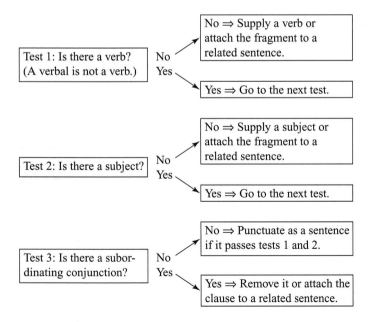

Test 1: Is there a verb? (A verbal is not a verb.)

No ⇒ No ⇒ Supply a verb or attach the fragment to a related sentence.

Yes ⇒ Yes ⇒ Go to the next test.

Test 2: Is there a subject?

No ⇒ No ⇒ Supply a subject or attach the fragment to a related sentence.

Yes ⇒ Yes ⇒ Go to the next test.

Test 3: Is there a subordinating conjunction?

No ⇒ No ⇒ Punctuate as a sentence if it passes tests 1 and 2.

Yes ⇒ Yes ⇒ Remove it or attach the clause to a related sentence.

In English, both the independent and subordinate clauses must contain a subject and a predicate.

The students ^were^ helping to raise money for the earthquake victims. [independent clause]

In America we go to the store once a week, but in our home country ^we^ shop every day. [two independent clauses]

They stayed at the beach because they ^had^ a good time. [independent and subordinate clauses]

EXERCISE 2

Revise each item below to eliminate the sentence fragment. In each case, explain why you chose to revise as you did. If any fragment does not require revision, explain your reason for allowing it to stand.

1. During the late nineteenth century. Judge Roy Bean ruled the west Texas town of Langtry.
2. Judge Bean owned a saloon. Which doubled as his courtroom.
3. The majority of offenders brought to Bean's court were murderers. Because the judge's unmerciful rule over the Langtry territory discouraged lesser crimes.
4. The judge alone tried and sentenced murderers. Swiftly and harshly.
5. Although he never hanged anyone. Judge Roy Bean was renowned as "the hanging judge."

EXERCISE 3

The passage on the following page contains several fragments. Follow the guidelines in 2a and 2b to revise the passage so it contains no fragments. Give your reasons for revising each fragment as you did.

[1]Most of the kids in the/ neighborhood—Marcy, Jake, and Bernadette—owe their sense of security to the Barnwells, the older couple living at the end of the block. [2]Not just because Mrs. Barnwell takes the time to help them with their homework whenever their parents are at work. [3]The Saturdays at the park, the snacks Mr. Barnwell makes once in a while in the late afternoon, and the woodworking projects they encourage kids to begin and that sometimes are visible in their front yard. [4]These are just as valuable. [5]Their official roles as neighborhood babysitters are more complex than one might think. [6]Though it's easy to see that if you take the time to think about it. [7]You're not likely to forget it. [8]Some people report hearing that they never had children because they decided not to have any. [9]But that's not really what happened. [10]Unfortunately, they were unable to have them. [11]Making them both rather sad and leaving them with a lot of extra love to give. [12]In fact, the kind of disappointments we all have to face in some form. [13]They can alter, or change, the way we deal with other people, many times for the better. [14]People changing positively in the way they interact with the world. [15]People may become kinder to each other. [16]Because the most important things people have in this world are their relationships with others.

EXERCISE 4

Advertisements often use fragments. Find an advertisement from a local newspaper or magazine that contains several fragments. Rewrite the advertisement so that it contains only sentences; then write a short paragraph giving some reasons the advertiser may have had for using these fragments.

Comma Splices and Fused Sentences

A fused sentence and a comma splice are both composed of two (or more) improperly joined independent clauses. A fused sentence results from joining two independent clauses without using punctuation or a conjunction. A comma splice results from joining two independent clauses with a comma. This chapter will help you

- recognize a comma splice or a fused sentence and
- know when to separate clauses and when to join them.

Grammar checkers are somewhat better at finding comma splices than they are at finding fragments and considerably better than they are at finding fused sentences. When we ran this chapter through two such checkers, most (but not all) of the comma splices in the examples were flagged, but the checkers recognized only the fused sentences in 3b. None of the comma splices or fused sentences in the exercises were flagged.

A fused sentence (often called a "run-on sentence") or a comma splice (sometimes called a "comma fault") occurs only when you are writing compound or compound-complex sentences. (See 1f.) Not recognizing where a sentence begins and ends leads to these very similar problems.

Fused	The current was swift he swam to shore.
Comma splice	The current was swift, he swam to shore.

Both comma splices and fused sentences can be corrected by separating the clauses with a semicolon or a period or by joining them with a conjunction.

To separate independent clauses:	Examples:
1. Place a period after each clause.	The current was swift. **He** swam to shore.
2. Place a semicolon between clauses.	The current was swift; he swam to shore.
To link independent clauses:	**Examples:**
1. A comma can be inserted before *and, but, or, nor, for, so,* or *yet.*	The roads were icy, **so** they decided not to drive.
	They decided not to drive, **for** the roads were icy.
To relate clauses by subordination:	**Examples:**
1. One clause can be subordinated to the other.	The roads were so icy **that they decided not to drive.**
	Because the roads were icy, they decided not to drive.
2. One clause can become an introductory phrase.	**Because of the icy roads,** they decided not to drive.

A comma emphasizes similarity in idea and grammatical structure between the two clauses, and the conjunction specifies what kind of connection exists. The semicolon emphasizes the difference between ideas that are related and grammatically equal, such as two clauses. (Writers generally do not use the semicolon between parts that are not grammatically equal.) A period separates two grammatically equal but unrelated units of thought.

Subject + predicate,   **and**   subject + predicate.

Subject + predicate;   subject + predicate.

Subject + predicate.   Subject + predicate.

When the clauses are short, parallel in form, and unified in thought, a comma (instead of a semicolon or a period) can link independent clauses not joined by a coordinating conjunction.

They came, they fought, they died.

Ways to recognize independent clauses and distinguish them from phrases and subordinate clauses are explained in chapter 1, especially **1d** and **1e**.

Separating two independent clauses with a comma results in a *comma splice:*

We went to the beach, ₍but₎ they went to the park.

Using no punctuation at all between independent clauses results in a *fused* (or *run-on*) sentence:

Leslie is going to the gym ₍and₎ I'm attending a meeting.

Writers may not link independent clauses with a comma unless the first clause is followed by *and, but, for, or, nor, so,* or *yet.* If you wish to omit the coordinating conjunction, you must use a semicolon to link the clauses.

3a **A fused sentence or a comma splice may be revised in one of three ways.**

Fused sentences and comma splices may be revised by

- linking the clauses with a comma followed by *and, but, or, for, nor, so,* or *yet* (coordinating conjunctions),
- separating the clauses with a semicolon (see **14a**) or a period, or
- making one clause subordinate to the other.

Fused	Women no longer need to colonize the traditionally male professions they have already opened most of the doors to the desirable career paths.
Comma splice	Women no longer need to colonize the traditionally male professions, they have already opened most of the doors to the desirable career paths.
Revised	Women no longer need to colonize the traditionally male professions, **for** they have already opened most of the doors to the desirable career paths. [coordinating conjunction *for* added after the comma]
OR	Women no longer need to colonize the traditionally male professions; they have already opened most of the doors to the desirable career paths. [A semicolon separates the independent clauses.]
OR	Women no longer need to colonize the traditionally male professions. They have already opened most of the doors to the desirable career paths. [The clauses are punctuated as separate sentences.]
OR	**Because** women have already opened most of the doors to the desirable career paths, they no longer need to colonize the traditionally male

professions. [The second clause is subordinated to the first.]

Fused She didn't know what to say to his announcement she was not at a complete loss for words, either.

Comma splice She didn't know what to say to his announcement, she was not at a complete loss for words, either.

Revised She didn't know what to say to his announcement, **nor** was she at a complete loss for words, either. [Note the shift in the word order of subject and verb after the coordinating conjunction *nor.*]

OR She was **neither** ready with a response to his announcement **nor** at a complete loss for words. [This simple sentence has a compound complement.]

OR She didn't know what to say to his announcement; she was not at a complete loss for words, either. [A semicolon separates the independent clauses.]

OR She didn't know what to say to his announcement. She was not at a complete loss for words, either. [The clauses are punctuated as separate sentences.]

OR **Despite not knowing** what to say to his announcement, she was not at a complete loss for words. [One clause is reduced to a verbal phrase; see 30b.]

Fused I called for a reservation all the tables were taken.

Comma splice I called for a reservation, all the tables were taken.

Revised I called for a reservation, **but** all the tables

5. Many bats shriek and listen for returning echoes to determine the location of prey, this type of echolocation is most common.

6. These bats can deafen themselves so they shriek in pulses and freeze their middle ear bones.

7. Leaf-nosed bats have a more sophisticated location system, they emit a continuous sound and do not need to listen for echoes.

8. The frequency of the leaf-nosed bat's call could be harmful to its ears the bat is deaf and not affected.

9. Fruit bats do not use echolocation, it developed in the bat's ancestors approximately thirty million years ago.

10. Scientists have found fossilized species bats have been around for more than fifty million years.

3b **Independent clauses may also be separated by using a semicolon with a word such as *however, therefore,* and the like (conjunctive adverb). (See 14a.)**

Fused   Sexual harassment is not just a women's issue after all, men can be sexually harassed, too.

Comma splice   Sexual harassment is not just a women's issue, after all, men can be sexually harassed, too.

Revised   Sexual harassment is not just a women's issue; **after all,** men can be sexually harassed, too. [independent clause; transitional phrase, independent clause]

Fused   A century ago the wild West was tamed therefore, the stories it produced were no longer tales of cowboys and bandits.

Comma splice   A century ago the wild West was tamed, therefore, the stories it produced were no longer tales of cowboys and bandits.

Revised	A century ago the wild West was tamed; **therefore,** the stories it produced were no longer tales of cowboys and bandits. [independent clause; conjunctive adverb, independent clause]

Below are lists of frequently used conjunctive adverbs and transitional phrases.

Conjunctive Adverbs

also	however	next
anyhow	incidentally	otherwise
anyway	indeed	similarly
besides	instead	still
consequently	likewise	then
finally	meanwhile	therefore
furthermore	moreover	thus
hence	nevertheless	

Transitional Phrases

after all	even so	in the second place
as a result	for example	on the contrary
at any rate	in addition	on the other hand
at the same time	in fact	
by the way	in other words	

Unlike a coordinating conjunction, which has a fixed position between the independent clauses it links, many conjunctive adverbs and transitional phrases either begin the second independent clause or take another position inside it.

She believed that daily exercise has many benefits; **however,** she couldn't fit it into her schedule. [The conjunctive adverb begins the second independent clause; see 14a, page 212.]

She believed that daily exercise has many benefits; she couldn't, **however,** fit it into her schedule. [The conjunctive adverb (set off by commas) appears later in the clause.]

COMPARE

She believed that daily exercise has many benefits, **but** she couldn't fit it into her schedule. [The coordinating conjunction has a fixed position.]

E X E R C I S E 3

Write five correctly punctuated compound sentences using various conjunctive adverbs and transitional phrases to connect and relate independent clauses.

3c Divided quotations can trick you into making a comma splice. (See chapter 16.)

Comma splice   "Who won the Superbowl?" he asked, "what was the final score?"

Revised   "Who won the Superbowl?" he asked. "What was the final score?"

Comma splice   "Injustice is relatively easy to bear," says Mencken, "it is justice that hurts."

Revised   "Injustice is relatively easy to bear," says Mencken; "it is justice that hurts."

CHECKLIST for Comma Splices and Fused Sentences

Most of the time the advice in this list will help you find comma splices and fused sentences.

Common Sites for Comma Splices or Fused Sentences

1. With transitional phrases such as *however, therefore, for example*

2. When an explanation or example occurs in the second clause

3. When a positive clause follows a negative first clause

4. When a pronoun is the subject of the second clause

5. When a series of ideas is phrased as connected clauses

To Tell If a Sentence Is a Comma Splice or Fused Sentence

1. Notice how many pairs of grammatical subjects and verbs (1a–b) are in the sentence.
   a. Find the verbs.
   b. Match verbs to subjects.

2. Look for the punctuation that separates the pairs (if there are at least two).

3. If no punctuation separates them, you have a fused sentence.

4. If a comma separates them, you may have a comma splice.
   a. If there is a coordinating conjunction, the sentence is not a comma splice.
   b. If there is no coordinating conjunction, the sentence is a comma splice.

To Fix Comma Splices and Fused Sentences

1. Link clauses with a comma and a coordinating conjunction.

2. Separate the clauses by using a semicolon.

3. Separate the clauses by punctuating each as a sentence.

4. Subordinate one clause to the other.

5. Reduce one clause to an introductory phrase.

6. Rewrite the sentence integrating one clause into the other.

Exercise 4

Comma splices and fused sentences have been incorporated into the following paragraph. Revise it so that no comma splices or fused sentences remain. Mark sentences that need no revision with a check mark.

[1]"I really like magazines and newspapers," he said "I read the sections discussing world news and business because they make me think. [2]I read the sections discussing entertainment and gossip," he continued, "because the stories are either informative or so unusual that I can't put them down. [3]When I was in the hospital, I read the sections of the newspaper that discussed medical issues many articles in this section often focus on what can go wrong, this one, however, discussed the credentials and success rates of local hospitals."

[4]"I also read a lot of books, particularly in the evening it's a good way to relax and exercise my imagination. [5]There's not one genre or type I read religiously. [6]Someday, I'd like to read more science fiction books I always see them at the bookstore, but I haven't bought any yet."

Exercise 5

First, review chapter 2 and study chapter 3. Then, identify and mark the sentence fragments (SF), comma splices (CS), and fused sentences (FS) in the following passage. Next, write down why you classified them as you did, indicating how they could be revised. Put a check mark after each sentence that needs no revision.

[1]He looks frail, thin. [2]Almost vulnerable. [3]The baggy gray sweater I gave him for his birthday is loosely pulled around him like a cape his shoulders are stooped. [4]And he holds a book. [5]There is a sound, however, in my father's voice it is a tone of tired strength.

[6]We sit alone at the kitchen table only a few hours after the funeral. [7]"From day to day, we all must wear our painful experiences as a sign to others," he says with the vigor of pride and past victories, reading from the journal he's kept for the past fifty years, his constant companion. [8]"Here then is a glimpse of the sign

I send to you," he says, however he still smiles and speaks of healing, happiness, and the future. [9]He tells me stories about my mother. [10]The idea being that the stories we tell are important parts of the real lives we live. [11]After a few moments, he looks at me directly and leans in closer. [12]In a clear, quiet voice he says that in our stories, we can live with complete abandon. [13]In life, we must proceed slowly, gradually. [14]Primarily with balance and judgment. [15]Never with insensitivity.

Chapter 4
Adjectives and Adverbs

Adjectives and adverbs are modifiers; that is, they qualify, restrict, or intensify the meaning of other words. They also describe degrees of comparison. This chapter will help you

- recognize adjectives and understand how to use them (**4a**),
- recognize adverbs and understand how to use them (**4b**),
- use the comparative and superlative forms correctly (**4c**),
- know when to use a group modifier (**4d**), and
- revise double negatives (**4e**).

Grammar checkers are not reliable guides for finding errors with adjectives and adverbs. In this chapter, a grammar checker identified one example of an adjective where an adverb was called for but missed at least six others, found one double negative example but not the other, and found only two errors in the exercises.

Adjectives modify nouns and pronouns; **adverbs** modify verbs, adjectives, and other adverbs.

Adjectives	Adverbs
a **quick** lunch	eat **quickly**
armed squads	**heavily** armed squads
She looked **angry**.	She looked **angrily** at me.
the **most brilliant**	shines **more brilliantly**

In traditional grammar, the articles *a, an,* and *the* are often classified as adjectives.

> See **22a(1)** for the use of articles.

Because both adjectives and adverbs work as modifiers, often look very much alike, and generally occur near one another, they can be difficult to tell apart. To determine whether a word is an adjective or an adverb, you must consider its form and its function in a particular sentence. The following sections offer advice about doing that.

4a Adjectives modify nouns, groups of words functioning as nouns, or pronouns. They may function as subject or object complements.

Adjectives answer the questions *What kind?, How many?,* or *Which ones?*

young children

several men

writing class

> The English language does not allow adjectives to be pluralized. Thus, the same word can modify both a singular and a plural noun.
>
> sour oranges
>
> a sour lemon

(1) Adjectives can often be recognized by their endings.

Because many adjectives are formed from other parts of speech, you can often determine that a word is an adjective by looking at its ending; *-able, -al, -ful, -ic, -ish, -less,* and *-y* are commonly used to make an adjective from a noun or a verb.

accept**able**	angel**ic**	effort**less**
rent**al**	yellow**ish**	sleep**y**
event**ful**		

Certain adjectives formed from nouns have the *-ly* ending (*cost, costly*). Sometimes a verbal serves as an adjective: for instance, an infinitive or a participle ending in *-ing* or *-ed.*

a determin**ing** factor

a determin**ed** effort

a chicken **to eat**

And finally, adjectives generally, but not always, come before the words they modify.

When I write, I appreciate a **quiet** house.

Tom found the house **quiet.**

Nouns used as modifiers are almost always singular: *sophomore students, executive washroom.* Common exceptions are **man** and **woman,** which change to the plural when they modify a plural noun: *men doctors, women doctors.*

 In English, adjectives are customarily used in the following order, and having more than three adjectives is considered awkward:

Determiner   *the, a, an, this, these, those, our, my, much, many, five*

Evaluator	*fascinating, painful, sad*
Size	*large, small, tiny, miniscule*
Shape	*square, round, triangular*
Age	*young, old, aged, newborn, antique*
Color	*black, white, green, brown*
Nationality or geography	*Arabian, Cuban, Peruvian, Slavic*
Religion	*Jewish, Catholic, Protestant, Buddhist*
Material	*silk, paper, pine, rubber*

A fascinating old Cuban man visited our class.

Have you seen that ugly brick building?

Carolina baked the bread on a round Italian pizza pan.

(2) Adjectives used as subject or object complements are easily confused with adverbs.

An adjective used as a subject complement completes the meaning of the verb by describing the subject of the sentence. A common error is to use an adverb as a subject complement.

> *angry*
> The actor looked ⌃**angrily.** [explains something about *actor*]
>
> *angrily*
> The actor looked up ⌃**angry.** [explains something about *looked up*]

Adjectives that modify the direct object in sentences with such verbs as *call, consider, elect, find, make, name* are **object complements.** (When nouns are object complements, they do not modify the direct object: They elected George *president*.) (See 1b(3).)

> They found Collette **trustworthy.** [The adjective *trustworthy* refers to the direct object *Collette* and completes the meaning of the verb *found.*]

CAUTION Do not omit the *-d* or *-ed* of a past participle used as an adjective. (See **7b(3)**.)

The dog was too frighten_^to go to him. *[ed]*

E X E R C I S E 1

Using adjectives as complements, write two sentences that illustrate each of the following patterns.

Lemons	*taste*	*sour.*	
Subject +	linking + verb	subject complement.	
We	*found*	*her*	*uncooperative.*
Subject +	verb +	direct object	object complement.

4b Adverbs modify verbs, adjectives, and other adverbs.

Adverbs answer the questions *How?, When?,* or *Where?*

Leela played her part **perfectly.** I wanted to go home **early.** I put the cat **outside.**

Adverbs that modify verbs commonly describe how (manner), when (time), or where (place) the action occurred.

Manner	We walked **quietly.**
Time	We arrived **later.**
Place	We walked **home.**

Adverbs can also modify verbals (gerunds, infinitives, participles) and whole clauses. (See 1d, pages 24–25.) Whole clauses may even function as adverbs. (See 1e, pages 30–31.)

> **Walking rapidly** is good for you. [The adverb *rapidly* modifies the gerund *walking,* which serves as the subject.]

> **When I was seven years old,** my family began their tradition of spending every summer in Colorado. [An adverbial clause of time modifies the verb *began.*]

Because many adverbs are formed by adding *-ly* to an adjective, you can often spot them by looking for that ending.

> Monique wrote her name **careful**. [The adverb *carefully* modifies the verb *wrote.*]

> The plane departs at an unpleasant early hour. [The adverb *unpleasantly* modifies the adjective *early.*]

> The computer was priced **very** reasonable. [The adverb *very* modifies the adverb *reasonably.*]

The *-ly* ending is usually associated with adverbs formed from adjectives. A few adverbs have two acceptable forms (*quick, quickly; slow, slowly*). When in doubt, consult the dictionary for the label *adv.* and any usage notes.

Infinitives can also serve as adverbs.

> studied **to pass**   happy **to leave**   afraid **to speak**

Adverbs made from adjectives ending in *-y* change the *-y* to *i* before adding the *-ly.*

easy [adjective]   eas **i ly** [adverb]

If the adjective ends in *-le,* the *-le* is dropped before the *-ly* is added.

sim**ple** [adjective]   simp **ly** [adverb]

A number of words can function as either adjectives or adverbs—for example, *fast, well.* When in doubt, consult your dictionary for the labels *adj.* and *adv.* and any usage notes.

> She likes **fast** cars. [adjective]
>
> We ran **fast** to catch the bus. [adverb]

Most dictionaries still label the following as colloquial, meaning that you may hear it in conversation but should avoid it in writing: *sure* for *surely, real* for *really,* and *good* for *well.*

| **Conversational** | The Broncos played **real good** during the first quarter. |
| **Written** | The Broncos played **very well** during the first quarter. [appropriate in both written and conversational usage; see 19b] |

EXERCISE 2

Edit the following sentences to remove errors in the use of adverbs. To do so, convert any colloquial or other unacceptable modifier into an adverb acceptable in college writing. Put a check mark after each sentence that needs no editing.

1. The boat's engine roared loud throughout Puerto Vallarta Bay.
2. We were looking for the local known island protected as a wildlife refuge.
3. As we approached the island, the attendants brief illustrated snorkeling procedures.

4. Trained vacationers could scuba dive as long as they did so cautiously.

5. The man next to me explained that he didn't scuba dive as regular as he would like.

6. He was well trained and swam good.

7. When we reached the island, the majority of vacationers jumped eager from the boat.

8. With everyone participating in scuba diving and snorkeling, the boat seemed abnormal quiet.

9. My mother and I surely enjoyed watching everyone.

10. After an hour in the water, everyone returned to the boat so that we could reach our next destination as quick as possible.

4c **Many adjectives and adverbs change form to show relative quality, quantity, or manner (the degree of comparison).**

Both adjectives and adverbs show the quality, quantity, or manner of a single element (positive), or the relationship between two elements (comparative) or among three or more elements (superlative).

Positive: **large**	Comparative: **larger**	Superlative: **largest**
Positive: **quickly**	Comparative: **more quickly**	Superlative: **most quickly**

It is often difficult to know when to add the suffixes *-er* or *-est* to show degree and when to use *more/less* and *most/least*.

Generally, one-syllable adjectives and adverbs and two-syllable adjectives with the stress on the first syllable form the comparative by adding *-er* and the superlative by adding *-est.*

Adjectives and Adverbs

(If the base form of the word ends in *-y,* don't forget to change the *-y* to *-i* when adding the comparative or superlative ending: *lucky, luckier, luckiest.* See **18e(3)**.) Other longer adjectives and most adverbs form the comparative by using *more* (or *less*) and the superlative by using *most* (or *least*).

> tall, taller, tallest [one-syllable adjective]
>
> fast, faster, fastest [one-syllable adverb]
>
> pretty, prettier, prettiest [two-syllable adjective with stress on the first syllable]
>
> quickly, more/less quickly, most/least quickly [two-syllable adverb]
>
> fortunate, more/less fortunate, most/least fortunate [three-syllable adjective]
>
> rapidly, more/less rapidly, most/least rapidly [three-syllable adverb]

A few common modifiers have irregular forms.

> little, less, least
>
> good/well, better, best
>
> bad/badly, worse, worst
>
> far, further/farther, furthest/farthest (See the **Glossary of Usage**.)

When in doubt, consult your dictionary.

The chart below may help you sort out comparatives and superlatives in English.

Adjective and Adverb	Positive	Comparative	Superlative	Explanation
One syllable Adj. Adv.	thin quick	thinner quicker	thinnest quickest	*-er* and *-est* used with most one-syllable adj. and adv.
Two+ syllable Adj. Adv.	famous quickly	more famous more quickly	most famous most quickly	*more* and *most* used with two- (or more) syllable adj. and adv.
Irregular	bad good/ well far	worse better farther/ further	worst best farthest/ furthest	*Bad* has identical irregular forms for both adj. and adv. *Good/well* differs in the positive. *Far* is an adverb.

Some two-syllable adjectives can use both forms: *able, angry, clever, common, cruel, friendly, gentle, handsome, narrow, polite, quiet, simple.*

| **Better** | Representative Landor's maneuvers during the recess led to victory. |

Occasionally a group of words linked with hyphens (compound adjective) modifies a noun, regardless of the part of speech of the components. (See **18g**.)

I threw the **half-eaten** apple away.

The students did very well on a **harder-than-average** examination.

4e A double negative is incorrect.

Most words that express a negative are modifiers. The term **double negative** refers to the use of two negatives within a sentence or clause to express a single negation. The double negative was labeled incorrectly because in mathematics two negatives make a positive.

He didn't keep ~~no~~ records. OR He ~~didn't keep~~ no records.

any   *Kept*

Because *hardly, barely,* and *scarcely* already denote severely limited or negative conditions, using *not, nothing,* or *without* with these modifiers creates a double negative.

I could**n't hardly** quit in the middle of the job. OR I could**n't** ~~hardly~~ quit in the middl the job.

The motion passed with **~~not~~ scarcely** a protest. OR The motion passed with **~~not scarcely~~** a protest.

little

Rarely, the emphasis of a sentence requires the use of two negatives, but that construction is not considered a double negative.

It would**n't** be safe **not** to install smoke detectors. [This construction is permissible when the *not* is to be emphasized. Otherwise, the sentence should be revised.]

EXERCISE 4

After you have reread rules 4a through 4e and have studied the examples, correct all errors in the use of adjectives or adverbs in the sentences below. Also eliminate any awkward use of nouns as adjectives, and correct double negatives. Put a check mark after any sentence that needs no revision.

1. Gertrude Bell probably led a much fuller life than other women of her time.

2. The red-headed Bell was a wealthy, intelligent, young woman.

3. She was among the first women to graduate from Oxford and couldn't hardly be satisfied with domestic life.

4. Instead, Bell traveled to what were considered the most remotest countries in the world, saw the wonders of the Ottoman Empire, and explored the desert of Iraq.

5. Several of the Arab sheiks Bell met were surprised that she acted more manlier than womanly.

6. The Iraqi civil war gave Bell littler time to pursue archeology than usual.

7. She became an Arab rebellion supporter and was eventually made the social secretary by the king of Iraq.

8. Bell's travel in Iraq allowed her to socialize with novelist D. H. Lawrence and with the most important men in politics.

9. Winston Churchill invited Bell to the 1921 Cairo Conference because never had none of the participating men been to Iraq.

10. When the photo of the conference participants was taken, Bell looked real well in her feathered hat and silk dress among the thirty-six black-suited males.

Chapter

5

Pronouns and Case

This chapter explains

- what the various kinds of pronouns (personal, relative, indefinite, and so on) are and how to use them (**5a**),
- how the forms of pronouns are determined by case (**5b**), and
- how to handle case with compound constructions, *who* and *whom,* and other problem situations (**5c**).

Case refers to the form of a noun or pronoun that shows how it relates to other words in a sentence; for instance, in the phrase, *Martin's cat,* the possessive case of *Martin's* shows that Martin owns the cat. Most of what there is to say about case in English applies primarily to pronouns because a pronoun changes form to show this relationship. For example, the different case forms of the boldfaced pronouns below, all referring to the same person, show their different uses.

> **He** [the subject] wants **his** [modifier showing possession] cousin to help **him** [direct object].

He, the subject, is in the *subjective* case; *his,* showing possession, is in the *possessive* case; and *him,* the object, is in the *objective* case.

Pronouns also have singular and plural forms.

> **They** [plural subject] want **their** [plural modifier showing possession] cousins to help **them** [plural direct object].

Unlike pronouns, nouns do not change form except to become plural or to add -*'s* to show possession. In fact, moving a noun from one relationship to another changes the meaning of a sentence significantly.

Hugh wants his cousin to help him. He wants **Hugh's** cousin to help him. He wants his cousin to help **Hugh.**

Because grammar checkers can only count and compare and so cannot make judgments, they perform poorly when checking for case errors. When we ran this chapter through two grammar checkers, one of them found no errors at all, not even the deliberate errors such as the ones in exercise 5. The other did marginally better, finding most of the errors with reflexive pronouns, but it missed more than half of the *who/whom* errors. Just as bad, it incorrectly flagged *who's* (*who is*), suggesting *whom* instead, and unaccountably indicated that *they book* was a capitalization rather than a case error and should be corrected to *They book.* Most disturbing was the fact that although the grammar checker identified *Me and Jake brought it here* as an error, it suggested the revision *Jake and me* rather than *Jake and I.*

5a Understanding the various kinds of pronouns helps writers use them correctly.

Although English has several different kinds of pronouns, the important categories for studying case are *personal, relative, interrogative,* and *reflexive* pronouns.

(1) Personal pronouns identify the speaker, the person spoken to, and the person or thing spoken about.

The first-person pronoun (*I, we*) identifies the speaker, the second-person pronoun (*you*) identifies the person spoken to, and the third-person pronoun (*he, she, it, they*) identifies the person or thing spoken about. Personal pronouns change form to reflect their relationship to other words in the sentence. The subject of a sentence appears in the subjective case, the object appears in the objective case, and a word showing ownership appears in the possessive case.

Person	Subjective		Objective		Possessive	
	Singular	Plural	Singular	Plural	Singular	Plural
First person	I	we	me	us	my mine	our ours
Second person	you	you	you	you	your yours	your yours
Third person	he she it	they	him hers it	them	his hers its	their theirs

Notice that the second-person pronoun, *you,* has the same form for both singular and plural and for the subjective and objective cases. The possessive forms *mine, ours, yours, hers,* and *theirs* are used only as pronouns, never as possessive adjectives. The third-person pronoun *it* has the same form for the subjective and objective cases. All other forms of the personal pronoun reflect person, number, and case. (And the third-person singular forms also reflect the last vestige of gender in English. See **6b** and **19d(1)**.)

(2) Relative pronouns relate a subordinate clause to a noun in the main clause.

Relative pronouns (*who, whom, whoever, whomever, which, whose,* and *that*) introduce clauses that refer to a noun in the main clause.

Julieta, who is my sister, lives in Atlanta.

I suggested the remedy for **whoever** needed it. [*Whoever* is the subject of its own clause and is therefore in the subjective case.]

Who, whose, and *whom* ordinarily refer to people; *which* to things; and *that* to either. The possessive pronoun *whose* (in place of the awkward *of which*) sometimes refers to things.

The poem, **whose** author is unknown, has recently been set to music.

	Refers to People	Refers to Things	Refers to Either
Subjective	who	which	that
Objective	whom	which	that
Possessive	whose	whose (sometimes)	

CAUTION Do not confuse *who's* and *whose. Who's* is a contraction for *who is,* and *whose* indicates possession.

(3) Interrogative pronouns are used to ask questions.

The **interrogative** pronouns *who* and *whom*—like their relative pronoun counterpart *who*—change form to reflect their grammatical use in the sentence.

Who asked the question? [subjective case for the subject of the sentence]

She could not remember **whom** she gave the book to. [See 5c(2) for the approved use of the subjective case in such sentences.]

Which and *that* do not change form.

(4) Personal pronouns combine with *-self* to form the reflexive/intensive pronouns.

The reflexive pronouns *myself, ourselves, yourself, himself, herself, itself,* and *themselves* refer to the subject of the clauses in which they appear. Intensive pronouns are used primarily for emphasis and are indistinguishable in form from the reflexives.

> Jake saw a picture of **himself.** [reflexive]
>
> Jake, **himself,** brought it here. [intensive]

When these pronouns refer to a noun or pronoun already mentioned in the sentence, they always follow the person or thing to which they refer.

CAUTION Do not use *myself* or *me* in place of *I* in a compound subject.

> Jake and ~~myself~~ brought it here.
>
> ^Jake and I^
> ~~Me and Jake~~ brought it here.

Hisself and *theirselves,* although the logical forms for the reflexive pronouns (possessive plus -*self* as in *myself, yourself, herself*), are not accepted in college or professional writing. Instead, use *himself* and *themselves.*

> James and Jerry painted the house by ^themselves^ ~~theirselves~~.

Attempts to create a gender-neutral reflexive pronoun have resulted in such forms as *themself;* these forms are not accepted in college or professional writing either.

5b Pronouns change form to indicate the subjective, objective, or possessive case.

(1) Subjects of sentences and complements with linking verbs use subjective case.

A subject complement is a word that renames the subject. A linking verb is a form of *be* (*am, is, are, was, were*), a word expressing the senses (*look, sound, feel, taste, smell*), or a condition (*become, grow, prove, remain, seem, turn*). It relates the subject to the subject complement. (See **1b(3)**.) Pronouns that are the subjects of sentences use the subjective form.

Russell and ~~me~~ were in charge. [compound subject of the sentence, *I*

Russell and I, in the subjective case]

The ones in charge were ~~him and me~~. [compound subjective com- *he and I*

plement, *he and I,* in the subjective case]

Conversational English accepts *It's me* (*him, her, us, them*).

In English, the subject of a sentence must be stated using a noun phrase or a pronoun unless you are using an imperative. When the verb is an imperative, the pronoun is unstated, but understood. See **1b(1)**.

~~Threw~~ the ball. *He threw*

Look at me! [*You* is the unstated, understood subject of the imperative *look.*]

---

(2) Objects of all kinds use the objective case.

When a pronoun is a direct or an indirect object or the object of a preposition, it takes the objective case.

Direct object   Miguel loves **her.** [The direct object, *her,* is in the objective case. COMPARE Miguel loves Martha.]

| **Indirect object** | Miguel gave **her** his love. [The indirect object, *her,* is in the objective case. COMPARE Miguel gave Martha his love.] |
| **Object of a preposition** | Miguel cares deeply for **her**. [The object of the preposition, *her,* is in the objective case. COMPARE Miguel cares deeply for Martha.] |

(3) Modifiers are in the possessive case.

Modifiers that indicate ownership or a comparable relationship are in the **possessive case**. A few possessive pronouns (such as *mine* and *theirs*) sometimes function as nouns.

That book is **mine**. [COMPARE That book is my book.]

 Their and *they* can be confused in spoken English. *Their* is the possessive pronoun; *they* is in the subjective case. These must be distinguished in written English.

   their
   ~~they~~ book

   their
   ~~they~~ house

See the Glossary of Usage for confusion among *their, there, they're,* and *there're.*

5c   The case of a pronoun is determined by the pronoun's use in its own clause.

(1) Pronouns in compound constructions take the same case they would if the construction were not compound.

Multiple *subjects* or *subject complements* are in the subjective case.

I thought **he or Dad** would come to my rescue. [compound subject of the clause acting as a direct object]

It was **Maria and I** who solved the problem. [compound subject complement; see 5b(1)]

She and her father buy groceries on Saturday morning. [compound subject containing a possessive adjective that modifies one element]

The first-person pronoun *I* occurs last in a compound construction.

~~Me and~~ Ricardo *and I* are good friends.

Multiple *objects of prepositions* are in the objective case.

between Merrill and *me* ~~I~~

with Amanda and *him* ~~he~~

Multiple *objects of verbs or verbals* and *subjects of infinitives* are in the objective case.

Clara may appoint **you or me.** [direct object]

They lent **Tom and her** ten dollars. [indirect object]

He gets nowhere by scolding **Bea or him.** [object of the gerund]

Dad wanted **Sheila and me** to keep the old car. [subject of the infinitive]

You can test the case of any pronoun in a compound construction by eliminating the accompanying noun or pronoun and the conjunction.

(Lou and) I like to watch Star Wars movies. [subject]

They elected (George and) me to the board. [direct object]

Gabriel gave it to (Edwyn and) me. [object of the preposition]

If an appositive (a word that renames a noun or pronoun) follows a pronoun, normal case rules still apply.

We
~~Us~~ students need this.
∧

us
The director told ~~we~~ extras to go home.
∧

To test the case of a pronoun with an appositive, remove the appositive.

We
~~Us students~~ need this.
∧

us
The director told ~~we extras~~ to go home.
∧

E X E R C I S E **1**

Choose the correct pronoun in the parentheses in each of the following sentences. Explain your choice.

1. Two of my friends, Cherise and (she, her), started taking an ice-skating class.

2. The class met at the rink every other day, but (it, they) was closed on Sunday.

3. Cherise and Carol thought that the class helped (they, them) lose weight.

4. Cherise says the instructor was very helpful because (he, his) had taught the class for years.

5. After the first week of class, Carol was annoyed with Mark because of (him, his) complaining about the instructor.

6. Carol and (I, me, myself) agreed that Mark was probably trying to impress the female students, including (her, herself).

7. Nevertheless, Carol explained that the instructor paid as much attention to (he, him) as to (they, them).

8. By the end of the course, Mark and (they, them) were friends.

9. When Mark decided to take the next ice-skating course, (I, me) wondered if (he, him) and (I, me) would end up in that next class together.

10. Carol and Cherise, (they, themselves), said (they, them, themselves) would probably benefit from the second class as much as (we, us).

(2) When to use *who* or *whom* depends on how it is used in its own clause.

Who and *whom* are often misused. You may be able to avoid such misuse if you remember that the case form of *who* or *whoever* is determined by its grammatical function in its own clause. The subject of a verb in a subordinate clause takes the subjective case, even if the whole clause is used as an object.

> I remembered **who** won the Academy Award that year. [*Who* is the subject of the clause *who won the Academy Award that year.* The clause is the object of the verb *remembered.*]

> She offered help to **whoever** needed it. [*Whoever* is the subject of the clause *whoever needed it.* The clause is the object of the preposition *to.*]

When the pronoun is the direct object or the object of a preposition, *whom* is *always* the correct form. See **1b(2)** and **1c(6)**.

> They helped the people ~~who~~ *whom* they liked. [direct object]

> Gabriel happily greeted ~~whoever~~ *whomever* he met that day. [direct object]

> This is a friend ~~who~~ *whom* I write to once a year. [object of the preposition *to;* COMPARE I write *to him* once a year.]

> I don't know ~~who~~ *whom* he voted for. [object of the preposition *for;* COMPARE He voted *for him.*]

Hemingway's novel is titled *For **Whom** the Bell Tolls.* [objective case for the object of a preposition]

Although many writers still prefer the objective case, dictionaries have approved the use of *who* and *whoever* in sentences where they begin the clause.

I wondered **who** she gave the book to.

Who do you plan to vote for?

Give the book to **whoever** he wants to have it.

Who were you speaking of?

In college writing, it is better to use the traditional *whom* as the object even when it is the first word in a sentence.

Whom will they elect president?

Whom may be omitted (or *that* substituted) in sentences where no misunderstanding would result.

The friend he relied on moved away. [*whom* omitted after *friend*]
OR
The friend **that** he relied on moved away.

EXERCISE 2

Following the guidelines for college and professional writing, choose the appropriate form of the pronouns in parentheses. Remember to choose *whom* when the pronoun functions as an object and *who* when it functions as the subject of a verb or as a subject complement.

1. Robert Dover, (who/whom) has placed in the top five in dressage at the World Cup Finals, is a member of the United States Equestrian Team.
2. An equally successful member of the dressage team, (who/whom) the United States Equestrian Team has supported, is Carol Lavell.
3. The United States Equestrian Team finances teams (who/whose) members have attained high enough standards to represent the United States at international competitions.

4. The United States Equestrian Team was formed in the 1950s by sportsmen (who/whom) were interested in the sport of equestrian riding.

5. Members of the United States Equestrian Team include riders (who/whom) compete in dressage, show jumping, and other driving and riding sports abroad.

6. The organization's training program allows visits by interested individuals (who/whom) arrive when the stables are open.

7. The organization considers supporting (whoever/whomever) can provide their own horses and exhibit the skills to win.

8. Amateurs and professionals (who/whom) apply to the United States Equestrian Team are evaluated by (whoever, whomever) the organization accepts as skilled judges.

9. The American Horse Shows Association can nominate a professional rider (who/whom) it thinks would be an asset to the United States Equestrian Team.

10. (Whoever, Whomever) the organization finances for competition must surely be thankful that supporters, (whoever, whomever) they may be, were able to make contributions to the United States Equestrian Team.

EXERCISE 3

Using the case form in parentheses, convert each pair of sentences in the following paragraph into a single sentence.

EXAMPLES

I understand the daredevil. He motorcycled across the Grand Canyon. (who)

I understand the daredevil who motorcycled across the Grand Canyon.

Evelyn consulted an astrologer. She had met him in San Francisco. (whom)

Evelyn consulted an astrologer whom she had met in San Francisco.

A gerund is a verbal used as a noun.

> The man's **sitting** (gerund acting as subject) at the desk annoyed us. [The gerund tells us that it was the act of sitting that annoyed us.]

Notice that the possessive case precedes gerunds, but not participles.

EXERCISE 4

Find and revise all pronoun forms in the following paragraph that would be inappropriate in college English. Put a check mark after each sentence that needs no revision.

[1]Marcie and Chris wanted Elizabeth and I to go to the movies with them. [2]In fact, they wanted us—Elizabeth and I—to choose the movie we would all see. [3]As for Elizabeth and I, we both like movies, but Chris and Marcie like them more than we. [4]Marcie didn't know this, however, and she strongly urged us to come with them. [5]Moreover, Elizabeth and I, stammering a response, did not suggest to Chris and her that we really didn't want to go with them. [6]Eventually, I whispered to Elizabeth, "It looks like those two are going to force you and me to go to the movies even though they could go by themselves." [7]She replied, "Although we really don't have to go, they would probably be mad if we didn't." [8]Obviously, we two had wanted to do something other than go to the movies, but neither of us actually spoke up. [9]Unfortunately, the movie was really awful, and Chris and Marcie enjoyed the movie no more than we did, although they generally enjoy movies more than us. [10]When all was said and done, though, it was Elizabeth and I who I blamed for us having a bad time.

Chapter

6 Agreement

A verb and its subject agree (match) when their forms indicate that they are both either singular or plural. A pronoun and its antecedent (the noun that the pronoun refers to) agree when they are both singular or plural and have the same gender. This chapter gives guidance on how to handle the following trouble spots:

- the present tense of verbs with singular subjects (**6a**),
- complicated sentence structure (**6a(1)**, **6a(3)**, and **6a(5)**),
- agreement of verbs with relative pronouns (**6a(6)**) and with titles (**6a(10)**),
- agreement of verbs with indefinite pronouns (*everyone, no one, everybody*) or singular generic nouns (*a teacher, a student, an employee*; **6b(1)**) as antecedents (see **19d(1)** on sexist language), and
- compound (*Ted and I*) (**6b(2)**) and collective-noun (*committee, audience*) (**6b(3)**) antecedents.

Notice in the examples below that the singular subject takes a singular verb and that the plural subject takes a plural verb. (If you cannot easily recognize verbs and their subjects, see **1a** and **1b**.)

Singular	The **car** in the lot **looks** shabby. [*car looks*]
Plural	The **cars** in the lot **look** shabby. [*cars look*]

Except for forms of *be* and *have* (*you were, he has eaten*), verbs in other tenses do not change form to indicate the number and person of their subjects. (For a list of various forms of *be* and the subjects they take, see page 111 in chapter **7**.)

When a pronoun has an antecedent, these two words usually agree in number. (See chapter 28.)

Singular   A **wolf** has **its** own language. [*wolf—its*]

Plural   **Wolves** have **their** own language. [*wolves—their*]

A pronoun also agrees with its antecedent in gender (masculine, feminine, or neuter). (See 6b.)

the **boy** and **his** sister [masculine antecedent]

the **girl** and **her** brother [feminine antecedent]

the **garden** and **its** weeds [neuter antecedent]

 The possessive pronouns—*his, her, its, their, my, our, your*—agree with their antecedents, not with any noun they may modify.

6a   Verbs must agree with their subjects.

Agree means that if a subject is plural, the verb must have a plural form, and if the subject is singular, the verb must have a singular form. (If you cannot easily recognize verbs and their subjects, see 1a–b.)

Singular   The **rose** in the vase **is** beautiful.

Plural   The **roses** in the vase **are** beautiful.

Because only present tense verbs change form to indicate the number and person of their subjects, most problems with subject-verb agreement occur when present tense is used. It is easy to confuse the endings of *verbs* (where *-s* indicates **singular**) with those of *nouns* (where *-s* indicates **plural**).

Subject + *s*	Verb + *s*
The **students need** attention.	The **student needs** attention.
Zinnias bloom best in the sun.	A **zinnia blooms** best in the sun.

If the subject of your sentence is singular but is not *I* or *you*, the verb needs the *-s* ending.

That talk show host ask**s** silly questions. [The sound of the *-s* may be masked in speech if the word that follows begins with an *s*.]

 English requires the addition of an *-s* to make most nouns plural and to form third-person singular verbs (except when the verb includes a helping verb).

She **walks** very fast. She **can walk** very fast.

Grammar checkers often create more agreement problems than they solve. While they do flag agreement errors, they are only occasionally correct, and they frequently flag correct sentences and make bizarre "corrections." For instance, one grammar checker flagged *What I think is my own business* from this chapter and suggested that *is* should be changed to *am* to agree with *I*.

Because a grammar checker cannot distinguish between verbs in separate clauses, it compares *think* to *I* and finds correct agreement. So far, so good, but it soon gets in trouble because it next compares *is* with the immediately preceding noun or pronoun, which happens to be *I*. It reports an agreement error and suggests that *is* should be changed to *am* to agree with *I*.

If you understand subject-verb agreement, you may find a grammar checker useful for finding errors you have overlooked in proofreading. If, however, you are not confident about subject-verb agreement, using a grammar checker can be risky. It will pay you to be alert for situations that lead to agreement errors.

---

(1) Agreement errors are frequent when other words come between the subject and the verb.

The **rhythm** of the pounding waves **is** calming. [*Waves* is the object of a prepositional phrase, not the subject.]

All of the dogs in the neighborhood **were barking.** [*Dogs* and *neighborhood* are both objects of prepositions. *All* is the subject. (See **6a(7).**)]

Phrases such as *accompanied by, along with, as well as, in addition to, including, no less than, not to mention,* and *together with* generally introduce a prepositional phrase and do not affect the number of the subject.

Her **salary** together with tips **is** just enough to live on.

Tips together with her salary **are** just enough to live on.

(2) Agreement errors often occur when subject and verb endings are not clearly sounded in rapid speech.

Economists seem concerned. [might sound like "Economist seem" concerned, but the former is correct]

She ask Sybil first. ^asks

(3) Compound subjects joined by *and* need a plural verb.

My two best **friends** and my **fiancé hate** each other.

The **coach** and the **umpire were** at home plate.

Writing on a legal pad and **writing with a computer are** not the same at all. [gerund phrases—COMPARE "Two actions are not the same."]

A compound subject that refers to a single person or unit takes a singular verb.

> The **founder and president** of the art association **was** elected to the board of the museum.
>
> The **writer and director** of *The Thin Red Line* **is** Terence Malik.

(4) Agreement errors are common with subjects joined by *either . . . or.*

Subjects linked by *either . . . or, neither . . . nor*, and *or* agree with the singular form of the verb unless these subjects are clearly plural. In the examples below, all subjects are clearly singular and agree with the singular forms of the verbs.

> John or Doris **writes** to us regularly.
>
> Neither Carol nor Ted **is** excluded from the meeting.
>
> Either Patty or Tom **was** asked to preside.

If one subject is singular and one is plural, the verb agrees with the subject closer to the verb.

> Neither the basket nor the **apples were** expensive.
>
> Neither the apples nor the **basket was** expensive.

The verb also agrees in person with the nearer subject.

> Either Frank or **you were** going to hire her anyway.
>
> Either you or **Frank was** going to hire her anyway.

(5) Inverted word order or *there* + *verb* constructions can lead to agreement errors.

VERB + SUBJECT

> Hardest hit by the subzero temperatures and snow **were** the large **cities** of the Northeast.

There + **VERB** + **SUBJECT**

There **are** several **ways** to protect yourself from a tornado.

(6) Using relative pronouns (*who, which, that*) as subjects can lead to agreement errors.

Stoddard Hall, which is the computer science building, is always open.

It is the **doctor who** often **suggests** a diet.

Those are the **books that are** out of print.

This is the only **store that gives** triple coupons. [COMPARE Only one store gives triple coupons.]

It is not bigger discounts but **better service that makes** a store successful. [COMPARE Better service (not bigger discounts) makes a store successful.]

The Starion is the only **one** of the new models **that includes** air conditioning as standard equipment. [*That* refers to *one* because only one model offers air conditioning without charging extra. It is logically singular.]

(7) Agreement errors are frequent with *either, one, everybody, all, any, some, none,* and other indefinite pronouns.

Each, either, everybody, one, and *anyone* are considered singular and so require singular verbs.

Either of them **is willing** to shovel the driveway.

Each has bought a first-class ticket.

Everybody in our apartment building **has** a parking place.

Other indefinite pronouns such as *all, any, some, none, half,* and *most* can be either singular or plural, depending on whether they refer to a unit or quantity (singular) or to a collection of individuals (plural).

Wendy collects comic books; **some are** very valuable. [plural reference; COMPARE Some comic books are very valuable.]

The bank would not take all the money because **some was** foreign. [singular reference; COMPARE Some money was foreign.]

Singular subjects that are preceded by *every* or *each* and that are joined by *and* agree with a singular verb.

Every cat and dog in the county **has** to be vaccinated.

Each fork and spoon **has** to be polished.

Placing *each* after a plural subject does not affect the verb form.

The cat and the dog **each have** their good points.

Another problem arises when other words come between the pronoun and the subject it refers to.

None of those **are** spoiled. [*of those* indicates a group of individuals, thus a plural verb; COMPARE None of the food [a unit] is spoiled.]

Half or more of the population in west Texas is Hispanic. [*of the population* indicates a quantity or unit and thus requires a singular verb; COMPARE Half or more of the people [individuals] in west Texas are Hispanic.]

(8) Collective nouns and phrases often cause agreement difficulties.

Collective nouns and phrases refer to a group of individual things. Whether they require a singular or a plural verb depends on whether the sentence refers to the group as a whole or to the individual items in the collection.

Singular (Regarded as a Unit)	Plural (Regarded as Individuals or Parts)
Ten million gallons is a lot of oil.	**Ten million gallons** of oil **were spilled.**

The **majority is** very large. The **majority** of us **are** in favor.

The **number is** very small. A **number were** absent.

In American English, nouns that refer to a group as a whole (collective nouns) should not be treated as plural.

The committee ~~are~~ is meeting tonight.

Although the use of *data* and *media* as singular nouns (instead of *datum* and *medium*) has gained currency in conversational English, treat *data* and *media* as plural in college writing.

College and Professional Writing	Conversation
The media **have** shaped public opinion.	The media **has** shaped public opinion.
The data **are** in the appendix.	The data **is** in the appendix.

(9) Agreement errors are common when *what* is the subject of a linking verb.

Linking verbs include the forms of *be* (*am, is, are, was, were, being, been*), the verbs referring to the senses (*look, feel, smell, sound, taste*), and some others such as *appear, become, remain,* and *seem.*

Because the pronoun *what* is singular or plural depending on whether the word (or word group) it refers to is singular or plural, the verb agrees with its complement in sentences such as the following.

What I think **is** my own **business.**

What tastes best **is different** for each of us.

What our parents gave us **were memories** to be cherished.

(10) Agreement can be troublesome with titles of single works, words spoken of as words, and nouns plural in form but singular in meaning.

Dombey and Son **sticks** in the memory. [The novel itself, not the characters in it, sticks in the memory.]

Kids **is** a slangy way to say *children.*

Nouns that look like they are plural but are treated as singular include *economics, electronics, measles, mumps, news,* and *physics.*

Measles **is** a serious disease.

Economics **is** important for a business major.

Some nouns (such as *athletics, politics, series, deer,* and *sheep*) can be either singular or plural, depending on the meaning.

Singular	**Plural**
Statistics is an interesting subject.	Statistics are often misleading.
A series of natural disasters has occurred recently.	Two series of natural disasters have occurred recently.
The sheep strays when the gate is left open.	Sheep stray when the gate is left open.

Agreement

Four Steps to Subject-Verb Agreement

Is the verb present tense?	No	Agreement problems are unlikely.
	Yes	Look at the subject.

Is the subject a singular noun such as *book, tree,* or *hope*?	No	Use the form of the verb without *-s*.
	Yes	Use the form of the verb with *-s*.

Is the subject a singular pronoun?	No	Agreement problems are unlikely. Use the form of the verb without *-s*.
	Yes	Check to see whether the pronoun is third person.

Is the pronoun third-person singular?	No	Agreement problems are unlikely. Use the form of the verb without *-s*.
	Yes	Use the form of the verb with *-s*.

E X E R C I S E 1

In each sentence below, choose the correct form of the verb in parentheses. Make sure that the verb agrees with its subject according to the rules of college and professional writing.

1. Attitudes about money in adulthood, of course, (vary/varies).
2. Neither time nor affluence (remove/removes) the memory of childhood poverty.
3. Experiences of poor children (illustrate/illustrates) how significant money and status (is/are) in our society.
4. When paying the bills (is/are) problematic, the father and mother (bicker/bickers), which often (upset/upsets) the child.
5. Some adults (think/thinks) their mother or father (was/were) responsible for their attitude about money.
6. Their current understanding of their parents' past problems with money often (provide/provides) little solace.
7. A number of adults (overcome, overcomes) the stigma of being poor as children.
8. However, there (is/are) no sure way to predict which ones will succeed.
9. There (is/are) also evidence that (indicate/indicates) a portion of affluent children (develop/develops) unhealthy attitudes about money as well.
10. Problems of both types (is/are) less likely if one or more of the parents (talk/talks) to the children about money issues.

E X E R C I S E 2

Use each of the following to make a complete sentence. Be sure that subjects and verbs agree.

1. My books and my pen . . .
2. It is my mother who . . .
3. Everyone . . .

4. Neither the (singular subject) nor the (plural subject) . . .

5. The list of volunteers . . .

6b Pronouns agree with their antecedents in number and gender.

No currently available grammar checker can identify problems with pronoun-antecedent agreement. You need to rely on your own knowledge to recognize that a singular pronoun does not agree with a plural noun.

(1) Agreement is often difficult when the antecedent is a generic noun or indefinite pronoun.

Everybody has to live with ~~themselves.~~ *himself or herself* [Rephrased using a plural: *People have to live with themselves.*]

Each student has the combination to ~~their~~ *his or her* own locker. [singular compound phrase]

Singular   A lawyer represents **his or her** clients.

Plural   Lawyers represent **their** clients.

Because many consider the use of *his or her* awkward, it is usually best to rewrite your sentence so that the generic noun is plural. Further, a pronoun that refers to one of the following words should be singular: *man, individual, woman, person, everybody, one, anyone, each, either, neither, sort,* and *kind.*

Each of these companies had ~~their~~ *its* books audited.

When the gender of the antecedent is clear, use the appropriate personal pronoun.

> **Masculine**   John represents **his** clients.
> **Feminine**   Mary represents **her** clients.

When the gender of the antecedent is not clear or when the noun could refer to either men or women, rewrite the sentence to make the noun plural or use a form of *his or her* or *himself or herself.*

> College students who support themselves have little free time. [COMPARE A college student who supports *himself* or *herself* . . .]

When referring to a word such as *student,* which can include both men and women, you can avoid agreement problems by dropping the pronoun, by making the sentence passive, or by making the antecedent plural.

> Each student has the combination to a private locker. [no pronoun]
> The combination to a private locker is issued to each student. [passive]
> Students have the combinations to their private lockers. [plural]

In spoken language a sentence such as the following is considered easy and natural; in college and professional writing, however, it is still not accepted.

> Everyone who was invited to dinner, but they had already eaten. [sentence revised to avoid the agreement problem]

CAUTION Be careful not to introduce errors into your own writing because you are trying to avoid sexist usage. (See **19d.**)

(2) Joining words by *and* and by *or* or *nor* often leads to errors in pronoun-antecedent agreement.

Mark and Gordon lost **their** enthusiasm.
Did **Mark or Gordon** lose **his** enthusiasm?

If one of two antecedents joined by *or* or *nor* is singular and the other is plural, the pronoun usually agrees with the nearer antecedent.

> Neither the **president nor** the **senators** had announced **their** decision. [**Their** is closer to the plural antecedent **senators**.]

When it is awkward to follow this rule, as in "Roger or Melissa will bring her book," recast the sentence to avoid the problem: "Roger will bring his book, or Melissa will bring hers."

(3) Collective noun antecedents pose agreement problems.

When the antecedent is a collective noun, special care should be taken to avoid treating it as both singular and plural in the same sentence.

> The choir **is** writing ~~their~~ *its* own music. [Because the choir is working as a unit, it is regarded as singular.]

> The group of students disagree on methods, but **they** unite on basic aims. [Because the students in the group are behaving as individuals, the group is regarded as plural.]

Curing Problems with Pronoun-Antecedent Agreement

Antecedent	Singular	Plural	Option
Indefinite pronoun such as *anybody, each, everyone, either, someone*	√		
Collective noun such as *committee, audience*	√	(√ only if referring to individuals)	

| Word that refers to a member of a class—*a student, an employee,* etc. | √ |
| Compound construction such as *Martha and John, brother and sister* | √ (refers to nearest element) |

See **19d** for ways to avoid sexist language.

EXERCISE 3

There are usually at least two ways to revise the following sentences so that the pronouns agree with their antecedents. Try out as many ways as you can think of, and then choose the one you think is best. Place a check mark next to any sentence that is correct.

1. When I am busy studying, someone is always coming to the door wanting me to talk to them.
2. Everyone was asked to contribute to our campaign, but they had already given to another candidate.
3. If a politician campaigns hard for an election, they will often win.
4. The company's board of directors appointed its chairman yesterday.
5. Professor Graves wants everyone to bring their own bluebooks.
6. Do you think it is rude when a student makes an appointment and then they don't show up?
7. The group piled into the van, tugging sleeping bags and cooking pots after them.
8. Any student who works full time has to understand that their biggest problem is time management.
9. The student government organization, concerned about changes in the graduation requirements, were meeting with the vice president.

10. In the Midwest, everyone worries about tornadoes damaging their property.

EXERCISE 4

Keeping in mind the requirements of college writing, choose the correct pronoun or verb form in parentheses.

1. There (is/are) examples of European calligraphy in Trinity College's manuscript of the Irish *Book of Kells* and in the English *Lindisfarne Gospels,* which the British Museum (own/owns).

2. After the eighth century, either Carolingian miniscule script or Gothic script, (its/their) derivative, (was/were) most popular in European manuscripts.

3. In Asian calligraphy, there (is/are) a number of stylized scripts, but the syllabic script, which Kukai (is/was) now known to (has/have) invented in the ninth century, (reveal/reveals) (its/his/their) basis in Chinese characters.

4. A group of artists in the San Francisco area still (practice/practices) calligraphy, which each of the artists (use/uses) for unique purposes in (his/her/their) art.

5. Monica Dengo, among other calligraphy artists, (show/shows) (her/their) works of art in San Francisco, but (she/they) (is/are) best known for (her, their) use of Arabic scripts.

EXERCISE 5

All of the following sentences are correct. Change them as directed in parentheses, revising other parts of the sentence to make subjects and verbs and pronouns and antecedents agree.

1. A sign in the lab reads: "This computer does only what you tell it to, not what you want it to." (Change *this computer* to *these computers.*)

2. Perhaps this sign was put up by some frustrated students who were having trouble with their computer manuals. (Change *some frustrated students* to *a frustrated student.*)

3. The sign in the lab reminds me of similar problems. A chef, for example, whose vegetables or casserole is ruined in a microwave might think, "This oven reads buttons, not minds." (Change *vegetables or casserole* to *casserole or vegetables.* Change *This oven* to *These ovens.*)

4. Who knows what kind of label is attached to computer errors! (Change *kind* to *kinds.*)

5. A person has to learn how to use a computer, not how to program one. (Change *A person* to *People.*)

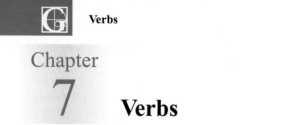

Chapter 7

Verbs

Being able to use verbs competently is an important part of being able to write clear and effective sentences. This chapter

- identifies the various kinds of verbs (**7a**),
- identifies the various forms of verbs (**7b**),
- explains the time relationships between verbs (**7c**),
- shows the relationship between the verb and the subject as well as the ways commands, possibilities, or wishes are expressed (**7d**),
- offers advice about *lie/lay* and *sit/set* (**7e**), and
- suggests ways to avoid confusing inconsistencies with verbs (**7f**).

You will, of course, encounter many terms as you work with the various forms and functions of verbs, but understanding the following five terms is basic to understanding explanations about verbs.

Tense refers to the form of the verb that indicates time—for example, present or past.

Person refers to whether the subject of the sentence is speaking (*I, we*—first person), spoken to (*you*—second person), or spoken about (*he, she, it, one, they*—third person).

Number refers to whether the subject of the sentence is one person or thing (singular) or more than one (plural).

Voice refers to the form of the verb that defines the relationship between the subject and the action (or state) of the verb.

Mood refers to the way a speaker or writer regards an assertion—as a statement, a command, or a condition not reflected in fact.

Grammar checkers cannot detect the subtle differences in the ways we use verbs because their decision process is based on matching and counting rather than on understanding. They catch some missing verbs, some helping verbs mismatched with main verbs, and some verbs lacking *-ed* endings, but they miss at least as many as they find. They can also identify some misused infinitives but seldom find misused present participles (**7b(2)**) or gerunds (**7c(2)**). They cannot distinguish between true passive verbs such as *have been seen* and a form of *be* followed by an adjective such as *have been healthy* and so frequently incorrectly flag passive constructions. Furthermore, they cannot tell when a passive construction is appropriate and so generally advise writers to "correct" them. They cannot find problems with improper tense forms or conditional sentences, and they occasionally flag properly used subjunctives as agreement errors.

7a Verbs change form depending on what kind of verbs they are and how they are used.

Verbs may be regular or irregular, or they may be helping verbs (auxiliaries). Verbs may be used as transitive or intransitive, or as linking verbs.

A **regular** or **irregular** verb	expresses action, occurrence, or existence (state of being).
An **auxiliary** verb	is a form of *be, have,* or *do* that combines with a verb to indicate voice, tense, or mood: Claudia **has studied** all night.

Modal auxiliary verbs	—*will, would, may, might, must, need, ought, shall, should, can, could, must, ought, dare, need, let* —are also considered auxiliaries and shade the meaning of the verb (its aspect).
A **transitive verb**	takes a direct object: Claudia **has studied** history [direct object].
An **intransitive verb**	does not take an object. Claudia **studies** hard.
A **linking verb**	relates the subject and a word referring to the subject (the complement). A linking verb may be a form of *be* (*am, are, is, was, were*), it may be a verb referring to the senses (*feel, look, smell, sound, taste*), and it may also be a verb that expresses existence or becoming (*appear, become, get, grow, prove, remain, seem, stay, turn*). Claudia **is** studious. She **sounds** authoritative. She **seems** responsible.

(1) Verb forms may be regular or irregular.

A **regular verb** is one that forms the past tense by adding a suffix that contains a *-d* or a *-t*.

Regular
laugh (*laughs*), *laughed*
hike (*hikes*), *hiked*
build (*builds*), *built*

Irregular verbs do not take the *-d* or *-ed* ending. They form their past tense by changing internally: *ran, spoke, thought.*

Irregular

run (runs), ran

speak (speaks), spoke

think (thinks), thought

(2) Auxiliary verbs combine with other verbs to indicate tense or voice.

When auxiliary verbs combine with other verbs, the meaning of the verb is altered in some subtle way. The auxiliary may express time or emphasis, or action in progress. For instance, *have* combines with the past form of a word that has features of both an adjective and a verb (a participle) to show the perfect tense—*have thrown, had thrown*—and forms of *be* combine with the past participle of a verb to form the passive voice (*has been thrown*—see page 115). *Be* also combines with the present participle (the *-ing* form of a verb) to show the progressive (an action in progress—*am throwing*). *Do* joins the present form of the verb to express emphasis (*does throw*) or negation, or to form questions.

CHECKLIST of Auxiliary Verbs			
Infinitive (base)	be	have	do
Present (first person)	am	have	do
Present (third person)	is	has	does
Second person and plural	are	have	do
Past singular	was	had	did

Past plural	were	had	did
Past participle	been	had	done
Present participle	being	having	doing

The present form of a verb may also be combined with another special kind of auxiliary verb, called a **modal auxiliary,** to make requests, give instructions, and express certainty, doubt, necessity, obligation, possibility, or probability: *we shall overcome, you can dream, she must sleep, they should laugh,* and so on.

Using Modal Auxiliaries

Aspect	Modal Auxiliary	+	Verb	Example
Ability	can, could	+	main verb	Annie *can pick* a flower next door.
Certainty, intention, probability	will	+	main verb	Annie *will pick* a flower next door.
Necessity	must	+	main verb	Annie *must pick* a flower next door.
Obligation	should, ought to	+	main verb	Annie *should pick* a flower next door.
Permission	may, can, could	+	main verb	Annie *may pick* a flower next door.
Possibility	could, might	+	main verb	Annie *could pick* a flower next door.

The present form of a verb combines with *shall* or *will* to show the future tense. (See the Glossary of Usage for the limited use of *shall*.)

> Annie **will pick** flowers next door tomorrow. [future tense]

In formal writing, *can* refers to ability; *may* refers to permission. (See the Glossary of Usage.)

> I **can** borrow the car to go to the movie. [ability]
>
> **May** I borrow the car? [permission]

Although the auxiliary always precedes the basic verb, other words may intervene.

> **Have** the members **paid** their dues?
>
> Television **will** never completely **replace** newspapers.

Using Auxiliary Verbs

Be + the present participle	progressive; tense determined by the tense of *be*	Cherise *is watering* the roses.
Be + the past participle	passive voice	The roses *were watered.*
Do + the present tense form	emphatic; tense determined by the tense of *do*	Cherise *did water* the roses.
Have + the past participle	perfect tenses	Cherise *has watered* the roses.
Modal + the present tense form	*can, could, may, might, must, shall, should, will, would*	Cherise *can water* the roses. Cherise *should water* the roses.

EXERCISE 1

Fill in the blank with an auxiliary combined with the base form, present participle, or past participle of the verbs listed in the right-hand column.

EXAMPLE

One _is driving_ the other back.   drive

1. A southeasterly storm _____.   approach

2. The air traffic controller _____ it for   watch
   the past fifteen minutes.

3. He _____ that the storm is violent,   hear
   so he _____ nervous.   become

4. The plane _____ new instructions or   need
   _____ an alternate path.   require

5. The controller _____ the flight path,   change
   and the pilot _____ the change, even   make
   if it _____ time-consuming.   seem

6. Indeed, the storm _____ delays.   cause

7. Unfortunately, delays _____ to stack   tend
   up like dominoes.

8. In other airports, controllers _____   experience
   their own delays because bad weather
   and maintenance _____ the flight   affect
   schedules.

9. Holiday passengers everywhere _____   scramble
   to find hotels for the night.

10. Neither the pilots nor the controllers
    _____ until the passengers _____   rest, land
    safely on the ground.

(3) The forms of *be* are highly irregular.

The most irregular verb in the English language is *be*. It has eight forms: *am, are, is, was, were, be, been, being.*

That may **be** true.

He **was being** difficult.

Following is a list of forms of *be* used with various subjects in the present and past tenses.

	First Person	Second Person	Third Person
Present	I am	you are	he/she/it is [singular]
	we are	you are	they are [plural]
Past	I was	you were	he/she/it/ was [singular]
	we were	you were	they were [plural]

Be can serve as a linking verb between a subject and its complement. (See **1b**.)

Gabriel **is** a very good student.

CAUTION Some dialects accept the use of *be* in place of *am, is,* or *are* (the present forms of *be*). They also accept the use of *be* with the present participle (**7a(2)**) to indicate habitual action or its omission to indicate simple action. College and professional writing (the contexts for formal written English), however, require the conventional forms of *be,* as shown in the list above.

She ̭be a fine hockey player. [*be* instead of *is*]

is

He ̭be walking to class. [Habitual action—he always walks to class.]

walks

He $\overset{is}{\wedge}$ walking to class today. [Simple action—his walking today was unusual.]

 In constructions where the subject is equivalent to a complement, do not omit the verb.

Going to the beach $\overset{is}{\wedge}$ a lot of fun.

Siriphan $\overset{is}{\wedge}$ very homesick.

EXERCISE 2

Complete the following sentences by using a form of the verb in the right-hand column.

1. Marcia _____ to work overtime this week.   be willing

2. She always _____ her vacation in June.   take

3. The money _____ a big help with the expenses.   be

4. She _____ to Barbados on a cruise.   go

5. She _____ relatives there.   have

(4) Verbs may be transitive, linking, or intransitive.

A noun or a pronoun follows a **transitive verb** and completes its meaning (a direct object). A transitive verb can also be made passive. (See 7b(1).) An **intransitive verb** does not accept a direct object, and it cannot be made passive. One kind of intransitive verb, a **linking verb,** uses a noun, pronoun, or adjective to complete its meaning, but it cannot be made passive. (See the Glossary of Terms.) Other intransitive verbs do not use either direct objects or subject complements. These are often called the **intransitive complete** verbs.

Transitive	The hammer **bent** the nail. [*Nail,* the direct object, receives the action of *hammer.*]
Linking	The bell **looks** fragile. [The subject complement, *fragile,* refers to *bell.*]
Intransitive	The bell **rang** repeatedly. [The adverb *repeatedly* modifies the verb.]

Some verbs can be transitive or intransitive, depending on the sentence.

| Transitive | Darlene **studies** the book. [*book*—direct object] |
| Intransitive | Darlene **studies** all night. [complete—no object or complement] |

A dictionary will indicate whether a verb is transitive or intransitive, or whether it can be either.

 English recognizes two kinds of verbs, those that express states of being (sometimes called **stative** verbs) and those that express action (**dynamic** verbs). Some verbs have two meanings, one stative, the other dynamic.

| Stative | I have [possess] time to waste. |
| Dynamic | I was having [experiencing] trouble understanding him. |

 7b **The conjugation of a verb is based on its principal parts.**

A **conjugation** is a table of the various forms of a verb.

Verbs

(1) The tables that follow illustrate the important parts of a verb.

The following conjugation of the verb *see* shows the relationships among tense, person, voice, and mood. (See **7c** and **7d**.) It also shows how auxiliary verbs help make a verb passive and form the perfect tenses.

Indicative Mood

		Active Voice		Passive Voice	
		Singular	*Plural*	*Singular*	*Plural*
Present tense	**1st**	I see	we see	I am seen	we are seen
	2nd	you see	you see	you are seen	you are seen
	3rd	one (he/she/it) sees	they see	one (he/she/it) is seen	they are seen
Past tense	**1st**	I saw	we saw	I was seen	we were seen
	2nd	you saw	you saw	you were seen	you were seen
	3rd	one (he/she/it) saw	they saw	one (he/she/it) was seen	they were seen
Future tense	**1st**	I shall (will) see	we shall (will) see	I shall (will) be seen	we shall (will) be seen
	2nd	you will see	you will see	you will be seen	you will be seen
	3rd	one (he/she/it) will see	they will see	one (he/she/it) will be seen	they will be seen

Present perfect tense	**1st**	I have seen	we have seen	I have been seen	we have been seen
	2nd	you have seen	you have seen	you have been seen	you have been seen
	3rd	one (he/she/it) has seen	they have seen	one (he/she/it) has been seen	they have been seen
Past perfect tense	**1st**	I had seen	we had seen	I had been seen	we had been seen
	2nd	you had seen	you had seen	you had been seen	you had been seen
	3rd	one (he/she/it) had seen	they had seen	one (he/she/it) had been seen	they had been seen
Future perfect tense (seldom used)	**1st**	I shall (will) have seen	we shall (will) have seen	I shall (will) have been seen	we shall (will) have been seen
	2nd	you will have seen	you will have seen	you will have been seen	you will have been seen
	3rd	one (he/she/it) will have seen	they will have seen	one (he/she/it) will have been seen	they will have been seen

Imperative Mood

Active Voice	Passive Voice
see	be seen

Subjunctive Mood

Active Voice	Passive Voice
see	see

The subjunctive is difficult to distinguish from other forms of a verb except for the subjunctive forms of *be*. (See 7d(2).)

If I **were** you, I would quit. [See 7d(2).]

(2) Verbs have at least three principal parts.

The three principal parts of verbs are the base form—or simple present—(*see*), which is the same as the infinitive (*see*); the past form (*saw*); and the past participle (*seen*). (A participle is a verb form that can function as an adjective. The *to* in *to see* is an infinitive marker, not precisely part of the infinitive.) Some consider the present participle (*seeing*) to be a fourth principal part. (See principal parts in the Glossary of Terms.)

The **present form** can be a single-word verb (*demand*) or a combination of a single-word verb and a helping verb (*is demanding, can demand*). Unless the verb is irregular, the **past form** can also be a single-word verb with *-d* or *-ed* (*demanded*). (See page 123.) It can be combined with helping verbs (*might have demanded*).

Part I of this checklist of principal parts lists regular and irregular verbs that are sometimes misused. Part II lists some verbs that allow more than one form for the past tense or the past participle, and part III lists some troublesome verbs that are easy to confuse and tricky to spell.

CHECKLIST of the Principal Parts of Verbs		
Part I: Principal Parts of Verbs Sometimes Misused		
Present	**Past**	**Past Participle**
arise	arose	arisen
ask	asked	asked

attack	attacked	attacked
bear	bore	borne/born
begin	began	begun
blow	blew	blown
break	broke	broken
bring	brought	brought
burst	burst	burst
choose	chose	chosen
cling	clung	clung
come	came	come
do	did	done
drag	dragged	dragged
draw	drew	drawn
drink	drank	drunk
drive	drove	driven
drown	drowned	drowned
eat	ate	eaten
fall	fell	fallen
fly	flew	flown
forgive	forgave	forgiven
freeze	froze	frozen
give	gave	given
go	went	gone
grow	grew	grown
happen	happened	happened
know	knew	known
ride	rode	ridden
ring	rang	rung
rise	rose	risen

run	ran	run
see	saw	seen
shake	shook	shaken
speak	spoke	spoken
spin	spun	spun
spit	spat	spat
steal	stole	stolen
sting	stung	stung
swear	swore	sworn
swim	swam	swum
swing	swung	swung
take	took	taken
tear	tore	torn
throw	threw	thrown
wear	wore	worn
weave	wove	woven
wring	wrung	wrung
write	wrote	written

Part II: Verbs with Options for the Past or Past Participle

awaken	awakened OR awoke	awakened
dive	dived OR dove	dived
get	got	got OR gotten
hang (things)	hung	hung
hang (people)	hanged	hanged
shrink	shrank OR shrunk	shrunk OR shrunken
sing	sang OR sung	sung
sink	sank OR sunk	sunk
spring	sprang OR sprung	sprung

stink	stank OR stunk	stunk
strive	strove OR strived	striven OR strived
wake	woke OR waked	woken OR waked

Part III: Principal Parts of Troublesome Verbs

Present	Past	Past Participle	Present Participle
lay	laid	laid	laying [*to put down; transitive*]
lead	led	led	leading
lie	lay	lain	lying [*to recline; intransitive*]
loosen	loosened	loosened	loosening
lose	lost	lost	losing
pay	paid	paid	paying
set	set	set	setting [*to place; transitive*]
sit	sat	sat	sitting [*to rest on the buttocks; intransitive*]
study	studied	studied	studying

EXERCISE 3

Respond to the questions in the past tense with a verb in the past tense; respond to the questions in the future tense with a verb in the present perfect tense (*have* or *has* + a past participle). Follow the pattern of the examples.

EXAMPLES

Did she criticize Don?   *Yes, she criticized Don.*

Will they take it?   *They have already taken it.*

1. Did they buy a computer?
2. Will I break it?

3. Did she throw away the manual?
4. Will he lose the document?
5. Did the cursor freeze?
6. Will the service center give advice?
7. Did you see the vendor agreement?
8. Will they begin repairs?
9. Did she leave an invoice?
10. Will you pay by check?

(3) Participles used alone cannot function as the verb in a predicate.

Participles such as *rising* or *shrunk* are never used alone as the verb of a sentence. When an *-ing* or an *-en* form or an irregular participial form such as *shrunk* is part of the verb, it always has at least one helping verb. Whether the *-ed* form is a verb or a past participle depends on the context. Both the past and present participles can work as modifiers, and they can also form part of the verb.

Sentences with Participles	Sentences with Simple Verbs
We could see heat waves *rising* from the road. [present participle]	Heat waves *rise* from the road. [simple present tense verb]
I was wearing jeans *shrunk* in the wash. [past participle]	We *shrank* those jeans in the wash. [simple past tense verb]
We ate pastries baked yesterday. [past participle]	We baked pastries yesterday. [simple past tense verb]

Be especially careful not to confuse nouns modified by participles with actual sentences. (See 2a.)

CAUTION Although it is easy to remember a clearly pronounced *-d* or *-ed* (*added, repeated*), it is sometimes harder to remember a needed *-d* or *-ed* in such expressions as *supposed to* or *used to* when the sound is not emphasized in speech. (See **4a**.)

Yesterday, I ~~ask~~ *asked* myself if the judge was ~~prejudice~~ *prejudiced*.

He ~~use~~ *used* to smoke.

I am not ~~suppose~~ *supposed* to be the boss.

She ~~talk~~ *talked* to Ellen yesterday.

E x e r c i s e 4

Look at one of your recent writing assignments. Underline all the verbs. Do all the verbs that require an *-ed* ending have one? If not, revise those sentences.

7c **Verb Tense makes time relationships clear.**

Verbs usually change form to show whether an action happened in the present, the past, or the future. This change of form is called **tense,** and through tense a verb can show, for example, that one action began yesterday and is still going on but that another action began yesterday and ended yesterday. Tenses are based on primary forms called principal parts (*ask, asked, asked*). (See **7b**.) Although English verbs change form only for the present and past tenses, three simple tenses and three perfect tenses are generally recognized. A **perfect tense** refers not only to the time in which the action began but also to the time in which it is completed.

Simple Tenses

Present   We often write letters. [based on the base form *write*]

Past   After graduation, we wrote letters. [change of form to show past tense]

Future   We will write letters after graduation. [future time expressed using an auxiliary]

Perfect Tenses

Present   We have written letters since graduation. [time expressed using an auxiliary with the past participle]

Past   We had written letters after graduation. [time expressed using an auxiliary with the past participle]

Future   We will have written letters before graduation. [time expressed using an auxiliary with the past participle]

When used as part of a verb, the present participle, as well as the past participle, always has at least one auxiliary. When a participle is used with a form of *be,* the verb is referred to as being in the **progressive** form. When a participle is used with a form of *do,* the verb is referred to as being in the **emphatic** form. Transposed, a form of *do* also signals a question.

It **is beginning** to snow. It **was snowing.** [progressive]

I **do respect** you. She **did answer** the question. [emphatic; COMPARE **Did** she **answer** the question?]

 Unlike the simple present, which expresses activities without reference to a specific moment in time, the present progressive expresses action that is occurring at the moment the speaker makes the statement.

I boil eggs.   The act of boiling eggs is habitual.

I am boiling eggs.   The act of boiling eggs is occurring now.

(1) Tense forms may be used to show a wide variety of time references.

Tense is not the same as time. Although tenses refer to time (see page 121), the tense forms often do not reflect divisions of actual time. For instance, as the following examples show, the present tense form is certainly not restricted to present time. It can refer to past and future occurrences as well. Furthermore, auxiliaries and other words in the sentence such as adverbs can also indicate time. In addition to the simple present, the present tense can be used to show habitual action, a timeless truth, or, with an adverb, future time.

> Dana **uses** common sense. [habitual action]
>
> Blind innocence **sees** no evil. [timeless truth]
>
> The new supermall **opens** tomorrow. [present with an adverb denoting the future]

The present tense is also commonly used to give a sense of immediacy to historical actions and to refer to what an author writes.

> In 1939 Hitler **attacks** Poland. [historical present]
>
> Joseph Conrad **writes** about what he **sees** in the human heart. [literary present]

The past tense refers to a definite time in the past not extending to the present, to action completed in the past, or to continuing action in the past.

> They **played** a good game. [action completed in the past]
>
> Adolpho **played** well in those days. [action contained in the past]
>
> We **were learning** to use a computer. [continuing action in the past]

Future time denoting sometime after the present is shown by combining a base form with a form of *will*.

> We **will see** the movie. [some time after now]
>
> We **will be spending** June in the mountains. [continuing action in the future]

The perfect tenses—those combining a form of *have* with the base form of the verb—express actions that began at an unspecified time in the past and that may continue into the present (present perfect), actions that occurred entirely before a specific time in the past (past perfect), and actions that will begin before a specific time in the future (future perfect).

She **has used** her savings wisely. [up to now—present perfect]

I **have seen** the movie. [some unspecified time before now—present perfect]

Terese **had planned** to meet with me before class. [specific time in the past—past perfect]

Our bumpers **will have rusted** by the time he changes his mind. [specific time in the future—future perfect]

Sometimes the simple past can replace the past perfect.

Tawanda **had talked** [*or* **talked**] to me before class started.

The future perfect is almost always replaced by the simple future.

After graduation, I **will have seen** [*or* **will see**] my dreams come true.

Exercise 5

For each sentence, explain the differences in the meaning of the tense forms separated by slashes.

1. The Asian elephant roams/does roam/had been roaming freely in the jungles of Thailand.
2. The elephant's harsh habitat and treatment in domesticity have endangered/will have endangered the species very soon.
3. The Thai Elephant Conservation Center has treated/had treated hundreds of cases in its hospital since 1994.
4. Some of the afflicted elephants ate/did eat/were eating bananas containing amphetamines.

5. In *Gone Astray: The Care and Management of the Asian Elephant in Domesticity,* Richard Lair wrote/writes about the disappearing Thai jungle and the rapidly declining numbers of Asian elephants.

(2) Tense forms should appear in a logical sequence.

Combinations of tense forms can make very fine distinctions in relation to actual time.

When the speaker **finished,** everyone **applauded.** [Both actions took place at the same definite time in the past.]

Collette **has worked** nights because she **needed** extra money. [Both forms indicate action at some time before now, but *needed* indicates a time before the action indicated by *has worked.*]

When I **had been** here for two weeks, I **learned** that my application for financial aid **had been denied.** [The first *had* before *been* indicates a time before the action described by *learned.* The second *had been* indicates action completed before that indicated by *learned.*]

Infinitives

The present infinitive expresses action occurring at the same time as, or later than, that of the main verb; the present perfect infinitive shows action that occurred before the time shown by the main verb.

I want **to show** you my new trick. [present infinitive—at the same time as the main verb *want*]

He preferred **to go** home. [present infinitive—at a time later than *preferred*]

I would like **to have won** first place. [present perfect infinitive—at a time before the main verb *would like;* COMPARE "I wish I *had won.*"]

Infinitive and Gerund Phrases after Verbs

Certain verbs are followed by infinitives and others by gerunds. (Gerunds are verbal forms that function as nouns.)

I offered **to help** her.

I avoided **calling** her.

Some of the most common verbs followed by a gerund are *appreciate, avoid, consider, delay, discuss, enjoy, finish, keep (on), mention, mind, postpone, suggest.*

I **mind missing** the party.

Some of the most common verbs followed by an infinitive are *agree, appear, ask, decide, expect, intend, need, plan, pretend, promise, refuse, want.*

I **decided to go** home.

Some verbs that are followed by a noun or a pronoun + an infinitive are *advise, allow, ask, encourage, expect, force, invite, remind, require, want.*

I **encouraged** Mac **to study** with her.

The verb *go* is followed by the gerund in certain expressions that for the most part concern recreational activities.

Let's **go swimming.**

Participles

The present form of participles expresses action occurring at the same time as that of the main verb, while the present perfect form indicates action that took place before that of the main verb.

> **Planning** for the election, he decided what he should advocate. [The *planning* and *deciding* were simultaneous.]

> **Having built** the house themselves, they felt a real sense of pride. [The *building* took place first; then came their sense of pride.]

EXERCISE 6

In the following paragraph, insert the appropriate form of the word in parentheses so that the events in the paragraph form a logical sequence.

¹Last night I (go) (see) the college's spring revue. ²When I (arrive) at the auditorium, everyone (stand) in line (wait) (get) in. ³As soon as the doors (open), everyone (rush) (find) their seats. ⁴I (find) mine right away and (sit) down, but I (stand) up often for all the other people who (sit) in my row. ⁵After the lights (dim), the music (begin), and the curtains (opening), the cast (begin) (sing) and (dance), and I (lose) all track of time until the curtain (come) down for the intermission. ⁶After the intermission, an entirely different cast (perform) from the one that (begin). ⁷I (be) (startle) until I (remember) the article in the campus paper that (report) how a dispute between the producer and the director (be settle).

7d Verbs have voice and mood.

(1) Voice indicates the relationship between the action (or state) of the verb and the subject.

Two kinds of relationships between the action or state of the verb and the subject are possible: active and passive. For transitive verbs, **active voice** emphasizes the subject as the *doer* of the action. **Passive voice** deemphasizes the doer of the action and makes the subject the *receiver* of the action. (See 29d(1) and the Glossary of Terms.) To make an active verb passive, use the appropriate form of *be* with the base verb. **Intransitive verbs** are used only in the active voice.

Active	The interviewer rejected Tom's application. [The subject *interviewer* acts on the object *application.*]
Passive	Tom's application was rejected by the interviewer. [The subject *application* is acted upon.]
OR	Tom's application was rejected. [The prepositional phrase identifying the doer of the action could be omitted.]

In the examples above, the subject and the object of an active verb (the actor and the receiver of the action) switch places when a verb becomes passive. The subject of a passive verb receives the action. This transformation to passive voice is possible only with verbs that accept a direct object, that is, **transitive verbs.**

Most writers choose the active voice because it is clearer, more precise, more concise, and more vigorous than the passive. Many also prefer the active voice because, unlike the passive, it allows people to take responsibility for their actions. Careful writers generally reserve the passive voice for occasions when the agent (the person or thing doing the act) is unknown or unimportant, or when the action itself is more important than the agent. This use of the passive is reflected in scientific writing, where the experiment is more important than the experimenter. (See 29d(1).)

E X E R C I S E 7

Rewrite each of the following sentences to make active verbs passive and passive verbs active.

1. The local team won the first game in the tournament.

2. Our basketball team was selected by the NCAA.
3. The 7'6" center dropped the ball in the basket every time.
4. Every time he did that the fans cheered him loudly.
5. His teammates passed the ball to him whenever they could.

(2) A speaker's or writer's attitude about what he or she is saying is referred to as *mood*.

The **indicative mood** makes statements—a definite attitude; the **imperative mood** issues commands or requests—an insistent attitude; and the **subjunctive mood** expresses situations that are hypothetical or conditional—a tentative attitude.

Indicative	Dannice calls me every day.
Imperative	Call me every day, Dannice!
Subjunctive	It is important that Dannice call me every day.

The subjunctive mood, though rare, still occurs in certain fixed expressions such as *God bless you* and is also used with certain verbs, to express wishes and certain other hypothetical meanings.

Forms for the subjunctive

For the verb *be:*

PRESENT, singular or plural: **be** [archaic except in fixed expressions such as the following]
   so **be** it
   be that as it may

PAST, singular or plural: **were**
   as it **were**
   If I **were** you . . .

For all other verbs with third-person singular subjects, the subjunctive omits the characteristic *-s* ending.

> PRESENT, singular only: **see** [The *-s* ending is dropped.]

> *Examples*
> We asked that the hotel **give** us a different room.
> Suppose we **were** to leave before she does.
> Should the witness **avoid** the question, the judge will be angry.

> *Alternatives in indicative mood*
> When we ask, the hotel **gives** us a different room.
> After we **leave,** she will leave.
> If the witness **avoids** the question, the judge will be angry.

Should and *would* (past forms of *shall* and *will*) are also used for the subjunctive.

Subjunctives are used under the following conditions.

1. **After *that* with such verbs as *demand, insist, move, recommend, request, suggest***

   > I demand that the parking ticket **be** voided.

   > I suggested that she **move** to a new apartment.

   > The committee requested that we **adjourn.** [COMPARE The committee wanted to adjourn.]

2. **To express wishes or a hypothetical, highly improbable, or contrary-to-fact condition in *if* or *as if* clauses**

   > I wish I **were** in Ashville.

   > If I **were** you, I'd accept the offer.

   > Eat as if every meal **were** your last.

In the past half century, the use of *will* and *would* has become almost universally accepted in constructions that used to take the subjunctive. *Shall* is still used in such questions as "Shall we go?"

   > I wish she **would** leave.

   > I am worried that I **will** be late.

3. **As *had* rather than *would have* in clauses that begin with *if* and that express an imagined condition**

> If he ~~would have~~ *had* arrived earlier, he wouldn't have lost the sale.

> OR

> *Had* ~~If~~ he ~~would have~~ arrived earlier, he wouldn't have lost the sale.

EXERCISE 8

Explain the use of the subjunctive in each of the following sentences. Then revise each sentence so that it is appropriate for either a formal business letter or an informal letter to a friend and state the reason(s) for any changes you make.

1. Had the sales been higher, we would have received a larger raise.
2. She insisted that Victor be heard.
3. I wish that Inez were here.
4. If there should be a change in policy, we would have to make major adjustments.

EXERCISE 9

Compose five sentences illustrating at least three uses of the subjunctive.

7e *Sit* and *set, lie* and *lay,* and *rise* and *raise* are often confused.

You will pick the correct form most of the time if you remember that you can *set, lay,* or *raise* something, but that you yourself *sit, lie,* or *rise.* Thinking of these verbs in pairs and learning their principal parts can help you remember which form to use. *Sit, lie,* and *rise* are intransitive; *set, lay,* and *raise* are transitive.

Present	Past	Past Participle	Present Participle	Examples
Intransitive				
sit	sat	sat	sitting	**Sit** down. You **sat** up. **Sitting** down, I thought it over.
lie	lay	lain	lying	**Lie** down. He **lay** there for hours. It **has lain** next to the shed for months. **Lying** down, I fell asleep.
rise	rose	risen	rising	I **rise** before daybreak. I **rose** even earlier yesterday. I **have** always **risen** at seven. I am **rising** earlier each day.
Transitive				
set	set	set	setting	I **set** the clock. I **set** it down. It had been **set** there. We were **setting** the pieces on the tray.
lay	laid	laid	laying	We **lay** those aside. I **laid** the pencils next to the pads. She **was laying** our tests next to our seats.
raise	raised	raised	raising	I **raise** the window each night. I **raised** the window last night. I am **raising** the window to clear the smoke.

Set, lay, and *raise* mean "to place or put something somewhere." For example, to *set* the table means to *lay* the silverware next to the plates. *Sit, lie,* and *rise,* the intransitive verbs of the pairs, mean "be seated," "get into a horizontal position," or "get up." For example, *you sit down* or *lie down* or *rise up.*

EXERCISE 10

Without changing the tense, substitute the appropriate form of *sit/set, lie/lay,* or *rise/raise* for the italicized verbs in the following sentences.

1. Last week they *established* their plans for the trip.
2. I often *rest* on the old stone wall and watch the sunset.
3. I *lifted* the window shade.
4. I try to *get up* in time to work out each morning.
5. After he weeded the garden, Chen decided to *nap* on the front porch.
6. I *am putting* your book on the front porch.
7. I have *slept* here for at least three hours.
8. Oliver was *sprawling* on the couch when I arrived.
9. Marcella *got up* in time to see me off.
10. Kalynda was *adjusting* her watch.

7f Unnecessary shifts in tense or mood can confuse readers.

Writers deliberately use a variety of tenses when they write about actions or events happening at different times. (See also 27a.) In other situations, however, changing tenses, mood, or voice can be distracting to the reader. Most shifts occur with literary or historical topics. Literary action occurs in fictional time and by convention is referred to in the present tense. Historical events may be referred to in the historical present. (See 7c(1).)

> He *came* to the meeting and ~~tries~~ tried to take over. [shift in tense from past to present corrected by making both verbs past]

Shifts can make reading a passage difficult.

The *Padshahnama* ~~was~~ *is* [It still exists.] an ancient manuscript that is owned by the Royal Library at Windsor Castle. This manuscript ~~will detail~~ *details* [the literary present] the history of Shah-Jahan, the Muslim ruler who ~~has~~ [The action was completed many years ago.] commissioned the building of the Taj Mahal during his reign in India. Battles, court scenes, and the adventures of Shah-Jahan's sons are among the significant events depicted in the *Padshahnama*. Shah-Jahan ~~is~~ *was* imprisoned [Use of the literary present here conflicts with the past tense later in the sentence.] for the last eight years of his life by his son, Awrangzeb, who was the new Mughal ruler.

E XERCISE 11

Look carefully at the following passages to note any errors or inconsistencies in tense and mood or other problems with verb usage and revise as needed.

Passage A

[1] It is hard for me to realize that it were only three years ago that I first begin to send e-mail to my friends. [2] Today I got most of my mail (except for bills) online, and I also did much of my other business online, too. [3] For instance, I can paying my bills electronically since I had an account at an electronic bank, and I can also ordering almost anything I wanted from a catalog that I could have looked at on the World Wide Web. [4] I even buys my last car online. [5] Of course, I go to a dealer and drove a model that I like first, but then I order the car on the Web. [6] It was less expensive, and I didn't have the hassle of dealing with a pushy salesperson.

Passage B

[7]One of the best things about the electronic revolution is the way it was changing the academic world. [8]My World Civilizations class meets online in a special chat room calls a MOO (for Multiple-user dungeon Object: Oriented), and we also will look at the various sites on the World Wide Web that showed pictures of archeological digs (like the one on the Mayans), architecture, and so on. [9]Taking a history class this way makes it lived for me. [10]It also makes my Shakespeare class more interesting. [11]I will look at the William Shakespeare pages on the World Wide Web and can find comments that famous scholars will make and citations to books and articles that helped me understanding the plays better. [12]I don't think I will have taken the time to go to the library for the same material—and it wouldn't have been as much fun to look at, either.

Mechanics

Chapter

8

Document Design

This chapter contains information on presenting your writing so that it is as readable as possible. As the volume of information grows, so does the importance of its delivery—the visual design that gives readers the cues that lead them to the information they require and that enable them to read it efficiently.

This chapter gives guidance on

- using the proper materials (8a),
- layout, headings, and graphics (8b),
- appropriate form for electronic documents (8c), and
- proofreading for matters of format (8d).

Visual design sends messages to readers. A dense, tightly packed page with narrow margins signals difficult material. Ample white space signals openness and availability. White space frames the material on the page, preventing it from seeming oppressive and burdensome and so contributes to ease in reading, regardless of the difficulty of the content. But too much white space can send a negative message: For instance, a triple-spaced research paper with huge margins announces that the writer has little to say.

Because the way you design your documents tells a reader a great deal about you, a well-designed letter of application and résumé can mean the difference between being hired and not being hired. (See 39b(4–5).) Similarly, a well-designed research paper can make a difference in how favorably a professor regards the quality of your work.

8a Using the proper materials enhances readability.

(1) Enhance readability with good quality paper and neat binding.

Use good 20-pound white $8\frac{1}{2}$-by-11-inch paper (neither onion-skin nor erasable bond); this kind of paper is suitable for use with typewriters, word processors, and most printers linked to a computer. If you use a printer that requires continuous sheets, choose paper that allows clean removal of pin-feed strips and separation of sheets. If you write your papers by hand, use regular $8\frac{1}{2}$-by-11-inch lined white notebook paper and follow your instructor's recommendations.

Use a paper clip or a staple to fasten pages. Do not use any other method of binding pages unless you are specifically asked to do so.

(2) Electronic documents should follow a consistent format.

If you submit your work electronically (for instance, by e-mail, on a bulletin board, in a Web document, or on some kind of re-movable disk), follow your instructor's directions exactly. If you use a disk, make sure that you use the proper size, density, and format. Most machines now accept only $3\frac{1}{2}$-inch high-density disks, but if your reader has a machine that uses only double-density disks, you must accommodate that restriction. Macin-tosh disks will not work on PCs unless they are specifically re-formatted. Label disks clearly. If you submit your work via e-mail or a bulletin board, use the subject line correctly and en-sure that your work is free of errors before you send it. What-ever the requirements, the computing facilities to meet them are likely to be available on campus at no cost.

(3) Type, fonts, and justification are best kept simple.

Although laser and ink jet printers can print different typesizes and styles (fonts) on a single page, most academic papers should be printed using a font that looks like typewriter type, such as Courier, or a simple proportional font such as Times Roman. It is usually best to avoid the sans serif fonts such as Arial because they are hard to read. Fancy display fonts such as PTBarnum or *Script* are seldom appropriate, and using a variety of fonts detracts from the content. Although word processing makes it easy to use italics or boldfacing for emphasis, resist the temptation. (See 10f.) Also, resist the impulse to justify your right margins (make them straight). Unless your printer has proportional spacing, it justifies the right margin by inserting spaces between words so that every line is the same length; the irregular spacing within the line can be distracting and at times can even mislead readers. Because college classes often simulate professional writing situations and since publishers and editors of learned journals generally request that manuscripts not be justified, it is usually inappropriate to justify the right margin of academic documents even if the printer has proportional spacing. Justification may be appropriate if a document will not be reformatted before being printed, as is the case with some business documents or documents intended for desktop publishing.

Pages from a good ink jet or laser printer are always acceptable. If you have a dot matrix printer, you should set the program (or the printer) for letter-quality or near-letter-quality print because readers find print that shows separate dots hard to read. Further, before you start, make sure that the printer cartridge has enough ink or toner to complete your document. If you use a typewriter or dot matrix printer, the ribbon must be fresh enough to type clear, dark characters. If your instructor accepts handwritten papers, write in blue or black ink on one side of the paper only.

8b Clear and orderly arrangement contributes to ease in reading.

The advice here follows the guidelines in the *MLA Handbook for Writers of Research Papers,* fifth edition (New York: Modern Language Association, 1999). If your instructor requires another style manual, check the most recent edition of that manual. (See the list of style manuals, page 559.)

(1) Effective layout makes documents easy to read.

Word processing software can be set to lay out pages exactly to your specifications: It can number your pages, print a certain number of lines per page, and incorporate appropriate word divisions. Software also allows you to vary the spacing between lines, but unless your instructor agrees to different spacing, observe the conventions of college writing and double-space all papers. Leave margins of one inch (or no more than one and one-half inches) on all sides of the text to give your reader room for comments and to prevent a crowded appearance. The ruled vertical line on notebook paper marks the left margin for handwritten papers. You can adjust the margin control on a typewriter to provide the margins you need.

(2) Indentation signals a change of ideas.

The first lines of paragraphs should be uniformly indented. You can set your word processing software to indent the first lines of all paragraphs one-half inch. (Indent five spaces on a typewriter, or one inch if writing by hand.) Indent block quotations one inch from the left margin (ten spaces on the typewriter). (See 16b.)

(3) All pages should be numbered.

Place Arabic numerals—without parentheses or periods—at the right margin, one-half inch from the top of each page. Put your last name immediately before the page number so that your instructor can identify a page that gets misplaced.

(a) The first page

Unless your instructor requests a title page, place your name, your instructor's name, the course and section number, and the date in the top left-hand corner (one inch from the top and one inch from the left edge of the page), double-spacing after each line. You should also double-space between the lines of a long title and center all titles. The page number should appear in the upper right-hand corner.

Begin your first paragraph on the second line below the title (the first double-spaced line). (See the models in chapters 33, 38, and 39.) Most research papers do not require a title page, but if you use one, follow your instructor's directions about the form.

If your instructor does want a title page, put the title of your paper first, followed by the subtitle, if any. Begin the title approximately two inches below the top of the page; center it and double-space it if it is longer than a single line. About halfway down the page, center your name. Then space down approximately the same amount and type such information as the course and section number, the professor's name, and the date.

MLA Style (First page)   **Title Page**

```
                              Bohn 1

Dietrich Bohn
Dr. Miller
English 299, Section 4
30 June 1999
Rigoberta Menchú and Representative Authority
     The 1983 publication of Rigoberta
Menchú's I, Rigoberta Menchú, has done much
to help her work to improve human rights in
her native country, Guatemala. Recently,
however, there has been a great deal of
controversy--especially since the 1999
publication of David Stoll's Rigoberta Menchú
and the Story of All Poor Guatemalans--
surrounding the truth of Menchú's
autobiography. Stoll, an anthropologist at
Middlebury College in Vermont, proves that
Menchú did not tell the whole truth about
her life in the book that made her famous.
When Menchú told her story, her goal was to
call international attention to the plight
"of all poor Guatemalans." She achieved this
goal by changing her story to make it more
compelling to her audience. These changes
have undermined her authority as a
representative figure and threaten to damage
her cause as well. The example of
I, Rigoberta Menchú shows why it is wrong to
fictionalize an autiobiographical account
that claims to speak for a whole people.
```

```
            Rigoberta Menchú and
            Representative Authority




                Dietrich Bohn




            English 299, Section 4
               Professor Miller
                30 June 1999
```

(b) Subsequent pages

Place your name and the page number in the upper right-hand corner, one-half inch from the top. Begin your text at the left margin, one inch from the top and double-space throughout.

(4) Headings help organize complex information.

Headings are particularly useful for helping the reader manage information in research papers, technical and business reports, and other kinds of complex documents. (See 39b.) Headings can also highlight the organization of a long block of information or make it easy to combine several brief statements to avoid choppiness.

If you use headings, make them consistent throughout your document, and if you have two levels of headings, treat all occurrences of each level alike. For instance, headings in this book follow a pattern similar to that of an outline. The main rules are identified by a number and letter set against the left margin and followed by subdivisions marked by numbers in parentheses. Further subdivisions are set flush with the left margin and, depending on the level of the division, appear in bold type of various sizes.

(5) Graphics aid understanding.

Visual examples help most readers understand complex information more readily. **Tables** organize information into columns and rows so that relationships are more easily noted. They are also particularly good for presenting numeric information. When you design a table, be sure to label all of the columns and rows accurately and give your table a title and a number.

Table 1

Mean Annual Temperature in Reno, Nevada

Month	Temp.	Month	Temp.
January	40	July	79
February	43	August	85
March	50	September	80
April	60	October	65
May	70	November	53
June	72	December	44

Charts and **graphs, drawings, maps,** and **photographs** demonstrate relationships among data and spatial concepts or call attention to particular points, people, objects, or events.

They are referred to as **figures. Pie charts** are especially useful for showing the relationship of parts to a whole.

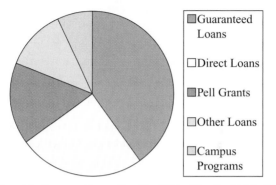

Fig. 1. Financial aid sources. Source: *Chronicle of Higher Education* 12 Feb. 1999: A31.

Graphs show relationships over time. For instance, a graph can show increases or decreases in enrollment or in student achievement or highlight differences in financial trends.

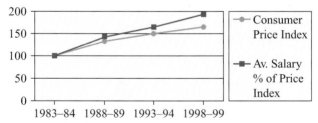

Fig. 2. Increase in buying power of faculty salaries, 1983–99. Source: *Chronicle of Higher Education* 26 Mar. 1999: A50.

Bar charts as on the next page show other kinds of correlations. They might illustrate stock market performance over several decades or the relative speeds of various computer processors.

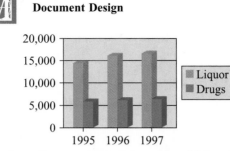

Fig. 3. Arrests on college campuses for liquor and drug violations. Source: *Chronicle of Higher Education* 28 May 1999: A1.

Other kinds of graphics such as **diagrams** and **drawings, maps,** and **photographs** help readers understand other kinds of concepts—dimensions and specific details, spatial relationships, emotional impact, and so on.

Map

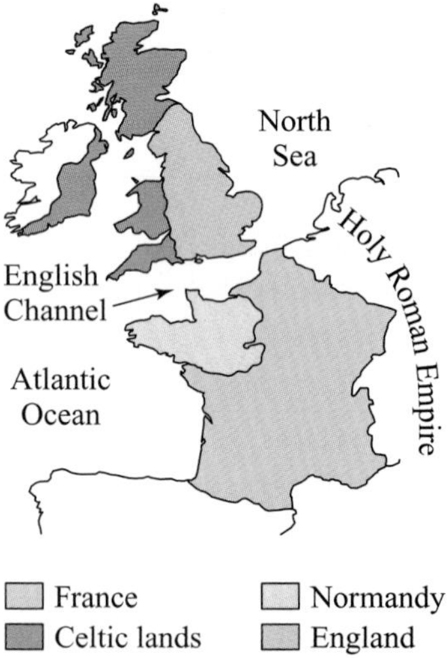

Fig. 4. Normandy circa 1066.

Diagram

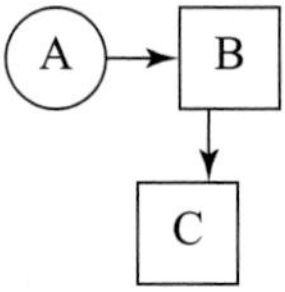

Fig. 5. A to C.

Drawing

Fig. 6. Window caulking.

Remember that each visual element you use should be numbered (for example, Table 1, Fig. 4). Table numbers and labels appear before the table, and table sources as well as figure numbers and labels are placed after the material they illustrate. If there are many illustrations, consider placing all of them in an appendix. Occasionally, text will also flow around a table or a figure, especially if it is otherwise difficult to place the image near the text it illustrates.

Fig. 7. *Goldengrove Unleaving.*

8c The appropriate form for electronic documents can vary.

Electronic documents may be presented on the Internet, on your campus network, on a class or organization's electronic bulletin board, or even on a disk that you hand to your instructor or fellow student. Electronic documents, which are usually easy to modify, permit new kinds of collaboration and use of materials.

(1) E-mail requires special care to avoid misunderstandings.

In the past few years, e-mail has become an important medium for communication. It is much less formal than a letter or a memo but more enduring than conversation in that it can be edited, saved, and filed. It also fosters speedy and convenient communication. E-mail uses a format like that of an interoffice memo, with "TO" and "SUBJECT" lines for entering the address of the person you are writing to and the topic of your message. (See also **39b(1)**.)

Using e-mail puts concern for the audience (**32a(2)**) in the foreground and requires special care to communicate ideas clearly. Experienced users have developed guides (referred to as **netiquette**) to help new users avoid some common hazards. Some standard advice appears below.

Design Hints for Bulletin Board Postings and Electronic Mail

1. Keep line length short. Because some users have monitors that display only forty characters in a line, it is considerate to keep your messages concise, your paragraphs short, and your subject focused.
2. The subject line of your message is like a title. Keep it short and descriptive.
3. Use a signature line at the end of each message. Your signature should include your name, your position and affiliation (if any), and your e-mail address. It can also include your postal address and telephone number if you wish, but it should not be longer than four lines.
4. Use capitals as you would in an ordinary typewritten document; that is, use mixed upper- and lowercase letters. Full capitals in electronic communications are understood as shouting. If you wish to stress a word, you can enclose it in asterisks, but do so *sparingly*.
5. Respect copyright. Anything not specifically designated as public domain is copyrighted, including e-mail messages from friends. Credit any quotations, references, and sources. (See also **38d**.)

(2) The World Wide Web offers new ways to present ideas.

The World Wide Web provides opportunities for designing new kinds of documents. It contains **pages** that a reader can view using a **browser.** (A browser is a computer program that fetches the text and graphic images that make up a Web document—a page—and enables the user to view them.) Web pages can be dynamically linked to other Web pages to form a new sort of document set that is very different from a book. Whereas the author of a book chooses which information a reader should see first, the Web permits users to determine the sequence in which they will view it. The information, however, may be much the same. Some instructors occasionally permit students to construct Web pages in lieu of submitting papers.

Constructing a Web page is not technically difficult if you have the right equipment. Web pages are written in a fairly simple language called HyperText Markup Language (HTML). Although it is fairly easy to learn to write HTML code, you can make adequate Web pages using HTML-capable word processing software or a recent version of a Web browser. For instance, two leading word processing programs allow users to save documents as HTML files. Both of the leading browsers also have Web page–editing components that you can use to build fairly complex pages without knowing how to do any HTML coding at all. (The Web page that appears later in this chapter was developed using one of them.) The planning that goes into making the page and the choices you make while you are building it are more important than knowing HTML.

When you plan a Web page, you make the same kinds of rhetorical choices that you make when you plan an essay or a term paper: you decide what your rhetorical stance will be—identify your audience and your purpose, determine the context for the page (for instance, whether it is to be part of a class Web site or perhaps developed from a deep personal interest in the subject), and decide on the tone you will take. When you write an essay, you make a list or an outline of points you will address (32d); when you construct a Web page, you also determine what information you will include and design a strategy for presenting it.

A Web document can be linear, like an essay, presenting each of its points in sequence; it can be hierarchical, branching out at each level; or it can be radial, allowing the reader to decide the final sequence of points.

Linear

Hierarchical   **Radial**

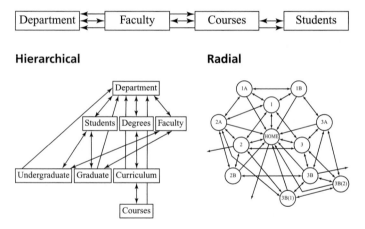

Web pages generally use about half as much text as paper pages. On a Web page, placement of the information, use of numbered lists, and visual elements substitute for directly stated transitional expressions and extensively described examples. A Web page should normally not exceed a couple of screens of carefully spaced information surrounded by meaningful white space—space that is not occupied by either text or images. To achieve that goal, group related points and provide space between groups. Typically, the top part of the page—the upper part of the first screen—should identify the document: the title, a visual element, a few bulleted points. Browsers show the top of the page first, and it should be distinctive enough to make the reader want to explore more.

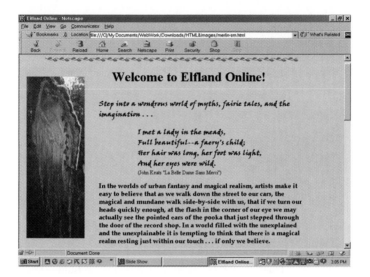

Kay Robinson's first design for this page displayed a large amount of text on this first screen, but she revised it by moving text down the page so it would appear when the user scrolled to the next screen (not shown).

You can usually expect to find the connections to other parts of the document or other sites—the site map—toward the bottom of the first page. Kay, however, put hers on the first screen—a sensible decision for this page. At the bottom of every page are the links to other sites, the date created or modified, and any copyright information. If your personal safety is assured, it can be a good idea to include an e-mail address where readers can contact you about the document. However, for security reasons, Kay chose not to reveal her e-mail address.

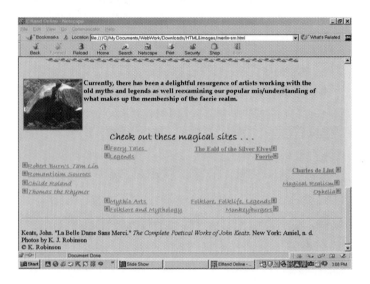

If you use visual elements—and you probably should—keep them under 30k (kilobytes) in size. Graphics larger than that slow down the loading of your Web page and place an undue burden on the user's Internet connection. Similarly, choose the background and text colors with care. Dark backgrounds can be dramatic, but a dark background with light text will print a blank page. It is usually better to select a light background with black, dark blue, or dark green text. Colors can be meaningful: red commands attention, blue recedes, green is usually comforting, and yellow can be alarming. Consider which color combination of background and text is most appropriate for your purpose. Consider also how many colors you will use. Many designers recommend no more than three (although you can use varying intensities of each—for example, light blue, medium blue, dark blue). Backgrounds with designs can make text very difficult to read, so make sure you choose one that enhances your text rather than overwhelms it.

Select a clear, easy-to-read font. HTML does not support the wide variety of fonts available to you in a word processing program. Even if you can find fancier fonts suitable for titles and other display elements, a simple font such as Ariel or Times Roman is probably best for most of your text. And bear in mind that the eye best accommodates about sixty characters per line. Much more makes text hard to read, so you need to select a font size accordingly.

The external links on your page are part of your text, so you will want to consider very carefully how many and what kind of links you include. Make sure that you have a clear reason for using them because readers get frustrated when links take them to irrelevant (albeit interesting) information, and they will associate your page with that frustration rather than with the good information you provide.

Finally, you must get permission for any text or graphics you draw from another source. Much of the information on the Web is free, but it requires acknowledgment. That warning also applies to visual elements. Furthermore, because publishing an address on your page can send many viewers to that particular remote site and perhaps bog down its server, you should use the contact information provided for that site to ask permission to link.

For more detailed help with designing a Web site, you might look at some of the following.

Tim Berners-Lee, the creator of the World Wide Web, is the author of this Web-based design manual.

http://www.w3.org/Provider/Style/Introduction.html

Jeff Glover, the Web manager for XOOM.COM, has good advice to offer at his Web site.

http://jeffglover.com/ss.html

Check out library science professor Alastair Smith's list of nearly four dozen Web site evaluation guides.

http://www.vuw.ac.nz/~agsmith/evaln/evaln.htm

Be aware that Web addresses may change. There are often forwarding mechanisms, but when there are not, you may still be able to find the page by dropping the last element of the address and trying again. You may need to do that several times. If that doesn't work, you may be able to find the page by running a search (**37d(2)**) or, as a last resort, looking at the links on other Web sites.

CHECKLIST for Designing Web Pages

1. Organize your page before you construct it. Otherwise, you are likely to become hopelessly muddled.

2. Write the page so that it can be viewed with or without pictures. While graphics greatly enhance the experience of moving from page to page, many people lack a connection that will allow them to receive graphics.

3. Limit each page to two or three screens of information. Instead of forcing your reader to scroll endlessly down your page, create additional pages and link to them.

4. Make all of the pages in a single Web document consistent. For example, you should not give your home page a blue background and the various pages linked to it pink, green, and yellow ones. You can create a template to use for all of the pages in the document.

5. Use graphics sparingly. Graphic files are typically very large and take a long time to transfer. A reader who does not have fast equipment may well abandon your beautiful, graphics-rich document for one that is less lovely but faster to access.

6. Be careful not to crowd your page with text. Just as books with narrow margins and dense type can be intimidating, so can a similarly constructed Web page. Set pages up so that they can be scanned quickly on a single screen and provide a link to other screens.

7. Understand the difference between a paper page and a Web page. Each has its advantages and disadvantages. Quick access to dozens or even hundreds of topics is easier with a Web browser than with a book, but few of us would care to curl up with a video monitor. Take advantage of the capabilities of the tool you are using.

8. Make your document easy to navigate. List sections of the document on your home page and include links to your home page from other pages in the site.

9. Include your name and the date you last worked on the page.

8d Proofreading provides quality control.

Proofreading differs from revising or editing. (See chapter 33.) **Revising** requires you to reconsider and possibly reorganize your ideas. **Editing** makes sure your prose is as clear, accurate, and stylistically consistent as possible. **Proofreading** pays particular attention to the conventions of grammar, mechanics, and punctuation, and to spelling errors that may have slipped through the editing process.

Proofreading also checks for and corrects layout errors and serves as a final check to make sure all necessary revising and editing have been done. Proofreading can be done manually or with a word processing program; doing both is insurance against error.

CHECKLIST for Proofreading Layout

Layout for Paper Documents

- Have you used proper margins? Are they all one inch wide or according to your instructor's specifications? Are paragraphs formatted consistently?

- Is each page numbered?

- Does the first page have the appropriate title and heading?

- Is the first line of each paragraph indented five spaces (or one inch if handwritten)?

- Is the print (or type or handwriting) dark, clean, clear, and legible?

- Are the lines double-spaced?

- Are all listed items numbered sequentially?

Layout for Electronic Documents

- Is the document too "text heavy"—that is, does each screen contain text of about the same density as a book? If so, consider revising to provide more white space.

- Are points graphically indicated by using bullets or by being otherwise divided into short blocks?

- Is there more than one type font? If so, consider revising. Are the type styles (bold, italic, and so on) used consistently throughout the document?

- Have you used a dark background with light type? If so, remember that to do so will not allow the user to print the page, since the light type will not show up in print.

- Have you used graphics effectively—images, lines, borders, bullets, and the like?

- Are any of your graphics larger than 30k? If so, try to shrink the image or choose a format with lower resolution.

- Are any links broken? If so, fix them.

- Have you provided a way back to the beginning of the document or to your home page?

- Have you identified yourself as the author and noted when the page was created or last revised?

- Have you run a spell checker?

Chapter

9

Capitals

Capital letters designate such things as proper names, peoples and their languages, geographical names, and certain organizations. Different styles for capitalization have been popular in the past, and no doubt others will be popular in the future. This chapter offers guidelines to help you know when and how

- to capitalize proper names (**9a**),
- to use capitals for titles of persons (**9b**),
- to capitalize words in titles of works (**9c**),
- to capitalize the pronoun *I* and the interjection *O* (**9d**),
- to capitalize the first word of directly quoted speech (**9e**), and
- to avoid unnecessary capitalization (**9f**).

If you have a special problem that is not covered here, look the word up in a good, recent dictionary (see **19a**). Dictionaries list not only words and abbreviations that begin with capitals but also acronyms that use full capitals. (Acronyms are words made from the first letters of the words in a term or from syllables of a term. See **11f**.)

Tom Cruise	Alabama	Rev.
Italians	Federal Express	NASA

A recent dictionary is also useful when the capitalization of a word depends on a particular meaning.

mosaic pictures BUT Mosaic Laws

on earth BUT the planet Earth

A style manual for the discipline in which you are writing is another useful guide for capitalization. (See page 559.)

When capitalizing a word is optional, consistently use the option you choose.

sunbelt OR Sunbelt   a.m. OR A.M.

Most grammar checkers are preset to identify capitalization errors in business writing. For college writing, however, they often give incorrect advice. It is true that they frequently flag words that should be capitalized, but they also frequently miss such words, and they rarely find words that are incorrectly capitalized. Be wary when you use them.

Current word processing programs usually correct common errors automatically. That feature can cause problems when you want to avoid capitalizing a word that is usually capitalized. For instance, the Auto-Correct feature will insist that you capitalize any word that follows the abbreviation *Jr.* It is a good idea to turn this feature off.

9a Proper names are capitalized and so, usually, are their abbreviations and acronyms.

As you study the following examples, notice that common nouns like *college, company, park,* and *street* are capitalized only when they are essential parts of proper names.

(1) Names and nicknames of persons or things and trademarks are capitalized.

Zora Neale Hurston	Flight 224	Honda Accord
John Paul II	Academy Award	Polaroid picture
Buffalo Bill	Pepsi	Scotch tape
Skylab	Nike	

(2) Names of peoples and their languages are capitalized.

African Americans	Latinos	English	Swahili
Asians	Poles	Korean	Urdu
Eskimos	Sikhs	Spanish	

Blacks, Whites OR blacks, whites [Whichever you choose, be consistent.]

(3) Geographical names are capitalized.

Arctic Circle	Havana	New Jersey
China	Iowa	Nigeria
Ellis Island	Lincoln Memorial	Seventh St.
Grand Canyon	Mississippi River	Yellowstone National Park

(4) Names of organizations, government agencies, institutions, and companies are capitalized.

B'nai B'rith	National Endowment for the Arts
Congress for Racial Equality	Howard University
International Red Cross	Museum of Modern Art
Phi Beta Kappa	Chicago Cubs
Internal Revenue Service	Ford Motor Company

(5) Names for days of the week, months, and holidays are capitalized.

| Wednesday | Tet | Fourth of July |
| August | Thanksgiving | Veterans Day |

The names of the seasons—spring, summer, fall, winter—are not capitalized.

(6) Designations for historical documents, periods, events, and movements are capitalized.

Declaration of Independence   Gulf War   Renaissance

Stone Age   Impressionism

(7) Names of religions, of their adherents, and of holy days, titles of holy books, and words denoting the Supreme Being are capitalized.

Christianity, Hinduism, Islam, Judaism

Christian, Hindu, Muslim, Jew

Bible, Book of Mormon, Koran, Talmud

Easter, Ramadan, Yom Kippur

Allah, Buddha, God, Vishnu, Yahweh

Some writers always capitalize pronouns referring to the Deity (except *who, whom, whose*). Others capitalize such pronouns only when the capital is needed to prevent ambiguity, as in "The Lord commanded the prophet to warn His people."

(8) Personifications are capitalized.

Then into the room walked Death. [COMPARE His death shocked everyone.]

Her heart belonged to Envy. [COMPARE She frequently experienced envy.]

(See also page 287.)

(9) Words derived from proper names are capitalized.

Americanize [verb]   Orwellian [adjective]

Marxism [noun]

When a proper name becomes the name of a general class of objects or ideas, it is no longer capitalized.

zipper [originally a capitalized trademark]

blarney [derived from the Blarney Stone, said to impart skill in flattery to those who kiss it]

If you are not sure whether a proper name or derivative has come to stand for a general class, look in a dictionary. Many such words can be treated with or without capitalization.

French windows OR french windows

Roman numeral OR roman numeral

When you can choose whether or not to capitalize a word, it is important to follow one option consistently.

(10) Abbreviations and acronyms or shortened forms of capitalized words appear in capitals.

AMEX, AT&T, B.A., CBS, CST, JFK, NFL, OPEC, UNESCO, YMCA [All of these are derived from the initial letters of capitalized word groups.]

(See also chapter 11 and 17a(2).)

9b Titles that precede the name of a person are capitalized but not those that follow it or stand alone.

Governor Christine Todd Whitman	Christine Todd Whitman, the governor
Captain Machado	Machado, our captain
Uncle Roy	Roy, my uncle
President Lincoln	the president of the United States

Words referring to family relationships are usually capitalized when the words substitute for proper names.

> Tell Mother I'll write soon. [COMPARE My mother wants me to write.]

9c The first, last, and all major words in titles are capitalized. (See 10a and 16c.)

In the style favored by the Modern Language Association (MLA) and in that recommended by the *Chicago Manual of Style* (*CMS*), all words in titles and subtitles are capitalized, except articles, coordinating conjunctions, prepositions, and the *to* in infinitives (unless they are the first or last word). The articles are *a, an,* and *the;* the coordinating conjunctions are *and, but, for, nor, or, so,* and *yet.* (A list of common prepositions can be found in chapter 1; see page 19.) MLA style favors lowercasing all prepositions, including long prepositions such as *before, between,* and *through,* which formerly were capitalized. APA style requires capitalizing any word that has four or more letters, including prepositions.

The Scarlet Letter	"How to Be a Leader"
From Here to Eternity	"What This World Is Coming To"
Men Are from Mars, Women Are from Venus [MLA and *CMS*]	
Men Are From Mars, Women Are From Venus [APA]	

In a title, MLA, APA, and *CMS* recommend capitalizing all words of a hyphenated compound except for articles, coordinating conjunctions, and prepositions unless the first element of the compound is a prefix.

> "The Building of the H-Bomb" [noun]
>
> "The Arab-Israeli Dilemma" [proper adjective]
>
> "Stop-and-Go Signals" [lowercase coordinating conjunction]

Because all three style manuals recommend that, in general, compounds with prefixes not be hyphenated except in special circumstances, the resulting single-word combinations follow the normal rules of capitalization. However, if misreading could occur (as in *un-ionized* or *re-cover*), if the second element begins with a capital letter (*pre-Christmas*), or if the compound results in a doubled letter that could be hard to read (*anti-intellectual*), all style manuals recommend hyphenating the compound. MLA and APA capitalize both elements of these compounds with prefixes, whereas *CMS* capitalizes only those elements that are proper nouns or proper adjectives. (While MLA does not specifically mention compounds with *self-*, both APA and *CMS* usually hyphenate *self-* compounds.)

> "Colonial Anti-Independence Poetry" [MLA]
>
> "Anti-Independence Behavior in Pre-Teens" [APA]
>
> "Anti-independence Activities of Delaware's Tories" [CMS]

However, in titles that appear in lists of references, APA style permits capitalizing only the first word and any proper nouns or proper adjectives.

9d   **The pronoun *I* and the interjection *O* are capitalized.**

> If I forget thee, O Jerusalem, let my right hand forget her cunning.
>
> —PSALMS

The interjection *oh* is not capitalized except when it begins a sentence.

9e The first word of every sentence (or unit written as a sentence) and of directly quoted speech is capitalized.

Procrastination is one of my specialties.

Oh, really! Do you want to become more efficient? Not right now.

Experienced cooks are usually ready to try something new. (You can learn from them.) [a parenthetical sentence]

Beth got out of the car and shouted, "Home at last!"

He says, "Stop dieting and start exercising." OR "Stop dieting," he says, "and start exercising." OR "Stop dieting," he says. "And start exercising."

One thing is certain: We are still free. [an optional capital after the colon; see 17d]

For the treatment of directly quoted written material, see chapter 16.

9f Unnecessary capitals are distracting.

(1) Capitalizing common nouns can distract your readers.

Do not confuse a common noun with proper nouns naming specific entities. A common noun preceded by the indefinite articles *a* and *an* or by such modifiers as *every* or *several* is not capitalized.

a speech course in theater and television [COMPARE Speech 324: Theater and Television]

a university, several high schools [COMPARE University of Michigan, Hickman High School]

However, always capitalize proper nouns, even when they are preceded by *a* or *an* or by modifiers such as *every* or *several*. In such cases, capitalized nouns name one or many of the members of a class.

a St. Bernard   every Virginian   several Canadians

(2) Using capitalization to indicate emphasis requires caution.

Occasionally, a common noun is capitalized for emphasis or clarity.

The motivation of many politicians is Power.

If you overuse this strategy, however, it will not achieve its purpose. There are other, better ways to achieve emphasis. (See chapter 29.)

Style Sheet for Capitalization

Capitals	No Capitals
the South	driving south
Southerners [geographical regions]	the southern regions [compass points]
Revolutionary War	an eighteenth-century war
a Chihuahua [a breed of dog named after a state in Mexico]	a poodle [a breed of dog]
a Ford tractor	a farm tractor
Washington State University	a state university
Declaration of Independence	a declaration of independence
German, Italian, Japanese	a language course
the PTA [OR the P.T.A.]	an organization for parents and teachers

Parkinson's disease [a disease named for a person]	flu, asthma, leukemia
the U.S. Army	a peacetime army
two Democratic candidates [a political party]	democratic procedures [refers to a form of government]
May	spring
Memorial Day	a holiday
Dr. Katherine Kadohata	every doctor, my doctor

EXERCISE 1

Write brief sentences using each of the following words correctly.

1. president
2. President
3. company
4. Company
5. west
6. West
7. avenue
8. Avenue
9. republican
10. Republican

EXERCISE 2

Insert capitals wherever needed.

¹my first semester in college was overwhelming. ²i failed economics and almost failed spanish and chemistry. ³one problem was that i was putting in too many hours at the bavarian inn, where i worked as assistant manager. ⁴the restaurant is popular because it is on the east side right across the street from the convention center. ⁵richard gross, the manager, was never around, and i usually had to work sundays and holidays as well as weekday nights. ⁶when other students were relaxing over thanksgiving, i was working overtime. ⁷my advisor finally told me, "this schedule isn't working for you. ⁸you should reduce the number of classes you're taking at dixon

college or cut back your hours at the restaurant." [9]when my grades came in january, i quit my job and took a special course on improving study habits. [10]i got a lot out of our textbook *focusing attention: how to manage time and improve concentration.* [11]next year I may transfer to metropolitan community college in minneapolis so that I can live closer to home.

Chapter

10   Italics

Italics are a typesetting convention. A word processing program allows you to follow the conventions of professional typesetters who use italics in the following ways. Italics identify or indicate

- the titles of separate publications (**10a**),
- foreign words (**10b**),
- the names of legal cases (**10c**),
- the names of ships and satellites (**10d**), and
- words used primarily as illustrations and algebraic expressions or statistical symbols (**10e**).

In print, italics are created by using a *font* style.

- In your word processing program, you have a number of fonts available—Courier, Times Roman, and Arial are three of the most common. *Italic* is a style available with most fonts.
- A grammar checker cannot indicate to you where you have used italics incorrectly because it is not programmed to identify fonts.

In handwritten or typewritten papers, you can indicate italics by underlining. In most situations, either italicizing or underlining is acceptable. If in doubt, follow the convention your audience expects. (See **32a(2)**.)

It was on *60 Minutes.*   It was on <u>60 Minutes</u>.

10a Italics identify the titles of separate works. (See 9c and 16c.)

A separate work is one published (or produced) as a whole rather than as part of a larger published work. A newspaper, for example, is a separate publication, but an editorial in that newspaper is not. Different conventions are used for indicating the title of the newspaper and the title of the editorial. (See 16c.) These conventions help readers gauge the size of a work and the relation between one work and another.

> Have you seen Russell Baker's "Disturbers of the Peace" in today's *New York Times*?

> I especially enjoyed "The Politics of Paradise" in Ellen Pagel's *Adam, Eve, and the Serpent*. [an essay in a book]

The titles of the following kinds of separate works are also italicized.

Books	*The Bluest Eye*	*A World Lit Only by Fire*
Magazines	*Wired*	*National Geographic*
Newspapers	*USA Today*	*Wall Street Journal*
Plays, films	*Othello*	*The Thin Red Line*
Television and radio shows	*Biography*	*Texaco Presents the Metropolitan Opera*
Recordings	*Hard Day's Night*	*Great Verdi Overtures*
Works of art	*Mona Lisa*	*David*
Long poems	*Paradise Lost*	*The Divine Comedy*
Comic strips	*Peanuts*	*Doonesbury*
Genera, species	*Homo sapiens*	*Rosa setigera*

In APA style, volume numbers in reference lists are italicized. (See **38h**.)

Memory & Cognition, 3, 635–647.

10f Used sparingly, italics occasionally show emphasis.

Sometimes, using italics for emphasis can contribute to clarity.

These *are* the right files. [making it clear that these files are, indeed, the correct ones]

If they take offense, then that's *their* problem.

Overuse of italics for emphasis (like overuse of the exclamation point) defeats its own purpose. If you find yourself frequently underlining (or italicizing) words, try substituting more specific (**20**) or forceful words (**29**) and varying sentence structure (**30**).

E X E R C I S E *1*

Identify and underline all words that should be italicized in the following sentences. Explain why each should be italicized.

1. To find information about museum collections and exhibits, I consulted Smithsonian Magazine, the New York Times, and several online museum Web sites.

2. While online, I visited the Web site for the Metropolitan Museum of Art to see Charles Demuth's painting The Figure 5 in Gold and Anthony Caro's sculpture Odalisque.

3. I didn't find any graphics of illustrated manuscripts on the Web site, but I did find the title page of William Blake's Songs of Innocence in my copy of Masterpieces of the Metropolitan Museum of Art.

4. I also found a photograph of a beautiful sheet from the Koran that illustrates the Arabic script known as the maghribi, or Western, style.

5. The picture of the Architeuthis dux displaying at the National Museum of Natural History caught my eye because this giant squid is the world's largest invertebrate.

6. I also read about the Smithsonian Institution's National Air and Space Museum, which houses the Freedom 7 spacecraft and the engine from the Saturn F-1.

7. The Web site for the Modern Art Museum's Celeste Bartos Film Museum explains that its collection includes such classics as The Great Train Robbery.

8. I would like to find multimedia clips of these films and other performances, such as Sunday in the Park with George and The Nutcracker, on the Internet.

9. I tried to find a clip of the Beatles' Hey, Jude at the Rock and Roll Hall of Fame and Museum site, but I found only a clip of John Lennon talking.

10. Since I wanted to create a Web site that led to interesting museum sites, I read about Internet copyright laws and The Washington Post Company v. Total News Inc.

Chapter
11

Abbreviations, Acronyms, and Numbers

Abbreviations, acronyms, and numbers are used in tables, notes, and bibliographies. They are also used in professional writing (see **39b**) and sometimes in college essays.

Abbreviations are usually marked with periods. Acronyms are not. An abbreviation is a shortened version of a word or phrase: *assn.* (association), *dept.* (department). An acronym is formed by the initial letters of a series of words or from the combination of syllables of other words: *AIDS* (**a**cquired **im**muno**d**eficiency **s**yndrome), *sonar* (**so**und **na**vigation **r**anging).

This chapter will help you learn

- how and when to abbreviate (**11a–e**),
- when to explain an acronym (**11f**), and
- how to decide if you should spell out a number or use numerals (**11g–h**).

11a Designations such as *Ms., Mr., Mrs., Dr.,* and *St.* appear before a proper name, and those such as *Jr., Sr.,* and *II* after.

Mrs. Adrienne Marcus	St. Paul
Mr. Julio Rodriguez	P. T. Lawrence, III
Ms. Gretel Lopez	Mark Ngo, Sr.
Dr. Sonya Allen	Erika C. Scheurer, Ph.D.

Avoid redundant designations.

Dr. Carol Ballou OR Carol Ballou, M.D. [NOT Dr. Carol Ballou, M.D.]

Most abbreviations form plurals by adding *-s* alone, without an apostrophe. Exceptions are made when adding an *-s* would create a different abbreviation: *Mr., Mrs.* When this is the case, consult a dictionary.

Use abbreviations for job titles (such as *Prof., Sen., Capt.,* or *Rev.*) only at the beginning of someone's name. When *Reverend* and *Honorable* are spelled out, they should be preceeded by *the*.

Rev. George T. Campbell OR the Reverend George T. Campbell

Hon. Julia F. Bennett OR the Honorable Julia F. Bennett

 In other languages, *the* is sometimes used before titles. American English omits *the* except when using *Reverend* or *Honorable*.

~~the~~ Dr. Sonya Allen

~~the~~ Professor Rodriguez

11b The names of streets, cities, states, countries, continents, months, days of the week, and units of measurement are usually written out in full.

To make sentences easy to read, write out in full the names that appear within them.

On a Tuesday in September, we drove ninety-nine miles to Minneapolis, Minnesota; the next day we flew to Los Angeles, where we stayed in a hotel on Wilshire Boulevard.

11c **Abbreviations are used for addresses in correspondence.**

Although words like *Street, Avenue, Road, Company,* and *Corporation* are usually written out when they appear in sentences, they are abbreviated in the address for a letter (see **39b(3)**) or other correspondence. Similarly, the names of states are also abbreviated when they are part of an address.

Sentence	Derson Manufacturing Company is located on Madison Street.
Address	Derson Manufacturing Co.
	200 Madison St.
	Watertown, MN 55388

When addressing correspondence within the United States, use the abbreviations designated by the United States Postal Service. (No period follows these abbreviations.)

Postal Abbreviations

AL	Alabama	IL	Illinois
AK	Alaska	IN	Indiana
AZ	Arizona	IA	Iowa
AR	Arkansas	KS	Kansas
CA	California	KY	Kentucky
CO	Colorado	LA	Louisiana
CT	Connecticut	ME	Maine
DE	Delaware	MD	Maryland
DC	District of Columbia	MA	Massachusetts
FL	Florida	MI	Michigan
GA	Georgia	MN	Minnesota
GU	Guam	MS	Mississippi
HI	Hawaii	MO	Missouri
ID	Idaho	MT	Montana

NE	Nebraska	RI	Rhode Island
NV	Nevada	SC	South Carolina
NH	New Hampshire	SD	South Dakota
NJ	New Jersey	TN	Tennessee
NM	New Mexico	TX	Texas
NY	New York	UT	Utah
NC	North Carolina	VT	Vermont
ND	North Dakota	VA	Virginia
OH	Ohio	VI	Virgin Islands
OK	Oklahoma	WA	Washington (state)
OR	Oregon	WV	West Virginia
PA	Pennsylvania	WI	Wisconsin
PR	Puerto Rico	WY	Wyoming

11d Abbreviations are used in bibliographies and other citations of research.

When used within a sentence, words such as *volume, chapter,* and *page* are written out in full.

I read the introductory chapter and pages 82–89 in the first volume of the committee's report.

In bibliographies, footnotes, and endnotes (see chapter 38), the following abbreviations are used.

abr.	abridged, abridgment
Acad.	Academy
anon.	anonymous
app.	appendix
Apr.	April
Assn.	Association
Aug.	August

biog.	biography, biographer, biographical
bk.	book
bull.	bulletin
c.	circa, about (for example, c. 1960)
CD	compact disc
CD-ROM	compact disc read-only memory
cf.	compare
ch., chs.	chapter, chapters
col., cols.	column, columns
Coll.	College
comp.	compiled by, compiler
Cong. Rec.	*Congressional Record*
cont.	contents OR continued
DAB	*Dictionary of American Biography*
Dec.	December
dept.	department
dir.	directed by, director
diss.	dissertation
div.	division
DNB	*Dictionary of National Biography*
DVD	digital videodisc
ed., eds.	edited by OR editor(s) OR edition(s)
enl.	enlarged (as in rev. and enl. ed.)
et al.	*et alii, et aliae* (and others)
Feb.	February
fig.	figure
FTP	File Transfer Protocol
fwd.	foreword, foreword by
gen. ed.	general editor
govt.	government

GPO	Government Printing Office
HR	House of Representatives
HTML	HyperText Markup Language
HTTP	HyperText Transfer Protocol
illus.	illustrated by, illustrator, illustration
inc.	incorporated OR including
Inst.	Institute, Institution
intl.	international
introd.	introduction, introduced by
Jan.	January
jour.	journal
KB	kilobyte
l., ll.	line, lines (omitted before line numbers unless the reference would be unclear)
mag.	magazine
Mar.	March
MB	megabyte
MOO	multiuser domain, object-oriented
ms., mss.	manuscript, manuscripts
n, nn	note, notes (used immediately after page number: 6n3)
natl.	national
n.d.	no date [of publication]
no., nos.	number [of issue], numbers
Nov.	November
n.p.	no place [of publication] OR no publisher
n. pag.	no pagination
Oct.	October
P	Press (used in documentation; see U)
p., pp.	page, pages (omitted before page numbers unless the reference would be unclear)

pref.	preface, preface by
pseud.	pseudonym
pt., pts.	part, parts
rept.	reported by, report
rev.	revision, revised, revised by OR review, reviewed by
rpt.	reprinted, reprint
sec., secs.	section, sections
Sept.	September
ser.	series
sic	thus, so; reproduced exactly as written (used to indicate an error reproduced without correction when quoting)
Soc.	Society
supp.	supplement
trans.	translated by, translator, translation
U	University (used in documentation; Wesleyan UP OR U of California P)
URL	uniform resource locator
vol., vols.	volume, volumes (omitted before volume numbers unless the reference would be unclear)
www	World Wide Web

11e Certain abbreviations have become so familiar they now substitute for words within sentences.

Some abbreviations are acceptable within sentences because they have come to function as the full equivalent of words. This is the case when the abbreviation has become a word in its own right or when it substitutes for words from another language.

(1) A clipped form is a word shortened from a longer word.

Because it functions as a word, a clipped form does not end with a period. Some clipped forms such as *rep* (for representative), *exec* (executive), or *info* (for information) are too informal for use in college writing. Others—such as *exam, lab,* and *math*—are becoming acceptable because they have been used so frequently that they no longer seem like abbreviations.

(2) Abbreviations designate time period and zone.

82 B.C. [OR B.C.E.] for before Christ [OR before the common era]	A.D. 95 [OR 95 C.E.] for *anno Domini,* in the year of our Lord [OR the common era]
7:40 a.m. [OR A.M.] for *ante meridiem,* before noon	4:52 EST [OR E.S.T.] for eastern standard time

Words designating units of time, such as *minute* or *month,* are written out when they appear in sentences. They can be abbreviated in tables or charts.

min.   mo.   yr.

(3) The abbreviation for the United States (U.S.) can be used as an adjective.

the U.S. Navy, the U.S. economy [COMPARE The United States continues to enjoy a strong economy.]

(4) Writers use initials in the names of individuals who are commonly referred to by their initials.

FDR   E. B. White

JFK   G. K. Chesterton

In most cases, however, first and last names should be written out in full.

Phyllis D. Miller

(5) Some abbreviations stand for expressions in Latin.

So that you can use these abbreviations correctly, the English equivalent is provided here in brackets.

cf. [compare]   et al. [and others]   i.e. [that is]
e.g. [for example]   etc. [and so forth]   vs. OR v. [versus]

11f Acronyms are usually spelled out the first time they are used.

Some acronyms have been used so frequently that they are likely to be recognized without explanation.

CBS   NASA   NFL   YMCA
IRA   NATO   SAT   UN

In most cases, however, experienced readers will expect you to identify an acronym the first time you use it.

FEMA (the Federal Emergency Management Administration) was criticized for its slow response to the victims of Hurricane Andrew.

OR

The Federal Emergency Management Administration (FEMA) was criticized. . . .

The ability to identify an acronym will vary from one audience to another. Some readers know that *HMO* stands for *health maintenance organization;* others may not. By spelling out such acronyms the first time you use them, you are providing a useful courtesy.

Exercise 1

Place a check mark next to those forms that are appropriate for use within the sentences of a college essay. Correct those that are not.

1. after 8 P.M.
2. 457 *anno Domini*
3. on St. Clair Ave.
4. two blocks from Water Street
5. in Nov.
6. in the second mo. of the yr.
7. in Calif.
8. at the UN
9. Mr. Robert Lyons
10. for a prof.

11g Depending on their size and frequency, numbers are written in different ways.

When you use numbers infrequently in a piece of writing, you can spell out those that can be expressed in one or two words and use figures for the others. When you use numbers frequently, spell out those from one to nine and use figures for all others. Very large numbers can be expressed by a combination of words and figures.

Always	over three inches
But	three-quarters of an inch OR .75 inches
Always	after 124 days
But	after thirty-three days OR after 33 days
Always	758 students
But	seven hundred students OR 700 students

In a discussion of related items containing both single- and double- or triple-digit numbers, use figures for all numbers.

Lana worked **7** hours last week, but Julio worked **22.**

If a sentence begins with a number, spell out the number.

Two hundred twenty-five contestants competed in the talent show.

Note that *and* is not used in this case. [NOT two hundred and twenty-five]

11h Some numbers follow special usages.

(1) Specific time of day can be indicated in either numbers or words.

4 p.m. OR 4:00 p.m. OR four o'clock in the afternoon
9:30 a.m. OR half-past nine in the morning

(2) Dates are usually indicated by both numbers and words.

November 8, 1962 OR 8 November 1962 [NOT November 8th, 1962]
December fourth OR the fourth of December OR December 4
the fifties OR the 1950s
the fourteenth century
in 1362
from 1998 to 2001 OR 1998–2001

Many languages invert the numbers for the month and the day, writing **18/9/01** for *September 18, 2001.* In American practice, the month precedes the day: **9/18/01.**

(3) Addresses require the use of numbers.

25 Arrow Drive, Apartment 1, Columbia, MO 78209 OR 25 Arrow Dr., Apt. 1, Columbia, MO 78209

21 Second Street

459 East 35 Street OR 459 East 35th Street

(4) Identification numbers are indicated numerically.

Channel 10   Edward III   Interstate 40   Room 222

(5) Pages and divisions of books and plays are indicated numerically.

page 15   chapter 8   part 2

in act 2, scene 1 OR in Act II, Scene I

(6) Decimals and percentages are indicated numerically.

a 2.5 average   12 percent   0.853 metric tons

(7) Large round numbers can be indicated with either numbers or words.

forty million dollars OR $40 million OR $40,000,000 [Figures are often used for emphasis.]

(8) In legal or commercial writing, numbers are often stated two ways.

The lawyer's fee will exceed two million (2,000,000) dollars.
OR
The lawyer's fee will exceed two million dollars ($2,000,000).

Languages differ in their use of the period and comma with numbers. American English marks any number smaller than one with a decimal point (period) and uses a comma to divide larger numbers into more understandable units. A comma between every third and fourth number separates thousands.

10,000 (ten thousand)

7.65 (seven and sixty-five one hundredths)

7,000.65 (seven thousand and sixty-five one hundredths)

In some other cultures, the decimal and the comma are reversed.

10.000 (ten thousand)

7,65 (seven and sixty-five one hundredths)

EXERCISE 2

Using accepted abbreviations and figures, change each item to a short-ened form.

1. in the first scene of the second act
2. four o'clock in the afternoon
3. on the seventh of April
4. Doctor Maria Simone
5. ten thousand two hundred sixty-three students

Punctuation

Chapter

12   The Comma

Punctuation lends to written language the flexibility that facial expressions, pauses, and variations in voice pitch give to spoken language. For instance, a pause after *sister* in the first example below makes it clear that the spoken sentence refers to only two people—the sister and a person named Mary Ellen. In the second example, a pause after *Mary* lets us know that the sentence refers to three people—the sister, Mary, and Ellen. In written language, a comma creates this pause.

When my sister called, Mary Ellen answered.

When my sister called Mary, Ellen answered.

But pauses are not a reliable guide for comma use because commas are often called for where we do not pause and pauses occur where no comma is called for. Knowing some basic principles works better. If you understand the following four principles, you will see through most of the mystery surrounding commas and find them easier to use consistently. This chapter will help you understand that commas

- come before coordinating conjunctions when they link independent clauses (**12a**),
- follow introductory adverbial clauses and, usually, introductory phrases (**12b**),
- separate items in a series (including coordinate adjectives) (**12c**), and
- set off nonrestrictive and other parenthetical elements (**12d**).

When we ran exercises 2 and 6 through the grammar checker, no missing commas were flagged for exercise 2 (in which you are to insert missing commas), and in exercise 6, the grammar checker was unsure whether a word or a comma was missing from one item.

12a Commas come before a coordinating conjunction that links independent clauses.

The coordinating conjunctions are *and, but, for, nor, or, so,* and *yet.* An independent clause is a group of words that can stand as a sentence. A comma must come before a coordinating conjunction that links two independent clauses.

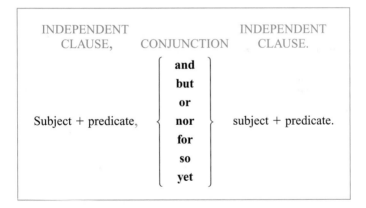

The minutes would pass, **and** then suddenly Einstein would stop pacing as his face relaxed into a gentle smile. —**BANESH HOFFMANN**

Samuel Coleridge-Taylor was an early twentieth-century British composer of African descent who wrote some beautiful symphonies, **but** today few know of his work.

Parents must give their children respect, **or** their children will not respect them.

From one point of view their migration was the fruit of an old prophecy, **for** indeed they emerged from a sunless world.

—N. SCOTT MOMADAY

I have not stopped hoping, **nor** have I stopped believing in the essential goodness of people.

They struggled to be the women society insisted they should be, **so** they often stifled their own creative urges.

The immigrants were officially prohibited from speaking in public, **yet** their silent protest was so compelling that those who wielded power had no choice but to pay attention.

When a sentence contains multiple clauses, a comma comes before each coordinating conjunction.

I chose to follow in the footsteps of my unconventional Aunt Esther, **and** I have never regretted my choice, **but** I think my mother was jealous of Aunt Esther, **and** I fear she never approved of me.

When the clauses are short, the comma can be omitted before *and, but,* or *or,* but not usually before *for, nor, so,* or *yet.* (See page 46.)

I liked my lessons **and** they made me confident enough to perform in front of others.

Nikki worked hard on back flips and dismounts, **for** she hoped to be a champion gymnast.

Sometimes a semicolon instead of a comma separates independent clauses, especially when the second one contains commas or when it reveals a contrast. (See 14a.)

Most people, according to my mother, skip cleaning in the corners; **but, she used to say,** they don't skip payday.

Not all coordinating conjunctions, however, are preceded by commas. A common slip is to place one before an *and* that links two verbs (a compound predicate) rather than two clauses.

> She **slapped** the hamburger patty onto the grill **and seasoned** it liberally before taking my order. [compound predicate—no comma before *and*]

EXERCISE 1

Follow 12a and insert the appropriate commas as you add coordinating conjunctions to link independent clauses in these sentences. (Remember that not all coordinating conjunctions link independent clauses and that *but, for, so,* and *yet* do not always function as coordinating conjunctions.)

1. A physician is accused of performing unnecessary surgery. Another hospital investigation is launched.
2. Families can choose to have their elderly relatives live with them at home. They may choose to house them in retirement centers.
3. Everyone in our class was assigned to an editing group. Only three of the groups could work together efficiently.
4. There are many customs for us to learn about. Our society has finally begun to appreciate its diversity.
5. We had not seen a bear before we went to Yellowstone. We had not seen a moose, either.

12b A comma usually follows introductory words, phrases, and clauses.

(1) A comma follows an introductory clause that precedes an independent clause.

INTRODUCTORY CLAUSE,
INDEPENDENT CLAUSE.

When you write, you make a sound in the reader's head.

—RUSSELL BAKER

Although the safest automobile on the road is expensive, the protection it offers makes the cost worthwhile. [adverbial clause preceding the independent clause]

If the omission does not make reading difficult, writers may omit the comma after an introductory clause when the clause is short.

When you sneeze you are responding to a nasal irritant.

A comma is usually unnecessary when the dependent clause follows the independent clause.

My grandmother's name will ensure me citizenship in the tribe **because it's on the Dawes roll.** [*Because,* a subordinating conjunction, introduces an adverbial clause.]

If a dependent clause is only loosely connected to an independent clause, a comma can precede it.

My grandmother is now retired, **although she was a banker for thirty years.**

(2) Commas follow introductory phrases before independent clauses.

INTRODUCTORY PHRASE,

or

INTRODUCTORY WORD,

} subject + predicate.

Prepositional phrases

From our porch, I could not hear what my father was saying, but I could hear the sound of my mother's laughter, throaty and rich with joy.

If the comma after an introductory prepositional phrase is not necessary to prevent misreading, it can be omitted.

> For safety the university installed call boxes linked directly to campus security.

Other types of phrases

> **Having traveled nowhere,** she believed the rest of the world was like her own small town; **having read little,** she had no sense of how other people think. [participial phrases before both independent clauses; see **1d–e**]

> The language difference aside, life in Germany doesn't seem much different from life in America. [absolute phrase; see **12d(7)**]

Introductory words

> **Furthermore,** the person responsible for breaking or damaging university equipment will be fined. [transitional expression; see page 53]

> **Well,** sit down and be quiet. [interjection]

> **Yes,** I bought my tickets yesterday. **No,** I didn't pay cash. [introductory *yes* or *no*]

Commas are not used after phrases that begin inverted sentences. (See **29f**.)

> With the hurricane came the tornadoes. [COMPARE Tornadoes came with the hurricane.]

> Of far greater concern than censorship of bad words is censorship of ideas.   —**DONNA WOOLFOLK CROSS**

EXERCISE 2

Insert a comma where needed in the following sentences. Explain why each comma is necessary. Put a check mark before any sentence in which no comma is needed.

1. If you are counting on a tax refund to give you a small nest egg you'd better have a backup plan.

2. As far as the IRS is concerned you probably aren't due one.

3. At the same time we understand why they think we all cheat on our taxes.

4. On the night of April 15 the lines at the post office drop boxes were half a mile long.

5. While waiting to put my tax return in the box I began to lose my temper.

6. Trying to find every possible deduction is still the main concern of almost every taxpayer.

7. With one hand on the wheel and the other on my tax return I followed hordes of taxpayers ahead of me docilely down the vehicle-clogged street.

8. Inside the glove box I always stash a small thermos of coffee as well as some cookies in case the wait is too long.

9. The wait still at least an hour from being over my Jeep was getting low on gas.

10. If you can remember to have a full tank before you go to mail your tax return.

12c Commas separate parallel items such as those in a series.

A series contains three or more parallel elements. (To be parallel, elements must be grammatically equal. See chapter 26.) The punctuation of a series depends on its form.

Pattern	Reason	Example
A, B, and C	Comma is preferred before *and*.	The melon was pink, sweet, and juicy.
A, B and C	Comma can be omitted before *and* when there is no danger of misreading.	The melon was pink, sweet and juicy.

A, B, C	Comma is essential when *and* is omitted.	The melon was pink, sweet, juicy.
A, A and B	Compound appositive (**12d(2)**) indicating only two elements	The melon was pink, rich and rosy as a sunset sky.

(1) Commas separate words, phrases, and clauses in a series.

A pet should be affectionate, trusting, obedient, and intelligent. [words in a series]

My job requires me to start work at 7 a.m., to drive to three different towns every day, and to carry heavy repair equipment upstairs. [phrases in a series]

My idea of a great vacation spot is one where no telephone rings, someone else fixes me great food, and I sit on the porch in the cool shade all day and read mystery novels. [clauses in a series]

If items in a series contain internal commas, you can make the meaning clear by separating the items with semicolons. (See **14b**.)

The main reasons I decided to replace my old car were that my fiancé, who is 6 feet 5 inches tall, couldn't sit in it; that I had over 100,000 miles on it; and that it needed a new transmission.

For special emphasis, writers sometimes use commas to slow the pace when coordinating conjunctions link all the items in a series.

We cannot put it off for a month, or a week, or even a day.

(2) Commas separate coordinate adjectives.

Coordinate adjectives are two or more adjectives that modify the same noun or pronoun. One test for coordinate adjectives is to switch them; another is to put *and* between them. If the meaning does not change, the adjectives are coordinate. Commas separate coordinate adjectives not linked by a coordinating conjunction.

> It is a **waiting, silent, limp** room. —EUDORA WELTY [*Waiting, silent,* and *limp* all modify *room.* COMPARE It is a silent, limp waiting room.]
>
> Walking along the **rushing, shallow** creek, I slipped on a rock and sank above my boot tops into a **small, still** pool. [*Rushing* and *shallow* modify *creek,* and *small* and *still* modify *pool.*]

EXERCISE 3

Using commas as needed, write sentences supplying coordinate adjectives to modify any five of the following ten word groups.

EXAMPLE

metric system   *Most countries use the familiar, sensible metric system to measure distances.*

1. onion bagel
2. country music
3. sirloin steak
4. oil painting
5. computer software
6. community college
7. basketball courts
8. high-rise buildings
9. pickup truck
10. state highway

12d Commas set off nonrestrictive and other parenthetical elements, as well as contrasted elements, items in dates, and so on.

Nonrestrictive clauses or phrases give nonessential information about a noun or pronoun. They can be omitted without changing the meaning.

To set off a nonrestrictive word or word group, use two commas, unless the element is placed at the beginning or end of the sentence. (Expressions that come at the beginning of a sentence are also treated in 12b.) Of course, not all words preceded and followed by commas are nonrestrictive.

> Some people lie, **as my grandmother observed,** because they don't know how to tell the truth. [COMPARE "As my grandmother observed, some people . . ." and ". . . tell the truth, as my grandmother observed."]

Restrictive clauses or phrases follow and limit the words they modify. They are essential to the clear identification of the word or words they refer to.

(1) Commas set off nonrestrictive clauses or phrases used as modifiers.

Clauses or phrases that *describe* rather than limit the meaning of the noun they modify are nonrestrictive. Set off by commas, they are nonessential parenthetical elements that may be omitted. Clauses that *limit* the noun are restrictive. Not set off by commas, they identify the noun or pronoun they modify by telling which one (or ones) and are essential elements that may not be omitted. In the first example below, "my sister" identifies the person the rest of the sentence is describing. As a result, any additional information serves only to describe "my sister." "Any sister," however, could be any woman who has a sibling, not just the writer's sister, and so needs a modifier that limits it to a specific person—a person who is a sister and who forgets birthdays.

	Nonrestrictive	Restrictive or Essential
Clauses	**My sister,** *who forgot my birthday,* is quite selfish.	**Any sister** *who forgets birthdays is quite selfish.*

	Mr. Jackson, *who won the teaching award*, lives next door.	**The man** *who won the teaching award* lives next door.
	We climbed **Mt. Rainier**, *which is over 15,000 feet high*.	We climbed **a mountain** *that is over 15,000 feet high*.
Phrases	**Our** new car, *covered in mud*, looks worn out.	**The** new car *covered in mud* looks worn out.

Sometimes only the omission or use of commas indicates whether a modifier is restrictive or nonrestrictive and thus signals the writer's exact meaning.

The party opposed taxes which would be a burden to working Americans. [opposition to levying taxes of a certain kind]

The party opposed taxes, which would be a burden to working Americans. [opposition to levying taxes of any kind, all of which would be a burden to working Americans]

Although traditionally writers have used *that* at the beginning of restrictive clauses, *which* has become acceptable if it does not cause confusion.

I like to drive a car that [or which] has fast acceleration and nimble handling.

(2) Commas set off nonrestrictive appositives.

Appositives can supply additional but nonessential details about a noun or pronoun (nonrestrictive), or else they limit the meaning of a noun or pronoun by indicating which one is meant (restrictive).

Nonrestrictive	Restrictive or Essential
Even Zeke Thornbush, **my friend**, let me down. [Knowing more than one Zeke is unlikely; therefore identifying Zeke as a friend is not essential.]	Even **my friend** Zeke Thornbush let me down. [Presumably the writer has more than one friend, so identifying Zeke is essential.]
The ringed planet, **Saturn**, can be seen at dawn. [Only one planet has rings, so *Saturn* is not essential information.]	The planet **Saturn** can be seen at dawn. [Several other planets might be seen at dawn, so *Saturn* is essential information.]

Abbreviations of titles or degrees after names are treated as nonrestrictive appositives.

> "Was the letter from Frances Evans, Ph.D., or from F. H. Evans, M.D.?"

Increasingly, however, *Jr.*, *Sr.*, *II*, and *III* are being treated as part of the name rather than as an appositive, and hence the comma is occasionally omitted.

E X E R C I S E 4

Set off nonrestrictive adjectival clauses or phrases and nonrestrictive appositives with commas. Put a check mark after any sentence that needs no commas.

1. I was able to take a class from Dr. Thompson who teaches Shelley and Keats.
2. I was able to take a class from the Dr. Thompson who teaches Shelley and Keats.
3. Lilacs which have a beautiful fragrance bloom in early spring.

4. Few people around here have ever heard of my home town a little place called Bugtussle.

5. Charles M. Duke Jr. and astronaut John W. Young landed the lunar vehicle near Plum Crater.

(3) Commas set off contrasted elements.

> Human beings, **unlike oysters,** frequently reveal their emotions. —GEORGE F. WILL

In sentences where contrasted elements are introduced by *not* and *but*, some writers put a comma before *but* while others do not. Generally, the comma before *but* emphasizes the contrast.

> Other citizens who disagree with me base their disagreement, not on facts different from the ones I know, but on a different set of values. —RENÉ DUBOS

> Today the Black Hills are being invaded again, not for gold but for uranium. —PETER MATTHIESSEN

(4) Commas set off geographical names, items in dates, and addresses.

Nashville, Tennessee, is the largest country and western music center in the United States.

I had to write to **Ms. Melanie Hobson, 2873 Central Avenue, Orange Park, FL 32065.** [no comma between the state abbreviation and the ZIP code]

Hunter applied for the job on **Wednesday, June 7, 2000,** but turned it down on June 12 because it paid only minimum wage.

OR

Hunter applied for the job on Wednesday, 7 June and turned it down on Monday, 12 June because it paid only minimum wage. [Commas are omitted when the date precedes rather than follows the month.]

(5) Commas set off parenthetical expressions.

Language, then, sets the tone of our society. —EDWIN NEWMAN

Much of the court and, **thus,** a good deal of the action are often invisible to a basketball player, so he needs more than good eyesight. —JOHN MCPHEE

When they cause little or no pause in reading, expressions such as *also, too, of course, perhaps, at least, therefore,* and *likewise* need not be set off by commas.

My awareness of the absurd has perhaps grown in recent years.

I'm trying to keep my spending to a minimum at least until I finish my degree.

(6) Commas set off mild interjections and words used in direct address.

Ah, that's my idea of a good meal. [interjection]

Now is the time, **my friend,** to stop smoking. [direct address]

(7) Commas set off absolute phrases.

An absolute phrase is a part of a sentence that is not grammatically connected to any other part.

His temper being what it is, I don't want a confrontation.

She was gazing out the window, **her breathing growing slower and slower.**

12e Commas are occasionally needed for ease in reading.

Some commas are necessary to prevent misreading. Without them the following sentences would confuse the reader, if only temporarily.

Still, water must be transported to dry areas. [COMPARE Still water . . .]

The day before, I had talked with her on the phone. [COMPARE I had talked with her . . . the day before.]

Someone predicted that by the year 2000, 3.5 million employees would be on the federal payroll. [COMPARE Someone predicted that by the year 2000 3.5 million . . .]

The earth breathes, in a certain sense.   —LEWIS THOMAS   [COMPARE The earth breathes in moisture.]

Sometimes a comma replaces a clearly understood word or group of words.

Scholars often see the humor in mistakes; pedants, never.

EXERCISE 5

Explain the reason for each comma used, and point out which commas are optional and which are a matter of stylistic preference.

1. When we left Chicago, we settled in rural Ohio, but by then my brother was already lost.
2. My belief is that as children grow up, they benefit more from friendships than from parenting.
3. Whatever Martha cooked tasted like a little bit of heaven, and she acquired a fine local reputation as a first-class chef.
4. As Fran Lebowitz put it, "Alas, I do not rule the world and that, I am afraid, is the story of my life—always a godmother, never a god."
5. If all else fails, try making somebody else's day a little more cheerful.

EXERCISE 6

For humorous effect, the writer of the following paragraph deliberately omits commas that can be justified by the rules in this chapter. Identify where commas might be inserted to contribute to ease in reading. Compare your version with someone else's and comment on any differences you find.

[1]The commas are the most useful and usable of all the stops. [2]It is highly important to put them in place as you go along. [3]If you try to come back after doing a paragraph and stick them in the various spots that tempt you you will discover that they tend to swarm like minnows into all sorts of crevices whose existence you hadn't realized and before you know it the whole long sentence becomes immobilized and lashed up squirming in commas. [4]Better to use them sparingly, and with affection precisely when the need for one arises, nicely, by itself.   —LEWIS THOMAS, *The Medusa and the Snail*

E X E R C I S E   7

Explain each comma in the following paragraph (from *Time* magazine).

[1]Yet punctuation is something more than a culture's birthmark; it scores the music in our minds, gets our thoughts moving to the rhythm of our hearts. [2]Punctuation is the notation in the sheet music of our words, telling us when to rest, or when to raise our voices; it acknowledges that the meaning of our discourse, as of any symphonic composition, lies not in the units, but in the pauses, the pacing and the phrasing. [3]Punctuation adjusts the tone and color and volume till the feeling comes into perfect focus. [. . .] [4]A world which has only periods is a world without inflections. It is a world without shade. [5]It has a music without sharps and flats. [6]It has a jackboot rhythm. [7]Words cannot bend and curve. [. . .] [8]A comma, by comparison, catches the gentle drift of the mind in thought, turning in on itself and back on itself, reversing, redoubling and returning along the course of its own sweet river music, while the semicolon brings clauses and thoughts together with all the silent discretion of a hostess arranging guests around her dinner table. [. . .] [9]Punctuation, then, is a matter of care. [10]Care for words, yes, but also, and more important, for what the words imply.   —PICO IYER

Chapter

13   Unnecessary Commas

Unnecessary (or misplaced) commas send false signals that can confuse a reader. Although a comma ordinarily signals a pause, not every pause calls for a comma. As you read the following sentence aloud, you may pause naturally at several places, but no commas are necessary.

> It is a paradox of our time in the West that never have so many people been so relatively well off and never has society been more troubled.   —BARBARA TUCHMAN

This chapter can help you avoid unnecessary commas that

- separate the main sentence elements (13a),
- are used improperly with a coordinating conjunction (13b),
- set off words that are not parenthetical (13c),
- set off restrictive elements (13d), and
- are used improperly in a series (13e).

13a   Commas do not separate the subject from its verb or the verb from its object.

Although speakers often pause after the subject or the object of a sentence, that pause should not be reflected by a comma.

> Most older students⊙ must hold a job in addition to going to school. [separation of the subject (*students*) and verb (*must hold*)]
>
> The lawyer said⊙ that I could appeal the speeding ticket. [separation of the verb (*said*) and the direct object (a noun clause: *that I could . . .*)]

13b Commas do not follow coordinating conjunctions, and they immediately precede them only when they link independent clauses. (See chapter 3 and 12a.)

It is incorrect to use a comma after a coordinating conjunction (*and, but, for, nor, or, so, yet*). Writers also sometimes put an unnecessary comma before a coordinating conjunction that does not link independent clauses.

> For three decades the Surgeon General's office has warned us about the dangers of smoking but⊙ millions of people still smoke. [separation of the conjunction (*but*) and the subject of the clause (*millions of people*)]

> I fed the dog⊙ and put it out for the night. [separation of compound verbs (*fed* and *put out*)]

13c Commas set off only those words and short phrases that are clearly parenthetical.

Parenthetical words and phrases are those that are nonessential—such as asides or interpolations.

> Martha was born⊙ in Miami in 1976. [The phrase, *in Miami,* modifies *born,* an integral part of the sentence.]

> Perhaps⊙ the valve is not correctly calibrated. [*Perhaps* is not a parenthetical element.]

13d Commas do not set off restrictive (necessary) clauses, phrases, or appositives. (See 12d.)

A restrictive clause, phrase, or appositive (12d(2)) is essential to the meaning of the sentence.

Everyone⊙who owns an automobile⊙ needs to have collision insurance. [The *who* clause is essential; people who do not have cars do not need collision insurance.]

With strains of bagpipes in the background, crowds watched two men⊙ carrying lances charge each other on horseback. [The men carrying lances were being watched, not just any two men.]

13e　Commas do not precede the first item of a series or follow the last (including a series of adjectives modifying the same noun—coordinate adjectives).

Field trips were required in a few courses, such as⊙ botany, geology, and sociology. [No comma is needed before the first item of the series (*botany*).]

I've always wanted a low-slung, fast, elegant⊙ convertible. [No comma is needed after the last item in the series (*elegant*).]

E X E R C I S E　1

Study the structure of the following sentences, and then give a specific reason why there is no comma after each italicized word. Be prepared to explain your answers in class.

[1]At the age of *eighty* my mother had her last bad fall, and after *that* her mind wandered free through time. [2]Some days she went to *weddings and* funerals that had taken place half a century earlier. [3]On *others* she presided over family *dinners* cooked on Sunday *afternoons* for children who were now gray with age. [4]Through all *this* she lay in *bed* but moved across time, traveling among the dead decades with a *speed* and ease beyond the gift of physical science.　—RUSSELL BAKER

EXERCISE 2

Change the structure and punctuation of the following sentences according to the pattern of the examples.

EXAMPLE

A fishing boat saw their distress signal, and it stopped to offer aid. [an appropriate comma; see **12a**]

A fishing boat saw their distress signal and stopped to offer aid.

[The second main clause is reduced to a part of the compound predicate, so the comma is no longer needed.]

1. Our employers gave us very good annual evaluations, and they also recommended us for raises.
2. Much modern fiction draws on current psychological knowledge, and it presents very believable characters.
3. Kim has had several jobs to put herself through college, and she has worked hard at all of them.

EXAMPLE

If a person suffers physical abuse, he or she should notify the police. [an appropriate comma; see **12b(1)**]

Any person who suffers physical abuse should notify the police.

[The introductory adverbial clause is converted to a restrictive clause, so the comma is no longer needed.]

4. When people make requests rather than give orders, they generally get cooperation.
5. If older folks want younger folks to take advice, they would do well to listen to what the young people say.

Chapter

14 The Semicolon

A stronger mark of punctuation than the comma, the semicolon connects sentence elements that are grammatically equal such as two independent clauses (1e). This chapter can help you understand that semicolons

- link closely related independent clauses (14a),
- separate parts of a sentence containing internal commas by acting as a stronger mark than the comma (14b), and
- do not connect independent clauses with phrases or dependent clauses (14c).

Mary said she was hungry; Hugh thought she wanted to go out to dinner. [closely related clauses]

Watching stupid, sentimental, dull soap operas; eating junk food like french fries, cheeseburgers, and milkshakes; and just doing nothing are my favorite vices. [parts containing internal commas]

14a Semicolons connect independent clauses not linked by a coordinating conjunction.

Two or more related sentences (or independent clauses) can be linked by a semicolon, connected by a comma and one of the coordinating conjunctions (*and, but, for, nor, or, so, yet*), or punctuated as separate sentences.

MAIN CLAUSE	;	MAIN CLAUSE.
Subject + predicate	;	subject + predicate.
Many Web sites are interesting	;	some are not accurate.
MAIN CLAUSE	, (AND, BUT)	MAIN CLAUSE.
Subject + predicate	, (and, but)	subject + predicate.
Many Web sites are interesting	, but	some are not accurate.
MAIN CLAUSE	.	MAIN CLAUSE.
Subject + predicate	.	Subject + predicate.
Many Web sites are interesting	.	Some are not accurate.
MAIN CLAUSE	; (HOWEVER, THEREFORE),	MAIN CLAUSE.
Subject + predicate	; (however, therefore),	subject + predicate.
Many Web sites are interesting	; however,	some are not accurate.

In the box above, semicolons indicate a close connection between the ideas, conjunctions indicate a more distant connection, and periods separate them. If you read the sentences in the box aloud, you can hear different intonation patterns for each.

This principle also applies to sentences that combine several different kinds of clauses (compound-complex sentences). (See 14b.)

When you read your first science fiction novel, the details seem bizarre and so unrealistic that you may have difficulty becoming engaged in the tale; the familiar universe has been replaced by an unfamiliar—and often threatening—one.

Sometimes a semicolon (instead of the usual comma) comes before a coordinating conjunction when a writer wants to emphasize the contrast between the two ideas being joined. (See 12a, page 192.)

Politicians may refrain from negative campaigning for a time; but when the race gets close, they can't seem to resist trying to dredge up personal dirt to use on their opponents.

Occasionally, a comma separates short, very closely related main clauses.

I am thrilled by a symphony, I ignore a film score; I respond to the form, I don't notice music that lacks a structure. [A semicolon is used between pairs of independent clauses joined by commas.]

When placed between independent clauses, a semicolon comes before words such as *for example, however, on the contrary, therefore* (conjunctive adverbs). (See 3b and the list on page 53.)

Some french fries are greasy; **however,** others are not. I like them any way you fix them.

A comma after a conjunctive adverb or transitional expression can be omitted if the adverb is essential to the sentence or if the comma is not needed to prevent misreading.

Like jazz, rap is a uniquely American form of music; indeed it can be said that both forms are uniquely African American.

When the second main clause explains or expands the first, a colon is sometimes substituted for the semicolon. Either is acceptable. (See 17d(1).)

14b Semicolons separate elements that themselves contain commas.

The chief attorney for a major manufacturer was accused of several felonies which included concealing evidence that the company knew there was a lethal defect in one of its products; persuading an employee to lie about the callous, profit-driven refusal to fix the defect; and actually shredding important, irreplaceable legal documents.

EXERCISE 1

Substitute a semicolon for any comma that could result in misreading.

1. Many of today's popular authors are sports figures, players on professional football and basketball teams, actors in Hollywood and on television, and notorious figures in the news.
2. Callie based her argument on the philosophy of Bertrand Russell, the famous logician, philosopher, and pacifist, the theories of Noam Chomsky, the father of transformational linguistics, and evidence collected by Carl Rogers, a clinical psychologist interested in counseling.

14c Semicolons do not connect parts that are grammatically unequal, such as phrases and clauses.

Semicolons do not connect clauses with phrases. (See 1d–e.)

We consulted Alinka Kibukian/ the local meteorologist.

Needing them to provide summer shade/ we planted two of the largest trees we could afford.

Semicolons do not connect a main clause with a subordinate clause.

I learned that he would not graduate this term; which really surprised me.

I really should trade this car in; although I can still drive it.

EXERCISE 2

Find the semicolons used between parts of unequal rank and punctuate appropriately. Do not change properly used semicolons.

1. I like to season my scrambled eggs with two things; a sprinkling of garlic salt and a dusting of pepper.

2. Elaine always bought her pants and shirts at thrift stores; no expensive trendy fashions for her; then she put together some of the most outrageous outfits I have ever seen.

3. Walking late at night; holding hands with my boyfriend; just listening to the street sounds; are what I would rather be doing than anything else.

4. Many times I've had to run for the morning bus; after I've arrived at the bus stop only a minute late; the bus has just been pulling away.

5. Although he knows he should finish his homework first; he still wants to go to the movies right now.

Chapter 15   The Apostrophe

Apostrophes are part of the words they are used in, whereas other punctuation marks follow the words they are used with. This chapter discusses how apostrophes

- show possession (except with personal pronouns) (15a),
- mark omissions in contractions (15b),
- form certain plurals (15c), but not others, and
- are not used to show the possessive form of personal pronouns (15d).

15a   Apostrophes show possession—ownership— for nouns and some indefinite pronouns (*everyone, somebody*).

An apostrophe marks the possessive case, and the possessive case shows ownership: *Tonya's car.* The possessive case of nouns and of indefinite pronouns such as *anyone, everybody, no one,* and *somebody* (see 15a(1)) is indicated by an apostrophe followed by an *-s,* or sometimes just the apostrophe alone. (See 15a(2).)

Al's pie   someone's car

Sometimes a phrase beginning with *of* and ending with *'s* shows possession (often called a **double possessive**).

that book of LaShonda's [LaShonda owns or wrote the book.]

that book of LaShonda [The book is about LaShonda.]

A possessive can follow the word it explains or identifies (modifies).

> Is that new computer Ana's or Kim's? [COMPARE Ana's or Kim's computer.]

A grammar checker is good at finding some kinds of apostrophe errors, but not so good at finding others. It does not reliably flag problems with possessives, and it usually hedges the advice it gives, saying that you have a "possible" error. Furthermore, it does not tell you whether the apostrophe goes before the *-s* or after it, or whether you need an *-s* at all. But a grammar checker is usually right about missing apostrophes in contractions such as *can't* or *don't*.

---

(1) Singular nouns (including people's names), indefinite pronouns, and acronyms add the apostrophe and -s.

the dean's office	NASA's goal	Yeats's poems
anyone's computer	Dickens's novels	Parrish's paintings

(2) Plural nouns (including people's names) ending in -s add only the apostrophe.

the boys' game	the babies' toys	the Joneses' house

Plurals that do not end in -s add the apostrophe and -s.

men's lives	women's cars	children's swing set

(3) To show joint ownership or to make a compound noun possessive, the apostrophe and -s are added to the last word only.

Olga and Nadia's house [COMPARE Olga and Nadia's houses—they jointly own more than one house.]

her mother-in-law's telephone

Walter Bryan Jr.'s letter [To avoid confusion, no comma follows *Jr.'s* although *Jr.* is usually set off by commas; see **12d(2)**.]

(4) Individual ownership is indicated by adding the apostrophe and *-s* to each name.

Tamiko's and Sam's apartments [different apartments]

(5) Sometimes an apostrophe shows time relationships, indicates an academic degree, or is used before gerunds. (See **1d(2)**.)

an hour's delay   in a week's time   bachelor's degree

Lucy's having to be there seemed unnecessary.

Proper names of organizations and geographical locations are not consistent in using the apostrophe or the apostrophe and *-s*. Follow local usage.

Devil's Island   Devils Tower   Devil Mountain

E X E R C I S E *1*

Follow the pattern of the examples as you change the modifier after the noun to a possessive form before the noun.

EXAMPLES

proposals made by the committee   *the committee's proposals*

poems written by Keats   *Keats's poems*

1. the mansion of Elvis Presley
2. a hat belonging to somebody else
3. shoes for children
4. the glossary of that book
5. an error made by the math professor
6. the coat belonging to Maurice Champaign, Jr.
7. the sounds of the video game and dishwasher

8. worth fifty cents
9. a paper written by David and Jennifer
10. the description of the child

15b The apostrophe marks omissions in contractions and numbers.

don't   they'll   class of '98

 Many instructors do not permit contractions in college writing, so you can safely write out the two words and omit contractions altogether: *do not, they will.*

15c The apostrophe and -*s* form the plurals of letters, numbers, and words referred to as words.

The apostrophe and -*s* are used to make the plural of a letter of the alphabet or an abbreviation followed by a period.

his *p*'s and *q*'s   Ibid.'s   Ph.D.'s

To prevent confusion, an '*s* can also be used to show the plural of capital letters and of words referred to as words.

too many *A*'s   all of the *if*'s and *and*'s

If there is no possibility of confusion, either '*s* or -*s* forms such plurals as the following.

the 1990's OR the 1990s   the VFW's OR the VFWs
his 7's OR his 7s   the &'s OR the &s
her *and*'s OR her *ands*

Who's is the contraction for *who is. Whose* is the possessive form of the relative pronoun *who.*

Who's [Who is] responsible? **Whose** responsibility is it?

15d   Personal pronouns and plural nouns that are not possessive do not take an apostrophe.

Each personal pronoun (*I, we, you, he, she, it, they*) has its own form to show possession (*my, mine, our, ours, your, yours, his, her, hers, its, their, theirs*).

A friend of **theirs** knows a cousin of **yours.**

An apostrophe is not used with *-s* to indicate plurals of words that are not possessive case.

The **Smiths** are home.   Idaho **potatoes** are on sale.

Do not confuse *it's* with *its. It's* is a contraction for *it is. Its* is the possessive form of *it.* Whenever you write *it's,* you should be able to substitute *it is.*

Its motor is small.	**It's** [it is] a small motor.
The dog enjoys **its** bone.	**It's** [it is] the dog's bone.
The board made **its** plan.	**It's** [it is] the board's plan.
Its name is Spot.	**It's** [it is] named Spot.

E X E R C I S E   2

In the sentences below, insert apostrophes where needed. If a sentence does not need an apostrophe, put a check mark by it.

1. Pictures of the class of 97 fill Marks photo album.
2. There are two is and two ls in *illustrious.*
3. NASAs space flights still capture many peoples imaginations.
4. My fathers unexpected mood swings are making me nervous.

5. Many peoples beliefs had changed by the 1960s.

6. Upon graduation, several of my brothers friends received gifts from their grandparents.

7. Cherise likes fencing; its technical dimensions intrigue her.

8. "Its just one MDs diagnosis, right?" Jamal inquired.

9. Theres a big gap between Lenas age and theirs.

10. People often mistake my car for someone elses.

Chapter
16   **Quotation Marks**

Quotation marks are always used in pairs. The first mark indicates the beginning of the quotation, and the second indicates the end. Any other marks associated with the quotation follow the rules explained in this chapter. After studying this chapter, you will have a better understanding of

- direct quotations (**16a**),
- long quotations set in indented blocks (**16b**),
- certain titles (**16c**),
- words used in a special sense (**16d**),
- overuse of quotation marks (**16e**), and
- the conventions of quotation marks (**16f**).

16a   Quotation marks set off most quotations, dialogue, and thoughts.

Double quotation marks set off direct quotations, but not indirect ones. Single quotation marks enclose a quotation within a quotation.

(1) Double quotation marks enclose direct quotations.

"People are trapped in history," writes James Baldwin, "and history is trapped in them." [Quotation marks enclose only the quotation, not expressions like *she said* or *he replied.* Place the period inside the quotation marks. See **16b(1)** and **16f**.]

(2) Quotation marks are not used with indirect quotations.

James Baldwin claims that people cannot escape history and that history cannot exist without people. [Quotation marks are not used for indirect quotations.]

(3) Single quotation marks enclose quotations within quotations.

"Then Elena said 'get out of my life,' " Martin complained. [The comma appears inside the quotation within a quotation; the period goes at the end of the sentence. (See page 225 for how to punctuate a quotation within a quotation presented as an indented block.)]

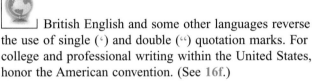

British English and some other languages reverse the use of single (') and double (") quotation marks. For college and professional writing within the United States, honor the American convention. (See **16f.**)

Other usage	The police officer said, 'When I saw the thief running away, I shouted, "Stop! You are under arrest." '
American English	The police officer said, "When I saw the thief running away, I shouted, 'Stop! You are under arrest.' "

In direct quotations, reproduce all quoted material exactly as it appears in the original, including capitalization and punctuation. If the quoted material contains an error, Modern Language Association (MLA) style advises you to insert *sic* (Latin for "thus" or "so"). If you put *sic* at the end of the quotation, enclose it in parentheses; if you put it after the error inside the quotation, enclose it in brackets. (See **17g.**)

"Although some ancient texts have been under-understood" (*sic*), Marzik explains, "we now have the capability to decipher them completely."

Marzik explains, "Although some ancient texts have been under-understood [*sic*], we now have the capability to decipher them completely."

If the quoted material contains a reference that would be unclear once the material is taken out of context, explain the reference in one or two words immediately after the reference. (See 38b.)

The speaker said, "These ancient texts [the *Mabinogion* and some bardic fragments] have not been well understood, but we are beginning to decipher them now."

Indicate an omission within a quotation by the use of ellipsis points enclosed in brackets. (See 17i.)

The speaker said, "Some ancient texts have not been well understood [. . .], but we are beginning to decipher them now."

(4) Dialogue is enclosed in quotation marks.

Dialogue is directly quoted conversation. When quoting conversation, write what each person says, no matter how short, as if it were a separate paragraph. It helps to include expressions such as *he said,* as well as closely related bits of narrative, in the same paragraph as the direct quotation.

Through an interpreter, I spoke with a Bedouin man tending nearby olive trees. "Do you own this land?" I asked him.

He shook his head. "The land belongs to Allah," he said.

"What about the trees?" I asked. He had just harvested a basket of green olives, and I assumed that at least the trees were his.

"The trees, too, are Allah's," he replied.

> I marveled at this man who seemed unencumbered by material considerations . . . or so I was thinking when, as if in afterthought, he said, "Of course, I own the *olives.*"   —HARVEY ARDEN

When quoting more than one paragraph by a single speaker, put quotation marks at the beginning of each new paragraph. However, use only one set of closing quotation marks, at the end of the last paragraph.

(5) Thoughts are enclosed in quotation marks.

Double quotation marks set off thoughts as if they were stated.

> "I won't make that mistake again," I thought.

16b Long quotations are indented.

Although short quotations are run into the text, indentation sets off long quotations of prose and poetry. In this case the indentation shows that you are quoting, so quotation marks are not used. (See 38f(2), page 617.)

(1) Prose is indented one inch from the left margin.

When using the MLA style of documentation (38e), set off any quotation consisting of more than four lines by indenting all lines one inch (or ten spaces). When using the American Psychological Association (APA) style (38h), set off quotations of forty words or more by indenting all lines five to seven spaces (one-half inch). When using either MLA or APA style, double-space the lines in the block.

In MLA style, do not indent the first line of a single quoted paragraph or less. Indent each first line of two or more quoted paragraphs three spaces. In APA style, indent the first line of the second and subsequent paragraphs five to seven spaces.

A colon may introduce a long quotation if the quotation is not an integral part of the structure of the preceding sentence. However, if the quotation continues the sentence structure of the preceding sentence, use the punctuation that sentence calls for, even if the result is no punctuation before the blocked quotation. Use internal quotation marks only if they appear in the original. Place the page number on which the quotation is found in parentheses after the final period (parenthetical citation). Use no punctuation after the closing parenthesis of the citation.

> Metal coins replaced bartering. Then paper money became more convenient to use than metal coins not only because it is easy to handle but also because, as Cetron and O'Toole say in *Encounters with the Future,* it has other advantages:
>> Printing more zeros is all it takes on a bill to increase its value. Careful engraving makes it easy to recognize and difficult to counterfeit. The fact that private individuals cannot create it at will keeps it scarce. Karl Marx once said that paper money was valued "only insofar as it represents gold" but that may never have been true. (188)
>
> Today, checks and credit cards are even more convenient than paper money.

(2) Poetry is indented one inch from the left margin.

Except for very special emphasis, enclose a quotation of three (or fewer) lines of poetry in quotation marks and run it into the text as you would a short prose quotation. Indicate the divisions between lines by a slash with a space on each side. (See 17h.)

> In "The Collar," George Herbert, frustrated because his faith seems to have no immediate rewards, exclaims "Sure there was wine / Before my sighs did dry it; there was corn / Before my tears did drown it."

Passages of more than three lines should be set off—double-spaced and indented one inch (or ten spaces).

> In Sonnet 138 Shakespeare addresses his fickle lady:
>> When my love swears that she is made of truth,
>> I do believe her, though I know she lies,
>> That she might think me some untutored youth,
>> Unlearned in the world's false subtleties. (1–4)

If unusual spacing is part of the poem, reproduce the spacing as nearly as possible. If a quotation begins with part of a line, do not put the quoted material at the left margin but rather place it approximately where it would occur in the full line. Use quotation marks only if they appear in the original. Numbers in parentheses placed two spaces after the end of the quotation can be used to indicate the line numbers.

> In "The Collar," George Herbert is frustrated because his faith seems to have no immediate rewards:
>> Sure there was wine
>> Before my sighs did dry it; there was corn
>> Before my tears did drown it.
>> Is the year only lost to me?
>> Have I no bays to crown it,
>> No flowers, no garlands gay? all blasted?
>> All wasted? (10–16)

16c Quotation marks enclose the titles of short works such as stories, essays, poems, songs, episodes of a radio or television series, articles in periodicals, and subdivisions of books.

Lon Otto's *Cover Me* contains such wonderful stories as "Winners" and "How I Got Rid of That Stump." [short stories]

"Nani" is my favorite of the poems by Alberto Ríos that we studied this semester. [short poem—see 10a for titles of long poems]

I always want to laugh when I hear "Big Girls Don't Cry." [song]

Coral Browne starred in "An Englishman Abroad," part of the *Great Performances* series. [episode in a television series]

Did you read William Gibson's "Disneyland with the Death Penalty" when it appeared in *Wired*? [article in a periodical]

Use double quotation marks to enclose the title of a short work appearing in a longer italicized (underlined) title. Use single marks for such a title within a longer title enclosed in double quotation marks.

Interpretations of "*The Secret Sharer*"

"Cynicism in Hardy's 'Ah, Are You Digging on My Grave?' "

16d Used sparingly, quotation marks may enclose words intended in a special or ironic sense.

His "gourmet dinner" tasted as if it had come out of a grocer's freezer. [COMPARE His so-called gourmet dinner tasted as if it had come out of a grocer's freezer. The use of *so-called* eliminates the need for quotation marks.]

And I do mean good and evil, not "adjustment and deviance," the gutless language that so often characterizes modern discussions of psychological topics.   —CAROL TAVRIS

Either quotation marks or italics can be used in definitions. (See also 10e.)

Ploy means "a strategy used to gain an advantage."

Ploy means *a strategy used to gain an advantage.*

16e Overusing quotation marks detracts from readability.

Quotation marks are not needed when they call attention to clichés or to a *yes* or a *no,* or when they highlight dubious usage.

(1) Quotation marks do not call attention to a cliché. (See 20c.)

Highlighting a cliché in this way emphasizes a writer's unwillingness to think of a fresh expression.

A good debater does not beat around the bush.

(2) Quotation marks do not enclose *yes* or *no* in indirect discourse.

I have to learn to say no to people who ask me to do more than I should.

(3) Quotation marks do not indicate questionable diction.

A wimp can't say no to anyone. [Neither *wimp,* a slang term, nor *no* is set off with quotation marks.]

16f Follow American printing conventions for using various marks of punctuation with quoted material.

(1) Commas and periods are placed inside quotation marks.

Generally speaking, commas go inside closing quotation marks; so do periods if the quotation ends the sentence.

"Lou," she said, "let's go someplace after class." [comma and period inside the quotation marks]

Aaron declared, "I'm nearly finished with 'The Machine Stops.' " [period inside the closing marks, both single and double]

The period goes at the end of the sentence if other words follow the end of the quotation.

"I don't know why my CD player doesn't work," she said. [Note that the comma goes inside the closing quotation marks.]

The period goes after a parenthetical citation when it follows a quotation that ends a sentence. For example, in MLA-style documentation, a page number in parentheses follows a quotation (see 38e(1)) unless it is a block quotation. (See pages 587–89.)

In their biography of Bill Gates, *Hard Drive,* Wallace and Erickson explain, "What sustained the company was not Gates' ability to write programs, to 'crank code' [. . .]. Gates sustained Microsoft through tireless salesmanship" (152). [The first ellipsis mark appears outside the single quotation mark to show that a part of the original sentence is omitted. The final period follows the parenthetical citation.]

(2) Semicolons and colons are placed outside the quotation marks.

Semicolons and colons always go outside the quotation marks.

She spoke of "the gothic tale"; I immediately thought of "The Dunwich Horror": H. P. Lovecraft's masterpiece is the epitome of "gothic."

(3) Question marks, exclamation points, and dashes are placed outside the quotation marks unless they are part of the quotation.

When a question mark, an exclamation point, or a dash is part of the quoted matter, it goes inside the quotation marks. When it is not, it goes outside. When a quotation containing one of these marks ends your own sentence, you do not add an additional end mark either inside or outside the quotation marks.

Inside the quotation marks:

Pilate asked, "What is truth?"

Gordon replied, "No way!"

"Achievement—success!—" states Heather Evans, "has become a national obsession."

Why do children keep asking "Why?" [a question within a question—one question mark inside the quotation marks]

Outside the quotation marks:

What is the meaning of the term "half-truth"?

Stop whistling "All I Do Is Dream of You"!

She exclaimed, "I'm surprised at you!"—understandable under the circumstances.

E X E R C I S E 1

Write a page of dialogue between two friends who are disagreeing about songs or stories. Punctuate the quotations carefully.

E X E R C I S E 2

Insert quotation marks where they are needed. Then, for practice, change any direct quotations to indirect and any indirect quotations to direct.

1. Have you read Amy Tan's essay Mother Tongue?
2. I was disturbed by the article Who Owns the Law?

3. Andy said, Have people ever asked me Do you revise what you write? Yes, lots of times, and when they do, I tell them that my motto is A writer's work is never done.

4. Here, stoked means fantastically happy on a surfboard.

5. Although running keeps me trim, Claudia claimed, it also gives me energy.

6. In a short story called Everyday Use, Alice Walker explores the meaning of family heritage.

7. Luis explained that he enjoys music the most when he can listen to it when he is alone.

8. Connie said that she thought Mike really lived according to the saying, All I want is more than my share.

9. *Women's Ways of Knowing* begins with a chapter entitled To 21.

10. I remember hearing a hilarious parody of the old song YMCA titled HTML.

Chapter 17

The Period and Other Marks

Periods, question marks, exclamation points, colons, dashes, parentheses, brackets, slashes, and ellipsis points are important in writing and in transferring meaning from spoken to written language. (For use of the hyphen, see 18g.) In the sentences below, the marks in color signal meaning and intonation.

Look around you! The world is beautiful. Can't you see it?

Paul Fussell writes of *The Boy Scout Handbook* (1979), "But the best advice is ethical: 'Learn to think.' 'Gather knowledge.' . . . 'Respect the rights of others.' "

According to Edward Hoagland, far from feeling that life's "contest is unfair; [turtles] keep plugging, rolling like sailorly souls — a bobbing infirm gait, a brave, sea-legged momentum — stopping occasionally to study the lay of the land."

This chapter will help you understand how to use

- end punctuation—the period (17a), the question mark (17b), and the exclamation point (17c),
- the colon (17d),
- the dash (17e), parentheses (17f), brackets (17g), the slash (17h), and
- ellipsis points (17i).

The MLA (Modern Language Association) and APA (American Psychological Association) style manuals state specifically that only one space follows all punctuation marks: the period, the question mark, the exclamation point, the colon, the ending parenthesis and bracket, and each of the dots in ellipsis points. No spaces precede or follow the hyphen or dash.

Be wary of the advice—or lack of advice—grammar checkers offer about punctuation. When we ran this chapter through a grammar checker, it flagged no errors at all, not even the deliberate ones in the exercises and some of the examples.

17a Periods punctuate certain sentences and abbreviations.

(1) The period marks the end of a declarative or a mildly imperative sentence.

A *declarative sentence* is a statement. An *imperative sentence* is a command. If a command is forceful, it could be called a *demand.*

We are first and foremost fellow human beings. [declarative]

Respect your heritage. [mild imperative]

"Go home," he ordered. [declarative sentence with a quotation containing an imperative]

She asks how people can belittle the heritage of others. [declarative sentence containing an indirect question]

"How can people belittle the heritage of others?" she asked. [declarative sentence containing a direct quotation that happens to be a question]

"I'm as good as you are!" he shouted. [declarative sentence with a quotation containing an exclamation]

(2) Periods follow some abbreviations.

Dr.   Jr.   a.m.   p.m.   vs.   etc.   et al.

Periods are not used with all abbreviations (for example, *MVP, mph, FM*). (See chapter 11.) If you do not know whether an abbreviation uses a period, check a desk dictionary. Dictionaries often list options, such as *USA* or *U.S.A., CST* or *C.S.T.*

Only one period follows an abbreviation that ends a sentence.

> The study was performed by Ben Werthman et al.

17b The question mark follows direct (but not indirect) questions.

A command is sometimes stated as a question and is followed by a question mark: Would you pass the salt?

An indirect question is phrased as a statement and so ends with a period.

> What in the world is Jennifer doing? [direct question]
>
> They want to know what Jennifer is doing. [indirect question]
>
> Did you hear them ask, "What is Jennifer doing?" [A direct question within a direct question is followed by one question mark inside the closing quotation mark. See 16f.]
>
> What is Jennifer doing? thinking? hoping? [A series of questions having the same subject and verb can be treated as elliptical; that is, only the first item needs to include both the subject and verb.]

Declarative sentences sometimes contain direct questions.

> He asked, "Did Cisneros publish a collection of stories in 1991?" [Put a question mark inside quotation marks when it concludes a direct question. See 16f(3).]
>
> When the question comes up, Why don't you invest in the stock market? we answer that we live on a budget. [A question mark follows the question not enclosed in quotation marks. The comma follows an adverbial clause (see 12b). Capitalize the word beginning a formal question.]

A question mark inside parentheses shows that the writer is not sure whether the preceding word, figure, or date is correct.

Chaucer was born in 1340(?) and died in 1400.

Do not punctuate an indirect question with a question mark.

She asked him if he would go.

17c An exclamation point can be used after a word or group of words that is emphatic or shows strong feeling.

Wow! Amazing! That was the best movie I've ever seen!

When a direct quotation ends with an exclamation point, no comma or period is placed immediately after it.

"Get off the road!" he yelled.

He yelled, "Get off the road!"

Use the exclamation point sparingly. Overuse diminishes its value, and emphasis can be achieved in other ways (see chapter 29). A comma is better after mild interjections, and a period is better after mildly exclamatory expressions and mild imperatives.

Oh, someone took my seat.

How moving that final scene was.

EXERCISE 1

Illustrate the chief uses of the period, the question mark, and the exclamation point by composing and punctuating brief sentences of the types specified.

1. a declarative sentence containing a quoted exclamation (17a, 17c)

2. a mild imperative (17a)
3. a direct question (17b)
4. a declarative sentence containing an indirect question (17b)
5. a declarative sentence containing a direct question (17b)

17d   The colon calls attention to what follows, and it also separates time, scriptural references, and titles and subtitles.

A colon generally signals that what follows is important. Leave only one space after a colon.

(1) A colon directs attention to an explanation or summary, a series, or a quotation.

> I am always seeking the answer to the eternal question: How can we be joined to another person—spouse, parent, child—yet still remain ourselves?

The colon can introduce a second independent clause that explains or expands the first.

> For I had no brain tumor, no eyestrain, no high blood pressure, nothing wrong with me at all: I simply had migraine headaches, and migraine headaches were, as everyone who did not have them knew, imaginary.   —JOAN DIDION

A colon also sometimes follows one sentence to introduce the next.

> They were concerned mainly about speed: not only did they need a very fast computer, but also they had to have a very fast Internet connection.

Style manuals are fairly consistent on whether to capitalize the first word of a passage that follows a colon (9e). All style manuals agree that after a colon you should capitalize the first letter of a rule or principle or of a quoted sentence. MLA and *The Chicago Manual of Style* permit the use of a lowercase letter when other material follows a colon; APA also permits the use of a lowercase letter unless what follows the colon is a complete sentence.

> Claire Safran points out two of the things that cannot be explained: "One of them is poltergeists. Another is teenagers."

Be especially careful not to use an unnecessary colon between a verb and its complement or object, between a preposition and its object, or after *such as*.

Unnecessary colon	The winners were: Asa, Vanna, and Jack.
Use instead	There were three winners: Asa, Vanna, and Jack.
OR	The winners were as follows: Asa, Vanna, and Jack.
OR	The winners were Asa, Vanna, and Jack.
Unnecessary colon	How fast a computer can run on the Internet depends on some of its parts, such as: its modem, its hard disk, and its video card.
Use instead	How fast a computer can run on the Internet depends on the speed of its modem, its hard disk, and its video card.

(2) A colon separates figures in time references as well as titles and subtitles.

We are to be there by 11:30 a.m.

I just read *Women's Ways of Knowing: The Development of Self, Voice, and Mind.*

Many writers prefer to use a colon in scriptural references: He quoted from Psalms 3:5. However, MLA recommends periods

(Psalms 3.5), and recent biblical scholarship follows this practice as well.

(3) A colon follows the salutation of a business letter.

Dear Dr. D'Angelo: Dear Faustine:

(4) The colon also appears in bibliographic data. (See chapter 38.)

E X E R C I S E 2

Punctuate the following sentences by adding colons.

1. While surfing the Internet, I looked for online versions of each of the following books *Always Coming Home, The Dispossessed,* and *The Left Hand of Darkness.*
2. Four cities noted for their tourist appeal are these Paris, Rome, New York, and London.
3. By 730 p.m. he had watched three movies *Roman Holiday, Casablanca,* and *Raiders of the Lost Ark.*
4. For months she has argued with her parents over this concept animals have the right to live full, pain-free lives.
5. The medication the doctor prescribed caused Mario to experience one negative side effect it made him sleepy.

17e   **The dash marks a break in thought, sets off a parenthetical element for emphasis or clarity, and sets off an introductory series.**

In handwriting indicate a dash by an unbroken line the length of two hyphens—approximately one-eighth of an inch; on a typewriter, by typing two hyphens with no spaces; and on a keyboard, by typing two hyphens, which most word processing programs convert automatically to an em dash (—).

Use dashes sparingly, not as easy or automatic substitutes for commas, semicolons, or end marks.

(1) A dash marks a sudden break in thought, an abrupt change in tone, or faltering speech.

When we were in first grade, my friend Charlotte finally learned to read every page in her primer——by gluing all of them together.

I know who she is, Mrs.——Mrs.——Mrs. Somebody——the Mayor of Gilpin——or Springtown.

(2) A dash sets off a parenthetical element for emphasis or (if it contains commas) for clarity.

In many smaller cities of this nation, cable television operators——with the connivance of local government——have a virtual monopoly.

Those deep feelings of friendship that are so difficult to express——feelings of appreciation, of understanding, of love——are really the feelings we should tell our friends about most directly.

(3) A dash occurs after an introductory list or series.

In the main part of the following sentence, *all* points to or sums up the meaning of the list.

"Keen, calculating, perspicacious, acute and astute——I was all of these."   —MAX SCHULMAN

17f Parentheses set off nonessential matter and enclose numerals or letters used for lists.

Use parentheses to set off information that mainly illustrates or supplements the main part of the sentence or nonessential (parenthetical) information.

Scores on the Scholastic Aptitude Test (SAT) have been declining for some years. [first-time use of an acronym; see 11f and the **Glossary of Terms**]

> Bernard Shaw once demonstrated that, by following the rules (up to a point), we could spell fish this way: ghoti.   —JOHN IRVING [an explanatory parenthetical expression]

> In general, a sound argument contains (1) a clear statement of its point placed near the beginning and (2) a refutation of opposing positions, usually right after the point statement. [In long sentences especially, parenthetical enumeration highlights the points.]

In the next example the entire sentence is parenthetical. (See 9e.)

> If we refuse to talk "like a lady," we are ridiculed and criticized for being unfeminine. ("She thinks like a man" is, at best, a left-handed compliment.)   —ROBIN LAKOFF

Use parentheses sparingly; the elements they enclose should still read smoothly in the sentence as a whole.

Dashes, parentheses, and commas are all used to set off parenthetical matter, but they express varying degrees of emphasis. Dashes set off parenthetical elements sharply and usually emphasize them.

> But in books like Piri Thomas's *Down These Mean Streets* and Pedro Pietri's *Puerto Rican Obituary,* there was suddenly a literature by Puerto Ricans, in English and decidedly in——and against—— the American grain.   —JUAN FLORES

Parentheses usually deemphasize the elements they enclose.

> But in books like Piri Thomas's *Down These Mean Streets* and Pedro Pietri's *Puerto Rican Obituary,* there was suddenly a literature by Puerto Ricans, in English and decidedly in (and against) the American grain.

Commas separate elements, usually without emphasizing them.

> But in books like Piri Thomas's *Down These Mean Streets* and Pedro Pietri's *Puerto Rican Obituary,* there was suddenly a literature by Puerto Ricans, in English and decidedly in, and against, the American grain.

17g **Brackets set off insertions (such as *sic*) in or alterations to quoted matter (including many ellipses) and replace parentheses within parentheses. (See 16a(3).)**

Parker Pilgrim has written, "If he [Leonard Aaron] ever disapproved of any of his children's friends, he never let them know about it." [An unclear pronoun reference is explained by the bracketed material.]

Not every expert agrees. (See, for example, Katie Hafner and Matthew Lyon's *Where Wizards Stay Up Late* [New York: Simon, 1996].)

[I]f the network was ever going to become more than a test bed [. . .], word of its potential had to spread.   —KATIE HAFNER **and** MATTHEW LYON   [The first pair of brackets indicates the *I* is changed from a lowercase letter; the second pair encloses an ellipsis showing that a word or words have been omitted.]

17h **The slash occurs to mark line divisions in quoted poetry and between terms to indicate that either term is applicable.**

Between terms, there are no spaces before or after a slash, but a space is placed before and after a slash used between lines of poetry.

I noticed that there is yet another book out on writer/critic John Ciardi.

Wallace Stevens refers to the listener who, "nothing himself, beholds / Nothing that is not there and the nothing that is."

Extensive use of the slash to indicate that either of two terms is applicable (as in *and/or, he/she*) can make writing choppy. You can use *or* instead of the slash.

When combined terms modify a noun, link the terms with a hyphen: *east-west differences*. (See 18g.)

EXERCISE 3

Punctuate each of the following sentences by supplying commas, dashes, parentheses, brackets, or slashes. Be ready to explain the reason for every mark you add, especially those you choose for setting off parenthetical matter.

1. Loyalty, courtesy, and courtly love these were the most important concepts for chivalric knights.

2. In the ten years between 1960 and 1970, two of the city's biggest buildings were erected downtown The Tower of Freedom 1961 and the Municipal Auditorium 1967.

3. A car's optional features an automatic transmission instead of a standard one a CD player instead of a factory radio power windows instead of manually operated ones can increase its price.

4. For fifty years after the Civil War, political decisions in this country were still made on the basis of the old North South divisions.

5. This strange statement appeared in the entertainment section of the local newspaper: Because of an unforeseen technical problem sic this evening's main feature will be delayed by one hour.

17i Ellipsis points (three equally spaced periods) mark an omission from a quoted passage or a reflective pause or hesitation.

(1) Ellipsis points mark an omission within a quoted passage.

The *MLA Style Manual*—but not the *Publication Manual of the American Psychological Association*—recommends enclosing ellipsis points in brackets to distinguish those showing omitted material from those used by the author. (See also 17g.) In any case, make sure your omission does not change the meaning of the material you quote.

> **Original**   To bring rowing to minorities, it's important to first understand why they aren't rowing. The first clue is that not long ago programs spent as much energy keeping minorities out of rowing as they now expend to attract them.   —TINA FISHER FORDE

Omission within a quoted sentence

Noting that "programs spent [. . .] energy keeping minorities out of rowing," Tina Fisher Forde explains one reason for the small numbers of minorities in rowing.

Omission at the beginning or end of a quoted sentence

Neither ellipsis points nor capitals are used at the beginning of a quotation, whether it is run into the text or set off in a block. However, if the original of the quoted material begins with a capital letter, a bracketed ellipsis may be used to show that the capital does not indicate the beginning of a sentence.

An omission that coincides with the end of your sentence requires a period in addition to the three bracketed ellipsis points. Put a space between the last word quoted and the bracket and then include the three spaced ellipses. Close the bracket and place the period immediately after it. With a parenthetical reference, the period comes after the second parenthesis instead.

Tina Fisher Forde claims that in the past rowing programs worked hard at "keeping minorities out of rowing [. . .]."

OR rowing [. . .]" (19).

Omission of a sentence or more

A period before the bracketed ellipsis points marks the omission of a sentence or more (even a paragraph or more) within a quoted passage. If the quoted material ends with a question mark or exclamation point, three bracketed ellipsis points are added and the mark is placed immediately after the closing bracket.

Original   I long ago stopped wondering why major thunderstorm activity is preferred to major thunderstorms. It is because of the national affection for unnecessary word activity. Once upon a time, weathermen spoke of showers.   —EDWIN NEWMAN

Of the tendency toward wordiness, Edwin Newman writes, "I long ago stopped wondering why major thunderstorm activity is preferred to major thunderstorms. [. . .] Once upon a time, weathermen spoke of showers. [A sentence of eleven words has been omitted from the original, and a sentence comes before and after the period and ellipsis points.]

Of the tendency toward wordiness, Edwin Newman writes, "[M]ajor thunderstorm activity is preferred to major thunderstorms [. . .] because of the national affection for unnecessary word activity." [Five words have been omitted from the first sentence and four from the second. The ellipses link the sentences.]

To indicate the omission of a full line or more in quoted poetry, use spaced periods covering the length of either the line above it or the omitted line.

She sang beyond the genius of the sea.
[. . . . .]
The song and water were not medleyed sound
Even if what she sang was what she heard,
Since what she sang was uttered word by word.

—WALLACE STEVENS

(2) Although ellipsis points can mark a reflective pause or hesitation, they should not be overused.

Love, like other emotions, has causes . . . and consequences.

—LAWRENCE CASLER

(3) Ellipsis points to show a pause can also come after the period at the end of a sentence.

The van is loaded. Our adventure is about to begin. . . .

EXERCISE 4

Punctuate the following sentences by supplying appropriate end marks, commas, colons, dashes, parentheses, and ellipses. Do not use unnecessary punctuation. Be prepared to explain the reason for each mark you add, especially when you have a choice of correct marks (for example, commas, dashes, or parentheses).

1. I keep remembering what my father used to say jokingly "Some day you'll grow up and have kids who will treat you the way you treat me"

2. For his birthday Matthew requested the following gifts a Spider Man action figure a water gun some new athletic shoes

3. "Good and" can mean "very" "I am good and mad" and "a hot cup of coffee" means that the coffee not the cup is hot

4. Many small country towns are very similar a truck stop a gas station a crowded diner

5. Gretchen Jordan's best friend sat at the back of the church where she wouldn't be seen and cried quietly through the entire wedding

6. As my grandmother used to say "Love trust and considerate behavior are all necessary for a good marriage"

7. I imagine that the tickets will seem expensive to all my friends employed or unemployed who want to go to the Lollapalooza concert

8. "Is he is he okay" I stammered

9. She believed the best way to age gracefully was to look at the world through a child's eyes not to act like a child

10. "Mark" I yelled "Mark how could you have done such a thing" I tried to hurry out the door before he could respond but he caught up with me

D

Spelling and Diction

Chapter 18
Spelling, the Spell Checker, and Hyphenation

This chapter explains how to improve your spelling and how to use hyphens. It covers in detail

- using a spell checker (**18a**),
- spelling words according to pronunciation (**18b**),
- spelling words that sound alike (**18c**),
- using affixes (prefixes and suffixes) correctly (**18d–e**),
- dealing with *ei* and *ie* (**18f**), and
- using hyphenation to link and divide words (**18g**).

Spelling problems are highly visible, and misspellings may make a reader doubt whether the writer can present information clearly and correctly. Therefore, always proofread to detect misspellings or typographic errors. (See **33d**.)

One way to improve your spelling is to record correctly the words you have misspelled and study them. Another is to develop your own tricks to help you remember. For example, you might remember the spelling of *separate* by reminding yourself that it has *a rat* in it or the spelling of *attendance* by remembering that it includes *dance*.

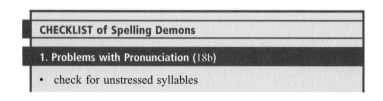

CHECKLIST of Spelling Demons

1. Problems with Pronunciation (18b)

- check for unstressed syllables

- consider the spelling of the root word

- consider alternate pronunciations for spelling clues

2. Problems with Words That Sound Alike—Homophones (18c)

- possessives and contractions: *your, you're*

- single words versus two-word phrases: *maybe, may be*

- *-nce* versus *-nts: instance, instants*

- other words that sound alike: *accept, except*

3. Problems with Affixes (18d–e)

- prefixes: *moral, immoral*

- suffixes
  - final *e: bride, bridal*
  - doubling final consonant: *drop, dropping*
  - changing *y* to *i: defy, defies*
  - retaining final *l: real, really*
  - plural forms: *toys, boxes, men, criteria*

4. Confusion of *ei/ie* (18f)

- sounds spelled *ei*

- sounds spelled *ie*

If you have trouble with spelling, consult your dictionary. Watch out for restrictive labels such as *British* or *chiefly British* and use the American form.

American	theater	fertilize	color	connection
British	theatre	fertilise	colour	connexion

In college or professional writing, do not use spellings labeled *obsolete* or *archaic, dialectal* or *regional,* or *nonstandard* or *slang.*

| **Not** | afeared | heighth | chaw | boughten |
| **But** | afraid | height | chew | bought |

If your dictionary lists two unlabeled alternatives, either form is correct—for example, *fulfill* or *fulfil, symbolic* or *symbolical.* The first option listed is usually the more common form.

18a Spell checkers can be valuable tools, but they must be used with caution.

Some people often feel that they no longer need to worry about spelling because computers have spell checkers to correct errors. While a spell checker can be helpful, it does not solve all spelling problems. For example, the computer cannot tell when you confuse such words as *principal* and *principle* because it cannot know which meaning is called for.

In addition, there are times when you will be writing in-class papers or essay exams. Spelling errors in such material can give your reader a poor initial impression and cause your work to be taken less seriously or your grade to be lowered. For those reasons, a basic knowledge of spelling is always important. Furthermore, if you misspell what you search for on the Web, you won't find what you need.

THE TRUTH ABOUT SPELL CHECKERS

A spell checker will not catch

- typographical errors when the error makes a word (such as *was* for *saw*).

- misspellings such as *could of* or *would of* for *could have* or *would have* (those that result from mistaking words that are not stressed in speech).
- misspellings that result from using the wrong member of a pair of words (homophones) that sound alike (such as *their/there*) although it will sometimes flag such words to question your usage. When that happens, look the word up in the dictionary (again) to be sure. Spell checkers often give incorrect advice.
- words that are correctly spelled but wrongly used such as *affect* for *effect.* As with homophones, spell checkers will occasionally flag such words, but you are much safer doing your own checking. You can set the search-and-replace function of your word processor to look for each word and then make sure you have used it correctly.

A spell checker will usually catch

- a letter dropped or added when a prefix is added.
- misspellings of irregular words or those that change the vowel of the root word when a suffix is added, but you will have to watch carefully to catch those the spell checker misses.
- words that are not in its dictionary. Either it will not tell you how to spell them, or it will suggest erroneous alternatives.

18b Spelling often does not reflect pronunciation.

Many words in English are not spelled as they are pronounced, so we often cannot rely on pronunciation for correct spelling. One trick you might use is to be aware of how the word would sound if it were pronounced as it is spelled. Following is a list of such words with the trouble spots boldfaced.

accident**all**y	can**di**date
athlete	congra**tu**lations

February	nu**cl**ear
gen**er**ally	**per**spire
govern**m**ent	Real**t**or
mo**d**ern	stren**gth**

Many unaccented syllables have acquired a neutral vowel sound—usually an indistinct "uh" sound in spoken English, although the spelling can use any one of the vowels (*a, e, i, o, u*). In dictionaries, this neutral vowel sound is often represented by a special symbol /ə/ called a *schwa,* as in *confidence,* /**ˈkähn-fə-dən(t)s**/.

It is sometimes helpful to think of the spelling of the root word as a guide to correct spelling.

| confidence, confide | exultation, exult |
| different, differ | indomitable, dominate |

Even a simple word, such as *often,* sometimes has alternate pronunciations (**ôf′ən, ôf′tən**). One of these alternates might be a better guide to spelling. Here are examples of other such words.

| everybody | literature | veteran |
| interest | sophomore | which |

CAUTION Words like *have, and,* and *than* are often not stressed in speech and are thus misspelled. A spell checker will not catch these misspellings.

I would ~~of~~ rather had fish ~~then~~ soup ~~an~~ salad.
      have   *than*   *and*

18c The meanings of words that sound alike are determined by the spelling.

Words such as *forth* and *fourth* or *sole* and *soul* are homophones: They sound alike but have vastly different meanings and spellings. Be careful to choose the right word for your context. A spell checker will not catch such errors.

Many frequently confused spellings can be studied in groups.

(1) Contractions and possessive pronouns are often confused.

In contractions, an apostrophe indicates an omitted letter. In possessive pronouns, there is no apostrophe.

Contraction	Possessive
It's my turn next.	Each group waits **its** turn.
You're next.	**Your** turn is next.
There's no difference.	**Theirs** is no different.

(See 15b and 15d.)

(2) Single words and two-word phrases may be confused.

A number of words function both as single words and as two-word phrases with different meanings. Following are examples of such words.

He wore **everyday** clothes.	He wears them **every day.**
Maybe we will go.	We **may be** going.

You **ran into** my car.	We can **run in to** check it.
Nobody was there.	The police found **no body.**

Other examples are *anymore, any more; awhile, a while; everybody, every body;* and *everyone, every one.*

CAUTION *A lot* and *all right* are still spelled as two words; *alot* and *alright* are considered incorrect, although *alright* is often used in newspapers and magazines. (See the Glossary of Usage.)

(3) Singular nouns ending in *-nce* and plural nouns ending in *-nts* are easily confused.

Assistance is available.	I have two **assistants.**
For **instance,** Jack can go.	They arrived **instants** ago.
My **patience** is frayed.	Some **patients** waited for hours.

The following list contains words that sound exactly alike (*break/brake*), ones that sound alike in certain dialects (*horse/hoarse*), and ones that are similar in sound, especially in rapid speech (*believe/belief*), but have different meanings. The spell checker cannot identify words that are correctly spelled but wrongly used. In general, the words listed here present common spelling rather than usage problems. You may understand the distinction in meaning between the terms in most of the following pairs but sometimes confuse the spelling because they sound so much alike. If you are unsure about the difference in meaning between any pair of words, consult the Glossary of Usage, the Index, or your dictionary.

Words Whose Spellings Are Frequently Confused

accept, except	advice, advise
access, excess	affect, effect
adapt, adopt	aisles, isles

alley, ally
allude, elude
already, all ready
altar, alter
altogether, all together
always, all ways
amoral, immoral
angel, angle
ante-, anti-
ascent, assent
ask, ax
assistance, assistants
baring, barring, bearing
began, begin
believe, belief
board, bored
break, brake
breath, breathe
buy, by, bye
canvas, canvass
capital, capitol
censor, censure, sensor
choose, chose
cite, site, sight
clothes, cloths
coarse, course
complement, compliment
conscience, conscious
council, counsel
cursor, curser
dairy, diary
decent, descent, dissent
desert, dessert
device, devise
discreet, discrete
dominant, dominate
dyeing, dying

elicit, illicit
emigrate, immigrate
envelop, envelope
fair, fare
faze, phase
fine, find
formerly, formally
forth, fourth
forward, foreword
gorilla, guerrilla
have, of
hear, here
heard, herd
heroin, heroine
hole, whole
holy, wholly
horse, hoarse
human, humane
idea, ideal
instance, instants
its, it's
knew, new
later, latter
lay, lie (See 7e.)
lead, led
lessen, lesson
lightning, lightening
lose, loose
marital, martial
maybe, may be
midst, mist
minor, miner
moral, morale
of, off
passed, past
patience, patients
peace, piece

persecute, prosecute
personal, personnel
perspective, prospective
plain, plane
pray, prey
precede, proceed
predominant, predominate
presence, presents
principle, principal
prophecy, prophesy
purpose, propose
quiet, quit, quite
raise, rise (See 7e.)
respectfully, respectively
right, rite, write
road, rode
sat, set (See 7e.)
sense, since

shown, shone
stationary, stationery
straight, strait
than, then
their, there, they're, there're
threw, through, thorough
throne, thrown
to, too, two
tract, track
waist, waste
weak, week
weather, whether
were, wear, where, we're
which, witch
who's, whose
your, you're

18d Adding a prefix to a base word changes the meaning but does not alter its spelling.

Prefixes are added to the beginning of the base word, called the **root.**

necessary, **un**necessary   moral, **im**moral

 No letter is added or dropped when a prefix is added. This type of misspelling is usually detected by a spell checker.

18e Adding a suffix to the end of the base word may require changing its spelling.

resist, resist**ant**   beauty, beaut**iful**

Spelling, however, is irregular and follows certain conventions. This type of misspelling is usually detected by a spell checker.

(1) Dropping or retaining a final *e* depends on whether the suffix begins with a vowel.

A word ending in an unpronounced *e* drops the final *e* before a suffix beginning with a vowel.

bride, brid**al**	come, com**ing**
combine, combin**ation**	prime, prim**ary**

A word ending in an unpronounced *e* retains the final *e* before a suffix beginning with a consonant.

entire, entire**ly**	rude, rude**ness**
place, place**ment**	sure, sure**ly**

Some exceptions are *awful, duly, likable, ninth, truly, wholly.*

To keep the /s/ sound in *ce* or the /j/ sound in *ge,* keep the final *e* before *-able* or *-ous.*

courage**ous**	manage**able**	notice**able**

(2) Final consonants are usually doubled when a suffix begins with a vowel.

Double the final consonant before a suffix beginning with a vowel if (a) the consonant ends a one-syllable word or a stressed syllable and (b) the consonant is preceded by a single vowel.

drop, dro**pp**ing	BUT	droop, droo**p**ing
admit, admi**tt**ed	BUT	picket, picke**t**ed

(3) The final *y* is changed or retained depending on whether the suffix begins with a vowel.

Change the *y* to *i* before suffixes—except *-ing.*

defy:	**defies, defied, defiance**	BUT	**defying**
modify:	**modifies, modified, modifier**	BUT	**modifying**

Most verbs ending in *y* preceded by a vowel do not change the *y* before *-s* or *-ed: stay, stays, stayed*. Similarly, nouns like *joys* or *days* retain the *y* before *-s*. The following spelling irregularities are especially troublesome: *lays, laid; pays, paid; says, said*.

(4) A final *l* before *-ly* is retained.

cool, coolly	real, really
formal, formally	usual, usually

E X E R C I S E   **1**

Add the designated suffixes to the following words.

EXAMPLES

-er, -ness, -ly: late   *later, lateness, lately*
-ing, -ed: rebel   *rebelling, rebelled*
-ing: lose, guide, rise   *losing, guiding, rising*

1. -ous: courage, continue
2. -ly: like, sure, safe
3. -ing, -ed, -ance: admit
4. -ment, -ed, -ing: manage
5. -able: notice, manage, desire
6. -ed, -ing, -ment: conceal
7. -ing, -ed, -ful: care, use, hope
8. -ing, -ed, -er: play, jog
9. -ed, -ing, -ly: complete
10. -ed, -ing: pay, plan

(5) The plural of nouns is formed by adding *-s* or *-es* to the singular.

scientists	sisters-in-law [chief word pluralized]
tables	the Smiths [proper names]
toys	

For nouns ending in an *f* or *fe,* change the ending to *ve* before adding -*s* when the sound of the plural changes from *f* to *v: thief, thieves; life, lives;* BUT *roof, roofs.*

For nouns ending in *s, z, ch, sh,* or *x,* add -*es* when the plural adds another syllable.

box, box**es**	peach, peach**es**
crash, crash**es**	the Rodriguez**es**

Nouns ending in *y* preceded by a consonant add -*es* after changing the *y* to *i.*

company, compan**ies**	ninety, ninet**ies**

Although usage varies, most nouns ending in *o* preceded by a consonant add -*es.* Some words, like *nos/noes, mottos/mottoes,* and *zeros/zeroes,* can add -*s* or -*es.* Consult a dictionary if you have a question.

echo**es**	hero**es**	potato**es**	veto**es** [-*es* only]
auto**s**	memo**s**	piment**os**	pro**s** [-*s* only]

Certain irregular nouns do not add -*s* or -*es* to form the plural.

Singular	woman	goose	sheep	child
Plural	women	ge**e**se	sheep	child**ren**

Words derived from other languages generally form their plurals as they did in their original languages. If you are uncertain about how to make any word plural, look in the dictionary.

Singular	criterion	alumnus, -a	analysis	datum	species
Plural	criteria	alumn**i**, -**ae**	analyses	data	species

EXERCISE 2

Supply plural forms (including any optional spellings) for the following words. If a word is not covered by the rules, use your dictionary.

1. half   2. speech   3. phenomenon

4. woman	10. genius	16. bush
5. potato	11. passerby	17. hero
6. theory	12. halo	18. Kelly
7. radius	13. tomato	19. church
8. bath	14. leaf	20. life
9. story	15. scarf	

18f   *Ei* and *ie* are often confused.

When the sound is /i/ (as in *me*), write *ie* except after *c,* in which case write *ei.*

> chief   priest   yield

> BUT after *c* conceit   perceive   receive

When the sound is other than /i/, you should usually write *ei.*

> eight   foreign   heir   rein   their   weight

Some exceptions include *either, neither, friend,* and *species.*

18g   Hyphens can link or divide words.

Hyphens not only link, or make a compound of, two or more words that function as a single word, but they also divide words at the end of a line.

Grammar checkers are of limited use with hyphens. They often, but not always, can identify compound words and suggest a correct spelling such as *double-space* instead of *doublespace.* Grammar checkers can also recognize and flag fractions and compound numbers to alert you to a missing hyphen, but they will usually misdiagnose a hyphen used to avoid ambiguity or a hyphenated prefix such as *ex-* or *anti-*.

---

(1) Hyphens link two or more words to form a compound that functions as a single word.

Nouns	We planted forget-me-nots and Johnny-jump-ups.
Verbs	She speed-read the paper.
	I double-checked.
	He hard-boiled the egg.

Some compounds are listed in the dictionary with hyphens (*eye-opener, cross-examine*), others are written as two words (*eye chart, cross fire*), and still others are written as one word (*eyewitness, crossbreed*). When in doubt, consult your dictionary.

CAUTION Do not confuse the hyphen with the dash, which is key-boarded as a double hyphen with no spaces before and after. (See 17e.)

Hyphenate two or more words serving as a single adjective before a noun. (See 17h.)

> a well-built house [COMPARE a house that is well built]
>
> He has that get-it-done, make-it-happen attitude.

In a series, hyphens can carry over from one item to the next.

> eighteenth- and nineteenth-century houses

Omit the hyphen in the following cases:

- after an adverb ending in -*ly* (*quickly frozen foods*),
- in chemical terms (*sodium chloride solution*), and
- in a modifier using a letter or numeral as the second element (*group C homes, type IV virus*).

Hyphenate spelled-out fractions and compound numbers from *twenty-one* to *ninety-nine* (or *twenty-first* to *ninety-ninth*).

one-eighth   eighty-four   twenty-third

Also hyphenate combinations of figures and letters (*mid-1990s*), as well as nine-digit ZIP codes (*Dallas, TX 75392-0041*).

Hyphenate to avoid ambiguity or an awkward combination of letters or syllables between a prefix and root or a suffix and root.

re-sign the petition [COMPARE resign the position]
de-emphasize

In addition, hyphenate between a prefix and a capital letter and between a noun and the suffix -*elect*.

anti-American   President-*elect*

Otherwise, in general, do not hyphenate prefixes or suffixes.

E xercise 3

Refer to 18g(1) and to your dictionary as you convert each phrase to a compound or to a word with a prefix. Use hyphens when needed.

EXAMPLES

a movie lasting two hours   *a two-hour movie*
glasses used for water   *water glasses*

1. an antique couch covered in velvet
2. a brush for teeth
3. diplomats who solve problems
4. in the shape of an O
5. a house twenty years old
6. a garage for three cars
7. a holiday lasting four days
8. a light used at night
9. a highway with four lanes
10. lightbulbs costing ten dollars

(2) Hyphens break words at the ends of lines.

If you must divide a word at the end of a line, use a hyphen to separate syllables.

Word processing programs have a feature called automatic hyphenation, which can hyphenate words at the ends of lines, but it often does so improperly and unnecessarily. It is safer to hyphenate the words yourself and double-check when proofreading.

In dictionaries, spaces usually divide words into syllables: **re al ly, pre fer, pref er ence, sell ing, set ting.** But not every division between syllables is an appropriate place for dividing a word. The following principles are useful guidelines.

Do not divide abbreviations, initials, capitalized acronyms, or one-syllable words.

p.m. [NOT p.-m.]	USAF [NOT US-AF]
through [NOT thr-ough]	UNESCO [NOT UNES-CO]

Do not create one-letter syllables by putting the first or last letter of a word at the end or beginning of a line.

~~o mit~~ *omit*   ~~a ble~~ *able*   ~~bo a~~ *boa*

Do not put the last two letters of a word at the beginning of a line.

~~dat ed~~ *dated*   ~~does n't~~ *doesn't*   ~~safe ly~~ *safely*   ~~grav el~~ *gravel*   ~~tax is~~ *taxis*

Divide hyphenated words only at the hyphen.

mass-| produce   father-| in-law   OR   father-in-| law

Divide words between two consonants that come between vowels, except when the division does not reflect pronunciation.

pic-| nic   dis-| cuss   thun-| der   BUT   co-| bra

Divide words between those consonants that you double when adding *-ing*.

set-| ting   jam-| ming   plan-| ning   [COMPARE sell-| ing]

(3) Three hyphens in lists of works cited indicate that the author is the same as in the previous entry. (See 38e(2).)

Booth, Wayne C. *Modern Dogma and the Rhetoric of Assent.* Chicago: U of Chicago P, 1974.
---. *The Rhetoric of Irony.* Chicago: U of Chicago P, 1982.

EXERCISE 4

Write a list of five cues that help you remember certain difficult spellings. Share your devices with other students in the class.

EXERCISE 5

Edit the following paragraph for misspellings and correct usage of the hyphen.

[1]My friends and I recently watched a videotape of *First-Knight,* a movie that is principly located in the make believe city of Camelot. [2]Of course, we had all heard the story of Lancelot and Guinevere, too of the most famous lovers in all of fiction, and their troubled relationship with King Arthur. [3]Despite this fact, we liked the movie because it successfully communicatid the various phenomena associated with the conflict between love and loyalty. [4]One scene in which this conflict is most readly apparent occurs after Guinevere marries Arthur. [5]When her former home is attacked, Guinevere becomes concerned for her family's safety and, not

surprisingly, both men come to her rescue: Arthur, because
Guinevere is his wife and because he loves her; and Lancelot,
because Arthur is his king and because he also loves Guinevere.
[6]Fortunately, Arthur's military strategies and Lancelot's individual
prowess lead to the invaders' defeat, even if only temporarily,
proving that victory depends not on the sighs of an army, but on its
skill and cooperation. [7]In fact, all of the issues concerning love and
loyalty portrayed in the movie's storyline are timeless and will
be as important in the twenty first century as they were in the
eighth. [8]Nevertheless, although the film maker did a good job of
conveying such significant issues, some of my friends didn't like the
fact that the costumes worn by the actors and actresses were
historically inaccerate.

Chapter

19 Good Usage

A writer's indispensable tool for finding information about the acceptable uses of language is a good college dictionary. Whereas a thesaurus can alert you to possible synonyms and is an important aid to writing, a dictionary furnishes the meaning of a word, its pronunciation, and its part of speech, as well as the word's plural forms and verb tenses. Although a dictionary includes words appropriate in colloquial as well as in college and professional writing (often referred to as edited American English or EAE), it also includes usage labels and short usage paragraphs to distinguish between the two. Words labeled **dialect, slang,** or **nonstandard,** as well as words no longer in common use labeled **archaic** or **obsolete,** are usually inappropriate for college and professional writing. If a word has no label, it is acceptable. (See the Glossary of Usage.)

In this chapter, you will learn about

- dictionaries (19a),
- language for different audiences and occasions (19b),
- clear, simple style (19c), and
- inclusive writing (19d).

Dictionaries

Because language is constantly changing, it is important to choose a desk dictionary, not a pocket dictionary, with a recent copyright date. Many are available, either in paperback or on CD-ROM; both usually include the same information. Pocket dictionaries, which are useful for spelling and quick definitions, omit important information on usage and derivation. Reliable dictionaries include:

The American Heritage Dictionary
Funk & Wagnalls Standard College Dictionary
Merriam-Webster's Collegiate Dictionary
The Random House Dictionary
Webster's New World Dictionary

Occasionally, you may need to refer to an unabridged or a special dictionary.

Unabridged Dictionaries

The Oxford English Dictionary. 2nd ed. 20 vols. 1989–.
CD-ROM. 1994.
*Webster's Third New International Dictionary of the English
Language.* 1995.

Special Dictionaries

Bryson, Bill. *The Facts on File Dictionary of Troublesome
Words.* 1985, 1987.
Cowie, A. P., and R. Mackin. *Oxford Dictionary of Current
Idiomatic English.* Vols. 1–2. 1975, 1984.
Follett, Wilson. *Modern American Usage: A Guide.* 1998.
Morris, William, and Mary Morris. *Harper Dictionary of
Contemporary Usage.* 2nd ed. 1985, 1992.
Onions, C. T. *Oxford Dictionary of English Etymology.* 1966.
Partridge, Eric, and Paul Beale. *Dictionary of Catch Phrases.*
1992.
———. *Dictionary of Slang and Unconventional English.* 8th
ed. 1985.
Roget's International Thesaurus. 1999.
Merriam-Webster's Collegiate Thesaurus. 1995.
Merriam-Webster's Dictionary of English Usage. 1993.

⌐ The following dictionaries are recommended for
nonnative speakers of English.

Longman Dictionary of Contemporary English. 1996.
(*Longman Dictionary of American English,* 1997, is the
American abridgment.)

Longman Dictionary of English Language and Culture. 1992.

The Newbury House Dictionary of American English. 1996.

Oxford Advanced Learner's Dictionary of Current English. 1998. (*Oxford ESL Dictionary,* 1994, is the American edition.)

Two excellent resources for ESL students are the following.

Longman Language Activator. 1993. (This book supplies definitions, usage, and sample sentences: it is a cross between a dictionary and a thesaurus.)

Swan, Michael. *Practical English Usage.* 1995. (This is a practical reference guide to problems encountered by those who speak English as a second language.)

Inexpensive collections that include a dictionary, thesaurus, usage guide, and certain other reference works are beginning to be available on a single CD-ROM disk.

CAUTION   Most word processing programs also include a thesaurus. When using a computer thesaurus, do not merely substitute one word for another without understanding subtle differences in meaning. In listing synonyms, dictionaries often point out such distinctions.

19a   Dictionaries provide information beyond the definition of a word.

Reading the introductory material and noting the meaning of any special abbreviations will help you understand the information your dictionary provides. The following sample entry from the tenth edition of *Merriam-Webster's Collegiate Dictionary* provides important information. Almost all desk dictionaries provide the same information, although possibly in a different order. *Answer* is listed twice in the following entries—first as a noun and then as a verb.

Part of speech

Pronunciation

Syllabication

Origin

Spelling ——— ¹**an·swer** \'ant(t)-sər\ *n* [ME, fr. OE *andswaru* (akin to ON *andsvar* answer); akin to OE *and-* against, *swerian* to swear—more at ANTE-] (bef. 12c) **1 a :** something spoken or written in

Date of first occurrence

reply to a question **b :** a correct response **2 :** a reply to a legal charge or suit : PLEA; *also* : DEFENSE **3 :** something done in response or reaction ⟨his only ~ was to walk out⟩ **4 : a** solution of a problem **5 :** one that imitates, matches, or corresponds to another ⟨television's ~ to the news magazines⟩

Usage of definition #3

vb. forms ——— ²**answer** *vb* **an·swered; an·swer·ing** \'an(t)s-riŋ, 'an(t)-sə-\ *vi* (bef. 12c) **1 :** to speak or write in reply **2 a :** to be or make oneself responsible or accountable **b :** to make amends : ATONE **3 :** to be in conformity or correspondence ⟨~ed to the description⟩ **4 :** to act in response to an action performed elsewhere or by another **5 :** to be adequate : SERVE ~ *vt* **1 a :** to speak or write in reply to **b :** to say or write by way of reply **2 :** to reply in rebuttal, justification, or explanation **3 a :** to correspond to ⟨~s the description⟩ **b :** to be adequate or usable for : FULFILL **4** *obs* **:** to atone for **5 :** to act in response to ⟨~ed the call to arms⟩ **6 :** to offer a solution for; *esp* : SOLVE—**an·swer·er** \'an(t)-sər-ər\ *n*

syn ANSWER, RESPOND, REPLY, REJOIN, RETORT mean to say, write, or do something in return. ANSWER implies the satisfying of a question, demand, call, or need ⟨*answered* all the questions⟩. RESPOND may suggest an immediate or quick reaction ⟨*responded* eagerly to a call for volunteers⟩. REPLY implies making a return commensurate with the original question or demand ⟨an invitation that requires you to *reply*⟩. REJOIN often implies sharpness or quickness in answering ⟨"who asked you?" she *rejoined*⟩. RETORT suggests responding to an explicit charge or criticism by way of retaliation ⟨he *retorted* to the attack with biting sarcasm⟩.

Synonyms and distinctions with usage examples

Spelling, syllabication, and pronunciation

Dictionaries describe both written and spoken language. You can check spelling and word division (syllabication), as well as the pronunciation of unfamiliar words. A key to sound symbols appears at the bottom of the entry pages and also in the introduction. Alternative pronunciations usually represent regional differences.

Parts of speech and inflected forms

Dictionaries label the possible uses of words in sentences—for instance, *tr. v., adj.* These labels identify the various ways that nouns, verbs, and modifiers change form to indicate number, tense, and comparison.

Word origin/etymology

The origin of a word—also called its derivation or etymology—can be useful in understanding its meaning and appreciating the many cultures that have influenced, and continue to influence, the English language.

Date of first occurrence

The date (*bef. 12c*) in parentheses in the sample is the first known occurrence of the word in written English.

Definitions

Definitions are listed in different order in different dictionaries. The sample lists the oldest meaning first. Often, meanings are ordered according to how common they are.

Usage

Most dictionaries give guidance on usage through discussion and quotations showing how the word has been used in context.

Synonyms

Dictionaries always list synonyms, sometimes with detailed explanations of subtle differences in meaning. When discussions such as the one in the sample are used in conjunction with a thesaurus, they are extremely helpful. The entry for the word *answer* lists five one-word synonyms. The entry for each synonym has a cross-reference to the entry for *answer*.

EXERCISE 1

Study the definitions for the following pairs of words, and write a sentence to illustrate the subtle differences in meaning in each pair.

1. clemency-mercy
2. provoke-excite
3. vampire-necrophile
4. ingenuous-innocent
5. putrefy-rot

6. courageous-fearless
7. charm-charisma
8. practicable-viable
9. liberate-free
10. insolent-rude

19b Language varies according to the audience, the place, and the purpose.

There is a difference between the words used in conversation (colloquialisms) or informal writing, such as a personal journal (32), and the more formal language appropriate for college and professional writing. In speech, you sometimes use dialect words or words that only persons from your own area, profession, or generation might understand. In writing, it is important to select words that are meaningful to your audience.

The words you choose will vary from situation to situation, place to place, and occupation to occupation. It is unlikely that anyone would use the same kind of language to discuss a traffic fine with a judge and with a family member or best friend. The discussions with the judge would probably be relatively formal, while those with the family member or friend would be less so. These are differences of register—the variety of language used in specific social contexts. The language used for college or professional writing is appropriate for most situations. Specific situations may, however, call for other kinds.

(1) Colloquial (or conversational) words are rarely used in college and professional writing.

Words labeled **colloquial** (or **conversational**) are common in speech and used by writers in dialogue and informal writing. Such words may be used for special effect in academic writing, but in general unlabeled words are preferred. For example, conversational terms such as *dumb, belly button,* or *kid* can be revised to read *ignorant, navel,* or *tease.*

Although contractions, such as *it's* and *aren't,* are common in English, many instructors consider them inappropriate for college writing.

(2) Slang is not acceptable in college and professional writing.

Slang is usually defined as words belonging to a particular age group, locality, or profession. Slang, in fact, covers a wide range of words that are variously considered breezy, racy, excessively informal, facetious, or taboo. Sometimes they are newly coined or highly technical. Slang is usually avoided in college writing, however, because it may be misunderstoond or can easily become dated.

(3) Regionalisms are not appropriate in college and professional writing.

Since their meaning may not be widely known, regional or dialectal usages, such as *tank* for *pond,* are normally avoided in writing to an audience outside the region where they are current. Speakers and writers can safely use regional words known to the audience they are addressing, however.

(4) Nonstandard usage should be avoided in college and professional writing.

Words and expressions labeled **nonstandard** should not be used in college and professional writing, except possibly in direct quotations. For example, *ain't* should not be used for *am not,* nor should "He done ate" be used for "He has already eaten."

(5) Archaic and obsolete words are inappropriate in modern writing.

All dictionaries list words (and meanings for words) that have long since passed out of general use. Such words as *rathe* (early) and *yestreen* (last evening) are still found in dictionaries because they occur in our older literature and so must be defined for the modern reader, but they should not be used.

A number of obsolete or archaic words—such as *worser* (for *worse*) or *holp* (for *helped*)—are still in use but are now nonstandard.

(6) Technical words should be avoided when writing for nonspecialists.

The careful writer will not refer to an organized way of finding a subject for writing as a *heuristic* or a need for bifocals as *presbyopia.* Of course, the greater precision of technical language makes it desirable when the audience can understand it, as when one physician writes to another.

Jargon is technical language tailored specifically for a particular occupation. Technical language can be an efficient shortcut for specialized concepts, but you should use jargon only when you can be sure that both you and your readers understand it.

19c A clear, straightforward style is preferable to an ornate one.

An ornate or flowery style makes reading slow and calls attention to your words rather than your ideas. Although different styles are appropriate for different situations—depending, for example, on purpose, audience, and context (32a)—you should usually keep your writing simple and straightforward.

Ornate   The majority believes that the approbation of society derives primarily from diligent pursuit of allocated tasks.

Simple   Most people believe that success results from hard work.

 In the United States, a plain, straightforward style is valued for its simplicity and clarity, but it may not always be considered gracious by other cultures shaped by different traditions. Do not hesitate to honor your own culture; by making careful choices regarding diction and tone, it is possible to be both straightforward and polite.

EXERCISE 2

Without using slang or regionalisms, rewrite the following passages for a friendly audience that likes a simple, straightforward style.

1. Expert delineation of the characters in a work of fiction is a task that is difficult to facilitate.

2. In an employment situation, social pleasantries may contribute to the successful functioning of job tasks, but such interactions should not distract attention from the need to complete all assignments in a timely manner.

3. Commitment to an ongoing and carefully programmed schedule of physical self-management can be a significant resource for stress reduction.

4. The Center for Automotive Maintenance recommends regular monitoring of fluids necessary for internal combustion vehicles and increasing the allocation level of such fluids when necessary.

5. Students troubled by dysfunctions in interpersonal relationships can receive support from information specialists in the counseling division of health services.

19d Writing should be inclusive and not stereotype groups according to race, class, age, orientation, or gender.

Be aware of your audience and make sure that you choose language that includes all of its members. Take care, as well, to use the terms preferred by various groups. You can get some guidance from books such as Marilyn Schwartz's *Guidelines for Bias-Free Writing* (1995), but the best plan is to look at reputable regional newspapers, check prestigious national magazines, look in a recent dictionary, or ask people of various ages (and if possible various regions) who belong to that particular group.

A grammar checker can find racist or sexist words such as those ending in *-ess* or *-man* and almost always flags *mankind.* Unfortunately, it also erroneously identifies appropriate uses of such words as *female, woman,* and *girl* as sexist, but not similar uses of *male* or *boy.* Good sources for information about African American English and nonsexist language can be found on the Internet at http://www.cal.org/ebonics/ and http://www.stetson.edu/~history/nongenderlang.html.

---

(1) Sexist language demeans both men and women.

Making language inclusive (that is, avoiding sexist terms) means treating men and women equally. For example, many feel that women are excluded when *man* is used to refer to both men and women.

> **Man's** achievements in the twentieth century are impressive.

Sexist language has a variety of sources. Easiest to spot is the kind that results from true contempt for the opposite sex—not simply vulgar terms, but also language that denigrates, such as referring to people by their body parts. More difficult to recognize is the sexist language that results from stereotyping. We must become aware that it is stereotyping to refer to a male teacher or a woman lawyer. We are less likely to notice the kind of stereotyping that occurs from such statements as "*room mother* for the third grade" or "The *drunk* couldn't find *his* car." Most difficult is sexist usage embedded in the language itself—the use of *he* to refer to both men and women and terms such as *mankind.*

Being alert for possible uses of sexist language and knowing how to find it and revise it will go far toward gaining the approval of your audience, whatever its demographics. As the following list illustrates, revising to remove sexist language is relatively straightforward.

- **Generic *he:*** A doctor should listen to *his* patients.

  A doctor should listen to **his or her** patients. [use of the appropriate form of *he or she*]

Doctors should listen to **their** patients. [use of plural forms]

Listening to patients **is important for** doctors. [eliminating the pronoun by revising the sentence]

- **Occupational stereotype:** Glenda, a female engineer at Howard Aviation, won the best-employee award.

  Glenda, an engineer at Howard Aviation, won the best-employee award. [removal of the unnecessary gender reference]

- **Terms such as *man* or those with *-ess* or *-man* endings:** Labor laws benefit the common *man*. *Mankind* benefits from philanthropy. The *stewardess* brought me some tomato juice. The *fireman* rescued the kitten from the tree.

  Labor laws benefit **working people.** [A neutral term replaces the stereotype.]

  Everyone benefits from philanthropy.

  The **flight attendant** brought me some tomato juice.

  The **firefighter** rescued the kitten from the tree.

- **Patronizing labels:** The CEO said he would ask his *girl* to schedule the appointment.

  The CEO said he would ask his **secretary** (or **assistant**) to schedule the appointment.

- **Stereotyping gender roles:** I was told that the university offers free tuition to faculty *wives*.

  I was told that the university offers free tuition to faculty **spouses.**

- **Inconsistent use of titles:** *Mr. Holmes* and his *wife* Mary took a long trip to China.

  Mr. and Mrs. Holmes took a long trip to China.

  Peter and Mary Holmes-Wolfe took a long trip to China. OR **Peter Holmes** and **Mary Wolfe** took a long trip to China.

• **Unstated gender assumption:** Have your *mother* make your costume for the school pageant.

Have your **parents** provide you with a costume for the school pageant.

(2) References to race and ethnicity must be handled with care and sensitivity.

Stereotyping is harmful whether it occurs in a racial or ethnic context or not. Even positive stereotypes can be harmful because they exclude those to whom the stereotype does not apply. All Native Americans are not concerned about the land, nor are all Asian Americans exceptional engineering students or all African Americans talented athletes. Similarly, not everyone who has a talent for organization is German American, nor are all Italians good cooks, or all racists White. In most situations, it is unnecessary to identify someone's race or ethnicity, just as it is unnecessary to make gender-specific references.

Further, because language changes, the terms used to refer to various racial and ethnic groups also change from time to time and from place to place. Although people of African descent are no longer referred to as *colored* or *Negro,* those terms persist in the names of important organizations such as the National Association for the Advancement of Colored People and the United Negro College Fund. And today, whether to refer to *African Americans* or *Blacks* is sometimes a question of which generation your audience belongs to. People of Spanish-speaking descent in different parts of the nation have different preferences about whether to say *Latino/Latina, Chicano/Chicana,* or *Hispanic, Latin American, Mexican American,* or *Puerto Rican.* Many descendants of indigenous peoples prefer *Native American* to *American Indian,* and *Asian American* has supplanted *Oriental.* Use the term the group itself prefers.

(3) Sensitivity to matters of ability, age, class, religion, occupation, and orientation is appreciated.

Although referring to persons with physical disabilities as *handicapped* may be demeaning, being overly cautious about references to disabilities is equally demeaning. For example, avoiding such phrases as "I see what you mean" when a blind person is in the audience can be as demeaning as presenting a chart without explanation. Older people may respond positively when they are called *mature,* but many dislike being called *senior citizens* as much as young people would resent being called *junior citizens.*

Statements such as "We celebrate the major holidays—Christmas, Easter, the Fourth of July" with no mention of Yom Kippur or Ramadan are insensitive and exclusionary. Terms such as *faggot* or *dyke* perpetuate hate. Although some attempts to enhance the prestige of manual labor—such as the fictitious term *deforestation technician* to describe a member of a logging team—could be considered elitist and patronizing, using legitimate, inclusive terms for various occupations such as *housekeeper* instead of *maid* shows sensitivity. Labels such as *soccer mom*, *yuppie*, or *redneck* are clearly class references that reduce individuals to types. In all instances, avoid the stereotyping that uncritical use of language can create: people with cancer are not *victims,* a *long-time companion* may or may not be a partner in a same-sex relationship, and *inner-city residents* are just as likely to be the rich and famous as members of a particular ethnic group.

E X E R C I S E   3

Make the following sentences inclusive by eliminating all sexist language.

1. She was a published authoress as well as a fine actress.

2. The reporter interviewed President Berrier and his secretary, Rosa Gonzales.

3. Both Louise, a skilled pianist, and Erik, a handsome man, played with the local symphony last Friday night.

4. The ladies took a tour of the city while the executive managers met for a business conference.

5. The repairman came to fix the refrigerator.

6. My uncle has never married and his sister is a spinster.

7. Rosalind is a stay-at-home mom.

8. The guest list included the corporate executives and their wives.

9. If everyone realizes his personal potential, society will prosper.

10. These students are particularly interested in studying mankind and his technological advancements.

EXERCISE 4

Rewrite the following paragraph in language appropriate for a paper in an English composition class. Consult the Glossary of Usage or a dictionary to determine appropriate usages.

[1]I've been blessed by having a large amount of friends throughout my life, but as far as friends go, Melinda is one of the best. [2]We've had alot of fun together through the years. [3]Several years ago, however, I found a job where I could move up the ladder of success, so I moved away, knowing that Melinda and myself would keep in touch. [4]Even though my leaving saddened us both, it didn't effect our basic friendship at all. [5]We write to each other most every week, and not long ago, I made a surprise visit to her, and I stayed for a week. [6]If she had known I was arriving that afternoon, she would have taken off of work to meet me at the airport. [7]Even though we stay in touch, I still miss her; hopefully we'll be able to see each other again soon.

Chapter

20   Exactness

Good writing often consists of short, familiar, carefully chosen words. When drafting (see chapter 32), choose words that express your ideas and feelings. When revising (see chapter 33), make those words exact, fresh, and natural. Use the words you already know effectively, but add to your vocabulary to increase your options for choosing the exact word that suits your purpose, audience, and occasion.

Make new words your own by

- mastering their denotations and connotations and by writing clear definitions (20a),
- understanding how to use idioms (20b), and
- using fresh, clear expressions (20c).

20a   Accurate and precise word choice conveys meaning efficiently.

(1) Accuracy is essential.

The **denotation** of a word indicates what it names, not what it suggests. For example, the noun *beach* denotes a sandy or pebbly shore, not suggestions of summer fun. Inaccurate usage misstates your point, inexact usage diminishes it, and ambiguous usage confuses your reader. Select words that state your point exactly.

The speaker ~~inferred~~ *implied* that our enrollment had increased significantly this year. [*Infer* means "to draw a conclusion from evidence."

For example: From the figures before me, I inferred that our enrollment had increased significantly this year. *Imply* means "to suggest," so *implied* is the exact word for the sentence as drafted.]

Jennifer spends too much money on video games, ~~and~~ *but* she works hard to earn it. [*And* adds or continues; *but* contrasts. In this case, negative and positive information are contrasted.]

The lecture will focus on *motivating* ~~inspiring~~ athletes. [*Inspiring* is ambiguous in this context because the lecture could be about "how to inspire athletes" or "athletes who are inspiring."]

(2) Connotations enrich meaning.

The **connotation** of a word is what the word suggests or implies. *Beach,* for instance, may connote natural beauty, warmth, surf, water sports, fun, sunburn, crowds, or even gritty sandwiches. Context has much to do with the connotations a word evokes; in a treatise on shoreline management, *beach* has scientific, geographic connotations, whereas in a fashion magazine, it evokes images of bathing suits. In addition to being influenced by context, most readers carry with them a wealth of personal associations that can influence how they respond to the words on the page. The challenge for writers is to choose the words that are most likely to evoke the appropriate connotations from their readers.

One of the reasons I am recommending Mr. Krueger for this job is that he is so *persistent* ~~relentless.~~ [*Relentless* has negative connotations that are inappropriate for a recommendation.]

I love the *aroma* ~~odor~~ of freshly baked bread. [Many odors are unpleasant; *aroma* sounds more positive, especially in association with food.]

He gets into trouble sometimes because he is so *naive* ~~innocent~~. [*Inno-cent* suggests virtue; *naive* suggests a lack of judgment.]

Your ability to understand connotations will improve as your vocabulary increases. When you learn a new word that seems to mean exactly what another word means, study the context in which each word is used. As you learn new words, use them in your writing. If you are confused about connotations, consult a good ESL dictionary or ask a native speaker whether these words have different connotations.

(3) Specific, concrete words are usually stronger than general, abstract ones.

A **general** word is all-inclusive, indefinite, and sweeping in scope. A **specific** word is precise, definite, and limited in scope.

General	Specific	More Specific/Concrete
food	fast food	cheeseburger
entertainment	film	*Titanic*
place	city	Atlanta

An **abstract** word deals with concepts, with ideas, with what cannot be touched, heard, or seen. A **concrete** word signifies particular objects, the practical, and what can be touched, heard, or seen.

Abstract	democracy, loyal, evil, hate, charity
Concrete	mosquito, spotted, crunch, grab

Some writers use too many abstract or general words, leaving their writing vague and lifeless. As you select words to fit your context, you should be as specific and concrete as you can. For example, instead of the word *bad,* consider using a more precise adjective.

bad planks:	rotten, warped, scorched, knotty, termite-ridden
bad children:	rowdy, rude, ungrateful, perverse, spoiled
bad meat:	tough, tainted, overcooked, contaminated

To test whether or not a word is specific, you can ask one or more of these questions about what you want to say: Exactly who? Exactly what? Exactly when? Exactly where? Exactly how? As you study the following examples, notice what a difference specific, concrete words can make in expressing an idea and how specific details can expand or develop it.

Vague   She has kept no reminders of performing in her youth.

Specific   She has kept no sequined costume, no photographs, no fliers or posters from that part of her youth.

—LOUISE ERDRICH

Vague   He realized he was running through the cold night.

Specific   He found himself hurrying over creaking snow through the blackness of a winter night.   —LOREN EISELEY

Vague   When I was younger, I could eat more without getting fat.

Specific   When I worked on farms as a boy, loading hay bales onto wagons and forking silage to cows, shoveling manure out of horse barns, digging postholes and pulling barbed wire, I could eat the pork chops and half-dozen eggs my neighbors fed me for breakfast, eat corn bread and sugar in a quart of milk for dessert at lunch, eat ham steaks and mashed potatoes and three kinds of pie for supper, eat a bowl of hand-cranked ice cream topped with maple syrup at bedtime, and stay skinny as a junkyard dog.

—SCOTT RUSSELL SANDERS

As these examples show, sentences with specific details are often longer than sentences without them. But the need to be specific does not necessarily conflict with the need to be concise. (See chapter **21**.) Simply substituting one word for another can often make it far easier to see, hear, taste, or smell what you are hoping to convey.

I ~~had an accident~~ while trying to ~~catch a fish~~.
(handwritten: fell out of the canoe) *(handwritten: land a muskie)*

Occasionally, a skillful writer can achieve a dramatic effect by mixing concrete and abstract terms, as in the following example.

> We inhaled those nice big fluffy fumes of human sweat, urine, effluvia, and sebaceous secretions.   —TOM WOLFE

And all writers use abstract words and generalizations when these are vital to communicating their ideas, as in the following sentence.

> At its best, [art] reveals the nobility that coexists in human nature along with flaws and evils, and the beauty and truth it can perceive.
> —BARBARA TUCHMAN

Abstract words are exact when they are used to express abstractions—words like *immortal, inexhaustible, soul, spirit, compassion, sacrifice,* and *endurance.* When you use abstract words and generalizations, make sure you do so deliberately and with good reason.

(4) Figurative language can contribute to exactness.

Commonly found in nonfiction prose as well as in fiction, poetry, and drama, figurative language uses words in an imaginative rather than a literal sense. Simile and metaphor are the chief **figures of speech.** A **simile** is the comparison of dissimilar things using *like* or *as.* A **metaphor** is an implied comparison of dissimilar things not using *like* or *as.*

Similes

He was **like a piece of rare and delicate china** which was always being saved from breaking and finally fell. —ALICE WALKER

The thick blood welled out of him **like red velvet,** but still he did not die. —GEORGE ORWELL

She sat **like a great icon** in the back of the classroom, tranquil, guarded, sealed up, watchful. —REGINALD MCKNIGHT

[The moth] burned for two hours without changing, without swaying or kneeling—only glowing within, **like a building fire glimpsed through silhouetted walls, like a hollow saint, like a flame-faced virgin gone to God,** while I read by her light, kindled, while Rimbaud in Paris burns out his brain in a thousand poems while night pooled wetly at my feet. —ANNIE DILLARD [a series of similes describing a moth caught in a candle flame]

Metaphors

His **money was a sharp pair of scissors** that snipped rapidly through tangles of red tape. —HISAYE YAMAMOTO

We refuse to believe that **the bank of justice** is bankrupt.
—MARTIN LUTHER KING, JR.

It was gurgling out of her own throat, **a long ribbon of laughter,** like water. —SANDRA CISNEROS [a metaphor and a simile]

For the canyon traps light, rehearses all the ways a thing can be lit: **the picadors of light jabbing the horned spray of the Colorado River;** light like caramel syrup pouring over the dusky buttes; the light almost fluorescent in the hot green leaves of seedlings. —DIANE ACKERMAN [In this stunning metaphor, the river is described as the bull and the light as the horsemen who prepare the bull for the bullfighter; the metaphor is then followed by a simile for *light*—"like caramel syrup."]

Single words are often used metaphorically.

These roses must be **planted** in good soil. [literal]

Keep your life **planted** wherever you can put down the most roots. [metaphorical]

We always **sweep** the leaves off the sidewalk. [literal]

He seems likely to **sweep** her right off her feet. [metaphorical]

Similes and metaphors are especially valuable when they are concrete and point up essential relationships that cannot otherwise be communicated. Similes and metaphors can also be extended throughout a comparison paragraph, but be careful not to mix them. (See 23c.)

Other common figures of speech include **personification** (attributing to nonhumans characteristics possessed only by humans), **paradox** (a seemingly contradictory statement that actually makes sense when you think about it), and **irony** (a deliberate incongruity between what is stated and what is meant). In addition, experienced writers often enjoy using **overstatement, understatement, images,** and **allusions.** Figures such as these can contribute to lively, memorable writing even if they do not always contribute to exactness. (See 39a(5).)

E x e r c i s e 1

Choose five of the ten items below as the basis for five original sentences containing figurative language, exact denotations, and appropriate connotations.

1. the look of her hair
2. a hot summer day
3. studying for an exam
4. your favorite food
5. buying a car
6. an empty street
7. college athletes
8. a heavy rain
9. a traffic jam
10. the way he talks

20b Exact word choice requires an understanding of idioms.

An **idiom** is an expression whose meaning is peculiar to the language or differs from the individual meanings of its elements.

Be careful to use idiomatic English, not unidiomatic approximations. *She talked down to him* is idiomatic. *She talked under to him* is not. Occasionally, the idiomatic use of prepositions proves difficult. If you do not know which preposition to use with a given word, check the dictionary. For instance, *agree* may be followed by *about, on, to,* or *with.* The choice depends on the context. Writers sometimes have trouble with expressions such as these:

Dealing with Troublesome Idioms

Instead of	Use
abide **with**	abide **by** the decision
according **with**	according **to** the source
bored **of**	bored **by** it
comply **to**	comply **with** rules
conform **of/on**	conform **to/with** standards
differ **to**	differ **with** them
in accordance **to**	in accordance **with** policy
independent **to**	independent **of** his family
happened **on**	happened **by** accident
plan **on**	plan **to** go
superior **than**	superior **to** others
type **of a**	type **of** business

Many idioms—such as *all the same, to mean well, eating crow, raining cats and dogs*—cannot be understood from the individual meanings of their elements. Some like *turning something over in one's mind* are metaphorical. Such expressions cannot be meaningfully translated word for word into another language. Used every day, they are at the very heart of the English language. As you encounter idioms that are new to you, master their meanings just as you would when learning new words.

Grammar checkers can find some unidiomatic expressions, mainly unidiomatically used prepositions attached to verbs. But they do not find all of them. Further, grammar checkers will not flag a nonsense sentence such as the following, "These books must be broiled in the hope" but will flag a sentence like "Is a squirrel in the tree" pointing out that "*Is* usually begins a question." The problem, however, may not be an omitted question mark but an omitted expletive such as *there.* If English is not your first language, a grammar checker can occasionally help, but even if your grasp of English is very fluent, it can be tricky to use.

When learning how to use idioms, study how writers use them. The context in which idioms appear will often help you understand their meaning. For example, if you read, "I never eat broccoli because I can't stand it," you would probably understand that *not to be able to stand something* means *to dislike something intensely.* As you learn new idioms from your reading, try making a list and using them in your own writing. If you are confused about the meaning of a particular idiom, check an idiom dictionary.

Exercise 2

Write sentences using each of the following idioms correctly. Use your dictionary when necessary.

1. hang up, hang out
2. differ from, differ with
3. wait on, wait for
4. get even with, get out of hand
5. on the go, on the spot

20c Fresh expressions are more distinctive than worn-out ones.

Such expressions as *bite the dust, breath of fresh air,* or *smooth as silk* were once striking and effective. Excessive use, however, has drained them of their original force and made them **clichés.** Some **euphemisms** (pleasant-sounding substitutions for more explicit but possibly offensive words) are not only trite but wordy or awkward—for example, *correctional facility* for *jail* or *pre-owned* for *used.* Many political slogans and the catchy phraseology of advertisements soon become hackneyed. Faddish or trendy expressions like *whatever, impacted, paradigm, input,* or *be into* (as in "I am into exercising") were so overused that they quickly became clichés.

Nearly every writer uses clichés from time to time because they are so much a part of the language, especially the spoken language. But experienced writers often give a fresh twist to an old saying.

> I seek a narrative, a fiction, to order days like the one I spent several years ago, on a gray June day in Chicago, when I took a rollercoaster ride on the bell curve of my experience.   —GAYLE PEMBERTON   [COMPARE frequent references elsewhere to being on "an emotional roller coaster"]

Variations on familiar expressions from literature or the Bible, many of which have become part of everyday language, can often be used effectively in your own writing.

> Now is the summer of my great content.   —KATHERINE LANPHER [COMPARE Shakespeare's "Now is the winter of our discontent. . . ."]

Good writers, however, do not rely too heavily on the words of others; they choose their own words to communicate their own ideas.

EXERCISE 3

From the following list of trite expressions, select five that you often use or hear and replace them with carefully chosen words or phrases. Then use them in sentences.

EXAMPLES

beyond the shadow of a doubt   *undoubtedly*

slept like a log   *slept deeply*

1. a crying shame
2. after all is said and done
3. at the crack of dawn
4. bored to tears/death
5. in the last analysis

6. avoid like the plague
7. beat around the bush
8. the powers that be
9. in this day and age
10. the bottom line

20d The use of the first and second persons can help writers be exact.

Although there are times when it is inappropriate, the use of *I* when you are writing about personal experiences is both appropriate and natural. It is also the clearest way to distinguish your own views from those of others or to make a direct appeal to readers. However, if you frequently repeat *I feel* or *I think*, your readers may think you don't understand much beyond your own experience.

The second person (*you*) is a way to connect with readers. It can also be less wordy and more precise than the third-person alternatives.

EXERCISE 4

Study the following paragraph and prepare to discuss in class your response to the author's choice of words—his use of exact, specific language to communicate his ideas.

¹A single knoll rises out of the plain of Oklahoma, north and west of the Wichita range. ²For my people, the Kiowas, it is an old landmark, and they gave it the name Rainy Mountain. ³The hardest weather is there. ⁴Winter brings blizzards, hot tornadic winds arise in the spring, and in summer the prairie is an anvil's edge. ⁵The grass turns brittle and brown, and it cracks beneath your feet. ⁶There are green belts along the rivers and creeks, linear groves of hickory and pecan, willow and witch hazel. ⁷At a distance in July or August the steaming foliage seems almost to writhe in fire. ⁸Great green and yellow grasshoppers are everywhere in the tall grass, popping up like corn to sting the flesh, and tortoises crawl about on the red earth, going nowhere in plenty of time.

—N. SCOTT MOMADAY, "The Way to Rainy Mountain"

Chapter 21 Conciseness

Using words economically is fundamental to writing clearly because unnecessary words or phrases distract readers and blur meaning. Good writers know how to make their points concisely. This chapter discusses how to

- avoid redundant and unnecessary words (**21a**)
- combine sentences (**21b**),
- use repetition for emphasis (**21c**), and
- use pronouns and elliptical constructions to eliminate repetition (**21d**).

In some situations, repeating a word or phrase can be useful. (See **26b**, **29e**, and **31b(3)**.) But in most cases, repetition is a sign of inefficiency.

Wordy	In the early part of August, a hurricane was moving threateningly toward Houston.
Concise	In early August, a hurricane threatened Houston.
Repetitious	This excellent baker makes excellent bread.
Concise	This baker makes excellent bread.

21a Every word should count; words or phrases that add nothing to the meaning should be omitted.

(1) Redundancy contributes to wordiness.

Restating a key point in different words can help readers understand it. (See **38c(3)**.) But there is no need to explain the meaning of readily understood terms by using different words that say the same thing or to emphasize a word by rephrasing it. If you do, your work will suffer from redundancy: repetition for no good reason.

Ballerinas auditioned ~~in the tryouts~~ for *The Nutcracker.*

Each actor has a unique talent ^for ~~and ability that he or she uses in his or her~~ acting.

Although they are usually small ~~in size,~~ women gymnasts are extremely strong.

Useless Words in Common Phrases

yellow [in color]
at 9:45 a.m. [in the morning]
[basic] essentials
bitter [-tasting] salad
but [though]
connect [up together]
because [of the fact that]
[really and truly] fearless
fans [who were] watching TV

circular [in shape]
return/refer [back]
rich [and wealthy] nations
small [-size] potatoes
to apply [or utilize] rules
[true] facts
was [more or less] hinting
by [virtue of] his authority
the oil [that exists] in shale

Avoid grammatical redundancy, such as double subjects (*my sister [she] is*), double comparisons ([*more*] *easier than*), and double negatives (*could[n't] hardly*).

(2) Unnecessary words should be deleted.

Beware of empty or vague words such as *area, aspect, element, factor, field, kind, situation, thing,* or *type.* Replace such inexact words with exact ones that say precisely what you mean.

The tax increase involved many ~~factors.~~ complex issues.

~~In the event that~~ *If* taxes are raised, ~~expect~~ *voters will* complaints ~~on the part of the voters.~~

Some One- or Two-Word Replacements for Common Expressions

at all times	**always**
at this point in time	**now**
by means of	**by**
for the purpose of	**for**
in an employment situation	**at work**
in spite of the fact that	**although**
on account of the fact that	**because**
somewhere in the neighborhood of $2,500	**about $2,500**

One exact word can say as much as many inexact ones. (See 20a.)

spoke in a low and hard-to-hear voice	**mumbled**
persons who really know their particular field	**experts**

(3) Expletives often indicate wordiness.

There followed by a form of *be* is an expletive—a word that signals that the subject will follow the verb. (See 29f.) Because expletives shift emphasis away from the subject, they can result in unnecessary words. They can also be imprecise because they substitute a form of *be* for a forceful verb.

~~There were three~~ *Three* children ~~playing~~ *were* in the yard.

The *it* construction is also an expletive when *it* has no word to refer to and is followed by a form of *be*.

Learning to ski

~~It~~ is easy ~~to learn to ski~~.

The *it* construction is necessary only when there is no logical subject. For example: *It is going to snow.*

Exercise 1

Substitute one or two words for each of the following phrases and use your choice in a sentence.

1. in this day and age
2. has the ability to sing
3. was of the opinion that
4. in a serious manner
5. prior to the time that
6. did put in an appearance
7. located in the vicinity of
8. has a tendency to break
9. during the same time that
10. involving too much expense

Exercise 2

Revise each of the following sentences to make them more concise.

1. There are three possible dates that they might release the film on.
2. During our trip to Seattle, many ridiculous things happened that were really funny.
3. It looked to me as if the bridge could be dangerous because it might not be safe.

ITEM CHARGED

Patron: Marissa Finder
Patron Barcode:

Patron Group: SMWC Undergrad

Due Date: 11/7/2004 11:59 PM

Title: Jerome Biblical
                   commentary, edited by
                   Raymond E. Brown,
                   Joseph A. Fitzmyer [and]
                   Roland E. Murphy. With
                   a foreword by Augustin
                   Cardinal Bea.

uthor:
all Number: 220.7 .B879j
numeration:
hronology:
opy: 1
em Barcode:

4. Many seriously ill patients in need of medical attention were diagnosed by physicians on the medical staff of the hospital.

5. In the frozen wastes of the southernmost continent of Antarctica, meteorites from outer space that fell to earth thousands of years ago in the past were exposed to view by erosion by the deteriorating ice.

21b Combining sentences or simplifying phrases and clauses can eliminate needless words.

Note the differences in emphasis as you study the following examples.

~~The grass was like a carpet. It~~ *A carpet of blue-green grass* covered the whole playing field.

~~The color of the grass was blue green.~~

Some ~~phony~~ unscrupulous brokers are *cheating* ~~taking money and savings from~~ elderly ~~old~~ people ~~who need that money because they planned to use it as a retirement~~ *out of their* pension*s*.

21c Repetition is useful only when it contributes to emphasis, clarity, or coherence. (See also 26b, 29e, and 31b(3).)

~~Your teacher is unlike my teacher.~~ Your teacher likes teaching better than mine ~~does~~.

She hoped he understood that *her comment did not reflect her feelings* ~~the complaint she made was not the way that she really felt about things.~~

We will not rest until we have pursued **every** lead, inspected **every** piece of evidence, and interviewed **every** suspect. [In this case, the repetition of *every* is useful because it emphasizes the writer's determination.)

21d **Pronouns and constructions that omit words that will be understood by the reader without being repeated (elliptical constructions) can eliminate needless repetition. (See chapter 28.)**

Instead of repeating a noun or substituting a clumsy synonym, use a pronoun. If the reference is clear (see 28b), several pronouns can refer to the same antecedent.

> The hall outside these offices was empty. ~~The hall~~ *It* had dirty floors, and ~~the~~ *Its* walls ~~of this corridor~~ were covered with graffiti.

An **elliptical construction** helps the writer of the following sentence be concise.

> Speed is the goal for some swimmers, endurance [is the goal] for others, and relaxation [is the goal] for still others.

Sometimes, as an aid to clarity, commas mark omissions that avoid repetition.

> My family functioned like a baseball team; my mom was the coach; my brother, the pitcher; and my sister, the shortstop.

As these examples show, parallelism reinforces elliptical constructions. (See chapter 26.)

EXERCISE 3

Revise the following sentences to eliminate wordiness and needless repetition.

1. The bricks on our new house are red in color and in spite of the fact that they are new the look of these bricks is a used, beat-up appearance.
2. America has two main kinds of business. Americans need to pay attention to getting justice for all, and they also need to be sure that everyone is treated alike.

3. Because of the fact that my parents thought my fiancé was really a terrific guy, I put a lot of effort into trying to work through my conflicts with him.

4. I couldn't understand her response to my paper because of the illegible handwriting that could not be read.

5. Our skating coach made the recommendation saying that my pairs partner and I should put more time into our practicing.

Chapter

22 Clarity and Completeness

Clarity in writing depends on more than grammar. Clarity results from critical thinking (**35**), logical development (**32**), and exactness of diction (**20**) at least as much as it does from correct use of grammar. However, some grammatical issues can cloud otherwise clear writing. This chapter will help you

- use articles, pronouns, conjunctions, and prepositions for clarity (**22a**),
- include all necessary verbs and auxiliaries in a sentence (**22b**), and
- complete comparisons (**22c**) and intensifiers (**22d**).

Regarding completeness, in speaking we sometimes have a tendency to drop—or "swallow"—unemphatic words. If you give too much weight to "writing like you talk," you may find that you omit these words from your writing because you simply do not hear them. These words are necessary in writing, however, to make your meaning clear.

We ^had better study hard. [Often not heard in speech, *had* must be included in writing.]

A grammar checker will sometimes alert you to a missing word, but it will just as often fail to. It may also tell you that an article is missing when it is not. You are better off proofreading your work yourself. (See **8d**.)

22a Articles, pronouns, conjunctions, or prepositions are sometimes necessary for clarity and completeness.

(1) Omitting an article (*a, an, the*) can confuse your reader.

The following sentence is a good example. Unless it is edited, it could mean that either one person or two people are "standing nearby"; it is ambiguous.

> **A** friend and ^*a*^ helper stood nearby.

Indefinite Articles

Review material on count and noncount nouns. (See 1c(2).)

The indefinite articles *a* and *an* are used with singular countable nouns in the following situations.

- with descriptive or general nouns

  a house   **an** orange

- with something mentioned for the first time

  Our history professor assigned **an** exam for next Monday.

- with the meaning of *one,* not *more*

  I chose **a** piece of fruit from the basket.

- with reference to a member of a group

  a novel

Use *a* before a consonant sound: **a** yard, **a** university. Use *an* before a vowel sound.

> **an** apple   **an** hour

Plural count nouns use words such as *some* or *any*. (See
6a(7).)

some magazines   **any** books

 Definite Articles

The definite article *the* is used with singular or plural
noncount nouns to indicate a specific person, place, or
thing in the following situations.

- when the noun has been previously introduced or when you
  and the reader know what you are referring to

  We must leave **the** building now.

  We will have a quiz tomorrow. **The** quiz will cover
  chapters 1 and 2.

- when the noun is unique

  the Vietnam Memorial

- when an ordinal number (fourth, sixth) or superlative (least,
  best) comes before the noun

  the eighth day of the month   **the** least expensive

Omission of the Article

The article is omitted entirely in a number of cases and is
optional in others. Some general directions for omitting
the article follow.

- with another determiner

  Sign up for this new course.

- before a noncount noun

  Let's have ice cream and cake.

- before a plural countable noun that does not refer to a specific item

  Buy oranges and apples.

- before a plural noun that has a general meaning

  Everyone wants benefits.

- in certain common expressions

  go to school, go to class, go to college, go to bed

(2) When conjunctions or prepositions are omitted, clarity suffers.

In the following example, the *of* is often omitted in speech but never in writing.

We had never tried that type $_\wedge$ film before. *(of)*

When your sentence has a compound verb (two verbs), you may need to supply a different preposition for each verb to make your meaning clear.

I neither believe $_\wedge$ nor approve of those attitudes. *(in)*

In the following sentence, use a comma when the conjunction *and* is omitted.

Habitat for Humanity built the house, (**and**) then later painted it. [COMPARE Habitat for Humanity built the house and later painted it. (See **13b**.)]

22b Verbs and auxiliaries that are sometimes omitted in speech are necessary in writing to avoid awkwardness or to complete meaning.

The revision eliminates the awkwardness in the following sentence.

Voter turnout has never $_\wedge$ and will never be 100 percent. *(been)*

Although *is* may not be heard in speech, it is included in writing.

Lamont is strong and very tall.

In sentences such as the following, omitting or including the second verb is optional.

The storm was fierce and the thunder (**was**) deafening.

22c Complete comparisons are needed to explain meaning if it is not suggested by the context.

He is taller **than his brother.**

Most people think television is more violent **than it used to be.**

Comparisons can be completed by other words or phrases in the sentence, by other sentences in the paragraph, or by the context.

In the next century, people will need more education.

22d The intensifiers *so, such,* and *too* need a completing phrase or clause.

My hair is **so** long **that I must get it cut today.**

Julian has **such** a hearty laugh **that it makes everyone feel good.**

It is just **too** much **for me to try to do.**

Although not appropriate in college or professional writing, the omission of a completing phrase often occurs in writing that approximates speech after intensifiers such as *so, such,* and *too* when they are used for emphasis.

My hair is **so** long.

Julian has **such** a hearty laugh.

It is just **too** much.

EXERCISE 1

Supply the words needed for formal writing in the following sentences.

1. They always have and always will go to the coast for vacation.
2. Cars with standard transmissions are better.
3. Rogelio likes his hardcover books better.
4. The airline passengers better pay attention to the safety guidelines.
5. Siobhan been trying to make her research paper more persuasive.

EXERCISE 2

Insert words where needed.

1. The snow in the plains region is as heavy as the mountains.
2. Chris stronger than my father.
3. The auditorium was already packed with people and still coming.
4. I had an unusual party my last birthday.
5. The students are angered and opposed to the administration's attempts to change university policy.

Chapter

23 Sentence Unity: Consistency

Good writing is unified and sticks to its purpose. It is consistent throughout, with no shifts in grammatical structure, tone, style, or viewpoint. This chapter can help you understand how to revise

- unrelated ideas (23a),
- a series of details into a clear sequence (23b),
- mixed metaphors and constructions (23c), and
- faulty predication (23d–e).

23a Relating ideas clearly in a sentence helps the reader.

Occasionally, sentences need an additional phrase or two to establish such relationships as time sequence, location, and cause.

Unrelated   An endangered species, tigers live in India where there are many people. [unity thwarted by a gap in thought]

Related   An endangered species, tigers live in India **where their natural habitat is shrinking because of population pressures**. [The added phrase makes the cause-and-effect relationship between the tigers' habitat and their endangerment clear.]

Exercise 1

All the sentences below contain apparently unrelated ideas. Adding words when necessary, rewrite each sentence to indicate a logical relationship between the ideas. If you cannot establish a close relationship, put the ideas in separate sentences.

1. The coffee at the diner is incredibly bad, and most of the customers seem to buy it often.
2. Dr. Roberts has an unusual and innovative teaching style, and I was unable to attend her class last week.
3. Her friends ski on the mountain in the winter, and in the summer earn money by working at odd jobs they avoid doing the rest of the year.
4. Enrique gave his mother a new coat for Christmas, and she went to dinner with his father.
5. There are lots of problems with the new supervisor at work, but I like to avoid them and talk to her one-on-one.

23b Arranging details in a clear sequence makes your point clear.

The amount of detail in the first sentence is excessive. Although detail usually makes writing more interesting, too much of it can be distracting. Do not include details that are not necessary to develop your point.

Excessive	When I was only sixteen, I left home to attend a college that was nearby and that my uncle had graduated from twenty years earlier.
Clear	I left home when I was only sixteen to attend a nearby college. [If the detail about the uncle is important, include it in another sentence. If not, delete it.]

When getting rid of excessive details, remember that length alone does not make a sentence ineffective. Sometimes you may need a long sentence in which every detail contributes to the central thought. Parallel structure (see chapter 26), balance, rhythm, effectively repeated connectives, and careful punctuation can make even a paragraph-length sentence interesting and coherent.

> The rediscovery of fresh air, of home-grown food, of the delights of the apple orchard under a summer sun, of the swimming pool made by damming the creek that flows through the meadow, of fishing for sun perch or catfish from an ancient rowboat, or of an early morning walk down a country lane when the air is cool—all of these things can stir memories of a simpler time and a less troubled world.   —CASKIE STINNETT, *The Wary Traveler*

E X E R C I S E 2

Revise each sentence in the following passage to eliminate excessive detail.

¹I have never seen a place that was as filled with history that had been passed along by various family members who cherished every moment of it. ²Finally I returned to the place where I had lived for years which had been built decades before my birth.
³The old farm, considered a model of technological advances only thirty years before, but then in need of paint and repairs, as is so often the case with places long inhabited, had to be renovated for future use. ⁴Because of this, when I was eight years old, sleeping in the bedroom at the far north corner of the main house, because the larger bedrooms were occupied by my older brothers and sisters, my parents decided that they wanted to move us to a more modern home located in the suburbs of the city. ⁵The renovation of the old farm lasted only a few years, which really seemed much longer than that but made us appreciate our history, as many fail to do, until it is too late.

23c **Careful writers avoid mixed metaphors and mixed constructions.**

(1) A mixed metaphor combines different images and creates an illogical comparison.

Mixed   If you are on the fast track up the corporate ladder, it is best to keep working as hard as you can.

Revised   If you are on the fast track to a brilliant corporate career, it is best to keep working as hard as you can.

(2) Mixed constructions are illogical.

A sentence that begins with one kind of construction and shifts to another is a **mixed construction.** (See 23d–e and chapter 27.) Mixed constructions often omit the subject or the predicate.

Mixed   When Simon plays the didgeridoo sounds like a wounded cow. [adverbial clause + predicate; no subject]

Revised   When Simon plays the didgeridoo, it sounds like a wounded cow. [adverbial clause + main clause]

OR   Simon's playing makes the didgeridoo sound like a wounded cow. [subject + predicate]

Mixed   It was a young, frolicsome puppy but which was generally well behaved.

Revised   It was a young, frolicsome puppy, but it was generally well behaved. [main clause + independent clause]

23d Faulty predication can lead to problems.

Faulty predication occurs when the subject and predicate do not fit together logically.

Faulty	One book I read believes in eliminating subsidies. [A person, not a thing, believes.]
Revised	The author of one book I read believes in eliminating subsidies.
Faulty	One kind of prejudice is a salesclerk, especially after she or he has ignored an elderly customer. [The ignoring of the customer, not the salesclerk, is an example of prejudice.]
Revised	One kind of prejudice is a salesclerk's ignoring an elderly customer.

23e Faulty predication in definitions is illogical.

(1) Faulty construction of definitions can make writing difficult to read.

Constructions combining *is* with *when, where,* or *because* are often illogical since forms of *to be* signify identity or equality between the subject and what follows.

Faulty	The reason the package arrived so late is because he didn't mail it soon enough.
Revised	The package arrived so late because he didn't mail it soon enough.
Faulty	The Internet is when you look at text and images from across the world.
Revised	The Internet allows you to look at text and images from across the world.

Faulty   A grocery store is where people go to buy food.

Revised   A grocery store is a place where people go to buy
              food.

(2) Definitions clarify the precise meaning of words. (See chapter 32e(7).)

A short dictionary definition may be adequate when you need
to define a term or convey a special meaning that may be unfamiliar to the reader.

Here *galvanic* means "produced as if by electric shock." (See 16d.)

Giving a synonym or two may clarify the meaning of a term.
Such synonyms are often used as appositives.

Machismo, confidence with an attitude, is described in the article.

Writers frequently show—rather than tell—what a word means
by giving examples.

Many homophones (*be* and *bee, in* and *inn, see* and *sea*) are not
spelling problems.

Words often have a number of meanings. It must be clear to
the reader which meaning you are using.

In this paper, I use the word *communism* in the Marxist sense of social organization based on the holding of all property in common.

By stipulating your meaning in this way, you set the terms of
the discussion.

You can also formulate your own definitions of the concepts
you wish to clarify.

Knowledge is seasoning for the mind's palate.

Clichés could be defined as thoughts that have hardened.

A formal definition first states the term to be defined and puts it into a class, then differentiates it from other members of its class.

A *phosphene* [term] is a luminous visual image [class] that results from applying pressure to the eyeball [differentiation].

E X E R C I S E 3

Define any two of the following terms in full sentences using first (a) a short dictionary definition, then (b) a synonym, and finally (c) an example.

1. psychotic
2. honesty
3. bowie knife
4. reverence
5. elegant
6. wetlands
7. racism
8. liberal
9. terrify

Chapter 24

Subordination and Coordination

Subordination and coordination establish clear structural relationships among ideas and help readers follow your train of thought. (See 1e and 2b.) This chapter offers advice on revising

- short, choppy sentences (24a),
- long, stringy sentences (24b), and
- faulty or excessive subordination (24c).

Subordinate means "being of lower structural rank." Subordinate structures such as phrases, appositives, or subordinate clauses make the ideas they express appear less important than the ideas expressed in independent clauses, whether those ideas are really less important or not. In the following sentences, two facts of equal importance are alternately made subordinate. The subordinate clauses are italicized, and the independent clauses are boldfaced.

Subordinate Clause	Main Clause
After they ran the obstacle course,	**they splashed water on their faces.**
After they splashed water on their faces,	**they ran the obstacle course.**

Notice that when the clauses are reversed, the meaning of the sentence changes. In the following sentence, the subordinate clause contains the vital information; the independent clause simply gives it a context.

The weather service announced *that a tornado was headed straight for town.* [The subordinate clause is the direct object of the sentence.]

Coordinate means "being of equal structural rank." When two ideas are grammatically equal, as in the following example, they are expressed in coordinate structures such as two independent clauses.

	Main Clause			Main Clause	
SUBJECT	**+ PREDICATE,**	**and**	**SUBJECT**	**+ PREDICATE.**	
They	ran the obstacle course,	and	they	splashed their faces with water.	

Coordination also gives ideas equal structural emphasis.

a **stunning** and **unexpected** conclusion [coordinate adjectives]

in the attic or **in the basement** [compound prepositional phrases]

(See **1d** and **1e** for an explanation of the difference between phrases and clauses and the difference between main and subordinate clauses.)

24a Careful subordination can combine a series of related short sentences into longer, more effective units.

Choppy I was taking eighteen hours of course work. I wanted to graduate in three years. It turned out to be too much. I also had a full-time job at the newspaper. I just couldn't do both. I needed the money. I needed the extra course in order to graduate early. I felt bad about the whole thing. I had to drop one of my courses. I had to have the money from my job. I had to pay my tuition.

Revised I was taking eighteen hours of course work because I wanted to graduate in three years, but it turned out to be too much. Since I already had a full-time job at the newspaper, I just couldn't do both. I needed the money, but I needed the extra course in order to graduate early. Even though I felt bad about the whole thing, I had to drop one of my courses because I had to have the money from my job in order to pay my tuition.

When combining a series of related sentences, select the main idea, express it in the structure of a simple sentence (**SUBJECT + PREDICATE**), and use some of the following subordinate structures to relate the other ideas to the main one.

(1) Related sentences can be reduced to adjectives or adjectival phrases.

Choppy The road was slick with ice. It looked shiny and black. It was very treacherous.

Better **Slick with ice,** the **shiny, black** road was very treacherous. [participial phrase and coordinate adjectives]

(2) Related sentences can be reduced to adverbs and adverbial phrases.

Choppy Season the ground beef with garlic and Italian herbs. Use a lot of garlic. Go lighter on the herbs. Brown it over low heat.

Better **After seasoning** the ground beef **heavily** with garlic and **lightly** with Italian herbs, brown it **slowly.** [an adverbial phrase and adverbs]

OR   Season the ground beef **heavily** with garlic and **lightly** with Italian herbs, and brown it **slowly.** [adverbs]

Choppy   His face was covered with white dust. So were his clothes. The man looked like a ghost.

Better   **His face and clothes white with dust,** the man looked like a ghost. [The first two sentences are combined in an absolute phrase—a grammatically unconnected part of a sentence.]

(3) Related sentences can be reduced to appositives and contrasting elements.

Choppy   Philip's meanness was a small-minded act. It was noticed. But it was not criticized.

Better   Philip's meanness—**a small-minded act**—was noticed **but not criticized.** [an appositive and a contrasted element]

(4) Related sentences can become subordinate clauses.

Subordinate clauses are linked and related to main clauses by subordinating conjunctions and relative pronouns. These subordinators signal whether a clause is related to the base sentence by **time** (*after, before, since, until, when, while*), **place** (*where, wherever*), **reason** (*as, because, how, so that, since*), **condition** (*although, if, unless, whether*), or **additional information** (*that, which, who, whose*). (See pages 21 and 74 for lists of subordinators.)

Choppy   The thunderstorm ended. Then we saw a rainbow. It seemed to promise a pleasant evening.

Better   **When the thunderstorm ended,** we saw a rainbow, **which seemed to promise a pleasant evening.** [adverbial clause and adjectival clause]

24b Using subordination and coordination is preferable to stringing several main clauses together.

Do not overuse coordinating connectives like *and, but, however, or, so, then,* and *therefore.* For ways to revise stringy or loose compound sentences, see **30c.** Methods of subordination that apply to combining two or more sentences also apply to revising faulty or excessive coordination in a single sentence.

(1) Subordination can make one idea more prominent than another.

In the following examples, the main idea, expressed in the independent clause, is boldfaced; the other idea, expressed in the subordinate clause, is italicized.

Stringy	**Jim had a good job** and **he lost the election,** but **he really didn't mind.** [three independent clauses strung together]
Better	*Since he already had a job,* **Jim didn't really mind losing the election.** [one subordinate clause and one main clause]
Stringy	**I can't float. I just sink. I even hold my breath.** [three loosely related sentences]
Better	*Even though I hold my breath,* **I seem to sink rather than float.** [one subordinate clause and one independent clause]

(2) Coordinate elements give ideas equal importance.

The tornado hit, and the town was leveled. [equal grammatical emphasis on the tornado and the town]

COMPARE The town was leveled when the tornado hit. [Subordinating *the tornado* emphasizes *the town.*]

OR The tornado hit, leveling the town. [Subordinating *the town* emphasizes *the tornado.*]

(3) Subordinate or coordinate elements connect ideas logically.

When

ₐI slammed the car door on my hand, ~~and~~ I broke three fingers. [Subordinate to show a cause-and-effect relationship between ideas.]

OR

I broke three fingers because I slammed the car door on my hand.

The gasoline tank sprang a leak, *so* ~~and~~ all hope of winning the race was lost.

Can you mail the letter when

ₐ~~Are~~ you walking to school ~~or mailing the letter~~?

 CAUTION When introducing a single adjectival clause, do not use *but* or *and* before *which, who,* or *whom.*

Leela is a musician ~~and~~ who can play several instruments.

24c Faulty or excessive subordination can confuse the reader.

Faulty   Chen was only a substitute pitcher, winning half of his games.

Better   Although Chen was only a substitute pitcher, he won half of his games. [*Although* establishes the relationship between the ideas.]

Excessive   Some people who are not busy and who are insecure when they are involved in personal relationships worry all the time about whether their friends truly love them.

Better	Some insecure, idle people worry about whether their friends truly love them. [two subordinate clauses reduced to adjectives]

Exercise 1

Observing differences in emphasis, convert each pair of sentences below to (a) a simple sentence, (b) a compound sentence consisting of two main clauses, and (c) a complex sentence with one main clause and one subordinate clause. Be prepared to discuss the most effective revision.

1. Mara likes to take a small afternoon nap after finishing her homework. She is a dedicated and talented student.
2. The house was very ancient and gloomy. It was a grand Victorian home on the edge of town.
3. David was driving to San Francisco. On the way, his truck broke down.
4. After the guests left the party the hosts cleaned the living room. Then they washed the dishes before going to bed.
5. The kids couldn't concentrate in the living room studying their Spanish homework that they had to finish. They stopped their studying and went outside.

Exercise 2

Revise the following passage using effective subordination and coordination.

¹Bennett Hall is a residence unit at our college and it is an old building. ²It is nearer to my classes than the other dorm rooms would be since it is only a five-minute walk to the center of campus. ³It has large, spacious bedrooms. ⁴It is a good distance away from the football stadium and it offers a great deal of privacy to its residents. ⁵There's little noise. ⁶My room is on the far corner of the building. ⁷It faces east. ⁸It has a balcony overlooking the yard below. ⁹There are dark green shrubs that are covered with small white flowers. ¹⁰The place is comfortable and I enjoy living there.

Chapter 25

Misplaced Parts and Dangling Modifiers

Keeping related parts of a sentence together and avoiding modifiers that do not logically refer to another word in the sentence (dangling modifiers) make the meaning of the sentence clearer to your reader. This chapter offers advice on

- placing modifiers near the words they modify (**25a**) and
- making sure modifiers have a word in the sentence to refer to (**25b**).

A grammar checker will often catch split infinitives (which are now generally regarded as acceptable), but it did not catch the ones in this chapter. Nor do grammar checkers catch dangling or misplaced modifiers. Neither the dangling elements in the exercises nor those in the examples were flagged by the two grammar checkers we used.

25a Placing modifiers near the words they modify clarifies meaning.

The meaning of the following sentences changes according to the position of the modifiers.

Natasha went out with **just** her coat on.

Natasha **just** went out with her coat on.

Just Natasha went out with her coat on.

The student **who fell** had tried to help his friend.

The student had tried to help his friend **who fell.**

(1) To keep the meaning clear, place modifiers such as *almost, even, hardly, just, merely, nearly,* and *only* immediately before the words they modify.

The truck ~~only~~ costs *only* $2,000.

He ~~even~~ works *even* during his vacation.

(2) Prepositional phrases should be placed to indicate clearly what they modify.

Arne says *in the first paragraph* that he means to leave the country ~~in the first paragraph~~.

(3) Adjectival clauses should be placed near the words they modify.

I put the chair *that I had recently purchased* in the middle of the room ~~that I had recently purchased~~.

(4) "Squinting" constructions should be revised so they refer clearly to either a preceding or a following element.

The next day I agreed ~~the next day~~ to help him.

OR

I agreed ~~the next day~~ to help him *the next day*.

(5) Some constructions that split an infinitive are awkward and should be revised.

A split infinitive occurs when a word comes between *to* and the verb: *to carelessly purchase*. When such constructions are awkward, as in the following example, they should be revised.

The jury was unable ~~to~~, under the circumstances, ∧*to* convict the defendant.

Today, even the most conservative authorities generally agree that splitting an infinitive is occasionally not only natural but also desirable.

He forgot to **completely** close the gate. [COMPARE He forgot **completely** to close the gate.]

E X E R C I S E   *1*

Revise the following sentences, placing the modifiers in correct relation to the words they modify.

1. The evening news carried the story of the army's failure to rescue the soldiers in every part of the country.
2. Olivia wore her favorite coat almost until the sleeves were threadbare.
3. The tornado only destroyed two buildings.
4. My sister returned this morning from her vacation at the beach on the plane.
5. Mark neglected to, because he was forgetful, set his alarm.
6. Sandy broiled steaks for the neighbors with lots of garlic on them.
7. The sitcom appearing on last night's television schedule which is new is really funny.
8. Nelda made it clear why coming to class late was wrong on Tuesday.
9. Jack went to work in his restaurant uniform on the bus.
10. At the coffee house the employees serve steaming coffee to customers in big coffee cups.

25b Modifiers that refer to no particular word in the sentence need revising.

Dangling modifiers are primarily verbal phrases that do not modify any particular words or phrases in the sentence. Although any misplaced word, phrase, or clause can be said to dangle, words in the sentence can be rearranged, or words can be added, to make the meaning clear.

(1) Dangling participial phrases should be revised. (See 1d.)

Dangling   *Tuning the television to CNN,* the State of the Union speech reached millions of voters. [no clear word for *Tuning the television* to refer to]

Revised   *Tuning the television to CNN,* **millions** of voters listened to the State of the Union speech. [referent supplied—*millions*]

Placed after the main independent clause, the participial phrase in the revision below refers to the subject.

Dangling   The afternoon passed very pleasantly, *lounging* in the shade and *reminiscing* about our childhood. [An *afternoon* cannot *lounge* or *reminisce.*]

Revised   **We** passed the afternoon very pleasantly, *lounging* in the shade and *reminiscing* about our childhood. [subject supplied]

(2) Dangling phrases containing gerunds or infinitives should be revised. (See 1d(1).)

Dangling   On *entering* the stadium, the size of the crowd surprised Theo. [*Size* cannot *enter.*]

Revised   On *entering* the stadium, **Theo** was surprised at the size of the crowd. [subject supplied]

Dangling	*To write* well, good books must be read. [*Books* do not *write*.]
Revised	*To write* well, **I** must read good books. [subject supplied]

(3) Dangling elliptical adverbial clauses should be revised. (See 1e(2).)

Elliptical clauses imply words that are not stated.

Dangling	*When only a small boy,* my father took me with him to Chicago. [*Father* is not a *small boy.*]
Revised	*When* **I was** *only a small boy,* my father took me with him to Chicago.

Sentence modifiers (see the Glossary of Terms) are considered standard usage, not danglers. (See also 1c(5).)

First, I will learn to dance.

Marcus played well in the final four games, **on the whole.**

EXERCISE 2

Revise the following sentences to eliminate dangling modifiers. Put a check mark after any sentence that needs no revision.

1. Dusk having fallen, the kids went inside.
2. Our conversation ended by exchanging phone numbers and promising a visit in the near future.
3. Leaving the house, the front door was locked.
4. The colors should be vivid to paint memorable pictures.
5. Having repeated their vows, the minister married the couple.
6. By following the rules of the road, accidents are less likely to happen.
7. In determining an appropriate college, considering the degrees offered is important.

8. After working on assignments for three hours, the rain began.

9. Knowing how to drive is necessary before getting a driver's license.

10. Even though expecting a large reward, the money wasn't the main motive.

Chapter
26 Parallelism

Parallelism contributes to ease in reading by making ideas that are parallel in meaning parallel in structure. It also provides clarity and rhythm. This chapter comments on

- balancing similar grammatical elements (**26a**),
- clarifying parallel structure (**26b**), and
- dealing with correlative constructions (**26c**).

Parallel elements appear in lists or series, in compound structures, in comparisons, and in contrasting elements.

I like to swim, to dance, and *to have* ~~having~~ fun.

OR

I like swimming, dancing, and *having* ~~to have~~ fun.

Many parallel elements are linked by a coordinating conjunction (such as *and, but,* or *or*) or by correlatives (such as *neither . . . nor, whether . . . or*). Others are not. In the following examples, verbals used as subjects and complements are parallel in form.

To define flora is **to define** climate. —*NATIONAL GEOGRAPHIC*

Seeing is **believing.**

Ideas that are equal in importance should be presented in parallel structures.

We are not so much what we eat as *what* ~~the thoughts~~ we think.

OR

We are not so much ~~what~~ *the food* we eat as the thoughts we think.

If elements are not parallel in thought, rather than trying to make them parallel in structure, rethink the sentence.

We can ^eat ~~choose ham, tuna salad,~~ or ^we can watch television.

Parallel structures are also used in outlines to indicate elements of equal importance. (See **32d(2)**, page 417.)

26a Similar grammatical elements need to be balanced.

For parallel structure, balance nouns with nouns, prepositional phrases with prepositional phrases, and clauses with clauses. In the examples that follow, repetition emphasizes the balanced structures.

(1) Balance parallel words and phrases.

The Africans carried with them a pattern of kinship
that emphasized ‖ **collective survival,**
‖ **mutual aid,**
‖ **cooperation,**
‖ **mutual solidarity,**
‖ **interdependence,**
and ‖ **responsibility for others.**

—JOSEPH L. WHITE

She had ‖ **no time to be human,**
‖ **no time to be happy.**

—SEAN O'FALLON

(2) Balance parallel clauses.

I remember Iyatiku's sister, Sun Woman,
‖ **who held so many things in her bundle,**
‖ **who went away to the east.**

—PAULA GUNN ALLEN

(3) Balance parallel sentences.

When I stepped up with my left foot, I squelched.
When I stepped up with my right foot, I gurgled.

EXERCISE 1

Write three sentences: one containing parallel words, one containing parallel phrases, and one containing parallel clauses. Use the examples in 26a as models.

26b Parallel structures need to be clear to the reader.

Repeating a preposition, an article, the *to* of the infinitive, or the introductory word of a phrase or clause can make parallel structure clear.

For about fifteen minutes I have been stalking about my house,

hands ‖ **on** my hips,
a scowl ‖ **on** my face,
‖ **trying to** remember where I put my car keys,
‖ **trying to** keep from shouting at everyone who loves me.

The reward rests not ‖ **in** the task
but ‖ **in** the pay.   —JOHN KENNETH GALBRAITH

I was happy in the thought
‖ **that** our influence was helpful
and ‖ **that** I was doing the work I loved
and ‖ **that** I could make a living out of it.   —IDA B. WELLS

26c Conjunctions such as *both . . . and* (correlatives) require parallel structures.

Correlatives (*both . . . and, either . . . or, neither . . . nor, not only . . . but also, whether . . . or*) link sentence elements that are always parallel.

Whether at home or at work, he was always busy.

The team not   practices

Not only practicing at 6 a.m. during the week, but the team also scrimmages on Sunday afternoons.

OR

does the team practice   it

Not only practicing at 6 a.m. during the week, but the team also scrimmages on Sunday afternoons.

EXERCISE 2

Make the structure of each sentence parallel.

1. He uses his computer for writing and to play games.
2. She was praised by her supervisor and her secretary admired her.
3. I started swimming, running, and lifted weights.
4. My mother said that she wanted me to pick up some things from the store and for me to be home by dinner.
5. The student was not only diligent but also enjoyed having fun.
6. I couldn't decide whether to buy the new car or take a vacation.
7. John and I have put the images on the Web and are available for viewing at http://www.folks.net.
8. Her true pleasure is playing the piano rather than in the library.
9. He is intelligent but a coward.
10. She found that her son had more time to do his work and it was better quality.

Chapter
27 Consistency: Avoiding Shifts

Abrupt, unnecessary shifts—for example, from past to present tense, from singular to plural, from words acceptable in college writing to slang, or from one perspective to another—make reading difficult and obscure your meaning. This chapter gives advice on how to avoid shifts

- in tense and mood (**27a**),
- in person and number (**27b**),
- between direct and indirect discourse (**27c**),
- in tone and style (**27d**), and
- in perspective and point of view (**27e**).

27a Shifts in verb tense or mood interfere with clarity.

Unless the actions occur at different times, keep verb tense consistent. Make sure you do not confuse the reader by needlessly switching from indicative to subjunctive mood (**7d**) or by changing person in the middle of a sentence.

Arlo **believed** in nuclear power, while Mary ~~believes~~ *believed* in solar power. [Both verbs should be in the same tense.]

If I **were** not so stupid and he ~~was~~ *were* not so naive, we would have known better. [Both verbs should be in the subjunctive mood.]

When using the literary or historical present (see **7c** and **39a**), avoid slipping into the past tense.

Hamlet **sees** his father's ghost, **kills** Polonius, and ~~died~~ *dies* in the final act. [All of the verbs should be in the present tense.]

27b Consistency in person and number contributes to ease in reading. (See chapter 28.)

If ~~a person is~~ *you are* looking for a job, **you** should have a good résumé. [Both subjects are in the second person.]

The **team** is counting on winning ~~their~~ *its* game. [Both *team is* and *its* are singular.]

27c Shifts between direct and indirect discourse make writing less clear. (See also 26a.)

Direct discourse quotes what is said—exactly. Indirect discourse reports what someone said without quoting the exact words. Similarly, an indirect question is a question phrased as a statement, while a direct question is one phrased as a question.

Janet wondered how Alex broke the computer and why ~~didn't he~~ *he didn't* tell her himself.

My professor said, "You're late" and "Would ~~I~~ *you* please be on time?"

27d Consistent tone and style contribute to ease in reading.

When writers shift tone (33a(3)), they change the way they signal the attitude they have toward their subject or their readers.

When writers shift styles, they change the attitude they have toward their readers.

> The journalists who contend that the inefficiency of our courts will lead to the total elimination of the jury system are ^*a group of eccentrics* ~~a bunch of nuts.~~

27e Inconsistent perspective and viewpoint make writing less clear.

Make sure that the actions you describe can actually be performed or that the events you report are logically ordered.

> Standing in the valley, I could see our troops at the crest of the hill^,
> *later, standing*   *I could see*
> and ^on the other side of the ridge, ^the enemy in full retreat.

EXERCISE 1

Correct all unnecessary shifts. Put a check mark after any sentence that needs no revision.

1. First sauté the garlic in olive oil and then you should add the crushed tomatoes.
2. Then I chopped onions and slice a pound of sausage.
3. Barney likes reading but watching TV is also liked.
4. If there are any complaints, you might inquire, "Why should they be complaining?" and ask that they adopt a better attitude.
5. Marguerite spent her evenings reading popular novels and her days were devoted to studying.
6. Even though his mother may not approve, he used to go visit his friends anyway.
7. They had reached a point where it is difficult for one to stop.
8. Like a shark through the waves, our distinguished gray-haired hostess glided through the throngs of people on the dance floor.

9. Drive the car to the auto shop, and then it should be left there for repairs.

10. My sister asked me if I had met my friend at the airport and will she be staying with us while she's in town.

Exercise 2

Revise the following paragraph to eliminate all unnecessary shifts.

[1]Downtown Charities will be holding its annual Wine and Dine event at the Municipal Convention Center in Santa Theresa on Saturday, July 10. [2]The evening featured a wine tasting, four-course gourmet dinner, chamber music, silent auction, and fashion show. [3]All ticket and silent auction proceeds have benefited the Downtown Homeless Shelter, a nonprofit organization devoted to providing safe lodging and hot meals to local homeless persons. [4]Sponsors will include Vintner's Cellar Fine Wines, Français Culinary Institute, and Fashion Importers of America. [5]For more information, call the box office at the convention center.

Chapter
28   Pronoun Reference

Pronouns refer to the nouns immediately preceding them. Clarity involves making sure that pronoun references or usage is not

- ambiguous or unclear (**28a**),
- remote or awkward (**28b**),
- broad or implied (**28c**), or
- impersonal (**28d**).

Each boldfaced pronoun below clearly refers to an italicized noun or pronoun—its **antecedent**—which can be a word group as well as a single word.

> Nevertheless, it is the same dedication to family that has always tied *women* to the home that today urges **them** into the workplace.

> A cow-calf operation keeps *cattle* year-round in the same pastures where **they** are bred, born, and raised.

> Thus, *being busy* is more than merely a national passion; **it** is a national excuse. —NORMAN COUSINS

Without any loss of clarity, a pronoun can often refer to a noun that follows it.

> Unlike **their** ancestors, the *soldiers* of today's infantry do not travel on their feet.

The meaning of each pronoun should be immediately obvious. To avoid confusion, repeat the antecedent, use a synonym for it, or rewrite your sentence.

28a Ambiguous or unclear pronoun references can confuse a reader.

When a pronoun could refer to either of two possible antecedents, the ambiguity confuses, or at least inconveniences, your reader. Two ways to make the antecedent clear are to rewrite the sentence or to replace the pronoun with a noun.

Quinn pointed out *that because Roy's* to Roy that since his cat was shedding *Roy* he had cat hair all over his suit. [Otherwise, it is not clear who owns the cat and who has cat hair on his suit.]

The books *that* were standing on the shelf that needed sorting. [The ambiguous reference creates a silly sentence; the books, not the shelf, needed sorting. The sentence can also be rewritten to move the problem phrase closer to its antecedent: The books that needed sorting were standing on the shelf.]

A pronoun may sometimes clearly refer to two or more antecedents.

Jack and Jill met **their** Waterloo.

28b Remote or awkward references can confuse a reader.

If a pronoun is too far away from its antecedent, the reader may have to backtrack to get the meaning. A pronoun that refers to a modifier (a word that identifies or explains another word) or to another pronoun in the possessive case (5b(3)) can also obscure meaning. Rewriting the sentence to bring a pronoun and its antecedent closer together or substituting a noun for the obscure pronoun will clarify meaning.

Remote	The *sophomore* found herself the unanimously elected president of a group of animal lovers, *who* was not a joiner of organizations. [*Who* is too far removed from its antecedent *sophomore.* See **25a(3)**.]
Better	The **sophomore, who** was not a joiner of organizations, found herself the unanimously elected president of a group of animal lovers.
Obscure	Before Ellen could get to the jewelry store, **it** was all sold. [*It* could refer to *store* but probably should refer to *jewelry.*]
Better	Before Ellen could get to the jewelry store, all the **jewelry** was sold.
Awkward	The Kiwanis Club sells tickets for the **fireworks** on the Fourth of July **that** it sponsors. [The pronoun refers to a distant antecedent.]
Better	The Kiwanis Club sells tickets for the fireworks that it sponsors on the Fourth of July.

Exercise 1

Revise each of the following sentences to eliminate ambiguous, remote, or obscure pronoun references.

1. The Laughlins' argument with the Kendalls did not end until they invited them to a picnic by their pool.
2. In Mary's letter she did not mention what the argument was about.
3. On the gas grill the various buttons and knobs seldom confuse cooks that are clearly labeled.
4. Mary waved to Mrs. Laughlin as she was coming through the gate.
5. The garden is peaceful. Near the pool hibiscus grow in profusion loaded with bright pink flowers and spreading their green leaves. It is cleaned daily.

28c Careless use of broad or implied references makes writing unclear.

Pronouns such as *it, such, this, that,* and *which* may refer to a specific word or phrase or to the sense of the whole clause, sentence, or paragraph.

Specific The **glow** was enough to read by, once my eyes adjusted to **it.** —MALCOLM X [*It* refers to *glow.*]

Broad Some people think that the fall of man had something to do with sex, but *that*'s a mistake. —C. S. LEWIS [*That* refers to the sense of the whole clause.]

When used carelessly, broad references can interfere with clear communication. To ensure clarity, make each pronoun refer to a specific word. Unless the meaning is clear, avoid reference to the general idea of a preceding clause or sentence.

When class attendance is compulsory, some students feel that education is being forced on them. This ^*perception* is not true. [*This* has no antecedent.]

Express the idea referred to rather than merely implying it.

He wanted his teachers to think he was above average, as he could have been if he had used ^*his intelligence* it to advantage. [*It* has no expressed antecedent.]

My father is a music teacher. ^*Teaching music* It is a profession that requires much patience. [*It* has no expressed antecedent.]

28d Impersonal *it* is generally not accepted in college or professional writing.

Awkward	It was no use trying.
Revised	**There was** no use trying.
OR	**Trying was** useless.

Avoid the awkward placement of *it* near another *it* with a different meaning.

Awkward	It would be simpler to stay in the old apartment, but it is too far from my job. [The first *it* is an expletive (see Glossary of Terms), while the second refers to *apartment.*]
Revised	Staying in the old apartment would be simpler, but it is too far from my job.

E X E R C I S E 2

Revise the following sentences as necessary to make all references clear. Put a check mark after any sentence that needs no revision.

1. Sandra did not pay the parking ticket, which turned out to be a mistake.
2. If you are told to report to the courthouse, they will fine you.
3. Collette told Li that she was a good friend.
4. In the book it says that the author disapproves of elephant hunters.
5. Sally decided to let her driver's license expire, which she came to regret.
6. Almost everyone has trouble parallel parking, but this is not true when you know the trick.
7. Although it would be unwise for me to buy the new computer now, it is a powerful machine.
8. Marilyn decided not to attend the reunion which was a disappointment for our grandparents.

9. When building railroads, the engineers planned embankments for fear that flooding would cover them and make them useless.

10. When the termite eggs are hatched, they grow wings and fly around the country in swarms.

Chapter

29   Emphasis

You can emphasize ideas by using subordination and coordination (chapter 24), parallelism (chapter 26), and exact word choice (chapter 20) and also by writing concisely (chapter 21). This chapter presents additional ways to emphasize material, such as

- placing words at the beginnings of sentences (29a),
- using periodic sentences (29b),
- arranging ideas in climactic order (29c),
- using forceful verbs (29d),
- repeating words (29e),
- inverting sentence order (29f),
- balancing sentence elements (29g), and
- varying sentence length (29h).

29a   Placing words at the beginning or end of a sentence emphasizes them.

Because words at the beginning or end of a sentence—especially the end—receive emphasis, place the ones you want to emphasize in these positions whenever possible.

In today's society, most ~~good~~ jobs require a college education ~~as part of the background you are supposed to have~~.
Good *today*

~~I could hear the roar of traffic~~ outside my hotel room in Chicago ~~when I was there~~.
Traffic roared

As these examples show, you can often make your sentences more concise (see chapter 21) by revising them so that important words fall at the beginning or the end. Sometimes, however, you may need to add a few words to make a sentence emphatic.

Because the semicolon (see chapter 14) used between main clauses is a strong mark of punctuation, the words placed immediately before and after it tend to be emphasized.

Also, the colon and the dash often precede an emphatic ending. (See also 17d and 17e.)

> In short, the freedom that the American writer finds in Europe brings him, full circle, back to himself, with the responsibility for his development where it always was: in his own hands.
>
> —JAMES BALDWIN

> Until fairly recently, the pattern was that the father and sons worked, and, to whatever extent their earnings allowed, the mothers and daughters were supposed to display culture, religion, luxury, and other assorted fine feelings of society—in addition to seeing that the housework got done.   —JUDITH MARTIN

EXERCISE 1

Placing important words carefully, revise the following sentences to improve the emphasis.

1. A computer has become essential to write with.
2. Marsha is very successful and a tireless worker, in my opinion.
3. They say Woodbury has decided to spend more money on schools; soon its surrounding towns may invest more in education also.
4. There was a sign in the motel office announcing that there was a state park about a mile away, more or less.
5. In a sense, music has the power to unleash the imagination for us.

29b A periodic sentence surrounded by cumulative sentences is emphasized.

In a **cumulative sentence,** the main idea (the independent clause or sentence base) comes first; less important ideas or details follow. In a **periodic sentence,** however, the main idea comes last, just before the period.

Cumulative	History has amply proved that large forces can be defeated by smaller forces superior in arms, organization, morale, and spirit.
Periodic	That large forces can be defeated by smaller forces superior in arms, organization, morale, and spirit is one important lesson of history.
Cumulative	Memory operates by way of the senses, by way of detail, which is the stuff of fiction, the fabric of good stories. —DAVID HUDDLE
Periodic	In a day when movies seem more and more predictable, when novels tend to be plotless, baggy monsters or minimalist exercises in interior emotion, it's no surprise that sports has come to occupy an increasingly prominent place in the communal imagination. —MICHIKO KAKUTANI

Both types of sentences can be effective. Because cumulative sentences are more common, however, the infrequently used periodic sentence is often the more emphatic.

29c When ideas are arranged from least to most important, the last idea receives the most emphasis.

They could hear the roar of the artillery, the crash of falling timbers, the shrieks of the wounded.

Benefiting from much needed rest, moderate medication, and intensive therapy, he eventually recovered.

The applicants relaxed when they saw that she was charming, friendly, and kind.

Violating this principle can achieve a humorous effect when a writer shifts suddenly from the dignified to the trivial or from the serious to the comic. This effect is appropriate only when a writer intends to be humorous, however.

Contemporary man, of course, has no such peace of mind. He finds himself in the midst of a crisis of faith. He is what we fashionably call "alienated." He has seen the ravages of war, he has known natural catastrophes, he has been to singles bars. —WOODY ALLEN

EXERCISE 2

Arrange the ideas in the following sentences from what you consider to be least to most important.

1. Juan was known for his wisdom, humor, and efficiency.
2. She majored in communications because she wanted to understand people, inspire them, and influence them.
3. Unless we rebuild downtown, the city will become dangerous, unattractive, and unlivable.
4. I bought my share of supplies for the picnic: ribs, mustard, paper plates, and pickles.
5. Alcoholism destroys families, ruins health, and leads to erratic behavior.

29d Active, forceful verbs can add emphasis to sentences.

(1) Active voice is more emphatic than passive voice. (See 7d.)

Active voice emphasizes the *doer* of the action by making the doer the subject of the sentence. **Passive voice** emphasizes the *receiver* of the action, minimizes the role of the doer, and results in wordier sentences. One sign of passive construction is that a form of the verb *to be* is added to the action conveyed by another verb in the sentence.

Active	Sylvia won the race.
Passive	The race was won by Sylvia.
Active	All citizens should insist on adequate medical care.
Passive	Adequate medical care should be insisted on by all citizens.

Because whoever or whatever is responsible for the action is no longer the subject, sentences in the passive voice are often less precise. It is grammatically correct but stylistically undesirable to write "The race was won." Such a sentence does not tell the reader who the winner was. Politicians sometimes favor the passive voice because it allows them to avoid responsibility—hence constructions like "a meeting has been called" or "your taxes have been raised."

The passive voice is appropriate, however, when the doer of an action is unknown or unimportant.

Passive	The television set was stolen. [The thief is unknown.]
Passive	We couldn't watch the Super Bowl because our television set had been stolen. [Given the emphasis of the sentence, the identity of the thief is unimportant.]

When reporting research or scientific experiments, writers often choose to use the passive voice to preserve their objectivity and to emphasize the work being done on a project rather than who is doing it.

Passive	The experiment was conducted under carefully controlled conditions over several months.

Unless they have a strong reason to use the passive voice, good writers prefer the active voice because it is clearer and more emphatic.

(2) Action verbs and forceful linking verbs are more emphatic than forms of *have* or *be*.

When used without an action verb, forms of *have* or *be* rob your writing of energy and forcefulness. The real action often lies in a verbal phrase or in the object or complement.

Our college ~~is~~ always *wins* ~~the winner of~~ the conference. [The subject complement—*winner*—contains the real action conveyed more forcefully by the verb *win*.]

The meat *smells* ~~has a~~ rotten ~~smell.~~ [The action needs to come in the verb—*smells*—rather than in the noun serving as subject complement—*smell.*]

You can *solve* ~~be more effective at solving~~ a problem *more effectively if you* ~~by~~ understanding it first. [The objects of the prepositions (*solving, understanding*) contain the action conveyed more forcefully by verbs.]

Exercise 3

Make each sentence more emphatic by substituting active voice for passive or by substituting a more forceful verb for a form of *have* or *be.* You may sometimes need to invent a doer for the action.

1. A motion was made to expel you from school.
2. Every weekday afternoon, questionable values are taught by soap operas and talk shows.
3. The sales manager is responsible for supervising a staff of fifteen.

4. A bowl was broken when the dishes were being washed.
5. Every worker has the desire for respect.

29e Repeating important words gives them emphasis.

Although good writers avoid *unnecessary* repetition (see chapter 21), they also understand that *deliberate* repetition emphasizes key terms.

> We forget all too soon the things we thought we could never forget. We forget the loves and the betrayals alike, forget what we whispered and what we screamed, forget who we are.
>
> —JOAN DIDION

When you decide to repeat a word for emphasis, make sure that it is a word worth emphasizing, that it conveys an idea central to your purpose.

29f Inverting the standard word order of a sentence gives it emphasis.

> At the feet of the tallest and plushiest offices lie the crummiest slums. —E. B. WHITE [COMPARE "The crummiest slums lie at the feet of the tallest and plushiest offices."]
>
> Basic to all the Greek achievement was freedom. —EDITH HAMILTON [COMPARE "Freedom was basic to all the Greek achievement."]

When you invert standard word order for emphasis, you should make sure your sentence has not become so awkward or artificial that it is difficult to read.

29g A balanced construction gives a sentence emphasis.

A sentence is balanced when grammatically equal structures—usually main clauses with parallel elements—express contrasting (or similar) ideas. (See 26a.) A balanced sentence emphasizes the contrast (or similarity) between parts of equal length and movement.

> Love is positive; tolerance negative. Love involves passion; tolerance is humdrum and dull. —E. M. FORSTER

29h A short sentence following one or more long ones is emphasized.

> In the last two decades there has occurred a series of changes in American life, the extent, durability, and significance of which no one has yet measured. No one can. —IRVING HOWE

EXERCISE 4

Revise each sentence for emphasis. Be prepared to explain why your revision provides appropriate emphasis in the context you have in mind.

1. I gave him the letter, two weeks ago, when he asked me.
2. Scouting develops a person morally, mentally, and physically.
3. The tornado devastated Iowa on a hot and humid day.
4. As the station is reached, the train is seen coming around the bend.
5. In college she devoted herself to studying hard, making new friends, going to parties, and working part-time.
6. He thought about the children, he considered the budget, he reflected on past experience, and a decision was reached by him.

7. Lots of angry protestors were all around us for a while.

8. It is usually required by the state that cars be inspected before their registration can be renewed each year.

9. We will give our hearts, we will donate our money, and we will share our time.

10. The paintings in the exhibit were unoriginal, but the use of color was appealing in them.

Chapter

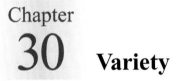

30 Variety

Varying the kinds of sentences you use can make your writing lively and distinctive, but relying too heavily on a few familiar structures often makes writing predictable. If you experiment with sentence structure, you make it more likely that readers will pay attention to what you write. Some of the ways to vary sentence structure that are covered in this chapter are

- combining choppy sentences (**30a**),
- varying sentence beginnings (**30b**),
- avoiding stringy compound sentences (**30c**),
- inserting words or phrases between the subject and the verb (**30d**), and
- using questions, commands, or exclamations instead of statements (**30e**).

Both of the following paragraphs express the same ideas in virtually the same words, both use acceptable sentence patterns, and both are grammatically correct. Variety in sentence structure and length, however, gives one paragraph a stronger rhythm than the other.

Not Varied

The land is small, subdued. Its colors are low in key. The salt marshes and the low houses at their margins have a comforting dimension, and the woods beyond, the hidden ponds, and the suddenly revealed harbors do, too. You should, however, look outward. The sea is always there. The sea is a great presence, for it is fraught with sublimity. You may in some places not actually see the ocean, but you can sense its proximity and catch whiffs of its tang. You hear or seem to hear its distant roar and rut. [five simple sentences and three compound ones]

Varied

The land is small, subdued; its colors are low in key. The salt marshes, the low houses at their margins, the woods beyond, the hidden ponds, the suddenly revealed harbors have a comforting dimension. But look outward and there is always the sea, a great presence fraught with sublimity. Even where you cannot actually see the ocean, you sense its proximity, catch whiffs of its tang, hear or think you hear its distant roar and rut. —EDWARD B. GARSIDE [This paragraph contains four sentences of varying length and structure: one simple, two compound, and one complex. The sentences begin with subjects, a coordinating conjunction, and an adverb.]

If you have difficulty distinguishing between various types of sentence structure, review the fundamentals treated in chapter 1, especially 1b.

Although grammar checkers will identify long sentences, they cannot determine whether such a sentence is appropriate or whether it contributes to variety. Identifying long sentences can help writers recognize and revise rambling sentences or avoid comma splices and fused sentences.

30a **A series of short, simple sentences sounds choppy. (See 29h.)**

To avoid the choppiness produced by this kind of construction, you can lengthen some sentences by showing how the ideas are subordinate or coordinate. (See chapter 24.)

Choppy   The Maine coast and the Oregon coast look very much alike. The houses by the water, however, are different. It's a matter of architectural style.

Effective	Although the Maine coast and the Oregon coast look very much alike, the architectural style of the houses by the water is different. [use of subordination to combine sentences]
Choppy	Some people study everything on the menu. Next they ask about how various dishes are made. Then they think things over for a few minutes. Finally they order exactly what they had the last time. The idea is to seem interested in food without taking any risks.
Effective	To seem interested in food without taking any risks, some people study everything on the menu, ask how various dishes are made, think things over, and end up ordering exactly what they had the last time. [use of coordination to combine sentences]

Occasionally, as the example below illustrates, a series of brief, subject-first sentences can be used for special effect.

Although it had been an easy enough day, much like any other, something seemed wrong just before dinner. I felt hot. My chest hurt. The room began to tilt. [The feeling of a heart attack is conveyed by a series of abrupt sentences.]

EXERCISE 1

Convert each series of short, simple sentences into a single sentence. Use no more than one coordinating conjunction in each.

1. It was the bottom of the ninth inning. The score was tied. The bases were loaded. There were two outs.
2. Eileen bought a laptop. It has plenty of memory. She is still getting used to the keyboard.
3. He made an interesting argument. Employers should offer flexible working hours. Giving people more flexibility will improve morale.
4. My car needs new tires. It also needs a brake job. I should probably get it tuned up also.

5. Shopping for clothes can be fun. You have to have time to try things on. Otherwise you might make mistakes.

30b **Writing sounds monotonous when too many sentences begin the same way.**

Most writers begin more than half their sentences with the sub-ject—far more than any other construction. Although this pat-tern is normal for English sentences, relying too heavily on it can make your writing dull. Experiment with the following al-ternatives for beginning sentences.

(1) Begin with an adverb or an adverbial clause.

> **Finally,** an ancient rattling, clanking pickup rounded the corner and lurched down the street toward us. [adverb]

> **Although the rules of the game have not changed much,** bas-ketball is a faster, rougher game than it was when Wilt Chamber-lain played. [adverbial clause]

> **When you first start writing**—and I think it's true for a lot of beginning writers—you're scared to death that if you don't get that sentence right that minute it's never going to show up again. —TONI MORRISON [adverbial clause]

(2) Begin with a prepositional or verbal phrase.

> **Out of necessity** they stitched all of their secret fears and linger-ing childhood nightmares into this existence. —GLORIA NAYLOR [prepositional phrase]

> **To be really happy,** most of us have to give something of our-selves—not money, but our time and energy—to help others. [in-finitive phrase]

> **Looking north from the summit of Quandary Peak,** we see a serrated pattern of snowcapped summits marching toward the Canadian border. [participial phrase]

(3) Begin with a sentence connective—a coordinating conjunction, a conjunctive adverb, or a transitional phrase.

In the following examples, each sentence connective shows the relationship between the ideas in each set of sentences. (See also **31b(4)**.)

Many restaurants close within a few years of opening. **But** others, which offer good food at reasonable prices, become well established. [coordinating conjunction]

Difficulty in finding a place to park is one of the factors keeping people from shopping downtown. **Moreover,** public transportation has become too expensive. [conjunctive adverb]

This legislation will hurt the economy. **In the first place,** it will cost thousands of jobs. [transitional phrase]

(4) Begin with an appositive, an absolute phrase, or an introductory series. (See 24a.)

A town of historic interest, Santa Fe also has many art galleries. [appositive]

His fur bristling, the cat attacked. [absolute phrase]

Light, water, temperature, minerals—these affect the health of plants. [introductory series; see **17e(3)**]

EXERCISE 2

Rewrite each sentence so that it begins with an appositive, an absolute phrase, or an introductory series.

1. Customers were waiting an hour before the store opened because advertisements had convinced them that the best merchandise would go fast.
2. A field full of abandoned cars stretched before them.
3. He began to write poetry using scraps of paper while he was in prison.

4. *Gilligan's Island,* a mindless series from the sixties, illustrates a number of stereotypes that are strangely enduring.
5. The printer at my office works twice as fast as the one I have at home and provides a greater variety of fonts.

30c Stringing simple sentences together to make a compound sentence is less effective than experimenting with structure.

Although compound sentences are often useful, they can be ineffective as well. If you normally write short, simple sentences and then revise by just linking those sentences with *and* or *but,* your writing will still lack variety. Remember that subordination is as important as coordination. (See chapter 24.) To revise an ineffective compound sentence, you can use one of the following methods.

(1) Make a compound sentence complex.

Compound	Seafood is nutritious, and it is low in fat, and it has become available in greater variety.
Complex	Seafood, which is nutritious and low in fat, has become available in greater variety.

(2) Use a compound predicate in a simple sentence.

Compound	She deftly trapped the kitten, and then she held it so that its legs were against her palm, and next she strapped a tiny collar around its neck.
Simple	She deftly trapped the kitten, held it so that its legs were against her palm, and strapped a tiny collar around its neck.

(3) Use an appositive.

Compound	J. P. Webb was an old-fashioned construction engineer, and he built two of the most spectacular roads in Summit County.
Simple	J. P. Webb, an old-fashioned construction engineer, built two of the most spectacular roads in Summit County.

(4) Add a prepositional or verbal phrase.

Compound	The snow was thick, and we could not see where we were going.
Simple	In the thick snow, we could not see where we were going.
Compound	The plane pulled away from the gate on time, and then it sat on the runway for two hours.
Simple	After pulling away from the gate on time, the plane sat on the runway for two hours.
Compound	The town is near the interstate, and it attracted commuters, and its population grew rapidly.
Simple	The town, located near the interstate, attracted commuters and grew rapidly in population.

(5) Use additional conjunctions to increase the number of compounds.

Experienced writers sometimes achieve interesting effects by exaggerating what could be considered a flaw. By using a number of conjunctions in close succession, you can slow the pace and dignify material that might otherwise seem unremarkable.

> I was on Fire Island when I first made that sauerkraut, and it was raining, and we drank a lot of bourbon and ate the sauerkraut and went to bed at ten, and I listened to the rain and the Atlantic and felt safe. —JOAN DIDION

EXERCISE 3

Using the methods illustrated in 30c, revise these compound sentences.

1. My sister became frustrated in her job, so she quit after a few months, and now she is collecting unemployment and feeling that she made a mistake.
2. Annuals can add color to your garden, and many of them are inexpensive, but you have to do a lot of replanting.
3. First semester was difficult, and I almost dropped out of school, but I learned how to plan my time, and then my grades improved.
4. Greg is always talking about taking a vacation, but he never does it, and he is overworking himself.
5. Coffee shops are popular meeting places, and they have improved the standard of coffee served in town, but there are too many of them, and I wonder how they can all stay in business.

30d Occasionally using words or phrases to separate the subject and verb can vary the conventional subject-verb sequence.

Although it is usually best to keep the subject next to the verb so that the relationship between them is clear (see 1a), breaking this pattern on occasion can lead to variety. In the following examples, subjects and verbs are in boldface.

Subject-verb	**Great Falls was** once a summer resort, but **it has become** a crowded suburb.
Varied	**Great Falls,** once a summer resort, **has become** a crowded suburb.
Subject-verb	The **fans applauded** every basket and **cheered** the team to victory.

| Varied | The **fans,** applauding every basket, **cheered** the team to victory. |

An occasional declarative sentence with inverted word order can also contribute to sentence variety. (See 29f.)

EXERCISE 4

Using the methods illustrated in 30d, vary the conventional subject-verb sequence in these sentences.

1. The video store is across the street from the high school, and it attracts many students.
2. His ability to listen is an acquired skill that makes him a good counselor.
3. Mark was hurrying to get home before the storm broke, but he flooded the engine of his car.
4. The manager identified with the employees, so she supported their decision to reduce overtime.
5. The customers were frustrated by the lack of service and walked out of the restaurant.

30e When surrounded by declarative sentences, a question, an exclamation, or a command adds variety.

What was Shakespeare's state of mind, for instance, when he wrote *Lear* and *Antony and Cleopatra*? It was certainly the state of mind most favourable to poetry that there has ever existed.   —VIRGINIA WOOLF   [Woolf's answer follows the initial question.]

Now I stare and stare at people, shamelessly. Stare. It's the way to educate your eye.   —WALKER EVANS   [A one-word imperative sentence provides variety.]

Exercise 5

Prepare for a class discussion on the sentence variety in the following paragraph.

[1]It is too much that with all those pedestrian centuries behind us we should, in a few decades, have learned to fly; it is too heady a thought, too proud a boast. [2]Only the dirt on a mechanic's hands, the straining vise, the splintered bolt of steel underfoot on the hangar floor—only these and such anxiety as the face of a Jock Cameron can hold for a pilot and his plane before a flight, serve to remind us that, not unlike the heather, we too are earth-bound. [3]We fly, but we have not "conquered" the air. [4]Nature presides in all her dignity, permitting us the study and the use of such of her forces as we may understand. [5]It is when we presume to intimacy, having been granted only tolerance, that the harsh stick falls across our impudent knuckles and we rub the pain, staring upward, startled by our ignorance.   —BERYL MARKHAM

Writing

Chapter
31

Working with Paragraphs

An essential unit of thought in writing, paragraphs stand in relation to and in the context of all the other paragraphs that surround them. But even if writers seldom write paragraphs that stand alone, analyzing single paragraphs can help writers understand patterns of development that also apply to the whole essay (chapters 32 and 33). Furthermore, understanding how to revise paragraphs for greater unity and coherence helps writers effectively organize their thoughts. This chapter will help you write

- unified paragraphs (31a),
- coherent paragraphs (31b),
- well-developed paragraphs (31c), and
- transitions between paragraphs (31b(4)).

Good paragraphs contribute to the development of the main idea of an essay in ways similar to those in which sentences contribute to the development of an idea in a paragraph. (See 31c and 31d.) The beginning of a paragraph is indented (or preceded by an extra line of white space) to signal the reader that a new idea or a new direction for an idea follows.

For easy reference, all the paragraphs in this chapter are numbered. In paragraph 1, observe how

- the sentences relate to a single main idea (showing *unity*),
- ideas progress easily from sentence to sentence (showing *coherence*), and
- specific details support the main idea (showing *development*).

1   *The exactness of her house was inhuman.* This glass went here and only here. That cup had its place and it was an act of impudent rebellion to place it anywhere else. At twelve o'clock the table was

set. At 12:15 Mrs. Cullinan sat down to dinner (whether her husband had arrived or not). At 12:16 Miss Glory brought out the food. —MAYA ANGELOU, *I Know Why the Caged Bird Sings*

This paragraph has **unity** because each sentence supports the main idea (in italics); it has **coherence** because each sentence leads logically to the next. And even though this is a relatively short paragraph, it is **developed** because the main idea is supported by several details.

Paragraphs have no set length. Typically, they range from 50 to 250 words and average perhaps 100 words. Paragraphs in books are usually longer than those in newspapers and magazines.

Although one-sentence paragraphs are occasionally used for emphasis, short paragraphs often indicate inadequate development. Long paragraphs, too, can reveal problems in your writing, especially if they exhaust one point or combine too many points.

Transitional paragraphs (see 31b(4)), as well as introductory and concluding paragraphs (see 33a(4–5)), serve other purposes.

31a Paragraphs should be unified.

In a unified paragraph, each sentence helps develop the main idea. Unity is violated when a sentence unrelated to the main idea is part of the paragraph. Consider the following example.

2   New York has a museum to suit almost any taste. The Metropolitan Museum and the Museum of Modern Art are famous for their art collections. Other important collections of art can be found at the Frick, Guggenheim, and Whitney Museums. Visitors interested in the natural sciences will enjoy the Museum of Natural History. Those interested in American history should visit the Museum of the City of New York. *Getting around the city is easy once you have mastered the subway system.* Part of Ellis Island has

become a museum devoted to the history of immigration. Exhibits devoted to social and cultural history can also be found at the Jewish Museum and the Asia Society.

In this paragraph, the italicized sentence about the subway system violates the unity of a paragraph devoted to museums. If pertinent to the essay as a whole, public transportation in New York could be discussed in a separate paragraph.

Because the act of writing often generates unexpected ideas, some of which may be unrelated to your main idea, you should study the unity of your paragraphs. You are likely to discover that you have wandered off track at some point—probably because a new idea occurred to you before you had finished discussing an earlier one. Even experienced writers frequently discover that this has happened to them. It is a normal part of drafting (see chapter 32) and can be corrected through revision (see chapter 33).

The following strategies can help make your own paragraphs stronger.

(1) A topic sentence expresses the main idea of a paragraph.

Stating the main idea in a single sentence, often called a **topic sentence,** will help you achieve unity. As a critical reader (see chapter 35), you will find that this sentence may appear at any point in a paragraph. Because they try to avoid using the same patterns over and over, experienced writers organize paragraphs in different ways at different times. But if you are new to writing or making a special effort to improve the unity of your paragraphs, place your topic sentences at the beginning.

(a) The topic sentence often appears at the beginning of a paragraph.

Placing the topic sentence at the beginning helps readers grasp your main point immediately and helps you stay focused as you develop the paragraph. For example, the topic sentence of paragraph 3 (in italics) announces the idea that writing involves bringing out what might otherwise be hidden.

3   *We write to expose the unexposed.* If there is one door of the castle you have been told not to go through, you must. Otherwise, you'll just be rearranging furniture in rooms you've already been in. Most human beings are dedicated to keeping that one door shut. But the writer's job is to see what's behind it, to see the bleak unspeakable stuff, and to turn the unspeakable into words—not just any words but if we can, into rhythm and blues.

—ANNE LAMONT, *Bird by Bird*

(b) The topic sentence sometimes appears at the end of a paragraph.

Occasionally, the topic sentence is placed near the end of the paragraph, especially when the writer progresses from specific examples to a generalization as in paragraph 4.

4   In the warmth of the inner Solar System a comet releases clouds of vapor and dust that form the growing head and then leak into the tail, which is the cosmic equivalent of an oil slick. Pieces of the dust later hit the Earth, as meteors. A few survivors among the comets evolve into menacing lumps of dirt in tight orbits around the sun. *For these reasons comets are, in my opinion, best regarded as a conspicuous form of sky pollution.*

—NIGEL CALDER, "The Comet Is Coming"

(c) The topic sentence sometimes appears at both the beginning and the end of a paragraph.

When you want to emphasize the main idea, you can begin and conclude a paragraph with two versions of the same idea. By restating the topic sentence at the end, you can also reinforce the unity of a long paragraph. In paragraph 5, both the first sentence and the last convey the idea that food is at the heart of life in Vienna.

5　　*The biggest challenge to cope with in Vienna is the food.* The basic traditional diet consists of meat, mostly beef or pork, potatoes, dumplings and cabbage. There are all sorts of soups and many kinds of freshly baked breads, including croissants, which the Viennese invented and exported to France during the reign of Louis XVI. And, as if the main courses weren't heavy enough, there are the desserts—puddings, strudels, crepes, pancakes, mousses and cakes, all topped with great gobs of whipped cream. Eating in Vienna is wonderfully satisfying, as if you had achieved a notable physical breakthrough, like climbing Pike's Peak or competing in the Boston Marathon. *You will look in vain in Vienna for joggers; it's a city dedicated to culinary self-indulgence.*

　　　—**WILLIAM MURRAY,** "In Vienna, Elegance Comes Readily to Mind"

(d) A single topic sentence can serve for a sequence of two or more paragraphs.

When you write a topic sentence that introduces ideas that can be developed in separate paragraphs, that sentence can establish the unity of more than one paragraph. In this case, as in paragraphs 6 and 7, be sure to write a topic sentence that clearly prepares readers for a discussion that will be subdivided.

6　　*There are two families of poisonous snakes in the United States, both of them native to our part of the south.* The first, *Elapida,* which includes cobras, mambas, and other deadly Old World snakes, are represented in the New World by eastern and western coral snakes. Coral snakes are shy, beautiful, and extremely dangerous. Their venom is a neurotoxin that attacks the central nervous system, particularly automatic functions such as breathing and heartbeat. Fortunately, coral snakes are reclusive by nature. They seldom bite, and when they do, their small mouths and fixed fangs make it difficult for them to latch on to humans.

7　　　The second family of poisonous snakes, the *Crotalida,* contain pit vipers—rattlesnakes, copperheads, and cottonmouths. The pits for which these snakes are named are infrared-heat-sensing organs that lie between the nostrils and eyes. With them, the snakes hunt their warm-blooded prey by seeking out body heat. The pit vipers are efficient killers, with large flexible mouths; long, retractable fangs; and venom that attacks and destroys cells and tissue. Victims die of internal hemorrhaging, cardiovascular shock, or kidney and respiratory failure. —DENNIS COVINGTON, *Salvation on Sand Mountain*

(e) Some paragraphs are unified without having a topic sentence.

When narrating events or describing a scene (see 32e), writers can omit a topic sentence if all of the details and examples within a paragraph help convey a clear impression. Note how paragraph 8 conveys what it is like to live with a relative who is dying at home.

8   When my mother began using the electronic pump that fed her liquids and medication, we moved her to the family room. The bedroom she shared with my father was upstairs, and it was impossible to carry the machine up and down all day and night. The pump itself was attached to a metal stand on casters, and she pulled it along wherever she went. From anywhere in the house, you could hear the sound of the wheels clicking out a steady time over the grout lines of the slate-tiled foyer, her main thoroughfare to the bathroom and the kitchen. Sometimes you could hear her halt after only a few steps, to catch her breath or steady her balance, and whatever you were doing you were instantly suspended by a pall of silence. —CHANG-RAE LEE, "Coming Home Again"

The author could have added a topic sentence about anxiety or about how the sounds in a house change when there is serious illness. But the details here are powerful enough to speak for themselves. They combine to tell readers: When you are living with a mother who is dying but still trying to take care of herself, the sound of her effort is both reassuring and troubling.

EXERCISE 1

Photocopy a page or two from a piece of writing you like and mark the topic sentences. Be prepared to explain your choices.

Exercise 2

Write a paragraph with a topic sentence at the beginning, another with the topic sentence at the end, and a third with the topic sentence at the beginning and restated at the end. If you get stuck, here are a few suggestions to get you started.

1. The biggest benefit to working out is . . .
2. You know you are in trouble when . . .
3. Discrimination can be defined as . . .
4. When I am awake in the middle of the night . . .
5. To hold my attention, a movie must . . .

(2) In a unified paragraph, every sentence relates to the main idea.

The most common way to unify a paragraph is to make each sentence support the main idea. In paragraph 9, each sentence develops what the writer means by the italicized topic sentence.

9   *Celebrity is modern myth, an attempt by studying the lives of others to find answers for ourselves.* The pantheon changes but always is full of incarnate human gods, sacred marriages, taboos, kings killed when their strength fails, human scapegoats, expulsion of embodied spirits. Supermodels, rock and TV stars, shaman-priests, and Elvis are examples of contagious magic, the myths created by many. Myths were explanations, and Elvis still explains how the lowly can rise, how the high can fall, how the magician can enchant, how the ritual can thrill and the man-god convince each he has come only for them.

        —JULIE BAUMGOLD, "Midnight in the Garden of Good and Elvis"

As you check your paragraphs for unity, use the following strategies to solve problems.

Strategies for Improving Paragraph Unity

Eliminate	Any information that does not clearly relate to the main idea should be cut.
Add	If the relationship between the main idea and certain details might not be clear to your reader, add a phrase or a sentence to make their relevance clear.
Separate	If more than one major idea appears in a single paragraph, separate them and develop them in different paragraphs.
Rewrite	If you want to convey more than one idea in a single paragraph but had not originally planned to do so, rewrite your topic sentence so it includes both ideas and establishes a relationship between them.

EXERCISE 3

Note how each sentence in the following paragraph expresses a different major idea. Select one and use it as a topic sentence to develop a unified paragraph with specific details and examples.

10   ¹People don't always understand how hard it is to go to college while you're trying to support yourself and your kids. ²After the divorce, I had to get a different kind of job to support my kids, but jobs with the right hours are hard to find if you don't have any real education, so I had to take a job as a cook. ³My mom keeps the kids during the day while I go to school, but I have to get a sitter to take care of them while I work the dinner shift. ⁴I try to study in between when I get home from school and when I have to go to work, but the kids are usually all over me wanting attention. ⁵So, what I don't get done then I have to do after I get off work which is pretty late in the evening. ⁶Then, I have to be up to get the kids fed before I go to class. ⁷It doesn't leave much time for study or for my kids either.

31b Clearly arranged ideas and effective transitions foster coherence.

A paragraph can be unified (see 31a) without being coherent. In a unified paragraph, every sentence relates to the main idea. In a coherent paragraph, each sentence leads to the next. The following paragraph (11) has unity but lacks coherence.

11   The inside of the refrigerator was covered with black mold, and it smelled as if something had been rotting in there for years. I put new paper down on all the shelves, and my roommate took care of lining the drawers. The stove was as dirty as the refrigerator. When we moved into our new apartment, we found that the kitchen was in horrible shape. We had to scrub the walls with a wire brush and plenty of Lysol to get rid of the grease. The previous tenant had left behind lots of junk that we had to get rid of. All the drawers and cabinets had to be washed.

Although every sentence in this paragraph concerns cleaning the kitchen after moving into an apartment, the sentences are not arranged in any meaningful pattern.

A paragraph is coherent when the relationship among the ideas is clear and the progression from one sentence to the next is easy for the reader to follow. To achieve this goal, arrange ideas in a clearly understandable order and link sentences by using transitional devices such as pronouns, repetition, conjunctions, phrases, and parallel structure. These devices also ease the transitions between paragraphs.

(1) Organization helps create coherence.

To show readers how each sentence in a paragraph leads to the next, writers arrange their ideas in a clear sequence of some kind. Study the following patterns and consider which ones to adopt in your own writing.

(a) In chronological order, you report events according to the order in which they occurred.

Chronological order, one of the simplest ways to arrange ideas in a paragraph, is useful when you are telling a story or explaining a process. Paragraph 12 uses chronological order.

12   Standing in line at the unemployment office makes you feel very much the same as you did the first time you ever flunked a class or a test—as if you had a big red "F" for "Failure" printed across your forehead. I fantasize myself standing at the end of the line in a crisp and efficient blue suit, chin up, neat and straight as a corporate executive. As I move down the line I start to come unglued and a half hour later, when I finally reach the desk clerk, I am slouching and sallow in torn jeans, tennis shoes and a jacket from the Salvation Army, carrying my worldly belongings in a shopping bag and unable to speak.

                    —JAN HALVORSON, "How It Feels to Be out of Work"

(b) By arranging ideas in order of importance, you help readers grasp the points you want to emphasize.

When you arrange ideas according to **order of importance (the climactic pattern),** you go from most to least important or from least to most important. (See also **29c.**) This pattern is especially useful in expository and persuasive writing (see **32a(1)** and chapter **36**), both of which involve helping readers understand logical relationships (such as what has caused something to happen or what kinds of priorities should be established).

In paragraph 13, the author focuses on a hierarchy of intelligence, moving from lower to higher forms of life.

13   An ant cannot purposefully try anything new, and any ant that accidentally did so would be murdered by his colleagues. It is the ant colony as a whole that slowly learns over the ages. In contrast, even an earthworm has enough flexibility of brain to enable it to

be taught to turn toward the left or right for food. Though rats are not able to reason to any considerable degree, they can solve such problems as separating round objects from triangular ones when these have to do with health or appetite. Cats, with better brains, can be taught somewhat more, and young dogs a great deal. The higher apes can learn by insight as well as by trial and error.
—GEORGE RUSSELL HARRISON, *What Man May Be*

(c) Moving from the specific to the general or from the general to the specific also establishes a logical sequence of ideas.

To move from **specific to general,** a paragraph may begin with a striking detail or series of details and conclude with a summarizing statement as in paragraph 14; to move from general to specific, it may begin with a statement or idea, which is then supported by particular details, as in paragraph 15.

14   This winter, I took a vacation from our unfinished mess. Getting back into it was tough, and one morning, I found myself on my knees before the dishwasher, as if in prayer, though actually busting a water-pipe weld. To my right were the unfinished cabinets, to my left the knobless backdoor, behind me a hole I'd torn in the wall. There in the kitchen, a realization hit me like a 2-by-4: for two years I'd been working on this house, and there was still no end in sight. *It had become my Vietnam.*   —ROBERT SULLIVAN, "Home Wrecked"

15   It was not the only disappointment my mother felt in me. In the years that followed, I failed her so many times, each time asserting my own will, my right to fall short of expectations. I didn't get straight As. I didn't become class president. I didn't get into Stanford. I dropped out of college.   —AMY TAN, "Two Kinds"

One common form of the general-specific pattern is **topic-restriction-illustration,** in which the writer announces the topic, restricts it, and illustrates the restricted topic. In paragraph 16, the writer announces the topic—studying a novel—restricts it in the second sentence, and then illustrates the restriction with an example.

16   The result of the proper study of a novel should be contemplation of the mystery embodied in it, but this is a contemplation of the mystery of the whole work and not of some proposition or paraphrase. It is not the tracking-down of an expressible statement about life. An English teacher I knew once asked her students what the moral of *The Scarlet Letter* was, and one answer she got was that the moral of *The Scarlet Letter* was, think twice before you commit adultery.

> —**FLANNERY O'CONNOR,** "The Teaching of Literature"

(d) Opening with a question or problem to which the rest of the paragraph responds is another way to achieve coherence.

In the **question-answer** pattern illustrated by paragraph 17, the first sentence asks a question that the supporting sentences answer.

17   What's wrong with the student-union book shop? Everything. It's interested in selling sweatshirts and college mugs rather than good books. Its staff often is incompetent and uncivil. The manager may not be intelligent enough even to order a sufficient number of copies of required textbooks for the beginning of a term. As for more lively books—why, there are masses of paperbacks, perhaps, that could be procured at any drugstore; there are a few shelves or racks of volumes labeled "Gift Books," usually lavishly illustrated and inordinately costly, intended as presents to fond parents, but there are virtually no book books, of the sort that students might like to buy.

> —**RUSSELL KIRK,** "From the Academy: Campus Bookshops"

In the **problem-solution** pattern, the first sentence (or two) states the problem and the rest of the paragraph suggests the solution, as illustrated by paragraph 18.

18　　That many women would be happier not pursuing careers or intellectual adventures is only part of the truth. The whole truth is that many people would be. If society had the clear sight to assure men as well as women that there is no shame in preferring to stay non-competitively and non-aggressively at home, many masculine neuroses and ulcers would be avoided, and many children would enjoy the benefit of being brought up by a father with a talent for the job instead of by a mother with no talent for it but a sense of guilt about the lack.　—BRIGID BROPHY, "Women"

Paragraphs 12 through 18 illustrate the most frequently used patterns for organizing paragraphs in college writing. Using any of these patterns will help readers follow your thinking. (For additional paragraphs, see **32e** and **33a(4–5)**.)

E X E R C I S E 4

Find examples of three different kinds of paragraph development. Identify the order of ideas (chronological, climactic, general to specific, specific to general, topic-restriction-illustration, question-answer, problem-solution). Explain in writing how each paragraph follows the pattern and organization you have identified.

(2) Grammar contributes to coherence.

In addition to arranging their sentences in a clear pattern, writers also create coherent paragraphs by ensuring that each new sentence builds on either the subject or the predicate of the preceding one. (See chapter **1**.) In one common pattern, links are established between the subject of the topic sentence and all subsequent sentences in the paragraph, as the following diagram suggests.

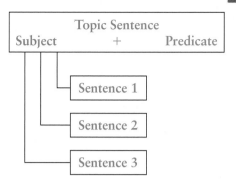

Note how all sentences after the first in paragraph 19 refer back to **Women,** the subject of the topic sentence.

19   **Women** from all classes protested these abusive and discriminating practices. These **protesters** banded together and marched through the streets of their country demanding equality with men. And these **women** were labeled feminists. **They** wanted the right to vote, **they** wanted the right to fair working conditions and fair wages, and **they** wanted the right to live their lives in the manner they chose without ostracism from society. Yes, these **women** (and a few like-minded men) were called feminists.

                           —CAROL JOHNSON, "What Is a Feminist?"

Writers can also link each new sentence to the preceding one by linking predicates or, as in paragraph 20, by creating links through both subjects and predicates.

20   Sir Robert Falcon Scott, who died on the Antarctic peninsula, was never able to bring himself to use dogs, let alone feed them to each other or eat them. Instead he struggled with English ponies, for whom he carried hay. Scott felt that eating dogs was inhumane; he also felt, as he himself wrote, that when men reach a Pole unaided, their journey has "a fine conception" and "the conquest is more nobly and splendidly won." It is this loftiness of sentiment,

this purity, this dignity and self-control, which makes Scott's
farewell letters—found under his body—such moving documents.

—ANNIE DILLARD, "An Expedition to the Pole"

Subject Links	**Predicate Links**
Sir Robert Falcon *Scott*, who died on the Antarctic peninsula,	was never able to bring himself to use dogs, let alone feed them to each other or eat them.
Instead *he*	struggled with English ponies, for whom he carried hay.
Scott felt that eating dogs	was inhumane;
he also felt, as he himself wrote, that when men reach a Pole unaided, their journey	has "a fine conception" and "the conquest is more nobly and splendidly won."
It is this loftiness of sentiment, this purity, this dignity and self-control,	which makes Scott's farewell letters—found under his body— such moving documents.

—ANNIE DILLARD, "An Expedition to the Pole"

(3) The use of transitional devices such as pronouns, repetition, transitional words and phrases, and parallel structures improves coherence.

Many of the same kinds of transitions link sentences within paragraphs and paragraphs within an essay or paper: pronouns, repetition of key words or ideas, conjunctions and other transitional phrases, and parallel structures. (See also chapters 23 and 26.)

(a) Pronouns help establish links between sentences.

In paragraph 21, the writer links sentences by using the pronouns *their* and *they.* Although these same two pronouns are used repeatedly, their referent, "easy victims," is always clear.

21   Several movements characterize easy victims: **their** strides were either very long or very short; **they** moved awkwardly, raising **their** left legs with **their** left arms (instead of alternating them); on each step, **they** tended to lift **their** whole foot up and then place it down (less muggable sorts took steps in which **their** feet rocked from heel to toe). Overall, the people rated most muggable walked as if **they** were in conflict with **themselves; they** seemed to make each move in the most difficult way possible.
            —CARIN RUBENSTEIN, "Body Language That Speaks to Muggers"

**(b) Repetition of words, phrases, or ideas can link a
    sentence to those that precede it.**

In paragraph 22, the repetition of the key word *wave* links the sentences and also provides emphasis. (See **29e**.)

22   The weekend is over, and we drive down the country road from the cottage to the pier, passing out our last supply of **waves.** We **wave** at people walking and **wave** at people riding. We **wave** at people we know and **wave** at people who are strangers.
            —ELLEN GOODMAN, "Waving Goodbye to the Country"

**(c) Conjunctions and other transitional phrases also
    contribute to coherence.**

Conjunctions and transitional phrases demonstrate the logical relationship between ideas. In the following sentences, notice the subtle changes in the relationship between two clauses when they are linked by different conjunctions.

He laughed, and she frowned.

He laughed while she frowned.

He laughed because she frowned.

He laughed, so she frowned.

He laughed; later, she frowned.

Here is a checklist of some frequently used transitional connections arranged according to the kinds of relationships they establish.

CHECKLIST of Transitional Connections	
Alternative and addition	or, nor, and, and then, moreover, besides, further, furthermore, likewise, also, too, again, in addition, even more important, next, first, second, third, in the first place, in the second place, finally, last
Comparison	similarly, likewise, in like manner
Contrast	but, yet, or, and yet, however, still, nevertheless, on the other hand, on the contrary, conversely, even so, notwithstanding, in contrast, at the same time, although this may be true, otherwise, nonetheless
Place	here, beyond, nearby, opposite to, adjacent to, on the opposite side
Purpose	to this end, for this purpose, with this object
Result or cause	so, for, therefore, accordingly, consequently, thus, thereupon, as a result, then, because, hence
Summary	to sum up, in brief, on the whole, in sum, in short, in any event
Repetition	as I have said, in other words, that is, to be sure, as has been noted
Exemplification	for example, for instance, in the case of
Intensification	in fact, indeed, to tell the truth
Time	meanwhile, at length, soon, after a few days, in the meantime, afterward, later, now, then, in the past, while

(d) Parallel structures can establish the relationship between two or more sentences.

Parallelism is the repetition of a sentence pattern or of other grammatical structures. (See also chapter 26.) In paragraph 23, the first three sentences are structured the same way.

> When you're three years old [. . .], that's expected.
>
> When you're six [. . .], you deserve some credit [. . .].
>
> When you're nine [. . .], you should be applauded [. . .].

Repeating this pattern emphasizes the close relationship among the ideas.

23   When you're three years old and stick mashed potatoes up your nose, that's expected. When you're six and make your bed but it looks like you're still in it, you deserve some credit for trying. When you're nine and prepare the family meal but the casserole looks worse than the kitchen, you should be applauded for your effort. But somewhere along the line, some responsible adult should say, "You're too old for this nonsense."

—**DAN KILEY,** *The Peter Pan Syndrome:*
Men Who Have Never Grown Up

E X E R C I S E 5

Improve the coherence of paragraph 11 (page 370) by rearranging the sentences in it and adding transitional phrases.

E X E R C I S E 6

Revise the following paragraph so that the thought flows smoothly from one sentence to the next. Add pronouns and linking devices, and revise the sentences to create parallel structure and to repeat key phrases.

24   [1]The Internet offers a number of benefits to businesses and consumers. [2]Internet presence allows businesses to introduce their new products in a timely fashion. [3]They can more effectively beat

their competition to sales. ⁴Their presence on the Internet offers businesses a cheap and effective method of advertising. ⁵They save money on printing and mailing advertisements and can reach consumers worldwide. ⁶Corporations can link their catalogs on their Web sites. ⁷People can order the products through the Internet. ⁸Consumers save time and money by browsing Internet catalogs and ordering products directly from the companies. ⁹The use of the Internet by businesses and consumers saves time and money. ¹⁰It strengthens the relationship between businesses and consumers.

EXERCISE 7

Examine paragraphs from your own writing and find two that could be more coherent. Revise them using different strategies for creating coherence.

(4) Transitions establish the relationship between paragraphs.

Transitions between paragraphs are as important as transitions between sentences and are achieved by many of the same devices—repetition of words or ideas, conjunctions and other transitional phrases, and parallel structures. Such devices are usually evident in the first sentence of a paragraph.

One of the easiest ways to create a transition is to repeat a word or idea from the last paragraph in the first sentence of the new one, as in paragraphs 25 and 26. (The italics in this example was added.)

25   For those who pray or chant with great perseverance, there is the suggestion that their *waiting* has been converted into purposefulness.

26   Of course, we do not just *wait* for love; we *wait* for money, we *wait* for the weather to get warmer, colder; we *wait* for the plumber to come and fix the washing machine [. . .].

—EDNA O'BRIEN, "Waiting"

Paragraphs 27 and 28 show how you can use a transitional phrase (italicized) to connect paragraphs.

27   Children need help in becoming civic-minded citizens of the digital age, in figuring out how to use the machinery in the service of some broader social purpose than simple entertainment. They need guidance in managing their new ability to connect instantly with other cultures. They need reminders about how to avoid the dangers of elitism and arrogance.

28   *But more than anything else,* it's time to extend to children the promise of the fundamental idea that Locke, Thomas Paine, Thomas Jefferson, and others introduced to the world three centuries ago: That everyone has rights. That everyone should be given as great a measure of freedom as possible. That all should get the opportunity to rise to the outer limits of their potential.

                    —JON KATZ, "The Rights of Kids in the Digital Age"

You can use parallel structures to demonstrate relationships between paragraphs, as in paragraphs 29 and 30.

29 ‖ I understood that when I graduated
  ‖ I would get a job at *Glamour* or *Mademoiselle*
    ‖ where I would meet a dashing young lawyer,
      ‖ fall in love,
      ‖ get married,
      ‖ have 2.5 children, and
      ‖ play bridge all day
        ‖ like my mother did.
  ‖ But the Sixties gave me new goals.

30 ‖ I discovered that when I married,
  ‖ I had to keep my job at *Rolling Stone*
    ‖ where I met my unemployable poet-husband,
      ‖ got promoted,
      ‖ had 1 child, and
      ‖ did the housework late at night
        ‖ like my mother's maid had.

                    —SUSAN ALLEMEIR, "Divorcaversarey"

Sometimes a transitional paragraph serves as a bridge between two paragraphs. Ordinarily, such a paragraph is short (often consisting of only one sentence) because the writer intends it to be merely a signpost, as in paragraphs 31 through 33.

31   I'd met him, and his girlfriend, at a Valentine's party given by a mutual friend. For months I had arisen at dawn each Saturday and Sunday to bike fourteen miles across the busy city to reach his house. I spent the day with him and rode back. He came to visit me in his car (a souped-up, cherry red GTO in need of a new muffler—I heard the muffler's growl two blocks distant and my heart executed an involuntary backflip). After he left, I lectured myself. *I'm in control. We're just friends.*

32   Then he began to visit my dreams.

33   Too many of these dreams and I biked fourteen miles to his house, then invited him to go on a bike ride. I rode as far as we could go and farther to exhaust myself and him, and when I had ridden past exhaustion I found I was still driven by the energy of love and I sat down and said, "There's something I have to tell you. Something you ought to know."

—**FENTON JOHNSON,** *Geography of the Heart*

31c Details and examples can develop paragraphs.

A short paragraph is not necessarily weak. It may be transitional (as in paragraph 32), or its brevity may be a means of emphasizing a key idea. But if you frequently write short paragraphs—paragraphs that end after three or four sentences of average length—think about why.

Students sometimes fall into the habit of writing short paragraphs because they are afraid that they will be told to "break up" long ones. There are certainly times when a paragraph becomes so long that it is hard for readers to make their way through it, times when a writer has become repetitive or insisted on giving a dozen examples when half that number would do. These are paragraphs that take up more than a page. But if you go to the other extreme and have four or five paragraphs on a single page, your writing is going to seem choppy. Experienced writers recognize that there is a middle ground between these extremes. They may write some paragraphs that are only three or four lines long and others that fill the whole page. But most of their pages will consist of two or three well-developed paragraphs, each of which is **unified** (31a) and **coherent** (31b).

The most common reason for paragraphs that are too short to be satisfying is that the writer has become frustrated, distracted, or impatient—abandoning a train of thought rather than developing it. Although there will be times when you can combine two short paragraphs (which may be next to each other or located in different parts of an essay), there will be many more occasions when you need to make a short paragraph longer by developing the idea it was meant to convey. Most short paragraphs need to be developed with more specific details or examples (see 20a).

(1) You can develop a paragraph by supporting the topic sentence with details.

A good paragraph gives readers something to think about. You will disappoint them if you end a paragraph too soon. Consider paragraph 34.

34   Father Whalen was my favorite priest. I got to work with him when I was an altar boy. He was really good at his job, and I will always remember him.

Although this paragraph is **unified** and **coherent,** it is short on detail. In what sense was Father Whalen good at his job? If he really does live on in memory, what exactly is it about him that can be remembered?

Now consider a well-developed paragraph by an experienced writer.

35   *Working with Whalen was a pleasure; he was a real artist, someone who could have made his mark in any field.* He had all

the tools—good hands, nimble feet, a sense of drama, a healthy ego, the unnerving itch to be loved that all great performers have. He did not rush his movements, mumble, or edit his work. He was *efficient,* yes—he'd send the right hand out for the chalice as his left hand was carving a blessing in the air, that sort of thing—but every motion was cleanly executed and held in the air for the proper instant, and he had astounding footwork for such a slab of meat. He was one or two inches over six feet tall, 250 pounds maybe, big belly sliding around in his shirt, but he was deft on the altar and could turn on a dime in the thick red carpet. He cut a memorable double pivot around the corners of the altar table on his way to his spot, and he cut that sucker as cleanly as a professional skater before a Russian judge.

—BRIAN DOYLE, "Altar Boy"

Notice how the series of details in paragraph 35 supports the topic sentence (italicized). Developed with detail, the paragraph remains unified and coherent. There is no need to "break it up"; readers can see how one sentence leads to another, creating a clear picture of the man being portrayed.

(2) You can develop a paragraph by providing examples that illustrate your topic sentence.

Like details, examples also contribute to development by making specific what might otherwise seem general and hard to grasp. Details describe a person, place, or thing; examples illustrate an idea with information that can come from different times and places. In college writing, you will be expected to provide examples to support your ideas. (See 35c and 36c(2).)

Paragraph 36 uses several closely related examples (as well as details) to support the topic sentence with which it opens.

36   *The civility that lingers on in Japan is the most charming and delightful aspect of life here today.* Taxi drivers wear white gloves, take pride in the cleanliness of their vehicles, and sometimes give a discount if they mistakenly take a long route. When they are sick,

Japanese wear surgical masks so they will not infect others. The Japanese language has almost no curses, and high school baseball teams bow to each other at the beginning of each game.

—NICHOLAS KRISTOF, "In Japan, Nice Guys (and Girls) Finish Together"

You can also use one striking example, as in paragraph 37, to clarify your idea.

37   Glamour's lethal effect on the psyche is also caught in the language that commonly describes its impact: "dressed to kill," "devastating," "shattering," "stunning," "knockout," "to die." Perhaps it's not surprising that Rita Hayworth's famous pinup pose in which she's kneeling in a silk negligee on satin sheets was taped to the bomb that was dropped on Hiroshima.

—JOHN LAHR, "The Voodoo of Glamour"

EXERCISE 8

Develop one of the following sentences with enough details or examples (or both) to make an interesting paragraph.

1. Summer is my favorite time of year.
2. It was the filthiest room I had ever seen.
3. The class was so boring that I wanted to drop it.
4. I grew up in a friendly neighborhood.
5. Public speaking can be stressful.

EXERCISE 9

Examine your own writing and select a paragraph you think needs additional details or examples. Rewrite that paragraph.

31d Revising can improve paragraph logic and effectiveness.

At some point in the process of drafting an essay (see chapter 32), you may stop to assess the logic and effectiveness of your paragraphs. Although this activity is a normal part of revising and editing (see chapter 33), it can occur at almost any time during your writing, and it can be repeated as frequently as necessary. When you rework paragraphs, consider the questions in the following checklist.

CHECKLIST for Revising Paragraphs

- Do all the ideas in the paragraph belong together?

- Is the paragraph coherent? Do the sentences focus on the topic? Do they link to previous sentences? Is their order logical?

- Are sentences connected to each other with easy, effective, and natural transitions? Is the paragraph linked to the preceding and following ones?

- Is the paragraph adequately developed? Are any necessary ideas left out?

- If there are problems, can analyzing the strategy used to develop the paragraph help solve them?

EXERCISE 10

Prepare for a class discussion of the following paragraphs (38, 39, and 40) by identifying what the main ideas are (see 31a), how they are developed, and how sentences are arranged in a coherent pattern.

38   In sharp contrast to high school, I now possessed a large number of varied and decidedly wonderful friends, whom I valued immeasurably. Through them I discovered what it was to love people. There was an art to it, I discovered, which was not really all that different from the love that is necessary for the making of art. It required the effort of always seeing them for themselves and not as I wished them to be, of always striving to see the truth of them. —LUCY GREELY, *Autobiography of a Face*

39   Vin was a dreamy, boozy Celt, seldom there when you needed him, but often charming. When he wasn't squeezed by the vice of depression, Vin laughed frequently and cried occasionally, but mainly he talked his way through life, telling wonderful stories— many of them true. Cliff was a practical, abstemious New England Yankee, always there for you, but not much fun. Though Cliff was frugal with words and emotions, he was a man who meant what he said. Cliff gave an honest day's work for his pay and he never questioned the right of an employer to set the wage rate, but Vin jumped from job to job, avoided heavy lifting and complained about exploitation. Vin was prodigal, unreliable, and winning: "Let a smile be your umbrella," he told me, "and you'll have a wet face." Cliff, suspicious of joy, was circumspect and austere: "There's a right way and a wrong way to do everything," he told me repeatedly. Cliff was morning, a glaring sun, and Vin was night, a blue moon. The alternating presences filled my sky. Now they stood together, upon a hill, in late-summer twilight, playing the same game, while I carried their golf bags.

—SHAUN O'CONNELL, "A Memory of Two Fathers"

40   Desire I think has less to do with possession than with participation, the will to involve oneself in the body of the world, in the principle of things expressing itself in splendid specificity, a handful of images: a lover's body, the roil and shimmer of the sea overshot with sunlight, a handful of cherries, the texture and weight of the word. The word that seems most apt is *partake;* it comes from Middle English, literally from the notion of being a part-taker, one who participates. We can say we take a part *of* something but we may just as accurately say we take part *in* something; we are implicated in another being, which is the beginning of wisdom, isn't it—that involvement which enlarges us, which engages the heart, which takes us out of the routine limitations of self.   —MARK DOTY, *Heaven's Coast*

Chapter 32

Planning and Drafting Essays

Experienced writers understand that writing is a process. This chapter discusses many of the activities involved in that process:

- understanding your rhetorical situation (32a),
- finding good topics (32b(1)),
- focusing your ideas (32b(2)),
- writing a clear thesis statement (32c),
- organizing your ideas (32d), and
- using development strategies (32e).

As you plan and draft an essay, you may need to return to a specific activity several times. For example, drafting may help you see that you need to go back and collect more ideas, change your thesis, or even start over with a new one. Rather than seeing repeated effort as a sign of failure, experienced writers consider it an opportunity to improve. (See chapter 33.) They know that writing effective essays requires work, but the effort is worthwhile. Working out your ideas and making them clear to readers will help you gain new insights and enjoy a sense of genuine accomplishment.

32a Writers must understand their purpose, audience, and context.

Purpose	What a writer hopes to achieve in a piece of writing
Audience	Who will read the piece in question

| **Context** | Where and when the exchange between writer and audience takes place |

Your purpose should be appropriate for both the audience and the context. Consider, for example, how your speech changes depending on the person to whom you are speaking and where you are. You would not convince a prospective employer to hire you if you spoke the same way you talk to your closest friend. Nor would you speak the same way to your friend regardless of the context: where and when the conversation takes place, as well as the social factors that can influence it. Meeting a friend for coffee when she is excited about getting a new job would generate words different from the ones you would use the first time you see her after she has suffered a serious loss. You should demonstrate similar flexibility when making appropriate choices for different essays. The combination of purpose, audience, and context is called your **rhetorical situation.** Assess your rhetorical situation when you are planning an essay and remember it when you are revising your drafts (see chapter 33).

(1) *Purpose* means your reason for writing.

The clearer your purpose, the better your writing is likely to be. To clarify your purpose, it helps to ask yourself if you want to

- express how you feel about something,
- amuse or entertain readers,
- report information to readers,
- explain the significance of information,
- persuade readers to agree with you, or
- convince readers to undertake a specific action.

When classified according to purpose, nonfiction writing is often described as **expressive, expository,** or **persuasive.**

Expressive writing emphasizes the writer's feelings and reactions to people, objects, events, and ideas. Personal letters and journals are often expressive, as are many essays. The following example (paragraph 1) comes from an essay designed to convey how the author feels about the relationship he had with his father. (For ease of reference, each of the sample paragraphs in this chapter is numbered.)

1   At just about the hour when my father died, soon after dawn one February morning when ice coated the windows like cataracts, I banged my thumb with a hammer. Naturally I swore at the hammer, the reckless thing, and in the moment of swearing I thought of what my father would say: "If you'd try hitting the nail it would go in a whole lot faster. Don't you know your thumb's not as hard as that hammer?" We were both doing carpentry that day, but far apart. He was building cupboards at my brother's place in Oklahoma; I was at home in Indiana putting up a wall in the basement to make a bedroom for my daughter. By the time my mother called with the news of his death—the long distance wires whittling her voice until it seemed too thin to bear the weight of what she had to say—my thumb was swollen. A week or two later a white scar in the shape of a crescent moon began to show above the cuticle, and month by month it rose across the pink sky of my thumbnail. It took the better part of a year for the scar to disappear, and every time I noticed it I thought of my father.

—SCOTT RUSSELL SANDERS, "The Inheritance of Tools"

Expository writing, or referential writing as it is sometimes called, focuses the reader's attention on objects, events, and ideas rather than on the writer's feelings about them. Textbooks, news accounts, scientific reports, and encyclopedia articles are often expository, as are many of the essays students are expected to write in college. When you report, explain, clarify, or evaluate, you are practicing exposition. The following paragraph comes from an article that explains what happens to people when exposed to severe cold.

2   But those who understand cold know that even as it deadens, it offers perverse salvation. Heat is a presence: the rapid vibrating of molecules. Cold is an absence: the dampening of the vibrations.

At absolute zero, minus 459.67 degrees Fahrenheit, molecular action ceases altogether. It is this slowing that converts gases to liquids, liquids to solids, and renders solids harder. It slows bacterial growth and chemical reactions. In the human body, cold shuts down metabolism. The lungs take in less oxygen, the heart pumps less blood. Under normal temperatures, this would produce brain damage. But the chilled brain, having slowed its own metabolism, needs far less oxygen-rich blood and can, under the right circumstances, survive intact.

—PETER STARK, "As Freezing Persons Recollect the Snow"

Persuasive writing is intended to influence the reader's attitudes and actions. Most writing is to some extent persuasive; through the choice and arrangement of material, even something as apparently straightforward as a résumé can be persuasive. However, writing is usually called persuasive if it is clearly arguing for or against a specific position (see chapter 36). In paragraph 3, note how the author calls for better management of national parks.

3   We must protect our national parks, for our families and for our future. The only way that we can ensure that our priceless heritage of national parks and other public lands is still here for our grandchildren is through responsible federal management. We must not abandon the guiding principles of the national parks set down in 1916: Our parks must remain "dedicated to conserving unimpaired . . . natural and cultural resources and values . . . for the enjoyment, education and inspiration of this and future generations."   —MELANIE GRIFFIN, "They're Not for Sale"

Writers frequently have more than one purpose. For example, it is often necessary to report information when you are trying to persuade. There is nothing wrong with having more than one purpose. The challenge is to be sure that you *have* a purpose. If you have more than one purpose, you should be using one to help you achieve the other—which is very different from writing without a purpose or simply losing sight of your original purpose.

CHECKLIST for Assessing Purpose

- If you are writing in response to a specific assignment, what is your instructor's purpose in giving it?

- Are you expected to fulfill a given purpose, or can you define your own?

- Are you trying primarily to express how you feel? Are you writing to improve how well you understand yourself or trying to help others understand you better?

- Are you trying to be entertaining? What do you hope to accomplish by treating your subject humorously?

- Are you writing primarily to convey information? Are you trying to teach others something that they do not know already or to demonstrate that you have knowledge in common?

- Are you writing primarily to persuade your readers? Do you want them to stop a certain behavior or to undertake a specific action?

- Do you have more than one purpose in writing? Can you achieve all of them? Are any in conflict?

- Are you trying to show your instructor that you have specific writing skills?

E X E R C I S E   1

Select one of the following subjects and write a description of how you would approach the subject if you were writing an essay that would be primarily (a) expressive, (b) expository, or (c) persuasive.

1. summer	4. computers	7. working
2. children	5. rain	8. music
3. cars	6. fast food	9. housing

(2) *Audience* **refers to those who will read your writing.**

Understanding your audience will help you decide on the length and depth of your essay, the kind of language to use, and the examples that will be the most effective. Audiences vary considerably, and so do writers. Some writers like to plan and draft essays with a clear sense of audience in mind; others like to focus on the audience primarily when they are revising (see chapter 33). At some point, however, you must think clearly about who will be reading what you write and ask yourself whether your choices are appropriate for this audience.

(a) Specialized audiences

A **specialized audience** has a demonstrated interest in your subject. If you are writing about the harm caused by alcohol abuse, members of organizations such as Alcoholics Anonymous or Mothers Against Drunk Driving would constitute a specialized audience. So would nutritionists, police officers, or social workers. These audiences would have different areas of expertise and possibly different agendas, so it would be unwise to address each of them exactly the same way. In each case, however, you could assume that your audience has a special interest in your subject and some knowledge of it.

When writing for specialized audiences, you need to consider how much and what sort of information, as well as what methods of presentation, are called for. You can adjust your tone and the kind of language you use as you tailor your presentation to their expertise and attitudes. (See 19b.) If you provide a detailed explanation of basic terms or procedures, an audience of experts might decide that your work is too elementary and choose to read something else instead. But if you can provide the same audience with new information—or a new way of understanding the familiar—the attention you receive is likely to be favorable. The average reader would probably be confused by the language in the following paragraph because it was written for a specialized audience of linguists who are already familiar with the terminology of their discipline.

4   The notions of illocutionary force and different illocutionary acts involve really several quite different principles of distinction. [. . .] So we must not suppose what the metaphor of "force" suggests, that the different illocutionary verbs mark off points on a single continuum. Rather, there are several different continua of "illocutionary force," and the fact that the illocutionary verbs of English stop at certain points on these various continua and not at others is, in a sense, accidental. For example, we might have had an illocutionary verb "rubify," meaning to call something "red." Thus, "I hereby rubify it" would just mean "It's red." Analogously, we happen to have an obsolete verb "macarize," meaning to call someone happy.

—J. R. SEARLE, "Speech Acts: An Essay in the Philosophy of Language"

Many of the papers you write in college—in history, economics, and psychology for example, as well as in English—are for a specialized audience. When you write an essay for a college course, you can assume that your instructor is already familiar with the material. For example, if you are writing an essay about a novel assigned by your English instructor, it is not necessary to summarize the plot unless you have been specifically asked to do so. You can assume that this specialized audience already knows what takes place. Instead of telling your audience what he or she already knows, use your essay to communicate your interpretation of the material you have both read (see 39a).

No one knows everything about a subject, and a specialized audience is usually pleased to learn something new. However, writing for members of a specialized audience does not necessarily demand that you know more than they do. At times it may be sufficient to demonstrate that you understand the material and can discuss it appropriately. Moreover, a specialized audience for one subject would not be a specialized audience for another.

(b) Diverse audiences

A **diverse audience** consists of readers with different levels of expertise and interest in your subject. For example, if you are writing an essay about computer software that will be read by other students in a first-year composition course, you will probably discover that some of your readers know more about software than others.

When writing for a diverse audience, you can usually assume that your readers have interests different from yours but share a willingness to learn about new material if it is presented clearly and respectfully by someone who is taking the trouble to identify with them. Consider how the following description from an introductory linguistics textbook explains a concept that the author of the comparable passage on page 394 assumed to be already understood by a specialized audience.

5   The study of how we do things with sentences is the study of **speech acts.** In studying speech acts, we are acutely aware of the importance of the *context of the utterance.* In some circumstances *There is a sheepdog in the closet* is a warning, but the same sentence may be a promise or even a mere statement of fact, depending on circumstances. We call this purpose—a warning, a promise, a threat, or whatever—the **illocutionary force** of a speech act.

—VICTORIA FROMKIN and ROBERT RODMAN, *An Introduction to Language*

To attract the attention of a diverse audience, look for what its members are likely to have in common despite their differences. For example, are they all students at the same school or residents of the same state? Do they all work full- or part-time? Do they believe in the importance of exercise or worry about conflicts in personal relationships? The key to communicating successfully with diverse readers is to find some way to draw them together on common ground and join them there.

One way to envision a diverse audience is to think in terms of educational level. Instead of writing for students in general, you could ask yourself whether the audience you most want to reach is composed primarily of students in their first or fourth year of college. With one of these audiences in mind, you could emphasize common concerns and lessen the risk of excluding readers whose lives, in other respects, are quite different from yours. By considering the educational level of your audience, you will also find it easier to make appropriate choices in diction (see chapters **19** and **20**) and detail (see **31c**). For example, an upper-division textbook in linguistics presents a somewhat more complete approach to speech acts than an introductory text.

6   Every speech act has two principal components: the utterance itself and the intention of the speaker in making it. First, every utterance is represented by a sentence with a grammatical structure and meaning; this is variously called the **locution** or the utterance act. Second, speakers have some intention in making an utterance, something they intend to accomplish; that intention is called an **illocution,** and every utterance consists of performing one or more illocutionary acts.

   —EDWARD FINEGAN and NIKO BESNIER, *Language: Its Structure and Use*

You could also envision a diverse audience defined by some other common ground—such as gender. If you look through popular magazines, you can easily find articles written for either men or women. However, when writing for a gender-specific audience, do not make the mistake of assuming that all men or all women think the same way or share the same values. Further, there is a big difference between consciously choosing to write for a gender-specific audience and accidentally ignoring gender differences when writing for an audience that includes men and women.

Sometimes you may not know much about your audience. When this is the case, you can often benefit from imagining a thoughtful audience of educated adults. Such an audience is likely to include people with different backgrounds and cultural values (see **39a(2)b**), so be careful not to assume that you are writing for readers who are exactly like you. A useful technique, in this case, is to imagine yourself in conversation with a small group of specific persons who have diverse backgrounds but nevertheless share an interest in your topic. Even if your actual readers are sometimes less thoughtful than your ideal readers, they may rise to the occasion, when treated respectfully, and assume the role you have projected for them. To a considerable extent, the language you use will determine whether diverse readers feel included or excluded from your work. Be careful to avoid jargon or technical terms that would be understood only by a specialized audience. If you must use a specialized term, explain what you mean by it. (See **19b(6)**).

(c) Multiple audiences

Writers often need to address multiple audiences. At work, you might need to write a memo or a letter that will be read not only by the person to whom it is addressed but also by other people who receive copies (see **39b**). The readers in a multiple audience can have distinctly different expectations. If, for example, you are asked to evaluate the performance of an employee you supervise and send copies to both that person and your boss, one part of your audience is probably looking for praise while the other is looking to see whether you are a competent supervisor.

The use of e-mail for communication (see **39b**) has increased the likelihood of writing for a multiple audience because messages can be easily forwarded—and not always with the writer's permission. Other electronic texts, such as those generated by Listserv dialogues, MOOs, or online conversation through a Web site, can also reach a multiple audience. When writing texts for electronic submission, consider whether anyone outside your immediate audience could take an interest in your work.

When writing essays in college, you may also find yourself writing for multiple audiences. The most common example is drafting an essay that will be discussed by a small group of fellow students and read by your instructor. If you choose to write an essay for a diverse audience and submit it to an instructor who is a specialist on your subject, you are actually writing for multiple audiences. This kind of writing requires you to consider a variety of attitudes and positions (see 36c). Doing so is helpful when planning your essay and bringing different points of view to bear as you prepare to revise it (see chapter 33).

CHECKLIST for Assessing Audience

- Who is going to be reading what you write?

- What do you know about the members of this audience? What characteristics can you safely assume about them?

- What values do you share with them?

- How do you differ from them?

- How much do they already know about your topic?

- What kind of language is appropriate for them?

- How open are they to views that may be different from theirs? Are they likely to prefer hearing you restate what they already know or learning something new?

- How professional would they expect you to seem?

- What do you *not* know about your audience? What assumptions would be risky?

- Are you writing with one audience in mind and then expecting a different audience to read what you have written? If so, have you clearly indicated the audience you have in mind so your readers can imagine that they are part of it?

E x e r c i s e 2

Choose a recent class and write a description of it that would be read by (a) a member of your family, (b) the instructor, or (c) the dean of your school. Then write a second description that would be read by all three.

(3) *Context* means the circumstances under which writers and readers communicate.

Context includes time and place. An essay written outside class may be very different from one written in a classroom even if both are written for the same instructor and in response to the same question. What you are able to write has been influenced by time and place, and your audience is likely to take this into account—by expecting more from you when you have more time and better working conditions. Similarly, an instructor may expect more from an essay written at the end of the course than from one written at the beginning.

Context is also influenced by social, political, religious, and other cultural factors (see 39a(2)b). Your background and beliefs often shape the stance you take in your writing. An essay written shortly before Christmas, for example, could be influenced by both your own anticipation of that event and whether or not you think your audience shares that anticipation. Or a political crisis, such as the outbreak of war or the collapse of a nation's economy, could prompt you to reconsider the purpose of an essay you are drafting. Writers can benefit by considering whether factors such as these have led them to make assumptions about their audience that may or may not be accurate.

When you read the work of other writers, you will sometimes find examples in which the context is specifically stated, as in the following passage.

7   In the twenty-second month of the war against Nazism we meet here in this old Palace of St. James, itself not unscarred by the fire of the enemy, in order to proclaim the high purposes and resolves of the lawful constitutional Governments of Europe whose countries have been overrun; and we meet here also to cheer the hopes of free men and free peoples throughout the world.

—WINSTON CHURCHILL, "Until Victory Is Won"

Often, however, the context must be inferred. Whether you choose to state your context or not, it is essential that you consider it.

CHECKLIST for Assessing Context

- Under what circumstances are you writing this essay? If you are free to choose the time and place in which you write, have you set aside a time when you are likely to do good work and found a site where you can work without distractions?

- Under what circumstances will your essay probably be read? If it is going to be one of many essays in a pile on someone's desk, can you help that person quickly see the purpose of your work and how it responds to your assignment?

- How has your response to this assignment been influenced by what else is going on in your life? Are you satisfied with this response, or does it put you at risk? Can you make any changes in your schedule that will allow you to focus more attention on this assignment?

- Have you been asked to write an essay of a specific length? If length has not been specified, what seems appropriate for your audience?

- What document design (see chapter 8) is appropriate for this context?

32b Writers find appropriate subjects and decide how to focus them.

Whether you are assigned a subject or are free to choose your own, you must consider what you know—or would like to learn about—and what is likely to interest your audience (see 32a(2)). You must also decide how to focus your subject so that you can develop it adequately within the time and space available to you.

When you take a writing course, you might be asked to choose your own subject. In this case, you should consider your interests and your experience. The first step toward interesting an audience in your subject is to be interested in it yourself. Often the best subject is one drawn from your own experience, because experience has given you knowledge of the subject. Thinking about hobbies, sports, jobs, places, trips, and relationships can often help you discover a subject that is important to you and likely to interest readers if you write about it with a clear purpose and well-chosen detail (see chapter 20 and 31c and 32a(1)).

More often, however, you will be asked to write essays about subjects outside your personal experience but within your college experience. For instance, you may have a paper due for a course in ancient history. If you are not limited to a specific question, you would be responsible for choosing your subject—but it would have to be one related to the course. Just as you do when you write about personal experience, you should make an effort to find material that interests you. Look in your textbook, particularly in the sections listing suggestions for further reading and study. Go through your lecture notes and examine the annotations you made in the works you read for the course. (See 38b.) Ask yourself whether there are any aspects of your subject you feel certain about and any others about which you would like to learn more. Writing about a subject is one of the best ways to learn about it, so use this assignment not only to satisfy your audience but also to satisfy yourself.

(1) There are several ways to search for a subject.

If you have a hard time finding something to write about—or have so many ideas that you have trouble choosing among them—try **journaling, freewriting, listing, clustering,** or **questioning.** Discussing assignments with other people can also help you generate ideas and decide on those likely to yield good essays. Use whatever methods produce results for you. Different methods may work best for different subjects; if you run out of ideas when using one method, switch to another. Sometimes, especially for an assigned subject remote from your own interests and knowledge, you may need to try several methods.

(a) Journaling

Keeping a journal is a proven way to generate subjects for essays. Although there are many different kinds of journals, students often benefit from writing in a personal journal or a writer's notebook every day.

In a **personal journal,** you reflect on your experience. Instead of simply listing activities, meals, or weather reports, you use writing to explore how you feel about what is happening in your life. You might focus on external events, such as what you think about a book or a film, or focus on your inner life by exploring changes in mood or attitude. Writers who keep a personal journal usually write for their own benefit; they are their own audience and do not share what they write with others. But in the process of writing this journal—or reading it—they may discover subjects they can use for essays.

Like a personal journal, a **writer's notebook** also includes responses to experience. In this case, however, the emphasis is on sorting through what you are learning. Students often benefit from keeping a writer's notebook in which they respond exclusively to what they are reading. They record quotations that seem especially meaningful, evaluate the strengths and weaknesses of a particular text, summarize the material, note points they agree with, and jot down questions they would like to raise in class or pursue in an essay. (See 38b and 38c(4).) In addition to helping you discover subjects for essays, a writer's notebook can help you become a better reader.

Some writers keep both a personal journal and a writer's notebook. Others keep only one—or create a combination of the two. In either case, they feel free to write quickly without worrying about spelling, grammar, or organization.

(b) Freewriting

When freewriting, writers record without stopping whatever occurs to them during a limited period of time—often no more than ten minutes or so. They do not worry about whether they are repeating themselves or getting off the track; they simply write to see what comes out. No matter how bad the writing may be, the process helps them discover ideas they did not realize they had. The entries in a personal journal or writer's notebook may be freewritten, but freewriting is not limited to journaling. You can take out a sheet of paper and freewrite whenever you have a few minutes to spare. Some writers use colored marking pens to identify different topics generated by this activity.

In directed freewriting, writers begin with a general subject area and record whatever occurs to them about this subject during the time available. When asked by his English teacher to write about whatever he remembered about high school, Peter Geske wrote the following example of directed freewriting during five minutes of class time. This was the first step toward drafting his essay, three different versions of which appear in chapter 33.

Write about high school? I can't believe this topic. This is a waste of time. I came here to learn not to sit around doing busy work. Does he think we're all eighteen? A good five years older than anybody else in this class and stuck in a dead-end job. I hate that job. Guess that's why I'm here but I don't see how writing about high school is going to help. All those stupid cliques and teachers who were real losers. Rodriguez was o.k. At least he listened. Who else? I don't know what to say but I'm supposed to keep on writing and my hand is getting tired. Well at least we're doing something. Unlike all those classes that were out of control. Kleinberg never said anything when kids brought knives and flashed them right in front of him. And that zombie who taught chemistry. Reading from the textbook all the time without even looking at us. Maybe she was afraid of us. Am I afraid to be back in school? I sure hope no one reads this. The only thing good about high school was sports. Reynolds wouldn't let us get away with anything. A tough guy who cared. You always knew what to expect from him.

As the color coding shows, this freewrite generated at least four possible writing topics about high school: cliques, unqualified teachers, good teachers, and sports. Some of these topics overlap. Sports, for example, could be combined with cliques if athletes kept to themselves; or a good teacher might be contrasted with a bad one. However, the focus could also be narrowed to a single teacher or even to a single aspect of that teacher's performance—such as the inability to control the class. Within a few minutes, this writer has discovered that he has more to say than can be addressed in a single essay.

(c) Listing

One way to gather ideas about your writing topic is to make an informal list, a process also known as **brainstorming.** The advantage to listing is that, like outlining, it lets you see individual items at a glance rather than having to pick them out of a block of writing. It also encourages the establishment of relationships. Jot down any ideas that come to you while you are thinking about your subject. Do not worry if the ideas come without any kind of order, and do not worry about the form in which you write them down; grammar, spelling, and diction are not important at this stage. Devote as much time as necessary to making your list—perhaps five minutes, perhaps an entire evening. The point is to collect as many ideas as you can.

Peter made the following list after he had decided to focus his essay on the quality of the education he received at his high school.

```
geometry with Kleinberg
sophomore English with Mrs. Sullivan
American history with Mr. Rodriguez
out-of-date books
a terrible library
out-of-control classes
failing chemistry
good grades in English and history
blow-off courses
     social problems
     sex education
     speech
partying throughout senior year
too many students in each class
useless computers
```

This list may appear chaotic, but earlier items suggest later ones, and a review of the whole list may indicate items that need to be rearranged, added, or deleted. As you look through the list, you will find some ideas that are closely related and could be grouped together. For instance, items about school facilities can easily be grouped together, as can items about specific courses. Toward the end of his list, Peter began to establish some relationships by developing a sublist of courses he found useless. Order and direction are beginning to emerge.

For an example of a list written and revised under pressure, see page 468.

(d) Clustering

Instead of listing ideas in a column, you can try arranging them as they occur in a kind of map that shows how they relate to one another. To try clustering, write your main subject in the middle of a blank sheet of paper and then draw a circle around it. Surround that circle with others containing related ideas, and draw a line between each of them and the main subject. As you think of additional ideas or details, place them in new circles and connect them with lines to the circles to which they are most closely related (as in the example on page 407). Doing so will establish various ways of exploring your topic and provide a visual image of how these trains of thought connect. Although you are unlikely to pursue all of the directions you have charted once you narrow your focus (see **32b(2)**), the connections you have established can help you determine how you want to organize your essay (see **32d**).

(e) Questioning

Explore a subject by asking yourself some questions. There are two structured questioning strategies you might use—**journalists' questions** and a similar approach known as the **pentad** that encourages seeing relationships. **Journalists' questions**

Clustering

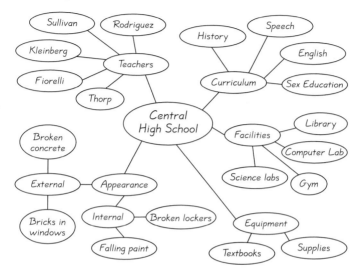

ask *Who?, What?, When?, Where?, Why?,* and *How?*; they are easy to use and can help you discover ideas about any subject. Using journalists' questions to explore the subject of high school education could lead you to think about *who* goes to public high school and *who* teaches there, *what* courses are offered, *when* education improves or deteriorates, *where* funding comes from and *where* teachers get their training, *why* some classes get overcrowded and *why* funds are short, and *how* education stimulates or *how* it fails.

The **pentad** considers the five dramatic aspects of a subject:

Act	what happens
Actor	who does it
Scene	the time, place, and conditions under which the event occurred
Agency	the method or circumstances facilitating the act
Purpose	the intent or reasons surrounding the act

Using this method can help you discover relationships among the various aspects of the subject. For example, consider something like "failing chemistry"—one of the ideas generated by Peter Geske in the list on page 405. What is the relationship between the act (failing a course) and the actors (the student who failed and the teacher who failed him)? Did the failure result from the inability of these two actors to perform well together? Or was the act related to the scene: an overcrowded classroom with out-of-date equipment?

(2) Writers need to focus their ideas.

Exploring the subject will suggest not only productive strategies for development, but also a direction and focus for your writing. Some ideas will seem worth pursuing, while others will seem inappropriate for your purpose, audience, or context. You will find yourself discarding ideas even as you develop new ones.

A simple analogy will help explain focus: When you want a picture of a landscape, you cannot photograph all that your eye can take in. You must focus on just part of it. As you aim your camera, you look through the viewfinder to make sure the subject is correctly framed and in focus. At this point you may wish to move in closer and focus on one part of the scene, or you may decide to change your angle, using light and shadow to emphasize some features of the landscape over others. You can think of your writing the same way—focusing and directing your ideas just as you focus and direct the lens of your camera—moving from a general subject to a more specific one.

For example, "high school" is too large and general a subject to make a good writing topic. However, some of the items that emerged in freewriting about this subject (page 404) and in the list that it elicited (page 405) can be grouped to form a topic that is both interesting and manageable. Or a single item, if well chosen, could lead to a sharply focused essay of some depth.

In addition to reviewing the ideas you have generated through strategies such as freewriting and listing, you can also discover a focus by thinking in terms of how strategies used to develop your ideas (see 32e) can take you in different directions. Working with "high school" as an example of a large subject that a writer would need to narrow, here are some questions inspired by considering development strategies.

a. *Narration.* What happened to me in high school? What is the story of my high school education?

b. *Process.* How do teachers teach? How do students spend their days? What was my learning process like?

c. *Cause and effect.* Why did I hate high school? How was I influenced by peers? Would I have done better in a different school district?

d. *Description.* What did my high school look like? What did a typical class look like? What was it like to be in study hall, the cafeteria, or the gym?

e. *Definition.* What is education? What is a good school? How demanding should a high school education be?

f. *Classification and division.* How could I classify the students or teachers in my high school? What is the significance of dividing students by year rather than by accomplishment? What group did I belong to?

g. *Example.* What was a typical day like? Who was my best teacher, and who was my worst?

h. *Comparison and contrast.* How did my school compare with a rival school? How does going to a public high school differ from going to a private high school? What did my two best teachers have in common?

The following sentence suggests a focus on comparison and contrast.

When I think of my last two English teachers, I can see how a teacher who cares about students differs from someone who is bored by them.

This sentence suggests cause and effect:

> The poor quality of the high school I attended can be traced to a shrinking tax base, a lack of parental interest, and an administrative failure to hold the school accountable to state standards.

Although you might need to combine two or more strategies to develop your work (see **32e**), thinking initially in terms of a single one can help you clarify your focus.

Because writing is a form of thinking, your focus may also emerge from writing your first draft and then assessing it. When you compare the draft of Peter Geske's essay on high school education (pages 445–47) with the final version of it (pages 457–60), you will see how drafting and revising can sharpen a writer's focus. (See chapter **33**.)

Whatever method you use to decide how to focus your work, your choice should be determined not only by your interests, but also by your purpose, the needs of your audience, and the time and space available.

CHECKLIST for Assessing a Topic

- Can you do justice to the topic in the space available to you? Should you narrow it?

- Do you know enough about it to be able to write about it at the length your instructor requires? Should you expand it?

- Are you interested in it?

- Could your audience be interested in it?

- Is it appropriate for the assignment?

- Are you willing to learn more about it?

EXERCISE 3

A. Choose a personal experience that might be an appropriate subject. Write a paragraph describing why you think it would be useful to share this experience with others. Identify your audience and
write a second paragraph describing how much information you
would need to include so that this audience would understand your
experience. Then, for your own reference, set some limits for yourself by making a separate list of anything about this experience
that you do not want to include because you wish to protect your
privacy or avoid embarrassing your audience.

B. Select an academic subject from one of your college courses and
write a paragraph describing how you would approach this subject
if you were writing for your instructor and how you would approach the same material if you were writing for ninth graders.

EXERCISE 4

Explore one of the subjects from exercise 3 by experimenting with
one of the following strategies: freewriting, listing, clustering, or questioning. Then consider how you could focus the ideas you have generated. To illustrate the different directions you could follow depending on your focus, write a list of at least ten questions.

32c A clearly stated thesis conveys your main idea.

If you have limited and focused your subject, you have gone a
long way toward developing an idea that controls the content
you include and the approach you take. Your controlling idea,
or thesis, also reflects how your purpose is appropriate for your
audience and context. (See 32a.)

(1) Essays usually include a thesis statement.

In college and many other kinds of writing, you will be expected to state your main idea succinctly. This **thesis statement**

contains a single idea, clearly focused and specifically stated, that grows out of your exploration of a subject. A thesis statement can be thought of as a central idea phrased in the form of an assertion. It is a claim (see 36c(1))—that is, it indicates what you claim to be true, interesting, or valuable about your subject.

An explicitly stated thesis statement helps keep your writing on target. It identifies the topic, the approach, and in some cases the plan of development. Note how the thesis statements below do all of these. The first is from an expressive essay.

> By the time that his children were growing up the great days of my father's life were over.   —VIRGINIA WOOLF, "Leslie Stephen"

With this apparently simple statement, the author has established that the topic is her father and indicated that she will discuss both early accomplishments and later decline while focusing primarily on his life within the family.

The following thesis statement for an expository essay divides "discipline" into three kinds.

> A child, in growing up, may meet and learn from three different kinds of discipline.   —JOHN HOLT, "Kinds of Discipline"

The main idea in a persuasive essay usually carries a strong point of view—an argumentative edge.

> Nothing better illustrates the low regard that the NCAA has often had for the rights of student-athletes than its random drug-testing policy.   —ALLEN L. SACK, "Random Tests Abuse Dignity"

You will probably try out several thesis statements as you explore your subject. Rather than starting with a preconceived thesis that you must then struggle to support, let it develop out of your thinking and discovery process and as you draft your paper. Your goal should be a claim that is neither self-evident nor too broad.

A clear, precise thesis statement will help unify what you write; it will guide many decisions about which details to keep and which to toss out. You can also use the thesis to guide your search for additional information you may need to strengthen your point. But it is important to allow your essay to remain flexible in the early stages. If you have information about your subject that is interesting but does not really help make your point, including it in your early drafts might lead you to a better essay by indicating a more profitable focus.

As you write, check your thesis statement frequently to see whether you have drifted away from it. Do not hesitate to change your thesis, however, if you find a more productive path or one you would rather pursue. Make whatever adjustments you need to ensure a unified essay. When you revise, test everything you retain against the thesis you have finally decided on—your original or a new version you have developed—and scrupulously discard anything that does not contribute. (See chapter 33.)

A thesis is usually stated in a declarative sentence with a single main clause—that is, in either a simple or a complex sentence (see 1e–f). If your thesis statement announces two or more coordinate ideas, as a compound sentence does, be sure that you are not losing direction and focus. If you wish to sharpen your thesis statement by adding information that qualifies or supports it, subordinate such material to the main idea.

Beware of vague qualifiers such as *interesting, important,* and *unusual.* Often such words signal that you have chosen a subject that does not interest you much; you would do better to rethink your subject to come up with something you care about. In a thesis statement such as "My education has been very unusual," the vague word *unusual* may indicate that the idea itself is weak and that the writer needs to find a stronger subject. However, this kind of vague thesis may disguise an idea of real interest that simply needs to be made specific: "Our family grew closer after my parents decided to teach me at home." The following examples show ways to focus, clarify, and sharpen vague thesis statements.

Vague   It is hard to make decisions.

Better Making financial decisions is difficult for me because I am confused by the number of investment choices that are available today.

Vague   Thomas Jefferson was a unique individual.

Better Believing in liberty but unable to free his own slaves, Thomas Jefferson suffered from a troubled conscience.

Vague   The media have a lot of influence on how people think.

Better The frequent use of unusually thin models in television and magazine advertisements has contributed to the rise of eating disorders among adolescent girls in the United States.

Thesis statements appear most often in the first or second paragraph, although you can put them anywhere that suits your purpose—occasionally, even in the conclusion. The advantage of putting the thesis statement in the first paragraph, however, is that your reader knows from the beginning what you are writing about and where the essay is going. Especially appropriate in college writing, this technique helps readers who are searching for specific information locate it easily. If the thesis statement begins the introductory paragraph, the rest of the sentences in the paragraph usually support or clarify it, as is the case in paragraph 8.

8   America is suffering from overwork. Too many of us are too busy, trying to squeeze more into each day while having less to show for it. Although our growing time crunch is often portrayed as a personal dilemma, it is in fact a major social problem that has reached crisis proportions over the past 20 years.

—BARBARA BRANDT, "Less Is More"

(2) A main idea is necessary even when a thesis statement is not required.

Some kinds of writing do not require a formulated thesis statement, but they do have a main, or controlling, idea. Writing without a thesis statement is sometimes acceptable when the main thrust is narrative or descriptive. A memoir or a journal, for example, is unlikely to have a thesis statement. And reports of information, such as a news story or a business memo (see 39b), frequently do not require a thesis. Yet even in cases such as these, your readers should be able to sense a clear direction and focus. You can help them understand your main idea by staying focused on it as you draft and revise.

CAUTION Many instructors expect every essay to have a clear thesis statement.

CHECKLIST for Assessing Your Thesis

- Is your thesis clear?

- Could it be more specific?

- Is it likely to interest your audience?

- Does it accurately reflect what you think?

- Can you support it?

- Will you be able to support it within the length specified for this essay?

- Is it placed where readers will be able to find it easily?

- Would your readers benefit from having it restated later in your essay?

32d Arranging ideas requires choosing an appropriate method or combination of methods.

Many writers need a working plan to direct their ideas and keep their writing on course. Some use informal written lists; others use formal outlines. Such plans are especially helpful for lengthy essays or documents (see chapter 38) and for writing under pressure (see chapter 34). Whatever method you choose, remember that you can always change your plan to suit any new direction your writing takes. The point is to have a way to direct your effort toward fulfilling your purpose.

(1) Informal working plans can be composed quickly.

An informal working plan need be little more than an ordered list that grows out of a collection of ideas. Look at the informal working plan that Peter Geske made as he prepared to write on the quality of his high school education.

Before he started his first draft, Peter reexamined his freewriting (page 404) and his first list of ideas (page 405). He decided to focus on evaluating the quality of the education he had received, rather than on other topics such as cliques or sports. Reviewing the items on his list, he noticed that his concerns could be grouped into three categories: facilities and supplies, curriculum, and teachers. He then formulated a tentative thesis and made an ordered list to chart the direction of his essay.

THESIS: Academic facilities and standards were so low at my high school that I learned very little while I was there and became discouraged about school.

1. Physical description of the school
2. Textbooks, computers, and other supplies
3. Class size
4. Courses that were a waste of time
5. Bad teachers
6. A few bright spots

When you make such a list, ideas might overlap. For example, it might not be possible to separate "courses that were a waste of time" from "bad teachers." Some ideas may drop out, and others may occur to you as you draft. But you have the beginning of a plan that can guide you.

As Peter continued to work on his essay, he made several changes in his original plan. For example, he decided to discuss class size before discussing textbooks and other supplies, added a conclusion, and then wrote an entirely different conclusion. Because writing is a process, changes of this sort are natural.

(2) Formal outlines can help writers develop ideas.

Writers sometimes find themselves required to follow a plan of organization that has been determined for them. The ancient Greeks, for example, developed a standard arrangement to help audiences follow whatever a speaker was saying because certain parts of a speech usually occurred in the same sequence. Even today, this **classical arrangement** proves useful for many writers—especially writers trying to persuade. For a description of classical arrangement, see pages 511–512.

Often, however, outlines grow out of the writing. Some writers can develop an excellent plan early in their writing process, turning a working list into a formal outline. Others discover that they need to rethink their original plan after they have actually done some writing. But whether it is written before the first draft or after it, a formal outline is often helpful when analyzing a draft and preparing to revise it. For example, if an outline shows only one subgroup under a heading, that section of the draft might need rethinking. It could be either unnecessary or inadequately developed, or it might belong under a different heading.

A structured outline uses indentation and numbers to indicate various levels of subordination. Thus, it is a kind of graphic scheme of your thinking. The main points form the major headings, and the supporting ideas form the subheadings. An outline of Peter's essay might begin as follows:

THESIS: Academic facilities and standards were so low at my high school that I learned very little while I was there and became discouraged about school.

I. Description of the school
   A. The building itself
      1. Run-down
         a. Exterior
         b. Interior
      2. Overcrowded
         a. Hallways
         b. Classrooms
   B. Facilities
      1. Terrible library
         a. Few books
         b. Poor access to the Web
      2. Inadequate labs
         a. Chemistry lab
         b. Biology lab
II. Description of programs
   A. Typical courses
      1. Math
         a. Using poor teaching methods
         b. Harassing students
      2. Chemistry
         a. Reading from the textbook
         b. Giving unfair tests
   B. Bright spots
      1. American history
         a. Analyzing the news
         b. Getting extra help
      2. English
         a. Reading good stories
         b. Doing creative writing

The types of outlines most commonly used are **topic** and **sentence outlines.** The headings in a **topic outline** are expressed in grammatically parallel phrases, as in the example above, while a **sentence outline** presents headings in complete and usually parallel sentences. A topic outline has the advantage of brevity and highlights the logical flow of your paper; a sentence outline forces you to think through your ideas more thoroughly. Here is how a sentence outline for Peter's essay might begin.

```
THESIS: Academic facilities and standards
were so low at my high school that I learned
very little while I was there and became
discouraged about school.

I. The school building hindered learning.
   A. The building was an eyesore.
      1. It was run-down and covered with
         graffiti.
      2. It was so overcrowded that it
         couldn't be kept clean.
   B. Facilities were inadequate.
      1. The library had few resources.
      2. Laboratories lacked equipment.
```

The headings in a sentence outline can often serve as topic sentences when you draft.

Regardless of the type of outline you choose, you will need enough headings to develop your subject fully within the boundaries established by your thesis.

32e Writers use various strategies to develop essays.

When drafting essays, you can benefit from techniques that help writers develop their ideas. The strategies discussed in this section can be used to frame entire essays by providing a way to organize ideas. For example, you could compose an essay devoted exclusively to defining a concept or explaining a process. More frequently, however, these strategies, or **modes** as they are sometimes called, are used to generate ideas and determine a focus (see **32b**) or to facilitate effective communication between writer and audience by developing a point that might otherwise be unclear. When drafting an essay, you may discover that you need to add a paragraph defining a term or explaining a process before you can expect your audience to understand your essay as a whole. Writers frequently use such strategies to fulfill their purpose.

These development strategies reflect the ways people think, and thinking is seldom straightforward. As a result, they are often used in combination. For example, a formal definition can be developed through both comparison and contrast, and narration can be developed through description. One mode is not inherently superior to another. What matters is that you choose a development strategy—or combination of strategies—that will satisfy your purpose and your audience within a particular context. Considering the expectations and needs of that audience (see **32a**) will help you determine which points to develop and which strategies can facilitate that development.

(1) Narrating a series of events tells readers what happened.

A narrative discusses a sequence of events, normally in the order in which they occur, to develop a particular point. This mode often uses time markers such as *then, later, that evening,* or *the following week.* (Longer narratives often begin in the middle of a sequence of events and contain flashbacks.) The narrative must be closely related to your main idea and must develop it. Drawn from an article that employs numerous strategies to convey information about self-damaging behavior, paragraph 9 uses narrative to convey a sense of what it is like to be a troubled adolescent.

9   Jill isn't sure how many aspirin she took, but estimates it was around 30. "That night was like the scariest night in my life," she says. "I was puking and sweating and had ringing in my ears and I couldn't focus on anything." Still, she slept through a second day before telling her parents what was really ailing her. They rushed her to a hospital, where she wound up in intensive care for three days with arrhythmia while IV's flushed out her system, and she was lucky not to have permanently damaged her liver.

—JENNIFER EGAN, "The Thin Red Line"

(2) Describing something to show how it looks, smells, or feels adds useful detail.

By describing a person, place, object, or sensation, you can make your material come alive. Descriptions are often visual, but they can appeal to senses other than just sight.

Description should suit your purpose and audience. In describing your car, for example, you would emphasize certain features to a potential buyer, others to a mechanic who is going to repair it, and still others to a friend who wants to borrow it. In paragraph 10, Kathleen Murphy makes her description of Clint Eastwood vivid by blending visual and auditory images and suggesting images of touch. Writing for an audience of movie-goers, Murphy seeks to convey what is attractive about the kind of masculinity Eastwood embodies in one of his early films.

10   His gait is that of a ghost or a predator, his poncho'd torso remaining strangely still, propelled ahead by the long legs, as though swimming upright in slow motion. Paradoxically, the hands of the remorseless gunfighter are those of a musician or a painter: elegant, long-fingered, with graceful wrists. In these formative stages of the Eastwood persona, his often nearly whispered vocal tones seem too pressured for ordinary speech. The silky, then

increasingly abrasive sibilance of his drawl, like sand or gravel shifting in water, works best for epigrams, cryptic ripostes, up-close seduction.

—**KATHLEEN MURPHY,** "The Good, the Bad, and the Ugly:
Clint Eastwood as Romantic Hero," *Film Comment*

(3) Explaining a process shows readers how something happens.

Process paragraphs, in explaining how something is done or made, often use both description and narration. You might describe the items used in the process and then narrate the steps chronologically, as in paragraph 11. Add an explanation of process to your draft if doing so can illustrate a concept that might otherwise be hard for your audience to grasp. Although few readers are likely to be eager to play with an egg, Martin Gardner teaches them how in order to convey scientific knowledge in easily understandable terms.

11   The best of all scientific tricks with an egg is the well-known one in which air pressure forces a peeled hard-boiled egg into a glass milk bottle and then forces it out again undamaged. The mouth of the bottle must be only slightly smaller than the egg, and so you must be careful not to use too large an egg or too small a bottle. It is impossible to push the egg into the bottle. To get the egg through the mouth you must heat the air in the bottle. That is best done by standing the bottle in boiling water for a few minutes. Put the egg upright on the mouth and take the bottle off the stove. As the air in the bottle cools it contracts, creating a partial vacuum that draws the peeled egg inside. To get the egg out again invert the bottle so the egg falls into the neck. Place the opening of the bottle against your mouth and blow vigorously. This will compress the air in the bottle. When you stop blowing, the air expands, pushing the egg through the neck of the bottle and into your waiting hands.   —**MARTIN GARDNER,** "Mathematical Games"

(4) Showing cause or effect establishes why something happens or what it results in.

Writers who explore causes raise the question *Why?* and must answer it to the satisfaction of their audience. Be sure to avoid the fallacy of assuming that since one event precedes another it necessarily caused it. (See **35h(8)**, false cause.) Paragraph 12 provides several reasons why drinking remains popular on many college campuses. The author is a dean who wants his audience to support programs designed to reduce alcohol abuse. By listing some of the reasons why such programs can fail, he establishes that his goal will not be easily achieved.

12   Regrettably, certain realities impede the process of educating the young about the dangers of alcohol. First, the vast majority of young adults feel invulnerable. Second, learning in the abstract has little relationship to actual behavior. Third, as we seek to educate about alcohol we are focused not so much on imparting knowledge as we are, in effect, trying to change attitudes, and we all know how difficult that is in people of any age.

                                              —DAVID WINER, "Drinking on Campus:
                                            An Old Practice That Begs for New Solutions"

Writers can also demonstrate effects, as in paragraph 13, which discusses some results of protecting an endangered species.

13   The alligator's turnaround since that time has made national news. Protection and strict controls on interstate shipment of gator hides have worked: the animals have come back strong. Every so often, one will eat a poodle or take up residence in the water hazard on the sixteenth hole. Fish-and-game people are then called out to lasso the uncomprehending reptile and move it to an out-of-the-way place. There is even some limited commerce again in the skins. At least one entrepreneur is ranching alligators, just as though they were cattle or mink. Not long ago, someone in Florida was killed by an alligator in what I suspect must have been a well-deserved attack. —GEOFFREY NORMAN, "Gators"

(5) Comparing or contrasting helps readers see similarities or differences.

A comparison points out similarities, and a contrast points out differences. When drafting, consider whether a comparison would help your readers see a relationship that they might otherwise miss or whether a contrast would establish useful distinctions. When writing a definition, for example, you might help readers by showing how a word or phrase differs from language that seems similar.

When writing to explain cultural differences that continue to cause misunderstanding in our country, Arthur L. Campa contrasts the values of English and Spanish colonizers in paragraph 14.

14   Anglo-American culture was absolutist at the onset; that is, all the dominant values were considered identical for all, regardless of time and place. Such values as justice, charity, and honesty were considered the superior social order for all men and were later embodied in the American Constitution. The Spaniard brought with him a relativistic viewpoint and saw fewer moral implications in man's actions. Values were looked upon as the result of social and economic conditions.

—**ARTHUR L. CAMPA,** "Anglo vs. Chicano: Why?"

Two valuable kinds of comparisons are **metaphor** and **analogy.** A **metaphor** is a figure of speech. (See **20a(4)**.) An **analogy,** often used in argument, makes a point by comparing a complex or unfamiliar concept to a simple or familiar one or by comparing two familiar concepts that are not ordinarily thought to be similar. In paragraph 15, Nelson Mandela draws an analogy between leadership and gardening.

15   In some ways, I saw the garden as a metaphor for certain aspects of my life. A leader must also tend his garden; he, too, plants seed, and then watches, cultivates, and harvests the result. Like the gardener, a leader must take responsibility for what he cultivates;

he must mind his work, try to repel enemies, preserve what can be preserved, and eliminate what cannot succeed.

—NELSON MANDELA, "Raising Tomatoes and Leading People"

However, it is important that you do not assume that because two things are alike in some ways that they are alike in all ways. (See 35h(6), false analogy.)

(6) Classifying or dividing material can give order to it.

To classify is to categorize things in large groups that share certain common characteristics. **Classification** is a way to understand or explain a subject by establishing how it fits within a category or group. For example, a book reviewer might classify a new novel as a mystery—leading readers to expect a plot that inspires suspense. **Division,** however, breaks objects and ideas into smaller parts and examines the relationships among them. Divided into chapters, a novel can also be discussed by focusing on such components as plot, setting, and theme (see 39a).

Classification and division represent two different perspectives; ideas can be put into groups (classification) or split into subclasses (division) on the basis of a dividing principle. Classification and division often work together. As in paragraph 16, they help clarify differences.

16   To ensure a safe and productive workplace, as well as to protect their companies from liability, managers need to understand that sexual harassment can take different forms. In a *quid pro quo* case, sexual favors are extorted through a threat: "Yield to my demands or you will be penalized." Harassment of this kind is clearly against the law, as is any activity that can be classified as "hostile environment." If an employee can demonstrate that she or he has been subjected to a series of incidents in which lewd language or gestures are used to intimidate and management has failed to intervene, your company can be liable for damages. Other

complaints, which fall under "offensive behavior," may or may not be redressable under the law but still require prompt and thoughtful responses from management.

—SARAH DETTINGER, "Sexual Harassment in the Workplace"

(7) Defining an important term clarifies meaning.

By defining a concept, a term, or an object, writers increase clarity and focus discussion. Definition locates a concept, a term, or an object in a class and then differentiates it from other members of that class: "A concerto [the term] is a symphonic piece [the class] performed by one or more solo instruments and orchestra [the difference]." The difference distinguishes the term from all other members of the class. Paragraph 17 defines volcanos by putting them into a class ("landforms") and by distinguishing them ("built of molten material") from other members of that class. The definition is then clarified by examples.

17   Volcanos are landforms built of molten material that has spewed out onto the earth's surface. Such molten rock is called lava. Volcanos may be no larger than small hills, or thousands of feet high. All have a characteristic cone shape. Some well-known mountains are actually volcanos. Examples are Mt. Fuji (Japan), Mt. Lassen (California), Mt. Hood (Oregon), Mt. Etna and Mt. Vesuvius (Italy), and Paricutín (Mexico). The Hawaiian Islands are all immense volcanos whose summits rise above the ocean, and these volcanos are still quite active.

—JOEL AREM, "Rocks and Minerals"

Definitions can be clarified and extended by details and examples, as in paragraph 17, or by synonyms and etymology (the history of the word). Synonyms are often only one or two words enclosed in commas immediately following the term.

Sophomores, second-year students, derive their name from two Greek words meaning "wise fool."

Use these strategies to make your essay as a whole more understandable to your audience. Make sure, however, that you are using them to support your thesis and purpose. If a paragraph or two devoted to definition or another mode is contributing to the main idea of your draft, then it is contributing to development. If you added these paragraphs simply because you ran out of other things to say or wish to demonstrate a pattern of organization, then you will probably need to drop them as you revise the essay as a whole (see chapter 33).

32f   Your first draft allows you to continue exploring your topic and to clarify what you think.

Get your ideas down quickly. Spelling, punctuation, and usage are not as important in the first draft as they are in the final one. Your first draft may be disappointing, but it gives you something you can improve on later. If you are not sure how to begin, you could start by simply stating your thesis and the main points you hope to cover. Similarly, you could conclude by restating your thesis or summarizing your main points. Later, when you revise this first draft, you can experiment with other ways of introducing and concluding an essay (see 33a(4–5)).

Keep your plan in mind as you draft. If you find yourself losing track of where you want to go, stop writing and reread what you have. You may need to revise your plan, or you may simply need to reorient yourself. If you are stuck and do not know what to write next, referring to your plan can help.

Instead of letting a snag cause you to stop drafting, you could move ahead in your plan and write paragraphs that will appear later; the intervening material may occur to you if you keep on writing. For example, if you have trouble writing the introduction, start with a supporting idea you feel sure of and write until you reach a stopping point. When you are actually writing, you will probably think more efficiently. You can then move on to another part that will be easy to write—another supporting idea or even the conclusion. What is important is to begin writing, to write as quickly as you can, and to save your early work so that you can refer to it as you revise (see chapter 33).

Although some writers like to draft in longhand, using a word processing program when drafting offers distinct advantages: You can easily move from drafting one part to another, knowing that you can scroll up or down when drafting generates new ideas. And when you save a draft in an electronic file, you are well positioned for revising your work later.

Finally, bear in mind that writing is a form of thinking. As you draft, you are likely to discover that you had more to say than you realized. If you are confident in your plan, you may choose to suppress any idea that is not directly related to what you had intended to cover. Writers often benefit, however, from developing an unexpected idea. When drafting leads you to a place you did not intend to visit, give yourself permission to explore if you sense that you are making a useful discovery. You can consider how to integrate this material into your plan when you prepare to revise, or you may simply choose to delete it.

E X E R C I S E 5

Write a one-page description of the process you usually follow when planning and drafting an essay. Then write a second page reporting how satisfied you are with the results of the process. Indicate what seems to work for you and what you might need to change.

Chapter 33

Revising and Editing Essays

To **revise** means "to see again." This activity, which is at the heart of writing well, implies that you take a fresh look at your draft—rethinking what you have written and what you still need to write by distancing yourself from your work and evaluating it from a reader's point of view. To **edit** means to polish a piece of writing by making word choice more precise (**20a**), prose more concise (chapter **21**), and sentence structure more effective (chapters **29** and **30**), in addition to eliminating any errors in grammar, punctuation, and mechanics. Although revising and editing can overlap, they are essentially very different activities. Inexperienced writers sometimes think they are revising when they are really editing. Most writers need to do both.

Revising usually comes before editing. This does not mean that you cannot correct errors as you move along, especially if doing so makes you more confident or comfortable. But the more time and energy you invest in editing early on, the harder it may be to make major changes that would enrich your essay. When something looks perfect on the surface, it can be tempting not to touch it. Even if you do some editing as you draft, you should be willing to rearrange paragraphs and make significant cuts and additions as you revise.

This chapter will help you revise and edit your essays by discussing how to

- consider your work as a whole (**33a(1–2)**),
- evaluate your tone (**33a(3)**),
- write a good introduction (**33a(4)**),
- write a good conclusion (**33a(5)**),
- choose an appropriate title (**33a(6)**),

- work effectively in a writing group (**33b**),
- edit to improve style (**33c**), and
- proofread to eliminate errors (**33d**).

33a   Revision is essential to good writing.

In one way or another you revise throughout the writing process. For example, even in the earliest planning stages, as you consider a possible subject and then discard it in favor of another, you are revising. Similarly, after choosing a subject, you might decide to change your focus or emphasize some new part of it. That, too, is a kind of revision. And, of course, you are revising when you realize that a sentence or a paragraph you have just written does not belong where it is, so you delete or move it.

Nevertheless, experienced writers usually revise after they have completed a draft—no matter how much they may have revised while planning and drafting. They not only revise certain sentences and paragraphs, but also they review the draft *as a whole.* Although some writers do so immediately after drafting, while their minds are still fully engaged by their topic, they also usually benefit from setting their draft aside for a time so that later they can see their work more objectively. Whenever possible, plan your writing process so that you can put a draft aside, at least overnight, and then see it later with fresh eyes.

Because revision is an ongoing process, writers often print several different versions when composing with a computer. By labeling each version—or at least dating each hard copy—you can keep track of how your work is evolving.

---

(1) Everything on the page benefits from reconsideration.

When you review your essay as a whole, ask yourself whether your main point comes through clearly and whether you ever digress from it. (See 32c.) Writers frequently get off track as they generate ideas through the act of writing. Now is the time to eliminate those side trips. It is also wise to make sure you are developing a point rather than simply repeating the same thing in different words—or, as sometimes happens, contradicting yourself by saying two very different things.

Revising also demands paying close attention to the needs and expectations of your readers. (See 32a(2).) Have you provided examples or other details that will interest your audience? Are your ideas clearly expressed in language appropriate for that audience? Will your audience understand the purpose of your essay? In other words, revising successfully requires that you examine your work both as a writer and as a reader. As a writer, you must ask yourself whether you have succeeded in saying what you wanted to say. As a reader, you must ask yourself whether what is clear to you will also be clear to your audience.

Moreover, you should examine your paragraphs to make sure they are unified, coherent, and well developed (see chapter 31). Assess how well each paragraph leads to the next, whether you need to rearrange any, and whether your transitions are effective (see 31b(4)).

CAUTION When you move or delete paragraphs, check to see whether your new arrangement works and whether you need to write new transitions.

(2) What is not on the page can be even more important than what is there.

One of the most challenging tasks in revision is to see whether you have left out something that your audience might expect or that would strengthen your essay as a whole. Your best ideas will not always surface in your first draft; you will sometimes have an important new idea only after you have finished your draft and taken a good look at it. No matter how good a draft looks, ask yourself whether something is missing.

Inexperienced writers sometimes end an essay prematurely because they cannot think of anything else to say. One way to get past this block is to use such strategies as listing and questioning (pages 405–08). Another way is to share your work with others and ask them to let you know whether there is anything they find confusing or want to know more about (see 33b).

(3) Your tone helps you fulfill your purpose.

Tone reflects your attitude toward your subject and must be appropriate to your purpose, audience, and context. When revising, experienced writers consider how they sound. They may find that they sound confident and fair minded and decide that this is exactly how they want to present themselves. They may also discover that they sound sarcastic, angry, apologetic, arrogant, or bored and then decide to change their tone when they revise. Writers who sound arrogant or bored are unlikely to impress readers favorably, but almost any other tone can be effective at times. Your challenge, when revising, is to make sure that your tone contributes to how you want your readers to respond. Although humor might be effective in an argument designed to persuade others to stop eating junk food, it would be offensive in a report on world hunger.

Consider the difference in tone between the following two writers, both of whom are trying to persuade people to support capital punishment. Paragraph 1 is from a successful journalist who amused and provoked readers of his newspaper column, while paragraph 2 is from a book by a university professor. Both are discussing what they learned from Aristotle about anger and revenge. (For ease of reference, each of the sample paragraphs in this chapter is numbered.)

1   A keeps a store and has a bookkeeper, B. B steals $700, employs it in playing at dice or bingo, and is wiped out. What is A to do? Let B go? If he does he will be unable to sleep at night. The sense of injury, of injustice, of frustration will haunt him like pruritus. So he turns B over to the police, and they hustle B to prison. Thereafter A can sleep. More, he has pleasant dreams. He pictures B chained to the wall of a dungeon a hundred feet underground, devoured by rats and scorpions. It is so agreeable it makes him forget his $700. He has got his *katharsis.*

—**H. L. MENCKEN,** "The Penalty of Death"

2   Anger is expressed or manifested on those occasions when someone has acted in a manner that is thought to be unjust, and one of its origins is the opinion that men are responsible, and should be held responsible, for what they do. Thus, as Aristotle teaches us, anger is accompanied not only by the pain caused by the one who is the object of anger, but by the pleasure arising from the expectation of inflicting revenge on someone who is thought to deserve it. [. . .] Anger is somehow connected with justice, and it is this that modern penology has not understood; it tends, on the whole, to regard anger as a selfish indulgence.

—**WALTER BERNS,** *For Capital Punishment*

When Peter Geske revised the first draft reprinted later in this chapter (pages 445–47), he decided to change his tone after one of his readers commented that he sounded sarcastic and another commented on his anger. Although sounding angry or sarcastic might be appropriate in some rhetorical situations (see 32a), Peter felt that he sounded harsher than he intended.

EXERCISE 1

A. Reread the passages by H. L. Mencken and Walter Berns and then write a short analysis of how these men sound. Be sure to identify specific words or phrases that led you to attribute this tone to them.
B. Study the first draft of Peter Geske's essay (pages 445–47) and then study his final version (pages 457–60). Write a short paper comparing the tone of these two versions.

(4) Introductions establish an essay's topic and capture the attention of readers.

An effective introduction arouses a reader's interest and indicates the subject and tone of the essay (see **32b** and **33a(3)**). For long or complex essays especially, a good introduction also charts the direction the essay will follow so that readers know what to expect.

Introductions have no set length; they can be as brief as a couple of sentences or as long as a couple of paragraphs or more. Although introductions appear first in the essay, experienced writers may compose them at any time during the writing process. Moreover, introductions often change when writers revise. Because getting started can be difficult, writers sometimes draft openings that are inefficient, misleading, or dull. When they study what they have drafted, they usually find ways to introduce their ideas more effectively. The introduction often contains the thesis statement (see **32c**), which may need to be clarified through revision. Writers must also decide how to locate the thesis statement within an introduction that leads to it or develops it.

You can arouse the interest of your audience by writing introductions in a number of ways.

(a) Start with an interesting fact or unusual detail.

3   A new Census Bureau report predicts that there will be 383 million Americans in the year 2050. That's 128 million more than there are now, and 83 million more than the bureau was predicting just four years ago, when it appeared that the U.S. population would peak and stabilize at around 300 million.

—**MICHAEL KINSLEY**, "Gatecrashers"

(b) Use an intriguing statement.

4   After smiling brilliantly for nearly four decades, I now find myself trying to quit. Or, at the very least, seeking to lower the wattage a bit.   —**AMY CUNNINGHAM**, "Why Women Smile"

(c) Open with an anecdote.

5   As I walked out the street entrance to my newly rented apartment, a guy in maroon high-tops and a skateboard haircut approached, making kissing noises and saying, "Hi, gorgeous." Three weeks earlier, I would have assessed the degree of malice and made ready to run or tell him to bug off, depending. But now, instead, I smiled, and so did my four-year-old daughter, because after dozens of similar encounters I understood he didn't mean me but *her.*

—BARBARA KINGSOLVER, "Somebody's Baby"

(d) Begin with a question your essay will answer.

6   In a series of futuristic commercials, AT&T paints a liberating picture of your not-too-distant life, when the information superhighway will be an instrument of personal freedom and a servant to your worldly needs and desires. But is the future of cyberspace really so elegant, so convenient? Or does it represent a serious threat to your privacy and your freedom?

—ERIK NESS, "BigBrother@cyberspace"

(e) Start with an appropriate quotation.

7   When the Reverend Jerry Falwell learned that the Supreme Court had reversed his $200,000 judgment against *Hustler* magazine for the emotional distress he had suffered from an outrageous parody, his response was typical of those who seek to censor speech: "Just as no person may scream 'Fire!' in a crowded theater when there is no fire, and find cover under the First Amendment, likewise, no sleazy merchant like Larry Flynt should be able to use the First Amendment as an excuse for maliciously and dishonestly attacking public figures, as he has so often done."

—ALAN DERSHOWITZ, "Shouting 'Fire!'"

(f) Open with an illustration.

8   Libby Smith knows what it is like to be a victim of gay bashing. First, there were the harassing telephone calls to her home. Then, one evening last March as she went to get her book bag out

of a locker at the University of Wisconsin at Eau Claire, she was attacked by two men.

—MARY CRYSTAL CAGE, "Gay Bashing on Campus"

(g) Begin with general information about the subject or show how you came to choose it.

9   Anyone new to the experience of owning a lawn, as I am, soon figures out that there is more at stake here than a patch of grass. A lawn immediately establishes a certain relationship with one's neighbors and, by extension, the larger American landscape. Mowing the lawn, I realized the first time I gazed into my neighbor's yard and imagined him gazing back into mine, is a civic responsibility. —MICHAEL POLLAN, "Why Mow? The Case Against Lawns"

(h) Simply state your thesis.

10   Even today, when the American landscape is becoming more and more homogeneous, there is really no such thing as an all-American style of dress. A shopping center in Maine may superficially resemble one in Georgia or California, but the shoppers in it will look different, because the diverse histories of these states have left their mark on costume.

—ALISON LURIE, "American Regional Costume"

Whatever type of introduction you choose to write, use your opening paragraph to indicate your subject, engage readers' attention, and establish your credibility (see **35d**).

(5) An effective conclusion helps readers understand the most important points of an essay or why those points are significant.

When revising, consider whether your draft ends abruptly or seems to trail off. Writers sometimes stop drafting before they have come to a conclusion that draws their ideas together. On other occasions, they sometimes go on too long—drafting additional paragraphs after what is, in effect, the end of the essay or paper in terms of its focus (see 32b). An essay should not merely stop; it should finish. Some suggestions follow.

(a) Conclude by rephrasing the thesis.

11   Such considerations make it clear that it's time for schools to choose between real amateurism and real professionalism. They can't have a little of both. From now on, in college sports, it's got to be poetry or pros.   —LOUIS BARBASH, "Clean Up or Pay Up"

(b) Direct attention to larger issues.

12   My antibody status does not matter to you. Certainly it matters—with absolute enormity—to me. But what I'd like you to remember is the blood on the subway, the click of the refrigerator door, the woman in black so elegant and uneasy, First Avenue at gritty, gorgeous dusk, the brilliance of that bad art in the examining room, the pores of the doctor's face—all of them declaring, by their very existence: As long and as well as you can, live, live.

—DAVID GROFF, "Taking the Test"

(c) Encourage your readers to change their attitudes or to alter their actions.

13   Our medical care system is in trouble and getting worse. While the experts try to figure out how to achieve utopian goals at affordable prices, let's do something practical about the suffering on our doorsteps. Primary care is the most affordable safety net we can offer our citizens. By all means, let's continue the debate about universal, comprehensive insurance to cover all medical costs, but, in the meantime, let's provide primary health care to all uninsured Americans—now!

—GORDON T. MOORE, "Caring for the Uninsured and Underinsured"

(d) Conclude with a summary of the main points covered.

14   Viewed in this light, Josef Mengele emerges as he really was: a visionary ideologue, an efficiently murderous functionary, a diligent careerist—and disturbingly human.

—ROBERT JAY LIFTON, "What Made This Man?"

(e) **Clinch or stress the importance of the central idea by referring in some way to the introduction.**

Introduction

15   I read *The National Enquirer* when I want to feel exhilarated about life's possibilities. It tells me of a world where miracles still occur. In the world of *The National Enquirer,* UFOs flash over the Bermuda Triangle, cancer cures are imminent, ancient film stars at last find love that is for keeps. Reached on The Other Side by spiritualists, Clark Gable urges America to keep its chin up. Of all possible worlds, I like the world of *The National Enquirer* best. [. . .]

Conclusion

16   So I whoop with glee when a new edition of *The National Enquirer* hits the newsstands and step into the world where Gable can cheer me up from The Other Side.

—**RUSSELL BAKER,** "Magazine Rack"

Whatever strategy you choose, provide readers with a sense of closure. Bear in mind that they may be wondering, "So what? Why have you told me all this?" Your conclusion gives you an opportunity to respond to that concern. If there is any chance that readers may not understand your purpose, use your conclusion to clarify why you asked them to read what they have just read (see 36e(6)).

(6) A good title fits the subject and tone of an essay.

The title is the reader's first impression and, like the introduction, should fit the subject and tone of the paper. Writers who are confident that they have chosen a subject likely to interest their audience might choose a title that simply announces their topic: "How to Pay for a Good College" or "The Art of the Nap." Other writers might draw attention with a title that involves a play on words, as in "Cents and Sensibility" or

"Dressed to Thrill." A good title could also take the form of a question designed to arouse the reader's curiosity, as does "Who Killed the Bog Men of Denmark? And Why?"

Some writers like to choose a title before they draft because they find that a good title helps clarify their direction. Others choose the title later in the writing process. Whenever you decide to title your essay, a good way to begin is to try condensing your thesis statement without becoming too general. Reread your introduction and conclusion, and examine key words and phrases for possible titles. Try to work in some indication of your attitude and approach. And when revising your essay as a whole, consider whether you need to revise your title as well.

E X E R C I S E 2

Choose an article or chapter from a work you recently read, and evaluate the introduction and conclusion. What writing strategies do they reveal, and how effective are they? Write an alternative introduction and conclusion using different strategies.

CHECKLIST for Revising Essays

- Is the purpose of the work clear (32a(1))? Does the work stick to its purpose?

- Does the essay address the appropriate audience (32a(2))?

- Is the tone (33a(3)) appropriate for the purpose, audience, and context?

- Is the subject focused (32b(2))?

- Does the essay make a clear point (32c)? Is this point well supported? Do the relationships expressed in the essay clearly relate to this point?

- Is each paragraph unified and coherent (31a and 31b)? Are the paragraphs arranged in a logical, effective order (31d)? (See the paragraph checklist on page 386.)

- Does the essay follow an effective method or combination of methods of development (32e)?

- Is the introduction effective (33a(4))?

- Is the conclusion appropriate for the essay's purpose (33a(5))?

33b Writers benefit from sharing their work with others.

Because writing is a form of communication, writers benefit from checking to see whether they are communicating their ideas effectively. When they consult with readers and ask for honest responses to their work, writers usually gain a clearer sense of how they can improve their drafts.

(1) Clearly defined evaluation standards help both writers and reviewers.

Whether working in a writing group or with a single reader such as a tutor or your instructor, it is important to have agreed-on evaluation standards that are understood by all concerned. Without such an understanding, you may get advice that is inappropriate or unhelpful.

Instructors usually indicate their evaluation standards in class, on assignment sheets, or in separate handouts. Being mindful of these standards when reviewing a draft is essential. For example, if your instructor has told you that he or she will be evaluating the paper in question primarily in terms

of whether you have a clear thesis (32c) and adequate support for it (36c(2)), you could be at risk if you ignore these
criteria because you are focusing on sentence length and variety (chapter 30) or on whether or not you have a good title
(33a(6)).

While working with the evaluation criteria that have already
been indicated for an assignment, writing groups must often
negotiate how to use their time efficiently and productively so
that every member of the group gets help within a limited time
period. Groups often benefit from reviewing evaluation criteria at the beginning of a working session and using them to indicate where they should focus their attention. Writers who raise
specific concerns about their drafts (see 33b(2)) that are clearly
related to the assignment in question can also help focus the
group's attention.

If your instructor asks you to develop your evaluation criteria, or if you are working within an independent writing group
that gathers outside the classroom, the checklist on pages
439–40 can help you get started. Using it as a draft, you would
then need to establish which issues deserve priority and whether
there are any others that need to be added.

(2) You can help readers review your work by telling them about your purpose and your concerns.

When submitting a draft for review, you can increase the
chances of getting the kind of help you want by introducing
your work and indicating what your concerns are. You can do
so orally within a writing group that has gathered to review
drafts. Or when this is not possible, you can attach a cover letter—sometimes called a "writer's memo"—to your draft. In either case, adopting the following model can help your reviewers give you useful responses.

Topic and purpose	Tell your readers what your topic is, why you have chosen it, and what you hope to accomplish by writing about it. Indicate your thesis (see **32c**), and explain in a sentence or two why you have taken this position. Providing this information gives readers useful direction.
Strengths	Identify those parts of the draft that you are confident about. Doing so directs attention away from any area that you do not want to discuss and saves time for all concerned.
Concerns	Being clear about your concerns is essential to effective problem solving. Let your readers know exactly what kind of help you want from them. For example, if you are worried about your conclusion, say so. Or if you are afraid that one of your paragraphs may not fit the focus of the draft as a whole, direct attention to that paragraph in particular. You are most likely to get useful help when you ask for the kind of help you want, and indicating your concerns tells readers that it is safe to discuss them with you.

When given orally, an orientation along these lines should take only a minute or two. In a cover letter, a single page consisting of three paragraphs should be sufficient.

(3) When you submit a draft for peer review, some responses may be more helpful than others.

When you write about your ideas, you are putting part of yourself on paper. So hearing honest criticism of those ideas can be difficult. Even experienced writers sometimes feel anxious when they submit their work for evaluation.

Before asking for responses to a draft you are planning to revise, it can be useful to remind both your readers and yourself that the work in question is *only a draft*. You may know this, and your readers may know this, but saying it out loud is helpful because the message signals readers that it is safe for them to criticize and reassures you that these readers are responding to a piece that is not yet finished.

Some readers may retreat into silence because they do not know what to say or settle for identifying a minor error in order to look as if they are being helpful. Others may be unnecessarily assertive, giving you more advice than you had bargained for and insisting that you follow it. But if you allow yourself to hear what other people have to say about your work, more often than not you will get helpful responses.

When reading or listening to responses to a draft, try not to become defensive. If you cut other people off, you may miss the advice that could have been the most useful to you. After your reviewers have finished, however, you are responsible for evaluating the responses you received—rejecting those that would take you in a direction you do not want to pursue and honoring those that would help you fulfill your purpose (see 32a). Remind yourself that you are the author of the draft in question and that you get the final say about what goes into an essay with your name on it. And it's a rare writer who pleases everyone.

(4) You can help other writers by giving a thoughtful response to their work.

When you are asked to read a draft written by someone else, ask what concerns the writer has about it. Read the draft carefully before you respond—at least twice, if time allows. When you respond, be specific. Be sure to respond to the concerns the writer has expressed. If you see other problems in the draft, ask whether the writer wants to know about them. Praise whatever the writer has done well, and identify what you think could be improved. In either case, draw attention to passages that illustrate what you mean.

Whenever possible, frame your comments as a personal response rather than as a universal judgment. For example, if you tell a writer, "Your second page is confusing," you are putting yourself in the position of speaking for all readers. If, on the other hand, you say, "I have trouble following your organization on page two," you alert the writer to a potential problem while speaking only for yourself.

Remember that it is possible to be honest without being unkind. You will not be helping a writer if you ignore problems in a draft you are reviewing. On the other hand, dwelling on every problem and insisting that another writer follow all of your advice can also be unhelpful. In this case, the writer may feel that you are taking over. Help others write the papers they want to write, not the paper you want to write.

(5) Peer review usually improves as writers gain experience and build trust.

After freewriting, listing, and organizing his ideas into a working plan (see 32d), Peter Geske submitted the following draft for review by other students three weeks into an introductory composition class. His assignment was to write an essay (of approximately one thousand words) evaluating how well his high school education had prepared him for college. His audience was defined as "the class": twenty-four students, most of whom were working either full- or part-time and commuting to school from diverse sites in a large metropolitan area. Because the students in his group were having their first experience with peer review and were working without agreed-on evaluation criteria, they were able to give Peter only limited help. Although the comments that follow his draft are not ideal, they represent the range of responses you might receive in a similar situation. As writing groups gain experience and members employ the strategies outlined in 33b(1–4), responses usually become more helpful.

As you read this draft, remember that it is only the first draft. Revisions of this draft are reprinted later in this chapter.

Peter Geske
English 101, sec. 2
                    High School
     In today's society education is becoming
more and more important. The children of
today need education to get good jobs and
keep up with this fast paced modern society.
Nobody ever explained this to my teachers
though. High school was the worst. The
teachers at my school were losers and didn't
know what they were doing. The building was
falling apart also and their was alot of
violence in it.
     Central was built about a hundred years
ago and that's probably the last time it got
a coat of paint. The walls were cracked and
we used to flick off loose paint chips all
the time. On the outside it looked like a
prison. It used to have big windows but they
got bricked up to save energy. There was
also graffiti all over the place. No trees
anywhere but plenty of broken cement and
crumbling asphalt.

The school had at least twice as many kids squeezed into it than it was designed for. Even with plenty of people cutting to party, every classroom was crowded. Sometimes at the beginning of the year there wasn't even a desk for everyone. Computers were a joke. We had one small lab for two thousand students and they were these old machines that you couldn't run good programs on. If you wanted to use the internet you had to go to the library and there was always somebody else using the terminal there which was the only one in the school with access to the Web.

Science equipment was also bad. I really hated my chemistry teacher but maybe she wouldn't of been so bad if we had a decent lab.

Once you got past your sophomore year you could do pretty much what you wanted to. You were supposed to take English every year and you had to take math and science too. You also had to take blow off courses you could sleep through like social problems where Mr. Thorp used to talk about the problems his kids were having and how students today aren't as good as they used to be. But juniors and seniors could take lots of electives and you could pass your English requirement by reading science fiction or taking a course where you did nothing but watch tapes on a VCR.

The teachers were the worst. They couldn't control their classes and everybody took advantage of that. Mr. Kleinberg was my geometry teacher. He wore these green socks everyday and I swear it was always the same pair. When you got close to him it was really gross he smelled so bad. Kids never paid attention to him and he would usually start screaming at one person while knives were being pulled in another corner and other kids were strung out on drugs. My chemistry teacher was just as bad. Her name was Mrs. Fiorelli and she was real skinny. All she would ever do was read from the textbook. Her class was out of control also and when somebody would try to ask a question she would just keep on reading. She gave these killer tests though and I ended up flunking her course not that I need to know chemistry for anything.

It wasn't all bad though. Mr. Rodriguez taught American history and he was cool. He tied the textbook to current events which made it more interesting and also was good about giving extra help. My English teacher sophomore year was also ok. I liked some of the books we read and getting the chance to be creative.

This is just my opinion. There might be other kids who had a good experience at Central and maybe someday I'll laugh about it.

CAUTION The preceding paper is an early draft. Do not consider it a model essay. It is reprinted here so that you can see how it improved through revision. For later versions of this paper, see pages 450–52 and 457–60.

Here are some of the comments Peter received when he distributed this draft to other students without indicating whether he had any specific questions or concerns about it. Before revising, Peter had to weigh these comments and decide for himself which were the most useful.

Good paper! I think you should say more about science equipment though because that paragraph is so short. Also you mention your chemistry teacher in that paragraph and then talk about her again later on. Maybe keep all the chemistry stuff together

I really liked your paper especially the description of Mr. Kleinberg because I could really picture him. Great details! I had a teacher just like that. His name was Mr. Percovich, and he couldn't control his class either. I had him for biology my junior year. I hated him!

The only thing that bothered me about your paper is how you mention teachers first and then the building in your first paragraph, but then you talk about the building first in your paper. You should improve your organization.

Great paper! I wouldn't change a thing!

I really liked how you draw attention to bad teaching and overcrowded schools. These are important problems. But I think you need to add a thesis statement at the end of your first paragraph. Also, you sound kind of sarcastic when you pick on the personal appearance of your math and science teachers. Was that really a big issue for you?

You sound like you really care about this topic, and that made me care too. Are you sure you want to sound so angry though? And I get kind of confused at the end. You come on so strong through the whole paper and then you back off in your conclusion. The last paragraph didn't work for me because it sounds like you are apologizing for writing the paper.

EXERCISE 3

Reread "High School" and the comments it received. Identify the comments that you think are the most useful and then add two of your own.

EXERCISE 4

Compose an evaluation sheet, with specific questions and guidelines, that could help other students provide useful responses when asked to provide peer review in a writing course.

After Peter Geske had time to reconsider his first draft and to think about the responses he received from readers, he made a number of changes. Here is what his paper looked like midway through its revision. (For his final draft, see pages 457–60.)

Peter Geske

English 101, sec. 2

High School *Title?*

In today's society education is becoming more and more important. The children of today need education to get good jobs and keep up with this fast paced modern society. Nobody ever explained this to my teachers though. High school was the worst. The teachers at my school were losers and didn't know what they were doing. *Picture a building that looks like a run-down warehouse or prison. That's what my high school looked like.* The building was falling apart also and their was alot of violence in it. *Standards were so low that I learned very little and became discouraged about school.*

Central was built about a hundred years ago and that's probably the last time it got a coat of paint. The walls were cracked and we used to flick off loose paint chips all the time. On the outside it looked like a prison. It used to have big windows but they got bricked up to save energy. There was also graffiti all over the place. There were No trees anywhere but plenty of broken cement and crumbling asphalt. *First outside then in* *Inside combine somehow*

move up The school had at least twice as many kids squeezed into it than it was designed for. Even with plenty of people cutting to party, every classroom was crowded *over because* . Sometimes at the beginning of the year there wasn't even a desk for everyone. Computers were a joke. We had one small lab for two thousand students and they were these old machines *Make a new paragraph on equipment?*

that you couldn't run good programs on. If you wanted to use the internet you had to go to the library and there was always somebody else using the terminal there which was the only one in the school with access to the Web.

Science equipment was also bad. I really hated my chemistry teacher but maybe she wouldn't of been so bad if we had a decent lab.

add to teacher paragraph

have

Once you got past your sophomore year you could do pretty much what you wanted to. You were supposed to take English every year and you had to take math and science too. You also had to take blow off courses you could sleep through like social problems where Mr. Thorp used to talk about the problems his kids were having and how students today aren't as good as they used to be. But juniors and seniors could take lots of electives and you could pass your English requirement by reading science fiction or taking a course where you did nothing but watch tapes on a VCR.

Save this?

The teachers were the worst. They couldn't control their classes and everybody took advantage of that. Mr. Kleinberg was my geometry teacher. He wore these green socks everyday and I swear it was always the same pair. When you got close to him it was really gross he smelled so bad. Kids never paid attention to him and he would usually start screaming at one person while knives were being pulled in another corner and other kids were strung out on drugs. My

because her chemistry teacher put her to sleep? science together!

nodding off from

chemistry teacher, ~~was~~ just as bad. Her name
was Mrs. Fiorelli, and she was real skinny. ~never did anything~ ~except~
~All she would ever do was~ read from the text-
book. Her class was out of control also and
when somebody would try to ask a question
she would just keep on reading. She gave
these killer tests ~~though~~ and I ended up
~~flunking~~ *failing* her course not ~~that~~ *because I learned so little in it* ~~I need to know~~
~~chemistry for anything.~~

It wasn't all bad though. Mr. Rodriguez *who*
taught American history ~~and he~~ was ~~cool. He~~
~~tied the textbook to~~ current events which
made it more interesting ~~and~~ also was good
about giving extra help. *Mrs. Sullivan who taught* My English teacher *creative writing* *good*
sophomore year was also ok. I liked some of
the books we read and getting the chance to
be creative. *But these were the exceptions to the rule.*

As I look back on my high school years, I am amazed that I learned ~~This is just my opinion. There might be~~
anything except how to party. Now that I am in college, I wish I had gone to a ~~other kids who had a good experience at~~
better high school. ~~Central and maybe someday I'll laugh about~~
~~it.~~

33c Editing makes ideas clearer and more engaging by refining the style in which they are presented.

After you are satisfied with the revised structure of your essay
and the content of your paragraphs, edit individual sentences
for clarity, effectiveness, and variety (see chapters 22 through
30). Consider combining choppy or unconnected sentences and

reworking long, overly complicated ones. If you overuse some structures, say, introductory prepositional phrases, try to experiment with other patterns. Eliminate any needless shifts in grammatical structures, tone, style, or point of view.

Examine your diction, and make sure the words you have used are the best choices for this particular essay. If any words leap out as much more formal or informal than your language as a whole, replace them with words that are more consistent with your style. Eliminate any unnecessary words (see chapter 21). If you have experimented with words new to your vocabulary, make sure that you have used them accurately.

Check whether your punctuation is correct and whether you have followed standard conventions for mechanics. Even if you have already used a spell checker (see 18a), use it again because new errors may have been introduced in the revision process. Remember also that such programs are never foolproof. Double-check that you are using words like *there* and *their* or *who's* and *whose* correctly—and remember that even words that you have spelled correctly might be the wrong words in a specific sentence.

CHECKLIST for Editing

Sentences

• Are ideas related effectively through subordination and coordination (24)?

• Are all sentences unified (23)?

• Do any sentences contain misplaced parts or dangling modifiers (25)?

• Is there any faulty parallelism (26)?

- Are there any needless shifts in grammatical structures, in tone, or in style (27)?

- Are ideas given appropriate emphasis within each sentence (29)?

- Are the sentences varied in length and in type (30)?

- Are there any fragments (2)? Are there any comma splices or fused sentences (3)?

- Do all verbs agree with their subjects (6a)? Do all pronouns agree with their antecedents (6b)?

- Are all verb forms appropriate (7)?

Diction

- Are any words overused, imprecise, or vague (20c, 20a)? Are all words idiomatic (20b)?

- Have all unnecessary words and phrases been eliminated (21)? Have any necessary words been left out by mistake (22)?

- Is the vocabulary appropriate for the audience, purpose, and context (19b, 32a)?

- Have all technical words that might be unfamiliar to the audience been eliminated or defined (19b(6))?

Punctuation and Mechanics

- Is all punctuation correct (12–17)? Are any marks missing?

- Are all words spelled correctly (18)?

- Is capitalization correct (9)?

- Are titles identified by either quotation marks (16c) or italics (10a)?

- Are abbreviations (11) appropriate and correct?

33d Proofreading can help you avoid irritating or confusing your readers with careless errors.

Once you have revised and edited your essay, format it carefully (see chapter 8). It is then your responsibility to proofread it. Proofreading means making a special search to ensure that the product you submit is error-free. Your proofreading may alert you to problems that call for further editing, but proofreading is usually the last step in the writing process.

Thanks to the computer, you can easily produce professional-looking documents with clear fonts and consistent margins. Showing that you care about presentation indicates that you respect your audience and care about your work. (See chapter 8.) Remember, however, that presentation is only one aspect of a successful project. A paper that looks good could still have problems. No matter how beautiful your paper looks when you print it out, proofread it carefully.

Also watch for three common word processing errors: accidentally leaving a word out, leaving in a word that you meant to delete, or inserting in the wrong place a passage that you moved. Errors of this sort are especially common now that so much writing is done on computers. A spell checker can alert you to repeated words, but you have to proofread to see whether deleting or moving material led to other errors. For example, when deleting a phrase you may have accidentally left one of its words in the text.

Because the eye tends to see what it expects to see, many writers miss errors—especially minor errors, such as a missing comma or apostrophe—even when they think they have proofread carefully. It is usually wise to proofread more than once, and many writers find that they benefit from reading their work aloud as they proofread.

An extra pair of eyes can also be helpful, so you might ask a friend to help you. This is very different, however, from abdicating your own responsibility. If someone else helps you proofread, this check should be in addition to yours. Moreover, if you ask someone to proofread your work, remember that you are asking for only an error-check. If you want a more thoughtful response that could help you revise, you need to ask for it at an earlier point in the process (see 33b(2)).

To use the proofreading checklist that follows, it helps to refer to the chapters and sections cross-referenced in this handbook and also to keep your dictionary handy (see 19a) to look up any words you are uncertain about. Then read your words aloud slowly, pronouncing each syllable carefully. Some people find they benefit from reading through the paper several times this way, checking for a different set of items on each pass. Finally, you should first make sure your paper is properly formatted. (See 8b.)

CHECKLIST for Proofreading Text

Spelling (18)

- Are all words spelled correctly? Have you run a spell checker?

- Have you double-checked the words you frequently misspell or any the spell checker might have missed (for example, homonyms or misspellings that still form words, such as *form* for *from*)?

- Have you consistently used the American spelling of words that have more than one option (*theater/theatre*)?

- Have you double-checked the spelling of all foreign words and all proper names?

Punctuation (12–17)

- Does each sentence have appropriate closing punctuation, and have you used only one space after each period (17a)?

- Is all punctuation within sentences appropriately used and correctly placed (comma, 12; semicolon, 14; apostrophe, 15; other internal marks of punctuation, 17; hyphen, 18g)?

- Are quotations carefully and correctly punctuated (16, 17g, and 17i)?

Capitalization and Italics (9–10)

- Does each sentence begin with a capital letter (9e)?

- Are all proper names, people's titles, and titles of published works correctly capitalized (9a–c)?

- Are quotations capitalized properly (9e and 16a)?

- Are italics used properly (10)?

33e The final draft reflects the care the writer took.

After the intermediate draft reprinted on pages 450–52, Peter continued to revise his essay. Each subsequent draft became stronger. Here is the final draft he eventually submitted.

```
Peter Geske
Professor Henrikson
English 101, Section 2
12 May 2000
                School Daze
    Picture a run-down building that looks
like a warehouse and feels like a prison.
You approach through a sea of broken cement
```

and crumbling asphalt. There are no trees near the building, although a few tufts of uncut grass struggle to grow in a yard of baked-down dirt. Many of the windows have been bricked in, and the ground floor is covered with graffiti. Inside, inadequate lights reveal old tiles, broken lockers, and flaking paint. The school is empty because it is only seven o'clock. Within an hour, however, it will be overcrowded with students who are running wild and teachers who do not know how to respond. You have entered Central High School, the institution where my education suffered because of poor facilities and low standards.

Built a hundred years ago, Central had a good reputation when the neighborhoods around it were prosperous. Now it is the worst high school in the city, and the school board seems to have given up on it. The more run-down it gets, the worse the morale gets, and as morale gets lower, the school goes farther downhill.

After the condition of the building itself, the most obvious problem at Central is the overcrowding. Almost every classroom is filled to capacity, and sometimes there are more students than desks--especially at the beginning of the school year when most people are still showing up for school. The situation gets a little better by Columbus Day, because kids soon discover that one of the advantages of going to Central is that they can skip school without anybody caring.

Our textbooks were usually ten years out of date. And if more expensive supplies ever made it through the door, they did not last long. We had only one computer lab for two thousand students, and it was equipped with old machines that could not access the Internet. Science supplies were almost as bad. In the chemistry lab, for example, there was never enough equipment for individual experiments even when we were teamed with a lab partner. We were put in groups of four and had to wait half the class period before we got the chance to work. By then, most people had checked out. What usually happened is that one person would do the work, and the rest of the team would coast on those results.

My chemistry teacher, Mrs. Fiorelli, is a good example of another problem at Central: bad teachers. All she would ever do was read from the textbook. When somebody would try to ask a question, she would just keep reading. Then she would turn around every few weeks and give difficult tests. It was as if she hated us and wanted to punish us when she couldn't ignore us any longer.

I had many other teachers who were just as bad. Mr. Kleinberg, my geometry teacher, could not control the class. When we got out of control--which was every day--he would start screaming at one person (usually a girl who wasn't doing anything) while other students were flashing knives and plenty were nodding off from drugs. Would you be surprised to hear that I now have a problem with both science and math?

To be fair, I did have some good teachers at Central: Mr. Rodriguez, who taught American history, and Mrs. Sullivan, who taught creative writing. But they were the exceptions. For every good teacher, there were at least three who should consider a career change. And for every course in which you might actually learn something, there were two blow-off courses in which all you had to do was read science fiction, watch tapes on a VCR, or listen to some guy talk about the problems he was having with his own kids.

As I look back at the four years I spent at Central, I am amazed that I learned anything at all. By the time I reached senior year, all I wanted to do was party. I had lost interest in school--which explains why I have been working in a warehouse for the past five years instead of going straight to college. Now that I am here, I sure wish I were better prepared.

EXERCISE 5

Compare the three versions of "School Daze" reprinted in this chapter, and summarize how Peter revised his work. If he showed his final draft to you before handing it in for a grade, what would you tell him?

Chapter 34
Writing under Pressure

Some writers feel under pressure no matter how much time they have because they suffer from writing anxiety. Strategies for reducing such anxiety include freewriting frequently (32b), making writing a normal part of the day by keeping a journal (32b), and learning that most writing situations allow time for a process (chapters 32 and 33) rather than a one-time shot at perfection. The focus of this chapter, however, is how to write well under the pressure of time constraints. It includes advice on

- managing deadlines (34a),
- overcoming writer's block (34b), and
- taking essay tests (34c).

It is not always possible to engage in a writing process that stretches over a period of weeks or even days. Sometimes writers must quickly respond to e-mail (see 39b(1)) or prepare a proposal for presentation at a hastily convened meeting. Working students and single parents sometimes cannot devote as much time as they would like to every writing assignment. And almost all students are faced at some point with essay examinations that must be written in two hours or less. The key to succeeding in such situations is to use the time you have as efficiently as possible.

34a Make deadlines work for you.

You will almost always be working with deadlines whether on papers with a specified due date, or on in-class writing assignments or essay exams. Late papers will lead to penalties, and unless you learn to manage your time on in-class writing assignments and essay exams, you will not be able to adequately demonstrate your knowledge of the subject or your writing ability.

Preparing ahead of time always helps. Although an essay exam may not occur until midterm, preparation should begin on the first day of class. Decide what is most important about the material you are learning, and pay attention to indications that your instructor considers certain material especially important. Ask questions whenever you are uncertain. Be sure to read the instructions and questions carefully.

The best preparation for in-class writing assignments is to write frequently for your own benefit—note taking, regular journal writing, and freewriting. By regularly exercising your own writing, you will be able to write more fluently when forced to write quickly.

If you are writing a paper that is due in one, two, or more weeks, it is especially important to start early. If you are free to choose your own topic, select it soon so that you can be thinking about it. Make deadlines work for you by establishing your own. Set deadlines for writing a first paragraph and a first draft; set a third deadline for revising and editing. Try writing an introductory paragraph (33a(4)), but be aware that you will probably alter this writing or abandon it in your final paper. Just the act of writing, however, will generate ideas. If you spread your work out during this period, you will find that your mind will be forming ideas when you are washing dishes, taking a shower, walking to class, or even while you are sleeping. Keep a small notebook handy to jot down notes.

34b There are strategies for overcoming writer's block.

Writer's block can occur at any time to any writer no matter how experienced. The only difference between your writer's block and that of experienced writers is that they have developed their own strategies for overcoming it. Sometimes it helps to step away from the work. Although you may not be aware of it, your mind will continue to develop ideas for your writing.

Plan your time carefully. The stress that results from a looming deadline can be a major contributor to writer's block. Indeed, students have many demands on their time—papers due in other courses, books that must be read, exams that are scheduled, as well as the demands of family or outside employment. Often students feel that instructors are unaware of such responsibilities, but instructors also have many responsibilities of their own and understand the need to set priorities. It is important that you allot time for each task and distinguish between what you must do and what you would like to do, and then budget your time accordingly. Often you may not be able to give as much time to every assignment as you might like.

One cause of writer's block is the striving for perfection. You certainly wish to make your paper as perfect as you possibly can, but remember that perfection is a goal that even experienced writers seldom reach. You are better off turning in completed work that is less than perfect than no work at all. Understand that sometimes, because other responsibilities have claimed more of your time than you allocated to them, or because you found the subject you were assigned less interesting than you had hoped, or for any of a host of other reasons, your final draft may not be the best that you think you are capable of. There is always the nagging thought that if you had more time—weren't having to go to your job, or study for an exam for another course—you could do better. Do the very best you can given your circumstances and move on. Deadlines and due dates are a reality that must be honored by all writers.

There are several ways to work through writer's block.

CHECKLIST for Overcoming Writer's Block

- Develop your own strategies for overcoming writer's block.

- Allot your time carefully.

- Prioritize your responsibilities and assign time for each activity.

- Set up regular writing habits; write at the same time and the same place whenever possible.

- In an out-of-class assignment, do not worry about getting the wording exactly right in the first draft. You can revise later.

- Do not stop the flow of your writing by worrying about mechanical problems (spelling or punctuation) in your first draft. You can check such errors later.

- In an essay exam try to sit in the same place in the classroom where you have sat all semester.

34c Essay tests require special preparation.

(1) Set up a time schedule.

Check the number of questions on the exam and the number of points for each question and then figure what percentage of the time you should allot to each question. When no points are specified, you can tell which questions the instructor considers important if he or she recommends spending more time on one than on another. If one question will count more heavily than the others, pace yourself with this fact in mind.

Allow some time at the end for revising and proofreading your answers. For example, suppose that you are expected to complete the examination in a fifty-minute class period. If there are three questions and one of them is worth half of the available points, and the rest are split between the other two, allow about twenty minutes for the larger question and ten minutes for each of the others. That leaves you about ten minutes to go back over your answers. When you have used up the time you have allotted for a question, leave room to complete it later and go on to the next whether you are finished or not. Even if you cannot complete every question, partial answers to every question will usually gain you more points than complete answers to only some of the questions. Furthermore, you can use the ten minutes you saved to put the finishing touches on any incomplete answers.

(2) Read instructions and questions carefully.

Students who normally write well sometimes do poorly when writing in-class essays and essay exams because they are in such a rush to begin writing that they hurry through the instructions without reading them carefully or, if there are choices, they do not adequately consider which question best suits them. Before you start writing, read the instructions carefully and note specific directions. For example, realizing that you must "answer questions A *and* B" is very different from believing that you must "answer question A *or* B."

Invest a few minutes in studying the questions so that you do not make a false start and waste time. When asked to answer more than one question, decide whether they are likely to overlap. If you accidentally drift into answering more than one question at a time, you might find yourself with nothing more to say when you get to the next section.

Another good idea is to reframe the question in your own words. Does your version match the question? If so, you can feel confident that you understand what is demanded of you and go ahead. If not, you have probably missed the point and will need to rethink your approach.

Most questions contain specific instructions about how, as well as what, to answer. Be alert for words like *compare, define, argue,* and *cause* that identify your task and provide cues for organizing your response. Other terms like *discuss* or *explain* are less specific, but they may be linked to words like *similar* or *differ* (which signal a comparison or contrast), *identify* (which signals a definition or description), or *why* (which signals the need to identify causes). Also, note language indicating whether you are being asked to report information or to offer your own views. Words like *think, defend,* and *opinion* signal that you are expected to frame a thesis (see **32c**) and support it.

CHECKLIST of Terms Used in Essay Questions

When you are asked to demonstrate your mastery of the information being tested, it is a good idea to know exactly what approach your instructor expects. Most essay examinations contain a sentence that begins with one of the following words and ends with a reference to the information you are to demonstrate your grasp of.

Compare (and contrast)	Examine the points of similarity (compare) and difference (contrast) between two stated things. See **32e(5)**.
Define	State the class to which the item to be defined belongs (see **32e(7)**) and what distinguishes it from the others of that class.
Describe	Use details in a clearly defined order to sketch the item that you are asked to describe. See **32e(2)**.

Discuss	Examine, analyze, evaluate, state pros and cons—in short, this direction gives you wide latitude to address the topic in a variety of ways and is thus more difficult to handle than some of the others, since you must choose your own focus. It is also the term that appears most frequently. See 31c and 32e.
Evaluate	Appraise the advantages and disadvantages of the topic. See 39a(2)c.
Explain	Clarify, make plain, and interpret the topic (see 31c(1)), reconcile differences, or state causes (see 32e(4)).
Illustrate	Offer concrete examples or, if possible, figures, charts, and tables to explain the topic. See 31c(1–2).
Summarize	State the main points in a condensed form; omit details, and curtail examples. See 38c(4).
Trace	Narrate a sequence of events, describe progress, or explain a process. See 32e(1–4).

(3) Decide how to organize your response.

Although time constraints may keep you from creating an out-line, you should always be able to find time to draft an informal working plan (see 32d). Identify the thesis you will offer, then list the most important points you plan to cover. These might occur to you randomly, and you might subsequently decide to rearrange them, but the first step is to create a list that does justice to your topic. When you have finished the list, you should review it and delete any points that seem irrelevant or not important enough to discuss in the time allowed. Then number the remaining points in a logical sequence determined by chronology (reporting events in the order in which they occurred), by causation (showing how one thing led to another), or by order of importance (going from the most important point to the least important). An alternative plan is to arrange your points in order of increasing importance, but this can be risky when writing under pressure: if you run out of time sooner than you expected, you may not get to your most important point.

Here is an example of an edited list quickly composed during the first few minutes of an essay exam. It was jotted down in response to the following question: "Some readers believe that *Huckleberry Finn* is racist. Discuss the treatment of race in this novel. Do you think the book is racist? If so, why? If not, why not?"

THESIS: Huckleberry Finn is not racist. The best character in the book is black, and a white boy comes to understand this.

tie
to gether {

5. use of racist language
1. treatment of Jim
4. Huck's go to hell speech
~~Jim in jail~~
6. reproducing authentic dialogue
3. Jim protects Huck in the storm — mention the snake bite
7. the scene where the slaves get sold ← if time allows
2. Jim as Huck's true father

The language of an assignment sometimes tells you how to organize it. For example, consider the following task.

> Discuss how the building of railroads influenced the development of the American West during the second half of the nineteenth century.

At first glance, this assignment might seem to state the topic without indicating how to organize a discussion of it. To *influence,* however, is to be responsible for certain consequences. In this case, the building of railroads is a cause, and you are being asked to identify its effects (see **32e(4)**). Once you have recognized this, you might decide to discuss different effects in different paragraphs.

Here is another example.

> Consider the concept of the unconscious as defined by Freud and by Jung. On what points did they agree? How did they disagree?

The reference to two psychoanalysts, coupled with words like *agree* and *disagree,* indicates that your task is to compare and contrast. You could organize your response to this question by first discussing Freud's ideas and then discussing Jung's— preferably covering the same points in the same order. Or you could begin by establishing similarities and then move on to differences. There is almost always more than one way to organize a thoughtful response. Devoting at least a few minutes to planning your organization can help you demonstrate what you know.

(4) State main points clearly.

Instructors who read essay exams and in-class essays are usually looking to see how well students have understood assigned material. Stating your main points clearly will help them make that evaluation. In a weak essay, important points may be buried where they can be overlooked, while minor or irrelevant points are prominent. Make your main points stand out from the rest of the essay by identifying them somehow. For instance, you can use transitional expressions such as *first, second, third;* you can underline each main point; or you can create headings to guide the reader. By the time you have drafted most of your essay, you should know what your key points are. Because the act of writing often generates new ideas, these points may differ from those you had originally planned to make. Use your conclusion to summarize your main points. If you tend to make points that differ from those you had in mind when you started, try leaving space for an introduction at the beginning of the essay and then drafting it after you have drafted the rest.

(5) Stick to the question.

Always answer the exact question as directly as you can. Sometimes you may know more about a related question than the one assigned. Do not wander from the question being asked to answer the question you wish had been asked. Similarly, make sure that you follow your thesis as you answer the question; do not include irrelevant material. If you move away from your original thesis because better ideas have occurred to you as you write, go back and revise your thesis (see **32c**). If you drift into including irrelevant material, draw a line through it.

(6) Revise and proofread.

Save a few minutes to reread your answer. Make whatever deletions and corrections you think are necessary. If time allows, think about what is not on the page by asking yourself if there is anything you have left out that you can still manage to include. Unless you are certain that your instructor values neatness more than competence, do not hesitate to make corrections. Making corrections will allow you to focus on improving what you have written, whereas recopying your answer just to make it look neat can be an inefficient use of time (and possibly leave you with only half your essay recopied when the time is up). Make sure, however, that your instructor will be able to read your changes. Clarify any illegible scribbles. If you have added ideas in the margins, in each case draw a line to a caret ($\land$) marking the exact place in the text where you want additions or corrections to be placed. Finally, check spelling, punctuation, and sentence structure (see 33d).

EXERCISE 1

Write three questions that you might be asked on an essay exam for a course you are currently taking. Then choose the question you like best and write a description of how you would organize your response.

EXERCISE 2

Bring in an old exam from another course. If the writing posed any difficulties for you, be prepared to identify and discuss them.

Chapter

35 Reading and Thinking Critically

To read and think critically means to distinguish between ideas that are credible and those that are less so. In addition to reading for content by identifying the key points in a text, critical readers think about what they read and evaluate it. Critical thinking is essential for critical reading. It is also essential when evaluating research (37), writing arguments (36), and undertaking other types of writing (38 and 39).

Critical readers know that they cannot believe everything they read. They understand that different writers discussing the same topic and drawing on the same evidence can reach significantly different conclusions. Instead of routinely agreeing with the writer who seems to reinforce reassuringly familiar beliefs, critical readers are likely to discover that different writers have each revealed a part of what may ultimately prove to be true. The challenge for readers, then, is to identify which ideas make more sense than others and to determine the extent to which those ideas are reliable and useful. To do so, they consider the values and assumptions of the writers they read, asking themselves what each writer expects them to believe. Critical readers think about where they agree or disagree with the assumptions of others. In addition, they study language carefully because they understand that writers influence readers by using a range of rhetorical strategies that may not be apparent at first glance.

Because thinking and reading critically involve making well-reasoned choices, these closely related skills are among the most valuable you can acquire. You can master them through practice, just as you have mastered other skills.

This chapter will help you

- prepare for reading a text critically (35a),
- distinguish facts from opinions (35b),
- decide whether claims are supported by evidence (35c),
- evaluate a writer's credibility (35d),
- use inductive reasoning (35e),
- use deductive reasoning (35f),
- use the Toulmin approach to reasoning (35g), and
- recognize logical fallacies (35h).

35a Previewing can help you read a text critically.

To **preview** reading means to assess how difficult a text will be and what you are likely to learn from it. When you understand what a task demands, you are more likely to complete it successfully. Comprehending what you read is the first step toward reading critically. After all, you cannot determine the merits of a text without understanding its content.

When you page through a magazine looking for articles that seem interesting, you are, in a sense, previewing it. A simple preview of this sort can help you identify what you want to read, but it might also lead you to an article that disappoints you. A more systematic preview can give you better results, especially when you are undertaking college reading assignments. Look for the following features.

Title   Titles and subtitles often reveal the focus of a work and sometimes even its thesis, so they are usually worth noting. (See 33a(6).) If the title provides little information (as may be the case when a writer uses a clever phrase to attract attention), do not assume that the work itself will be useless. When you look at other parts of it, you are likely to get a clearer sense of the work as a whole.

Directories   Books usually have features that direct readers to specific sections within them. A *table of contents* identifies the chapters within a book; an *index,* at the back, lists the specific topics covered. Checking these directories can help you determine whether the book will have the kind of information you are looking for and, if so, exactly where you can find it. A *bibliography,* or list of works cited, indicates how much research is involved; it can also direct you to other useful sources. In both books and periodicals, look for lists that reveal information about contributors.

Length   A long work may contain more information than a short one, but it may also take longer to read. When you consider length, you can estimate how much time you should set aside for reading. By checking length, you can also estimate whether a work is long enough to include useful content or so short that it probably skims the surface of the subject it addresses.

Visual aids   The extent to which visual aids are useful varies, because different readers have different learning styles. Nevertheless, a quick check for graphs and illustrations can help you decide whether the work has the kind of information you need. Because visual aids break up what might otherwise be large blocks of densely written text, they can also signal points where you might pause.

Summaries   Both books and articles often contain summaries, and reading a summary can help you decide whether the work as a whole will be helpful. Reading a summary can also help you follow a difficult text because you then know its major points in advance. Summaries can often be found in the *preface* of a book, as well as in introductory and concluding chapters. Scholarly articles often begin with a summary identified as an *abstract.* Within articles, the introductory and concluding paragraphs often include summaries. (See **37d(1)c**.)

In addition to looking for these features in the work you are previewing, look inside yourself as well so that you can prepare to read critically. Assess how much you already know about the subject. If the work looks difficult and you are unfamiliar with the subject matter, you may benefit from doing some preliminary reading by downloading a less demanding work from an electronic indexing service or the World Wide Web (see **37d**). You should also consider whether you have values or opinions that could interfere with your ability to pay close attention to views that may be different from yours. Sometimes it is easy to hear only what you want to hear or see only what you want to see. Without abandoning your values, you can increase your capacity for critical reading by being alert for occasions when you are tempted to dismiss new ideas prematurely.

To preview college reading assignments, ask the questions in the following checklist.

CHECKLIST for Previewing a Text

- How long is this work, and how long are different sections of it? Does the organization seem straightforward or complex? How much time will I need to read this piece carefully?

- What do I already know about the subject? Can I keep this knowledge in mind as I read so I can establish some immediate connections with the text?

- Do I have any strong feelings about this subject that could interfere with my ability to understand how it is treated in this text?

- Do I know anything about this author, and if so, can I trust what he or she writes? If the author is unfamiliar to me, is there any biographical information in the source that will help me assess his or her credibility? (See **35d**.)

- What can I learn from the title? Is there a subtitle? If there are subheadings in the text, what do they reveal about the organization?

- What do the table of contents and index indicate about what is in the book? Does this article include an abstract?

- Are there graphs, figures, or other visual aids? If so, how can this material be useful to me?

- Is there a bibliography that will indicate how extensive and current the research is?

- Does the introduction or conclusion reveal the author's thesis? (See **32c**.)

- Has the author included a summary near the conclusion or at the end of any of the subsections?

- Would it be easier for me to understand this text if I read something else first?

In addition to asking yourself these questions, you can also benefit from scanning specific sentences and phrases. Although the central idea of a paragraph can occur anywhere within it (see **31a(1)**), it often appears in the first or last sentence. By reading these sentences, you can get a sense of a work's content and organization.

The main outline of a text can also be determined by words that indicate sequencing, such as "There are *three* advantages to this proposal. . . . The *first* is. . . . The *second* is. . . ."

In addition, you can scan for key phrases that writers use to signal important points. The phrase *in other words,* for example, signals that a writer is about to paraphrase a point just made—probably because it is important (see **38c(3)**). Other key phrases include *in the following article* (or chapter), which can signal a statement of the author's focus or purpose; and *in summary, in conclusion,* and *the point I am making,* which signal a restatement or clarification of the author's thesis. Further, words like *therefore* and *thus* signal that a point is being made about the information just presented.

Previewing is a way to make reading easier and more meaningful. It can also help you select appropriate material when you do research (see chapter 37). But remember that previewing a text is not the same as reading all of it closely.

35b **Critical readers distinguish between fact and opinion.**

As you acquire information through reading, you may believe that you are acquiring **facts**—reliable pieces of information that can be verified through independent sources or procedures. Facts are valued because they are believed to be true. **Opinions** are assertions or inferences that may or may not be based on facts. When opinions are widely accepted, they may seem to be factual when actually they are not.

Facts are not necessarily more valuable than opinions; a thoughtful and well-informed opinion may have more merit than a page of random facts. But accepting opinions unsupported by facts can lead you to faulty conclusions that damage your credibility because you will look as if you are not thinking seriously about the material in question. By distinguishing facts from opinions, you are more likely to use both kinds of information effectively.

To distinguish between fact and opinion, ask yourself questions about what you have read: Can it be proved? Can it be challenged? How often is the same result achieved? (See 35c.)

If a statement can consistently be proved true, then it is a fact. If it can be disputed, then it is an opinion.

Fact   Spinach contains iron.

Opinion   Americans should eat more spinach.

To say that spinach contains iron is to state a well-established fact; it can be verified by consulting published studies or by conducting laboratory tests. But to say that Americans need to eat more spinach is to express an opinion that may or may not be supported by facts. When considering the statement "Americans should eat more spinach," a critical reader might ask, "What is spinach good for? How important is iron? Do *all* Americans suffer from iron deficiency? Is spinach the only source of iron?" Exploring any of these questions could lead to discovering differences of opinion as well as learning some facts.

Because the facts themselves can change, critical readers and thinkers need to remain flexible as they distinguish between fact and opinion. The erroneous belief that the sun revolves around the earth was once considered a fact, and Newtonian physics was once believed to be indisputably true. Describing what can easily happen in research, a distinguished physician writes that a good scientist must be prepared for the day when his or her life's work is suddenly called into question.

> All the old ideas—last week's ideas in some cases—are no longer good ideas. The hard facts have softened, melted away and vanished under the pressure of new hard facts.
>
> —LEWIS THOMAS, "The Art of Teaching Science"

No matter how knowledgeable, any person who is unwilling to assimilate new information and question old ideas cannot expect to meet the challenges of a rapidly changing world. Researchers studying AIDS, for example, must maintain their intellectual dexterity so they can adapt as new information becomes available. Or, to use another example, the ease with which students can now access information on the World Wide Web has encouraged many teachers to develop new methods of instruction.

The line between fact and opinion is not always clear. What seems to be factual could be the result of inadequate research or assumptions that are so widely held that they have not been challenged in a long time. And opinions sometimes reflect extensive life experience. Critical readers are thus prepared to ask themselves what kind of verification would be necessary to determine the reliability of the information in question. In some cases, verification would be easy; in others it might be much more difficult. Reliability depends not on the ease with which data can be verified, but on whether verification is possible. Whether they are examining fact or opinion, critical readers ask, "What kind of evidence is necessary, how could that evidence be obtained, and what would happen if conflicting evidence is discovered?"

E X E R C I S E 1

Determine which of the following statements seem to be fact and which seem to be opinion. In each case, what kind of verification would you expect before accepting the statement as reliable? Explain your decisions in writing and be prepared to discuss your choices in class.

1. Willa Cather won the Pulitzer Prize for fiction in 1923.
2. Women often earn less money than men holding the same position.
3. New Yorkers are unfriendly.
4. You cannot write well unless you know how to write correctly.
5. A college diploma is necessary for jobs that pay well.
6. The capital of California is Sacramento.
7. Running is good for your health.
8. The United States won the Second World War.
9. Water freezes at 32 degrees Fahrenheit.
10. John F. Kennedy was assassinated by Lee Harvey Oswald.

35c Critical readers look for evidence.

Critical readers expect writers to support their claims with ample evidence consisting of facts and other data such as personal experience and observation. When you are reading a work that makes a specific point, ask yourself whether the writer has provided evidence that is accurate, representative, and sufficient. Examine critically any information that writers present. Accurate information should be verifiable. Recognize, however, that a writer may provide you with information that is accurate but unreliable because it is drawn from an exceptional case or a biased sampling. If, for example, you are reading an argument about airline safety that draws all its information from material distributed by a major airline, the evidence cited is unlikely to represent the full range of data available on this topic.

Similarly, examine polls and other statistics carefully. How recent is the information, and how was it gathered? In 1936, a poll conducted by the *Literary Digest* predicted the election of Alf Landon, but Franklin D. Roosevelt won by a landslide. The poll was nonrepresentative and therefore faulty because it was limited to people who owned cars or had personal telephone service. During the worst economic depression in American history, Americans who had cars and personal telephones were financially secure and likely to vote against Roosevelt, who advocated increased government spending on domestic programs. Even with representative polls, however, statistics can be manipulated. Do not accept them uncritically.

To decide how much evidence is appropriate, consider the nature of the claim. (See 36c(1).) A writer who makes an absolute claim will need to provide more evidence than a writer who makes a moderate one. Absolute claims assert that something is always true or false, completely good or bad, while moderate claims are more limited.

Absolute claim	Nurses at Memorial Hospital are incompetent.
Moderate claim	Nurses at Memorial Hospital are failing to fulfill some of their responsibilities.
Absolute claim	Ronald Reagan was the best president we ever had.
Moderate claim	Reagan's foreign policy helped bring about the collapse of the Soviet Union.

Moderate claims are not necessarily superior to absolute claims. After all, writers frequently need to take a position strongly in favor of or against something. But the stronger the claim, the stronger the evidence needed to support it. Be sure to consider the quality and significance of the evidence (see 37c)—not just its quantity.

35d Readers must evaluate a writer's credibility.

Critical readers look for evidence that helps them determine whether an author is well informed and fair minded. To determine how credible a writer is, ask yourself the questions in the following checklist.

CHECKLIST for Evaluating Credibility

- Does the writer support claims with evidence?

- Does the writer reveal how and where evidence was obtained?

- Does the writer recognize that other points of view may be legitimate?

- Does the writer use sarcasm or make personal attacks on opponents?

- Does the writer reach a conclusion that is in proportion to the amount of evidence provided?

- Does the writer have credentials that invest the work with authority?

- Does the writer seem biased? (See 37c.)

As you evaluate credibility, consider the writer's *ethos* (see 36d(1)) by asking whether he or she has good knowledge of the subject, good character, and good will toward the audience. Thoughtful writers support their claims with evidence (see 35c and 36c) and reach conclusions that seem justified by the amount of evidence provided. They reveal how and where they obtained this evidence (38a, 38b, and 38d), and their tone (33a(3)) is appropriate for their purpose, audience, and context (32a). Moreover, they show that they have given fair consideration to views with which they disagree (see 36c(3)).

If you are uncertain about a writer's credibility or are simply interested in learning more about this person's professional standing, you can often obtain additional information by searching an electronic indexing service or the World Wide Web (see 37d).

Exercise 2

Evaluate the credibility of the following excerpt from an argument against gun control written by a newspaper columnist who once served as a public relations specialist for the National Rifle Association.

[1]The gun control issue, then, is never a question of what the government "allows" us to own. [2]The Constitution states that

government has *no authority* over the firearms ownership of the people. [3]The people, not the government, possess an absolute right in the area of gun ownership. [4]If you or I want to own an AR-15 or any other gun, it is none of the government's business *why* we want it, and certainly none of its business to presume that we may be up to no good. [5]In a free society, the salient question is *never* whether the government can trust the people but always whether the people can trust their government. [6]The history of the Second Amendment makes this point ever so clear. [7]You could spend a lifetime studying the writings of the Founding Fathers and would never find among any of them the kinds of sentiments expressed by our 20th-century gun controllers—sentiments that reflect a profound distrust for a free people. [8]You would not find a single person among all the founders of our nation who was worried about firearms in the hands of the citizenry. [9]The very idea is preposterous.

—ROGER KOOPMAN, "Second Defense"

35e Critical thinkers understand inductive reasoning.

When writers use **inductive reasoning,** they begin with a number of facts or observations and use them to draw a general conclusion. Most of us use inductive reasoning to make decisions in daily life. For example, if you get indigestion several times after eating sauerkraut, you might conclude that eating sauerkraut gives you indigestion. This use of evidence to form a generalization is called an **inductive leap,** and the leap should be in proportion to the amount of evidence gathered. It is reasonable to stop eating sauerkraut if it consistently makes you ill—especially if you have sampled sauerkraut from more than one source (since different preparations could change the effect). But if you conclude that no one should ever eat sauerkraut, your claim would be too large for the amount of evidence in question.

Because induction involves leaping from discovering evidence to interpreting it, this kind of reasoning can help writers reach probable, believable conclusions, but not some absolute truth that will endure forever. Making a small leap from evidence to a conclusion that seems probable is not the same as jumping to a sweeping conclusion that could easily be challenged. Generally, the greater the weight of the evidence, the more reliable the conclusion.

Science's use of inductive reasoning is known as the **scientific method.** For instance, early medical studies equated diets high in fat with coronary artery disease. The scientific community reserved judgment since the early studies were based on only a small sample, but later studies involving larger numbers of subjects confirmed the early reports. Although everyone with coronary artery disease cannot be studied, the sample is now large enough and representative enough for scientists to draw the conclusion with more confidence. Nevertheless, a critical thinker would still examine the available evidence carefully and ask a number of questions about it. If the research had been conducted primarily on men, would the conclusions be equally applicable to women? Are the conclusions equally applicable to people of all races? To what extent have the researchers controlled all variables? Does the evidence support the conclusion that has been drawn, or should it be modified? Because scientists are critical thinkers who ask such questions, they are often motivated to do further research.

When used in persuasive writing (see chapter 36), inductive reasoning often employs examples. When writers cannot cite all the instances that support their conclusions, they choose the ones most closely related to the point they are making (see 31c).

An inductively reasoned essay can be organized in different ways (see 36e). You might begin by identifying a problem that needs to be solved, then provide evidence about the problem or a proposed solution, and then reach a reasonable conclusion. Or you could begin with what you have concluded by presenting it in the form of a topic sentence (31a(1)) or a thesis statement (32c) and then provide evidence that supports that claim.

35f Critical thinkers understand deductive reasoning.

When writers use **deductive reasoning,** they begin with generalizations (premises) and apply them to a specific instance to draw a conclusion about that instance. For example, if you know that all soldiers must complete basic training and that Martha has enlisted in the army, then you could conclude that Martha must complete basic training. This argument can be expressed in a structure called a **syllogism.**

Major premise	All soldiers must complete basic training.
Minor premise	Martha has become a soldier.
Conclusion	Martha must complete basic training.

Sometimes premises are not stated.

Martha has enlisted in the army, so she must complete basic training.

In this sentence, the unstated premise is that all soldiers must complete basic training. A syllogism with an unstated premise—or even an unstated conclusion—is called an **enthymeme.** Enthymemes are frequently found in written arguments (see chapter 36) and can be very effective. For example, the argument "We need to build a new dormitory because the ones we have are seriously overcrowded," contains the unstated premise that dormitories should house only the number of people they were designed for. Writers with a good sense of audience understand that readers can lose interest in a discussion of what can be safely assumed.

Critical thinkers, however, should examine enthymemes with care since the omitted statement may be inaccurate. "Samuel is from Louisiana, so he must like Cajun food" contains the unstated major premise that "Everyone from Louisiana likes Cajun food." This premise is unacceptable because there is no reason to assume that everyone from a particular region shares the same taste in food—even if the food in question happens to be a local specialty. As a critical reader, you must accept the truth of the premise in order to agree with the conclusion.

A deductive argument must be both true and valid. A **true** argument is based on well-backed premises generally accepted by your audience. A **valid** argument is based on logical thinking. The conclusion in the following syllogism is valid because the conclusion follows logically from the major and minor premises, but it is not true because the major premise is not generally accepted.

Major premise	All redheads are brilliant.
Minor premise	Jane is a redhead.
Conclusion	Therefore Jane is brilliant.

Because syllogisms can be logical without being true and because they are too absolute for questions that do not have absolute answers, they are often more effective as exercises in critical thinking than as outlines for written arguments. Nevertheless, familiarity with syllogistic reasoning can often help you understand and evaluate arguments. Although you may have occasion to use deduction in your own writing, this kind of thinking is especially useful for critical reading.

E X E R C I S E 3

Supply the missing premise in the following statements and determine whether the reasoning is both valid and true.

1. He must be a nice person. He smiles all the time.
2. She is a good writer. She is easy to understand.

3. We need to restrict the use of water. We are suffering from a severe drought.

4. Omtronic Co. must be well managed. Its earnings have grown steadily over the past few years.

5. Dr. Kordoff must be a good teacher. Her classes always fill up quickly.

EXERCISE 4

Study the following excerpt from "The Declaration of Independence." Identify the assumptions on which this argument is based and be prepared to explain how one assumption leads to another.

[1]We hold these truths to be self-evident, that all men are created equal, that they are endowed by their Creator with certain unalienable rights, that among these are life, liberty and the pursuit of happiness. [2]That to secure these rights, governments are instituted among men, deriving their just powers from the consent of the governed. [3]That whenever any form of government becomes destructive of these ends, it is the right of the people to alter or to abolish it, and to institute new government, laying its foundation on such principles and organizing its powers in such form, as to them shall seem most likely to effect their safety and happiness.

—THOMAS JEFFERSON

35g The Toulmin method is an alternative approach to reasoning.

Another way of using logic is the method devised by Stephen Toulmin in *The Uses of Argument* (New York: Cambridge UP, 1964). To create a working form of logic suitable for the needs of writers, Toulmin drew on deductive reasoning but put less emphasis on the formal conventions of a syllogism. His approach sees argument as the progression from accepted facts or evidence (**data**) to a conclusion (**claim**) by way of a statement (**warrant**) that establishes a reasonable relationship between the two. For example, in the argument,

> Since soldiers are required to complete basic training, and since Martha has become a soldier, Martha must complete basic training,

the claim is that Martha must complete basic training, and the data consist of the fact that she has become a soldier. The warrant, that soldiers are required to complete basic training, ties the two statements together, making the conclusion follow from the data.

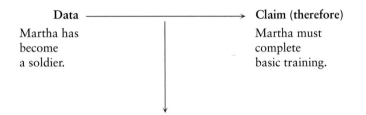

Data ——————————————→ **Claim (therefore)**

Martha has become a soldier.

Martha must complete basic training.

Warrant (since)
Soldiers must complete basic training.

Of course, few arguments are as simple as this. For instance, Martha may have been exempted from basic training because she has a special skill for which there is an urgent need. In such cases, writers can make allowances for exceptions. Qualifiers such as *usually, probably,* and *possibly* show the degree of certainty of the conclusion, and rebuttal terms such as *unless* allow writers to indicate exceptions.

> **Since** Martha is a soldier, she **probably** completed basic training **unless** an exception was made for her.

When using the Toulmin model to analyze written arguments, critical readers are often able to identify the claim, the data, and the qualifiers more easily than they can find the warrant. Like the unstated premise in an enthymeme (see 35f), the warrant is often assumed or implied but not explicitly stated. To determine a writer's warrant, recognize that warrants can take different forms. A warrant may be

- a matter of law or requirement (such as regulations for military service published by the Department of Defense),
- an assumption that the data came from a reliable source (see 35d and 37c),
- an assumption that what is true of a sample is true of a larger group, or
- a moral, political, or economic value that is widely accepted in the writer's culture.

In addition, the Toulmin model requires that warrants have **backing,** or support. The backing may or may not appear within a written argument, but a writer should be able to produce it to support a warrant that has been questioned. Writers who assume that they are drawing their evidence from reliable authorities, for example, should be able to cite the credentials of those authorities. And those who base their argument on the law or another written code that has been widely agreed on should be able to cite the exact statute, precedent, or regulation in question.

Like deductive reasoning, the Toulmin method of reasoning can help you read critically by providing a means of analyzing written arguments.

EXERCISE 5

Analyze the argument in the following excerpt by asking yourself the following questions.

A. What is the conclusion or claim?
B. What data support the claim?
C. What is the warrant that underlies the argument?

¹The movement to make English the official language of the United States is in no way a put-down of other languages or cultures. ²But it is the language used predominantly by the print and electronic media; it is the tongue in which government at every level is conducted. ³To be an effective citizen one ought to vote, and to do so intelligently one must be well informed. ⁴Candidates, of course, present the issues and outline their platforms in English.

—YOLANDA DE MOLA, "The Language of Power"

EXERCISE 6

Review the excerpt from "The Declaration of Independence" in exercise 4. What kind of backing could be offered to support the warrants you find there?

35h Critical thinkers recognize logical fallacies.

Fallacies are lapses in logic that can result from relying on faulty premises, from misusing or misrepresenting evidence, or from distorting the issues. They can be the result of poor thinking, but they can also be a deliberate attempt to manipulate— as suggested by the origin of the term *fallacia,* which is Latin for "deceit."

Many fallacies are what logicians call *non sequiturs,* which is Latin for "it does not follow." Any conclusion that is based on a faulty premise—or does not follow from its premises—can be described as a *non sequitur.* For example, the statement "Billy Joe is honest, therefore, he will get a good job" is a *non sequitur* because it rests on a faulty premise: many honest people do not get jobs. (See **35f**.) Both logicians and rhetoricians find it useful, however, to distinguish different kinds of fallacy. Here are some of the major ones. Be alert for them in your reading, and try to avoid them in your thinking.

(1) *Ad hominem* **is a personal attack on an opponent that draws attention away from the issues under consideration.**

Faulty   He is unfit to be governor because he drank too much when he was a college student. [Whether or not this candidate drank too much when he was young may reveal something about his character, but voters might decide that he now has political skills and principles that could benefit the state.]

(2) *Appeal to tradition* **is an argument that says something should be done a certain way simply because it has been done that way in the past.**

Faulty   We should not allow women to join this club because we have never let women join before. [Times change; what was acceptable in the past is not necessarily acceptable in the present.]

(3) *Bandwagon* **is an argument saying, in effect, "Everyone's doing or saying or thinking this, so you should too."**

Faulty   Everyone cheats on exams, so why shouldn't you? [The majority is not always right.]

(4) *Begging the question* **is a statement that assumes what needs to be proved.**

Faulty   We need to fire the thieves in the police department. [If there are thieves working in the police department, this point needs to be established.]

(5) *Equivocation* **is an assertion that falsely relies on the use of a term in two different senses.**

> **Faulty** We know this is a natural law because it feels natural. [When first used, *natural* means principles derived from nature or reason; when used again, it means easy or simple because of being in accord with one's own nature.]

(6) *False analogy* **is the assumption that because two things are alike in some ways, they must be alike in others.**

> **Faulty** Bill Collins will be a good senator because he used to be a good quarterback. [The differences between playing football and serving in the Senate are greater than the similarities.]

(7) *False authority* **is the assumption that an expert in one field can be a credible expert in another.**

> **Faulty** The defense budget must be cut, as the country's leading pediatrician has shown. [Pediatric medicine is unrelated to economics or political science.]

(8) *False cause* **is the assumption that because one event follows another, the first is the cause of the second— sometimes called** *post hoc, ergo propter hoc* **("after this, so because of this").**

> **Faulty** Our new school superintendent took office last January, and crime has increased 14 percent. [The assumption is that the school superintendent is responsible for the increase in crime, an assumption unlikely to be true.]

(9) *False dilemma* **means stating that only two alternatives exist when in fact there are more than two (sometimes called the *either/or* fallacy).**

> **Faulty** We have only two choices: to build more nuclear power plants or to be completely dependent on foreign oil. [Other possibilities exist.]

(10) *Guilt by association* **is an unfair attempt to make someone responsible for the beliefs or actions of others.**

> **Faulty** Judge Barlow must be dishonest because she belongs to the same club as that lawyer who was recently disbarred. [People can belong to the same club—or live in the same neighborhood—without engaging in the same behavior.]

(11) *Hasty generalization* **is based on too little evidence or on exceptional or biased evidence.**

> **Faulty** Ellen is a poor student because she failed her first quiz. [Her performance may improve in the weeks ahead or be good in all her other subjects.]

(12) *Oversimplification* **is a statement or argument that leaves out relevant considerations about an issue to imply that there is a single cause or solution for a complex problem.**

> **Faulty** We can eliminate hunger by growing more food. [Increasing the amount of food produced does not guarantee that the hungry will have access to it.]

(13) *Red herring* **means dodging the real issue by drawing attention to an irrelevant one (sometimes called** *ignoring the question***).**

> **Faulty** Why worry about overcrowded schools when we ought to be trying to attract a professional hockey franchise? [Professional sports have nothing to do with overcrowded schoolrooms.]

(14) *Slippery slope* **is the assumption that if one thing is allowed, it will be the first step in a downward spiral.**

> **Faulty** Handgun control will lead to a police state. [Handgun control has not led to a police state in England.]

What looks like a logical fallacy may be acceptable under some circumstances, however. Although personal attacks on an opponent (*ad hominem* arguments) should normally be avoided, a writer may have good reason to question someone's character. For example, if a candidate for public office has been cheating on his income tax, a writer may decide that voters should be advised of this information because it raises issues of public trust and accountability. Similarly, people should normally make their own decisions and not simply go along with the crowd (*bandwagon* arguments). But if you are part of a team that is working on a collaborative project and achieving consensus is essential to getting the job done, your teammates could legitimately point out that everyone else has agreed to the plan that you have rejected.

Be alert for logical fallacies and examine them critically within the arguments in which they occur. When you think you have found one, decide whether it is fallacious and, if it is, how seriously it affects your judgment of the writer's credibility (see **35d**). Do not assume that identifying a fallacy means that you can automatically dismiss whatever a writer has to say. In some cases, credibility may be undermined; in others, a writer could remain credible despite a lapse in reasoning.

EXERCISE 7

For each of the following statements, write one or two sentences in which you explain the flaw in reasoning. Then identify circumstances under which you might find these statements convincing.

1. You should vote for Jonathan because everyone else is.
2. We must either build more prisons or crowd more prisoners into existing cells.
3. This car must be reliable; it's the kind my dentist drives.
4. If we censor pornography, we will ultimately lose freedom of speech.
5. I know that store is badly managed. One of the salespeople there was rude to me once.
6. If women dressed more conservatively, they wouldn't get raped.
7. You can't trust a guy like that; his brother was found guilty of tax evasion.
8. We should cut welfare because people on welfare are getting too many benefits.
9. The union is arguing for a cost-of-living raise, but its leaders are all a bunch of crooks.
10. Children would do a lot better at school if they didn't spend so much time watching television.

EXERCISE 8

Read the following paragraph and identify the logical fallacies you find in it. Then, adopting the point of view of someone opposed to animal experimentation, write two or three paragraphs responding to the argument offered here.

[1]As the Oscar-winning director Scavan Kleck has argued, "Animal experimentation saves lives." [2]Isn't the life of a little girl more important than the life of a chimpanzee? [3]We have to choose:

we can either experiment on animals to find cures for life-threatening diseases or we can stand by helplessly while thousands of children die. [4]Experimentation is necessary because research is important. [5]And why should we worry about what happens to animals in laboratories when the real problem is how people treat their pets? [6]Advocates of animal rights are a bunch of sentimental vegetarians who don't care what happens to children, and they will never be satisfied with banning painful experiments on animals. [7]If they succeed in getting legislation passed that restricts experimentation, it's only a question of time before the sale of meat is prohibited. [8]Just look at the trouble they've already caused. [9]The cost of research has soared since people started protesting against animal experimentation.

Chapter
36   Writing Arguments

When writing an argument, you plan, draft, revise, and edit a document that is appropriate for your audience and context. (See chapters 32 and 33.) In addition, you read and think critically (see chapter 35) and consider what it would take to persuade your audience to agree with you. This chapter will help you write persuasively by discussing how to

- understand the purpose of your argument (36a),
- choose an appropriate subject (36b),
- take a position or make a claim (36c(1)),
- provide evidence to support your claim (36c(2)),
- establish that you are fair minded and well informed (36d),
- decide whether it would be appropriate to appeal to the feelings of your audience (36d), and
- organize your ideas (36e).

As you proceed, you should understand the importance of arguing ethically and treating your opponents with respect. Argument is a way to discover truth and negotiate differences. It should not be used to punish or ridicule people with whom you happen to disagree.

36a   Different arguments have different purposes.

When writing an argument, you should always consider your purpose. It may be to pursue the truth until you have formed an opinion that seems reasonable. Or it may be to persuade an audience to agree with an opinion that you already hold. Readers often expect the introduction to an argument to establish its purpose. Your conclusion can also emphasize your purpose.

When you are writing to pursue the truth, you are writing **to inquire.** In conversation, you probably have ample experience with argument as a means of inquiry. For example, when you meet with a friend to talk about a decision one of you needs to make, you are using argument as inquiry. Such an argument does not involve quarreling; it is shaped instead by the give-and-take of dialogue as different ideas are exchanged. Philosophers and rhetoricians call this kind of serious conversation **dialectic.** Many of the great works of ancient philosophy take the form of a dialogue written along these lines. You might practice dialectic by actually writing a dialogue between two speakers or by simply listing the pros and cons of differing views until you arrive at a conclusion that seems true to you.

If you have already reached a conclusion to which you are committed, then your purpose is probably to **convince** other people to accept your position to some extent. This purpose can take at least four different forms.

- If there is little likelihood that you can convince your readers to change a strongly held opinion, then you could be achieving a great deal by simply convincing them that your position deserves to be taken seriously.
- If the members of your audience are not firmly and absolutely committed to a position, then you might write in the hope of convincing them to agree with you.
- If they agree with you in principle, then you might convince them to undertake a specific action—such as voting for the candidate you are supporting.
- If, however, there are fundamental differences within your audience, then you might write to reduce the extent of their conflict by establishing common ground and negotiating a compromise.

EXERCISE 1

Study the following paragraph and decide what the author's purpose seems to be. Then write a paragraph stating that purpose and the grounds that led you to your conclusion.

[1]I am not advocating the erection of a wall against immigration. [2]Instead a more generous immigration policy should go hand in hand with greater punishment of illegal entrants, including fines and possibly jail terms. [3]Greater legal immigration is not only desirable in its own right but would reduce the number who seek to enter illegally. [4]Not surprisingly, illegal entry generally expands when a country contracts the number of immigrants accepted.

—GARY S. BECKER, "Illegal Immigration"

36b Argument assumes the existence of differing views.

If there are no differences, there is no need to argue. The first step toward finding a subject for argumentation is to consider issues that inspire different opinions. If most people already share the same opinion—believing, for example, that it is nice to sit by a fireplace on a cold winter night—then there is little point in writing an argument espousing this view. Widely held opinions could become topics for expressive or expository essays (see 32a(1)), such as "Why I Love Fireplaces" or "How to Build Your Own Fireplace," but they lack the element of controversy found in an appropriate topic for argumentation.

Behind any effective argument is a question that can generate more than one reasonable answer. If you ask "Is there poverty in our country?" almost anyone will agree that there is. But if you ask "Why is there poverty in our country?" or "What can we do to eliminate poverty?" you will hear very different answers. Answers differ because people approach questions with different assumptions and also because they acquire different kinds of information. In other words, people work from different premises or warrants (see **35f** and **35g**) and often look primarily for evidence that supports what they assume to be true. Be careful not to do so when preparing your own arguments. To be persuasive, you must demonstrate that you have given fair consideration to diverse views (see **36c(3)**).

When you write an argument, you are either looking for an answer to a question or showing that you have found the answer you want your audience to accept. Choose a question that needs an answer, then focus (see **32b**) on the part of this question you will address in your essay. Consider your own values and assumptions and how they differ from those of your audience so that you can decide what you can take for granted and what you will need to establish.

A good subject may occur to you if you note how you respond to the views of others. Your response to a class discussion or material you have read for class could lead to a good essay. When you are free to choose your own subject, you should be able to think of many suitable ones if you stay abreast of current events by reading newspapers or following the news online. Even if you are doing something as simple as listening to a television commentator, you might find yourself agreeing or disagreeing with what you hear, and a good essay could be developed from this response. To find a subject, you can also try methods such as freewriting and listing (see **32b(1)**).

When you think you have found a suitable subject, you can benefit from asking yourself the following series of questions.

CHECKLIST for Assessing a Subject

- Is there more than one possible answer? Would anyone be likely to disagree with me?

- Do I know enough about this subject? Can I find out what I need to know?

- Have I narrowed the subject so that I can do justice to it in the space I have available?

- Do I have a purpose in writing about this subject?

- Are the subject and purpose appropriate for my audience?

If you can answer "yes" to all these questions, you can feel confident about your subject and move further into the writing process. If you answer "no" to any of them, use them for further planning. You may well find a good way to narrow your subject, for example, or clarify your purpose as you explore your subject (see 32b). And you can learn more about your subject by searching for information in your library or on the World Wide Web (see chapter 37).

36c A persuasive argument is well developed.

You should explore your subject in enough depth to be able to take a clear position on it and to acquire enough evidence to support that position. In addition, you should consider the reasons why other people might disagree with you and be prepared to respond.

(1) An argument takes a position or makes a claim.

When making an argument, writers take a position on the subject they have chosen. When writing to inquire, this position is likely to appear in the conclusion. When writing to convince, it can appear at almost any point (see 36a and 36e).

The position or stand you take is the main idea, or thesis (see 32c) of your argument. This idea is called the **claim** or the **proposition.** Your claim states what you want your audience to accept or do. Make your claim clear to your audience.

Claims vary in extent; they can be absolute or moderate, large or limited (see 35c). They also vary in kind. Rhetoricians traditionally recognize three kinds of claim.

(a) *Substantiation* **claims assert that something exists.**

Without making a value judgment, a substantiation claim makes an assertion that can be supported by evidence.

> Graduates of our law school often have difficulty finding a job.
>
> There is bumper-to-bumper traffic on Highway 94 during rush hour.

(b) *Evaluation* **claims assert that something has a specific quality.**

According to an evaluation claim, something is good or bad, effective or ineffective, attractive or unattractive, successful or unsuccessful.

> Our law school is failing to produce well-trained attorneys.
>
> Our current transportation system is inadequate.

(c) *Policy* **claims call for a specific action.**

When making policy claims, writers call for something to be done.

> We must find the funds to hire better faculty for our law school.
>
> We need to build a light-rail system linking downtown with the airport and the western suburbs.

Arguments about social issues such as abortion, health care, and affirmative action usually make a policy claim, but such claims are also common in everyday life. Policy claims typically draw on substantiation and evaluation claims: you cannot persuade an audience to do something without first demonstrating that there is a problem that needs to be fixed. In some college essays, you may need to make only a substantiation or evaluation claim. When writing about literature, for example (see 39a), you might need only to evaluate a character.

(2) Effective arguments are well supported.

You must have at least one reason for the claim you make in an argument, and it must be established in your paper. You must also convey any other significant reasons for your position, as well as the values and assumptions that support your thinking.

When you are exploring your subject, make a list of the reasons that have led to your belief without trying to edit them (32b(1)). When you are ready to begin drafting (32f), think critically (chapter 35) about the reasons on your list. Some may need to be eliminated because they overlap; others, because you would have trouble supporting them or because they seem trivial. You can then base your argument on the remaining reasons. If additional reasons occur to you as you write, you can easily add them to your list or incorporate them immediately into your draft.

Although it is possible to base your case on a single reason, it can be risky. If your audience does not find this reason persuasive, you have no other support for your case. When you show that you have more than one reason for believing as you do, you increase the likelihood that your audience will find merit in your case. For example, suppose you believe in capital punishment and write an argument favoring it on the grounds that it deters crime. Readers who are aware of evidence showing that the death penalty does not deter crime could find your argument well written but dismiss it nevertheless. If you introduce other reasons for supporting the death penalty, then you make a more complex case that cannot be dismissed so readily.

Sometimes, however, you might have only one good reason for your position. If so, do not be discouraged. A well-developed discussion of a single good reason can be more persuasive than a superficial discussion of several. To develop an argument for which you have only one good reason, explore the reasons behind your reason: the values and assumptions behind your argument—your premise or warrants (see **35f** and **35g**). By demonstrating the thinking behind the single reason on which you are building your case, you can still create a well-developed argument.

Whether you have one reason or several, be sure to provide sufficient evidence from credible sources to support your claim:

- facts,
- statistics,
- examples, and
- testimony.

Be sure also to show readers *why* your evidence supports your claim. Do not assume that the relationship between claim and evidence will be clear to others simply because it is clear to you. Make the connection explicit so that your audience can understand your thinking. (See **35c**, **35d**, and **37c**.)

(3) Effective arguments respond to diverse views.

In addition to listing reasons for believing as you do, you should make a list of reasons why people might disagree with you. Good arguments are never one sided. If you want to be persuasive, you must demonstrate that you are familiar with other views. The most common strategy for doing so is to introduce reasons why others believe differently and then show why you do not find these reasons convincing. In classical rhetoric, this strategy is called **refutation.** By showing not only the reasons for your position but also the weakness of the objections that can be made against it, you bolster your case significantly.

As you consider opposing views, you are likely to discover some you cannot refute. Do not be surprised to discover that other people's views have merit. Issues are often controversial precisely because good arguments can be made by all sides. When you find yourself agreeing with a point raised on another side of the issue, you can benefit from offering a **concession.** By openly conceding that you agree with opponents on a specific point, you show that you are fair minded (see **35d**) and increase your credibility. Concessions also increase the likelihood that opponents will find merit in your case. It is hard to persuade people to agree with you if you insist that they are entirely wrong. If you admit that they are partially right, they are more likely to admit that you could be partially right as well.

Arguments that are exchanged electronically—by e-mail or in discussion groups—can easily become one sided when writers forget that they are using the computer to communicate with other human beings. It is tempting, under such circumstances, to treat others disrespectfully. This temptation should be resisted. Even if you cannot see your readers or expect to meet them face-to-face, you will be more persuasive if you imagine that they are in the same room with you.

When deciding what arguments to refute and what points to concede, consider how long your essay will be and what you know about the audience you are trying to persuade. In a short argument, you will probably need to limit yourself to a brief discussion of opposing views. In a longer one, you can afford to explore such views more fully. In either case, however, think about what your audience is likely to feel or believe and write with those assumptions in mind. Address the most important concerns of your readers. You may lose their attention if you spend time refuting arguments that do not concern them.

Although it is considered rude in some cultures to disagree openly with authority or to state your own views frankly, American readers are accustomed to directness. Consider the expectations of your audience (see **32a**) and write with them in mind.

E X E R C I S E 2

The following paragraph is taken from an argument by Martin Luther King, Jr., in which he defended the struggle for civil rights against the public criticism of a group of prominent clergymen. Write a short analysis of this paragraph in which you note (a) an opposition argument to which he is responding, (b) a refutation that he offers to this argument, (c) a concession that he makes, and (d) any questions that this excerpt raises for you.

[1]You express a great deal of anxiety over our willingness to break laws. [2]This is certainly a legitimate concern. [3]Since we so diligently urge people to obey the Supreme Court's decision of 1954 outlawing segregation in the public schools, at first glance it may seem rather paradoxical for us consciously to break laws. [4]One may well ask: "How can you advocate breaking some laws and obeying others?" [5]The answer lies in the fact that there are two types of laws, just and unjust. [6]I would be the first to advocate obeying just laws. [7]One has not only a legal but a moral responsibility to obey just laws. [8]Conversely, one has a moral responsibility to disobey unjust laws. [9]I would agree with St. Augustine that "an unjust law is no law at all."

—MARTIN LUTHER KING, JR., "Letter from Birmingham Jail"

Different kinds of appeals are often necessary.

If people were entirely rational, persuasion could be achieved through the logical use of evidence (see 35e–h). But because people are often caught up in their own concerns, feel threatened by differences, or see argument as a kind of combat, they may not even hear what you say—no matter how logical it may be. Getting a fair hearing is essential if you want your views to be understood. Theories of argument, from the ancient world to the present, offer advice on how to gain this hearing.

(1) There are three classical appeals.

Aristotle and other important thinkers in the ancient world believed that persuasion is achieved through a combination of three appeals: ethos, logos, and pathos. **Ethos** (an ethical appeal) means demonstrating that you have good character, good will toward the audience, and good knowledge of your subject. **Logos** (a logical appeal) is the effective use of critical thinking and the judicious use of information. It is what you employ when you support your claims, make reasonable conclusions, and avoid logical fallacies (see 35h). Both logos and ethos are essential to effective argumentation. **Pathos** (an emotional appeal) involves using language that will stir the feelings of your audience. Although pathos can be misused by people who wish to obscure thought, it can be effective when used to establish empathy. When you are trying to be persuasive, remember that human beings have feelings as well as thoughts. Appeal to these feelings if you can, but do not rest your entire case on them.

To illustrate how a writer can use all of these appeals, here are three additional excerpts from Martin Luther King, Jr.'s "Letter from Birmingham Jail," the argument quoted on page 506.

(a) Ethical appeals establish a writer's credibility.

In his opening paragraph, King shows that his professional life is so demanding that he needs more than one secretary. He also shows that he wishes to engage in "constructive work," that he has good will toward his audience, and that he will argue in good faith.

> My Dear Fellow Clergymen:
>
> While confined here in the Birmingham city jail, I came across your recent statement calling my present activities "unwise and untimely." Seldom do I pause to answer criticism of my work and ideas. If I sought to answer all the criticisms that cross my desk, my secretaries would have little time for anything other than such correspondence in the course of the day, and I would have no time for constructive work. But since I feel that you are men of genuine good will and that your criticisms are sincerely set forth, I want to try to answer your statement in what I hope will be patient and reasonable terms.

(b) Logical appeals help an audience think clearly.

To help his audience understand why segregation is wrong, King defines key terms.

> Let us consider another example of just and unjust laws. An unjust law is a code that a numerical or power majority group compels a minority group to obey but does not make binding on itself. This is *difference* made legal. By the same token, a just law is a code that a majority compels a minority to follow and that it is willing to follow itself. This is *sameness* made legal.

(c) Emotional appeals can reinforce an argument.

As he moves toward his conclusion, King evokes feelings of idealism and also of guilt.

> I have travelled the length and breadth of Alabama, Mississippi and all the other southern states. On sweltering summer days and

crisp autumn mornings I have looked at the South's beautiful churches with their lofty spires pointing heavenward. I have beheld the impressive outlines of her massive religious-education buildings. Over and over I have found myself asking: "What kind of people worship here? Who is their God? [. . .] Where were their voices of support when bruised and weary Negro men and women decided to rise from the dark dungeon of complacency to the bright hills of creative protest?"

—MARTIN LUTHER KING, JR., "Letter from Birmingham Jail"

The full text of this argument includes other examples of ethos, logos, and pathos. Classical appeals often occur throughout an argument, not just in separate paragraphs. Look for these appeals in the arguments you read and employ them in your own.

(2) Rogerian appeals emphasize showing other people that you understand them.

Rogerian argument derives from the work of Carl R. Rogers, a psychologist who believed that many problems are the result of misunderstanding causing a breakdown in communication. In his book *On Becoming a Person* (1961), Rogers argues that people often fail to understand each other because of a natural tendency to judge and evaluate, agree or disagree. He emphasizes the importance of listening carefully to what others say and understanding their ideas. His model calls for having the courage to suspend judgment until you are able to restate fairly and accurately what others believe. When each person in a conflict demonstrates this ability, the likelihood of misunderstanding is significantly reduced. One of the advantages of this model is that it can be initiated by a single person in a potentially explosive situation. Another advantage is that it can help foster personal growth.

Skills such as paraphrasing and summarizing (see 38c (3–4)) are essential to Rogerian argument. Although this model can be used to achieve a number of goals, it is especially useful when building consensus. A writer making a Rogerian argument says, in effect, "I have heard your concerns, and I am responding to them to the best of my ability. I am also offering some ideas of my own from which we can both benefit. I want to work with you and will not try to push you around." This emphasis on being fair minded and nonconfrontational gives **ethos** (see **36d(1)**) an essential place in Rogerian argument. Because it emphasizes the importance of listening and speaking respectfully, a Rogerian approach to communication is also useful when writing groups discuss how to revise drafts. (See **33b**.)

To demonstrate that you have given fair consideration to the views of others, you begin a Rogerian argument by paraphrasing these views and demonstrating that you understand the thinking behind them. Then you introduce your own position and explain why you believe it has merit. Because Rogerian argument is designed to build consensus, you conclude by showing how everyone concerned about the issue could benefit from adopting your proposal. (See pages 512–13.)

The summary of benefits with which a Rogerian argument concludes gives you the opportunity to draw your argument together and appeal to your audience without simply restating what you have already said. The following example comes from the conclusion to an argument on public education. Note how the author shows how students, teachers, and the public at large could benefit from adopting her proposal.

> Reducing maximum class size in our secondary schools from thirty students to twenty-five will not solve all the problems in our system, but it will yield important benefits. Students will get more individualized instruction. Better able to give their full attention to the students who remain with them, teachers will gain greater job satisfaction. And in an era when events like the recent killings in Littleton, Colorado, raise legitimate concerns about the safety of public schools, an improved student-teacher ratio reduces the risk of a troubled student being overlooked—a comfort to parents as

well as educators. Finally even those citizens who do not have children will benefit, because in the long run everyone gains from living in a community where people are well educated.

—LAURA BECHDEL, "Space to Learn"

36e There are several ways to organize an argument.

You can begin by outlining or by writing your first draft and then deciding how to better organize it as you revise (chapter 33). In either case, you can organize your argument deductively (35f) by working to a conclusion that is entailed by your premise or inductively (35e) by moving toward a conclusion that is not entailed by your premise.

Unless your instructor asks you to demonstrate a particular type of organization, no one type is unquestionably right for every written argument. The decisions you make about organization should be based on what would be most effective when writing about your subject in a specific context for the audience you have in mind. (See 32a.) Writers often develop a good plan simply by listing the major points they want to make (32d(1)), deciding what order to put them in, and then deciding where to respond to counterarguments (36c(3)). They must also decide whether to place their thesis or proposition at the beginning, in the middle, or at the end of their argument.

There are, however, a few basic principles that are useful to remember.

(1) Classical arrangement works well if your audience has not yet taken a position on your issue.

One way to organize your argument is to follow the plan of classical rhetoric. This plan assumes that an audience is prepared to follow a well-reasoned argument.

Introduction	Introduce your issue and capture the attention of your audience. Try using a short narrative or a strong example. (See 33a(4).)
Background information	Provide your audience with a history of the situation, state how things currently stand. Define any key terms. Even if you think the facts speak for themselves, draw the attention of your audience to those points that are especially important and explain why they are meaningful.
Proposition	Introduce the position you are taking. Frame it as a thesis statement or claim. (See 32c and 36c(1).)
Proof	Discuss the reasons why you have taken your position. Provide facts, expert testimony, and any other evidence that supports your claim.
Refutation	Show why you are not persuaded by the arguments of people who hold a different position. Concede any point that has merit but show why this concession does not damage your own case.
Conclusion	Summarize your most important points and appeal to your audience's feelings.

Use this plan if it seems appropriate for your rhetorical situation (see 32a).

(2) Rogerian arrangement can help calm an audience strongly opposed to you.

To write an argument informed by Rogerian appeals (pages 509–11), you can be guided by the following plan.

Introduction	Establish that you have paid attention to views different from your own. Build trust by stating these views clearly and fairly.
Concessions	Reassure the people you hope to persuade by

showing that you agree with them to an extent and do not think they are completely wrong.

Thesis   Now that you have earned the confidence of your audience, state your claim or proposition.

Support   Explain why you have taken this position and provide support for it.

Conclusion Conclude by showing how your audience and other people could benefit from accepting your position. Indicate the extent to which this position will resolve the problem you are addressing. If you are offering a partial solution to a complex problem, concede that further work may be necessary.

When following this plan, you will find that some parts require more development than others. For example, while you may be able to make concessions within a single paragraph or to state your own position in one, you are likely to need several paragraphs to support your thesis.

(3) Refutation and concessions are most effective when placed where readers will welcome them.

Classical arrangement places refutation toward the end of an argument and works well for an audience familiar with this plan. But if you wait until the end of your argument to recognize views that differ from yours, readers unfamiliar with classical arrangement may have already decided that you are too one-sided—and may even have stopped reading. When writers are taking a highly controversial stand on a subject that has inspired strong feelings, they sometimes begin by responding to these strongly held views. A variation on classical arrangement allows writers to begin by refuting these views on the grounds that readers would be unwilling to hear a new proposition unless they are first shown what is wrong with their current thinking.

In a Rogerian argument, a writer would begin by reporting these views fairly and identifying what is valuable about them. The strategy in this case is not to refute the views in question but to concede that they have merit—thus putting the audience at ease before introducing a thesis or claim that might be rejected if stated prematurely. (See pages 509–11.)

Under other circumstances, however, some readers may react negatively to a writer who responds to opposing arguments before offering any reasons to support his or her own view. These readers want to know where an argument is headed. For this reason, writers often choose to state their proposition at the beginning of the argument and offer at least one strong reason to support it before turning to opposing views. They sometimes keep at least one other reason in reserve, so that they can discuss it after responding to opposing views instead of ending with an emphasis on refutation.

Unless you are required to follow a specific plan, you should respond to opposing views when your audience is most likely either to expect this discussion or to be willing to hear it. You must assess your readers carefully (see 32a), determining what opinions they are likely to have about your subject and how open they are to new ideas. If your audience is receptive, you can place refutation and concessions after launching your own case. If your audience adheres to a different position, you should respond to their views toward the beginning of your essay.

(4) Separate reasons are best discussed in separate paragraphs.

You can list several reasons in a single paragraph if its purpose is to summarize why you hold your position. Writers sometimes also include several reasons in a single paragraph near their conclusion if these reasons consist of additional advantages that do not call for detailed discussion. But if you try to develop two separate reasons in the same paragraph, it may lack unity and coherence. (See chapter 31.) When readers look at any paragraph, they should be able to see how it advances the argument that is being made. Discussing separate reasons in separate paragraphs can help readers follow your argument.

Whatever organizational plan you follow, you will usually need at least a full paragraph to develop any reason for your claim (see 36c(1)), and some reasons could easily take several paragraphs. You might need two paragraphs to explain one reason and only one to explain another, either because one is more important or because you have more to say about one than the other. But no matter how many paragraphs you write, or how long any one of them may be, make sure that every paragraph is unified and coherent (see 31a–b).

(5) You can begin a paragraph with a view different from yours.

If you follow this strategy, the rest of the paragraph is available for your response, and readers make only one shift between differing views. If you begin a paragraph with your view, then introduce an opponent's view, and then move back to yours, readers must shift direction twice and may miss the point. If you wait until the very end of a paragraph to respond to a different view, you could deny yourself the space you need to respond.

(6) Your conclusion can reinforce your purpose.

If you are writing to inquire, you might conclude with the truth you have reached. If you are writing to convince others, you might end by restating your position and summarizing your reasons for holding it. Ideally, however, a good conclusion does more than repeat points that have already been made. When considering how to conclude an argument, it is often useful to imagine readers who are interested in what you have to say but unsure about what you expect from them. "So what?" they might ask. "How does all this affect me, and what am I supposed to do about it?" When writing to persuade others, you could conclude with a paragraph that indicates how opposing parties in a conflict could all gain from accepting the position you have argued. Your conclusion could also emphasize a specific action that you want your audience to take (see 33a(5)). Or you could conclude with an ethical or emotional appeal (see 36d(1)).

EXERCISE 3

Study the editorial page of any newspaper for two or three days. Choose an editorial or letter to the editor that strikes you as effective. Bring copies of it to class, and be prepared to discuss how it is organized and what kind of appeals it includes.

36f **You can improve your ability to write persuasively by studying the arguments of other writers.**

The following paper illustrates one student's response to an assignment in persuasive writing. As you read it, consider whether the author has argued her case effectively.

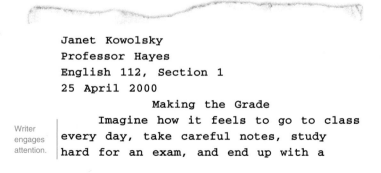

Janet Kowolsky
Professor Hayes
English 112, Section 1
25 April 2000

Making the Grade

Writer engages attention.

Imagine how it feels to go to class every day, take careful notes, study hard for an exam, and end up with a grade that is even lower than you feared. Then imagine that this has happened in your favorite subject and you limp back to your room wondering whether you should change your major or maybe even drop out of school. College professors, especially those who have not been tested recently, might benefit from imagining this scene and considering how it would feel to take one of the tests they have devised under the same conditions their students experience.

Last semester I had four midterm exams and three finals. This semester I have already had another three exams, and more will be coming up in a few weeks. The results have been all over the place even though I studied hard for each of these tests. Surprisingly, some of my worst results have been in my best subjects. I have come to understand that performance on an exam is determined not only by how much you study for it and what the questions are like. It is also determined by the circumstances under which the exam is given.

Of the ten exams I have had so far, eight were taken in class and two were taken outside of class. The eight in-class exams differed in terms of how they were set up. Three involved studying like crazy without having any clear sense of what I would be asked to do. My teachers simply said to review everything we had covered so far because

Writer engages the attention of audience she hopes to persuade.

Writer identifies her audience.

Introduction of topic

Background

this exam was cumulative. The others were less stressful. When I was preparing for finals in December, my psychology professor and my biology professor distributed copies of previous exams so that my classmates and I could have a rough idea of what our exam was going to be like. That was helpful. This semester, my history teacher gave us a list of six questions a week before our midterm and told us she would choose three of them for our test. This was also helpful. I still had to study hard, because I wanted to be able to do a good job with any of these questions, but I had less anxiety preparing for the test.

Unfortunately, each of these exams had to be taken in a room crowded with other students and filled with tension. Whenever I wanted to pause to think, I would look around and see other people scribbling away and worry that I was falling behind. When people would start to leave early, I would become anxious-- thinking something must be wrong with me because I needed all the time that still remained. Then there were the many irritations and distractions: losing my concentration when someone arrived late and squeezed into the seat next to me, listening to people rummage in their backpacks for supplies, being asked if I had an extra pen, catching sight of other students passing material between them, and feeling like I was some kind of laboratory rat under the eye of the teacher monitoring the room.

Appeal to feeling

Two of my other tests were entirely different because they were take-home exams. One of these was in my introduction to literature class; the other was in calculus. Although these two exams were set up somewhat differently, they were both excellent. I think more professors should assign take-home exams.

Proposition or claim

Their big advantage is that you can work on them in a quiet place where you feel safe and comfortable. The questions on my two take-homes were challenging, but I did well on both of them because I was working in space that I selected. Because the circumstances are more comfortable does not mean that the exam itself has to be easy. If professors eliminated some of the stress of exam taking, they would be able to tell more accurately how much their students really know. Is that not the purpose of exams?

First reason in support of proposition

Writer raises a concern of her audience.

Some professors may be concerned that students will cheat if they take their exams at home. I have to admit that cheating could be a problem. However, students who really want to cheat can usually find a way of doing so on regular exams and other assignments. So avoiding take-home exams does not mean that cheating goes away. And take-

Writer anticipates an opposing argument and makes a concession.

Refutation | home exams can be designed to minimize cheating. My literature exam, for example, was an open-book essay exam. It was very useful to be able to look up quotes to back up what I wanted to say, but there is no way I could have passed the exam if I had not read the material and thought about it in advance.

Concession | Theoretically, somebody could probably get a friend to take an exam like this for him or her. But the same thing could happen when we have to write papers.

Refutation | When somebody cheats this way, the professor should be able to tell even if she was not there watching the person do it.

Writer raises a second opposing argument. | Another common argument against take-home exams is that they could become big productions. I have heard some students say that they would rather get an exam over with in two hours than have a take-home that takes as much work as writing another big paper. I understand these concerns. My literature teacher told us that we could take as long as we wanted on the exam just as long as we handed it in on time, and I ended up spending a whole morning on it.

Writ iden with oppe

Refutation | But my calculus professor insisted that we limit ourselves to the two hours we would get during the standard final exam period. We got to choose which two hours we would devote to the exam--and where we would take it--but the exam itself took no longer than any other exam.

In other words, take-homes can be designed in different ways to make them appropriate for different classes.

There are a number of other advantages to take-home exams. Finals are not scheduled during the same hours the class met, and this can be a problem for students who have jobs or children to care for. The take-home provides flexibility for such students by being sensitive to their needs. And just as they are more student-friendly, they are also more professor-friendly. Teachers do not have to hang around monitoring a classroom when they have lots of other things they could be doing. And more important, they get to read better exams. Would professors not be happier to see their students doing well than to see them doing poorly?

Take-home exams can be well designed or badly designed--just like any other assignment. But the flexibility they offer makes them preferable to traditional exams. Professors who have never offered a take-home exam should experiment with them. They will get a chance to do so soon, and I hope they will take advantage of it.

Chapter

37 Research: Finding and Evaluating Sources

The distinctive feature of a research assignment is that it requires you to obtain information in order to clarify your thinking. Good research skills are essential when you are required to write papers incorporating outside sources into a document that is clearly your own. (See chapter 38.) But these skills may help with other writing assignments as well, since you may need to obtain information even when you are not specifically required to do research. Moreover, good research skills are essential in most professions (see 39b), and there will be many occasions when you simply want to find something out for yourself.

An inquiring mind is the best equipment you can bring to research. But if you want to inquire efficiently, you need to develop specific skills in accessing and evaluating information. Without these skills, you may find yourself either without information you need or overwhelmed by more information than you can handle. These skills include knowing how to

- develop a research routine (37a),
- frame a research question (37b),
- evaluate the reliability of sources (37c),
- use a college or university library (37d(1)),
- use the World Wide Web (37d(2)),
- conduct surveys and interviews (37e), and
- compose a working bibliography (37f).

37a Writers need information.

Almost anything you write requires you to use information. Sometimes, you may discover that you have enough information from your own experience or observations. Other times, you may need to search a library or the World Wide Web (the Web) for material.

Because downloading images and texts from the Web is so easy (see 37d(2)), many students now go to it immediately and exclusively—overlooking other avenues that might give them better results. You can assume that there is information on the Web about most subjects. Sorting through hundreds of sites can be time-consuming, however. Before turning to the Web, consider whether material housed in your college library, and guidance from a reference librarian, would be useful during the early stages of your project (see 37d).

As you proceed, be aware of which sources are primary and which are secondary. **Primary sources** for topics in literature and the humanities are generally documents and literary works. In the social sciences, primary sources can be field observations, case histories, and survey data. In the sciences, primary sources are generally empirical—measurements, experiments, and the like. **Secondary sources** are commentaries on primary sources. So a review of a new novel would be a secondary source and so would a critical study of young adults based on survey data. Experienced researchers usually consult both primary and secondary sources, read them critically, and draw on them carefully. (See chapters 35 and 38.)

In addition to examining information that has already been published (either in print or on the Web), consider whether you would benefit from discussing your project with other people. An authority on your topic could be teaching at your college. Interview subjects could be close at hand or available through e-mail. Thoughtful conversation about your topic could be generated through an electronic discussion list (see 37e). And the instructor who assigned your project can help clarify what you need to do to complete it successfully.

(1) Different resources offer different advantages.

Much of the research that people do in their daily lives involves looking in different places to find answers to questions. If you plan to buy a new car, for example, you may read reviews published in magazines or on the Web, talk to people familiar with the cars that interest you, and take a test drive or two. A similar strategy may be appropriate for research assignments in school or at work: read, interview, and observe.

The following chart can help you see at a glance the advantages and disadvantages of different resources. (For additional information on developing a search strategy, see 37d.)

Resource Assessment Table

Library Catalog (see pages 534–36)

Advantages

It indexes books available on your campus. It may also link to catalogs at other schools. It identifies material that has been professionally edited, reviewed, and selected for purchase.

Disadvantages

It will not cover all books. A book you need may be checked out. Interlibrary loan may be necessary.

Electronic Indexes to Periodicals (see pages 537–46)

Advantages

They enable you to find material focused specifically on your topic. The most recent citations are identified first and direct you to current work in your field. They have a high percentage of credible sources.

Disadvantages

They provide citations to articles but usually not the full text of them. Articles must usually be located in library holdings or through interlibrary loan. Scholarly articles can be difficult reading for researchers unfamiliar with the field.

Web Sites (see pages 549–53)

Advantages

The Web contains a high volume of recent material. Many sites have links to other relevant sites. The full text can be downloaded and printed out on a personal computer.

Disadvantages

Researchers can be overwhelmed by the number of available sites and waste time investigating sites that prove unhelpful. A high percentage of sites lack credibility.

Conversation (see pages 554–56)

Advantages

Interviews can be conducted in person, by phone, or by e-mail and focus on a point you need to clarify. Dialogue can generate new ideas when you feel stuck.

Disadvantages

Ideas can be lost if not recorded. Misreporting is common. Sources may lack credibility.

(2) Establishing a research routine helps you use time efficiently.

Scheduling your time is especially important because research papers are usually assigned several weeks before they are due, and the temptation to procrastinate may be strong. Make sure to allow enough time for the long process of choosing a subject (32b), reading extensively, taking notes (38b), preparing a working bibliography (37f), developing a thesis (32c), outlining (32d(2)), drafting (32f), revising (33a), and editing (33c).

A **research log** can help you stay on schedule and keep you from having to do tasks over. It is a journal focused on everything related to your project: ideas for subjects, ways to refine topics, what you already know. Not only will a research log provide a central location for noting how your work is progressing, but also it can help you keep track of the tasks you have yet to do as well as any you need to do again.

Here is a sample form that can help you make a realistic schedule. You may need more (or less) time for each of these activities. Adjust your schedule to conform to the way you work best.

Activity	Days Needed	Date Completed
1. Explore the campus library	1	_____ ☐
2. Find a topic and develop a working hypothesis	2	_____ ☐
3. Establish a search strategy	1	_____ ☐
4. Develop a working bibliography	5	_____ ☐
5. Take notes	6	_____ ☐
6. Develop the thesis and outline	2	_____ ☐
7. Draft the paper	3	_____ ☐
8. Seek peer review	1	_____ ☐
9. Revise the paper	2	_____ ☐
10. Prepare the final draft	1	_____ ☐
11. Prepare the works-cited list	1	_____ ☐
12. Proofread	1	_____ ☐

37b Researchers focus their subject and frame it as a question that needs to be answered.

You find the **topic** for a research paper in much the same way as you find a topic for any piece of writing: you are assigned a topic or you choose a question that you would like to answer. (See 32b.)

The exploration methods discussed in 32b(1)—freewriting, listing, clustering, and questioning—can help you find an interesting topic. Focusing on a specific topic is important since one of your main objectives is to show your ability to write in some depth within the time allowed and (usually) the length specified. But be flexible. Even if you begin research with a focus already in mind, be prepared to revise it if preliminary research leads you to a related issue that interests you more.

As you focus your subject, think in terms of a **research problem:** a question or issue that can be resolved at least partly through research. It may lead you to a position you wish to argue (see chapter 36), but it should invite exploration rather than make a judgment. For example, the thesis "animal experimentation is wrong" is not a research problem because it is a conclusion rather than a question. Someone interested in animal research might begin with a question like "Are animals being treated responsibly in research labs?" or "Under what circumstances could animal experimentation be necessary?" Beginning with a question, rather than an answer, encourages researchers to look at diverse materials—not just material that reinforces what they already believe.

At this point, you might find it useful to make a **quick search.** Select two or three keywords from a subject you have in mind and enter them in an online index to periodicals (see **37d(1)b**). Check them in your library's main catalog (see **37d(1)a**) as well. Doing so will help establish whether there is enough material on your subject (or whether there is too much). The amount of pertinent material in your college library is also an important test. If you find hundreds of relevant sources, you should narrow the subject to one with a more manageable scope. However, if you have difficulty finding sources, chances are that your subject is too narrow and needs to be broader. Because the best research papers usually draw on different kinds of material, you should also reconsider any topic that would force you to rely exclusively on one type of source. A paper based only on newspaper articles, for example, could easily lack depth, and research drawn exclusively from books might overlook current information in the field. Similarly, relying solely on electronic sources is unwise since there are excellent sources in print that do not appear online.

EXERCISE 1

Consider the following subjects, each of which would need to be narrowed down for a ten-page paper. To experiment with framing a research problem, compose two questions about each of the following subjects.

1. illegal drugs
2. day care for children
3. racism
4. the job market
5. gender differences
6. eating disorders

37c Researchers look for reliable sources.

When you are doing research, one important consideration is always the reliability of your sources. (See **35d**.) As you discover sources, ask the questions in the following checklist.

CHECKLIST for Evaluating Sources
• What are the author's credentials?
• Do others speak of the writer as an authority?
• Does the work contain evidence indicating that the author is well informed?
• Does the work contain evidence that the author is prejudiced in any way?
• Is the work recent enough to provide up-to-date information?
• Does the work provide documentation to support important points?
• Does the work include a bibliography that can help you identify other sources?
• What can you discover about the company or organization that has published this work?

Book Review Digest, which contains convenient summaries of critical opinion on a book, could help you decide which books are most dependable. *Literary Marketplace* will provide basic information about publishers. You can usually assume that university presses demand a high standard of scholarship. Additional information about books and publishers can be found by searching the Web. A directory of publishers with sites on the Web can be obtained through Vanderbilt University (http://www.library.vanderbilt.edu/law/acqs/pubr.html).

As for periodicals, an article published in an **academic journal** (as opposed to a popular magazine) has usually been reviewed by experts before publication. Academic journals are usually published quarterly, which means that there are four issues a year; the time between issues allows for the careful selection and editing of articles. Pieces that appear in **general-circulation magazines** (the kind of magazines that appear weekly or monthly and that you might find in a supermarket or drugstore) may also be reliable, but they are usually written more quickly and chosen for publication by someone on the staff—not by an expert in the field.

Some general-circulation periodicals are straightforward about identifying their affiliations. For instance, *Mother Jones* reveals its liberal credentials on its masthead, which identifies its namesake as "Mary Harris 'Mother' Jones (1830–1930), orator, union organizer, and hellraiser," and through its rhetoric.

> When the bombs explode at abortion clinics, when the tax protesters turn their guns on federal agents, the cynical politicos who mixed the cocktail of national convulsion won't be around to take the blame. In their plush backstage parlors, they will shake their heads in perfunctory pity before getting back to the business of slapping backs, trading business cards, and stirring the next round of drinks. —WILLIAM SALETAN

Subscription forms for *Conservative Chronicle, The Capitalist's Companion,* and the Conservative Book Club published in *The American Spectator* reveal its political stance, but its rhetoric also makes it clear.

> Just when you think you've got the rules of politics figured out—that liberal Democrats won't give up the theory, rhetoric and practice of class warfare, for example, until you pry their cold, dead fingers from the wallets of the rich—along comes a one-two-three punch to send you reeling. —TOD LINDBERG

These are fairly obvious examples. At other times, however, an apparently well-reasoned article can reflect the values built into a periodical even if they are not readily apparent in the article itself. For example, an article on malpractice suits in the *Journal of the American Medical Association* is likely to be sympathetic to physicians.

Recognizing that periodicals may reflect the political values of their owners and editors does not mean, however, that you must necessarily distrust what you learn from them. Journals and newspapers can be committed to certain values and still have high standards for what they publish.

Distinguish between sources that are **committed** and those that are **biased.** A committed source represents a point of view fairly, while a biased source represents it unfairly. The difference is a matter of **ethos** (see **36d(1)**). It is possible to argue ethically for ideas you believe in; it is also possible to twist facts and misrepresent events to make your point. The same is true in publishing. If you read the *Wall Street Journal* over a period of several weeks, you will recognize that it has a conservative editorial policy and is sympathetic to business interests. This paper is also committed to honest reporting and clear writing, however, so the articles it prints may reflect conservative political positions and still be reliable. Bias appears when politics interfere with honest reporting so that important elements of a story are ignored, distorted, or suppressed. Be alert for such signs of bias as

- personal attacks on people,
- sarcastic language,
- sweeping generalizations unsupported by verifiable data,
- oversimplification of complex issues, and
- ignoring or belittling opposing views.

For additional signs of bias, see **35h**.

Understanding the distinction between "committed" and "biased" is especially useful when you navigate the Web. Many sites are created by organizations or individuals strongly committed to specific values and goals. If you visit the Web site for Planned Parenthood or the National Rifle Association, for example, you can expect to find information that advances the purposes of these organizations. Similarly, if you visit the Web site of the Emily Dickinson International Society, you can expect to find information presented in the hope of advancing interest in and scholarship about her poetry. A site designed by a teacher for a specific course is also likely to be committed to certain values that will be reflected not only in the grading and attendance policies but also in the texts chosen for study and the kind of writing assignments required. You can learn much from committed sites such as these. You need to read critically (see chapter 35) and remember that you are likely to encounter other points of view at other sites, but you should not assume that a site is biased just because it is committed. Look for the signs of bias listed above. It is natural to expect the Emily Dickinson site to be committed to Dickinson's work, but if your research then takes you to a site that ridicules people who prefer other poets or that makes unsupported claims about Dickinson's personal life, then you are visiting a site where commitment has degenerated into bias.

Evaluating electronic sources requires asking additional questions beyond those in the Checklist for Evaluating Sources on page 529. Since electronic sites can easily be kept up-to-date, look for evidence of frequent maintenance. Ask the following questions.

- How often is the site updated?
- Is the author acknowledged?
- Is the source located at an institution or sponsored by an organization about which information is available at other sites? Addresses including **.edu** (for education), **.gov** (for government), and **.org** (for organization) signal sources of this kind.
- Does the work include citations to other sources or, in the case of hypertext, links to other reliable documents?

Additional information on evaluating sites can be found at http://milton.mse.jhu.edu:8001/research/education/net.html (a site created and maintained by a librarian at Johns Hopkins University). Recognize, however, that the addresses for Web sites can change. When this happens, you will sometimes be linked to the new address; at other times, you will have to search for it.

As you read your sources, learn how to identify useful passages. Seldom will an entire Web site, book, or article be useful for a research paper. You will usually need to turn to many sources, rejecting some altogether and using only parts of others. You cannot spend equal time at every site you discover, nor can you always take the time to read a book completely. Use the table of contents and the index of a book, and learn to skim until you find the passages you need. When you find them, slow down, and read critically. (See chapter 35.)

EXERCISE 2

Imagine that you are conducting research on how Bill Gates made Microsoft a successful company. For this project, determine how reliable you would consider information drawn from the following sources.

1. *New York Times*
2. *Business Week*
3. *People Weekly*
4. *Harvard Law Review*
5. http://microsoft.com

EXERCISE 3

Do preliminary research for one of the subjects in exercise 1 or 2. Identify one source that seems reliable and another that seems biased. Write a one-page evaluation in which you assess the credibility of each.

37d　Researchers need to know how to locate information efficiently.

Experienced researchers understand that it is easy to waste time by looking for information in the wrong places or turning prematurely to resources they are not yet prepared to understand. Although different projects require different strategies—depending on what the nature of the topic is, how familiar you are with it, and how much time you have for research—you can usually benefit from beginning your search in your college library. If you turn to the library only toward the end of your search, however, you may have the frustrating experience of discovering exactly the right material and being unable to obtain it on short notice because it is checked out by someone else or must be obtained through interlibrary loan (an arrangement among local or regional libraries for exchanging books and photocopied articles). Weeks might pass before the material you need is either returned or shipped to your library.

(1)　Researchers know how to access information in libraries.

Libraries can provide you with diverse materials that have been carefully selected and organized. Moreover, libraries are staffed by information specialists who can help you find what you need. When you visit a library, be sure to look for both books and periodicals. Each requires a different system for retrieving information.

(a)　Books often contain the results of extensive research.

You locate a book by consulting the library's **main catalog,** which gives you the call number you need to find where the work is shelved. Most books are located in the **stacks.** Books put temporarily on **reserve** are located separately and can be checked out only for a short period, if at all. Reference books, encyclopedias, and indexes—materials that cannot usually be checked out of the library—are located in the **reference collection,** which may also include indexing information for electronic databases, either online or on CD-ROM.

Some libraries still maintain a **card catalog** consisting of cards arranged alphabetically in drawers. Cards for each book are filed alphabetically by author, title, and subject or subjects. Most libraries, however, have **computerized catalogs,** which save space and make research more efficient. A library catalog, then, whether computerized or kept on cards, identifies books by **author, title,** or **subject.** Most computerized catalog programs also allow researchers to locate sources by supplying the computer with other information, such as a keyword that may appear in the title or even a book's call number.

Although there may be a slight difference in format between the computerized entry and the catalog card, both provide essentially the same information: author, title, place of publication, publisher, date of publication, number of pages, and any special features such as a bibliography. Both also give the book's call number, which tells you exactly where the book is located.

If your library provides you with access to both card and computer catalogs, check with a librarian to see which is more current. Libraries that have computerized their catalogs may have stopped including new acquisitions in their card catalogs, and libraries that have only recently computerized their catalogs may not have their entire collection online.

An entry from a computerized catalog   In addition to providing the author, title, publisher, and date of publication, a computerized catalog entry also reveals the book's status—information that can save a researcher time when a book has been moved to a special collection or checked out by someone else.

Libraries use a number of different systems for computerizing catalogs. Some appear only on local networks, while others are Web-based to facilitate access from off campus. Expect to encounter variations on this example.

TUFTS UNIVERSITY	Search Tufts	Databases	Help	Hours	**Search Results** Startover

* Brief Record Hitlist * New/Refine Search * MARC Display * Download Full Citation for Record *

Previous Record Next Record

Record # 1

Author :	Nelson, Diane M., 1963-
Title :	A finger in the wound : body politics in quincentennial Guatemala / Diane M. Nelson.
Publisher :	Berkeley : University of California Press, [1999]
Paging :	xix, 427 p. : ill., maps ; 24 cm.
Subject Heading(s) :	Mayas—Ethnic identity.
	Mayas—Civil rights.
	Mayas—Politics and government.
	Body, Human—Political aspects—Guatemala.
	Body, Human—Symbolic aspects—Guatemala.
	Ladino (Latin American people)—Guatemala—Social conditions.
	Mestizaje—Guatemala—Social conditions.
	Popular culture—Guatemala.
	Sex role—Guatemala.
	Violence—Guatemala.
	Guatemala—Ethnic relations.
	Guatemala—Politics and government.
Description :	xix, 427 p. : ill., maps ; 24 cm.
Notes :	Includes bibliographical references (p. 383-406) and index.
ISBN :	0520212851 (pbk. : alk. paper)
LCCN :	98035061
Database Control # :	AGR-7713

Tufts   **Barcoded Items**

Location	Call Number	Material	Status
TISCH BOOK STACKS	F1435.3.E72 N45 1999 c.1	BOOK	Available

* Previous Record * Next Record *

* Brief Record Hitlist * New/Refine Search * MARC Display * Download Full Citation for Record *

Help

The information on a card catalog can help you decide whether you want to examine the book itself. The call number tells you where the library keeps it. When you go to the shelf where the book you are looking for is kept, you may find other relevant sources in the same place.

(b) **Magazines, journals, and newspapers often contain recent information on a subject.**

Periodicals (magazines, journals, and newspapers in print or on microform) are usually stored in a special section of the library. You can browse through current issues and often those of the past year. Older issues are usually stored elsewhere. To access information in periodicals, researchers use **electronic indexes.** Many periodicals are now also available online, and some allow for **full-text retrieval:** the option of downloading and printing out an article. Periodical literature is useful not only because it is timely but also because it has been professionally reviewed and edited.

A variety of periodical indexes (usually accessed at workstations within a library and increasingly via the Web) do for articles what the main catalog does for books: locate material by **subject, author,** or **keyword.** This information is stored electronically on CD-ROM and in online information storage and retrieval systems. To locate and retrieve information with these tools, you need a set of basic skills, as well as additional skills particular to each tool. These can be easily acquired through practice, just as you have already learned to use the computer for other purposes.

In addition to providing electronic access to periodical indexes, many college libraries also provide bound volumes of printed indexes, each of which covers a single year. (For a list, see page 543.) In either electronic or print form, each index includes many publications not listed in the others, so you may need to consult a number of indexes to find the information you need. Some of these may be unfamiliar to you, but they are worth mastering. Even if you have to visit the library to use them, and learn some new skills, the time will be well spent if it leads you to first-rate scholarship that would not appear on the Web.

Virtually every specialized field has its own periodicals, which usually provide much more detailed information than can be found in magazines or newspapers aimed at the general public. When conducting research, you should familiarize yourself with indexes that direct you to the kind of material being written and studied by professionals in your field.

Access to electronic information storage is provided by systems such as *FirstSearch,* which allow you to search in a large number of **databases** (collections of machine-readable information that you can retrieve using a computer). If your school does not subscribe to *FirstSearch,* check to see whether you have access to *SilverPlatter* or *Infotrac.* (See pages 540 and 544–46.) Other databases that may be available include full-text search and retrieval databases such as *EBSCO Academic Search Elite* for periodicals and *LEXIS-NEXIS* for legal documents and newspapers. Most permit users to restrict searches to a specific time period, language, and type of record.

Choosing an index   *FirstSearch* enables you to search through a number of databases. It arranges its indexes in thirteen subject areas: Arts and Humanities, Business and Economics, Conferences and Proceedings, Consumer Affairs and People, Education, Engineering and Technology, General and Reference, General Science, Life Sciences, Medicine and Health Sciences, News and Current Events, Public Affairs and Law, and Social Sciences. After you choose from among these, you are presented with additional choices. Covering more than forty indexes, *FirstSearch* is a highly useful tool for college research—and, as its name suggests, a good place to begin your search for periodical literature.

The introductory screen for *FirstSearch* prompts you to choose a database, and each subsequent choice brings up a new screen. To research a topic like social injustice in Guatemala as Dieter Bohn did for his paper (see 38f), you could click on the database for News and Current Events or Public Affairs and Law. To research what happens when young adults return home

to live with their parents, as Adrienne Harton did for her paper (see 38i), you could click on Social Sciences. Then, once you are in a database, you need to decide what kinds of records to search. By clicking **Article1st,** you could access "nearly 12,500 journals." By clicking **NewsAbs,** you could limit your search to a little "over 25 newspapers."

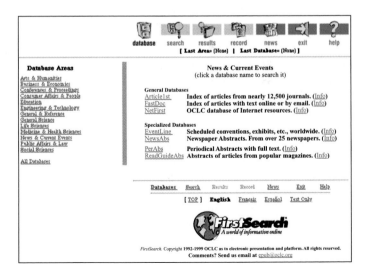

The databases available through *FirstSearch* vary from one library to another. Librarians choose which subscriptions best suit their institution's needs and budget, taking into account the offerings of other electronic indexes.

Most college libraries provide students with access to other indexing services. Many disciplines have their own indexes.

Literature	See the *MLA Bibliography*, which indexes articles and books written in most modern languages and is essential for research in English and American literature.
Education	See *ERIC*, which indexes articles and conference papers in all areas of education.
Psychology	See *PsychLit*, which provides short summaries, or abstracts, of articles in psychology in addition to the citations that will help you find the full article.
Life Sciences	See *Medline*, which provides abstracts of articles in medicine and biology from more than seven thousand journals.

These indexes and many others can be accessed through online service provided by *SilverPlatter*, to which many college libraries subscribe. Instructions for accessing indexes through *SilverPlatter* are usually posted near workstations equipped to handle it. See http://www.silverplatter.com/ for additional information about this service.

Selecting an appropriate index requires you to locate your topic within a discipline or grouping of disciplines. For example, if you are researching the causes of memory loss, you could go directly to *PsychLit*, which is devoted exclusively to scholarship in psychology. If you are researching cases in which students have opened fire on their high school classmates, you could also go to *PsychLit*. But if you recognize that sociologists and criminologists—as well as psychologists—are likely to have studied such cases, you might turn to *Social Science*

Abstracts, available through *FirstSearch,* for a broader range of material. On the other hand, searching a database devoted to business and economics is not likely to be useful for this topic.

Many databases are available on CD-ROM as well as on-line, but CD-ROM searching has one disadvantage: once published, the information cannot be updated without issuing a continuation. If you need up-to-the-minute information, you might need to search through one of the online information storage and retrieval systems to supplement what you find on CD-ROM.

Because electronic databases of scholarly materials are much easier to search and update than print versions, most libraries have switched to them. The databases in your library will look very much alike and can probably be searched using much the same set of commands. A different library, however, may subscribe to the same databases through a different service, and the commands and the screen designs may differ slightly. But if you learn to use one system, you can quickly learn to use another.

Searching an electronic index Whether your library provides indexing services online, via the Web, or on CD-ROM, you can use the following search strategy to locate periodical literature.

Basic Search Strategy

1. Identify the keywords used to discuss the topic.
2. Determine the databases to be searched.
3. Apply a basic search logic.
4. Log on and perform the search.
5. Identify the citations you want to keep.
6. Refine the search strategy if the first search returned too many or too few citations, or (worse) irrelevant ones.
7. Obtain the articles for which you have citations.

Identifying **keywords** for your topic, the first step in this strategy, echoes the beginning steps for locating information in your research process as a whole (see 37b). Many databases permit keyword searches of the entire database, not just **controlled terms** (a vocabulary of official descriptors used to retrieve information). Even if a keyword is not part of the controlled vocabulary, a database search may turn up **records** (or units of stored information) that use the keyword in titles or other parts of the record. If your search yields **no records,** try substituting a synonym or another closely related term for your keyword.

Basic search logic enables you to guard against retrieving too many or too few records. A search result that says, "Found: 2,493,508 records containing the descriptor 'film'" is as useless as one that reports, "Sorry, no records found." You can use certain words (called **logical** or **Boolean operators**) to broaden or narrow your search:

or   broadens a search—**young adults or single adults** finds all records that contain information about either category;

and   narrows a search—**young adults and single adults** returns only those records that contain both categories;

not   excludes specific items—**young adults and single adults not homeless** will exclude any records that mention homeless young single adults;

near   instructs the computer to find a link based on proximity of terms and prevents inclusion of widely separated terms—**young adults near single adults** lists only those references to both young adults and single adults that occur within a preset number of words (this option is often not available, however).

After you have logged on and performed your search, evaluate the records you have retrieved and discard any that are irrelevant. If you need to narrow or broaden your search, revise your selection of keywords and use them with logical operators.

Searching indexes in bound volumes   Although searching electronic indexes is more efficient than searching through bound and printed indexes, many college libraries continue to purchase bound volumes in addition to subscribing to comparable databases. The reason is simple: computers malfunction, networks go down, and Internet service is interrupted. Just as your computer may freeze some day, the entire system for a library can crash and be inoperable for several days. Bound volumes provide essential backup when computers are out of service. Searching through them takes more time than searching a database, but it is preferable to having your research disrupted. Some of the most useful ones, with their dates of beginning publication, are as follows.

Applied Science and Technology Index. 1958–.
Art Index. 1929–.
Biological and Agricultural Index. 1946–.
Business Periodicals Index. 1958–.
Cumulative Index to Nursing and Allied Health Literature (CINAHL). 1982–.
General Science Index. 1978–.
Humanities Index. 1974–.
Index to Legal Periodicals. 1908–.
Music Index. 1949–.
Philosopher's Index. 1967–.
Public Affairs Information Service (Bulletin). 1915–.
Social Sciences Index. 1974–.

When they publish electronic versions of their indexes, some publishers change the title: *Current Index to Journals in Education* (*CIJE*) and *Resources in Education* (*RIE*) are the bound volumes for research in education, while *ERIC* is the electronic version.

Consult the front of any bound volume for a key to the abbreviations used in individual entries.

(c) **Abstracting services provide summaries.**

An **abstract** is a short summary of a longer work. Articles in the social and natural sciences often begin with an abstract so that readers can quickly determine whether they wish to read the whole article. Abstracts can also be accessed electronically.

While bound printed indexes provide only a list of citations for articles, some of their electronic counterparts also provide abstracts. The bound volumes of the *Social Sciences Index,* for example, provide only the bibliographical information necessary for locating each article. *Social Science Abstracts* (available through *FirstSearch*) is now providing these citations, as well as short summaries of most articles.

InfoTrac, a widely used electronic index to articles in periodicals, now provides an abstracting service through its *Expanded Academic ASAP* database. Entering **menchu** (for Rigoberta Menchú, the subject of the research paper in 38f(2)), a student was able to locate numerous sources as can be seen on page 545. Moving the mouse to the entry for David Stoll and clicking produced both an abstract and the full text for this piece as can be seen on page 546.

Other **abstracting services** support specific academic discipines. Your library may have CD-ROMs for *Academic Abstracts, Biological Abstracts, Chemical Abstracts,* and *Psychological Abstracts.* When using one of these services, you can quickly scan the short summaries and decide which seem likely to be the most useful. As with *InfoTrac,* you can print out a list of citations, a list of citations with abstracts, and the full text of some of the articles you discover. Be aware, however, that abstracting services sometimes include material published in languages other than English. An abstract may be in English even if the article is not. When this is the case, the language in which the article was published is usually indentified within the abstract.

University of St Thomas Library

Return to:
Subject Guide   Expanded Academic ASAP

INFOTRAC
SearchBank

Citation List   New Database   New Search   Mark List

Citations 1 to 20
Subject: menchu, rigoberta

Limit
Search

☐   **Crossing Borders.** (Review) Tim Golden.
Mark   **The New York Times Book Review** April 18, 1999 v104 i16 p29 col 1 (30 col in)
View extended citation and retrieval choices

☐   **I, Rigoberta Menchu: An Indian Woman in Guatemala.** (Review) Peter Canby.
Mark   **The New York Review of Books** April 8, 1999 v46 i6 p28(6)
View extended citation and retrieval choices

☐   **A Lofty Liar.** (Nobel Peace Prize winner Rigoberta Menchu)(Brief Article) KARA J. PETERSON.
Mark
World Press Review April 1999 v46 i4 p33(1)
View text and retrieval choices

☐   **Nobel Winner Rejects 'Unjust' Allegations That She Lied.** (Rigoberta Menchu denies that she
Mark lied in book)(Brief Article) CALVIN REID.
Publishers Weekly March 8, 1999 v246 i10 p20(1)
View text and retrieval choices

☐   **In the end, the poor may decide.** (anthropologist challenges truth of Guatemalan's women's story)
Mark PAUL JEFFERY.
National Catholic Reporter March 5, 1999 v35 i18 p9(1)
View text and retrieval choices

☐   **Truth-telling and memory in postwar Guatemala: an interview with** Rigoberta Menchu.
Mark (winner of the 1992 Nobel Prize for Peace)(Interview) Jo-Marie Burt, Fred Rosen.
NACLA Report on the Americas March-April 1999 v32 i5 p6(4)
View text and retrieval choices

☑   **David Stoll on Rigoberta, guerrillas and academics.** (interview with author of book on
Mark Rigoberta Menchu)(Interview) Steven Dudley.
NACLA Report on the Americas March-April 1999 v32 i5 p8(2)
View text and retrieval choices

☐   **Peace Prize winner admits discrepancies.** (Rigoberta Menchu)
Mark   **The New York Times** Feb 12, 1999 pA12(L) col 1 (5 col in)
View extended citation and retriecval choices

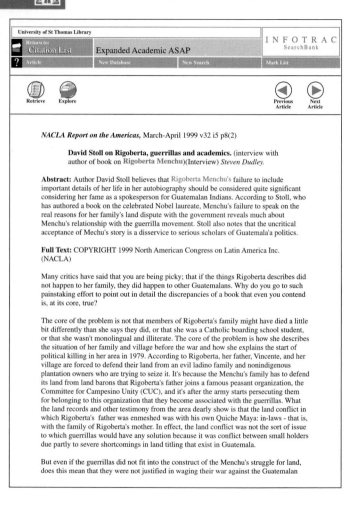

NACLA Report on the Americas, March-April 1999 v32 i5 p8(2)

David Stoll on Rigoberta, guerrillas and academics. (interview with author of book on Rigoberta Menchu)(Interview) *Steven Dudley.*

Abstract: Author David Stoll believes that Rigoberta Menchu's failure to include important details of her life in her autobiography should be considered quite significant considering her fame as a spokesperson for Guatemalan Indians. According to Stoll, who has authored a book on the celebrated Nobel laureate, Menchu's failure to speak on the real reasons for her family's land dispute with the government reveals much about Menchu's relationship with the guerrilla movement. Stoll also notes that the uncritical acceptance of Mechu's story is a disservice to serious scholars of Guatemala'a politics.

Many critics have said that you are being picky; that if the things Rigoberta describes did not happen to her family, they did happen to other Guatemalans. Why do you go to such painstaking effort to point out in detail the discrepancies of a book that even you contend is, at its core, true?

The core of the problem is not that members of Rigoberta's family might have died a little bit differently than she says they did, or that she was a Catholic boarding school student, or that she wasn't monolingual and illiterate. The core of the problem is how she describes the situation of her family and village before the war and how she explains the start of political killing in her area in 1979. According to Rigoberta, her father, Vincente, and her village are forced to defend their land from an evil ladino family and nonindigenous plantation owners who are trying to seize it. It's because the Menchu's family has to defend its land from land barons that Rigoberta's father joins a famous peasant organization, the Committee for Campesino Unity (CUC), and it's after the army starts persecuting them for belonging to this organization that they become associated with the guerrillas. What the land records and other testimony from the area dearly show is that the land conflict in which Rigoberta's father was enmeshed was with his own Quiche Maya: in-laws - that is, with the family of Rigoberta's mother. In effect, the land conflict was not the sort of issue to which guerrillas would have any solution because it was conflict between small holders due partly to severe shortcomings in land titling that exist in Guatemala.

But even if the guerrillas did not fit into the construct of the Menchu's struggle for land, does this mean that they were not justified in waging their war against the Guatemalan

(d) Reference works provide useful background.

When doing research, you may need to consult a variety of reference works. A general encyclopedia, such as *Encyclopaedia Britannica* (now available by subscription on the Web at http://www.eb.com/) can provide useful information, especially at an early stage in your research. And you will almost certainly need to consult a dictionary. (See 19a.) You may be able to access an electronic encyclopedia and dictionary through the software you are using before turning to the Web, where many other reference works can be located.

But despite the ease with which many reference works can now be accessed electronically, you may need to consult a specialized encyclopedia or dictionary in your college library to identify names and understand concepts in the books or articles you have discovered. Sources written for a specialized audience (see 32a(2)) will assume that readers do not need help with basic terms. Reference books can help you fill in the gaps that keep you from understanding the other sources you have found.

For a detailed list of reference books and a short description of each, consult *Guide to Reference Books* by Robert Balay and *American Reference Books Annual* (*ARBA*). For examples of reference works useful when writing about literature, see pages 695–96. A few of the most widely used reference books are listed here with abbreviated bibliographical information. Note that these are reference sources: refer to them for help, but do not rely on any of them as a principal source for a college paper.

Special Dictionaries and Encyclopedias

Dictionary of American History. Rev. ed. 8 vols. 1976–78. Supplements, 1996.
Dictionary of Art. Ed. Jane Turner. 34 vols. 1996.

Encyclopedia of American Foreign Policy. Ed. Alexander
DeConde. 3 vols. 1978.

Encyclopedia of Higher Education. Ed. Burton R. Clark and
Guy R. Neave. 4 vols. 1992.

Encyclopedia of Psychology. Ed. Raymond J. Corsini. 2nd ed.
4 vols. 1994.

Encyclopedia of Religion. Ed. Mircea Eliade. 16 vols. Also on
CD-ROM. 1996.

International Encyclopedia of the Social Sciences. Ed. D. E.
Sills. 8 vols. 1977. Supplements.

McGraw-Hill Encyclopedia of Science and Technology. 8th ed.
20 vols. 1997. Yearbooks.

The New Grove Dictionary of Music and Musicians. Ed. Stanley
Sadie. 20 vols. 1980. Reprinted with corrections in 1995.

Routledge Encyclopedia of Philosophy. Ed. Edward Craig and
Luciano Floridi. 10 vols. 1998.

Biographies

American National Biography. Ed. John A. Garraty and Mark C.
Carnes. 24 vols. 1999.

Biography and Genealogy Master Index. 1980–. Also on CD-
ROM. 1996.

Biography Index. 1946–.

Current Biography Cumulated Index. 1940–.

Dictionary of National Biography (British). 22 vols. 1882–1953.
Rpt. 1981. Supplements.

Dictionary of Scientific Biography. 16 vols. 1970–81.
Supplements.

Notable American Women: 1607–1950. 3 vols. 1971.
Supplements.

Notable Black American Women. 2nd ed. 1996.

Webster's New Biographical Dictionary. 1995.

Who's Who in America. 1899–. (See also Marquis's *Who's
Who Publications: Index to All Books.* 1976–, revised
annually.)

(2) Researchers need to know how to navigate the World Wide Web.

The Internet, an international network of computers linked through telephone and fiber-optic lines, is one of the most exciting tools available to you. Detailed instructions for gaining access to and using the Internet are beyond the scope of this handbook, but inexpensive, convenient help is readily available.

The computing center at your school may offer workshops that will teach you how to log on to the Internet, send an e-mail message, sign up with a newsgroup, or access the Web. Your library may also offer workshops on using the Web for research. If not, there is a good chance that someone you know can help get you started. You can also find useful introductions to the Internet in bookstores and computer superstores, as well as through online bookstores.

Nobody owns the Internet, and there is no charge to use it, but it is not really free. Companies, universities, the government, and other institutions bear most of the cost. You probably have access to the Internet through your academic computing account, especially if your school charges a computer users' fee. If you have a computer with a modem and your school has a data number you can dial, you can also probably do your Internet searching from home. If you are not connected to the campus network or your school does not support dial-up access, you may want to consider a local Internet service provider that offers unlimited access for a flat monthly fee.

The **World Wide Web** is a huge and rapidly expanding collection of information much of which—once located—is useful for research papers and some of which is not. The easiest way to find information on the Web is to use one of the many search systems (often called search engines), such as *AltaVista, InfoSeek, Lycos,* or *Yahoo!* After you type keywords into a text entry box, these engines will return a list of electronic documents (Web sites) that meet the searching criteria. Most search engines encourage the use of the logical operators *and, or,* and *not* to make the search as efficient as possible. (See page 542.)

Information about *AltaVista, Yahoo!,* and other search engines can be found at http://daphne.palomar.edu/TGSEARCH (a site created at Palomar College). There are important differences among search engines. Some, like *Yahoo!,* match keyword searches against Web sites submitted by owners and entered by human indexers (who also classify them into basic categories). Others, like *AltaVista,* are best known for their **spiders,** automatic programs that visit millions of Web sites to index the actual content of the pages, word by word.

Because of differences such as these, different search systems will return different results. One system may search only for the titles of documents, another may look at document links, and a few search the full text of every document they index. Furthermore, some search only the Web, whereas others search parts of the Internet (such as Usenet Newsgroups) that are not part of the Web. For these reasons, one engine may be better for academic information, another for general information, and yet another for business information. Until you are familiar with these tools, you should probably try them all and consult the help screens when necessary.

The following screen from *AltaVista,* one of the best-known systems, shows that this search engine located 3,764 Web sites on Rigoberta Menchú, the subject of the research paper in **38f.** Note that this engine provides a spell check, verifying, in this case, that the search was for Menchú (not *mensch,* a Yiddish word meaning "a good human being"). Note also that *AltaVista* offers a program for translating the text of Web sites from one language to another. But because accurate translation requires sensitivity to how the meaning of words can change depending on how they are used, translations generated by a computer may not be adequate for your needs.

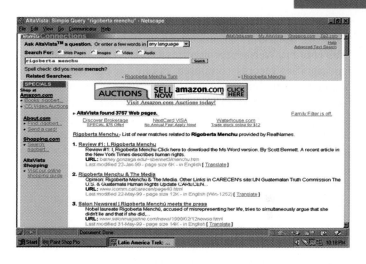

The result of the successful search will be a list of addresses or Uniform Resource Locators (URLs) you can use to access the page(s) you need. As you proceed with your research, keep a log in which you record what sites you visited on which days. Because sites change or even disappear, scholarly organizations such as the Modern Language Association (MLA) (see **38e**) and the American Psychological Association (APA) (see **38h**) require that bibliographies include the date of access as well as the date the site was posted. The posting date (or date when the site was last modified) usually appears on the site itself. When you print out material from the Web, you will usually find an access date on the top or bottom of the printout. When you take notes directly from the screen, however, you will have no record of the dates unless you write them down.

CAUTION Because anyone with access to a server can post information on the Web, a search can call up harebrained or tasteless information. However, a careful researcher can avoid unsuitable or unreliable material by thinking critically (see 35d and 37c). As you do so, distinguish between **Web access** and **Web content.** Web access signifies a delivery system. Web content signifies records composed strictly for the Web. For example, you can access *Encyclopaedia Britannica* on the Web, but it was not composed exclusively for the Web. Whether you access it online or in bound volumes, you are turning to a source that has a well-deserved reputation for credibility. But when you turn to someone's home page, you are looking at a document that does not exist outside the Web. Although many Web sources have excellent content, they seldom go through the kind of careful reviewing and editing that a good publisher requires.

Web pages are best viewed with a graphically capable browser. The example on page 553 shows one retrieved with *Netscape*, a widely used program that retrieves the pictorial elements intended to make Web pages pleasant to look at and easy to read. This page begins with an image accompanied by **links** to other pages. Identified by a different color from the text or by underlining, links can appear anywhere in a Web site. But they are especially likely to appear at the top or bottom of a given Web page. To follow a link, click on it with a mouse, touchpad, or trackball and wait until the new page appears on the screen. Scroll bars on the sides can be used to view more information. Many complex Web sites now have their own search buttons or links to a **site guide** to allow efficient examination of their own content.

The site on Rigoberta Menchú illustrated here provides access to an interview by her. Looking at this page, an experienced researcher would note a number of signs indicating a positive treatment of Menchú: a decorative border suggests sympathetic attention to her native culture. She is referred to by her first name and presented with a smiling face. And the text states, "Her life has been dedicated to bringing peace and justice to her country [. . .] " and also claims that she is "an inspiration." The site is committed to Menchú, and this stance must be taken into account when evaluating it for credibility (see 37c).

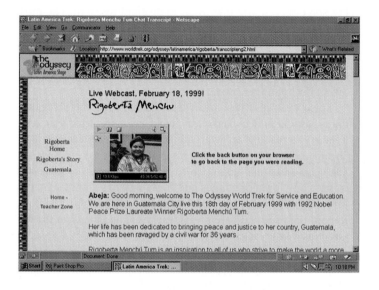

CAUTION Because computers have become so much a part of daily life, it is easy to take them for granted. Remember that the power that computers make available to you is also available to others. Protect yourself by being security conscious. Do not tell anyone your password, and change it if you have any reason to suspect that the security of your system has been breached.

Protect your equipment by guarding it against computer viruses, which lurk in every part of the Internet and can be extremely destructive to your data and your school's. Fortunately, good virus checkers are available at no charge. Ask your academic computing center for help. Everyone responsible for computers is eager to prevent the spread of viruses.

37e Field research involves interviewing, corresponding, observing, experimenting, and conducting surveys.

For some topics, you may want to do field research. The most common addition to library or Web-based research is an **interview.** The faculty at your college, business and professional people, and even relatives and friends can be appropriate interview subjects if they have relevant firsthand experience with the subject you are researching.

Since well-informed interviewers usually ask the best questions, you should consider an interview only after you have done some reading on your subject. Schedule interviews well ahead, and if you plan to use a tape recorder, ask permission. Take a professional approach to the interview: have pens and paper ready for taking notes and fresh batteries and blank tapes for your tape recorder. Dress appropriately and be punctual. Record the time and date of the interview on tape or at the beginning of your notes.

Begin with questions that are broad enough to give people room to reveal their own special interests; then follow up with more specific questions. Be prepared to depart from your list of questions whenever your subject says something of particular interest that would be useful to pursue. After the interview, send a thank-you letter if someone has been genuinely helpful.

Less formal than an interview, a dialogue with other people interested in your topic can also be useful. You may be able to enjoy such a dialogue with people on your campus or in your community. Researchers often benefit, however, from using the Internet as a tool for discussing ideas with people in other parts of the world.

 Discussion lists allow you to read messages posted to all the members of a group interested in a specific topic and to post messages yourself that those like-minded people will read. For instance, your instructor may belong to a specialized discussion list for composition teachers operated by the Alliance for Computers and Writing and called ACW-L. Participants discuss issues related to using computers to teach writing. Your instructor can send e-mail messages to the **Listserv address** that will redistribute them to hundreds of other writing teachers around the world. Similarly, your instructor can receive replies from anyone who subscribes to the list, but everyone will be able to read them.

Anyone who wants to discuss a topic can join a discussion list. To find out if there are any lists that might discuss the topic you are researching, visit http://www.liszt.com, a Web site that provides a directory for thousands of lists and instructions that can guide your search.

Discussion lists can also give you a means of conducting an informal **survey,** in which you ask a number of people the same set of questions and then analyze the results. But a survey limited to people who are already familiar with and discussing a topic will not be representative of other groups, such as the citizens of your state or region. (See 35c.) For some research questions (see 37b), you may get better results by designing a survey specifically for the kind of people whose views you wish to consider and directing it to that group.

You can administer a survey orally like an interview, or you can distribute a written questionnaire by mail or in person. Once you have a clear idea of what you want to find out, you may find the following checklist helpful.

CHECKLIST for Creating Survey Questions

- Does each question relate directly to the purpose of the survey?

- Are the questions easy to understand?

- Are they designed to elicit short, specific responses?

- Are they designed to collect concrete data that you can analyze easily?

- Are written questions designed to give respondents enough space for their answers?

- Are you able to present these questions to the population you want to survey?

In addition to interviews and surveys, you may also have occasion to draw directly on your own **experience** or **observations.** For example, if you have recovered from an eating disorder, your personal experience may be relevant to a research project on treating these disorders. Similarly, if you have lived in a dorm with people who have eating disorders, your observations of their behavior may be relevant. But check with your instructor to see whether experience, observations, or other field research is appropriate for the assignment on which you are working.

37f A working bibliography lists sources.

A working, or preliminary, bibliography contains information (titles, authors, dates, and so on) about the materials you think you might use. Write down the most promising sources you can find. Often, the sources you consult will have helpful bibliographies. Draw on them, but do not ignore other ways of discovering sources. Remember that you are responsible for conducting your own research.

Some people find it convenient to put each entry on a separate index card, which makes it easy to add or drop a card and to arrange the list alphabetically without recopying it. Others prefer to use a computer, which can sort and alphabetize automatically, making it easier for them to move material directly to their final paper.

It is also a good idea to follow consistently from the beginning the bibliographical form you are instructed to use. The MLA bibliographic style can be found in 38e and the APA style in 38h. Using the specified style from the start will save you time later, when you must compile a formal list of works cited that will appear at the end of your paper. Be sure to note the URL for Internet sites. Note MLA and APA style require that you include this information in bibliographies.

EXERCISE 4

Select a subject that you would like to become more knowledgeable about. Consult the main catalog in your library and at least one periodical index. Explore different ways of narrowing your subject. Then write a short essay in which you (a) report two potential ways of narrowing your subject, (b) explain which of the two you have selected for further research, (c) determine the number and quality of the sources that seem available, and (d) indicate what you hope to accomplish through this research project.

EXERCISE 5

Using at least two different search engines, look on the Web for information about your subject. Then write a short paper evaluating how well these engines served your needs.

EXERCISE 6

Prepare a working bibliography consisting of at least five sources in the documentation style your instructor requires.

Chapter 38

Research: Using and Citing Sources

To write well from sources, you need to activate your creative imagination (chapter 32), think critically (chapter 35), and discover relevant information (chapter 37). That effort can be undermined if you do not document your sources accurately—a skill that demands meticulous attention to detail. But no matter how many sources you use or how carefully you document them, remember that you are a *writer,* not simply a compiler of data. *You* are the most important presence in a paper that has your name on it.

This chapter will help you understand how to

- determine the purpose of a research paper (38a),
- take notes accurately (38b),
- use direct quotations (38c(2)),
- paraphrase (38c(3)),
- summarize (38c(4)),
- avoid plagiarism (38d),
- use MLA-style documentation (38e–f),
- use footnotes or endnotes (38g), and
- use APA-style documentation (38h–i).

Different disciplines usually employ different documentation styles, so there is no single way to document or to prepare a bibliography that can be used in every department of a college or university. Use the style your instructor specifies. The manuals listed below discuss documentation forms in detail. If you are asked to use one of these manuals, look for it in your library's reference collection, study it carefully, and make sure your notes and bibliography correspond exactly to the examples it provides.

Style Books and Manuals

American Chemical Society. *The ACS Style Guide: A Manual for Authors and Editors.* 2nd ed. Washington: Amer. Chem. Soc., 1998.

American Institute of Physics. *AIP Style Manual.* 4th ed. New York: Amer. Inst. of Physics, 1990.

American Mathematical Society. *A Manual for Authors of Mathematical Papers.* Rev. ed. Providence: Amer. Mathematical Soc., 1990.

American Medical Association. *American Medical Association Manual of Style.* 9th ed. Baltimore: Williams, 1997.

American Psychological Association. *Publication Manual of the American Psychological Association.* 4th ed. Washington: Amer. Psychological Assn., 1994.

Associated Press. *The Associated Press Stylebook and Libel Manual.* Rev. ed. Reading: Perseus, 1998.

The Chicago Manual of Style. 14th ed. Chicago: U of Chicago P, 1993.

Council of Biology Editors. *Scientific Style and Format: The CBE Manual for Authors, Editors, and Publishers.* 6th ed. New York: Cambridge UP, 1994.

Gibaldi, Joseph. *MLA Handbook for Writers of Research Papers.* 5th ed. New York: Modern Language Assn., 1999.

Harvard Law Review. *A Uniform System of Citation.* 16th ed. Cambridge: Harvard Law Review, 1996.

Linguistic Society of America. *LSA Bulletin,* Dec. issue, annually.

Turabian, Kate L. *A Manual for Writers of Term Papers, Theses, and Dissertations.* 6th ed. Chicago: U of Chicago P, 1996.

United States Geological Survey. *Suggestions to Authors of the Reports of the United States Geological Survey.* 7th ed. Washington: GPO, 1991.

United States Government Printing Office. *Style Manual.* Washington: GPO, 2000.

If your instructor does not require a specific documentation style, follow the one set forth by the discipline appropriate for your paper. When you do not know what type of documentation is appropriate, model your documentation on the style you find used in one of the journals in your field.

To provide further help, much of this chapter discusses the two documentation styles most widely used in college writing: MLA (Modern Language Association) style, used for papers in English and other modern languages (see **39a**), and APA (American Psychological Association) style, most often used for papers in psychology and other courses in the social sciences. For an example of CBE (Council of Biology Editors) style, variations of which are used in other natural sciences, see pages 732–41.

38a Research papers have a purpose.

A research paper, like any other paper, must have a purpose—and that purpose must be appropriate for your audience and context (see **32a**). Inexperienced writers sometimes assume that they are fulfilling the purpose of a research project by demonstrating that they have done some research. But research could be indicated simply by submitting a working bibliography (see **37f**) and a collection of notes. A research paper uses the results of research to make or prove a point. In other words, research papers are either **expository** or **persuasive.** (See **32a(1)**.)

If you have begun with a **research problem** (see **37b**), your paper will be expository if it explains

- the nature of the problem,
- its causes,
- its effects, or
- the way others are responding to it.

Your paper will be persuasive if it

- asks readers to recognize that a problem exists,
- offers a solution to the problem,

- calls on readers to undertake a specific action, or
- reconciles conflicting parties.

Exposition and persuasion can overlap. You may need to explain the effects of a problem, for example, before you can persuade readers to fix it. In other words, you may have more than one purpose, with one purpose serving to advance the other. As the writer of a research paper, what you need to decide is, "What is the most important goal I want to achieve in this project, and how can I best achieve it?"

As you work toward fulfilling your purpose, be sure to present yourself as thoughtful and fair-minded. Whether your audience consists of a single professor or some larger group, you must establish that you are a credible source (see **35d** and **36d(1)a**). To be credible in a research paper, you must show your audience that you have

- done serious research,
- understood what you have discovered,
- integrated research data into a paper that is clearly your own,
- drawn accurately on the work of others, and
- honored academic conventions for citing such work.

The rest of this chapter focuses on how to use sources to fulfill your purpose in writing a research paper. For information on how to conduct research, see chapter **37**.

38b Taking notes demands accuracy.

There are probably as many ways to take notes as there are note takers; some people are more comfortable taking notes on $8\frac{1}{2}$-by-11 paper, others on index cards, and still others in computer files. Each system has advantages and disadvantages, and you should match your choice to your project and your own work style.

Using a notebook

A ring binder into which you can insert pages of notes as well as photocopies is an excellent organizational tool, particularly if you arrange it to keep your working bibliography separate from notes and photocopies and if you have a system for sorting notes into the main subject categories your work covers. Identify the source on every page of notes, and use a fresh page for each new source.

Using photocopies

The easiest way to take notes is to make photocopies of excerpts from materials you think you might quote directly. On a photocopy you can mark quotable material and jot down your own ideas. Make sure you document the source on the photocopy, however.

Photocopied source with notes

The testimonials of Rigoberta Menchú and others, and the large number of indigenous combatants in the guerrilla organizations, suggest that many <u>Maya found them a hospitable site of struggle.</u> In turn, the revolutionary organizations were pushed by the incorporation of so many indigenous people (C. Smith 1990b, 271) to theorize the relations among class, ethnicity, and nationalism and to create more equal relations among Maya and ladino, supporting Mayan customs as much as possible given their mobility and attacking racism in self-criticism sessions (Simon 1988; Díaz-Polanco 1987; Harbury 1994; author interviews). <u>However many other indigenous people left the organizations,</u> some as part of larger splits, some fed up with what they perceived as <u>ongoing racist discrimination.</u> <u>What is undeniable is that despite the large numbers of Mayan combatants, there were no indigenous commanders representing the guerrillas in the peace talks,</u> and there are few ranking officials who are Maya.[29] *Diane Nelson, A Finger in the Wound (Berkeley: U of California P, 1999) 59.*

Check these sources?

Complex political situation— Link with Stoll

problem

evidence

Using notecards

In the past, researchers often took notes on index cards, which can still be useful if you are working in a library without your personal computer or if you prefer handwritten notes that you can rearrange as your research proceeds.

If you are using this system, show the author's name (and a short title for the work if the bibliography contains more than one work by that author) on each card, and include the exact page number(s) from which the information is drawn. If you put no more than a single note, however brief, on each card and a heading of two or three keywords at the top, you can easily arrange your cards as you prepare to write your paper.

Using computer files

If you have good keyboarding skills and are familiar with a word processing program, you may find it more efficient to use your computer for taking notes. This gives you the advantage of recording notes quickly and keeping them stored safely. Using a computer also makes it easy to copy and paste information into subject files and ultimately into the finished paper.

One problem with this method, however, is that you may go too fast and make mistakes. As a result, you may not digest the information in your source well enough to use it skillfully. Another problem is that you run the risk of plagiarism if you failed to note which records are direct quotations or paraphrases (see 38c(2–3)) and which are your own thoughts.

Be mindful of these risks, but do not let them discourage you. Problems can occur in any research method, especially if you get tired and try to cut corners. Experienced researchers choose the methods that give them the best results and, after considering what risks these methods may entail, take care to protect themselves. The following tips can help.

TIPS ON USING A COMPUTER TO TAKE NOTES

- Create a separate master folder (or directory) for your paper.
- Create folders within the master folder for your bibliography, notes, and portions of drafts.
- Keep all the notes for each source in a separate file.
- Use distinctive fonts or differentiators to distinguish your own thoughts from the thoughts of others whom you are paraphrasing.
- Place direct quotations in quotation marks.
- When taking notes, record exactly where the information came from.
- When you discover new sources, add them to your working bibliography (see **37f**).

Whatever system you use to create your notes, consider the questions in the following checklist.

CHECKLIST for Taking Notes

- Does every note clearly identify its source? Have you put the full bibliographic citation on the first page of every photocopy?

- Is the bibliographic information for the source of every note accurate? Double-check to be sure. Scrupulous care now can prevent a multitude of problems later on—such as being forced to leave out important information because you lost track of exactly where it came from.

- Have you taken down verbatim—that is, copied every word, every capital letter, and every punctuation mark exactly as it was in the original—any useful passage that you think you may later quote? Have you been especially careful to put quotation marks around any words you copy directly? Failure to do so as you take notes may lead to unintended plagiarism (see 38d) when you draft your paper.

- Have you used different type styles or different colors in computer files to make it easy to identify quoted text?

- When a source has sparked your own thoughts, have you identified both the source and the fact that the note is your own idea?

- Have you incorporated every source you are using into your working bibliography? (See 37f.)

38c Integrating sources fosters mastery of information.

Writers of research papers borrow information in three ways: quoting the exact words of a source, paraphrasing them, or summarizing them. With any of these methods, your writing will benefit if you are careful to integrate the material—properly cited, of course—into your own sentences and paragraphs. Whatever option you choose, make sure that you use sources responsibly.

A research paper that consists primarily of material taken from other writers is unlikely to be successful even if the sources are well chosen and meticulously cited (37 and 38d). Understanding how to evaluate sources (chapter 37) and take notes accurately (38b) is essential to research, but you must also understand how to integrate your research into a paper that is clearly your own. In a good paper, sources support a thesis (32c) that has grown out of the writer's research, but they do not obscure the writer's own ideas.

As you draft a research paper, remember that it is *your* paper. Integrate your source material—quotations, paraphrases, summaries—with your own statements rather than making the paper a patchwork of other people's comments. Make sure to use your own words and your own style throughout.

(1) Writers introduce and discuss the sources they use.

When experienced writers use borrowed material, they introduce it to readers by establishing the context from which the material came; for example, in a research paper about the value of vitamin C, readers might find it useful to know that the author of a quotation praising the vitamin was a Nobel laureate in chemistry. Similarly, you can introduce a paraphrase by making it clear why the information is important. An excellent way to introduce research is to use a phrase that indicates the author's attitude or the importance of the information. The following list of verbs that introduce quoted, paraphrased, or summarized information can be helpful in deciding how to integrate that information with your own ideas.

Sixty-Four Lead-In Verbs

acknowledge	charge	declare	illustrate
add	claim	deny	imply
admit	comment	describe	insist
advise	compare	disagree	interpret
agree	complain	discuss	list
allow	concede	dispute	maintain
analyze	conclude	emphasize	note
answer	concur	endorse	object
argue	confirm	explain	observe
ask	consider	express	offer
assert	contend	find	oppose
believe	criticize	grant	point out

reason	reply	see	suggest
refute	report	show	suppose
reject	respond	speculate	think
remark	reveal	state	write

Adding an adverb to one of these verbs can emphasize your attitude toward the material you are introducing: *persuasively* argue, *briefly* discuss, *strongly* oppose.

As a general rule, anything worth quoting is worth discussing, and the longer the quotation, the greater your responsibility to discuss it. Inexperienced writers often leave quotations and paraphrases sitting in their papers like undigested lumps of food from which no nourishment has been drawn. Experienced writers break those lumps down by showing what is significant about each source, that is, by identifying key terms, interpreting what someone else is saying, and indicating precisely where they agree or disagree.

The following examples of quotation, paraphrase, and summary show MLA documentation style. For additional information on MLA-style documentation, see 38e and 38f.

(2) Direct quotations draw attention to key passages.

A direct quotation should contribute an idea to your paper. Select quotations only if

- you want to retain the beauty or clarity of someone's words, or
- you need to reveal how the reasoning in a specific passage is flawed, and
- you plan to discuss the implications of what you quote.

Keep quotations as short as possible and make them an integral part of your text. (For examples of how this can be done, see 38f and 39a(7).)

Quote **accurately.** Enclose every quoted passage in quotation marks. Any quotation of another person's words except for well-known or proverbial passages should be placed in quotation marks or, if longer than four lines, set off as an indented block. (See 16b.)

Cite the exact source for your quotation. If you think your audience might be unfamiliar with a source, establish its authority by identifying its author the first time you refer to it. (Note that this citation is in MLA style.)

```
Mike Rose, a nationally recognized authority
on education, claims that learning is
facilitated not by fear but by "hope,
everyday heroics, the power and play of the
human mind" (242).
```

This reference clearly establishes that the quotation can be found on page 242 of a work by Mike Rose, additional information about which (such as the title and date of publication) would be found in a list of works cited at the end of the paper. (See 38e(2).)

CHECKLIST for Direct Quotations

- Have you copied all the words accurately?

- Have you copied all the punctuation accurately? (See 16f.)

- Do you need to observe a special form or special spacing? (See 16a and 16b.)

- Have you used ellipsis points correctly to indicate anything that is left out? (See 17i.)

- Have you avoided using ellipsis points *before* quotations that are clearly only parts of sentences?

- Have you used square brackets around everything you added to the direct quotation? (See 17g.)

- Have you used too many quotations? (Using too many quotations suggests inability to think independently or to synthesize material.)

(3) Paraphrasing enables you to convey ideas in your own words.

A **paraphrase** is a restatement of someone else's ideas in close to the same number of words. Paraphrasing enables you to demonstrate that you have understood what you have read; it also enables you to help your audience understand it. Paraphrase when you want to

- clarify difficult material by using simpler language,
- restate a crudely made point in more professional terms,
- use another writer's idea but not his or her words to demonstrate that you understood what you read, or
- create a consistent tone (see 33a(3)) for your paper as a whole.

Your restatement of someone else's words should honor two important principles: Your version should be almost entirely in your own words, and your words should accurately convey the content of the original passage. Moreover, you must indicate where the paraphrase begins and ends. Honoring these principles can be difficult, but if you rise to the challenge you will improve your skills in critical reading (see 35a–d) and demonstrate that you are in control of your material.

Using your own words

Unless you enclose an author's words in quotation marks, do not mix them with your own even if the sentence structure is different. Equally important, do not make the mistake of thinking that you can substitute synonyms for an author's words while you preserve his or her sentence structure. Both of these can be considered plagiarism (see **38d**) even if you cite the source because the citation does not reveal the full extent of your debt.

As you compare the source below with the paraphrases that follcw, note the similarities and differences in sentence structure as well as word choice. The parenthetical citations at the end of the paraphrases are in MLA-style documentation (see **38e(1)**).

Source (from "The Trouble with Wilderness," by William Cronon, in *Uncommon Ground: Toward Reinventing Nature* [New York: Norton, 1995], pp. 80–81)

> This, then, is the central paradox: wilderness embodies a dualistic vision in which the human is entirely outside the natural. If we allow ourselves to believe that nature, to be true, must also be wild, then our very presence in nature represents its fall. The place where we are is the place where nature is not.

Inadequate paraphrasing

```
Here is the main problem: wilderness is a
two-sided ideal in which people have no
place. When we convince ourselves that real
nature means the wilderness, then nature has
no people in it. This means that we could
never visit nature because as soon as we got
to a natural place it would no longer be
natural (Cronon 80-81).
```

Adequate paraphrasing

```
William Cronon has shown why it is
problematic to associate "nature" with
```

"wilderness." Wilderness means a place that
is unspoiled by human presence. When we
define nature as wilderness, we are
ultimately saying that people have no place
in nature (80-81).

CAUTION If you simply change a few words in a passage, you have
not adequately restated it. You may be charged with plagiarism if the wording of your version follows the original too
closely, even if you provide a page reference for the source. A
page reference after an inadequate paraphrase would acknowl-
edge the source of the idea but not the extent of your debt to
another writer's language.

Maintaining accuracy

Any paraphrase must accurately maintain the sense of the original. If you accidentally misrepresent the original because you
did not understand it, you are being **inaccurate.** If you deliberately change the gist of what a source says, you are being **unethical.** Compare the original statement below with the paraphrases.

Source (from "Second Reading," by Daniel D. Polsby, *Reason,* March 1996, p. 33)

> Generally speaking, though, it must be said that even among en-
> thusiasts who think about the Second Amendment quite a lot, there
> has been little appreciation for the intricate and nuanced way in
> which constitutional analysis is practiced, and has to be practiced,
> by judges and lawyers.

Inaccurate

People who care about the Second Amendment
don't really understand how hard judges and
lawyers have to work (Polsby 33).

Unethical

```
When writing about the Second Amendment,
Daniel Polsby has claimed that everybody else
who has written on this topic is stupid
(33).
```

Accurate

```
Daniel Polsby has claimed that public debate
over the meaning of the Second Amendment
seldom involves the kind of careful analysis
that judges and lawyers have to practice
when they try to interpret the Constitution
(33).
```

Source (from *Heaven's Coast,* by Mark Doty [New York: Harper, 1996], p. 159)

> We trivialize pain if we regard it as a preventable condition the spirit need not suffer. If we attempt to edit it out, will it away, regard it as our own creation, then don't we erase some essential part of the spirit's education? Pain is one of our teachers, albeit our darkest and most demanding one.

Inaccurate

```
Pain can never be prevented. It is
completely outside our control, but it makes
us grow stronger (Doty 159).
```

Unethical

```
Mark Doty argues that you are doing people a
favor when you hurt them (159).
```

Accurate

```
According to Mark Doty, pain cannot always
be alleviated. In a spiritual sense, however,
```

people can grow through suffering if they
are willing to learn from what is happening
to them (159).

(4) Summarizing enables you to convey ideas efficiently.

When you summarize, you condense the main point(s) of your
source. A summary omits much of the detail that a writer used
to develop the original but accurately reflects the essence of
that writer's work. In most cases, then, a summary reports a
writer's **main idea** (see 32d) and the most important support
given for it. Because summarizing enables writers to report the
work of others without getting bogged down in unnecessary detail, it is a highly useful skill in writing research papers.

A paraphrase (see 38c(3)) is usually close to the same length
as the original material. A summary must be shorter. When you
paraphrase, you are helping readers understand another writer's
work. When you summarize, you are saving space. The two
skills are closely related, however. To summarize, you must be
able to paraphrase. Although summaries consist primarily of
paraphrasing, they can also include short quotations, in quotation marks, of key phrases or ideas.

Source (from "What's Wrong with Animal Rights," by Vicki
Hearne, *Harper's,* Sept. 1991, p. 61)

> A human being living in the "wild"—somewhere, say, without
> having the benefits of medicine and advanced social organization—
> would probably have a life expectancy of from thirty to thirty-five
> years. A human being living in "captivity"—in, say, a middle-class
> neighborhood of what the Centers for Disease Control call a Met-
> ropolitan Statistical Area—has a life expectancy of seventy or more
> years. For orangutans in the wild in Borneo and Malaysia, the life
> expectancy is thirty-five years; in captivity, fifty years. The wild
> is not a suffering-free zone or all that frolicsome a location.

Summary

```
Because of the risks posed by living in the
wild, both humans and animals lead
significantly shorter lives under such
conditions than they do when cared for
within an "advanced social organization"
(Hearne 61).
```

⟨CAUTION⟩ If you retain some of another writer's phrasing when you are summarizing, be sure to put quotation marks around those words.

Exercise 1

Find a well-developed paragraph in one of your recent reading assignments. Then rewrite it in your own words and without repeating the sentence structure of the original. Make this paraphrase approximately the same length as the original. Then write a one-sentence summary of the same paragraph.

Exercise 2

Read Janet Kowolski's paper (pages 516–21) and then write a hundred-word summary of it that could serve as an abstract (see pages 543 and 665).

38d Plagiarism is a serious offense.

Taking someone else's words or ideas and presenting them as your own leaves you open to criminal charges. In the film, video, music, and software business, this sort of theft is called **piracy.** In publishing and education, it is called **plagiarism** or **cheating.** Whatever it is called and for whatever reason it occurs, it is illegal.

CAUTION Plagiarism is a serious offense. Carelessness is no excuse. Although the act may escape criminal prosecution, employers generally fire an employee who uses material illegally, and teachers often fail students who claim to have written material that was composed by someone else.

The *MLA Handbook for Writers of Research Papers,* 5th edition (New York: MLA, 1999) defines plagiarism as "intellectual theft" and advises

> At all times during research and writing, guard against the possibility of inadvertent plagiarism by keeping careful notes that distinguish between your own musings and thoughts and the material you gather from others. Forms of plagiarism include the failure to give appropriate acknowledgment when repeating another's wording or particularly apt phrase, when paraphrasing another's argument, or when presenting another's line of thinking.
>
>   You may certainly use another person's words and thoughts in your research paper, but the borrowed material must not seem like your own creation. (Gibaldi 30–31)

You would be putting yourself at a great disadvantage if you felt it was unsafe to draw on the work of others. One purpose of this chapter is to help you use such work responsibly so that you can enter into a thoughtful conversation with other writers. The challenge is to do this clearly so that your audience can distinguish among the different voices that have emerged through your research.

Honoring the principles discussed in this chapter will protect you from inadvertent plagiarism. There is, however, another form of plagiarism that is so blatant that no one could do it accidentally. That is to submit as your own an essay or paper written by someone else—obtained from a friend or a company that sells papers, or simply downloaded and printed off the World Wide Web. We do not need to linger on this kind of plagiarism because there is a clear way to avoid it: *Do not ever submit as your own a paper you did not write.*

In some countries, anyone who has purchased a book can quote from it without citing the source or requesting permission. The rationale is that the person bought the words when he or she bought the book. In the United States, that kind of thinking can get you into serious trouble.

You must give credit for all information you use except for two kinds: common knowledge and your own ideas. Common knowledge includes well-known dates and other facts: the stock market crashed in 1929; water freezes at 32 degrees Fahrenheit. It also includes information such as "The *Titanic* sank on its maiden voyage." This event has been the subject of many books and movies, and some information about it has become common knowledge: the *Titanic* hit an iceberg, and many people died because the ship did not carry enough lifeboats. But if you are writing a research paper about the *Titanic* and wish to include details about the ship's construction or the crew's behavior, then you are providing *un*common knowledge that must be documented.

After you have read a good deal about a given subject, you will be able to distinguish between common knowledge and the distinctive ideas or interpretations of specific writers. When you use the ideas or information these writers provide, be sure to cite your source.

As for your own ideas, if you have been scrupulous in recording your own thoughts as you took notes, you should have little difficulty distinguishing between what you knew to begin with and what you learned through your research and must therefore cite. Sometimes, however, researchers unconsciously absorb ideas and lose sight of the extent to which their thinking has been influenced by someone else. A research log can provide you with a clear record of what you knew at the outset, what you read, and how you reacted to your reading (see 37a(2)).

Source   (from "Returning Young Adults," by John Burnett and Denise Smart, *Psychology and Marketing* 11 [1994], p. 254)

> Both generations want their rights. The RYAs want the autonomy they have grown accustomed to and expect their parents to treat them like adults. The parents, meanwhile, have come to recognize their own rights. They may resent that the time, money, and emotional energy they planned to invest in themselves after the child's departure are instead allocated to the RYA.

Undocumented copying

```
Parents may resent that the time, money, and
emotional energy they planned to invest in
themselves after the child's departure are
instead allocated to the RYA.
```

Undocumented paraphrase

```
Parents may get upset when resources they
had planned to use on themselves must be
used to support an adult child who has
returned home.
```

Paraphrase with documentation

```
Marketing professors John Burnett and Denise
Smart note that young adults who return to
live at home can make their parents resent
supporting them with resources they had
planned to devote to themselves (254).
```

This idea is introduced with a reference establishing where the paraphrase begins. The sentence structure and phrasing have changed. A parenthetical citation marks the end of the paraphrase and provides the page number on which the source can be found.

Quotation with documentation

```
Marketing professors John Burnett and Denise
Smart note that parents "may resent that the
time, money, and emotional energy they
planned to invest in themselves after the
child's departure are instead allocated to
the RYA" (254).
```

Quotation marks show where the copied words begin and end, and the number in parentheses tells the reader the exact page on which the words appear. In this case, the sentence that includes the quotation identifies the authors. An alternative is to provide the authors' names within the parenthetical reference: (Burnett and Smart 254). If, after referring to the following checklist you cannot decide whether you need to cite a source, the safest policy is to cite it.

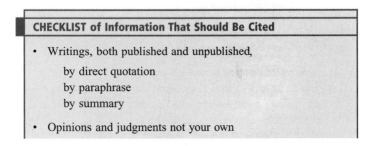

CHECKLIST of Information That Should Be Cited

- Writings, both published and unpublished,

    by direct quotation
    by paraphrase
    by summary

- Opinions and judgments not your own

- Statistics and other facts that are not widely known

- Images and graphics such as

  works of art
  drawings
  tables and charts
  graphs
  maps
  advertisements
  photographs

- Personal communication

  interviews
  letters
  e-mail

- Public electronic communication

  television and radio broadcasts
  films and videos
  recordings
  Web sites
  discussion lists

38e MLA-style documentation is required for research papers in literary studies and useful for other courses in the humanities.

With over thirty thousand members, the Modern Language Association supports teaching and scholarship in English and other languages spoken throughout the world. Its rules for documentation have been formulated with great care.

Directory of MLA-Style Parenthetical Citations

(1) Parenthetical citations tell readers where a writer has drawn material from a source.

Give proper credit by citing your sources. Traditionally, such citations took the form of notes numbered consecutively throughout the paper and placed either at the bottom of the appropriate page (footnotes) or all together at the end of the paper (endnotes). (See 38g.) Although some disciplines still use a note system, the MLA recommends placing citations in parentheses directly in the text. These parenthetical citations refer the reader to a list of works cited at the end of the paper. The advantage to this system is that it is easy for both writers and readers to use. The MLA suggests reserving numbered notes for supplementary or explanatory comments. Superscript numbers are inserted in the appropriate places in the text, and the notes are gathered at the end of the paper. (See pages 638–39).

The basic elements of the parenthetical citation are the author's last name and the page number of the material used in the source. However, it is not necessary to repeat any information that is already clearly provided. In other words, omit the author's name from the parenthetical citation if you have identified it in the text shortly before the material being cited. As you study the following examples, observe that common sense determines the information that must be included in a parenthetical citation. See also the discussion of punctuation and mechanics that follows these examples (pages 587–89).

Work by one author

```
Olivier creates Richard III's "central device
of coherence" by using a cyclical theme of
the crown (Brown 133).
```

In this citation, the author's name is included within the parentheses because it is not mentioned in the text. If there is only one work by Brown in the list of works cited, there is no need to place a title in the parentheses. However, a page number is included because the reference is to a specific passage. Note how the citation changes if the text includes more information about the source.

```
Constance Brown argues that in Richard III,
Laurence Olivier uses a cyclical theme of
the crown to create a "central device of
coherence" (133).
```

Work by two or three authors

```
High software prices mean that "education
must do without this resource, prices must
come down, or new strategies for development
must be devised" (Holdstein and Selfe 27).
```

Provide the last name of each author. Commas are necessary in a citation involving three authors, for example: (Bellamy, O'Brien, and Nichols 59).

Work by more than three authors

For a work by more than three authors, use the same form as the bibliographic entry (see pages 593–94), giving either the first author's last name followed by the abbreviation *et al.* (from the Latin *et alii,* meaning "and others") or all the last names. (Do not italicize or underline the abbreviated Latin phrase.)

```
In one important study, women graduates
complained more frequently about "excessive
control than about lack of structure"
(Belenky et al. 205).
```

OR

```
In one important study, women graduates
complained more frequently about "excessive
control than about lack of structure"
(Belenky, Clinchy, Goldberger, and Tarule
205).
```

Multivolume work

When you cite material from a multivolume work, include the volume number (followed by a colon and a space) before the page number.

```
As Katherine Raine has argued, "true poetry
begins where human personality ends"
(2: 247).
```

You do not need to include the volume number in the parenthetical citation if your list of works cited includes only one volume of a multivolume work.

More than one work by the same author

When your list of works cited includes more than one work by the same author, your parenthetical citations should include a shortened title that reveals which of the author's works is being cited in a particular instance. Use a comma to separate the author's name from the shortened title when both are in parentheses.

```
According to Gilbert and Gubar, Elizabeth
Barrett Browning considered poetry by women
to be forbidden and problematic
(Shakespeare's Sisters 107). That attitude
was based on the conception that male
sexuality is the "essence of literary power"
(Gilbert and Gubar, Madwoman 4).
```

This passage cites two different books by the same authors, Sandra M. Gilbert and Susan Gubar: *Shakespeare's Sisters: Feminist Essays on Women Poets* and *The Madwoman in the Attic: The Woman and the Nineteenth-Century Literary Imagination.* The authors' names are not necessary in the first citation since they are mentioned in the text; they are included in the second because their names are not mentioned in connection with *Madwoman.*

You can often avoid cumbersome references by including information in the text that might otherwise have to appear parenthetically.

```
In both The Madwoman in the Attic and
Shakespeare's Sisters, Sandra M. Gilbert and
Susan Gubar argue that the infrequent
appearance of women as literary figures is a
result of the repression imposed by male
sexuality.
```

In this case, no page reference is necessary because the works as a whole are being referred to. Titles and authors are clearly established in the sentence itself.

Works by different authors with the same last name

Occasionally your list of works cited will contain sources by two authors with the same last name—for example, rhetoricians Theresa Enos and Richard Enos. In such cases, you must use the first name as well as the last.

```
Richard Enos includes a thirteen-page
bibliography in Greek Rhetoric before
Aristotle (141-54). In her collection of
articles by prominent figures in modern
rhetoric and philosophy, Professing the New
Rhetorics, Theresa Enos mentions the
considerable contemporary reliance on pre-
Aristotelian rhetoric and includes an essay
on the subject by Michael Halloran (25, 331-
43).
```

In these references, the citation of more than one page "(141–54)" identifies continuous pages while "(25, 331–43)" indicates that the reference is to two separate sets of pages.

Indirect source

If you need to include material that one of your sources quoted from another work and cannot obtain the original source, use the following form.

```
The critic Susan Hardy Aikens has argued on
behalf of what she calls "canonical
multiplicity" (qtd. in Mayers 677).
```

A reader turning to the list of works cited should find a bibliographic entry for Mayers (which was the source consulted) but not for Aikens (because the quotation was obtained secondhand).

Poetry, drama, and the Bible

When you refer to poetry, drama, and the Bible, you must often give numbers of lines, acts, and scenes, or of chapters and verses, rather than page numbers. This practice enables a reader to consult an edition other than the one you are using.

Act, scene, and line numbers (all Arabic) are separated by periods with no space before or after them. The MLA suggests that biblical chapters and verses be treated similarly, although some writers prefer to use colons instead of periods in scriptural references. In all cases, the progression is from larger to smaller units.

The following example illustrates a typical citation of lines of poetry.

```
Emily Dickinson concludes "I'm Nobody! Who
Are You?" with a characteristically
bittersweet stanza:
          How dreary to be somebody!
          How public, like a frog
          To tell your name the livelong June
          To an admiring bog! (5-8)
```

Quotations of three lines or less are not indented (see 39a(6)).

The following citation shows that the famous "To be, or not to be" soliloquy appears in act 3, scene 1, lines 56–89 of *Hamlet.*

```
In Hamlet, Shakespeare presents the most
famous soliloquy in the history of the
English theater: "To be, or not to be
[. . .]" (3.1.56-89).
```

Biblical references identify the book of the Bible, the chapter, and the pertinent verses. In the following example, the writer refers to the creation story in Genesis, which begins with chapter 1, verse 1, and ends with chapter 2, verse 22.

```
The Old Testament creation story (Gen. 1.1-
2.22), told with remarkable economy,
culminates in the arrival of Eve.
```

Names of books of the Bible are neither italicized—under-lined—(see chapter 10) nor enclosed in quotation marks (see chapter 16), and abbreviation is preferred (see chapter 11).

Sources produced for access by computer

Although electronic sources are treated differently from print sources in your bibliography (38e(2)), many can be treated identically for parenthetical documentation in the text. An online book, for example, could easily have both an author and page numbers just like a printed book.

If an electronic source does not have page numbers but does provide another numbering scheme, use those numbers. If paragraphs are numbered, cite the number in question beginning with the abbreviation *par.* or plural *pars.* If screen numbers are provided, cite the screen, beginning with *screen.*

If the source includes no numbers distinguishing one part from another, then you must cite the entire source. In this case, to establish that you have not accidentally omitted a number, you can avoid using a parenthetical citation by providing what information you have within the sentence that introduces the material.

```
Raymond Lucero's Web site offers useful
advice for consumers who are concerned about
transmitting credit card information over the
Internet.
```

OR

```
Raymond Lucero's Shopping Online offers
useful advice for consumers who are concerned
about transmitting credit card information
over the Internet.
```

The Uniform Resource Locator (URL) for this site and additional information about it would be included in the list of works cited.

Punctuation and mechanics

Punctuation and numbers   Commas separate the authors' names from the titles (Brown, "Olivier's *Richard III:* A Reevaluation") and indicate interruptions in a sequence of pages or lines (44, 47). Hyphens indicate continuous sequences of pages (44–47) and lines (1–4). Colons separate volume and page numbers (Raine 2: 247); one space follows the colon. Periods separate acts, scenes, and lines in drama (3.1.56–89). Periods (or colons) distinguish chapters from verses in biblical citations (Gen. 1.1 or Gen. 1:1). (See 17d.)

Ellipsis points (see 17i) indicate omissions within a quotation and should be enclosed in brackets: "They lived in an age of increasing complexity and great hope; we in an age of [. . .] growing despair" (Krutch 2). Brackets (see 17g) also indicate interpolations within quotations also: "The publication of this novel [*Beloved*] establishes Morrison as one of the most important writers of our time" (Boyle 17).

When a question mark ends a quotation (see 17b), place it before the closing quotation mark; then add a period after the parenthetical citation.

```
Paulo Freire asks, "How can the oppressed,
as divided, unauthentic beings, participate
in developing the pedagogy of their
liberation?" (33).
```

The MLA favors Arabic numbers throughout, except when citing pages identified by Roman numerals in the source itself (such as the front matter of a book: Garner ix).

Placement of citations   Wherever possible, citations should appear just before a mark of punctuation in the text of the paper.

```
Richard Enos provides a bibliography of
sources for the study of Greek rhetoric
before Aristotle (141-54), and Theresa Enos's
edited collection, Professing the New
Rhetorics, includes Michael Halloran's essay
"On the End of Rhetoric, Classical and
Modern" (331-43).
```

Richard Enos's citation falls just before a comma; Theresa Enos's just before a period. However, in a sentence such as the following, the citations should follow the authors' names to keep the references separate.

```
Richard Enos (141-54) and Theresa Enos (25)
address classical rhetoric from very
different perspectives.
```

Lengthy quotations   When a quotation is more than four lines long, set it off from the text by indenting one inch (or ten spaces) from the left margin (see 16b).

Although the final punctuation mark comes *after* the citation in quotations fewer than four lines, it comes *before* the final punctuation mark in longer quotations set off by indentation.

```
Writing about how thousands of ethnic
minorities were persecuted and killed in the
Balkans during the 1990s, Susan Sontag asks
how European governments should respond when
another government commits genocide within
its borders:
            Imagine that Nazi Germany had had
            no expansionist ambitions but had
            simply made it a policy in the
            late 1930's and early 1940's to
            slaughter all the German Jews. Do
            we think a government has the right
            to do whatever it wants in its own
```

territory? Maybe the governments of
Europe <u>would</u> have said that 60
years ago. But would we approve now
of their decision? (55)

No indentation is necessary if you quote only one paragraph or
if you quote the beginning of a paragraph. When quoting more
than one paragraph, indent the first line of each paragraph by
three additional spaces.

(2) A complete list of the sources used in the paper helps readers to locate and evaluate them.

For MLA-style papers, the list of sources from which you have
cited information is called the **Works Cited.** (Other documentation styles differ from MLA in how they arrange and name
their reference lists—see **38h(2)** and **39b(6)**.) The works-cited
list appears at the end of the paper.

When you are ready to produce your final draft, you also
need to prepare the list of works cited. Eliminate from your
working bibliography (see **37f**) any sources that you did not
end up using and include every source that you did use.

- Arrange the list of works alphabetically by author.
- If a source has more than one author, alphabetize by the last name
  of the first author.
- Type the first line of each entry flush with the left margin and
  indent subsequent lines five spaces or one-half inch (a hanging
  indent).
- Double-space throughout.

As you study the following MLA-style entries, which cover
most of the types of sources you are likely to list, observe both
the arrangement of information and the punctuation. (See also
pages 178–81 for a list of abbreviations that are used in works
cited, notes, and tables.)

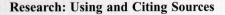

Books

Articles

Sources Viewed or Heard

Sources Produced for Access by Computer

Research: Using and Citing Sources

we a peice has 4r authors you can put 1st authors name, et al.

Most book entries consist of three units separated by periods.

Author	Title	Publication data

Lastname, Firstname. <u>Title Underlined</u>. City: Publisher, date.

1. *Author.* Give the last name first, followed by a comma and the first name.
2. *Title.* Underline the title of the book, and capitalize all major words. (See **9c**.) Always include the book's subtitle. Make underlining continuous, not separate under each word.
3. *Publication data.* Provide the city of publication, an abbreviated form of the publisher's name, and the latest copyright date shown on the copyright page. Type a colon after the city and a comma after the publisher. (To shorten the name of the publisher, use the principal name: Alfred A. Knopf becomes Knopf; Random House becomes Random; Harvard University Press becomes Harvard UP; University of Michigan Press becomes U of Michigan P.)

Book by one author

```
Smith, Jeanne Rosier. Writing Tricksters:
     Narrative Strategy and Cultural Identity
     in Maxine Hong Kingston, Louise Erdrich,
     and Toni Morrison. Berkeley: U of
     California P, 1997.
```

Use a colon to separate a main title from a subtitle. Capitalize all words in both the title and subtitle, except for articles, prepositions, and coordinating conjunctions (see **9c**). To cite books published by universities, abbreviate "University" and "Press" without periods. Indent all lines after the first by five spaces.

More than one work by the same author

```
Angelou, Maya. A Brave and Startling Truth.
     New York: Random, 1995.
---. Kofi and His Magic. New York: Potter,
     1996.
```

If you use more than one work by the same author, alphabetize the works by the first major word in each title. Give the author's name with the first title, but substitute three hyphens followed by a period for the name in subsequent entries.

Book by two authors

West, Nigel, and Oleg Tsarev. <u>The Crown
    Jewels: The British Secrets at the Heart
    of the KGB Archives</u>. New Haven: Yale
    UP, 1999.

Invert the name of the first author (or editor) and place a comma after it. Do not invert the second name.

Book by three authors

Spinosa, Charles, Ferdinand Flores, and
    Hubert L. Dreyfus. <u>Disclosing New
    Worlds: Entrepreneurship, Democratic
    Action, and the Cultivation of
    Solidarity</u>. Cambridge: MIT P, 1997.

List all three authors in the same sequence used in the book.

Book by more than three authors

When a book has more than three authors, MLA style allows writers either to give all names in full as they appear on the title page or to add the abbreviation *et al.* (for *et alii,* meaning "and others") after the first author.

Bell-Scott, Patricia, Beverly Guy-Sheftall,
    Jaqueline Jones Royster, Janet Sims-
    Wood, Miriam DeCosta-Willis, and Lucille
    P. Fultz, eds. <u>Double Stitch: Black
    Women Write about Mothers and Daughters</u>.
    New York: Harper, 1993.

OR

Bell-Scott, Patricia, et al., eds. <u>Double
    Stitch: Black Women Write about Mothers
    and Daughters</u>. New York: Harper, 1993.

Book by a corporate author

Institute of Medicine. <u>Blood Banking and
    Regulation: Procedures, Problems, and
    Alternatives</u>. Washington: Natl. Acad. P,
    1996.

Alphabetize by the first major word in the corporate name.

Book by an anonymous author

<u>Primary Colors: A Novel of Politics</u>. New
    York: Warner, 1996.

In the case of anonymous authors, begin the entry with the title. Do not use "Anonymous" or "Anon."

Book for which the editor appears as author

Warhol, Robyn R., and Diane Price Herndl,
    eds. <u>Feminisms: An Anthology of Literary
    Theory and Criticisms</u>. New Brunswick:
    Rutgers UP, 1993.

Edition after the first

Fromkin, Victoria, and Robert Rodman. <u>An
    Introduction to Language</u>. 6th ed. Fort
    Worth: Harcourt, 1998.

Work from an anthology (a collection of articles or other writings by different authors)

Bishop, Wendy. "Students' Stories and the
    Variable Gaze of Composition Research."

> Writing Ourselves into the Story:
> Unheard Voices from Composition Studies.
> Ed. Sheryl I. Fontane and Susan Hunter.
> Carbondale: Southern Illinois UP, 1993.
> 197-214.

Use this form for an article or essay that was first published in an anthology; use it also for a story, poem, or play reprinted in an anthology.

For an article or essay that was published elsewhere before being included in an anthology, use the following form.

> Chaika, Elaine. "Grammars and Teaching."
> College English 39 (1978): 770-83. Rpt.
> in Linguistics for Teachers. Ed. Linda
> Miller Cleary and Michael D. Linn. New
> York: McGraw, 1993. 490-504.

Note where the essay first appeared and then show where you read it. Use the abbreviation *Rpt.* for "reprinted." Both forms require you to cite the complete range of pages where the material can be found, not just the pages the researcher borrowed material from. In the second example, you must cite both the pages of the original publication (770–83 in this case) and the pages of the anthologized version (490–504).

Translated book

> Duras, Marguerite. The North China Lover.
> Trans. Leigh Hafrey. New York: New P,
> 1992.

Republished book

> Alcott, Louisa May. Work: A Story of
> Experience. 1873. Harmondsworth:
> Penguin, 1995.

The original work was published over a century before this paperback version. Use this form for books—even relatively recent ones—that have been reissued in a new format. (For reprinted articles, see "Work from an anthology," pages 594–95.)

Multivolume work

Odell, George C. D. <u>Annals of the New York
      Stage</u>. 15 vols. New York: Columbia UP,
      1927-49.

This multivolume work was published over a period of years. Cite the total number of volumes in a work when you have used more than one volume.

If you use only one volume, include the number (preceded by the abbreviation *Vol.*) after the title. If the number of volumes in the complete work is important, include it at the end of the entry.

Browning, Robert. <u>The Complete Works of
      Robert Browning: With Variant Readings
      and Annotations</u>. Ed. John C. Berkey and
      Allan C. Dooley. Vol. 6. Athens: Ohio
      UP, 1996.

Encyclopedia or almanac

Hile, Kenneth S. "Rudolfo Anaya."
      <u>Contemporary Authors</u>. New Rev. Ser.,
      1991.
Petersen, William J. "Riverboats and
      Rivermen." <u>Encyclopedia Americana</u>. 1999
      ed.

Full publication information is not necessary for a well-known reference work organized alphabetically. Use abbreviations to specify edition or series (such as New Rev. Ser. for New Revised Series). For sources that are more unusual, you should reveal more about the source.

Dreyer, Edward L. "Inner Mongolia."
 <u>Encyclopedia of Asian History</u>. Ed.
 Ainslee T. Embree. 4 vols. New York:
 Scribner's, 1988.

When an author's name is indicated only by initials, check the table of contents for a list of contributors. When an article is anonymous, begin your entry with the article title and alphabetize according to the first important word in the title.

Book in a series

Kelly, Richard Michael, and Barbara Kelly.
 <u>The Carolina Watermen: Bug Hunters and</u>
 <u>Boat Builders</u>. Twayne English Author
 Ser. 577. Winston-Salem: Blair, 1993.

When citing a book that is part of a series, provide the name of the series and the number designating the work's place in it (if any).

Introduction, foreword, or afterword to a book

Elbow, Peter. Foreword. <u>The Peaceable</u>
 <u>Classroom</u>. By Mary Rose O'Reilley.
 Portsmouth: Heinemann, 1993. ix-xiv.

Begin with the author of the introduction, foreword, or afterword. Include the name of the book's author after the title. Note the pages at the end, using Roman numerals if they appear as such in the work.

Pamphlet or bulletin

<u>Safety Data Sheet: Kitchen Machines</u>. Chicago:
 Natl. Restaurant Assn., 1970.

If the pamphlet has an author, begin with the author's name (last name first) as you would for a book.

Government publication

```
United States. Office of Management and
     Budget. A Citizen's Guide to the Federal
     Budget. Washington: GPO, 1999.
```

When citing a government publication, identify the government body (e.g., "United States," "Minnesota," "Great Britain," "United Nations") followed by the agency that issued the work. Underline the title of a book or pamphlet. Indicate the city of publication. Federal publications are usually printed by the Government Printing Office (GPO) in Washington, D.C., but be alert for exceptions.

When the name of an author or editor appears on a government publication, insert that name after the title and introduce it with the word *By* or an abbreviation (such as *Ed.* or *Comp.*) describing the person's contribution.

Articles

The documentation format for articles differs slightly from that for books. The three units are the same, and they are still separated by periods, but note the differences in treatment for titles and publication information.

Author	Title	Publication data

Lastname, Firstname. "Title of Article." <u>Journal</u> volume (year): pages.
Lastname, Firstname. "Title of Article." <u>Periodical</u> day/month/year: pages.

1. *Author.* Give the last name first, followed by a comma and the first name.
2. *Article title.* Type the article title in regular (Roman) face, and put it in quotation marks with the period inside the final quotation marks. Capitalize all major words in the title. (See 9c.)
3. *Publication data.* The exact kind of information differs according to the type of periodical, but all references provide the periodical title, the date of publication, and the page numbers on which the

article appeared. Continuously underline the periodical title, and capitalize all major words. (See 9c.) Note that no punctuation follows the periodical title and that a colon introduces the inclusive page numbers. If a periodical entry requires both a volume number and a date, put the date in parentheses.

Article in a journal with continuous pagination

A *journal* is a scholarly publication written for a specific profession, whereas a *magazine* is written for the general public.

```
Diaz, Gwendolyn. "Desire and Discourse in
     Maria Luisa Bombal's New Islands."
     Hispanofila 112 (1994): 51-63.
```

Citing a specific issue (e.g., fall 1994) is not necessary when a journal's pages are numbered continuously throughout the year.

Article in a journal with each issue paginated separately

```
Ray, Robert B. "How to Teach Cultural
     Studies." Studies in the Literary
     Imagination 31.1 (1998): 25-36.
```

When an issue is paginated separately (each issue begins with page 1), put a period after the volume number and add the issue number.

Article in a monthly magazine

```
Shenk, Joshua Wolf. "America's Altered
     States: When Does Legal Relief of Pain
     Become Illegal Pursuit of Pleasure?"
     Harper's May 1999: 38-49.
```

MLA style abbreviates the names of months (except for May, June, and July). Volume numbers are unnecessary because specific dates are given. A period goes between the last word in the title and the closing quotation marks unless the title ends with a question mark or exclamation point, in which case an additional punctuation mark would be redundant. A space (without punctuation) separates the magazine title from the date of issue.

Magazine articles are often interrupted by other articles. If the first part appears on pages 45–47 and the last on pages 213–21, give only the first page number followed by a plus sign: 45+.

Article in a weekly newspaper or magazine

```
Karps, Richard. "Risk's Rewards." Barrons 19
     Apr. 1999: 22-24.
Stille, Alexander. "The Man Who Remembers."
     New Yorker 15 Feb. 1999: 50-63.
```

Article in a daily newspaper

```
Leroux, Charles. "Reading Frenzy." Chicago
     Tribune 20 Apr. 1999, final ed., sec.
     2: 1+.
```

When it is not part of the newspaper's name, the name of the city should be given in brackets after the title: *Star Tribune* [Minneapolis]. If a specific edition is not named on the masthead, put a colon after the date and then provide the page reference. Specify the section by inserting the section number or letter immediately before the page number just as it appears in the newspaper: A7 or 7A. When an article is continued elsewhere in the section (but not on the next page), add + to indicate this continuation.

Editorial in a newspaper or magazine

```
Lewis, Anthony. "Deeper Than Politics."
     Editorial. New York Times 24 Apr. 1999,
     natl. ed.: A29.
```

If the editorial is not signed, begin the citation with the title.

Sources viewed or heard

Motion picture

<u>Shakespeare in Love</u>. Dir. John Madden.
        Miramax. 1998.

When you cite the contribution of a specific person, put the person's name first. Additional information can be included immediately after the title.

Fiennes, Joseph, perf. <u>Shakespeare in Love</u>.
        Screenplay by Marc Norman and Tom
        Stoppard. Dir. John Madden. Miramax.
        1998.

Radio or television program

"'Barbarian' Forces." <u>Ancient Warriors</u>. Narr.
        Colgate Salsbury. Dir. Phil Grabsky. The
        Learning Channel. 1 Jan. 1996.
Leavitt, David. <u>The Lost Language of Cranes</u>.
        Prod. Ruth Caleb. Dir. Nigel Finch.
        Great Performances. PBS. WNET, New York.
        24 June 1992.

Play performance

<u>Death of a Salesman</u>. By Arthur Miller. Dir.
        Robert Falls. Eugene O'Neill Theater,
        New York. 7 May 1999.

Cite the date of the performance you attended.

Musical composition

Puccini, Giacomo. <u>Turandot</u>.
Rachmaninov, Sergei. Symphony no. 2 in E
        minor, op. 27.

Begin with the composer and the name of the composition. If the composition is unnamed, identify it by the number given to it by the composer (Symphony no. 2). Add the key when it is specified by the composer and conclude with the work number (*opus* as in op. 27) if it is available.

If, however, you cite the published score of a musical composition, treat it like a book. Capitalize the abbreviations *no.* and *op.* when they are part of the title. Add the city of publication, publisher's name, and date of publication.

Compact disc sound recording

Franklin, Aretha. <u>Amazing Grace: The Complete Recordings</u>. Atlantic, 1999.

Provide the full title, including the subtitle. Adapt this form for other kinds of sound recording by including what kind it is (such as Audiocassette or LP), followed by a period, immediately before the name of the manufacturer.

If citing the recording of a specific song, begin with the name of the performer, and place the song title in quotation marks. Identify the author(s) after the song title. If the performance is a reissue from an earlier recording, provide the original date of recording (preceded by Rec.) immediately before the title of the compact disc.

Horne, Lena. "The Man I Love." By George and Ira Gershwin. Rec. 15 Dec. 1941. <u>Stormy Weather</u>. BMG, 1990.

Lecture

Mikolajczak, Michael. "T. S. Eliot's <u>The Waste Land</u>." Class lecture. English 212. University of St. Thomas, St. Paul. 30 Apr. 1999.

Use the title if available or provide a descriptive label for an untitled lecture and give the location and date.

Interview

```
Jones, Faustine. Personal interview. 16 Jan.
    2000.
```

Use this form for an interview you have conducted, giving only the name of the person you interviewed. If you did the interview over the telephone, substitute *Telephone interview* for *Personal interview.* If the interview was conducted by someone else, begin with the name of the interviewer, then state the title of the interview followed by the title of the source in which you found it.

Sources produced for access by computer

The information required to cite sources such as software programs or databases that can be distributed on diskettes or CD-ROM disks and the information required to cite online sources differ in two important ways. Citations to CD-ROM disks and diskettes generally should identify the publisher, the place, and the date of publication. Citations for information obtained online should state the electronic address and the date of access.

The main reason for citing any source is to give your readers enough information so that they can consult the source on their own. Because electronic sources change more frequently than print sources do, the date given for the creation or latest modification of a Web site and the date on which you accessed it are both important. Further, because sites may disappear overnight, it is wise to print out a hard copy of any site you use as a source.

The fifth edition of the *MLA Handbook for Writers of Research Papers* (1999) recognizes that "recommendations on electronic works are necessarily not definitive and will doubtless change as technology, scholarly uses of technology, scholarly uses of electronic materials, and electronic publication practices evolve" (Gibaldi 179). Check the MLA's Web site (http://www.mla) for updates on electronic citations.

This much, however, is certain: You must provide the correct **URL** for any Web site you use. By providing your readers with a complete address, including the access identifier (**http, ftp, telnet, news**), all punctuation marks, and both path and file names, you are telling them how to locate the source in question.

<http://stanfordmag.org.marapril99/>
<ftp://beowulf.engl.uky.edu/pub/beowulf>

Although it is also important to include other information, such as the author's name, the name of the site, and the date you accessed it, the complete address is essential. It substitutes for the publication data that help readers find print sources. Place the address within angle brackets < > so that it is clearly separated from any other punctuation in your citation. Divide the address after a slash when it cannot fit on a single line.

The information cited varies according to the kind of electronic source. Arrange that information in the following sequence.

1. *Author.* Give the last name first, followed by a comma and the first name.
2. *Work title.* Capitalize all major words in the title, and either underline it or place it within quotation marks (see **10a** and **16c**). Begin with the title when there is no author.
3. *Publication data.* For online services, this includes the date of publication, the name of the sponsoring organization, the date of access, and the network address. For a CD-ROM or diskette, include the city where the program was published, the name of the manufacturer, and the date of issue.

CAUTION The World Wide Web contains material that is uneven in quality. The *MLA Style Manual and Guide to Scholarly Publishing,* 2nd edition, cautions scholars to evaluate carefully the quality of any sources that they intend to use, print or electronic. For information on evaluating Web sites, see **37c**.

Online book

Many literary and historical works are available in electronic form, but not all electronically available versions are equally reliable. Be sure to use the most authoritative source. Note that the following example was published at a well-respected university.

```
Shakespeare, William. Richard III. The
     Complete Works of William Shakespeare.
     2 Aug. 1995. The Tech. MIT. 20 Apr. 1998
     <http://thetech.mit.edu/Shakespeare/
     History/kingrichardiii/
     kingrichardiii.html>.
```

In this case, the work was published on August 2, 1995, and accessed on April 20, 1998. Providing the date of publication tells readers how long the source has been available. Providing the date of access indicates how recently the site was still available, as well as the precise version used (since online sources can be updated after publication). Break URLs only at slashes.

Article in an online journal

```
Harnack, Andrew, and Gene Kleppinger. "Beyond
     the MLA Handbook: Documenting Sources on
     the Internet." Kairos 1.2 (1996).
     14 Aug. 1997 <http://www.english.ttu/acw/
     kairos/index.html>.
```

The date of access follows the volume and date of publication.

Article in an online magazine

```
Plotz, David. "The Cure for Sinophobia."
     Slate 3 June 1999. 8 June 1999 <http://
     www.slate.com/StrangeBedfellow/99-06-03/
     StrangeBedfellow.asp>.
```

Give the date of access after the date of publication even if you consult the source the same day it is posted.

Article in an online newspaper

"Tornadoes Touch Down in S. Illinois." New
  York Times on the Web 16 Apr. 1998.
  20 May 1998 <http://www.nytimes.com/
  aponline/a/AP-Illinois-Storms.html>.

Begin with the article title when an author is not identified.

Review in an online magazine or newspaper

Koeppel, Fredric. "A Look at John Keats."
  Rev. of Keats, by Andrew Motion. Nando
  Times News 16 Apr. 1998. 27 Aug. 1998
  <http://www.nando.net/newsroom/ntn/enter/
  041698/enter30_20804.html>.

Online government publication

United States. Dept. of State. Bur. of
  Democracy, Human Rights, and Labor.
  Guatemala Country Report on Human Rights
  Practices for 1998. Feb. 1999.
  1 May 1999 <http://www.state.gov/www/
  global/human_rights/1998_hrp_report/
  guatemal.html>.

Begin with the government responsible for this publication, followed by the division or agency that issued it. If a subdivision of a larger organization is responsible, name the larger division first followed by the subdivision. If an author is identified, provide the name(s) between the title and the date of issue.

Online work of art

```
Vermeer, Johannes. Young Woman with a Water
     Jug. c.1660. Metropolitan Museum of Art,
     New York. 27 Apr. 1999 <http://
     www.metmuseum.org/htmlfile/gallery/
     second/euro5.html>.
```

Place the date of the painting, sculpture, or photograph immediately after its title. If the precise date is not known, use the abbreviation *c.* (for circa) to indicate the approximate date attributed to it. Include the date of access after the name of the institution or organization making the work available for viewing.

Online map

```
"Virginia 1624." Map. Map Collections 1544-
     1996. Library of Congress. 26 Apr. 1999
     <http://memory.loc.gov/cgi-bin/map_...mp/
     ~ammmem_8kk3::&title=Virginia++>.
```

Include the word *Map* followed by a period immediately after the map's title.

Online cartoon

```
MacNelly, Jeff. "Doc's Union." Cartoon.
     Chicago Tribune 25 June 1999. 31 Mar.
     2000 <http://macnelly.com/editorial_image/
     macnelly_edtoon062599.html>.
```

E-mail

E-mail is treated much the same as personal letters and memos. Give the name of the writer, a description of the message (usually the subject line), the receiver of the message, and the date.

```
Peters, Barbara. "Scholarships for Women."
     E-mail to Rita Martinez. 10 Mar. 2000.
```

Academic discussion list

Whenever possible, cite an archived version of a posting to a discussion list to make it easier for your readers to find your source.

```
Schipper, William. "Re: Quirk and Wrenn
     Grammar." Online posting. 5 Jan. 1995.
     Ansaxnet. 12 Sep. 1996 <http://
     www.mun.ca/Ansaxdat/>.
```

Identify the name of the forum (in this case Ansaxnet, a group of scholars interested in England before 1100 C.E.) between the date of posting and the date of access.

Newsgroup

```
May, Michaela. "Questions about RYAs." Online
     posting. 19 June 1996. 29 June 1996
     <news:alt.soc.generation-x>.
```

Newsgroups are open forums, unconfined by a subscription list. Most have no moderator to ensure the quality of the postings, and messages are not usually retrievable after a few weeks. Ask whether your instructor wants you to make the source retrievable by including the e-mail address of the person who posted the item or by printing out the posting.

Synchronous communication

A synchronous group discussion, or a discussion occurring between a group of people at the same time, is like a conference call. Participants are usually screened, creating a smaller and more specialized group than the members of a discussion list. To cite a synchronous communication, include the writer's name, event description, original date, forum (e.g., Media-MOO), access date, and URL.

```
Galin, Jeff. Netoric's Tuesday Café
     discussion "Teaching Writing in the
     Digital Age: What Makes Teaching Good
     These Days?" 10 Sept. 1996. MediaMOO.
     10 Sept. 1996 <telnet://
     purplecrayon.media.mit.edu/8888>.
```

If the discussion is archived, substitute the electronic address of the archive, for example, a Web site.

```
Galin, Jeff. Netoric's Tuesday Café
     discussion "Teaching Writing in the
     Digital Age: What Makes Teaching Good
     These Days?" 10 Sept. 1996. MediaMOO.
     12 Sept. 1996 <http://www.cs.bsu.edu/
     homepages/siering/netoric.html>.
```

CD-ROM

For a source on CD-ROM, provide the author (if available) and the title, the publication medium, the place of publication, the publisher, and the publication date.

```
"About Richard III." Cinemania 96. CD-ROM.
     Redmond: Microsoft, 1996.
```

Publication on diskette

For publications on diskettes, provide the title, a descriptive label, the version number, the publisher or distributor, and the copyright date. Add other information at the end of the entry, including, if pertinent, the operating system and units of memory necessary to run the program. When a program is attributed to an author, insert the name (last name first) immediately before the title.

Hieatt, Constance, Brian Shaw, and Duncan
    Macrae-Gibson. <u>Beginning Old English:
    Exercise Disk</u>. Diskette. Vers. 6.4.
    Binghamton: OEN Subsidia, 1994.

Publication in more than one medium

<u>English Poetry Plus</u>. CD-ROM, diskette. New
    York: Films for the Humanities and
    Sciences, 1995.

 38f **Producing the final draft of a research paper
requires time and attention.**

After investing much time and effort into researching and drafting, writers sometimes fail to review their final draft carefully
enough because they have run out of time or energy. Planning
your time (see **37a(2)**) reduces the risk of being forced to submit a final draft that was prepared too quickly.

(1) Writing a good research paper requires revising, editing, and proofreading.

After writing and carefully documenting the first draft of your
paper, make needed revisions. An outline can help you determine whether your organization is logical (see **32d**). Revise
each paragraph to make its purpose clear, and edit each sentence to support its paragraph. Refer to chapters **8** and **33** as
needed, particularly the revising, editing, and proofreading
checklists. As you revise, make sure you continue to use your
sources carefully and responsibly (see **38b–d**). If you have questions about final manuscript form, refer to chapter **8** and to the
sample research paper in **38f(2)**.

The MLA recommends omitting a title page and giving the
identification on the first page before the title of the paper (see

page 613). Some instructors require a final outline along with the text of the paper; this serves as a table of contents. In this case, a title page is advisable. A title page usually gives the title of the paper, the author, the instructor's name, the name of the course and its section number, and the date—all attractively centered on the page. (For a sample title page that can be modified for an MLA-style paper, see the APA-style research paper in **38i**.)

(2) Studying a sample MLA-style research paper can help you prepare for writing your own.

After researching a case in which a Nobel Prize winner was found to have misrepresented the truth in the autobiography that made her famous, Dieter Bohn focused his paper on what this case reveals about the nature of credibility. As you study his paper, note how he develops his thesis, considers more than one point of view (**36c(3)**), and observes correct form for an MLA-style paper.

Websites
1. Author or editor   4. Name of Institutional org.
2. Title of Site   5. Date accessed
3. Date of last update 6.URL

f. Websites
Sheet: Nuclear Power. 27 Feb 1997, Federal Management.
1 May 1998 < URL>

serial
ven, Michael. Daliweb. Biography + Artistic Style: The
Surreal. 8 Feb. 1998. 1 May 1998 < URL>

Comments

A. All pages (including the first one) are numbered with Arabic numerals in the upper right-hand corner, one-half inch from the top. The page number is preceded by the author's last name. Notice that no period follows the page numbers.

B. The name of the author, the name of the professor, the course number, and the date of submission—appearing in that order—begin one inch from the top of the page and flush with the left margin. A margin of one inch is provided at the left, right, and bottom.

C. Double-space between the heading and the centered title of the paper. Double-space also separates the title from the first line of the text. (A title consisting of two or more lines is double-spaced, and each line is centered.)

D. The thesis statement for this paper is placed where readers can easily locate it. This thesis emerged through the process of writing the paper. Note the uncertainty Bohn reveals when exploring ideas before writing his first draft.

Excerpt from the research log of Dieter Bohn

```
The central issue is not whether or not
she told the truth (she clearly didn't)
but the implications of that. [. . .]
     I'm having a hard time [. . .]
because all the options seem to put me in
one camp or the other. I'm not entirely
happy with either. I don't want to say
that it was propaganda intended to further
the left's cause because I think there is
something to their cause. On the other
hand, condoning the lies in her book seems
tantamount to saying that it is okay to
distort the facts for a political agenda,
```

(continued on page 614)

Dieter Bohn   B
Professor Miller
English 299, Section 4
30 June 1999

Rigoberta Menchú and Representative Authority C

The 1983 publication of Rigoberta
Menchú's <u>I, Rigoberta Menchú</u> has done much
to help her work to improve human rights in
her native country, Guatemala. Recently,
however, there has been a great deal of
controversy--especially since the 1999
publication of David Stoll's <u>Rigoberta Menchú
and the Story of All Poor Guatemalans</u>--
surrounding the truth of Menchú's
autobiography. Stoll, an anthropologist at
Middlebury College in Vermont, proves that
Menchú did not tell the whole truth about
her life in the book that made her famous.
When Menchú told her story, her goal was to
call international attention to the plight
"of all poor Guatemalans" (<u>I, Rigoberta</u> 1).
She achieved this goal by changing her story
to make it more compelling to her audience.
These changes have undermined her authority
as a representative figure and threaten to
damage her cause as well. The example of
<u>I, Rigoberta Menchú</u> shows why it is wrong to D
fictionalize an autobiographical account that
claims to speak for a whole people.

In Guatemala, ladinos, or those of
European or mixed descent, make up
approximately fifty-six percent of the
population; the rest is composed mainly of

Comments

E. Bohn provides background information so that his audience can understand the political situation that inspired the book he has chosen to discuss. A parenthetical citation appears without a page reference because it is to a Web site without pagination or paragraphing. (See page 618.)

F. A parenthetical citation does not include the author's name when the author is clearly identified in the text, as is the case here.

Excerpt from the research log of Dieter Bohn (*continued from page 612*)

and even if the guerrillas for which
Menchú spoke were blameless (when I don't
think they are), I wouldn't want to accept
that.

The one thing I feel obligated to put
in this paper is that Menchú's book is <u>not</u>
an autobiography, but a consciously formed
story including her own life mixed with
what her allies would like construed as
the typical peasant experience in a
dictatorship. What I am hesitant about is
what to say about it. Condone it on the
basis of her great victimization mixed
with relativistic autobiographical theory?
Say it was wrong? Try to make no judgments
whatsoever? I don't know.

Anyway, that's where I'm at right
now.

different types of Amerindian, or Mayan, peoples ("Guatemala"). There has been tension E between these two ethnic groups; for many years, Mayans suffered under a series of oppressive ladino dictatorships. At the same time, there were several guerilla groups fighting the Guatemalan army, also composed mainly of ladinos but claiming to speak for Mayans. Caught in the middle were Mayan peasants, trying to survive in this difficult environment by cultivating mountainside fields and working on coastal plantations called <u>fincas</u>, most of which are owned by wealthy ladinos. It was out of this war-torn country that Rigoberta Menchú, a Mayan, traveled to Europe in January 1982 so that she could tell her story to anthropologist Elizabeth Burgos-Debray. After recording a week's worth of conversation with Menchú, Burgos-Debray converted those tapes into the book-length memoir known as <u>I, Rigoberta Menchú</u> (xv-xxi). F

3   In this book, Menchú recounts her upbringing, the murder of four members of her family, oppression by the Guatemalan army, and the guerilla resistance. Telling how she and her village organized to fight the oppression of ladino landowners, she describes events and feelings she claims were typical of what most Mayan peasants experienced. Filled with powerful language and stories about her fight against injustice, Menchú's book has received

Comments

G. Although the period normally *follows* the parenthetical citation, MLA style makes an exception for block quotations. For quotations indented one inch from the left margin, place the period *before* the parenthetical citation as shown here.

H. When two sources are cited within the same parentheses, they are separated by a semicolon.

I. Bohn establishes the credibility of a source by identifying a name that would be unfamiliar to this audience.

considerable attention because she tells such
a compelling story. For example, she
describes a confrontation between the people
of her village and the Guatemalan army:

> The people raised their weapons and
> rushed at the army, but they drew
> back at once, because there was the
> risk of a massacre. The army had
> all kinds of arms, even planes
> flying overhead. [. . .] But nobody
> thought about death. I didn't think
> that I might die, I just wanted to
> do something, even kill a soldier.
> (179)   G

4   Menchú's book became an international
bestseller (Grandin and Goldman 25; Wilson   H
A14). One of the many results of this
success has been the widespread use of
I, Rigoberta Menchú in university classrooms.
According to Charles Lane, an editor for The   I
New Republic, the book

> has become required reading in
> anthropology, women's studies, and
> Latin American history and politics
> courses at universities across the
> United States. [. . .] According to
> Menchú herself, it has inspired
> some 15,000 scholarly papers. It
> has been translated into twelve
> languages. (36)

        Another result of the book's success is
that Menchú has become an international
activist for human rights (Stoll, Rigoberta 5).

Comments

J. When a Web site or other source accessed by computer includes neither page nor paragraph numbers, the MLA advises writers to refer readers to the complete source, which can be found in the list of works cited. The MLA has never asked writers to create numbers for unnumbered texts. In the case of sources accessed by computer, specific passages can usually be located by performing a *find* on the Web site or in the electronic document by entering a few words from the quotation in question. For additional information on citing electronic texts, see pages 586–87 and 603–10.

K. Recognizing the controversy provoked by David Stoll's book on Menchú, Bohn establishes that another source has verified Stoll's findings. The quotation from Rohter is from an electronic source without page or paragraph numbers.

Bohn 4

All of this attention and acclaim eventually
helped Menchú win the 1992 Nobel Prize. In a
press release, the Norwegian Nobel Foundation
said that Menchú "stands out as a vivid
symbol of peace and reconciliation across
ethnic, cultural, and social dividing lines
[. . .]." Menchú's status as a symbol of   J
oppressed indigenous people was an especially
effective tool against the problems in
Guatemala. In 1995, the Guatemalan government
signed an agreement to stop violating human
rights (Stoll, <u>Rigoberta</u> 268). It did this
mainly because of international pressure--the
most significant result of Menchú's work.
Were it not for Menchú, many believe, the
human rights violations in Guatemala would
have passed largely unnoticed by the
international community (Grandin and Goldman
25). Now, although there are still problems,
the Guatemalan government cannot
indiscriminately kill peasants or destroy
their villages.

5   But the book that inspired so much of
this progress is misleading, as David Stoll
has shown. Larry Rohter, a reporter for the
<u>New York Times</u>, corroborated Stoll's account,   K

> Relatives, neighbors, friends and
> former classmates of Rigoberta
> Menchú [. . .] indicated that many
> of the main episodes related by Ms.
> Menchú have either been fabricated
> or seriously exaggerated.

Comments

L. In paragraph 6, a shortened version of the title appears within the parentheses because the works-cited list includes two works by Menchú. Ellipses within brackets indicate that Bohn has omitted part of Menchú's text. Bracketed phrases indicate that Bohn has inserted this information to make the source material clearer to his audience.

6   One of the major exaggerations that
Menchú made about her life as she told it in
her book concerns her childhood. She tells
us that most peasants try to eke out a
living from small farms in the mountains but
often cannot, and so travel down to the
fincas to work. The conditions in the fincas
are terrible; Menchú writes about working as
an eight-year-old:

>   I went on working and [. . .] for
>   two years they paid me only 20
>   centavos [equivalent to 20 U.S.
>   cents a day]. I picked more and
>   more coffee. It increased by one
>   pound, two pounds, three pounds. I
>   worked like an adult. Then,
>   finally, they started paying me
>   more. By the time I was picking 70
>   pounds of coffee [a day], they paid
>   me 35 centavos. (I, Rigoberta 35)

The workers were also exposed to toxins:
"They'd sprayed the coffee with pesticide by
plane while we were working, as they usually
did, and my brother couldn't stand the fumes
and died of intoxication" (Menchú, I,
Rigoberta 38). The conditions these workers
faced were terrible, and they were common to
most Guatemalan peasants. However, Stoll
discovered that Menchú never actually
experienced these conditions. Menchú's
surviving family members and neighbors say
that she spent most of her childhood in
Catholic boarding schools (Stoll, Rigoberta 160).

Comments

M. A superscript numeral in addition to a parenthetical citation indicates that an explanatory note will follow on a separate page at the end of the paper. (See page 639.)

In an earlier draft, Bohn had extended his discussion of what happened to Menchú's siblings by including the following passage describing the fate of a brother who was part of a group of prisoners burned alive by the military:

> They all had marks of different tortures. The captain devoted himself to explaining each of the different tortures. [. . .] You could only think that these were human beings and what pain those bodies had felt to arrive at that unrecognizable state. [. . .] Anyway, they lined up the tortured and poured petrol on them; and then the soldiers set fire to each one of them. (I, Rigoberta 177-79)

Bohn described this scene as "powerful enough to make even the hardest hearts sympathetic to Menchú's plight," but then went on to cite evidence showing that Menchú could not have witnessed this scene as she claims. When revising, he decided that he was dwelling too long on establishing how Menchú had misrepresented her story when he really wanted to focus on the political and ethical implications of these discrepancies. So he condensed this part of his paper and inserted an explanatory note. (See page 634.)

Nevertheless, Menchú did know from her interactions with other Guatemalan peasants what the conditions in the <u>fincas</u> were like, even if she did not experience them first-hand. Stoll himself points out that this is not an especially problematic change: "Even if the young Rigoberta did not watch her siblings die on a plantation, other Mayan children have" (<u>Rigoberta</u> 190).[1]

M

7   Unfortunately, there are other major fabrications that misrepresent the common experience of indigenous people. One change Menchú makes is the source of the land problems that many Mayans face. Menchú claims that her village was primarily fighting ladino landowners:

> We started thinking about the roots of the problem and came to the conclusion that everything stemmed from the ownership of the land. The best land was not in our hands. It belonged to the big landowners. Every time they see that we have new land, they try to throw us off it or steal it in other ways. (<u>I, Rigoberta</u> 116)

Although it is true that the rich plantation owners, the <u>finca</u> owners, owned much of the best land, in Menchú's particular case, her father's fight was not against ladino landowners, as Menchú asserts, but against other Mayans. She claims that "my father fought for twenty-two years, waging a heroic

Comments

N. Recognizing that his audience is unlikely to be familiar with the term, Bohn adds a bracketed explanation.

O. By using *sic* (Latin for *so* or *thus*) Bohn clarifies that this British spelling of *organize* appears in the source.

Bohn 7

struggle against the landowners who wanted to
take our land and our neighbors' land" (<u>I,
Rigoberta</u> 103). However, Stoll's research has
shown that people in Menchú's village agree
that her father's "most serious land dispute
was not with ladino plantation owners.
Instead, it was with K'iche [Mayan]
smallholders like himself: his in-laws"   N
(<u>Rigoberta</u> 30). This type of situation is
much more common than Menchú would like to
admit. Thus, her claim that the main problem
was between ladinos and Mayans is misleading;
the major land problems were actually between
Mayans and other Mayans.

8   Another disturbing fabrication is that
Menchú claims her village was united with
the guerillas against the army; instead, most
villages were actually stuck between both
forces. Menchú describes how her entire
village organized as guerilla fighters:
"Everyone came with ideas of how to defend
themselves. [. . .] We began to get a much
better idea of how to organise [sic] our
community" (<u>I, Rigoberta</u> 126). However, most   O
peasants were not on one side or the other,
but trapped between a guerilla movement they
did not wish to join and an army that was
killing everybody they thought was in
collusion with the guerillas (Stoll,
<u>Rigoberta</u> 110). Mayans were pressured into
joining one side or the other simply to keep
from getting killed.

Comments

P. Bohn cites additional sources to support his claim that relations between the guerillas and the Mayans were problematic. Note that he identifies both Nelson and Becker for his audience. The citation from Becker does not include a page reference because it is from an electronic text without page or paragraph numbers. (See page 618.)

9   By claiming that the guerillas formed spontaneously in the Mayan villages in response to oppression (<u>I, Rigoberta</u> 123), Menchú implies that guerilla warfare was inevitable. According to Stoll, "that view of the violence is incorrect" ("Literary"). The decision to fight was actually made by guerilla leaders who were ladino, not Mayan. Moreover, Diane Nelson, another anthropologist who has done research in Guatemala, argues that many Mayans felt the ladino leadership was racist. In <u>A Finger in the Wound</u>, Nelson writes that many "indigenous people left the [guerilla] organizations, [. . .] some fed up with what they perceived as ongoing racist discrimination" (59). Marc Becker, of the University of Kansas, also found evidence that the guerilla leadership "considered Indians to be politically and economically marginal to Guatemalan society with little promise of leading or contributing to a revolutionary uprising."

P

10   Menchú's version of events is significantly different from what actually happened. She changed what was a ladino-led attempt at an uprising to a version that sounded suspiciously like the perfect Marxist revolt: the lowest class becoming aware of its oppression and rising up. David Horowitz, a conservative columnist, noted this change and came to the conclusion that "the fictional story of Rigoberta Menchú is a piece of

Comments

Q. Summarizing the public debate over Menchú's work, Bohn balances a paragraph attacking her with a paragraph defending her. By doing so, he establishes that he has considered arguments from different sides—an essential strategy in persuasive writing. (See **36c(3)**.)

Communist propaganda designed to incite
hatred of Europeans and Westerners [. . .]"
(2). Others agree with Horowitz; in fact,
there is now a group calling itself
"Operation Remove Rigoberta" that is angry
about the influence Menchú has gained as a
result of her less-than-truthful book. This
group has used advertisements in college
newspapers as well as a Web site in a
campaign to remove the book from college
campuses ("Operation").

11   Against opinions such as this, John   Q
Beverly, of the University of Pittsburgh,
defends Menchú because he believes that she
was simply trying to gain support for her
cause, so her changes do not matter if they
are taken in that sense:

> [H]er primary purpose in making the
> text is not to humanize college
> students, or to give literary
> theorists something to argue over,
> but to act tactically through the
> text as a way of advancing the
> interests of the group or class
> represented in the testimonio
> [autobiography]. (138)

Stoll argues along the same lines. He claims
that she changed her story to make it more
compelling to a mass audience: "One of the
simplifying functions of solidarity imagery
is that it offers a single platform to
support" (Rigoberta 236). The Rigoberta
Menchú Tum Foundation, which Menchú founded,
has defended the book on the grounds that it

Comments

R. After summarizing three views (one of which is from a Web site without page or paragraph numbers), Bohn establishes what they have in common: a position he is challenging in this paper.

S. Paragraphs 11 and 12 include quotations from Web sites without page or paragraph numbers. (See page 618.) The bracketed *sic* indicates the absence of a period or semicolon in this position.

Interview with Dieter Bohn

After writing this paper for Professor Robert K. Miller, one of the authors of *Hodges' Harbrace Handbook,* Bohn met with Miller to discuss what the experience had been like from the writer's point of view. Excerpts from this interview appear below and also on pages 632, 634, and 636.

Miller: When you began this project, did you have a clear sense of how much work it would take?

Bohn: No. I knew it would be a lot. But I didn't really know what "a lot" meant. I was in the right ballpark for the research, but revising took much longer than I thought it would. When you care about the final product, you keep going back to try to get things right.

Miller: How many drafts did you write?

Bohn: Probably about five that were radically different. Twelve or thirteen if I could include versions that had small changes.

Miller: Did writing this paper for publication make it different from other papers?

Bohn: Yes. I felt more pressure to get the final draft right. The main difference is that I had to be absolutely sure that I was being true both to the facts and to myself. I was writing about someone who had misrepresented facts, and I wanted what I wrote to be true to the best of my knowledge.

(*continued on page 632*)

gained that support: "The path for which
Rigoberta Menchú opted [. . .] was that of
involving the conscience of the international
community." The Foundation asserts that
Menchú's account is not weakened by Stoll's
findings and that her goal of gaining
international attention is what was important
for that text. Thus, her foundation claims
that a precise use of the truth was not her
goal. In other words, all three defenders   R
essentially argue that, in this case, the
ends (international attention for Mayans)
justified the means (Menchú's fabrications).

12   Menchú is now attempting to sidestep the
political aspects of the controversy
surrounding her. In a recent interview she
spoke mainly about the problems of indigenous
peoples in a way that was clearly (and
probably purposefully) not Marxist in tone or
content: "Well I think it's not exactly a
conflict between the government and myself.
I'm not subject to any political party [sic]   S
I respect all the parties [. . .]"
("Webcast"). Menchú has asserted her
independence from the guerilla movement in
other ways. In a new autobiography, <u>Crossing
Borders</u>, she writes, "I am no philosopher. I
am simply a granddaughter of the Mayans
[. . .]" (87). This definition of herself is
significant. She claims to hold no
philosophical views, so that she is not tied
down by a political agenda. Yet she
identifies herself solely with the Mayan

Comments

T. The parenthetical citation establishes that Webb was quoted by Wilson; the list of works cited will thus have an entry for Wilson but not for Webb.

Interview with Dieter Bohn (*continued from page 630*)

Miller: Has working on this project had any impact on your writing process?

Bohn: Yes. I'm more willing to write things down, no longer afraid of a blank screen. I used to get blocked a lot. Now I know that whatever I put down I can later change.

Miller: Why did this topic appeal to you?

Bohn: It's current, and I don't often get to write about current controversies. What I like best though is that it really made me think. Usually I have a good sense of what I think when I start to write, but this topic forced me to keep thinking.

Miller: What was the most satisfying aspect of this project?

Bohn: I don't know, as it still isn't quite finished. I like my last two pages because they express what I came to think. That's probably what was most satisfying: having found a considered opinion and being able to put it out for others to read.

(*continued on page 634*)

people, which is, at many levels, a
political association--only it is a
slightly different arena of politics from the
guerilla associations. In the midst of the
controversy surrounding her,[2] Menchú has
tried to maintain her representative
authority as a Mayan by talking solely about
indigenous issues.

13   Ironically, while the book has been
attacked as being a piece of fiction, its
literary aspects have also been used to
defend it. The main argument has been that
Menchú is telling a deeper, more poetic
kind of truth. According to one critic,
"Menchú's reader must resist the temptation of
reading her _literally_, which would deny
her the capacity to represent herself _literar-
ily_ [poetically] and symbolically [. . .]"
(Handley 68). He argues that Menchú should
not be read as strictly nonfiction, but as a
subjective account of how she perceived what
happened to her. Others have gone even
further. Allen Carey Webb, of Western
Michigan University, has argued that, given
Menchú's terrible situation, her changes are
actually true in a deeper sense in that they
reflect what it was really like to be
oppressed (qtd. in Wilson A16).   T

14   This kind of defense, however, works
only so long as the "deeper truth" actually
corresponds to the changes Menchú made.
Unfortunately, it does not. Menchú's
autobiography does not represent a deeper
truth because it fails to meet the claim

Comments

U. Bohn balances recognition of Menchú's accomplishments with recognition of what he considers problematic, establishing that he understands the complexity of the case and wishes to avoid the kind of unfair attacks he found in some of the sources he read.

Interview with Dieter Bohn (*continued from page 632*)

Miller: What was the most frustrating part of this experience?

Bohn: Deciding what to put in the paper and what to leave out. I felt that I could have written four more papers with the amount of material I had.

Miller: Was there anything you left out that you hated to lose?

Bohn: The stuff about her brother. It was very moving. Also I wish I could have said more about the intricacies of life in her village.

Miller: After finishing a publishable draft, you remained part of the process of preparing that draft for publication—reviewing copyedited manuscript, galleys, and page proof. Are you glad you did so?

Bohn: Yes. It was very interesting because I didn't know the process. At first I was afraid that the paper would change, but that wasn't really an issue. So it was nice for me personally more than it was necessary for the paper itself.

(*continued on page 636*)

that Menchú herself makes for it: "My story
is the story of all poor Guatemalans. My
experience is the reality of a whole people"
(<u>I, Rigoberta</u> 1). Her story is not "the
reality of a whole people." Menchú claims
that there was solidarity among Mayans
against landowners, among Mayans with the
guerillas, and within the guerilla groups
themselves. The reality of the situation was
much more complicated, involving land
disputes, coercion, and racism.

15   When war and genocide are involved,
it is tempting to lie if doing so could
save lives. Along these lines, Menchú   U
oversimplified the situation as a means of
gaining support for her cause. That support
led to a peace agreement in Guatemala, so
she may have succeeded in saving lives. In
one sense, then, her success seems to
justify her means. However, other ends that
Menchú perhaps did not expect--international
attention of a different sort than she
wanted--resulted. Because her means involved
changing her story to fit what appears to be
a Marxist paradigm, her credibility as a
representative of the Mayans has been
damaged. The danger is that she has been so
successful in identifying herself with Mayans
that this damage could extend beyond Menchú's
person to the cause itself, equal rights for
indigenous people in Guatemala.

16   Although Menchú's misrepresentation of
the Mayan experience was understandable given
her situation, it was not right. Even if her

Comments

V. Bohn reaches a conclusion in which he reaffirms his thesis and establishes how his research has led him to improve his understanding of what writers can and cannot do.

Interview with Dieter Bohn (*continued from page 634*)

Miller: Would you do a project like this again?

Bohn: Yes, I would. For lots of reasons. I've learned so much about the subject and about writing. Most of all what it's like to engage in a scholarly debate that's important.

Miller: Any advice for students who are getting ready to write a research paper?

Bohn: Start early. Research a lot. But don't think you've got to finish all the research before you can write. It's also important to start writing early. You can go back and do more research as you get a clearer sense of what you need to find out.

changes were not discovered, they would have indirectly harmed her people. By fictionalizing what most Mayans went through, she caused the international community to act on false information. Too often this led to support for the guerilla movement rather than the Mayans. It is clear that Menchú was able to use her fame to accomplish some good results in Guatemala; unfortunately, the guerillas her book supported were not as noble as she made them out to be. In fact, in some cases the guerillas were exploiting the Mayans. Nelson concludes that in some cases, "the guerillas used the Maya[ns] as cannon-fodder [. . .]" (59). The good that Menchú eventually achieved came from building support for indigenous rights, not from her support of the guerilla movement.

17   Reflecting on this case raises the   V
question of whether it is ever right to fictionalize an autobiographical account. There is no easy answer, but what Menchú's story reveals is this: when the fictionalization deals not just with an individual, but--as Menchú puts it--with the "reality of a whole people," it is important to strive to tell the most accurate version of events possible. The reason is that the "whole people" may be affected by the story. Menchú did the exact opposite--she intentionally changed a story that she knew would be seen as representative. Her homeland and her people deserved a more truthful account.

Comments

W. Notes are coordinated with their location in the text by a super-script number that comes before the indented first line of the note and also at the appropriate location in the text.

According to the *MLA Handbook for Writers of Research Papers,* 5th edition

> In research papers, make all notes endnotes, unless you are instructed otherwise. As their name implies, endnotes appear after the text, starting on a new page numbered in sequence with the preceding page. Center the title *Notes* one inch from the top, double-space, indent one-half inch (or five spaces, if you are using a typewriter) from the left margin, and add the note number, without punctuation, slightly above the line. Type a space and then the reference. If the note extends to two or more lines, begin subsequent lines at the left margin. Type the notes consecutively, double-spaced, and number all pages. (Gibaldi 269)

See page 622 for part of an earlier draft that was summarized and became part of note 1.

Notes such as these provide writers with a way to incorporate material that they decide is too important to discard even if they cannot incorporate it within the paper iself because they need to focus their ideas (see **32b(2)**) and work within the length appropriate for a specific assignment. Responsible writers do not use explanatory notes as a means for preserving everything they decide to cut from their texts, because doing so could make excessive demands upon the good will of their audience (see **32a(2)**). When you decide to add explanatory notes, remember that you are asking readers to turn away from your main text in order to make a side trip. Evaluate each of these detours by asking yourself if they help you fulfill your purpose (see **32a(1)**).

Notes

W

[1] Many other changes that Menchú made to her story do not damage its credibility. An example is Menchú's claim to have witnessed the army burning her brother alive (<u>I, Rigoberta</u> 179). Stoll has shown that nobody was ever actually burned alive in the village where Menchú claims to have seen the torturing (<u>Rigoberta</u> 69). Still, Menchú's brother was murdered by the army, as were many other Mayans. Changes of this nature do not detract from its representative authority, as they are in line with common Mayan experience.

[2] There is not enough space in this paper to fully develop the controversy surrounding Menchú's politics. Many people have oversimplified Stoll's book by depicting it as little more than an accusation of lying. Some people have jumped to Menchú's defense, claiming that Stoll is a racist who is trying to silence Menchú. The important issue is that the very fact that the controversy exists raises serious questions about Menchú's credibility.

Comments

X. Center the title *Works Cited,* one inch down from the top of the page, and double-space between this title and the first entry.

Y. Include only those works you cited in the paper. If you consulted other sources but did not use them, do not include them in your list. Alphabetize entries according to the author's last name. Each entry should begin flush with the left margin. Lines after the first are indented five spaces (or one-half inch).

When citing two or more works by the same author, arrange them in alphabetical order determined by the first important word in the title. After providing the author's name in the first entry, additional entries for this same author are indicated by typing three hyphens, then a period followed by a space.

Works Cited X

Becker, Marc. "Ethnicity, Legitimacy, and the Y
State: Understanding Ethnic Movements in
Mexico, Guatemala, and Peru." <u>1997
Update on Latin America Conference</u>. 15
Mar. 1997. 30 Apr. 1999 <http://
falcon.cc.ukans.edu/~marc/update.html>.

Beverly, John. "The Real Thing (Our
Rigoberta)." <u>Modern Language Quarterly</u>
57.2 (1996): 129-39.

Burgos-Debray, Elizabeth. Preface.
<u>I, Riboberta Menchú</u>. 1983. New York:
Verso, 1996. xi-xxi.

Grandin, Greg, and Francisco Goldman. "Bitter
Fruit for Rigoberta." <u>The Nation</u> 8 Feb.
1999: 25-28.

"Guatemala." <u>The CIA World Factbook 1998</u>. 20
June 1999 <http://www.odci.gov/cia/
publications/factbook/gt.html>.

Handley, George. "It's an Unbelievable Story:
Testimony and Truth in the Work of
Rosario Ferre and Rigoberta Menchú."
<u>Violence, Silence, and Anger: Women's
Writing as Transgression</u>. Ed. Diedre
Lashgari. Charlottesville: UP of
Virginia, 1995. 62-79.

Horowitz, David. "I, Rigoberta Menchú, Liar."
<u>Salon</u> 11 Jan. 1999. 20 June 1999
<http://www.salonmagazine.com/col/horo/
1999/01/11horo.html>.

Lane, Charles. "Deceiving is Believing." <u>The
New Republic</u> 8 March 1999: 36-40.

Comments

Z. When citing Web sources, be scrupulously careful with the address and place it in angle brackets so that it will be clearly distinct from the rest of the entry. When the full address cannot fit on a single line, divide it after a slash.

"Live Webcast, 18 Feb. 1999! Rigoberta
      Menchú." <u>Latin America Trek</u> 18 Feb. 1999.
      25 Apr. 1999 <http://www.worldtrek.org/
      odyssey/latinamerica/rigoberta/
      transcripteng2.html>.

Menchú, Rigoberta. <u>Crossing Borders</u>. Trans.
      and ed. Anne Wright. New York: Verso,
      1998.

---. <u>I, Rigoberta Menchú</u>. Ed. Elizabeth
      Burgos-Debray. Trans. Anne Wright. 1983.
      New York: Verso, 1996.

Nelson, Diane. <u>A Finger in the Wound</u>.
      Berkeley: U of California P, 1999.

The Norwegian Nobel Foundation. "The Nobel
      Peace Prize for 1992." 18 June 1998. 27
      Apr. 1999 <http://www.nobel.se/laureates/
      peace-1992-press.html>.

"Operation Remove Rigoberta." <u>Front Page
      Magazine</u> 11 May 1999. 17 May 1999
      <http://www.frontpagemag.com/campaign/
      rigobertacampaign.htm>.

The Rigoberta Menchú Tum Foundation.
      "Rigoberta Menchú Tum: The Truth That
      Challenges the Future." Jan. 1999. 20
      June 1999 <http://
      ourworld.compuserve.com/homepages/rmtpaz/
      mensajes/m990120i.htm>.

Rohter, Larry. "Nobel Winner Accused of
      Stretching the Truth." <u>The New York
      Times on the Web</u> 15 Dec. 1998. 20 June
      1999 <http://www.nytimes.com/library/
      books/121598cambodian-memoir.html>.

Stoll, David. "Literary Truth." <u>National
    Public Radio Talk of the Nation</u>. 10
    June 1999. 14 June 1999 <http://
    search.npr.org/cf/cmn/
    cmnpsosfm.cfm?SegID:513367>.

---. <u>Rigoberta Menchú and the Story of All
    Poor Guatemalans</u>. Boulder: Westview,
    1999.

Wilson, Robin. "A Challenge to the Veracity
    of a Multicultural Icon." <u>The Chronicle
    of Higher Education</u> 15 Jan. 1999: A14-
    A16.

EXERCISE 3

Create an outline (see 32d(2)) for the sample MLA-style paper. Your
instructor will indicate whether you should create a sentence or a topic
outline.

EXERCISE 4

Read what the author of this paper says about the process of writing
it. (See pages 630, 632, 634, and 636.) Then write five questions you
would like to ask Dieter Bohn about the content of his paper.

Some disciplines use the note style of documentation.

Although the MLA has recommended parenthetical documentation since 1984 (and the influential *Chicago Manual of Style* since 1982), some disciplines in the humanities still use either footnotes or endnotes for documentation.

Both footnotes and endnotes require that a superscript numeral be placed wherever documentation is necessary. The number should be as close as possible to whatever it refers to, following the punctuation (such as quotation marks, a comma, or a period) that appears at the end of the direct quotation or paraphrase.

Footnotes should be single-spaced four lines below the last line of text on the same page where the documentation is necessary. Double-space between footnotes if more than one appears on any one page. **Endnotes** should be double-spaced on a separate page headed *Notes*. (For an example, see page 639.)

The following notes use the same sources as the ones in 38e(2). By comparing the model footnote with its corresponding works-cited entry, you will see differences between the two forms. (These numbered notes are arranged in a pattern for your convenience and are numbered sequentially, as your notes would be for documentation. But your notes, of course, would not begin with "book by one author" followed by "book by more than one author," and so on.)

Book by one author

¹ Jeanne Rosier Smith, <u>Writing Tricksters: Narrative Strategy and Cultural Identity in Maxine Hong Kingston, Louise Erdrich, and Toni Morrison</u> (Berkeley: U of California P, 1997) 143.

Indent one-half inch (or five spaces), then type the note number (without punctuation) followed by a space. Additional lines in a note should be flush with the left margin. Note that an abbreviation for "page" is not used before the page number at the end of the note.

Book by more than one author or editor

² Nigel West and Oleg Tsarev, <u>The Crown Jewels: The British Secrets in the Heart of the KGB Archives</u> (New Haven: Yale UP, 1999) 158.

If the book has more than two authors, use commas to separate the authors' names.

³ Charles Spinosa, Fernando Flores, and Hubert L. Dreyfus, <u>Disclosing New Worlds: Entrepreneurship, Democratic Action, and the Cultivation of Solidarity</u> (Cambridge: MIT P, 1997) 179.

Multivolume work

⁴ George C. D. Odell, <u>Annals of the New York Stage</u>, 15 vols.(New York: Columbia UP, 1949) 243.

⁵ Robert Browning, <u>The Complete Works of Robert Browning: With Variant Readings and Annotations</u>, ed. John C. Berkey and Allan C. Dooley, vol. 6 (Athens: Ohio UP, 1996) 114.

Editor as author

⁶ Robyn R. Warhol and Diane Price Herndl, eds., <u>Feminisms: An Anthology of</u>

Literary Theory and Criticisms (New Brunswick: Rutgers UP, 1993) 165.

Work in an anthology

[7] Wendy Bishop, "Students' Stories and the Variable Gaze of Composition Research," Writing Ourselves into the Story: Unheard Voices from Composition Studies, ed. Sheryl I. Fontane and Susan Hunter (Carbondale: Southern Illinois UP, 1993) 211.

Introduction, preface, foreword, or afterword to a book

[8] Peter Elbow, foreword, The Peaceable Classroom, by Mary Rose O'Reilley (Portsmouth: Heinemann, 1993) xii.

Article from a journal with continuous pagination

[9] Gwendolyn Diaz, "Desire and Discourse in Maria Luisa Bombal's New Islands," Hispanofila 112 (1994): 61.

Article from a magazine

[10] Alexander Stille, "The Man Who Remembers," New Yorker 15 Feb. 1999: 56.

Article from a newspaper

[11] Charles Leroux, "Reading Frenzy," Chicago Tribune 20 Apr. 1999, final ed., sec. 2: 1.

38h APA-style documentation is appropriate for research papers in psychology and most social sciences.

Directory of APA-Style Parenthetical Citations

(1) APA-style parenthetical citations include dates of publication.

In APA style, the basic elements of a parenthetical citation in the text are the author's last name, the year of publication, and the page number if the reference is to a specific passage in the source. If the author's name is mentioned in the text of the paper, give the date alone or the date and the page number in parentheses. In the following examples, note the details of punctuation and the treatment of the page number.

Work by one author

```
A prominent neurologist has concluded,
"Pushing back the age at which the wide-
spread form of Alzheimer's strikes--from, say,
age seventy to age ninety--would be nearly
tantamount to a cure" (Kosik, 1999, p. 17).
```

OR

Dr. Kenneth Kosik, a prominent neurologist, has concluded, "Pushing back the age at which the wide-spread form of Alzheimer's strikes--from, say, age seventy to age ninety --would be nearly tantamount to a cure" (1999, p. 17).

OR

Kosik (1999) has concluded, "Pushing back the age at which the wide-spread form of Alzheimer's strikes--from, say, age seventy to age ninety--would be nearly tantamount to a cure" (p. 17).

Unlike MLA style, APA style requires the abbreviation *p.* (or *pp.* for "pages") before the page reference. Use commas to separate the author's name from the date and the date from the page reference.

Work by two authors

There is evidence that students in second and third grade respond favorably to guidance from elementary school students in higher grades (Bowman & Myrick, 1987).

Use an ampersand (&) to separate the authors' names. A page number is not necessary when the reference is to an entire work—a common practice in writing within the social sciences.

Work by more than two authors

One study has shown that people who fear failure are not susceptible to hypnosis (Manganello, Carlson, Zarillo, & Teeven, 1985).

For works with *three to five authors,* cite all the authors in the first reference, but in subsequent references give only the last name of the first author followed by *et al.* ("Manganello et al." in this case). For works with *six or more authors,* provide only the last name of the first author followed by *et al.,* even in the first citation.

Anonymous work

Use a shortened version of the title to identify an anonymous work.

```
Chronic insomnia usually requires medical
intervention ("Sleep," 2000).
```

In this case, the author has cited a short article identified in the bibliography as "Sleep disorders: Standard methods of treatment."

Two or more works in the same parentheses

```
Opponents of animal experimentation have
traditionally argued that it is both
unnecessary and cruel (Mayo, 1983; Singer,
1975).
```

Use a semicolon to separate different studies, and arrange them in alphabetical order.

(2) An APA-style reference list follows specific conventions.

Format the "References" (alphabetical list of works cited) in the APA style your instructor specifies. (See the commentary on final manuscript style, pages 659–61.) As the fourth edition of the *Publication Manual* asserts, **final manuscript style** allows considerable freedom to format documents to enhance readability. Some instructors prefer that the first line of each entry in the references list be typed flush left and that subsequent lines be indented five spaces—called a **hanging indent.**

Other instructors prefer that you indent the first line of each entry five spaces and type subsequent lines flush with the left margin. The *Publication Manual* urges instructors to specify the style they prefer for the final manuscript.

The reference entries below have a hanging indent, but as the *Publication Manual* asserts, they could have been formatted just as correctly with an indented first line—the recommended approach for **copy manuscript** (see pages 659–61). Whichever format you use, be consistent and observe all details of indentation, spacing, and mechanics.

For additional information on APA-style documentation, visit the APA's Web site (http://www.apa.org).

Directory of APA-Style Entries for the Reference List

Books

Articles

Books

Most book entries consist of four units separated by periods:

1. *Author.* Give the author's last name and use initials for the first and middle names. For entries that contain more than one author, invert all names and put an ampersand (&) before the last one. (If two authors have the same last name and initials, spell out their first names and list the references in the alphabetical order of their first names.)
2. *Date.* Put the date in parentheses after the author's name. By including the date near the beginning of the entry, APA style draws attention to its importance.
3. *Title.* Capitalize only the first word in titles and subtitles. Do not capitalize other words (except for proper names that would be capitalized in other contexts). Separate titles and subtitles with a colon, and underline the title and any period immediately following it.
4. *Publication data.* Identify the city of publication. Add the two letter U.S. Postal Service abbreviations for states (for a list see pages 177–78) unless the city is one of the following: Baltimore, Boston, Chicago, New York, Philadelphia, and San Francisco. When a work is published outside the United States, add the country's name unless it is published in Amsterdam, Jerusalem, London, Milan, Moscow, Paris, Rome, Stockholm, Tokyo, or Vienna—in which case the city alone is sufficient. Give only enough of the publisher's name so that it can be identified clearly.

Book by one author

Riordan, C. H. (1997). <u>Equality and achievement: An introduction to the sociology of education.</u> New York: Longman.

More than one work by the same author

If you use more than one work by the same author, list the works in order of the publication date, with the earliest first. Repeat the author's name for each work.

Gates, H. L. (1992). <u>Loose canons: Notes on the culture wars.</u> New York: Oxford.

Gates, H. L. (1995). <u>Colored people: A memoir.</u> New York: Vintage.

Book by two or more authors

Fish, B. C., & Fish, G. W. (1996). <u>The Kalenjiin heritage: Traditional religious and sociological practices.</u> Pasadena, CA: William Carney Library.

Contrast APA style with MLA style, which inverts only the name of the first author in a multiauthor work. (See page 593.) Note also that APA style—unlike MLA style—calls for identifying the state unless a work is published in a major city associated with publishing. (See page 652.)

Edition after the first

Kelly, D. H. (1989). <u>Deviant behavior: A text-reader in the sociology of deviance</u> (3rd ed.). New York: St. Martin's.

Translation

```
Freud, S. (1960). Jokes and their
     relationship to the unconscious
     (J. Strachey, Trans.). New York: Norton.
     (Original work published 1905)
```

Cite the date of the translation. Include the date of the original publication in parentheses at the end of the entry. A period does not follow the original publication date. In text, use the following form: (Freud, 1905/1960).

Government document

```
Department of Transportation. (1996).
     Liability cost and risk analysis
     studies: Bus liability review for six
     transit systems (DOT-T-96-13).
     Washington, DC: Technological Sharing
     Program.
```

Treat the issuing agency as the author when no author is specified. Include a document or contract number (but not a library call number) if either number is printed on or in the document.

Work with no author

Use the first significant words of the title to cite anonymous materials in the text, underlining the title of a book. Unless Anonymous is specifically designated as the author of a work, do not use it for in-text citations or the list of references.

```
Directory of Mental Health Providers in
     Texas. (1996). Austin, TX: State
     Employees' Insurance Agency.
```

Articles

Capitalize only the first word and any proper nouns in article titles, and do not put quotation marks around titles. (If the article has a subtitle, use a colon to separate the title and the subtitle and capitalize the first word of each.) For an article in an edited book, provide both the title of the article and the title of the book in which it appears. Give the name of the editor and the complete page numbers for the article. For an anonymous article, place the article title where the author's name would normally appear, and alphabetize by the first important word in the title.

```
Boomerang age. (1990). American Demographics,
     12, 25-30.
```

The title of a journal is capitalized differently from article or book titles. Underline the journal title and continue the underlining so that it extends (without a break) to include the volume number and the commas preceding and following it. Include the issue number, when necessary, within parentheses but do not underline it. The point is to make volume and issue numbers visually distinct from the page reference (which is not preceded by *p.* or *pp.*).

Article in a journal with continuous pagination

```
Lenfant, C. (1996). High blood pressure: Some
     answers, new questions, continuing
     challenges. JAMA, 275, 1605-1606.
```

Article in a journal with each issue paginated separately

```
Kolakowski, L. (1992). Amidst moving ruins.
     Daedalus, 121(2), 43-56.
```

The issue number appears within parentheses and is not underlined.

Article in a monthly or weekly magazine

```
Levy, D. H. (1992, June). A sky watcher
     discovers comets and immortality.
     Smithsonian, 23, 75-82.
```

For a monthly magazine, give the year first, followed by a comma and the full spelling of the month. For a weekly magazine, provide the exact date: (2000, February 18).

Article in a newspaper

```
Dershowitz, A. M. (1999, December 18). Why
     justice had to get out of town. The New
     York Times, p. A31.
```

Article in a collection of articles by different authors

```
Chlad, F. L. (1991). Chemical storage for
     industrial laboratories. In D. A.
     Pipitone (Ed.), Safe storage of
     laboratory chemicals (pp. 175-191). New
     York: Wiley.
```

Book review

```
Becker, J. G. (1992). The dilemma of choice
     [Review of the book Psychiatric aspects
     of abortion]. Contemporary Psychology,
     37, 457-458.
```

When a review is titled, place the subject of the review in brackets after the review title. When a review is untitled, use the material in brackets as the title, but retain the brackets to show that this "title" is a description.

```
Pyles, A. R. (1997) [Review of Pre-adolescent
     female friendships]. School
     Psychologist, 2, 57-59.
```

Sources viewed or heard

Motion picture

Doran, L. (Producer), & Lee, A. (Director).
    (1995). <u>Sense and sensibility</u> [Film].
    London: Mirage.

Sound recording

Fellows, G. (Speaker). (1999). <u>Nutritional</u>
    <u>needs for women with AIDS</u> (Cassette
    Recording No. 8341). Cincinnati:
    Nutritionworks.

Sources produced for access by computer

While recognizing that standards for referencing information retrieved online are still evolving, the American Psychological Association suggests the following formats for references to electronic media. Note that APA recommends following the same sequence of information as provided for print sources. Any information, such as volume or page numbers, that is not available cannot be included. Information about how and when the source was retrieved appears at the end. Note also that the final period is omitted after URLs because trailing periods can cause difficulty in retrieving files.

> Lastname, I. (date). Title of article. *Name of periodical, volume number.* Retrieved [access date] from retrieval path
> Lastname, I. (date). Title of article or chapter. In *Title of full work.* Place: Publisher. Retrieved [access date] from retrieval path
> Lastname, I., Lastname, I., & Lastname, I. (date). *Title of full work.* Place: Publisher. Retrieved [access date] from retrieval path

To supplement this discussion of APA-style documentation for sources produced for access by computer, visit the American Psychological Association (http://www.apa.org).

Article in an online journal

```
Fairbairn, G. L. (1998). Suicide, language,
    and clinical practice. Philosophy,
    Psychiatry, 5. Retrieved December 3,
    1999 from the World Wide Web:
    http://muse.jhu.edu/journals/
    philosophy_p...y_and_psychology/v005/
    5.2fairbairn01.html
```

The date of publication appears immediately after the author's name. Include the access date after the volume number (or after the journal title when a volume number is unavailable). Do not put a period at the end of the citation as it might be mistaken for part of the electronic address.

Article in an online magazine

```
Py-Lieberman, B. (1999, November). The colors
    of childhood. Smithsonian. Retrieved
    December 19, 1999 from the World Wide
    Web: http://www.smithsonianmag.si.edu/
    smithsonian/issues99/nov99/
    object_nov99.html
```

Place the year before the month for the date of publication.

Article in an online newspaper

```
Azar, B. (2000, January). What's in a face?
    APA Monitor. Retrieved January 6, 2000
    from the World Wide Web:
    http://www.apa.org/monitor/sc1.html
```

Indicate the database through which the newspaper is accessed. If the newspaper can be downloaded from the World Wide Web, provide the address of the site.

World Wide Web page

```
Dorman, B., & Lefever, J. (1999, December
    28). The Autism Society Home Page.
    Bethesda, MD: Autism Society of America.
    Retrieved January 6, 2000 from the World
    Wide Web: http://www.autism-society.org/
```

When the name of the author (or creator) is not known, begin with the document title. Underline the document title, and provide additional information, if available, after the title (or after the date if the entry begins with the title). Conclude with the retrieval date and the retrieval path.

Cite e-mail, newsgroup, or bulletin board messages in the text but do not list them in the references. Not usually archived in any systematic way, these kinds of sources cannot be systematically retrieved and are regarded as ephemeral—short-lived and transitory.

38i Studying a sample APA-style research paper can help you understand how to write in the social sciences.

The fourth edition of the APA *Publication Manual,* 1994, specifies two different styles of manuscripts, the **copy manuscript** and the **final manuscript.** The *Manual* explains,

> The author of a thesis, dissertation, or student paper produces a "final" manuscript; the author of a journal article produces a "copy" manuscript (which will become a typeset article). The differences between these two kinds of manuscripts help explain why the requirements for theses, dissertations, and student papers are not necessarily identical to the manuscripts submitted for publication in a journal. (p. 331)

The copy manuscript style is used for a document that will be sent to a publisher and set in type. The final manuscript style should be used for such documents as student papers, lab reports, master's theses, and doctoral dissertations because they are final—that is, they will not be sent elsewhere for typesetting.

Copy manuscripts, the APA *Publication Manual* explains, "must conform to the format and other policies of the journal to which they are submitted" (p. 332). Final manuscript style, however, permits a "number of variations from the requirements described in the *Publication Manual*" (p. 332) and should conform to the requirements of an individual university, department, or instructor. The *Manual* further advises that it is not intended to cover scientific writing at an undergraduate level, because preferences for style at that level are diverse. Instructions to students to "use the *Publication Manual*" should be accompanied by specific guidelines for its use (p. 332).

Generally speaking, a **title page** includes three elements, all of which are double-spaced. The **running head** is a shortened version of the **title** and appears in the upper left-hand corner of the title page. It will also appear in the upper right-hand corner of every page, including the title page, which is counted as page 1. (If you use this title page as a model for a paper in MLA style, do not include the running head or the page number.) The title appears next in upper- and lowercase letters and is centered. The **author's name** or **byline** appears below the title and is followed by the author's affiliation. If an instructor asks that the course number be included, it will generally appear as the affiliation. Unless the instructor specifically requires it, the instructor's name and the date the paper is due are not included. (A copy manuscript, which is required when submitting work for publication, also includes an **abstract,** a 75- to 120-word summary of the paper. This is the range recommended by the *Publication Manual*.)

The body of the paper, the **discussion,** should normally be double-spaced and include in-text citations as specified in the *Publication Manual.* Variations in spacing to promote readability, however, are not only permitted, but encouraged.

A fourth essential component of the final manuscript, the **references,** is a list of all the references cited in the text. It does not usually include references that are not cited. However, any material that is especially pertinent or that informs the paper as a whole may be included if it is considered essential. When that is the case, the reference list becomes a bibliography. For additional examples of APA-style documentation, see the following student essay and the commentary on it printed on the left-hand pages.

Comments

A. A **title page** includes three double-spaced elements: running head, title, and author's full name and affiliation. Center the title and author horizontally (but not necessarily vertically).

B. The **running head** is a shortened version of the title. It appears in the upper right-hand corner of every page and the upper left of the title page, which is counted as page 1.

C. If an instructor asks that the course number be included, it generally appears instead of the affiliation. Unless specifically required, the instructor's name and the date the paper is due are not included.

Running head: GENERATION X B

Generation X: Moving Back Home A

Adrienne Harton

Texas Woman's University C

Comments

D. An abstract is a short summary of a paper. The APA *Publication Manual* requires that an abstract be supplied on the second page of any essay that is to be submitted for publication (copy manuscript style). Check with your instructor to see whether an abstract is required for your paper.

E. An APA-style abstract should be between 75 and 120 words. According to the APA *Publication Manual*, a good abstract is

- accurate,
- self-contained,
- nonevaluative,
- coherent, and
- readable.

Readers should be able to understand what a paper is about simply by reading the abstract. Devoted to summarizing the paper's content, the abstract does not include an evaluation of the paper's quality.

Abstract   D

During the last twenty years, young adults   E
returned to their parents' homes in record
numbers. Research indicates that education,
occupation, and personal lifestyle choices
all contributed to the economic hardships
that account for most of these cases. The
generation born between 1964 and 1980,
commonly referred to as Generation X, often
received more years of financial support from
parents than earlier generations enjoyed.
Further research will be needed to determine
if this trend continues.

Comments

F. The full title is centered on the top of the page beneath the running head. Double-space between the title and the first line of text (as in MLA style).

G. At the beginning of paragraph 2, Harton explains what "RYA" means. Thereafter, she uses the abbreviation without explanation. According to the APA *Publication Manual*:

> To maximize clarity, APA prefers that authors use abbreviations sparingly. Although abbreviations are sometimes useful for long, technical terms in scientific writing, communication is usually garbled rather than clarified if, for example, an abbreviation is unfamiliar to the reader. (p. 80)

The APA therefore recommends:

> A term to be abbreviated must, on its first appearance, be written out completely and followed immediately by its abbreviation in parentheses. Thereafter, the abbreviation is used in the text without further explanation (do not switch between the abbreviated and written-out forms of a term). (p. 83)

Generation X: Moving Back Home F

1   Jim and Carole Wilson appear to be a comfortable couple in their 50s, married for 30 years. The Wilsons own a home, drive nice cars, and were able to pay for a college education for all three of their children. The Wilsons deviate from the stereotypical couple, though, because one of their college-educated children has moved back home. Scott, the oldest child, quit his temporary job (waiting tables "while I look for something better") and resumed residence in his old bedroom. Unfortunately for parents like the Wilsons, this scenario has become increasingly common. Grown children are returning to the nest or sometimes never leaving at all. The primary impetus for this phenomenon is economic: Young adults are moving back home because they find it more convenient to live with their parents than to live on their own. By moving back home, they are able to pursue an education, find refuge when unemployed, save money so that they can pay off student loans, or simply enjoy a higher level of comfort than they can provide for themselves.

2   The Returning Young Adult (RYA) G phenomenon is a family development syndrome looked at as circular in the family's attempt to "launch" the young adult members into independence. The young adult leaves home to experience adult independent living, returns home, hopefully to leave again, this time successfully. The adults in question are

Comments

H. Note that the long quotation—a quotation of more than forty words—in paragraphs 2, 7, 9, and 11 is indented five spaces only, per APA style. (See **16b**.) Note also that APA, unlike MLA style, does not call for using brackets around ellipses.

I. Paragraph 3 describes RYA by using demographic evidence. Note that the definition of RYA in this paragraph restricts this classification to children who "actually did leave home but, because of the need for economic support, returned." A critical reader (see chapter **35**) might wonder how to classify adults who have decided to return to their parents' home because they need emotional support more than financial support.

usually in their twenties. According to
Natalie Schwartzberg (1991),

> American family young adulthood can be   H
> defined as usually beginning in the
> early twenties . . . when the young
> person is launched from the family of
> origin, and ending sometime in the early
> thirties, when the young adult is firmly
> ensconced in a job and is capable of
> intimacy. (p. 77)

As this quote suggests, emotional stability
is often linked to financial stability.
Unfortunately, many young adults have
difficulty achieving financial independence.
When they fail to attain a secure and
satisfying job, these adults choose to return
to what they perceive as the safety of their
parents' home. As a result, what Peck (1991)
defines as the "launching stage" becomes "one
of the most complex stages of the family's
life cycle" (p. 150).

3   Before analyzing the financial reasons   I
why people in their 20s are returning to
their parents' homes, researchers first
determine the characteristics of this group.
Burnett and Smart (1994) define RYAs: "To be
a true RYA, both the individual and parents
expected the child to leave home, the child
actually did leave home but, because of the
need for economic support, returned"
(p. 255). The RYA phenomenon is also called
the crowded nest or "boomerang effect." The
number of children in the RYA generation who
return to live with their parents seems

Comments

J. Paragraph 3 establishes that men are more likely than women are to return to their parents' home. A critical reader (see chapter 35) would note that there is a difference between the conclusions reached in "Boomerang age" and those reached by Burnett and Smart. See exercise 6 (page 684).

surprisingly high. "About 40 percent of young adults return to their parents' home at least once. Men and women are equally likely to return home until age 25, but men are more likely to return after that age" ("Boomerang age," 1990, p. 26). With almost half of the 20-something generation moving home, a family with two or more children can almost surely anticipate an RYA. Another intriguing statistic is that males "are more than twice as likely as females to live with their parents" (Burnett & Smart, 1994, pp. 257-258). Over 70% of those male RYAs have a yearly income of less than $10,000, also. From the data, researchers can typify the RYA as a male in his early 20s with a low-paying job or no job.

Determining the characteristics of the RYA's family is another important control. The RYA family often has an above-average income (Burnett & Smart, 1994, p. 254), which actually helps influence adult children to move home since most of them have not accumulated all the material comforts their parents have attained. Parents of young adults actually wield great influence in determining whether or not the child becomes an RYA. However, the economic circumstances of RYAs are almost always the deciding factor in moving back home. These characteristics of RYAs and their families suggest the need for further research on financial considerations, including the growing challenge of financing a higher education.

Comments

K. Paragraph 5 includes statistical evidence that will support Harton's analysis. Note that she relies heavily on one source, "Boomerang age" (which, however, is a statistical study from *American Demographics*). When introducing the Holtz study, Harton works the author's name into the text. Notice also that the page number follows the quote.

5   Education affects young adults in two
ways with regard to moving home. Either the
RYA is attending college and cannot afford to
live on his or her own, or the RYA chose not
to further his or her education and cannot be
self-sustaining on the paycheck alone. In the
first case, research shows that more young
adults are going to college, and almost half
of first-year college students have a job
("Boomerang age," 1990, p. 30). Furthermore,
many students start at 2-year colleges and so
take longer to finish, and students also now
take longer to choose a major. Such statistics
show that young adults are spending more time
in college than ever before. Living with one's
parents effectively decreases a student's
financial burden. Holtz (1995) claims, "The
average college undergraduate was taking more
than six years to earn a degree; fewer than
half graduated after the traditional four
years of study" (p. 124). An economic chain
reaction exists for college students living at
home. "Because people are delaying marriage,
they are living with their parents longer.
They are delaying marriage because they're
going to school. They're going to school
because most well-paying jobs now require a
college degree" ("Boomerang age," p. 26). Of
course, these RYAs have sound reasons for
living with their parents, but what about the
RYAs who are not continuing their education?

6   Some RYAs simply cannot afford to live
away from home on a small salary. The

Comments

L. Paragraph 6 includes a citation to a source with two authors.

M. The quotation at the end of paragraph 6 comes from a kind of electronic communication that the APA recognizes as acceptable for use within papers even if it cannot be included in the reference list. (See page 659.) Note that Harton includes the date of this communication.

N. Critical readers (see chapter 35) would note that the desire to maintain a certain lifestyle can be at odds with the need to pay bills. Such readers might ask: Could RYAs afford to maintain independent living if they were able to live more simply? Do young adults today expect to enjoy more material comforts than previous generations did?

typical 25-year-old working man has a median income less than the poverty level for a single person (Holtz, 1995, p. 158). Obviously, returning to one's childhood home makes sense whether the young adult is trying to save money or to maintain a particular lifestyle. While long-term prospects for the educated RYA are more promising, the average income for males without a college degree has fallen (Levy & Michel, 1991, p. 45). Many RYAs do not even have jobs. Whether RYAs' unemployment is a result of attending college or of a lack of proper education, the best financial decision to make is to move home with Mom and Dad. As one RYA explained in an online discussion: "I thought that I was being practical by studying business, but business life bores me. I need time to figure out what I really want" (J. Shaw, personal communication, November 18, 1999).

Jobs obviously affect economic situations of young adults. Some RYAs hold jobs and some do not, but for both groups, the dilemma is not having enough money to maintain a desired lifestyle and pay the bills too. One study notes, "As the U.S. economy shifts from manufacturing to services, it sharply reduces the number of entry-level jobs available to people who don't have much schooling" ("Boomerang age," 1990, p. 30). Another problem can be traced to the challenge of choosing a major in

college. As the business and technology
sectors grow faster than areas grounded in
liberal arts, college students can increase
their chances for long-term job security
by selecting a marketable major. But
unemployment can occur in any field, hence
the frequency with which some RYAs rely on
the parental safety net, as illustrated by
E. L. Klingelhofer (1989):

> The inability to find appropriate work
> has not been as catastrophic a burden
> as it once might have been because the
> parents were able to support the child,
> to help out, to tide him or her over.
> And, as the individual quest for work
> wore on and eventually, wore out, what
> had been thought of as a temporary
> arrangement imperceptibly became a
> permanent one. (p. 86)

Whereas unemployment once meant failure and
embarrassment, now it seems to be an
opportunity to return home.

8   Even for young adults with jobs, moving
home can be a solution to financial
problems. RYAs change careers with great
frequency. As research reveals, "Young adults
have the highest rate of occupational
mobility. Thirty percent of employed men aged
16 to 19, and 22 percent of those aged 20 to
24, changed occupations," compared with 10%
for all workers ("Boomerang age," 1990,
p. 52). Apparently, grown children choose to
live with their parents to find some
stability during professional uncertainty.

Furthermore, the jobs that young adults, even when college educated, obtain may not yield enough money to survive away from home. A college education can be very expensive, especially over 6 years. Some young adults who shoulder their entire college debts cannot afford to live away from home while paying student loans (Kuttner, 1995, p. M5). Regardless of whether an RYA has a job or not, the economic sense of moving back home exceeds the need for independence.

9   The final financial reason why grown children are returning to the nest encompasses personal lifestyle decisions: delayed marriage and middle-class comfort. The average age of marriage has steadily increased since the 1970s. Littwin (1986) concludes:

> Commitment to a relationship is just as difficult for them as commitment to a career or point of view. It is one act that might define them and therefore limit their potential. Besides, it is difficult to be in a relationship when you still don't know who you are. (p. 219)

10   With the option of moving home, young adults do not feel the pressure or the necessity to marry early. Even when people do marry early and divorce, research shows that many young adults return to their parents' homes to recover and stabilize (Klingelhofer, 1989, p. 86). RYAs can opt to live with their families as an alternative

Comments

O. Harton cites the personal communication from Coles in paragraph 11 in the text but, as with other nonrecoverable sources such as personal letters, e-mail, and bulletin board postings, does not list it in the references on page 683.

P. Harton's concluding paragraph (see 33a(5)) follows the traditional model of summarizing the preceding points and suggesting a direction for future study.

to marriage or to reestablish themselves after a divorce. In either scenario, the RYA is more financially stable than if he or she lived alone.

11   Some RYAs return to the nest to attain the material comforts of a middle- to upper-class home that they enjoyed and expected as dependents. Adult children now receive allowances, their own rooms, telephones, cars, personal freedom. Why should they leave the nest? For wealthier families, adult children moving home is a particular problem. Littwin (1986) says:

> The affluent, perfect parent is the ideal target for rebellion-and-rescue. . . . The young adult resents that he has been given so much that he cannot give himself. He has been cared for too well and too conscientiously. (p. 140)

A potential RYA, still a student at a private university and for whom his parents pay all expenses, recently complained about the constraints his full-time summer job placed on his lifestyle: "I don't see how you and Dad have any fun when you are working at least 50 hours a week. I want to enjoy my life." (L. Coles, personal communication, November 15, 1999). In an instant-gratification-seeking generation, returning to the nest is just easier than earning comfort.

O

12   In conclusion, young adults are moving back home for a variety of reasons. Of course, people of the 20-something generation

P

Comments

Q. A strong final statement, the quotation Harton uses to conclude her essay contains an implicit challenge to Generation X. Note also that it is introduced by a colon (see **17d(1)**).

would not be able to return home without
parental acquiescence. Future research will
reveal if RYAs develop a pattern of adult
dependence on their parents and whether this
pattern will hold true for children born
after 1980 (sometimes called Generation Y)
since this generation is coming of age in a
stronger economy. But for now, research
proves that grown children are moving
back home for a myriad of financial
considerations. And as one Gen X'er bemoans: Q
"We as a generation have yet to produce any
defining traits, except perhaps to show a
defeatist belief that we will do worse than
our parents" (Janoff, 1995, p. 10).

Comments

R. The reference list is organized alphabetically and begins on a new page. The last name is always given first, and initials are provided for first and middle names. The date of publication is always given parenthetically, immediately after the author's name. (See **38h(1)**.)

S. Observe the use of periods and commas, the style of capitalization for book and article titles, and the different capitalization style for journal titles. Underline book and journal titles, and carry continuous underlining of periodical titles through the volume number.

T. If Harton had used a copy manuscript format, which is required when submitting work for publication, she would have indented the first line of each entry five spaces. The first two entries would look like this:

> Boomerang age. (1990). <u>American Demographics, 12,</u> 25-30.
> Burnett, J., & Smart, D. (1994). Returning young adults. <u>Psychology and Marketing, 11,</u> 253-269.

U. According to the APA *Publication Manual:* "Authors should choose references judiciously and must include only the sources that were used in the research and preparation of the article" (p. 174). In this respect, APA style differs from MLA style because in MLA style a writer lists only sources that are actually cited in the paper. The reference to Cipriano indicates that Harton was influenced by this source even though she does not draw directly on it in the paper.

References

Boomerang age. (1990). <u>American Demographics, 12,</u> 25-30.

Burnett, J., & Smart, D. (1994). Returning young adults. <u>Psychology and Marketing, 11,</u> 253-269.

Cipriano, E. (1996). Who is this generation formerly known as x? <u>Seriously, 6</u>(1). Retrieved December 3, 1999 from the World Wide Web: FTP://spc.5yr.edu/ seriously/generation

Holtz, G. T. (1995). <u>Welcome to the jungle: The why behind "Generation X."</u> New York: St. Martin's Griffin.

Janoff, J. B. (1995, April 24). A gen-x Rip Van Winkle. <u>Newsweek, 127,</u> 10.

Klingelhofer, E. L. (1989). <u>Coping with your grown children.</u> Clifton, NJ: Humana Press.

Kuttner, R. (1995, June 25). The new elite: Living with mom and dad. <u>The Los Angeles Times,</u> p. M5.

Levy, F., & Michel, R. C. (1991). <u>The economic future of American families: Income and wealth trends.</u> Washington, DC: Urban Institute.

Littwin, S. (1986). <u>The postponed generation: Why American youth are growing up later.</u> New York: William Morrow.

Peck, J. S. (1991). Families launching young adults. In F. H. Brown (Ed.), <u>Reweaving the family tapestry: A multigenerational approach to families</u> (pp. 149-168). New York: Norton.

Schwartzberg, N. (1991). Single young adults.
     In F. H. Brown (Ed.), <u>Reweaving the</u>
     <u>family tapestry: A multigenerational</u>
     <u>approach</u> (pp. 77-93). New York: Norton.

EXERCISE 5

Do research to determine if the trend discussed by Harton has continued or if young adults are now moving more easily into independent living. Then write an abstract summarizing what you discover.

EXERCISE 6

Harton notes that men are more likely than women to return to their parents' home. Research the relationship between gender and independence, then write an APA-style paper reporting what you discover.

Chapter

39 Writing for Special Purposes

The information conveyed throughout this handbook will help you in different writing situations. The essentials of English grammar (1–4, 6–7, and 25) and the principles of effective sentence structure (23–24, 26, 29, and 30)—as well as conventions for using appropriate diction (19–22), punctuation (12–17), and mechanics (8–11 and 18)—are always relevant. Advice about planning and drafting (32), developing (31c and 32c), and revising and editing (33) applies to most writing that you will need to do in college and in your profession. Other advice, such as how to write arguments (36) and work with sources (38), applies to specific purposes. This chapter will introduce you to principles that govern two additional situations: writing about literature (39a) and effective business communication (39b).

It will help you understand

- vocabulary used for discussing literature (39a(1)),
- critical approaches for interpreting literature (39a(1)),
- personal responses to literature (39a(2)),
- essays about fiction (39a(3)),
- essays about drama (39a(4)),
- essays about poetry (39a(5)),
- special conventions for writing about literature (39a(6)),
- e-mail in the workplace (39b(1)),
- business memos (39b(2)),
- business letters (39b(3)),
- letters of application (39b(4)),
- résumés (39b(5)), and
- grant proposals (39b(6)).

39a Writing about literature increases your understanding of it.

Writing about literature involves exploring and focusing your subject (32b), formulating a thesis statement (32c) that can be supported from the work itself, and planning how to organize your thoughts so that your essay will have a sound structure. But it also involves being open to the possibility that reading and writing can improve your ability to understand experience—and possibly even change the way you see the world. The following principles can help you write thoughtfully about literature.

(1) Understanding literary terms helps writers discuss literature thoughtfully.

Like all specialized fields, literature has its own vocabulary. When you learn it, you are not just learning a list of terms and definitions. You are grasping concepts that will help you understand literature and write about it effectively.

(a) Words that define the elements of literature help readers to divide a work into components and see how those components relate to each other.

Setting **Setting** involves place—not just the physical setting, but also the atmosphere created by the author. It also involves time—not only historical time, but also the length of time covered by the action. A story set in San Francisco in 1876 will have a different setting from one set there in 2001 because the city has changed. Setting is important in both fiction and drama, as well as in many poems.

Plot The sequence of events that happen to **characters** is the **plot.** Unlike a narrative, which simply reports events, a plot establishes how events are related. Narrative asks, "What comes next?" Plot asks, "Why?" For example:

Narrative	The king died, and the queen died.
Plot	The queen was beheaded after she killed the king.

Depending on the author's purpose, a literary work may have a complicated plot or almost no plot at all. Plot is usually important in both fiction and drama, and it can also be an element of poetry, especially in long poems, such as *Paradise Lost.*

Characters   The **characters** carry the plot forward and usually include a main character, called a **protagonist,** who is in conflict with another character, with an institution, or with himself or herself. By examining a character's conflict, you can often discover the **theme.**

Characters can be understood by paying close attention to their appearance, language, and actions. Writing about fiction and drama often requires character analysis. Many poems also feature characters in conflict. "Home Burial" by Robert Frost, for example, reveals a conflict between a woman and her husband—both of whom speak in the poem.

Tone   Conveyed by diction and sentence structure, **tone** reveals a writer's or speaker's attitude toward events and characters or even, in some circumstances, toward readers. The tone of a story or poem may be somber, ironic, humorous, wry, or bitter. In a play, you are likely to discover that different characters have different tones. By determining the tone and the impact it has on you as a reader, you can gain insight into the author's purpose. (See 33a(3).)

Allusion   An **allusion** is a brief, unexplained reference to a work, person, place, event, or thing (real or imaginary) that serves to convey meaning compactly. Writing about the way she came to see her father, Sylvia Plath describes him in "Daddy" as a "man in black with a Meinkampf look." *Mein Kampf,* German for "my struggle," is the title of Hitler's political manifesto. Although Plath does not directly compare her father to Hitler, she links the two by making an allusion.

Symbols   Frequently used by writers of fiction, drama, and poetry, a **symbol** is an object, usually concrete, that stands for something else, usually abstract. On one level, it is what it is; on another, it is more than what it is. (For an example, see page 700.) When you write about a particular symbol, first note the lines in which it appears. Then think about what it could mean. When you have an idea, trace the incidents in the work that reinforce that idea.

Theme   The main idea of a literary work is its **theme.** Depending on how they interpret a work, different readers may identify different themes. To test whether the idea you have identified is central to the work in question, check to see if it is supported by the **setting, plot, characters, tone,** and **symbols.** If you can relate these components to the idea you are exploring, then that idea can be considered the work's theme.

A work may have more than one theme. When you believe you have identified the theme, state it as a sentence and be precise. A theme conveys a specific idea; it should not be confused with a topic.

Topic	family conflict
Vague theme	*King Lear* is about family conflict.
Specific theme	*King Lear* reveals a conflict between a father who yearns for respect and daughters who have lost confidence in his judgment.

For additional definitions of terms, see **39a(3–5)**.

(b) Critical approaches to literature help writers generate and focus ideas.

Writing papers about a literary work usually requires you to focus on the work itself and to demonstrate that you have read it carefully—a process known as **close reading.** Through close reading, you then offer an **interpretation** of what the work means to you.

Interpretations can be shaped by your personal response to what you have read, a type of critical theory that appeals to you, or the views of other readers, which you wish to support or challenge.

In recent years, there has been growing interest in **literary theory**—scholarly discussion that tries to explain how the meaning of literature can be determined. Literary theory ranges between approaches that seek to interpret a text almost exclusively based on the language and structure of the text itself and approaches that show how texts can be illuminated by considering them in light of historical, economic, or other social and cultural factors. Familiarity with literary theory can help you understand the books and articles you discover when you do research about literature (39a(2)e). It can also help you decide how you want to focus your own writing about literature.

Here are some of the prevailing critical approaches to literature.

Reader-response   Reader-response theory recognizes that individual readers can interpret what they read very differently because meaning is not fixed on the page. Meaning is constructed through a reader's interaction with a text, with different readers bringing different values and experiences, as well as different degrees of attention, to what they read. Moreover, the same reader can have different responses to the same work when rereading it after a number of years. For example, a middle-aged man might find Robert Frost's "Stopping by Woods on a Snowy Evening" more disturbing than it had seemed when he first read it in high school. Although a reader-response approach to literature encourages diverse interpretations, you must be able to support your interpretation by showing how your response interacts with the text to shape the meaning you describe. You cannot simply say, "Well, that's what this work means to me." You must show your audience the aspects or elements of the work that led you to that meaning.

Psychoanalytic   Psychoanalytic theories seek to explain human experience and behavior. These theories help readers to discern the motivations of characters as well as to envision the psychological state of the author as implied by the text. Writers who use the work of Sigmund Freud to explain why Hamlet is troubled by his mother's remarriage or why Holden Caulfield rebels at school (in *Catcher in the Rye* by J. D. Salinger) are adopting a psychoanalytic approach to literature. Critics who use the work of Carl Jung to explore archetypes (the original or essential forms of creation) are also using psychoanalytic theory to interpret literature.

Gender-based   Gender-based criticism focuses on the significance of gender or sexual orientation within a social context to determine the purpose of a text or to analyze its characters. Awareness of such approaches sometimes enables readers to understand the ways in which a text challenges prevailing assumptions in the period during which it was composed. A feminist critic, for example, might emphasize the oppression of women when interpreting *The Awakening,* by Kate Chopin. Another critic might draw on research into the nature of sexual desire and why some people are threatened by feelings different from their own to explain why Jake Barnes in Hemingway's *The Sun Also Rises* bonds with some men and is contemptuous of others.

Class-based   To explain the conflicts between characters in a work of literature, or a conflict between a character and a community or institution, class-based criticism draws on the work of Terry Eagleton and other theorists who have addressed the implications of social hierarchies and the role of money in human affairs. Such an approach could be used to explain why Lily Bart is unable to find a suitable husband in *The House of Mirth,* by Edith Wharton, or why a family loses its land in *The*

Grapes of Wrath, by John Steinbeck. A class-based approach called "Postcolonial Criticism" can be used to demonstrate how a text challenges the dominant powers in a particular time and place, asserting a drive toward the liberation of oppressed social groups.

Context-based   Context-based approaches interpret literature by considering the historical period in which a work was written and the cultural patterns that prevailed during that period. For example, recognizing that Willa Cather published *My Antonia* during World War I can help account for the darker side of that novel, just as understanding that *The Crucible,* by Arthur Miller, was, in part, a response to the McCarthy hearings can help explain why the play generated so much excitement when it was first produced. Critics who use a context-based approach known as "Cultural Studies" consider how a literary work interacts with other cultural artifacts (such as songs or fashion) from the period in which it was written.

(c) **The purpose of an essay about literature can be defined by specific terms.**

An interpretation that attempts to explain the meaning of one aspect of a work is called an **analysis.** To analyze a work of literature means to divide it into elements, examine such elements as setting and characters, and determine how one element contributes to the overall meaning. A common form of analysis is the **character analysis,** in which a writer interprets one or more aspects of a single character. An analysis could also focus on a single scene, symbol, or theme.

An interpretation that attempts to explain every element in a work is called an **explication** and is usually limited to poetry. When explicating William Wordsworth's "A Slumber Did My Spirit Seal," a writer might note that the *s* sound reinforces the hushed feeling of sleep and death in the poem. But it would also be necessary to consider the meaning of "slumber," "spirit," and "seal," as well as why the words are arranged as they are (as opposed to "A Slumber Sealed My Spirit" or "My Spirit Was Sealed by My Slumber").

An **evaluation** of a work determines how successful the author is in communicating meaning to readers. The most common types of evaluation are book, theater, or film reviews. You can also evaluate a work by focusing on how successfully one of its parts contributes to the meaning conveyed by the others. Like other interpretations, evaluation is a type of argument in which a writer cites evidence to persuade readers to accept a clearly formulated thesis. (See chapter 36.) An evaluation of a literary work should consider both strengths and weaknesses, if there is evidence of both.

CAUTION Although **summarizing** a literary work can be a useful way to make sure you understand it, do not confuse summary with analysis, interpretation, or evaluation. Those who have read the work are unlikely to benefit from reading a summary of it. Do not submit one unless your instructor has asked for it.

(2) Reading carefully and thinking critically about what you read will help you discover your topic.

You cannot write effectively about a work that you have not read. Begin the process of writing about literature by reading carefully and noting your personal response. Think critically about these impressions and be open to new ideas as you plan your essay.

(a) Writing about literature begins with active, personal engagement with what you read.

As you read, trust your own reactions. What characters do you admire? Did the work remind you of any experience of your own? Did it introduce you to a different world? Were you amused, moved, or confused? These first impressions can provide the seeds from which strong essays will grow. You may find, however, that you need to modify your initial impressions as you study the work more closely or as writing takes you in a direction you did not originally anticipate.

You can facilitate this engagement by **annotating** the texts you own—marking key passages and raising questions that occur as you read (see 38b). You can also benefit from **freewriting** about your first impressions or by keeping a journal in which you record your reactions to and questions about reading assignments (see 32b(1)). These methods of exploring a subject can help you discover what you think or what you want to understand. In addition to generating topics for writing, they provide a useful method for identifying questions you could raise in class. When you use these methods, do not try to edit yourself. Write whatever comes to mind without worrying about whether you are correct. You are exploring for your own benefit, and no one else has to see what you have written.

(b) **You can understand your personal response by considering how it is shaped by your identity.**

When reflecting on your personal response to a work of literature, you can clarify your thinking by considering how it could be shaped by the factors that make you who you are. For example, if you find yourself responding positively or negatively to a character in a novel or play, you could ask yourself whether this response has anything to do with your

- political beliefs,
- social class,
- geographic region,
- religion,
- race,
- gender, or
- sexual orientation.

Thinking along these lines can help you decide how to focus your paper and prepare you for understanding literary theory (see 39a(1)b).

(c) After choosing a subject, you need to develop it.

If your instructor asks you to choose your own subject, your first step should be to reflect on your personal response (see 39a(2)a–b). Reviewing your response may enable you not only to choose a subject, but also to formulate a tentative thesis. The purpose of your paper in this case would be to persuade readers to agree with you. Also, try some of the methods suggested in 32b to explore the work you plan to discuss. If you generate more than one possible topic, decide which one seems most original.

Choose a topic that would be interesting both to write and to read about. Readers are usually interested in learning what *you* think. If you choose an easy topic, you may find yourself repeating what many others have already said. As a rule, try to avoid writing the obvious, but do not let the quest for originality lead you to choose a topic that would be too hard to develop adequately.

Apply strategies of development (see 32e). You might **define** why you consider a character heroic, **classify** a play as a comedy of manners, or **describe** a setting that contributes to a work's meaning. Perhaps you could **compare and contrast** two poems on a similar subject or explore **cause-and-effect** relationships in a novel. Why, for example, does an apparently intelligent character make a bad decision?

(d) Rereading a work improves your understanding of it.

Not only does a literary work provoke different responses from different readers, but you can also have a significantly different response when rereading a work—even a work you think you understand already. Whenever possible, reread any work you are planning to write about. If its length makes this impractical, at least reread the chapters or scenes that impressed you as especially important or problematic.

If you have a tentative thesis, rereading a work will help you find the evidence you need to support it. You are likely to find evidence that you did not notice on your first reading or that will require you to modify your thesis. To establish yourself as a credible source (see 35d), use evidence appropriate for your purpose (see 35c) and present it fairly.

A good way to note evidence, ideas, and concerns is to annotate as you read. Because experienced readers are actively engaged with their reading, they often keep a pen or pencil handy so they can mark passages they may wish to study, ask about, or draw upon when writing. Adopt this practice in books that you own.

(e) Research can reveal how other readers have responded to a literary work.

Both writers and readers often favor papers that are focused on a person's individual response, analysis, interpretation, or evaluation. But by reading criticism that reveals what other readers think of a given literary work, you can engage in a dialogue. When you draw on the ideas of other people, however, remember that you must use those sources responsibly (see 38c–d) and that even when you incorporate them you must still advance a position that is clearly your own. Few readers enjoy papers that offer little more than a collection of quotations or paraphrases.

When you read criticism, remember that a work rarely has a single meaning. Three different critics may offer three radically different interpretations. Your responsibility is not to determine who is right but to determine the extent to which you agree or disagree with these differing views. Read critically (see chapter 35) and formulate your own thesis (see 32c).

Chapter 37 explains how to do research. To locate material on a specific writer or work, consult your library's catalog (37d(1)) and the *MLA Bibliography,* an index of books and articles about literature. An essential resource for literary studies, the *MLA Bibliography* can be consulted in printed volumes, through an online database search, or through access to a CD-ROM covering several years. (See pages 540–43.)

In addition to having books and articles about specific writers, your college or community library is also likely to have a number of reference books that provide basic information on writers, books, and literary theory. Works such as *Contemporary Authors, The Oxford Companion to English Literature,* and *The Princeton Handbook of Poetic Terms* can be useful when you are beginning your research or when your research has introduced you to terms you need to clarify.

You can also access information by searching the World Wide Web. Scholars and societies interested in specific writers sometimes create Web sites to encourage additional reading and discussion. (For an example, see exercise 4 on page 706.) Instructors teaching a specific work sometimes create chat rooms to foster online discussion. And contemporary writers may have home pages of their own. Links from these sites can lead you to additional information. As a general rule, however, a Web-based search should supplement but not replace the search for books and articles in the *MLA Bibliography.*

For an example of a paper that incorporates research about literature, see the essay by Dieter Bohn (see 38f(2)).

CAUTION Research is not appropriate for all assignments. Your instructor may want only your own response or interpretation. If your instructor has not assigned a research paper, ask whether one is acceptable.

(3) Essays about fiction help readers see that a good story has many dimensions.

Although the events have not happened and the characters may never have existed, serious fiction expresses truth about the human condition through such components as **setting, character,** and **plot** (see 39a(1)). Experienced readers consider how these components are tied together. The questions generated by the **pentad** (see pages 407–08) can be helpful in this respect. For example, you might ask how a character has been shaped by the setting in which she lives or how a key element of the plot is closely tied to this setting.

When thinking about the characters in a work of fiction, you can also benefit from considering whether they are **static** or **dynamic.** A static character remains the same, while a dynamic character changes in some way. Works of fiction could include both types. Often, however, the main character, or **protagonist,** is transformed by experience. Other characters may change as well. Being alert to how characters may be changing, and why, can help you understand the **theme** (see 39a(1)).

You must also consider how the story is being presented to you.

Point of view   The position from which the action is observed—the person through whose eyes the events are seen—is the **point of view.** It may be that of a single character within the story or of a narrator who tells it. Many works of fiction are told from a single point of view, but some shift the point of view from one character to another. Readers sometimes assume that the author of a work of fiction is the person who is telling the story when it is actually being presented by one or more of the characters. Since different characters are likely to have different strengths and weaknesses, as well as different needs and values, the point of view from which the work is told shapes how readers experience it, both initially and as they continue to read.

When a piece of fiction is conveyed by one of its characters, the point of view is **partially omniscient**—that is, partially all-knowing. A narrator who knows the thoughts of all characters is **omniscient.** A story told by a character who refers to herself or himself as "I" employs the **first-person** point of view. (Do not confuse this character with the author.)

When the narrator does not reveal the thoughts of any character, the work is being told from the **dramatic** or **objective** point of view.

As you read and write, ask yourself the following questions.

CHECKLIST for Analyzing Fiction

- From whose point of view is the story told?

- What is the narrator's tone?

- Who is the protagonist? How is his or her character developed? With whom or what is the protagonist in conflict?

- How does one character compare with another?

- What symbols does the author use?

- What is the theme?

- How does the author use setting, plot, characters, and symbols to support the theme?

EXERCISE 1

In consultation with your instructor, choose a short story and write an analysis in which you focus on one aspect of it.

(4) Essays about drama help readers understand texts written for public performance.

Although drama is written to be filmed or performed on a stage, it can also be read. In a performance, whether live or on film, the director and the actors imprint the play with their own interpretations; in a book or script, you have only the words on the page and the imagination you bring to them. Drama has many of the same elements as fiction. In particular, both involve **character, plot,** and **setting** (see 39a(1)). The primary difference is the method of presentation. In a novel you may find long descriptions of characters and setting, as well as passages that reveal what characters are thinking. In a play, you learn what a character is thinking when he or she shares thoughts with another character or presents a **dramatic soliloquy** (a speech delivered to the audience by an actor alone on the stage).

Dialogue   **Dialogue** is the principal medium through which we understand the characters when reading a play. Examine dialogue to discover motives, internal conflicts, and relationships among characters. In Ibsen's *A Doll's House,* for example, Nora's development can be traced through her speech. The play opens with her reciting lines like "Me? Oh, pooh, I don't want anything." It concludes with her deciding to leave her husband and declaring, "I must educate myself." In writing about drama, you might compare characters or analyze their development and its significance through their dialogue.

Stage direction   Plays are written to be performed, and when you see a performance, all you have to do is watch and listen. When you read a play, however, you need to imagine what a performance would be like. Reading **stage directions**—which are usually in italics, especially at the beginning of an act or a scene—will help you. The playwright may have described the setting, called for specific props, indicated how the actors should be dressed, and positioned actors on different parts of the stage. As the play unfolds, directions will also indicate when an actor enters or leaves the stage. If you read only the dialogue, skipping over the directions, you can easily lose track of who is on stage and why.

Paying attention to dialogue and stage direction can help you understand a play's **theme** as well as the **symbols** that help convey that theme (see 39a(1)). For example, at the beginning of *A Streetcar Named Desire,* by Tennessee Williams, one of the main characters buys a paper lantern to cover a naked light bulb. During the scenes that follow, she frequently talks about light, emphasizing her preference for soft, attractive lighting. At the end of the play, another character tears off the lantern, and still another tries to return the ruined lantern to her as she is being taken away to a mental hospital. Anyone seeing this play performed, or reading it carefully, would note that the lantern is a symbol. It is what it is (a real paper lantern), but it also stands for something more than it is (a character's determination to avoid harsh truths).

When you prepare to write about a play, ask yourself the following questions.

CHECKLIST for Analyzing Drama

- How are the characters depicted through dialogue?

- What is the primary conflict within the play?

- What motivates the characters to act as they do?

- Are there any parallels between different characters?

- How does setting contribute to the play's action?

- What is the theme?

- If there is more than one story in the play, how do they relate to each other?

EXERCISE 2

View a film or attend a play at your college or in a theater in your community. Write a short essay in which you identify the theme and show how the actions of the characters reveal that theme.

(5) Essays about poetry help readers understand how poets convey meaning through compressed language.

Poetry shares many of the components of fiction and drama. It too may contain a narrator with a point of view. Dramatic monologues and narrative poems may have plot, setting, and characters. But poetry is primarily characterized by its concentrated use of connotative **diction, imagery, allusions, figures of speech, symbols, sound,** and **rhythm.** Before starting to write a paper about a poem, try to capture its literal meaning in a sentence or two; then analyze how the poet transfers that meaning to you through the use of the following devices.

Speaker The first-person *I* in a poem is not necessarily the poet. It is more likely to be a character, or **persona,** that the poet has created to speak the words. In some poems, there may be more than one speaker. Although there are times when the poet may be the speaker, you usually need to distinguish between the two when writing about poetry.

Diction The term **diction** means "choice of words," and the words in poetry convey meanings beyond the obvious denotative ones. (See 20a(2).) As you read, check definitions and derivations of key words in your dictionary to find meanings beyond the obvious ones. How do such definitions and derivations reinforce the meaning of the poem? How do the connotations contribute to that meaning?

Simile A **simile** is a comparison using *like* or *as* to link dissimilar things. (See 20a(4).)

> you fit into me
> like a hook into an eye
>
> a fish hook
> an open eye

In these lines, Margaret Atwood uses sewing and fishing items to describe a disturbing personal relationship.

Metaphor   A comparison that does not use *like* or *as,* **metaphor** is one of the figures of speech most frequently used by poets. (See 20a(4).) In the following example from "Walking Our Boundaries," Audre Lorde uses a metaphor to describe how it feels to wait for a lover's touch.

> my shoulders are
> dead leaves
> waiting to be burned to life.

Imagery   The **imagery** in a poem is conveyed by words describing a sensory experience. Notice the images in the following lines from the poem "Meeting at Night," by Robert Browning, about a lover journeying to meet his sweetheart.

> Then a mile of warm sea-scented beach;
> Three fields to cross till a farm appears;
> A tap at the pane, the quick sharp scratch
> And a blue spurt of a lighted match,
> And a voice less loud, through its joys and fears,
> Than the two hearts beating each to each!

The heat and smell of the beach; the sounds of the tap at the window, the scratch of a match being lighted, the whispers, and the hearts beating; and the sight of the two lovers embracing— all of these images convey the excitement and anticipation of lovers meeting in secret.

Paradox   A **paradox** is a seemingly contradictory statement that makes sense when thoughtfully considered. In a poem about searching for religious salvation, John Donne writes,

"That I may rise and stand, o'erthrow me [. . .]." At first glance, the wish to be overthrown seems to contradict the desire to "rise and stand." On reflection, however, the line makes sense: the speaker believes that he will rise spiritually only after he has been overwhelmed by the God he is addressing.

Personification   The attribution to objects, animals, and ideas of characteristics possessed only by humans is called **person-ification.** In the following lines, Emily Dickinson personifies death, portraying it as a man driving a carriage.

> Because I could not stop for Death—
> He kindly stopped for me—
> The Carriage held but just Ourselves—
> And Immortality.

Hyperbole   **Hyperbole** is a deliberate exaggeration used for ironic or humorous effect. In "To His Coy Mistress," by Andrew Marvell, the speaker describes how much time he would invest in courting the woman he admires if life were not so short.

> An hundred years should go to praise
> Thine eyes, and on thy forehead gaze;
> Two hundred to adore each breast,
> But thirty thousand to the rest.

Understatement   Like **hyperbole, understatement** is used for ironic or humorous effect. In this case, however, a serious matter is treated as if it were a small concern. Writing in "Musée des Beaux Arts" about indifference to human suffering, W. H. Auden describes a painting in which a boy with wings is falling from the sky.

> In Breughel's *Icarus,* for instance: how everything turns away
> Quite leisurely from the disaster; the ploughman may
> Have heard the splash, the forsaken cry,
> But for him it was not an important failure; the sun shone
> As it had to on the white legs disappearing into the green

Water; and the expensive delicate ship that must have seen
Something amazing, a boy falling out of the sky,
Had somewhere to get to and sailed calmly on.

Sound   **Sound** is an important element of poetry. **Alliteration** is the repetition of initial consonants, **assonance** is the repetition of vowel sounds in a succession of words, and **rhyme** is the repetition of similar sounds either at the end of lines (end rhyme) or within a line (internal rhyme). When you encounter such repetitions, examine and analyze their connection to each other and to the meaning of a line, stanza, or poem. For instance, notice how the repetition of the *w* and the *s* sounds in the following lines from Elinor Wylie's "Velvet Shoes" sounds like the soft whisper of walking in a snowstorm.

Let us walk in the white snow
In a soundless space [. . .].

Whenever possible, read poetry aloud so you can hear it.

Rhythm   The regular occurrence of accent or stress that we hear in poetry is known as **rhythm,** which is commonly arranged in patterns called **meters.** Such meters depend on the recurrence of stressed and unstressed syllables in units commonly called **feet.** The most common metrical foot in English is the **iambic,** which consists of an unstressed syllable followed by a stressed one (prŏceéd). A second common foot is the **trochaic,** a stressed syllable followed by an unstressed one (fíftў). Less common are the three-syllable **anapestic** (ŏvĕrcóme) and the **dactylic** (párăgrăph). A series of feet make up a line to form a regular rhythm, as exemplified in the following lines from Coleridge's "Frost at Midnight."

Thĕ Fróst pĕrfórms ĭts sécrĕt mínĭstrý,
Ŭnhelpĕd bў ánў wínd. Thĕ ówlĕt's crý
Cămĕ loúd — ănd hárk, ăgáin! loúd ăs bĕfóre.

Note the changes in rhythm and their significance—the ways in which rhythm conveys meaning. The second line contains a

pause (**caesura**), which is marked by the end of the sentence
and which adds special emphasis to the intrusion of the owlet's
cry.

When you study a poem, ask yourself the following questions.

CHECKLIST for Analyzing Poetry

- What words have strong connotations?

- What words have multiple meanings?

- What images convey sensation?

- What figures of speech does the poet use?

- How does the poet use sound, rhythm, and rhyme?

- What does the poem mean?

- How do the various elements combine to convey meaning?

An essay about poetry need not necessarily explore all of these
questions, but considering them helps you understand what the
poet has accomplished—important preparation for whatever
the focus of your essay will be.

EXERCISE 3

Study the following poem. Then, paying close attention to the words
in it and how they are arranged, write an essay explaining what the
poem means to you.

The Sick Rose
O Rose, thou are sick!
The invisible worm
That flies in the night,
In the howling storm,

Has found out thy bed
Of Crimson joy,
And his dark secret love
Does thy life destroy.
                —WILLIAM BLAKE

Exercise 4

Do some research on William Blake by using the *MLA Bibliography* (page 695) or by visiting the William Blake Archive at the University of Virginia (http://jefferson.village.virginia.edu/blake/). Prepare a working bibliography (see 37f) consisting of five sources that discuss the poem in exercise 3.

(6) Using proper form shows your audience that you have written your paper carefully.

Writing about literature follows certain special conventions.

Tense   Use the present tense when discussing literature, since the author is communicating to a present reader at the present time. (See 7c(1).)

> In "A Good Man Is Hard to Find," the grandmother reaches out to touch her killer just before he pulls the trigger.

Similarly, use the present tense when reporting how other writers have interpreted the work you are discussing.

> As Henry Louis Gates has shown. . . .

Documentation   When writing about a work from a book assigned by your instructor, you may not need to give the source and publication information. However, if you are using an edition or anthology that is different from the one your audience is using, you should indicate this. One way of doing so is to use the MLA (Modern Language Association) form for works cited, as explained in section 38e(2), although in this case your bibliography might consist of only a single work. (See the example on page 713.)

An alternative way of providing this information is by acknowledging the first quotation in an explanatory note and then giving all subsequent references to the work in the body of the paper.

```
  ¹ Tillie Olsen, "I Stand Here Ironing,"
Literature: Reading, Reacting, Writing, ed.
Laurie Kirszner and Stephen Mandell, 3rd ed.
(Fort Worth: Harcourt, 1997) 154. All
subsequent references to this work will be
by page number within the text.
```

If you use this note form, you may not need a list of works cited to repeat the bibliographical information. Check with your instructor about the reference format he or she prefers.

Whichever format you use for providing publication data, you must indicate specific references whenever you quote a line or passage. References to short stories and novels are by page number; references to poetry are by line number; and references to plays are usually by act, scene, and line number. This information should be placed in the text in parentheses directly after the quotation, and the period or comma should follow the parentheses. (See 16b and 38e(1).)

Poetry For **poems** and **verse plays,** type quotations of three lines or less in the text and insert a slash (see 17h) with a space on each side to separate the lines.

```
"Does the road wind uphill all the way? /
Yes, to the very end"--Christina Rossetti
opens her poem "Uphill" with this two-line
question and answer.
```

Quotations of more than three lines should be indented one inch (or ten spaces) from the left margin, with double-spacing between lines. (See page 585.)

Author references   Use the full name in your first reference to the author of a work and only the last name in all subsequent references. Treat men and women alike: Dickens and Cather, not Dickens and Willa or Charles Dickens and Miss Cather.

(7) Studying another student's paper can help you clarify what you want to achieve in your own.

The following student essay illustrates a reader-response interpretation (see 39a(1)b) of a novel by Tim O'Brien assigned in the first semester of a first-year English course on writing about literature. When given the opportunity to choose his own topic for a paper on O'Brien's novel, Josh Otis decided to focus (see 32b(2)) on a specific friendship and to show how this friendship illustrates moral concerns.

Otis 1

Josh Otis
Professor Miller
English 199, Section 1
10 May 1999

    Friendship in The Things They Carried

1   In Tim O'Brien's novel The Things They
Carried, love blossoms in the death-filled
rain forests of Vietnam. Throughout the war,
soldiers are expected to remain indifferent,
for unless they are indifferent they risk
their own lives. Yet the friendship between

Otis 2

Kiowa and Tim runs so deep that it can only
be described as love. Their relationship
shows how a soldier who preserves his morals
and ability to feel compassion can help
another man survive immersion in death and
decadence.

2   Kiowa is an experienced soldier with a
strong sense of self, while Tim (not to be
confused with the author) is an inexperienced
young man thrust into the war and unsure
about whether he will succeed as a soldier.
Just after Tim arrives in Vietnam, there is
an incident in which the men find a dead
farmer in an abandoned village. One by one,
the soldiers go up and shake the old man's
hand, but Tim refuses. His refusal makes him
the object of harassment, but he persists.
That night Kiowa approaches him and says,

>   You did a good thing today. That
>   shaking hands crap, it isn't
>   decent. The guys'll hassle you for
>   a while, especially Jensen--but
>   just keep saying no. Should've done
>   it myself. Takes guts, I know that.
>   (257)

Kiowa's sense of what is morally sound and
his support of actions in accordance with
his beliefs help explain why he and Tim
become so close.

3   Kiowa carries a Bible with him, and
perhaps his faith is part of the reason that
he is able to behave honorably during a war.
Kiowa shares a religious conversation with

Henry Dobbins in the chapter titled "Church."
As the men are preparing to bivouac in an
abandoned pagoda (a Buddhist shrine), Kiowa
says, "It's bad news [. . .] you don't mess
with churches" (133). Kiowa is a man at war,
killing people, yet he still considers a
foreign religious shrine sacred. During the
conversation with Henry, Kiowa describes the
feeling of escape he gets when he is in a
church. "It feels good when you just sit
there," he explains, "like you're in a
forest and everything is really quiet, except
there's this sound you can't hear" (136).
These are the types of conversation Kiowa
has in The Things They Carried, meaningful
ones that deal with moral and religious
issues.

4 When Tim kills a young boy near My Khe
and freezes, staring at what he has just
done, Kiowa is supportive. This is a
traumatic moment for Tim. As he stares at
the dead boy, he is confronted with what he
has become: a killer. Although it is war,
and he is there to kill the enemy, killing
wasn't quite real until that moment. As a
soldier, Tim has heard all the terms
designed to distance men from the reality of
what they are doing--"zapped," "wasted." But
he fully understands that he has killed
someone. It is Kiowa who tries to help him
deal with the moral crisis he now faces.
Kiowa knew the import of what he was looking
at, that the dead boy could easily destroy

his friend's moral base. Kiowa tries to comfort Tim as he stares at the boy he has just killed. "Tim, it's a war. The guy wasn't Heidi--he had a weapon, right? It's a tough thing for sure, but you got to cut out that staring" (141). That is the voice of a friend, trying to help Tim deal with what is probably the most traumatic experience of his life. He offers other words, but all had the same end: trying to help a friend he loves make sense of the horror he has just created.

5   If Kiowa represents the moral center of this novel, then his death represents what can happen to morals in war. Like the morals of some of the men beside whom he fought, Kiowa is also fragile. Kiowa's death is as much an accident as an act of war. A young kid makes a mistake; he turns on a flashlight and marks their position for the enemy. In an instant, Kiowa is dead; the flick of a switch triggers the mortar rounds that kill him. The morals of the soldiers could also be destroyed by small, unintentional acts. Kiowa's body sinking in the mud represents what Vietnam did to the morals of many of these men; they were sucked under all the muck and decay that surrounded them. Once their morals were sucked away, it was a tough fight to pull them back, and sometimes, no matter how hard the men pulled, their morals could not be recovered.

6   Tim speaks of his loss in the chapter titled "Field Trip." In this chapter, Tim goes back to the field twenty years later to take his friend's moccasins and bury them under the muck in the spot where Kiowa had died so long ago. Tim says, "In a way, maybe, I had gone under with Kiowa, and now after two decades I'd worked my way out" (212). Tim works himself out by facing the battlefield, by being able to face his painful memories instead of burying them with his friend.

7   Throughout the book, O'Brien creates a combination of anger, grief, and fear so that readers can begin to imagine what American soldiers experienced. They killed and often died alongside their best friends and yet knew little about them. Most were very young and had not had their morals, faith, or emotions tested to any serious extent, let alone through killing other people and watching their friends die. These experiences created a strong bond between men of very different backgrounds. The bond between Tim and Kiowa was so strong that Tim goes back to the field twenty years later, willingly reliving the horror and death of his past, to take Kiowa his moccasins. As Tim wedges them into the muck, he thinks, "I wanted to tell Kiowa that he'd been a great friend, the very best, but all I could do was slap hands with the water" (212). Yet even that gesture was unable to capture for Tim the combined sense of love and loss he felt for his friend.

8   It took Vietnam veterans a long time to recover from the war, and it left some with scars that will never heal. In <u>The Things They Carried</u>, Tim O'Brien shows how these veterans were forced to dig long and hard through horror and squalor to make sense of what they had done. But throughout the ordeal they faced in recovering, nothing would help them more that the friendships they had forged in the fields and jungles of Vietnam.

Work Cited

O'Brien, Tim. <u>The Things They Carried</u>. New
     York: Penguin, 1991.

39b Effective business communication is necessary in most professions.

Effective business communication requires a strong sense of audience (see 32a), an ability to write clearly and efficiently (see chapter 21), and an understanding of business conventions. These conventions are changing as technology redefines the workplace. Thanks to fax machines and e-mail, for example, many business people find themselves writing more than ever. They also have to take responsibility for their own writing. Although there are still some executives who dictate a letter for someone else to edit and type, most business people are expected to write for themselves. The computers on their desks provide instant access to a wide range of written communication.

(1) E-mail provides efficient communication in the workplace.

When first introduced, e-mail was perceived as a vehicle for fast communication that did not need to be as carefully written as a memo or a letter, and it is still perceived that way in academic and research environments where the use of the powerful but user-unfriendly UNIX and VAX systems can make editing difficult. The speed with which you can send an e-mail message continues to be one of its advantages, but businesses now generally use sophisticated messaging programs such as cc:Mail or Lotus Notes that make correcting typographic errors in messages easier and, therefore, as important as it would be in any business communication.

E-mail is, however, a less formal medium than the traditional business letter or memo, so you will need to balance its implicit informality with a businesslike attention to detail. Since most businesses are hierarchical, the tone (see 33a(3)) of your e-mail should be suited to your own place in this hierarchy and the recipient's, that is, neither coldly formal nor overly familiar. Furthermore, in business, e-mail tends to be used for brief comments or requests and for social occasions (such as announcing a retirement party), whereas longer documents such as responses to reorganization plans and employee evaluations are generally still handled by letter or memo.

Be aware, also, that e-mail is not really private. Not only may your recipient keep your message in a file, print it out, or forward it to someone else, but it may remain on the company's main computer. Most businesses operate e-mail on their own networks, so the system administrator also has access to what you have written. You could be embarrassed or lose influence within your organization if your communication is poorly written. Present yourself well by reviewing every message to eliminate errors and inappropriate remarks.

Take care to spell your recipient's name correctly at the *To:* prompt, and be sure to enter an accurate and descriptive subject line. Busy people use the subject line to identify the messages they need to respond to immediately, those they can safely postpone for a few hours, and those they can postpone indefinitely. Because busy people receive many messages each day, it is a courtesy to include the relevant part of their original message when you reply to them. Furthermore, many people find unnecessary e-mail inefficient and time-wasting. Send copies to anyone who is mentioned in your message or who has some other legitimate reason for being included, but do not send out copies of your messages indiscriminately. (See also 8c(1).)

CHECKLIST for Business E-Mail

- Does my subject line describe the content of my message?

- Have I sent copies to everyone who should receive one? To anyone who need not?

- Is my tone appropriate for my audience and context? Have I refrained from using sarcasm or irony? If I have used humor, can I be sure that it will be understood?

- Do I sound like the kind of person I want or need to be while at work? Am I signaling that I am competent and resourceful, helpful and accommodating?

- Is my content clear, concise, focused, and accurate? Have I made any statements or errors that would embarrass me if copies of this message were distributed elsewhere?

- If I need a response, have I established the kind of response I need and when I need it? If I am responding, should I include enough of the original message so that my response is both clear and brief?

- Am I respecting the privacy of others, or am I forwarding a personal message without permission?

- Have I respected copyright law by crediting any quotations, references, and sources?

(2) Memos are useful when you want colleagues to study information or bring it to a meeting.

Like e-mail, memos are used to communicate a variety of information within an organization. Although e-mail is ideal for sending brief announcements and requests for information, many business writers prefer the more formal memo when communicating detailed information such as policy directives, activity reports, and monthly action reports. While the length of a memo varies according to its purpose, the basic format is relatively standard. A memo begins with essentially the same information provided by the message header of an e-mail. The person or persons to whom the memo is addressed appear in the first line, the person who wrote it in the second, the date in the third, and the subject in the fourth.

If the memo is long, it sometimes begins with a statement of purpose and then gives a summary of the discussion. This summary helps busy people decide which memos to read carefully and which to skim. The discussion is the main part of the memo and may benefit from the use of headings to highlight key parts. If appropriate, the memo closes with recommendations for action to be taken. You should clearly state in this part of the memo who is to do what and when. In the following example, excerpted from a longer memo, you can see how the writer opens with a statement of purpose.

An example of memo format

To: Regional Sales Managers
From: Alicia Carroll, National Sales Director
Date: January 26, 2000
Re: Performance review

Now that we have final sales figures for 1999, it is clear that sales are growing in the South and West, but declining in the Northeast and Midwest. These results can be traced to numerous factors and should not be seen as a reflection of individual performance. Each of you will soon receive a confidential evaluation of your work. The purpose of this memo is to share information and to outline goals for the coming year.

(3) Business letters convey formal communication, especially between a representative of a company and someone outside the company.

Standard business stationery is $8\frac{1}{2}$ by 11 inches for paper and 4 by 10 inches for envelopes. In the workplace, you usually use company letterhead that can be fed right into the office printer. If you are writing a business letter from home and do not have letterhead, use only one side of white, unlined paper. Or you can use your word processing program to create a professional-looking letterhead with your home address. On occasion, a business writer may handwrite a short note—either to provide a quick cover letter for forwarded material or to signal a personal relationship. In most cases, however, business letters should be word processed.

Check to see whether your company or organization has a policy about letter format. Most companies use a block format for regular correspondence (see pages 720–21), though an indented format (see pages 723–24) is sometimes used for personal business correspondence such as thank-you notes, congratulations, and the like.

A business letter has six parts: (a) heading; (b) inside address; (c) salutation; (d) body; (e) closing, which consists of the complimentary close and signature; and (f) added notations.

The **heading** gives the writer's full address and the date. Depending on your format, place the date flush left, flush right, or centered just below the letterhead. On plain stationery, place the date below your address. Arrange the letter so that it will be attractively centered on the page—flush with the left-hand margin, as in the letter on pages 721–25. Notice that the heading has no ending punctuation.

The **inside address,** placed two to six lines below the heading, gives the name and full address of the recipient. Use the postal abbreviation for the state name. (For a list of these, see **11c.**)

Place the **salutation** (or greeting) flush with the left margin, two spaces below the inside address, and follow it with a colon. When you know the surname of the addressee, use it in the salutation unless you are writing to someone who prefers to be addressed by first name. When writing to a woman, use *Ms.* unless this person has expressed a preference for *Miss* or *Mrs.* or can be addressed by her professional title.

Dear Ms. Samuelson:

Dear Dr. Gillespie:

Dear Mayor Rodriguez:

Dear Mr. Trudeau:

In letters to organizations or to persons whose name and gender you do not know, use the office or company name.

Dear Registrar: Dear Mobil Oil:

For the appropriate forms of salutations and addresses in letters to government officials, military personnel, and so on, check an etiquette book or the front or back of your dictionary.

In the **body** of the letter, single-space within paragraphs and double-space between them when using a block format; do not indent the first line of each paragraph. If you use an indented format, indent first lines five spaces and leave only a single space between paragraphs.

Follow the principles of good writing. Organize information so the reader can grasp immediately what you want. Be clear and direct; do not use stilted or abbreviated phrasing such as:

The aforementioned letter is on file.

Please send this to me ASAP.

The **closing** is double-spaced below the body. If your letter is in block style, type it flush with the left margin; if it is in indented style, align it with the date. Use one of the complimentary closes common to business letters, such as the following.

Formal	**Less Formal**
Very truly yours,	Sincerely,
Sincerely yours,	Cordially,

Place your full name four lines below the closing and, if you are writing on company or organization business, your title on the next line.

Notations, placed flush with the left margin two lines below your title, indicate any materials you have enclosed with or attached to the letter (*enclosure* or *enc., attachment* or *att.*), who will receive copies of the letter (*cc: AAW, PTN* or *c: AAW, PTN*), and the initials of the sender and the typist (*DM/cll*) if they are not the same person.

Model business letter (block format)

WDS WILLCOX, DAVERN, AND SMITH **529 LAKE SIDE BOULEVARD CHICAGO, IL 60605** 312-863-8916

Letterhead containing return address

September 6, 2000

Dr. Elizabeth Boroughs
Fairchild Clinic
1710 Sheridan Ave.
Lakewood, IL 60045

Inside address

Dear Dr. Boroughs: } Salutation

I have just given final approval to several organizational changes designed to ensure closer attention to the individual needs of our clients. Everyone here is excited about these changes, and I am writing to advise you of the one that will affect you most directly.

Effective the first of November, our certified public accountants will specialize in the areas in which they have the greatest expertise. Although we have always tried to direct clients to the accountant best suited to their needs, most staff members have had a diverse workload. This diversity worked well when the company was smaller, but it has become problematic during the past few years as we doubled the size of our staff in response to our growing list of clients.

As you probably know, tax laws have changed considerably in recent years. The new codes are complex, and interpretation continues to evolve. Given the complexity of the codes, the importance of guiding clients through effective tax planning, and the availability of highly trained personnel, accountants in our company will henceforth work within one of three divisions: corporate, small business, and individual.

Richard Henderson, who has prepared your taxes for the past three years, will now be working exclusively with individual clients. I have reviewed your tax records with him, and we agree that Grace Yee, one of our new associates, will give the Fairchild Clinic the best help we can offer. Although she is new to our staff, she comes to us with twelve years of experience, working mostly with medical groups.

You can expect to hear separately from both Rick and Grace, but I wanted to let you know myself that Willcox, Davern, and Smith remains committed to serving you and your business.

Sincerely,	Complimentary Close
Ted Willcox	Signature
Edward Willcox	Typed name
President	Title

EW/nfd } Notation

(4) Writing a good application letter can persuade a busy person to pay attention to your résumé.

Writing a letter of application is an essential step in applying for a job. This letter usually accompanies a résumé (see 39b(5)), and it should do more than simply repeat information that can be found there. Your letter provides you with the chance to sound articulate, interesting, and professional. Make the most of it.

Address your letter to a specific person. If you are responding to an advertisement that mentions a department without giving a name, call the company and find out who will be doing the screening. A misspelled name creates a bad impression, so make sure you spell that person's name correctly when you write.

In your opening paragraph, you should state the position you are applying for, how you learned about it, and—in a single sentence—why you believe you are qualified to fill it. Devote the paragraphs that follow to describing the experience that qualifies you for the job. If your experience is extensive, you can establish that fact and then focus on how you excelled in one or two specific situations. Mention that you are enclosing a résumé, but do not summarize it. Your goal is to get a busy person to read the résumé. Few people enjoy reading the same information twice.

In addition to stating your qualifications, you might also indicate why you are interested in this particular company. Demonstrating that you already know something about it will help you appear to be a serious candidate. Extensive information on most companies is available directly from them in their annual reports. You can also find information by searching *LEXIS-NEXIS* (page 538) and the World Wide Web (pages 549–53).

In your closing paragraph, offer additional information and make a specific request. Instead of settling for "I hope to hear from you soon," tell your reader how and where you can be reached and also mention any relevant information about your schedule during the next few weeks. Then try to arrange for an interview. At the very least, indicate that you are available for an interview and would enjoy the opportunity to exchange information.

Assume that your audience is busy and that there are many applications. These assumptions make it important for you to be concise (see chapter 21). A good letter of application should run between one and two pages, depending on your experience. As you revise (see chapter 33), delete anything that is nonessential.

To keep your letter under two pages, you may need to choose a smaller font than usual, but make sure the text is still easily readable.

Model application letter (indented format)

431 Felton Ave.
St. Paul, MN 55102
April 19, 2000

Mr. Thomas Flanagan
Tristate Airlines
2546 Ashton Ave.
Bloomington, MN 55121

Dear Mr. Flanagan:

I am writing to apply for the position of Assistant Director of Employee Benefits in the Human Resources Department of Tristate, as advertised in this morning's *Star Tribune.* My education and experience are well suited to this position, and I'd welcome the chance to be part of a company that has shown so much growth during a period when other airlines have been operating at a loss.

As you can see from my résumé, I majored in Business Administration with an emphasis in human resources. Whenever possible, I have found campus activities and jobs that would give me experience in working with people. As an assistant in the Admissions Office at the University of Southern Minnesota, I worked successfully with students, parents, alumni, and faculty. The position required both a knowledge of university regulations and an understanding of people with different needs.

I also benefited from working as an administrative intern last summer in the personnel division of Central Bank & Trust, a department that handles the benefits for almost three thousand employees. When I was working there, new computers were installed for the division. Because I have extensive experience with computers, I was able to help other employees make the transition. More important, I improved my knowledge of state law on health insurance and learned procedures for monitoring health benefits that are easily transferable.

I am very much interested in putting my training to use at Tristate and hope that we can schedule an interview sometime during the next few weeks. I will be here in St. Paul except for the week of May 7, but I will be checking my messages daily when I am out of town, and you should have no difficulty reaching me.

Sincerely,

Marcia Baumeister

Marcia Baumeister

enc.

(5) Writing an effective résumé can persuade employers to interview you.

A résumé is a list of a person's qualifications for a job and is enclosed with a letter of application. It is made up of four categories of information.

- Personal data: name, mailing address, telephone number, e-mail address, and (if available) fax number
- Educational background

- Work experience
- References

Most businesses appreciate résumés that highlight your experience and abilities.

Make your résumé look professional. Like the letter of application, the résumé is a form of persuasion designed to emphasize your qualifications for a job and get you an interview. Since there is usually more than one applicant for every job, your résumé should make the most of your qualifications. If you keep your résumé in a computer file, you can easily tailor it to each job you apply for so you can present your qualifications in the best light.

Writing a résumé requires planning and paying attention to detail. First, make a list of the jobs you have had, the activities and clubs you have been part of, and the offices you have held. Amplify these items by adding dates, job titles and responsibilities, and a brief statement about what you learned from each of them. Delete any items that seem too weak or tangential to be persuasive. (See 32b(2).)

Résumés can be organized in a number of ways. One is to list experience and activities in reverse chronological order, so that your most recent experience comes first. This is a good plan if you have a steady job history, without gaps that are hard to explain, and if your most recent experience is worth emphasizing because you have been in a position closely related to the position for which you are applying. If older experience is more directly relevant to the job for which you are applying, you can emphasize it by giving your work history chronologically. An alternative way to organize a résumé is to list experience in terms of job skills rather than jobs held. This plan is especially useful when your work history is modest or you are applying for a position in a new field but know you have the skills for the job.

Software programs that will prompt you to select the kind of résumé you need and then provide prompts for completing the different sections of it are available. When using a computer to write your résumé, you can also view it in its entirety on your screen and redesign it if necessary.

However you choose to organize your résumé, remember that presentation is important (see chapter 8). Although résumés were always expected to look professional, an unprofessional-looking résumé is even less likely to gain favorable attention now that electronic resources facilitate effective presentation. Your résumé is, in effect, going to someone's office for a kind of job interview, so make sure it is well dressed for the occasion. Use good-quality paper (preferably white or off-white) and a laser printer. Use boldface to mark divisions and experiment with different fonts. The design of your document should look professional, so resist the impulse to make it unnecessarily complicated. When in doubt, choose simplicity. For sample résumés, see pages 727–30.

CHECKLIST for Résumé Writing

- Make sure to include your name, address, and telephone number; an e-mail address or fax number could also be useful for employers wishing to contact you.

- Identify your career objective simply, without elaborating on future goals. Reserve a detailed discussion of your plans until asked about them during an interview (and even then make sure they enhance your appeal as a candidate). Try to match your qualifications to the employer's needs.

- Mention your degree, college or university, and pertinent areas of special training.

- Do not include personal data such as age and marital status.

- Even if an advertisement asks you to state a salary requirement, any mention of salary should usually be deferred until the interview.

- Whenever possible, make the relationship between jobs you have had and the job you are seeking clear.

- If you decide to include the names and addresses of references, include their phone numbers as well. List people who have agreed to write or speak on your behalf. Make sure these individuals understand the nature of the position you are seeking.

- To show that you are efficient, well organized, and thoughtful, use a clean, clear format.

- Make sure the résumé is correct by proofreading it carefully.

For further information on application letters, résumés, and interviews, consult a book on how to present yourself in a job search. Most bookstores have a section devoted to such material, and you can locate dozens of other titles by visiting an electronic bookstore.

Chronological résumé

Marcia Baumeister
431 Felton Ave.
St. Paul, MN 55102
(651) 228-1927
Marciab4@hotmail.com

CAREER OBJECTIVE:
A management position specializing in the
administration of employee benefits.

WORK EXPERIENCE:

Intern, Central Bank & Trust, June–August 1999.
Provided information to new employees, helped the personnel department get online with new information technology, and entered data for changes in medical benefits.

Student Assistant, Admissions Office, University of Southern Minnesota, January 1998–May 2000.
Responded to queries from parents and prospective students, conducted campus tours, planned orientation meetings, and wrote reports on recruitment efforts.

Tutor, University Writing Center, September 1997–May 2000.
Tutored students in business writing for six hours a week and worked as needed with other clients. Provided computer assistance, including ways to access information on the World Wide Web.

EDUCATION:

University of Southern Minnesota, B.S. with honors, 2000. Majored in Business Administration with an emphasis in Human Resources. Minors in Economics and Communications. Recipient of the 1999 Grable Award for university service.

Active in Management Club, Yearbook, Alpha Phi Sorority.

References available on request.

Emphatic résumé

Marcia Baumeister
431 Felton Ave.
St. Paul, MN 55102
(651) 228-1927
Marciab4@hotmail.com

CAREER OBJECTIVE:
A management position specializing in the administration of employee benefits.

MANAGEMENT SKILLS:
Familiarity with all contemporary models of effective management; good writing and communication skills; experience with planning and evaluating meetings; experience with programming and tracking information electronically; ability to teach computer skills.

EXPERIENCE IN HUMAN RESOURCES:
Assisted in the transfer of data on medical benefits for approximately three thousand employees at Central Bank & Trust in St. Paul; provided benefit information to employees; worked with students, parents, and faculty at the University of Southern Minnesota as an information specialist with an emphasis on student benefits.

ADDITIONAL EXPERIENCE:
Tutored students in writing, helped edit the yearbook, gave campus tours, and served as a liaison between my sorority and the university.

EDUCATION:

University of Southern Minnesota, B.S. with honors, 2000. Majored in Business Administration with an emphasis in Human Resources. Minors in Economics and Communication. Recipient of the 1999 Grable Award for university service.

EXTRACURRICULAR:

Active in Management Club, Yearbook, Alpha Phi Sorority.

References available on request.

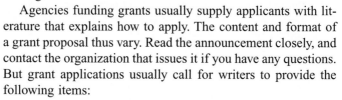

(6) Being able to write a grant proposal can improve your professional standing.

As a college student, business person, or community activist, you may have occasion to write a grant proposal: an application to a specific agency to fund a particular project. Grants are available to support academic research, creative writing, performance art, new businesses, and projects that can improve the quality of life in your community. Your campus may have a grants specialist who can advise you about funding opportunities. You can also find information about grants on the Internet. In addition, your college or community library may have directories of available grants, as well as books devoted to grant writing.

Agencies funding grants usually supply applicants with literature that explains how to apply. The content and format of a grant proposal thus vary. Read the announcement closely, and contact the organization that issues it if you have any questions. But grant applications usually call for writers to provide the following items:

- an abstract, or summary of the project,
- a narrative describing its purpose and nature,
- a description of the methodology that will be used,
- a schedule for completing the work, and
- a budget.

Writing a grant proposal usually involves writing for a diverse audience (see 32a(2)). Although the selection committee may include a member with expertise in your field, it is likely to include people with different kinds of expertise. For example, the selection committee of a foundation supporting work in the sciences may include physicists, chemists, biologists, and software engineers, as well as an administrator whose background may be in business or in the humanities. When you prepare a grant proposal, it is important to write clearly and simply—avoiding jargon and defining any technical terms you use.

Model grant proposal

The following proposal was written by a college junior seeking funding from a university that offers support for undergraduate research. The proposal includes graphics (see 8b(5)). While graphics are seldom required as part of a grant proposal, they can be useful. They also frequently appear in research papers written in the natural and social sciences (see 38h) as well as in professional writing such as sales reports and annual reviews. Many software programs are available to create graphics and import them into written text.

The complete proposal as originally submitted included a description of the academic course work that prepared the applicant for the research, a budget, a schedule, and approval from the faculty member who would supervise the work. These components have been omitted from the version reprinted here.

The documentation style in this proposal follows guidelines established by the Council of Biology Editors. Variations on this numbered system are common in writing in the natural sciences. For a list of manuals on documentation, see page 559.

The Behavioral Effects of a Mutant *Clock* Gene on Circadian Rhythms in Mice

Ethan Buhr
March 1999

Abstract

The earth's rotation causes a repeating pattern of light and dark in most environments. In turn, nearly all organisms have innate pacemakers or *biological clocks* that allow them to predict and adapt to these daily changes. In recent years, the mechanisms responsible for producing these circadian rhythms in mammals have been uncovered. The suprachiasmatic nucleus (SCN) of the hypothalamus has been localized as the site of the brain responsible for circadian rhythms. Within the SCN, certain genes have been identified as key players. Among these, the *Clock* gene has been the most actively studied. It has recently been shown that different versions of this gene may dictate day or night preference in humans ("lark" or "owl" behavior). Experiments aimed at characterizing the behavioral functions of the circadian systems in normal mice are currently under way in the lab where I work. The mice are first entrained (synchronized) to a 12-hour light and 12-hour dark cycle. They are then allowed to "free run" in complete darkness, and their activities are monitored. Light pulses of varying intensities and durations are then used to "shift" the circadian patterns of activity. These shifts are recorded and quantified to characterize the behavioral response of the circadian rhythm to light. These shifts are an assay of the light's effect on the underlying circadian pacemaker. This summer, our lab will receive mice with mutations of the *Clock* gene. I hope to conduct experiments similar to those under way to compare the circadian responses of mice with the mutant gene and mice with the normal gene. Understanding the effect of a mutation on this gene is crucial to understanding the gene's importance to the circadian pacemaker in mammals.

Introduction

Circadian neuroscience is a very active field of research, partly because of the immense impact that increased understanding of the mammalian circadian clock could have on human health (such as treatments for sleep disorders and seasonal depression), as well as on our understanding of circadian systems in general. The current interest in circadian neuroscience is also due to some recent discoveries linking several genes to the 24-hour rhythmicity of the mammalian circadian pacemaker. These genes undoubtedly play a major role in the oscillatory activity in the brains of all mammals. As a result, a huge research effort is focusing on the molecular mechanisms involved in these 24-hour timing systems.

Molecular mechanisms alone, however, are restricted in how much they can disclose about the importance of a gene. Just because the expression of a gene displays 24-hour rhythmicity, does that mean it is important in the circadian system? It is also important to consider behavioral characterizations of the system in concert with the molecular aspects of the clock mechanism. Only when both the behavioral and molecular aspects are understood can we truly grasp the workings of the system as a whole.

Current research is furthering our understanding of specific behavioral outputs of the circadian systems in mice. This research provides insight into how the "normal" circadian pacemaker functions in this animal. A current hypothesis is that a specific gene, *Clock*, is responsible for most of the mammalian circadian oscillation. To test this hypothesis, I plan to characterize the behavior of mice with mutant versions of the *Clock* gene. By comparing their activity rhythms (and the effects of light on these rhythms) with those of mice of the same species that have the normal *Clock* gene, we can determine exactly how important this gene is to the normal function of the mammalian circadian clock.

Narrative

Overview and Background

Most organisms have circadian rhythms of about 24 hours; these are driven by internal molecular clocks or pacemakers, which allow the organism to predict and adapt to daily changes in the environment. The specific mechanism has not been fully described. Recently, however, there have been tremendous advances in our understanding of the mechanisms that lie at the core of these physiological clocks.

The site in the mammalian brain considered to be the primary site of the circadian pacemaker is the suprachiasmatic nucleus (SCN) of the hypothalamus in the base of the brain (1–3). The SCN displays a distinct 24-hour pattern of neural activity both *in vivo* (in the body) and *in vitro* (in a petri dish) (1,2). Furthermore, when this area of the brain is damaged or missing, the animal loses all 24-hour rhythmicity, including sleep/wake cycles and hormonal rhythms (3).

This endogenous clock within the SCN is also *reset* by light. The response of neurons from the SCN of rats was measured electronically as light of varying intensities was shone on the animal, and a direct response of the SCN neurons to the light was clearly observed (2). Light resets the clock through defined pathways that are different from the pathways that mediate "pattern vision." In addition, circadian cycles in retinal-degenerate mice (mice that have no rod or cone photoreceptors) show responses to light identical to those seen for mice with normal retinas (4).

What exactly does light information do within the SCN that causes the resetting of the 24-hour clock? Many lines of research are focusing on the importance of several genes for this system. Four of the most important genes in the mammalian circadian system are called *Clock, Period, Timeless,* and *BMAL1* (5–11). The way these genes interact to cause 24-hour rhythms is still not understood. The most widely accepted hypothesis suggests that the expression of *Clock* and *BMAL1* genes induces the transcription of the *Period* gene (8,9). The resulting protein, PER, then inhibits further activity of the *Clock* gene in a negative feedback loop (see Figure 1) (6,7,11). Once the CLOCK protein levels fall, *Period* genes are no longer induced, and this, in turn, reduces the inhibition of the *Clock* gene.

This negative feedback model has been proposed to be the molecular mechanism underlying all mammalian circadian rhythms. An interesting study on the *Clock* gene in humans shows that people with different **alleles** of this gene show either a preference for night or day (that is, they are "morning people" or "night people") (10). The *Clock* gene thus appears to be a promising avenue for further study.

The research lab where I work focuses on characterizing the behavioral circadian activity of mice and the way the

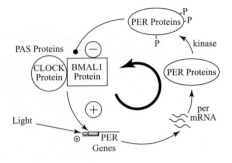

Figure 1
Proposed molecular mechanism for the mammalian 24-hour clock. Redrawn from
Dunlap, *Science* 1998;280:1549.

circadian pacemaker is reset by light stimulation. This is
examined by first synchronizing or entraining the mice to a 12-
hour light and 12-hour dark (12:12) cycle for at least 2 weeks.
The activity of the mice is recorded by a switch on the running
wheel in their cage, which is monitored continuously by
computer. Since mice are nocturnal, nearly all of their activity
is restricted to the dark phase of the 12:12 light-dark cycle (see
Figure 2).

Next, the mice are left in complete darkness for a week.
During this time, they are said to be "free running" (that is, their
circadian clock alone is controlling their activity rhythms).
Because the circadian clock of mice runs slightly shorter than
24 hours, in the absence of light cues their activity begins
slightly earlier each day. After a week of darkness, a light
stimulus (or "light pulse") is administered to each animal (this
day is marked with an arrow in Figure 2). On the day after the
light pulse, the mouse begins running on the wheel much later.
This "phase delay" of the circadian pacemaker is permanent,
and as can be seen in the figure, the mouse again runs slightly
earlier every day after the stimulus.

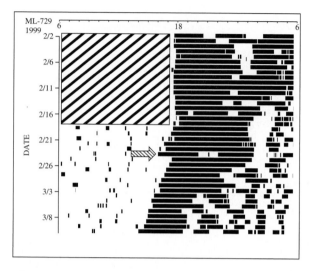

Figure 2
Running wheel activity record for a mouse. Each 24-hour day is displayed as a horizontal line on the record. The heavy bars indicate times of activity. Times of inactivity are blank. For the first half of this record, the mouse was maintained in a light/dark cycle (the hashed box indicates the light phase). After the light/dark cycle is discontinued, the circadian clock controls the mouse's activity rhythm. The arrow indicates a light pulse administered to the mouse, and a phase delay (resetting) of the circadian clock is clearly visible.

These phase shifts of the clock are quantified by measuring how many hours the mouse's cycle is delayed by the light pulse. In previous experiments that I have assisted with, our lab has demonstrated a direct correlation between the size of the phase delay and both the intensity and the duration of the light pulse. The higher the intensity of the light pulse, the larger the phase delays (Figure 3). This relationship is seen only up to a specific level, and then the system appears to saturate at a maximum response of approximately 100 minutes.

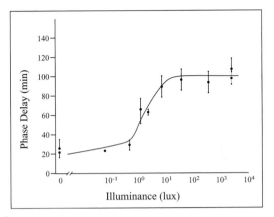

Figure 3
Phase shifts of the mouse circadian pacemaker as a function of the illuminance of the light stimulus. Each point represents the mean (+/-SEM) for a group of animals that received a light pulse of 15 minutes and the illuminance indicated.

The same is true for the duration of a light pulse. Figure 4 shows how phase delay is affected by the duration of the light pulse. This figure shows that as the light pulses get larger, the phase delay gets larger, but the effect is directly proportional only up to the saturation point.

The work described above characterizes mice with normal circadian systems. The work I am proposing will use mice with a mutant form of the *Clock* gene. It has been shown that this gene is necessary for normal circadian function, and mice without it lack circadian rhythmicity (6–11). However, the effects of this gene on *sensitivity to light* have never been characterized behaviorally. By comparing the light sensitivity of mice that have a mutant allele with the activity of mice that have the normal allele, we can determine the importance of this gene in resetting mammalian circadian rhythms. The results of this study will determine what effect (if any) the *Clock* gene has on the light entrainment and light responsiveness of the mouse circadian clock. This behavioral information is crucial for a general acceptance of the molecular mechanism of the mammalian circadian clock.

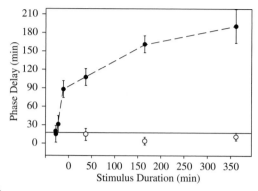

Figure 4
Stimulus response curve for phase delay versus light duration. Each point
represents the mean (+/−SEM) for a group of animals that received a light pulse of
9.9 lux and the duration indicated. Filled circles are for animals that received light
stimulation, and open circles are for mice that received only darkness for the
duration (as a control).

Methodology

　　To perform this study, I will use the equipment in the
neuroscience research lab at the University of St. Thomas. Mice
will be housed in individual cages with running wheels and
provided with appropriate food, water, and bedding.* The cages
will be stored in large environmental chambers that exclude all
outside light and have controllable lights and constant
ventilation. Electric switches connected to the running wheels
will send information into a computer, which records activity
throughout the experiment. The mice are first entrained to a
12-hour light and 12-hour dark schedule for at least 2 weeks.
Lights will then be turned off for the remainder of the
experiment. After a week of free run, each mouse will receive a

---

*All of the experiments and procedures described in this proposal have been
reviewed and approved by the University of St. Thomas Institutional Animal Care
and Use Committee (IACUC). A letter of approval from the IACUC is available upon
request. All of the proposed procedures will be carried out under the supervision of a
professor of biology at the University of St. Thomas. The animals will be maintained
in the University Animal Care Suite, which meets all U.S. Department of Agriculture
and U.S. Public Health Service requirements. These facilities are reviewed by the St.
Thomas IACUC committee twice a year.

single light pulse (white, fluorescent light) and then be returned to constant darkness for 2 weeks. Then, the behavioral response to the light stimulus will be measured.

Our experiments will test the light responsiveness using pulses of different intensities and durations for the *Clock*-mutant mice (mice with only a single allele of the *Clock* gene). Various intensities and durations of light will be administered to separate groups of mice (probably 4 to 6 mice per light level), following the same procedure as was used for the mice with the normal *Clock* gene to ensure that the results can be directly compared. This experiment will demonstrate for the first time how a mutant allele of the *Clock* gene affects the sensitivity of the mammalian circadian system to light.

Feasibility

This project can be completed using the resources and equipment at the University of St. Thomas. Dr. Dwight Nelson, who will be assisting and supervising me in every aspect of this experiment, has prepared to acquire the necessary mice.

Glossary of Terms

Allele A form of a certain gene. Most genes have multiple alleles or types that encode for different traits. (An allele for blue eyes would give a child blue eyes.)

Circadian rhythm Biological rhythms with daily cycles. The word "circadian" comes from the Latin *circa,* which means around, and *diem,* which means day. Circadian rhythms can be measured for almost any physical, behavioral, or cellular aspect, including sleep/wake, cell division, hormone levels, and cognitive ability.

Gene A portion of DNA of a single chromosome that encodes for a single protein.

Hypothalamus A part of the brain that lies at the base and contributes to the autonomic nervous system and endocrine function.

Lux A measure of the quantity of light corresponding to wavelengths detected by the human eye.

Mutant allele An allele of a gene that does not function or produce a functional protein.

Suprachiasmatic nucleus (SCN) A collection of neurons at the base of the hypothalamus. This nucleus is the site of the mammalian circadian pacemaker.

Transcription The translation of information from DNA to RNA and then to a protein.

References

1. Honma S, Shirakawa T, Katsuno Y, Namihira M, Honma K. Circadian periods of single suprachiasmatic neurons in rats. Neurosci Lett 1998;250:157–60.
2. Meijer JH, Watanabe K, Schaa J, Albus H, Detari L. Light responsiveness of the suprachiasmatic nucleus: long-term multiunit and single-unit recordings in freely moving rats. J Neurosci 1998;18(21):9078–87.
3. Weaver DR. The suprachiasmatic nucleus: 25-year retrospective. J Biol Rhyt 1998;13(2):100–12.
4. Foster RG, Provencio I, Hudson D, Fiske S, DeGrip W, Menaker M. Circadian photoreception in the retinally degenerate mouse (rd/rd). J Compar Physiol A 1991;169:39–50.
5. Allada R, White NE, Venus SW, Hall JC, Rosbash M. A mutant *Drosophila* homolog of mammalian *Clock* disrupts circadian rhythms and transcription of *period* and *timeless*. Cell 1998;93:791–804.
6. Bae K, Lee C, Sidote D, Chuang K, Edery I. Circadian regulation of a *Drosophila* homolog of the mammalian *Clock* gene: PER and TIM function as positive regulators. Mol Cell Biol 1998;18(10):6142–51.
7. Darlington TK, Wager-Smith K, Ceriani MF, Staknis D, Gekakis N, Steeves TDL, Weitz CJ, Takahashi JS, Kay SA. Closing the circadian loop: CLOCK-induced transcription of its own inhibitors *per* and *tim*. Science 1998;280:1599–1603.
8. Gekakis N, Staknis D, Nguyen HB, Davis FC, Wilsbacher LD, King DP, Takahashi JS, Weitz CJ. Role of the CLOCK protein in the mammalian circadian mechanism. Science 1998;280:1564–9.
9. Honma S, Ikeda M, Abe H, Tanahashi Y, Namihira M, Honma K, Nomura M. Circadian oscillation of BMAL1, a partner of a mammalian clock gene *Clock*, in rat suprachiasmatic nucleus. Biochem Biophys Res Communic 1998;250:83–7.
10. Katzenberg D, Young T, Finn L, Lin L, King DP, Takahashi JS, Mignot E. A CLOCK polymorphism associated with human diurnal preference. Sleep 1998;21(6):569–76.
11. Dunlap, J. An end in the beginning. Science 1998;280:1548–9.

EXERCISE 5

Choose one of the following.

1. In a letter, call the attention of your representative in city government to repairs needed on neighborhood streets.

2. Write a letter to an automobile company complaining about the performance of a car it manufactured.

3. Write a memo to the members of an organization you belong to recommending a change in procedures.

4. Prepare a résumé, and then write a letter of application for a position you are qualified to fill.

5. Think of an activity for which you would like to receive funding and imagine an agency to which you could apply for support. Then experiment with grant writing by drafting a four-page proposal.

Glossary of Usage

The following short glossary covers the most common usage problems. It also distinguishes between written and conversational English. An expression that may be acceptable in spoken English or in a letter to a friend is labeled **colloquial** or **informal** and is usually not acceptable in college or professional writing. College writing is sometimes referred to as "edited American English" or "academic discourse." The following labels are used in this glossary.

College and professional writing	Words or phrases listed in dictionaries without special usage labels; appropriate in college writing or in business.
Conversational	Words or phrases that dictionaries label *informal, slang,* or *colloquial;* although often acceptable in spoken language, not generally appropriate in college writing.
Unacceptable	Words or phrases labeled in dictionaries as *archaic, illiterate, nonstandard, obsolete, substandard;* generally not accepted in college writing.

You may also wish to consult 18c for a list of words that sound alike but have different meanings.

a, an   Use *a* before the sound of a consonant: **a** yard, **a** U-turn, **a** one-term president. Use *an* before a vowel sound: **an** empty can, **an** M.D., **an** ax, **an** X-ray.

accept, except   *Accept* means "to receive"; *except* means "to exclude": I **accept** your apology. All **except** Joe will go.

adapt, adopt   *Adapt* means "to change for a purpose"; *adopt* means "to take possession": You must **adapt** to extreme cold. The company will **adopt** a new policy.

adverse, averse   *Adverse* means "antagonistic" or "unfavorable"; *averse* means "opposed to": We would have gone had it not been for **adverse** weather conditions. After seeing the weather report, I was **averse** to going on the trip.

advice, advise   *Advice* is a noun, and *advise* is a verb: I accept your **advice.** Please **advise** me of the situation.

affect, effect   The verb *affect* means "to influence" or "to touch the emotions." The noun *effect* means "result of an action or antecedent": Smoking **affects** the heart. His tears **affected** her deeply. Drugs have side **effects.** The **effect** on sales was good. When used as a verb, *effect* means "to produce" or "to cause": The medicine **effected** a complete cure.

aggravate   Widely used for "annoy" or "irritate." Many writers, however, restrict the meaning of *aggravate* to "intensify, make worse": Noises **aggravate** a headache.

agree to, agree with   In idiomatic usage, *agree to* means "to accept" or "to consent"; *agree with* means "to come to an understanding" or "to suit": The customer **agreed** to our terms. George **agreed** to turn down the volume. I finally got Gina to **agree** with me. Vacation **agrees** with her.

ain't   Unacceptable in writing unless used in dialogue or for humorous effect.

all   The indefinite pronoun *all* is singular when it refers to a group as a unit and plural when it refers to individuals. All were present [refers to individuals—plural sense]. All is forgiven [refers to a quantity—singular sense].

allude, elude   The verb *allude* means "to refer to." The verb *elude* means "to avoid" or "to escape": Do you know what he **alluded** to? The suspect **eluded** capture.

allusion, illusion   An *allusion* is a casual or indirect reference. An *illusion* is a false idea or an unreal image: The **allusion** was to Shakespeare's *Twelfth Night*. His idea of college is an **illusion.**

alot   A misspelling of the overused and nonspecific phrase *a lot.*

already, all ready   *Already* means "before or by the time specified." *All ready* means "completely prepared": She is **already** in the car. The picnic supplies are **all ready** for you.

alright   Not yet a generally accepted spelling of *all right,* although it is becoming more common in journalistic writing.

altogether, all together   *Altogether* means "wholly, thoroughly." *All together* means "in a group": That book is **altogether** too difficult, unless the class reads it **all together.**

a.m., p.m. (OR A.M., P.M.)   Use only with figures: The show will begin at 7:00 **p.m.** COMPARE at seven *in the evening.*

among, between   These prepositions are used with plural objects (including collective nouns). As a rule, use *among* with objects denoting three or more (a group), and use *between* with those denoting only two: danced **among** the flowers, whispering **among** themselves; reading **between** the lines, just **between** you and me.

amongst   British English. Use *among* in college writing.

amoral, immoral   *Amoral* means "neither moral nor immoral." *Immoral* means "not moral": The behavior of animals is completely **amoral.** Some philosophers consider war **immoral.**

amount of, number of   Use *amount of* with a singular noncount noun: The **amount of** rain varies. Use *number of* with a plural count noun: The **number of** errors was excessive. See **number** and **1c(2)**.

and etc.   *Etc.* is an abbreviation of the Latin *et* ("and") *cetera* ("other things"). Omit the redundant *and.* See also **etc.**

and/or   This combination is appropriate in professional writing but acceptable in college writing only when the context calls for both *and* and *or* as well as either one singly: To write a comparison/contrast essay, examine the points of similarity **and/or** difference between two stated things.

angry at   Unacceptable for *angry with.*

another, other   *Another* is followed by a singular noun: **another** book. *Other* is followed by a plural noun: **other** books.

ante, anti   *Ante* is a prefix meaning "before," "in front of": They waited in the **anteroom.** *Anti* is a prefix meaning "opposed to," "hostile": There were **antiwar** riots.

anxious   Not to be used as a synonym for "eager."

anymore   Use *anymore* in negative sentences when the sense is "any longer," "now," or "these days." In positive sentences, use "now" instead. Sarah doesn't work here **anymore. Now** we have to recycle our trash.

anyone, any one; everyone, every one   Distinguish between each one-word and two-word compound. *Anyone* means "any person at all"; *any one* refers to one of a group. Similarly, *everyone* means "all," and *every one* refers to each one in a group: Was **anyone** hurt? Was **any one** of you hurt? **Everyone** should attend. **Every one** of them should attend.

anyplace   Conversational; use *any place* or *anywhere* for college writing.

anyways, anywheres   Unacceptable for *anyway, anywhere.*

apt, liable, likely   *Apt* is generally accepted and now used interchangeably with *liable* and *likely* before an infinitive. *Liable* is generally limited to situations that have an undesirable outcome: He is not **likely** to get sick. He is **liable** to get sick. (See **liable, likely.**) He is **apt** to get sick.

as   1. As a conjunction, use *as* to express sameness of degree, quantity, or manner: **As** scholars have noted . . . OR Do **as** I do. As a preposition, use *as* to express equivalence: I think of Tom **as** my brother. [Tom = brother] Use *like* to express similarity: Tom is **like** a brother.
2. Use *if, that,* or *whether* instead of *as* after such verbs as *feel, know, say,* or *see:* I do not know **whether** my adviser is right.
3. In subordinate clauses, use *because* to introduce a causal relationship and *while* to introduce a time relationship: **Because** it was raining, we watched TV. **While** it was raining, we watched TV.

assure, ensure, insure   *Assure* means "to state with confidence." *Ensure* and *insure* are sometimes used interchangeably to mean "make certain." *Insure* has the further meaning of "to protect against loss": Marlon **assured** me that he would vote for my ticket. I **ensured** (or **insured**) that Vincent had his tickets before I left home. Bing **insured** her car against theft.

as to   Imprecise; use the clearer word, *about:* He wasn't certain **about** the time.

at   Unacceptable in college writing when *at* follows *where,* even with intervening words. We did not know where the museum was ~~at.~~

at this point in time   Wordy for "now."

averse   See **adverse.**

awful   Unacceptable for the often overused adverb *awfully:* She is **awfully** intelligent.

awhile, a while   *Awhile,* an adverb, is not used as the object of a preposition: We rested **awhile.** [COMPARE We rested for **a while.**]

back up, backup   *Back up* means to reverse or to make an archival copy of work on a computer; *backup* is a noun that refers to such a copy: I had to **back up** to get out of the parking lot. I forgot to make a **backup** of my files before my hard drive crashed.

bad   Unacceptable as an adverb: Bill danced **badly.** Acceptable as a subject complement after sense verbs such as *feel, look, smell.* I feel **bad** when I have a cold. See **4a.**

because   Unacceptable in the expression *is because,* since *to be* signifies equality between the subject and what follows: The reason is ~~because~~ that it rained. See **23d.**

being as, being that   Wordy and imprecise; use *since, because.*

beside, besides   Always a preposition, *beside* usually means "next to," sometimes "apart from": The chair was **beside** the table. As a preposition, *besides* means "in addition to" or "other than": She has many books **besides** those on the table. As an adverb, *besides* means "also" or "moreover": The library has a fine collection of books; **besides,** it has a number of valuable manuscripts.

better   Unacceptable for *had better:* We **had better** run the spell check. See **had better.**

between   See **among, between.**

biannual, biennial   *Biannual* means twice in one year, while *biennial* means every two years: An equinox is a **biannual** event. The state legislature's meetings are **biennial** rather than annual.

breath, breathe   A common spelling error: *Breath* is a noun, and *breathe* is a verb.

bring, take   Both words describe the same action but from different standpoints. Someone *brings* something *to* the speaker's location, while someone else *takes* something *away* from the speaker's location: **Bring** your book when you come to class. I **take** my notes home with my book.

bunch   Conversational for "a group." In college writing, *bunch* is a noun referring to a natural cluster (a **bunch** of grapes) or a verb meaning "to make a group": Just **bunch** everything together and go.

busted   Unacceptable as the past tense of *burst*.

but what, but that   Conversational after expressions of doubt such as "no doubt" or "did not know." Use *that:* I do not doubt **that** they are correct.

can, may   *Can* refers to ability, and *may* refers to permission: I **can** [am able to] drive fifty miles an hour, but I **may** not [am not permitted to] exceed the speed limit. Contemporary usage allows *can* and *may* denoting possibility or permission to be used interchangeably.

can't hardly, can't scarcely   Unacceptable for *can hardly, can scarcely.*

capital, capitol   A *capital* is a governing city; it also means "funds." As a modifier, *capital* means "chief" or "principal." A *capitol* is a statehouse; the *Capitol* is the U.S. congressional building in Washington, D.C.

censor, censure   *Censor* (verb) means "to remove or suppress because of immoral or otherwise objectionable ideas": Do you think a movie ratings board should **censor** films that have too much sex and violence? A *censor* (noun) is a person who suppresses those ideas. *Censure* (verb) means "to blame or criticize"; a *censure* (noun) is an expression of disapproval or blame. The senate **censured** Joseph McCarthy.

center around   Conversational for "to be focused on" or for "to center on."

chairman, chairperson, chair *Chairman* is misused as a generic term. *Chairperson* or *chair* is generally preferred as the generic term.

cite, site, sight *Cite* means "to mention." *Site* is a locale. *Sight* is a view or the ability to see: Be sure to **cite** your sources in your paper. The president visited the disaster **site.** What a tragic **sight!**

climactic, climatic *Climactic* is an adjective that refers to a high point. *Climatic* refers to the *climate.*

coarse, course Homonyms; *coarse* refers to rough texture; *course* refers to a path or a plan of study: The jacket was made of **coarse** blue linen. Our **course** to the island was indirect. I want to take a **course** in how to make stained glass.

compare to, compare with *Compare to* means "regard as similar," and *compare with* means "examine to discover similarities or differences": The instructor **compared** the diagram **to** the finished product. The student **compared** the first draft **with** the second.

complement, compliment *Complement* means "to complete" or "to supply needs." *Compliment* means "to express praise." *Complimentary* means "given free," as in "**complimentary** tickets": Their personalities **complement** each other. Betsy **complimented** Jim on his award.

comprise, compose *Comprise* means "to contain." *Compose* means "to make up": The collection **comprises** many volumes. That collection **is composed** of medieval manuscripts.

conscious, conscience *Conscious* is an adjective meaning "awake" or "aware." *Conscience* is a noun meaning "the sense of right and wrong": His **conscience** made him **conscious** of his mistake.

consensus of opinion Redundant. Omit "of opinion."

consequently, subsequently *Consequently* means "as a result of"; *subsequently* means "following": The catcher missed the ball; **consequently,** the other team scored. **Subsequently,** they won the game.

contact Although often used in professional writing, this usage is considered imprecise in college writing; use *telephone, see, talk to, write to,* or the like.

continual, continuous *Continual* means recurring at regular intervals: He coughed **continually.** *Continuous* means recurring without interruption: He talked **continuously.**

convince, persuade *Convince* refers to a change of opinion or belief, while *persuade* refers to motivation to act: What does it take to **convince** you that you sing beautifully? I must **persuade** you to stop smoking.

could care less Avoided in college writing, this phrase is intended to express the speaker's complete lack of concern; however, it actually states the opposite. Use "couldn't care less."

council, counsel Homonyms; *council* is a noun meaning "an advisory or decision-making group." *Counsel* as a verb means "to give advice," and as a noun, "a legal adviser."

criteria, criterion *Criteria* is a plural noun meaning "a set of standards for judgment." The singular form is *criterion.*

data *Data* is the plural form of *datum,* which means "fact." Even though *data* is considered either singular or plural in common usage, it should be plural in college writing: When the **data are** complete, we will know the true cost.

differ from, differ with *Differ from* means "to be different," while *differ with* means "to disagree": To me, one country and western song scarcely **differs from** another. In that opinion, I **differ with** a number of my friends.

different than, different from Both are widely used, although *different from* is generally preferred in college writing.

discreet, discrete *Discreet* means "prudent," "having good judgment." *Discrete* means "distinct," "noncontinuous": A **discreet** inquiry may change an unpopular policy. The members of the audience came from three **discrete** groups.

disinterested, uninterested *Disinterested* means "impartial" or "lacking prejudice": a *disinterested* referee. *Uninterested* means "indifferent, lacking interest": A **disinterested** observer will give a fair opinion. An **uninterested** observer may fall asleep.

distinct, distinctive *Distinct* means "separate," "discrete." *Distinctive* means "characteristic," "noteworthy": There are two **distinct** kinds of rock in the wall. Each has **distinctive** features.

don't Unacceptable when used for "doesn't": My father **doesn't** dance.

drug Unacceptable as the past tense of *dragged.*

due to Usually avoided in college writing when used as a preposition in place of *because* or *on account of:* **Because of** holiday traffic, we arrived an hour late.

effect See **affect, effect.**

e.g. Abbreviation from Latin *exempli gratia,* meaning "for example." Replace with the English equivalent *for example* or *for instance.* Do not confuse with **i.e.**

elicit, illicit *Elicit* means "to draw forth." *Illicit* means "unlawful": It is **illicit** to **elicit** public funds for your private use.

emigrate from, immigrate to The prefix *e-* (a variant of *ex-*) means "out of." To *emigrate* is to go out of one's own country to settle in another. The prefix *im-* (a variant of *in-*) means "into." To *immigrate* is to come into a different country to settle. The corresponding adjective or noun forms are *emigrant* and *immigrant:* The Ulster Scots **emigrated from** Scotland to Ireland and then **immigrated to** the southern United States.

eminent, imminent *Eminent* means "distinguished"; *imminent* means "about to happen": Maria Hughes is an **eminent** scholar. The storm is **imminent.**

ensure See **assure, ensure, insure.**

enthused Conversational usage, not accepted in college writing. Use *enthusiastic.*

especially, specially *Especially* means "outstandingly"; *specially* means "for a particular purpose, specifically": This is an **especially** nice party. I bought this tape **specially** for the occasion.

-ess A female suffix now considered sexist, therefore unacceptable. Use *poet, author, actor,* and *waiter* or *server* instead of *poetess, authoress, actress,* and *waitress.*

etc. From the Latin *et cetera* meaning "and other things." In college writing, substitute *and so on* or *and so forth.* Since *etc.* means "and other things," *and etc.* is redundant.

eventually, ultimately *Eventually* means "at some future time," and *ultimately* means "farthest," "last," "fundamentally." The baby will **eventually** stop crying. His behavior was **ultimately** immoral.

every day, everyday As two words, *every day* is an adjective and a noun meaning "daily," but as one word, *everyday* is an adjective meaning "mundane," or "ordinary": It is an **every day** occurrence. These are **everyday** problems.

everyone, every one See **anyone, any one.**

except See **accept, except.**

expect Conversational; use *think, believe:* I **believe** our students are very happy here.

explicit, implicit *Explicit* means "expressed directly or precisely." *Implicit* means "implied or expressed indirectly": The instructions were **explicit.** There was an **implicit** suggestion in her lecture.

farther, further Generally, *farther* refers to geographic distance: six miles **farther.** *Further* is used as a synonym for *additional* in more abstract references: **further** delay, **further** proof.

feel In college writing, use *think* unless the subject is actual feelings.

female, male As nouns, avoid using these to refer to people. As adjectives, use with care to avoid sexist usage and/or sexual undertones: She is an interesting **woman.** He is an unusual **man.**

fewer, less *Fewer* refers to people or objects that can be counted; *less* refers to amounts that can be observed or to abstract nouns: **fewer** pencils, **less** milk, **less** support.

field Usually wordy or imprecise when used to refer to an academic or scientific discipline: We want to study ~~the field of~~ medicine. ~~My field is~~ I study feminist rhetoric.

firstly, secondly In college writing, use *first, second* instead.

flaunt, flout *Flaunt* means "to show off," and *flout* means "to defy": She **flaunted** her new wardrobe. Revolutionaries sometimes **flout** social conventions.

flunk Conversational for "fail."

former, latter *Former* refers to the first of two; *latter* to the second of two. If three or more items are mentioned, use *first* and *last:* John and Ian are both British; the **former** is from England, and the **latter** is from Scotland.

fun Conversational when used as an adjective. Use *fun* as a noun in college writing. We were having ~~a~~ **fun** ~~visit.~~

get Useful in many idioms but not appropriate in college writing in expressions such as the following: The baby's whining ~~got to~~ **annoyed** me. The puppy ~~got~~ **became** fat. Some of Frost's poems really ~~get to~~ **affect** me. I'm going to ~~get~~ **take revenge on** you for that.

go, goes Inappropriate in written language for *say, says:* I ~~go~~ **say,** "Hello!" Then he ~~goes~~ **says,** "Glad to see you!"

good, well *Good* is an adjective frequently misused as an adverb; *well* is an adverb: He dances **well.** He had a **good** time. *Well* in the sense of "in good health" may be used as a subject complement interchangeably with *good* in such expressions as "Pedro doesn't feel **well** (or **good**)."

good and Unacceptable as an intensifier in college writing: They were ~~good and~~ angry about the theft.

great Overworked for more precise words such as *skillful, good, clever, enthusiastic,* or *very well.*

had better (meaning *ought to*) Do not omit the verb *had:* We **had better** go home.

had ought (meaning *ought to*) Omit the verb *had:* We **ought to** go home.

half a, a half, a half a Use *half of a, half a,* or *a half.*

hanged, hung *Hanged* refers specifically to "put to death by hanging": She was **hanged** at dawn. *Hung* is the usual past participle: He had **hung** the picture.

hardly A negative, *hardly* cannot be used with another negative.

has got, have got Wordy; use *has* and *have* without *got:* I **have** ~~got~~ to study tonight.

he Used inappropriately as a generic term for both men and women. See **6b(1)** and **19d(1).**

he/she, his/her One solution to the problem of sexist language, these combinations are not universally accepted. In college writing, consider using *he or she, his or hers*. See **6b(1)**, **19d**.

herself, himself, myself, yourself These words (reflexive pronouns) cannot be subjects and can be direct objects only when they refer to the subject. See **5a(4)**.

hisself Use *himself.*

hopefully Means "with hope." Used inappropriately for *I hope* or *it is hoped.*

idea, ideal An *idea* is a thought; an *ideal* is a goal. They are not interchangeable: She had very high **ideals,** so she planned a career in health care.

i.e. Abbreviation for the Latin *id est,* meaning "that is." Use *that is* instead. Do not confuse with **e.g.**

if, whether Use *if* to mean "in the event that"; *whether* suggests alternatives: I can't go **if** you drive; **whether** I go depends on who is driving.

illusion See **allusion, illusion.**

imminent See **eminent, imminent.**

immoral See **amoral.**

impact Jargon when used to mean "have an effect": The new tax ~~impacts~~ affects everyone.

implement Jargon when used to mean "accomplish": We ~~implemented~~ accomplished our goals.

implicit See **explicit, implicit.**

imply, infer *Imply* means "suggest without actually stating," and *infer* means "draw a conclusion based on evidence": He **implied** that he was angry, but I **inferred** that he was frightened.

in, into *In* points to location, *into* to movement or a change in condition: We were **in** Atlanta. The prisoners were herded **into** a cell.

incredible, incredulous *Incredible* means "incapable of being believed," whereas *incredulous* means "incapable of believing": The tale of their journey was **incredible.** I was **incredulous** when I heard how much their trip cost.

individual, party Jargon when used to refer to a single person except when the person is being distinguished from a group or when used in legal writing. Who was that ~~individual~~ **person** I saw you with yesterday? I always thought Mrs. Smith was the guilty ~~party~~ **one.**

ingenious, ingenuous *Ingenious* means "creative or shrewd." *Ingenuous* means "innocent or unworldly": Terry's **ingenious** plan worked without complication. The criminal's **ingenuous** smile was misleading.

in regards to Unacceptable for *in regard to.*

inside of, outside of Wordy; use *inside* or *outside.*

irregardless Use *regardless.*

is when, is where *Because, when,* and *where* introduce adverbial clauses, and adverbial clauses cannot serve as subject complements. Revise the sentence or use a noun or noun clause instead: An essay ~~test is when~~ **requires** you **to** write answers in paragraphs. Economics ~~is where~~ **you the** study of money.

its, it's *Its* is a possessive pronoun, as in "The dog buried **its** bone." *It's* is a contraction of *it is,* as in "**It's** a beautiful day."

-ize An overused verb-forming suffix. Such recent coinages as *finalize, prioritize,* and *containerize* are generally unacceptable in college writing although they do appear in business writing.

kind, sort, type Used interchangeably. Singular forms are modified by *this* or *that,* plural forms by *these* or *those:* **This kind (sort, type)** of argument is unacceptable. **These kinds (sorts, types)** of arguments are unacceptable.

kind of a, sort of a Use *kind of* and *sort of:* This **kind of** ~~a~~ book sells well.

later, latter *Later* means "after a specific time," "a time after now"; *latter* refers to the second of two items: We will go **later.** Of the two versions, I prefer the **latter.**

lay, lie Use *lay* (*laid, laying*) in the sense of "put" or "place." Use *lie* (*lay, lain, lying*) in the sense of "rest" or "recline." *Lay* takes an object (to **lay** something), while *lie* does not. See also 7e.

| *Lay*—to put or place | He had **laid** the book on the table. | The man was **laying** the carpet. |
| *Lie*—to recline | He had **lain** down to take a nap. | The cat was **lying** on the bed. |

lead, led *Lead* has two meanings: as a noun, it means "a kind of metal," and as a verb, it means "to conduct." Use *led* for the past tense of the verb *lead:* After we **led** Joe to the old fountain, he asked us to **lead** him to some **lead** to use for repair.

learn Unacceptable for *teach, instruct, inform:* He **taught** me bowling.

leave Unacceptable for *let* in the sense of allowing: **Let** [NOT leave] him have the hammer.

lend, loan *Lend* is a verb meaning "to give temporarily." *Loan* is a noun meaning "something borrowed." In college writing, do not use *loan* as a verb: The banks **lend** money for mortgages. Most of us have student **loans** to repay.

less See **fewer, less.**

liable, likely *Liable* usually means "exposed" or "responsible" in an undesirable sense. *Likely* means "probably," "destined," or "susceptible": If you wreck the car, you are **liable** for damages. With her brains, she is **likely** to succeed.

like Although *like* is widely used as a conjunction in spoken English, *as, as if,* and *as though* are preferred for college English.

literally Often misused as an intensifier, *literally* means "actually" or "exactly as stated": I was ~~literally~~ **nearly** frozen after I shoveled snow for an hour.

lose, loose *Lose* is a verb: did **lose,** will **lose.** *Loose* is chiefly an adjective: a **loose** belt.

lots Conversational for *many, much.*

mankind Considered inappropriate because it excludes women. Use *humanity, human race.*

many, much *Many,* used with plural nouns, refers to numbers: **many** stores, too **many** cats. *Much,* used with singular nouns, refers to amount: **much** courage.

may be, maybe *May be* is a verb phrase; *maybe* is an adverb: The rumor **may be** true. **Maybe** the rumor is true.

may, can See **can, may.**

may of Use *may have.*

media, medium *Media* is plural: Some people think the **media** have sometimes created the news in addition to reporting it. *Medium* is singular: The newspaper is one **medium** that people seem to trust.

morale, moral *Morale* (a noun) refers to a mood or spirit: **Morale** was high. *Moral* (an adjective) refers to correct conduct or ethical character: a **moral** decision. *Moral* (as a noun) refers to the lesson of a story: the **moral** of the story.

most Use *almost* in expressions such as "almost everyone," "almost all." Use *most* only as a superlative: **most** writers.

much See **many, much.**

myself Use only when preceded by an antecedent in the same sentence: Li and **I** went swimming. BUT **I** made **myself** go swimming.

neither . . . nor, either . . . or Do not use *or* with *neither* or *nor* with *either.*

not . . . no/none/nothing Unacceptable when the two negatives have a negative meaning. I did **not** want ~~nothing~~ **anything** to do with them.

nothing like, nowhere near In college writing, use *not nearly:* My car is ~~nowhere near~~ **not nearly** as old as yours.

nowheres Unacceptable for *nowhere.*

number As subjects, *a number* is generally plural and *the number* is singular. Make sure that the verb agrees with the subject: **A number** of possibilities **are** open. **The number** of possibilities **is** limited. See also **amount of, number of.**

of Often mistaken for the sound of the unstressed *have:* They must ~~of~~ **have** [OR would **have**, could **have**, might **have**, ought to **have**, may **have**, should **have**, would **have**] gone home.

off of Use *off* in phrases such as "walked **off** ~~of~~ the field."

OK, O.K., okay Conversational usage. All three are acceptable spellings. It is usually better to replace *OK* with a more specific word.

on account of   Use the less wordy *because:* I went home ~~on account of being~~ **because I was** tired.

on the other hand   Use *however* or make sure this transitional phrase is preceded by "on the one hand."

ought   See **had ought.**

owing to the fact that   Wordy for *because.*

parameter   Overused and imprecise for "boundary," "perimeter."

party   See **individual.**

passed, past   *Passed* is the past tense of the verb *pass. Past* as a noun or adjective refers to a former time: We **passed** them in the street. Don't worry about **past** mistakes.

people, persons   In college writing, use *people* to refer to a general group, *person* to refer to an individual or group of individuals: A lot of **people** were at the concert last night. They will admit only one **person** at a time.

per   Used in business writing. Many writers reserve it for Latinisms such as *per capita, per se,* or *per cent/percent.*

percent, percentage   Use *percent* with a specific number: **60 percent.** Use *percentage* with an unspecified portion: The **percentage** of high school graduates attending college has increased in recent years.

phenomena   Plural form of *phenomenon.*

plenty   Conversational when used to mean *quite* or *sufficient* (as in "plenty good enough") or in place of *plenty of* (as in "plenty time").

plus   Acceptable as a preposition. Weak when used instead of the co-ordinating conjunction *and.* I telephoned ~~plus~~ **and** I sent flowers.

p.m.   See **a.m., p.m.**

practicable, practical   *Practicable* means "able to be put in to practice"; *practical* means "sensible," "useful": His plan was too complicated to be **practicable.** A colander is a **practical** utensil.

precede, proceed   To *precede* is to "go ahead of"; to *proceed* is to "go forward": His song will **precede** the fight scene. He will **proceed** with the song.

prejudice, prejudiced Use *prejudice,* a noun, when the word is the subject or an object; use *prejudiced,* an adjective, when the word modifies a noun or serves as a complement: **Prejudiced** people often are unaware of their **prejudices. Prejudice** is ugly in all its forms. She is not **prejudiced.**

pretty In college writing, *pretty* is not a qualifier. Unless the word means "attractive," use *quite, rather,* or *somewhat* instead: The mice were ~~pretty~~ **quite** tired after six hours in the maze.

previous to, prior to Wordy and pretentious for *before.*

principal, principle The adjective or noun *principal* means "chief" or "chief official." The noun may also mean "capital." The noun *principle* means "fundamental truth": The **principal** factor in the salary decision was his belief in the **principle** of sexual equality.

proceed See **precede, proceed.**

quotation, quote *Quotation* is a noun: You need a **quotation** here. *Quote* is a verb: He sometimes **quotes** lines from TV commercials.

raise, rear See **rear, raise.**

raise, rise Use *raise (raised, raising)* in the sense of "to lift or cause to move upward, to bring up or increase." Use *rise (rose, risen, rising)* in the sense of "to get up, to move or extend upward, ascend." *Raise* (a transitive verb) takes an object; *rise* (an intransitive verb) does not. See 7e.

> *Raise*—to lift   Retailers **raised** prices.
>
> *Rise*—to ascend   Retail prices **rose** sharply.

rarely ever Use either *rarely* alone or *hardly ever:* He **rarely** ~~ever~~ (or **hardly ever**) goes to the library.

real, really Use *real* as an adjective, *really* as an adverb. *Real* is often misused in expressions such as the following, where it is an adverb modifying the adjective *beautiful:* It is a ~~real~~ **really** beautiful day.

rear, raise *Rear* is preferred when speaking of bringing up children.

reason is because In college writing, substitute *that* for *because* or delete *reason is:* The reason the car won't start **is** ~~because~~ **that** the battery is dead. OR ~~The reason~~ The car won't start ~~is~~ **because** the battery is dead.

reason why　Redundant. Use *reason:* The **reason** I went home was that I was ill.

refer back　Redundant. Use *refer.*

regard, regarding, regards　Use *in regard to, with regard to,* or *regarding.*

relation, relationship　In college writing, use *relation* when linking things, *relationship* when linking people: We studied the **relation** between language and social change. My best friend and I were concerned about our **relationship.**

respectfully, respectively　*Respectfully* means "showing respect"; *respectively* means "in the order designated": I tried out a Chevy, a Ford, and a Plymouth, **respectively.** We always treated Ms. Bender **respectfully.**

sensuous, sensual　*Sensuous* refers to gratification of the senses in response to art, music, nature, and so on; *sensual* refers to gratification of the physical senses: Titian's paintings are very **sensuous.** A fine dinner can be a **sensual** experience.

shall, will　Traditionally *shall* was used with *I* or *we* to express future tense, and *will* was used with the other personal pronouns, but *shall* has almost disappeared in contemporary American English. *Shall* is still used in legal writing to convey obligation.

should, would　*Should* expresses obligation or condition: Students **should** not be rude in class. *Would* expresses wishes or habitual actions: If you **would** drive me to the library in Cedarville, I **would** have new books to read.

sit, set　Use *sit* in the sense of "be seated" and *set* in the sense of "to place something." *Set,* a transitive verb, takes an object. *Sit,* an intransitive verb, does not. See 7e.

Sit—be seated　　　　　Jonathon **sat** under the tree.

Set—place something　　Maria **set** the cookies on the table.

so　Overused as an intensifier; use a more precise modifier: She was ~~so~~ **intensely** focused.

some Conversational and vague when used as a substitute for such words as *remarkable, memorable:* She was ~~some~~ a remarkable athlete.

someplace Conversational for *somewhere.* The house is ~~someplace~~ **somewhere** in Kansas.

sometime, sometimes, some time *Sometime* is an adverb meaning "at an unspecified time"; *sometimes* is an adverb meaning "at times"; *some time* is an adjective-noun pair meaning "a span of time": Let's go to the movies **sometime. Sometimes** we go to the movies. They agreed to allow **some time** to pass before going to the movies together again.

sort, sort of See **kind, sort** and **kind of a, sort of a.**

stationary, stationery *Stationary* means "in a fixed position"; *stationery* means "writing paper and envelopes."

subsequently See **consequently.**

supposed to, used ~~to~~ In college writing, be sure to include the frequently unsounded *-d* at the end of these expressions.

sure Conversational when used as an adverb. Use *certainly* or *undoubtedly:* I ~~sure~~ **certainly** like your new hat.

sure and Use *sure to* instead: Be sure ~~and~~ **to** have the oil checked.

take See **bring, take.**

than, then Use *than* in comparisons: She is taller **than** I am. Use *then* in statements relating to time: I stopped and **then** I looked both ways.

that, which *That* has traditionally been used with a restrictive clause: The cup **that** is on the table is full [distinguishes a specific cup that is full]. *Which* has traditionally been used with a nonrestrictive clause: The cup, **which** is on the table, is full ["which is on the table" gives nonessential information]. Increasingly, however, writers are using these interchangeably and the distinction between them is becoming blurred. (See **12d.**)

their, there, they're, there're *Their* is the possessive form of *they; there* is ordinarily an adverb or an expletive; *they're* is a contraction of *they are; there're* is a contraction of *there are:* **There** is no explanation for **their** behavior. **They're** making trouble **there** on the ball field. **There're** no tickets left.

theirself, theirselves Use *themselves.*

them Unacceptable when used as an adjective; use *those* or *these* instead: ~~them~~ those apples.

then Sometimes incorrectly used for *than.* Unlike *then, than* does not relate to time: He's a better skater ~~then~~ than his brother.

these kind, these sort, these type, those kind See **kind, sort.**

they Unacceptable when used to indicate possession: They enjoyed ~~they~~ their vacation.

this here, that there, these here, them there Redundant; use *this, that, these, those.*

thru In college writing, spell out *through.*

thusly Use *thus.*

time period Redundant; use one word or the other, but not both.

to, too Distinguish the preposition *to* from the adverb *too:* When the weather is **too** hot to play ball, they go **to** the movies.

toward, towards Both acceptable. *Toward* is preferred in American usage.

try and Conversational for *try to:* I will **try ~~and~~ to** see him today.

type See **kind.**

unique Because it means "one of a kind," it is illogical to use *unique* with a comparative, as in *very unique.* Do not confuse with *unusual.*

uninterested See **disinterested.**

usage Not a substitute for *use of. Usage* refers to a customary practice and most often refers to language; *use of* refers to the employment of something: English teachers are concerned about verb **usage.** We had the **use of** the cabin for a week.

use to Should be *used to.*

utilize Often pretentious; *use* is preferred.

very Overused as an intensifier. Whenever possible, choose a stronger adjective or adverb: She was ~~very satisfied~~ **delighted** with her purchase.

wait on Unacceptable as a substitute for *wait for.*

ways Unacceptable for *way* when referring to distance: It's a long ~~ways~~ **way** from home.

well See **good, well.**

where Conversational as a substitute for *that:* I saw on TV ~~where~~ **that** she had been elected.

where . . . at, where . . . to Omit the superfluous *at, to:* **Where** is the library ~~at~~? **Where** are you moving ~~to~~?

which When referring to persons, use *who* or *that.* See **that, which.**

who, which, that *Who* refers to persons, *which,* to things. *That* generally refers to things but may refer to groups of people.

who, whom *Who* is used as the subject or subject complement in a clause, *whom* is used as an object: **Who** gave the money to **whom**?

whose, who's *Whose* indicates possession: **Whose** book is this? The mountain **whose** summit is over twelve thousand feet was difficult to climb. *Who's* is the contraction of *who is:* **Who's** going to the movie?

-wise An overused adverb-forming suffix. Business coinages such as *computerwise, advertisingwise,* or *cost-benefit-analysiswise* are generally unacceptable in college writing.

with regards to See **regard, regarding, regards.**

your, you're *Your* is the possessive of *you:* in **your** house. *You're* is a contraction of *you are:* **You're** gaining strength. See also **its, it's.**

Glossary of Terms

This glossary presents brief explanations of frequently used terms. Consult the index for references to further discussion of most of the terms and for a number of terms not listed.

@ The "at" sign that is part of every e-mail address; relates the user name to its internet location: <swebb@twu.edu>.

absolute phrase A grammatically unconnected part of a sentence—generally a noun or pronoun followed by a participle (and sometimes modifiers): We will have a cookout, **weather permitting** [noun + present participle]. **The national anthem sung for the last time,** the old stadium was closed [noun + past participle with modifier]. Some absolute phrases have the meaning (but not the structure) of an adverbial clause. See **1d(2)**, **24a**, and **30b(4)**. See also **phrase** and **sentence modifier.**

abstract A summary of the main points of a piece of writing, usually placed at the very beginning of the work.

abstract noun A noun that expresses qualities, concepts, and emotions that cannot be perceived through the senses: truth, justice, fear, future. See **20a(3)**.

accusative case See **case.**

acronym A word formed by combining the initial letters of a series of words: laser—*l*ight *a*mplification by *s*timulated *e*mission of *ra*diation, NASA—*N*ational *A*eronautics and *S*pace *A*dministration.

active voice The form of a verb indicating that the grammatical subject carries out the action: Emily *sliced* the ham. See chapter **7** and **29d(1)**. See also **passive voice, verb,** and **voice.**

adjective The part of speech modifying a noun or a pronoun. *Limiting adjectives* restrict the meaning of the words they modify: *that* pie, *its* leaves. *Descriptive adjectives* name a quality of a noun, including degrees of comparison: *red* shirt, *bigger* planes. *Proper adjectives* are derived from proper nouns: *Spanish* rice. See **9a**. Two or more adjectives separated by a comma, instead of by a coordinating conjunction, are referred to as *coordinate adjectives:* A *brisk, cold* walk. See **12c(2)**. *Interrogative adjectives* are used to ask questions: *Whose* book is it? See also **degree** and **predicate adjective**.

adjectival clause A subordinate clause used as an adjective: people *who bite their fingernails.* An adjectival clause may be restrictive. See **1e(2)**, **12d**, and **25a(3)**. See also **clause**.

adjectival phrase A phrase used as an adjective: The woman *carrying the large notebook* is my sister. See **1d(2)**. See also **phrase**.

adverb The part of speech modifying a verb, an adjective, or another adverb: *rapidly* approached, *too* bitter, *very graciously* accepted. An adverb may also modify a verbal, a phrase or clause, or the rest of the sentence: *Usually,* an artist does her best work when she is focusing *entirely* on the task at hand.

adverbial clause A subordinate clause used as an adverb. An adverbial clause may indicate time, place, cause, condition, concession, comparison, purpose, or result: *Although he is usually quiet* [concession], everyone listens to him *when he speaks* [time], *because he makes good suggestions* [cause]. See **1e(2)**, **12b(1)**, and **30b(1)**. See also **clause** and **conditional clause**.

adverbial conjunction See **conjunctive adverb**.

adverbial phrase A phrase used as an adverb. An adverbial phrase may indicate time, place, cause, condition, concession, comparison, purpose, or result. See **1d(2)** and **24a(2)**. See also **adverbial clause**.

agreement The correspondence in number and person of a subject and verb (*the dog barks, dogs bark*) or in number and gender of a pronoun and its antecedent (the *team* boarded *its* bus, the *members* carrying *their* bags). See chapter **6**.

allusion A brief, unexplained reference to a work or to a person, place, event, or thing that the writer expects the reader to be familiar with. See also **39a(1)**.

ambiguity The capability of being understood in two or more different ways: "Reading alone comforts me" could mean "*Reading by myself* comforts me" or "*Only reading* comforts me."

analogy A rhetorical device using the features of something familiar (and often concrete) to explain something unfamiliar (and often abstract), or similarities between things that are not usually associated.

analysis A separation of a whole into its constituent parts; for example, separating a literary work into its elements for study.

analytical reading A reader's active engagement by the writer's ideas and how those ideas are expressed, with attention to content and form.

angle brackets < > Used to enclose an Internet address to avoid interference from sentence punctuation.

antecedent A word or group of words that a pronoun refers to. The antecedent may follow (but usually precedes) the pronoun: *Pets* can be polite or rude, like *their* trainers. See chapter 28.

antonym A word that means the opposite of another: *follow* is the antonym for *lead.*

APA American Psychological Association. See 38h–i.

appeal The means of persuasion in argumentative writing; relies on reason, authority, and/or emotion.

appositive A noun or noun phrase placed next to or very near another noun or noun phrase to identify, explain, or supplement its meaning: Judith, *my friend.* Appositives may be restrictive. See 12d(2), 24a(3), 30b(4), and 30c(3).

appropriate Writing suitable for the audience, purpose, and occasion.

argument A kind of writing that uses various rhetorical strategies and appeals to convince the reader of the truth or falsity of a given proposition or thesis. See **appeal** and **thesis.**

article *The, a,* or *an* used as adjectives before nouns: *the* cups, *a* cup, *an* extra cup. *The* is a definite article. *A* (used before consonant sounds) and *an* (used before vowel sounds) are indefinite articles. See 22a.

audience The person or persons for whom the writing is intended. See 32a. A specific audience has considerable knowledge of the subject. A general (or diverse) audience consists of willing readers who are not experts on your topic.

auxiliary   A form of *be, have,* or *will* that combines with a verb to indicate voice, tense, or mood: *was* going, *had* gone, *will* go. Modals such as *will, would,* and *may* are also considered auxiliaries. See chapter 7 and 22b.

balanced sentence   A sentence with grammatically equal structures. See 29g.

bibliography   A list of books, articles, essays, or other material, usually on a particular subject.

binary   See **file.**

bookmark   To record the Internet address of a World Wide Web site you may wish to return to.

Boolean operator(s)   Words used to broaden or narrow computer database searches. These include *or, and, not,* and *near.* See page 542.

brainstorming   A method of generating ideas about a subject; involves listing ideas as they occur in a session of intensive thinking about the subject. See 32b.

browser   Software that finds and displays Web pages. Most browsers can display images as well as text.

bulletin board   An electronic message center.

cardinal number   See **number.**

case   The form or position of a noun or pronoun that shows its use or relationship to other words in a sentence. The three cases in English are the *subjective* (or nominative), which is usually the subject of a sentence; the *possessive* (or genitive), which indicates ownership; and the *objective* (or accusative), which functions as the object of a verb or preposition. See chapter 5 and 15a.

Oddly enough, a **hat** can keep your whole body warm [subjective].

Joe liked **Marilyn's** happy disposition [possessive].

Aaron bought a new **car** [objective].

cause and effect A rhetorical strategy by which a writer seeks to explain why something happened or what the results of a particular event or condition were or will be. See **32e(4)**.

CD-ROM Acronym for Compact Disk-Read Only Memory. CD-ROMs store large amounts of information—as much as 300,000 pages.

chat rooms Locations on the Internet where people who are online can have a conversation.

citation Notation (usually parenthetical) in a paper that refers to a source. See **38e(1)** and **38h(1)**.

chronological order The arrangement of events in a time sequence (usually the order in which they occurred).

claim A conclusion that a writer expects readers to accept. A claim should be supported by accurate and representative source material. See chapter **35**.

classification and division A rhetorical strategy in which a writer sorts elements into categories (*classification*) or breaks a topic down into its constituent parts to show how they are related (*division*). See **32e(6)**.

clause A sequence of related words within a sentence. A clause has both a subject and a predicate and functions either as an independent unit (*independent clause*) or as a dependent unit (*subordinate clause,* used as an adverb, an adjective, or a noun). See **1e** and chapter **24**. See also **sentence.**

I saw the moon. It was glowing brightly [sentences].

I saw the moon, for **it was glowing brightly** [independent clauses connected by a coordinating conjunction].

I saw the moon, **which was glowing brightly** [adjectival clause].

I saw the moon **because it was glowing brightly** [adverbial clause].

I saw **that the moon was glowing brightly** [noun clause—direct object].

cliché An expression that may once have been fresh and effective but that has become trite and worn out with overuse. See **20c**.

coherence The principle that all the parts of a piece of writing should stick together, one sentence leading to the next, each idea evolving from the previous one. See chapter **25** and **31b**.

collaborative writing A method of writing involving a cooperative effort between two or more persons.

collective noun A noun singular in form that denotes a group: *flock, jury, band, public, committee*. See **6a(8)**.

colloquialism A word or phrase characteristic of informal speech. "He's *grumpy*" is a colloquial expression describing an irritable person. See chapter **19b(1)**.

comma splice, comma fault A punctuation error in which two independent clauses are joined by a comma with no coordinating conjunction. See chapter **3**. Patricia went to the game, **and** her brother stayed home.

common gender A term applied to words that can refer to either sex (*parent, instructor, salesperson, people, anyone*). See **19d**.

common noun A noun referring to any or all members of a class or group (*woman, city, apple, holiday*) rather than to a specific member (*Susan B. Anthony, Las Vegas, Winesap, New Year's Day*). See **noun.**

comparative degree See **degree.**

comparison and contrast A rhetorical strategy in which the writer examines similarities and/or differences between two ideas or objects. See **32e(5)**.

complement A word or words used to complete the sense of a verb. Although the term may refer to a direct or indirect object, it usually refers to a subject complement, an object complement, or the complement of a verb like *be*. Susan is my *friend*. See **1b**.

complete predicate A simple predicate (a verb or verb phrase) with any objects, complements, or modifiers: We *ate the fresh homemade pie before the salad.* See **predicate.**

complete subject A simple subject (a noun or noun clause) with any modifiers: *Everyone at the picnic* liked the pie. See **1b**. See also **subject.**

complex sentence   A sentence containing one independent clause and at least one subordinate clause: *My neighbor noticed a stranger* [independent clause] *who looked suspicious* [subordinate clause]. See **1f(1)**, chapter **24**, and **30c(1)**. See also **clause.**

compound-complex sentence   A sentence containing at least two main clauses and one or more subordinate clauses: *When the lights went out* [subordinate clause], *there was no flashlight at hand* [independent clause], *so we sat outside and gazed at the stars* [independent clause]. See **1f(1)**. See also **clause.**

compound noun or compound adjective   Two or more nouns or adjectives that function as a single word: *northwest, milkshake, ice cream, brother-in-law; three-mile hike, school board policy.*

compound predicate   Two or more predicates having the same subject: Clara Barton *nursed the injured during the Civil War* and *later founded the American Red Cross.* See **2a** and **30c(2)**. See also **predicate.**

compound sentence   A sentence containing at least two independent clauses and no subordinate clause: *The water supply was dwindling* [independent clause], so *rationing became mandatory* [independent clause]. See **1f(1)**, **12a**, and **14a**. See also **clause.**

compound subject   Two or more subjects of the same verb: *Women, men,* and *children* call the crisis center.

concession   Agreeing with a point made by your opponent in response to your own argument. Doing so increases a writer's credibility, making the opposition more likely to agree with his or her argument.

conclusion   A sentence, paragraph, or group of paragraphs that brings a piece of writing to a satisfying close, usually by summarizing, restating, evaluating, asking a question, or encouraging the reader to continue thinking about the topic. See **33a(5)**.

concrete noun   Concrete nouns refer to things that can be experienced through the senses: *cologne, sunset, onions, thorns.* Concrete nouns make writing clear, vivid, and lively. COMPARE **abstract noun.**

conditional clause   An adverbial clause (beginning with such conjunctions as *if, unless, whether, provided*) expressing a real, imagined, or nonfactual condition: *If she does a good job,* I will pay her. See **7d**. See also **clause**.

conjugation   A set or table of the inflected forms of a verb that indicates tense, person, number, voice, and mood. See chapter **7**, pages 116–19.

conjunction   A part of speech (such as *and* or *although*) used to connect words, phrases, clauses, or sentences. *Coordinating conjunctions (and, but, or, nor, for, so, yet)* connect and relate words and word groups of equal grammatical rank: Color-blind people can usually see blue, *but* they may confuse red with green *or* with yellow. See **1c(7)** and chapter **26**. See also **correlatives.** *Subordinating conjunctions* (such as *although, if, when*—see the list on page 21) mark a dependent clause and connect it with a main clause: *When* Frank sulks, he acts *as if* he were deaf. See chapter **24**.

conjunctive adverb   A word (*however, therefore, nevertheless*) that serves not only as an adverb but also as a connective. See **3b**, **14a**, and **31b(3)**.

connective   A word or phrase that links and relates words, phrases, clauses, or sentences (*and, although, otherwise, finally, on the contrary, which, not only . . . but also*). Conjunctions, conjunctive adverbs, transitional expressions, relative pronouns, and correlatives function as connectives. See **31b(3)**.

connotation   The suggested or implied meaning of a word through the associations it evokes in the reader's mind. See **20a(2)**. See also **denotation.**

consonant   A class of speech sounds represented in English by any letter other than *a, e, i, o,* or *u.*

context   The surrounding information that helps give a particular word, sentence, or paragraph its meaning: *cabinet* means "a group of leaders" in a political context and "a place for storage" in a building context. *Context* also refers to circumstances surrounding the composition of a piece of writing—the occasion, the purpose, the audience, and what the writer and reader already understand about the topic. See **32a**.

contraction Condensing two words into one by adding an apostrophe to replace the omitted letter or letters: *aren't, don't*. Contractions are used primarily in spoken or colloquial written language.

contrast See **comparison and contrast**.

controlling idea The central idea of a paragraph or essay, often expressed in the paragraph's **topic sentence** or the essay's **thesis** statement. See **31a** and **32c**.

conventional Language that complies with the rules of written English as accepted by the academic and business communities, generally termed *correct*.

coordinating adjective See **adjective**.

coordinating conjunction One of seven connectives: *and, but, for, or, nor, so, yet*. See **1c(7)**, **12a**, chapter **24**, and chapter **26**. See also **conjunction**.

coordination The use of grammatically equivalent constructions to link ideas, usually (but not always) those of equal weight. See **12c(2)**, **24b**, and chapter **26**.

correlatives One of five pairs of linked connectives: *both . . . and; either . . . or; neither . . . nor; not only . . . but also; whether . . . or*. Correlatives link equivalent constructions: *both* Jane *and* Fred; *not only* in Peru *but also* in Mexico. See **26c**.

count, noncount nouns Individual, countable entities; cannot be viewed as a mass (*word, finger, remark*). Noncount nouns are a mass or a continuum (*hope, water*). See **1c(2)** and **noun**.

credibility The reliability of a person or evidence. See **35d**.

critical thinking/reading/writing The ability to analyze and synthesize ideas: to distinguish between fact and opinion, to recognize the importance of evidence and logic, to evaluate for credibility, and to avoid common fallacies. See chapter **35**.

cumulative sentence A sentence in which the subject and predicate come first, followed by modifiers. (Also called a *loose sentence*.) See **29b**.

cyberspace   William Gibson's term for virtual environments, now used generally to refer to the Internet.

dangling modifier   A word or phrase that does not clearly refer to another word or word group in the sentence. Even though ~~arriving~~ **we arrived** at the theater early, the movie started late. See 25b.

data   Accepted fact or evidence. In computer language, information stored in computer-readable form.

database   A kind of electronic filing system. Computer databases are usually organized hierarchically so that computers can find information more quickly. An *electronic database system* is a group of databases such as *Dialog* or *CARL Uncover.* Most such systems are *retrieval* databases—users can get information from them but cannot add to them.

declarative sentence   See **sentence.**

declension   A set or table of inflected forms of nouns or pronouns. See the examples on page 74.

deduction   A form of logical reasoning that begins with a generalization (*premise*), relates a specific fact to that generalization, and forms a *conclusion* that fits both. See 35f. COMPARE **induction.**

definition   A brief explanation of the meaning of a word, as in a dictionary. Also, an extended piece of writing, employing a variety of rhetorical strategies, to explain what something is or means. See 32e(7).

degree   The form of an adverb or adjective that indicates relative quality, quantity, or manner. The three degrees are *positive,* a quality of a single element; *comparative,* between two elements; and *superlative,* among three or more elements. Examples of sets of degree include *good, better, best* and *fast, faster, fastest.* See 4c.

demonstratives   Four words that point out (*this, that, these, those*): **Those** are as good as **these** [pronouns]. **Those** curtains have never been cleaned [adjective].

denotation   The literal meaning of a word as commonly defined. See 20a(1). See also **connotation.**

dependent clause   A subordinate clause. See **clause.**

description A rhetorical strategy using details perceivable by the senses to portray a scene, object, performance, and so on. See **32e(2)**.

determiner A word (such as *a, an, the, my, their*) that signals the approach of a noun: **the** newly mown *hay.*

development The elaboration of an idea through organized discussion filled with examples, details, and other information. See **31c**.

dialect A variety of language characteristic of a region or culture. Dialects are distinguished by vocabulary, pronunciation, and/or syntax: British English, Low German, Cantonese. See **19b(3)**.

dial-up access Refers to using a modem and a telephone line to connect a computer to a network.

diction The writer's choice of exact, idiomatic, and fresh words, as well as appropriate levels of usage. See chapters **19** and **20**.

direct address A name or descriptive term (set off by commas) designating the one or ones spoken to: Play it again, *Sam.*

direct discourse See **direct quotation.**

direct object A noun (or noun clause) naming *whom* or *what* after an active verb: Emily sliced the *ham.* See **1b(2)**. See also **object.**

direct quotation A repetition of the exact spoken or written words of others: "Where an opinion is general," writes Jane Austen, "it is usually correct." See **16a** and **38d**.

discussion list See **Listserv.**

documentation The citing of sources in a research paper to conform to a given style, such as MLA or APA. See chapter **38**.

domain name Part of an Internet address. Domain names consist of at least two elements, the host name and the domain, separated by dots, for example, *university.edu.* The Internet is organized into seven domains: commerce (.com), education (.edu), government (.gov), military (.mil), network management (.net), nonprofit organizations (.org), and the designations for other countries (.de for Germany, .uk for the United Kingdom, and so on).

double negative   The nonstandard combination of two negatives, which has a negative meaning: We ca*n't* do *nothing* about the weather. See **4e**.

download   Transferring files from the Internet to your computer and saving them.

draft, drafting   A working version of a piece of writing. The process of putting ideas into writing so they can be revised and edited. See **32e–f**.

edited American English (EAE)   The term adopted by the National Council of Teachers of English for the academic and business style expected in most college writing. EAE observes conventional rules of spelling, punctuation, mechanics, grammar, and sentence structure.

editing   Reworking sentences for clarity, sense, and conformity to conventional rules of spelling, punctuation, mechanics, grammar, and sentence structure.

electronic mail   See **e-mail.**

electronic resources   Online research tools that enable the computer user to access publicly available information. These may include CD-ROM, databases, and Internet access. See **CD-ROM, database, e-mail,** and **World Wide Web.**

electronic sites   Publicly available computer files that can be accessed through the Internet.

ellipsis   Three spaced periods that indicate material omitted from a quotation. See **17i**.

elliptical construction   The omission of an element essential to the grammar but not to the intended meaning: Cats are cleaner than pigs [are].

e-mail   Electronic mail; transfers messages over a communications network. E-mail may be limited to a single network but most often refers to messages sent via the Internet.

emoticon   A small icon made up of punctuation characters. It shows how a sender wants a message to be interpreted; e.g., a smiling emoticon (for example, :-), often called a smiley) indicates a joke.

emphasis   Special weight or importance given to a word, sentence, or paragraph by any of a variety of techniques. It may also mean stress applied to one or more syllables in a word. See chapters 29 and 18, respectively.

essay   A brief piece of nonfiction writing on a single topic in which a writer typically states the thesis in the introduction, develops several points in support of that thesis, and concludes.

ethos   Can be translated as "arguing honorably" and is employed when you tell others the truth and treat them with respect. See page 507, **logos,** and **pathos.**

etymology   The origin and historical development of a word; its derivation.

euphemism   An indirect or "nice" expression used instead of a more direct one: *correctional facility* instead of *jail.* See 20c.

evaluation   The process of finding and judging useful passages from source material. See chapter 37c.

evidence   Facts, statistics, examples, testimony, sensory details, and so on that support generalizations.

example   Any fact, anecdote, reference, or the like used to illustrate an idea. See 31c.

expletive   A signal of a transformation in the structure of a sentence that occurs without changing the meaning. The expletive *there* shifts the order of subject and verb in a sentence: *There* were over four thousand runners in the marathon. [COMPARE Over four thousand runners were in the marathon.] The expletive *it* transforms the main clause into a subordinate clause: It is apparent that the plane is late. [COMPARE Apparently, the plane is late.] See 6a(5).

expository writing   See **referential writing.**

expressive writing   Writing that emphasizes the writer's own feelings and reactions to a topic. See 32a(1).

fact   A reliable piece of information that can be verified through independent sources or procedures. A **fact** differs from an **opinion.** See **opinion.**

fallacy   A false argument or incorrect reasoning. See 35h.

FAQs or FAQ   Abbreviation for frequently asked questions. Usually an online archive containing answers to common questions about the purpose of an online service or program and methods of using it.

faulty predication   The use of a predicate that does not logically belong with a given subject: One superstition ~~is~~ **involves** a black cat. [The superstition is the belief about the cat, not the cat itself.] See **23d**.

figurative language   The use of words in an imaginative rather than a literal sense. See **20a(4)**.

file   A collection of computer-readable information. *Binary* files contain information readable only by computers unless the file is decoded. People can read *text* files (often called ASCII files) without having to decode them.

finite verb   A verb form that can function as the only verb in the predicate of a sentence: They *ate* a can of pork and beans. Verb forms classified as gerunds, infinitives, or participles cannot. See **predicate.** COMPARE **verbal.**

first person   See **person.**

flaming   Heated, confrontational exchanges on e-mail.

focus   The narrowing of a subject to a manageable size; also the sharpening of the writer's view of the subject. See **32b–c.**

formal writing style   The style of writing accepted in college and professional settings. You should consider the rhetorical situation (your audience, purpose, and occasion) to determine whether a college/professional style or a colloquial style is needed. You should master a style employing edited American English for most college and business writing. See chapter **19** and **32a.**

fragment   A group of words that begins with a capital letter and ends with a period but that lacks a subject, a predicate, or both. See chapter **2.**

freewriting   A method of finding a writing topic by composing for a specified length of time without stopping to reflect, reread, or correct errors.

freeware   Software available free of charge. Freeware programs are often available for downloading from the Internet; however, the computer user should be aware of the potential for downloading files infected with a computer virus. See **virus.**

FTP   Abbreviation for File Transfer Protocol. People use FTP for transferring files on the Internet.

function words   Words (such as prepositions, conjunctions, auxiliaries, and articles) that indicate the functions of other words in a sentence and the grammatical relationships between them.

fused sentence   Two or more sentences run together, with no punctuation or conjunctions to separate them. Also called a run-on sentence. Unacceptable in college and professional writing. See chapter 3. Patricia went to the game, **but** her brother stayed home.

gender   The grammatical distinction that labels nouns or pronouns as masculine, feminine, or neuter. In English, grammatical gender usually corresponds to natural gender.

general/specific, generalization   *General* words are all-embracing, indefinite, sweeping in scope: *food. Specific* words are precise, explicit, limited in scope: *spaghetti carbonara*. The same is true of *general* and *specific* ideas and of statements often called *generalizations* or *generalities*.

generalization   In argument, a conclusion drawn from facts and/or other evidence. Often used loosely to refer to statements that are too broad, indefinite, or sweeping in scope.

genitive case   See **case.**

gerund   A verbal that ends in *-ing* and functions as a noun. *Riding* a bike is good exercise.

grammar   The system of rules by which words are arranged into the structures meaningful in a language.

graphics   Images or pictures that can be displayed on a computer screen.

hardware   In computer terminology, the tangible components of the computer system such as the keyboard, the monitor, and the components inside the system box.

helping verb   A verb that combines with another verb to indicate voice, tense, or mood. See **7a**, **auxiliary**, and **modal**.

historical present   A tense used to describe events in literature or history that are permanently preserved in the present: The tragedy *is* that Iago *deceives* Othello. See **7c(1)** and **39a**.

home page   The introductory page for a Web site.

homophones   Words that have the same sound and sometimes the same spelling but differ in meaning (*their, there,* and *they're* or *capital* meaning funds and *capital* meaning government city). See **18c**.

HTML   Abbreviation for HyperText Markup Language, the system of codes embedded in a text whereby a browser can display that text as well as any accompanying images.

hyperbole   An intentional overstatement made for rhetorical effect. See **39a(5)**. COMPARE **understatement**.

hyperlink   Also called a hotlink. See **link**.

hypertext   Text encoded in HTML that is linked within a Web site and/or outside it.

idiom   A fixed expression (within a language) whose meaning cannot be deduced from its elements: *put up a fight; to mean well.* See **20b**.

illustration   In writing, the use of specific details to give substance and interest to a subject. See **31c**.

imperative mood   See **mood**.

inclusive language   The use of language in such a way that no group of people is ignored, insulted, or condescended to. It is an answer to sexist, racist, and classist language. See **19d**.

indefinites   The article *a* or *an* (*a* banana, *an* insect), as well as pronouns (*anyone, everybody*) and adjectives (*any* car, *few* problems, *several* questions) that do not specify distinct limits.

independent clause   See **clause**.

indicative mood   See **mood**.

indirect discourse   Information paraphrased or summarized from a source and, with attribution, integrated into a writer's own sentence.

indirect object   A word (or words) naming the one (or ones) indirectly affected by the action of the verb: Emily sliced *me* some ham. See **object.**

indirect question   A question phrased as a statement, usually a subordinate clause: We can ask *whether Milton's blindness was the result of glaucoma,* but we cannot be sure of the answer. See 27c.

indirect quotation   A report of the written or spoken words of another without using the exact words of the speaker or writer: The registrar said *that the bank returned my tuition check.* COMPARE **direct quotation.**

induction   A form of logical reasoning that begins with evidence and interprets it to form a conclusion. See 35e. COMPARE **deduction.**

infinitive   Usually made up of the word *to* plus the present form of a verb (called the *stem* of the infinitive). Infinitives are used chiefly as nouns, less frequently as adjectives or adverbs. They may have subjects, objects, complements, or modifiers: Lashanda wanted *to continue* the debate. [*Debate* is the object of the infinitive *to continue; to continue the debate* is the object of the verb *wanted.*]

infinitive phrase   A phrase that employs the infinitive form of the verb: *to go to the store, to run the race.* See **phrase.**

inflection   A change in the form of a word to show a specific meaning or grammatical function: **verb:** *talk, talks, talked;* **noun:** *dog, dogs, dog's, dogs';* **pronoun:** *he, him, his; they, them, their, theirs;* **adjective:** *thin, thinner, thinnest;* **adverb:** *rapidly, more rapidly, most rapidly.*

informal writing style   The style generally accepted for personal letters and other kinds of self-expression, but not generally appropriate in college writing; words or phrases that dictionaries label **informal, colloquial,** or **slang.** See chapter 19 and **formal writing style.**

informative writing   See **referential writing.**

intensifier   A modifier used for emphasis: *very* excited, *certainly* pleased. See **qualifier.**

intensive/reflexive pronoun   The *-self* pronouns (such as *myself, himself, themselves*). The *intensive* is used for emphasis: The teenagers *themselves* had the best idea. The *reflexive* is used as an object of a verb, verbal, or preposition: He blames *himself;* she bought a present for *herself.* An intensive or reflexive pronoun always refers to another noun or pronoun in the same sentence that denotes the same individual or individuals.

interjection   A word (one of the eight parts of speech) expressing a simple exclamation: *Hey! Oops!* (See **17c**.) When used in sentences, mild interjections are set off by commas: *Oh,* excuse me.

Internet   An international network of computers linked through telephone and fiber-optic lines that provides access to e-mail and the World Wide Web, among other things.

interpretation   Use of inductive reasoning to help understand facts in order to reach probable and believable conclusions and avoid sweeping conclusions that can be easily challenged. See **35e**.

interrogative   A word like *which, whose,* or *why* used to ask a question: *Which* is the more expensive? [pronoun] *Whose* lights are on? [adjective] *Why* are treasury bills a good investment? [adverb]

interrogative adjective   See **adjective.**

intransitive verb   A verb (such as *appear* or *belong*) that does not take an object: Sarah *ran* fast. See chapter **7**. See also **verb** and **transitive verb.**

introduction   The beginning of an essay, often a single paragraph, that engages the reader's interest and indicates, usually by stating the thesis, what the essay is about. See **33a(4)**.

invention   The process of using strategies to generate ideas for writing. See **32b** and **32e**.

inversion   A change in the usual word order of a sentence: Into the valley of death rode the six hundred. See **29f**.

IRC   Abbreviation for Internet relay chat, that is, chat rooms.

irony   A deliberate inconsistency between what is stated and what is meant. Irony can be verbal or situational. See **20a(4)**.

irregular verb   A verb that is not inflected in the usual way—that is, by the addition of -*d* or -*ed* to the present form to create the past tense and past participle. Examples include *begin, began, begun* and *lend, lent, lent.*

ISP Abbreviation for Internet service provider, a service that connects subscribers to the Internet.

jargon Technical slang, appropriate as a shortcut to communication when the audience is knowledgeable about the topic and the terms; it should be avoided in writing not intended for a specialized audience. See **19b(6)**.

journal A special-interest periodical (*Rhetoric Review, Environmental Legislation*). Also a notebook in which a writer records personal thoughts and experiences.

journaling Keeping a **journal.**

justification Inserting spaces between words so that every line is the same length and makes the right or left margin, or both margins, straight.

link A World Wide Web address that is embedded in a document and that allows users to move within a Web site or between sites by clicking on it; usually identified by color and underlining.

linkage data Information about links to and from a Web document; may be pertinent in evaluating an electronic source.

linking verb A verb that relates the subject complement to the subject. Words commonly used as linking verbs are *become, seem, appear, feel, look, taste, smell, sound,* and forms of the verb *be:* She *is* a writer. The bread *looks* burned. See **7a**.

listing An informal way of gathering ideas about a writing topic in which a writer lists any ideas he or she has about the subject. See pages 405–06.

Listserv A list of e-mail addresses to which messages can be automatically broadcast as if they were sent to a single user: a *discussion list* or a *mailing list.*

logic The presentation of ideas that shows a clear, predictable, and structured relationship among those ideas. See chapters **23** and **35**.

logical operator(s) See **Boolean operator(s).**

logos The logical use of language in effective arguments. See page 507, **ethos,** and **pathos.**

loose sentence   See **cumulative sentence.**

main clause   See **clause.**

main idea   The part of the paragraph or paper to which all the other ideas relate. See **32c, topic sentence,** and **thesis.**

mechanics   The form of words and letters, such as capitals, italics, abbreviations, acronyms, and numbers.

metaphor   An imaginative comparison between dissimilar things without using *like* or *as.* Frank is a *snake.* See **20a(4)** and **39a(5).**

misplaced modifier   A descriptive or qualifying word (modifier) placed in an awkward position, usually far away from what it modifies: I read that there was a big fire *in yesterday's newspaper.* I read in yesterday's newspaper that there was a big fire. [Place the modifier after the verb *read.*] Sometimes a misplaced modifier confuses the reader because it could qualify either of two words: To do one's best *sometimes* is not enough. *Sometimes* to do one's best is not enough. To do one's best is *sometimes* not enough. [Place the adverb closer to the verb.] See **25a.**

mixed construction   A garbled sentence that is the result of an unintentional shift from one grammatical pattern to another. *She is the woman wants to work here.* [Faulty combination of "She is the woman" and "The woman wants to work here" results in an unintentional shift.] See **23c(2).**

mixed metaphor   A construction that confuses two or more metaphors: He was *playing with fire* and got in *over his head.* See **23c(1).**

MLA   Modern Language Association. See **38e–f.**

modal   A helping verb (not conjugated) that shows ability (*can, could*); permission or possibility (*may, might*); determination, promise, or intention (*shall, should; will, would*); obligation (*ought*); or necessity (*must*).

modem   Acronym for *mo*dulator-*dem*odulator. A modem is a device that allows a computer to transmit data over telephone lines.

modifier   A word or word group that describes, limits, or qualifies another: a *true* statement, walked *slowly,* yards *filled with rocks,* the horse *that jumped the fence.* See chapters **4** and **25.**

MOO Multiple user dimension, Object Oriented; a text-based on-line space where many people can communicate simultaneously at scheduled times.

mood The way a speaker or writer regards an assertion—that is, as a declarative statement or a question (*indicative* mood); as a command or request (*imperative*); or as a supposition, hypothesis, recommendation, or condition contrary to fact (*subjunctive*). Verb forms indicate mood. See **7d(2)**.

narration A rhetorical strategy that recounts a sequence of events, usually in chronological order. See **32e(1)**.

netiquette Guidelines for proper behavior in e-mail correspondence, chat rooms, and so on.

network A group of two or more linked computer systems.

newsgroup An Internet discussion group that is accessible to anyone and that allows people to post messages about a specific topic.

nominalization The practice of using nouns instead of active verbs: She *made a list* of the schedule changes. [COMPARE She *listed* the schedule changes.] Excessive nominalization produces a wordy style.

nominative case See **case.**

nonfinite verb A verb form (verbal) used as a noun, adjective, or adverb. A nonfinite verb cannot stand as the only verb in a sentence. *To err* is human. *Seeing* is *believing.* See **1d** and **2a.** See also **verbal.**

nonrestrictive A word or word group set off by commas that is not necessary to the meaning of the sentence (parenthetical) and that can be omitted: My best friend, *Pauline,* understands me. See **12d.**

nonstandard Speech forms that are common in colloquial writing but that should be avoided in college and business writing. See **19b(4).**

noun A part of speech that names a person, place, thing, idea, animal, quality, or action: *Mary, America, apples, justice, goose, strength, departure.* A noun usually changes form to indicate the plural and the possessive case, as in *man, men; man's, men's.* See **1c(2).**

noun clause A subordinate clause used as a noun. See 1e. See also **clause.**

number The inflectional form of a word that identifies it as singular (one) or plural (more than one): *river–rivers, this–those, he sees–they see.* See 6a and 18e. *Cardinal numbers* express quantity: *two* (*2*), *thirty-five* (*35*). *Ordinal numbers* indicate order or rank: *second* (*2nd*), *thirty-fifth* (*35th*).

object A noun or noun substitute governed by an active verb, a verbal, or a preposition. See 1b(2–3) and 1c(6). Bill hit the **ball** [direct object]. She likes to grow **flowers** [object of a verbal]. I gave **him** the keys [indirect object]. They play ball in the **park** [object of a preposition].

object complement A word that helps complete the meaning of such verbs as *make, paint, elect, name.* An object complement refers to or modifies the direct object: They painted the cellar door *blue.* See 1b(3) and 4a. See also **complement.**

objective case See **case.**

online Connected to or having access to the Internet.

online server A server available for remote access. A server is a machine that houses software for delivering information on a *network.* See **network.**

opinion An idea that may or may not be based on fact. See 35b.

ordinal number See **number.**

overgeneralization Lacking specificity. See **general/specific, generalization.**

paradox A statement that seems contradictory but that may actually be true: "darkness visible," wise fool. See 39a(5).

paragraph Usually a group of related sentences unified by a single idea or purpose but occasionally as brief as a single sentence. The central, or controlling, idea of a paragraph is often explicitly stated in a *topic sentence.* A paragraph is marked by the indention of its first line or some other defining device.

parallelism The use of corresponding grammatically equal elements in sentences and paragraphs. It aids the flow of a sentence, making it read smoothly, and also emphasizes the relationship of the ideas in the parallel elements. We won *by practicing regularly* and *by playing well* [parallel prepositional phrases]. See chapter 26.

paraphrase A sentence-by-sentence restatement of the ideas in a passage, using different words. See 38c(3).

parenthetical documentation See **documentation.**

parenthetical element Nonessential words, phrases, clauses, or sentences (such as an aside) usually set off by commas but often by dashes or parentheses to mark pauses and intonation: *In fact,* the class, *a hardworking group of students,* finished the test quickly. See 12d, 17e(2), and 17f.

participle A verb form that may function as part of a verb phrase (was *thinking,* had *determined*) or as a modifier (a *determined* effort; the couple, *thinking* about their past). Participles may take objects, complements, and modifiers: The stagehand *carrying the trunk* fell over the threshold. [The participle *carrying* takes the object *trunk;* the whole participial phrase modifies *stagehand.*] See 7b(3) and 25b(1).

particle A word like *across, away, down, for, in, off, out, up, with* combined with a verb to form idiomatic usages in which the combination has the force of a single-word verb: The authorities refused to *put up* with him.

parts of speech The classes into which words may be grouped according to their form changes and grammatical relationships. The traditional parts of speech are *verbs, nouns, pronouns, adjectives, adverbs, prepositions, conjunctions,* and *interjections.* Each of these is discussed separately in this glossary. See also 1c.

passive voice The form of the verb showing that its subject is not the agent performing the action of the verb but is rather the goal of that action: The ham *was sliced* by Emily. See chapter 7 and 29d(1). See also **active voice.**

password A sequence of characters and/or numbers that allows a user access to an Internet service account, an informational Web site, a special-topic forum, and so on. Passwords are intended to provide security against unauthorized access.

pathos   The use of language in effective arguments to stir the feelings of an audience. See page 507, **ethos,** and **logos.**

pentad   A method of exploring a subject. The pentad considers the five dramatic aspects: the act, the actor, the scene, the agency (means), and the purpose (reason).

perfect tenses   The tenses formed by the addition of a form of *have* and showing complex time relationships in completing the action of the verb (the present perfect—*have/has eaten;* the past perfect—*had eaten;* and the future perfect—*will/shall have eaten*).

periodic sentence   A sentence in which the main idea comes last. See **29b**. COMPARE **cumulative sentence.**

person   The form of pronouns and verbs denoting or indicating whether one is speaking (*I am*—first person), is spoken to (*you are*—second person), or spoken about (*he is*—third person). In the present tense, a verb changes its form to agree grammatically with a third-person singular subject (*I watch, she watches*). See **6a** and **27b**.

personal pronoun   Any one of a group of pronouns—*I, we, you, he, she, it, they,* and their inflected forms—referring to the one (or ones) speaking, spoken to, or spoken about. See chapter **5.**

personification   The attributing of human characteristics to non-human things (animals, objects, ideas): "That night wind was breathing across me through the spokes of the wheel."   —WALLACE STEGNER. See **39a(5)**.

perspective   The manner in which a topic is addressed. A perspective can be static (still, frozen), dynamic (moving, radiating), or relative (compared to others).

persuasive writing   A form of writing intended chiefly to change the reader's opinions or attitudes or to arouse the reader to action. See **32a(1)**.

phrasal verb   A unit consisting of a verb plus one or two uninflected words like *after, in, up, off,* or *out* (see **particle**) and having the force of a single-word verb: We *ran out* on them.

phrase   A sequence of grammatically related words without a subject and/or a predicate. See **1d** and **2a**. See also **verbal.**

plagiarism   The use of another writer's words or ideas without acknowledging the source. Akin to theft, plagiarism has serious consequences and should always be avoided. See 38d.

plural   More than one. COMPARE **singular.**

pointing device   A device used to control the cursor (or pointer) on the display screen. To control the cursor with a *mouse,* the user rolls a small box-like device across a hard surface. The user turns a ball resting in a stationary holder to operate a *trackball* and moves a finger across a sensitive pad to use a *touchpad.*

point of view   The vantage point from which the topic is viewed. See 27e. It also refers to the stance a writer takes—objective or impartial (third person), directive (second person), or personal (first person).

positive   See **degree.**

possessive case   See **case.**

predicate   A basic grammatical division of a sentence. A predicate is the part of the sentence comprising what is said about the subject. The *complete predicate* consists of the main verb and its auxiliaries (the *simple predicate*) and any complements and modifiers: We *chased the dog all around our grandmother's farm.* [*Chased* is the simple predicate; *chased* and all the words that follow make up the complete predicate.]

predicate adjective   The adjective following a linking verb and modifying the subject. The bread tastes *sweet.* See 4a and **linking verb.**

predicate noun   A noun used as a subject complement: Bromides are *sedatives.* See 1b(3). See also **linking verb.**

predication   The act of stating or expressing something about the subject. See **faulty predication.**

prefix   An added syllable or group of syllables (such as *in-, dis-, un-, pro-*) placed before a word to form a new word: *adequate–inadequate.* A prefix ordinarily changes the meaning.

premise   An assumption or a proposition on which an argument or explanation is based. In logic, premises are either major (general) or minor (specific); when combined correctly, they lead to a conclusion. See 35f. See also **syllogism.**

preposition   A part of speech that links and relates a noun or noun substitute to another word in the sentence: The dancers leapt *across* the stage. [The preposition *across* connects and relates *stage* (its object) to the verb *leapt*.] See page 19 for a list of prepositions.

prepositional phrase   A preposition with its object and any modifiers: *in the hall, between you and me, for the new van.*

prewriting   The initial stage of the writing process, concerned primarily with planning.

primary source   In research or bibliographies, the source that provides firsthand facts.

principal parts   The forms of a verb that indicate the various tenses: the present (*give, jump*); the past (*gave, jumped*); and the past participle (*given, jumped*). See **7a**.

process, process writing   See **writing process.**

process analysis   A rhetorical strategy either to instruct the reader how to perform a procedure or to explain how something occurs. See **32e(3)**.

progressive verb   A verb phrase consisting of a present participle (ending in *-ing*) used with a form of *be* and denoting continuous action: *is attacking, will be eating.*

pronoun   A part of speech that takes the position of nouns and functions as nouns do. See **1c(3)**, chapter **5**, **6a**, **6b**, and chapter **28**.

proofreading   Checking the final draft of a paper to eliminate typographic, spelling, punctuation, and documentation errors. See **8d** and **33d**.

proper adjective   See **adjective.**

proper noun   See **noun.**

purpose   A writer's reason for writing. The purpose for nonfiction writing may be predominantly expressive, expository, or persuasive, though all three aims are likely to be present in some measure. See **32a**. See also **expressive writing, persuasive writing, and referential writing.**

qualifier   Any modifier that describes or limits: *Sometimes* movies are *too* gory to watch. Frequently, however, the term refers only to those modifiers that restrict or intensify the meaning of other words. See **intensifier.**

quotation   The exact words of another person repeated or copied. See **16a** and **38c(2)**.

reading preview   To scan a piece of writing for the main ideas. Critical readers use this method to scan a reading assignment quickly to determine an assignment's main purpose, thereby allowing them to think about it critically.

reciprocal pronoun   One of two compound pronouns expressing an interchangeable or mutual action or relationship: *each other* or *one another.*

record   A set of related information usable by a computer.

redundant   Needlessly repetitious, unnecessary.

referential writing   Writing whose chief aim is to clarify, explain, or evaluate a subject in order to inform or instruct the reader. Also called expository or informative writing. See **32a**.

reflexive pronoun   See **pronoun.**

refutation   Introducing reasons why others may believe differently followed by an explanation showing why these reasons are not convincing. See pages 513–14.

regular verb   A verb that forms its past tense and past participle by adding *-d* or *-ed* to the present form (or the stem of the infinitive): *love, loved; laugh, laughed.* See chapter **7**.

relative clause   An adjectival clause introduced by a relative pronoun: the programs *that provide services;* the teacher *who gives all A's.*

relative pronoun   A noun substitute (*who, whom, whose, that, which, what, whoever, whomever, whichever, whatever*) used to introduce subordinate clauses: He has an aunt **who** *is a principal* [adjectival clause introduced by the relative pronoun *who*]. OR **Whoever** *becomes treasurer* must be honest [noun clause introduced by the relative pronoun *whoever*]. See chapter **5**.

restrictive   A word, phrase, or clause that limits the word referred to by imposing conditions or by confining the word to a particular group or to a specific item or individual: Every student *who cheats* will be removed from the class. [The restrictive clause *who cheats* imposes conditions on—restricts—the meaning of *every student.* Only those students *who cheat* will be removed.] See **12d**. See also **nonrestrictive.**

retrieval database   A database system that allows users to search by keyword, author, or title and that may often provide the full text of a document.

revision   Part of the writing process. Writers revise by rereading and rethinking a piece of writing to see where they need to add, delete, move, replace, reshape, and even completely recast ideas.

rhetoric   The art of using language effectively. Rhetoric involves the writer's **purpose** (**32a**), the **audience** (**32a**), the discovery and exploration of a subject (**32b–c**), its arrangement and organization (**32d–e**), the style and tone in which it is expressed (**32a**), and the form in which it is delivered (chapter **8** and **32a**).

rhetorical question   A question posed for effect without expectation of a reply: Who can tell what will happen?

rhetorical situation   The relationship between the writer, the audience, and the context that determines the appropriate approach for a particular piece of writing.

run-on sentence   See **fused sentence.**

search engine   A program that searches documents for a specific word (keyword) and returns a list of all documents containing that word.

secondary source   A source that analyzes or interprets **primary source** material.

sentence   A grammatically independent unit of expression. A simple sentence contains a subject and a predicate. Sentences are classified according to structure (simple, complex, compound, and compound-complex) and purpose (declaratory, interrogatory, imperative, exclamatory). See chapter **1**.

sentence modifier   An adverb or adverb substitute that modifies the rest of the sentence, not a specific word or word group in it: *All things considered,* Middle America is a good place to live. OR *Yes,* the plane arrived on time.

server A computer that manages network resources; for example, a Web server, a network server, or a mail server.

sexist language Language that arbitrarily excludes one sex or the other or that arbitrarily assigns stereotypical roles to one sex or the other: A secretary should keep *her* desk tidy. [COMPARE Secretar*ies* should keep *their* desks tidy.] See **6b(1)**, **19d**, and **inclusive language.**

simile The comparison of two dissimilar things using *like* or *as.* Frank is as trustworthy *as a snake.* See **20a(4)** and **39a(5)**.

simple tenses The tenses that refer to present, past, and future time.

singular One. See **number.** COMPARE **plural.**

slang The casual vocabulary of specific groups or cultures, usually considered inappropriate for college and professional writing. Occasionally, slang can be effective if the writer carefully considers purpose and audience. See **19b.**

slash / The mark used to separate parts of an Internet address: <http://www.university.edu/mysite/mypage.html>.

snail mail Papers and packages sent by postal service; so called because it is much slower than e-mail.

software Computer programs that enable the user to perform specific tasks.

space order A concept often used to organize descriptive passages. Details are arranged according to how they are encountered as the observer's eye moves vertically, horizontally, from far to near, and so forth.

split infinitive The often awkward separation of an infinitive by at least one adverb: *to* quietly *go.* See **infinitive.**

squinting modifier An ambiguous modifier that can refer to either a preceding or a following word: Eating *often* makes her sick. See **25a(4).**

standard American English See **edited American English.**

stipulative definition A definition specifying that a particular sense of a term will be used: I use the term *sexist language* to mean language that demeans either sex. See **23e(2).**

style   An author's choice and arrangement of words, sentence structures, and ideas, as well as less definable characteristics such as rhythm and euphony. See 27d.

subject   A basic grammatical division of a sentence. The subject is a noun or noun substitute about which something is asserted or asked in the predicate. It usually precedes the predicate. (In imperative sentences subjects are implied, not stated.) The *complete subject* consists of the *simple subject* and the words associated with it: *The woman in the gray trench coat* asked for information [simple subject—*woman;* complete subject—*the woman in the gray trench coat*]. COMPARE **predicate.** The term may also refer to the main idea of a piece of writing.

subject complement   A word or words that complete the meaning of a linking verb and that modify or refer to the subject: The old car looked *shabby* [predicate adjective]. The old car was *an eyesore* [predicate noun]. See 1b, 4a, and 5b. See also **linking verb.**

subjective case   See **case.**

subjunctive mood   See **mood.**

subordinate clause   See **clause.**

subordinating conjunction   See **conjunction.**

subordination   The use of dependent structures (phrases, subordinate clauses) that are lower in grammatical rank than independent ones (simple sentences, main clauses). See chapter 24.

suffix   An added sound, syllable, or group of syllables placed after a word to form a new word, to change the meaning of a word, or to indicate grammatical function: *light, lighted, lighter, lightest, lightness, lightly.*

summary   A concise restatement briefer than the original. See 38c(4).

superlative degree   See **degree.**

syllogism   A three-part form of deductive reasoning. See 35f.

synonym   A word that has a meaning similar to that of another word.

syntax   Sentence structure; the grammatical arrangement of words, phrases, and clauses.

synthesis   Inductive reasoning whereby a writer begins with a number of instances (facts or observations) and uses them to draw a general conclusion. See **35e.**

tag question   A question attached to the end of a related statement set off by a comma: She's coming, *isn't she?* See **3a.**

Telnet   A program that connects a computer to a network server. The user then has access to programs and functions as if he or she were in the same physical location as the server.

template   A pattern that serves as a model. Some writers create a computer template (like a fill-in form) if they often use the same standard layout.

tense   The form of the verb that denotes time. Inflection of single-word verbs (*pay, paid*) and the use of auxiliaries (*am paid, was paid, will pay*) indicate tense. See chapter **7.**

thesis   The central point or main idea of an essay. It is one of the chief ways an essay is unified (see **unity**). A specific, clearly focused thesis statement helps the writer make all the other elements of the essay work together to accomplish his or her purpose. See also **32c.**

thread   A collection of messages on a single topic in a Listserv or newsgroup.

tone   The writer's attitude toward the subject and the audience, usually conveyed through diction and sentence structure. Tone affects the reader's response.

topic   The specific, narrowed idea of a paper. See **subject.**

topic sentence   A statement of the central thought of a paragraph, which, though often at the beginning, may appear anywhere in it. Some paragraphs may not have a topic sentence, although the main idea is clearly suggested.

touchpad   See **pointing device.**

trackball   See **pointing device.**

transitions   Words, phrases, sentences, or paragraphs that relate ideas and provide coherence by linking sentences, paragraphs, and larger units of writing. Transitions may be expressions (words or phrases such as *moreover, first, nevertheless, for example,* and so on) or structural features a writer uses, such as parallelism or repetition of key words and phrases. When they link larger units of writing, transitions may take the form of sentences or even brief paragraphs. See 31b.

transitive verb   A type of verb that takes an object. Some verbs may be either transitive or intransitive, depending on the context: They *danced* [transitive] the polka. They *danced* [intransitive] all night. See **verb** and **intransitive verb.**

truth   In deductive reasoning, the veracity of the premises. If the premises are true, the conclusion is true. An argument may be true but invalid if the relation between the premises is invalid. See 35f. See also **validity.**

unacceptable   Words or phrases labeled in dictionaries as *archaic, illiterate,* or *substandard;* generally not accepted in any kind of writing.

understatement   Intentional underemphasis for effect, usually ironic. See 39a(5). See also **hyperbole.**

Uniform Resource Locator   See **URL.**

unity   All the elements in an essay contributing to developing a single idea or thesis. A paragraph is unified when each sentence contributes to developing a central thought. See 31a and 32c.

URL   Abbreviation for Uniform Resource Locator, which identifies an Internet address, including the domain name and often a specific file to be accessed. For example, the URL for the Harcourt Web site includes the indicator that it is on the World Wide Web (http://www), the domain name (harcourtcollege) and the domain (com), all separated by periods: <http://www.harcourtcollege.com>. A slash following the domain indicates a subpage on a site. For example, the part of the Harcourt site that students and teachers can go to to find additional information is: <http://www.harcourtcollege.com/english>.

Usenet   A worldwide bulletin board system available on the Internet. It contains thousands of newsgroups on a wide variety of topics. People interested in a topic can subscribe to a newsgroup, where they can discuss the topic with like-minded people.

username   The element of an e-mail address that identifies a user to an Internet service provider.

validity   The structural coherence of a deductive argument. An argument is valid when the premises of a syllogism are correctly related to form a conclusion. Validity does not, however, actually refer to the truthfulness of an argument's premises. See 35f. COMPARE **truth.**

verb   A part of speech denoting action, occurrence, or existence (state of being). Inflections indicate tense (and sometimes person and number) and mood of a verb. Verbs may be either transitive or intransitive. See 1a and chapter 7. See also **inflection, mood, voice, transitive verb,** and **intransitive verb.**

verbal   A word that has the nature of a verb as well as being used as a noun, an adjective, or an adverb. Infinitives, participles, and gerunds are verbals. See **gerund, infinitive, nonfinite verb,** and **participle.** See also 1d.

verb phrase   See **phrase.** See also 1d.

virus   A destructive computer program that can replicate itself. Usually an executable program, a virus is generally transferred by infected disks or by infected files downloaded from the Internet or from bulletin boards. Viruses can also be transferred across networks.

voice   The form of a verb that indicates whether or not the subject performs the action denoted by the verb. See 7d, **active voice,** and **passive voice.**

vowel   A speech sound represented in written English by *a, e, i, o, u,* and sometimes *y.*

Web site   See **World Wide Web.**

word order   The arrangement of words in sentences. Because of lost inflections, modern English depends heavily on word order to convey meaning: Nancy gave Henry $14,000. Henry gave Nancy $14,000. Tony had built a garage. Tony had a garage built.

World Wide Web (WWW)   A system of Internet servers that store documents formatted in a special computer language (HTML). These documents are called *Web pages,* and a location containing several such pages is called a *Web site.* Web pages can provide links to other sites, as well as to graphics, audio, and video files. Users can jump to the linked sites by clicking on designated spots in the document. See pages 549–53.

writing process   The various activities of planning (gathering, shaping, and organizing information), drafting (setting down ideas in sentences and paragraphs to form a composition), revising (rethinking, reshaping, and reordering ideas), editing (checking for clear, effective, grammatically correct sentences), and proofreading (checking for correct spelling, mechanics, and manuscript form). The writing process sets no particular sequence for these activities but allows writers to return to any activity as necessary.

WWW   See **World Wide Web.**

Copyrights and Acknowledgments

Index

Numbers and letters in color refer to chapters and sections in the handbook; other numbers refer to pages.

English as a World Language Index

Entries in this index identify topics pertinent to dialects of English and English for nonnative speakers, as well as for speakers of American English. Numbers and letters in color refer to chapters and sections in the handbook; other numbers refer to pages.

CHECKLISTS